LUGARD

The Years of Adventure

1858–1898

F. D. Lugard, 1893

LUGARD

The Years of Adventure

1858-1898

THE FIRST PART OF THE LIFE OF
FREDERICK DEALTRY LUGARD
LATER LORD LUGARD OF ABINGER
P.C., G.C.M.G., C.B., D.S.O.

By

MARGERY PERHAM, C.B.E.

Fellow of Nuffield College, Oxford

COLLINS
ST JAMES'S PLACE, LONDON
1956

To My Sister

PRINTED IN GREAT BRITAIN
COLLINS CLEAR-TYPE PRESS: LONDON AND GLASGOW

INTRODUCTION

I TOOK up the work of writing this biography for three reasons.

The first was personal· Lord Lugard and I were friends. He was already an old man of seventy when I first met him but for the remaining seventeen years of his life he was vigorously active in colonial and especially African affairs. In this sphere we worked together in our different ways and at our different levels, he being the man of action, working with the experience and prestige of his long achievement, while I was the student. I hope to write a few pages about our friendship at the conclusion of this work so that readers may weigh as exactly as possible the allowance to be made for their having seen a man's life through the eyes of a friend. Here I will only say that my affection and admiration for a man to whose work, I think, history will accord the distinction of greatness did not lead me to agree with all his ideas or to endorse all his actions. By the end of his life he was not much interested in his future fame. But he knew that a biography would be written and that it would be based largely upon his personal collection of papers. He asked me to write it and as his brother, who was to be his executor, supported the wish, I agreed.

The other two reasons arise from what I have just said. I knew that, friendship aside, the story of his work in Africa must lie very close to my own studies of government in that continent. I have had the good fortune to walk in Lugard's footsteps, sometimes more than once and sometimes since I started the biography, in almost every part of Africa where he travelled and worked. It was clear that the record must be of the first importance for the history of Britain's dealings with Africa. His work there began in the adventurous period of exploration and of the anti-slavery struggle; it continued through that of the first occupation of Africa by chartered companies; it reached its climax in the creation of an official British administration. Finally, in his later life, Lugard wrote his classic on African government and devoted all his days and much of his nights to national and international dealings with Africa and to the promotion of African studies. I knew, therefore, that this biography could be much more than a personal story, since Lugard's life at once expressed and influenced Britain's policy in Africa for more than half a century.

Thirdly came the wider interest of the subject. As the world debate over colonialism grew more intense, Lugard, in his work and his ideas, stood out as a supreme type of that imperialism which had long been the pride

v

of his country and was now judged, by the major part of humanity, as something very near a crime. It seemed, therefore, that a full study of the life of such a man, living, as did so few of his generation of empire-builders, well into the modern period of imperial regression, might be a contribution to this important controversy.

Some explanation is needed of the form this book has taken. It is a long book. When I undertook to write it I had no idea of the volume of material I should find in Lugard's papers. These require a roomful of bookcases and cupboards and they allow, at some periods, the writing of an almost day-to-day account of his thoughts and acts. I considered that, where I could, it was worth giving this full account both for its personal and its public interest. I then found that much research in British and French archives and in British parliamentary history was needed in order to fit Lugard's actions into their diplomatic and political frame. As my other work, with the visits to Africa and elsewhere which it required, allowed me to give only a minor part of my time to the writing, I realized that it would be several years before I could be sure of finishing the work. Meanwhile Lugard's brother, Edward (Major E. J. Lugard, D.S.O., O.B.E.), who has put himself and all his material most devotedly to the service of this book, and other relatives and friends of Lugard, who are no longer young, were anxious to see at least some of the story between covers. It was therefore decided that the book must appear in two volumes, the first appearing as soon as it was finished. Lugard's life falls naturally into two parts. In the second part the wildest adventuring is over and he has become the governor. Though still, in Nigeria, a pioneer governor with lands to win and campaigns to direct, he is now the agent of the British government. This period begins neatly on January 1st, 1900 though it will be more convenient to make the break between the two volumes in 1898 just before Lugard was given his new appointment.

I hope that the second volume will follow in between twelve and eighteen months' time. More than half of it has been written already. Each volume, however, will be a self-contained story and will have its own index, maps, and list of authorities.

ACKNOWLEDGEMENTS & NOTES

MY THANKS go first to Major Lugard. He was his brother's *alter ego* in friendship and partnership. For long periods the two actually worked and travelled together; when apart they wrote—fortunately for the biographer—long letters to each other. I have profited also from the high standards of orderliness and exactitude they had learned at home and which had been reinforced by their military training. This meant that all papers were sent to me in perfect order—tied, docketed, dated. More than this, there have been no limits to the time and trouble Major Lugard has taken to help me in work that lay so near his heart, including the reading, at considerable cost to his eyesight and his feelings, of the enormous collection of private letters. Yet he never tried to influence my ideas. His unity with his brother was such that lack of approval here, or criticism there, or an intimate revelation elsewhere, hurt him more than if he had been himself the subject. Yet his almost absolute restraint from plea or protest has put me still further in his debt.

One of the happiest parts of writing a book of this kind is that the work creates contacts with other students of history arduously working in the same field, a little circle with whom mutual services, and sometimes also exciting discoveries of research, can be exchanged. Mr. H. B. Thomas, formerly editor of the *Uganda Journal*, and an historian of Africa as generous as he is conscientious, read through my draft with laborious and scholarly care. I am much in debt to Sir John Gray, now Chief Justice in Zanzibar, for help over the early history of Uganda. I gained much from Mr. Anthony Low who is writing a full-scale study of the earlier history of Uganda. Dr. Roland Oliver and Dr. A. J. Hanna most helpfully read some of the earlier chapters of the book. Miss de Kiewiet, first to investigate the Mackinnon Papers, generously shared with me some most valuable pieces of evidence. Mr. Sillery, late Resident Commissioner of Bechuanaland, read my chapters on his region. Mr. A. J. P. Taylor kindly read my Nigerian chapters with an eye to detect flaws in my diplomatic pattern. Lord Rennell of Rodd entrusted me with some of his father's letters. Lord Salisbury was good enough to allow me to study his grandfather's papers and to quote from them. Mr. Cuthbert Gedge, through the good offices of Mr. H. B. Thomas, gave me access to some of his father's letters.

Thanks are also due to the librarians who take so much more trouble than we have a right to ask in meeting the demands of research workers.

Acknowledgements & Notes

I have especially to thank those librarians who have helped me and my assistants in the Libraries of the Colonial Office, the Public Record Office, the Foreign Office Research Department, the British Museum, the Royal Empire Society, Rhodes House, and the Church Missionary Society. In Paris, gratitude is due to the chief archivist at the Ministry of Foreign Affairs.

I am grateful to the following for permission to reproduce illustrations in this book: Messrs. Elliott & Fry, Ltd. for the photograph of Lugard, 1893; Messrs. Faber & Faber, Ltd. for the photograph of Sir John Kirk; H.R.H. the Duchess of Kent for the portrait of Sir Francis de Winton; *Vanity Fair* for the cartoon of Lugard by Spy; *The Times* for the photograph of Flora Shaw; the National Portrait Gallery for the portrait of Sir George Goldie; *Punch* for the two cartoons; and Messrs. John Murray, Ltd. for the photograph of Sir James Willcocks. I am grateful to Messrs. William Blackwood & Sons, Ltd. for permission to reproduce from originals in F. D. Lugard, *The Rise of Our East African Empire* (1893), the two maps of Mengo and Environs, the map of Buganda, 1890, the March to the West, 1891 and the section of the chart showing Lugard's routes in western Uganda.

Finally I must thank my College which does all that is possible to enable its Fellows to pursue their research. I am especially grateful that I have been able to call freely upon research assistance and secretarial help. The greater part of this rather long-drawn-out task has fallen to Mrs. Giles Bullard (née Chadwick Brooks) and Miss Eleanor Glyn-Jones, but in the earliest stages Mrs. Richard Martin (née James) and in the latest Mrs. Hedley Bull were my assistants. These young graduates have given me much more than their due services: they have brought an enthusiastic interest, a sense of humour and a terrier-like pertinacity in hunting for elusive documents. With such help the laborious aspects of the work were lightened and the interesting parts made still more pleasurable.

Nuffield College
December 1955

MARGERY PERHAM

viii

CONTENTS

Contents

PART FOUR

THE NIGER 1894-1895

PART FIVE

THE KALAHARI 1895-1897

PART SIX

THE NIGER AGAIN 1897-1898

x

ILLUSTRATIONS

MAPS

MAPS

ABBREVIATIONS

A.A.E.	Archives des Affaires Etrangères
A.S.R.	*Anti–Slavery Reporter*
B.M.	British Museum, Additional Manuscripts
C.M.S.	Church Missionary Society
C.O.	Colonial Office Records
D.D.F.	*Documents Diplomatiques Français*
F.O.	Foreign Office Records
F.O.C.P.	Foreign Office Confidential Print
J.O. (Ch.) & (S.)	*Journal Officiel de la République française*, Débats parlementaires, Chambre des deputés et Senat
L.P.	Lugard Papers
M.P.	Mackinnon Papers
P.P.	Portal Papers
Q.V.L.	*The Letters of Queen Victoria*, Third Series, ėd. G. E. Buckle, vol. ii (1931)
S.P.	Salisbury Papers
Coupland I	R. Coupland, *East Africa and its Invaders* (1938)
Coupland II	R. Coupland, *The Exploitation of East Africa 1856–90* (1939)
Lugard I and II	F. D. Lugard, *The Rise of our East African Empire*, vols. i and ii (1893)

A complete list of sources is given on pages 717–23.

Any document whose source is not specified is in the Lugard Papers. Letters from this collection are not footnoted: the names and dates are given in brackets, L. being used for Lugard and E. J. L. for his brother Major Lugard, his most frequent correspondent.

Command Papers are given in full for the first reference and are afterwards referred to by their command number and date.

Quotations have been inserted in the original form except where mistakes in punctuation have been corrected.

PART ONE

Early Years 1858-1887

CHAPTER I

PARENTS AND CHILD

1858-1865 : Aet. 0-7

THERE ARE people still alive today who travelled from India to England in a sailing ship and took four months on the journey. Such a voyage at the age of five was the first great adventure in the life of Lugard, and it provides one way of measuring both the pace and the kind of change that has marked the last hundred years, the period which contained his life. For, though Lugard died in 1945, his elder sister, who was with him in the ship, is still vigorously alive as this is written, and can add her story of the voyage to the full account given in her mother's letters.

This mother, Mary Jane Lugard, was a brave woman, and she needed all her courage to embark from Madras in 1863 in the *Trafalgar*. This vessel was a dirty little troopship of only 1,000 tons, and Mary Jane was taking with her six children—her two step-daughters; her own three children, Agnes, seven years old, Frederick, five, Lottie, two; and another and seriously ailing infant, the charge of which she had undertaken. The mother was ill herself, broken down by the strain of working and child-bearing in southern India. It was only the warning that she would endanger her life by staying there any longer which had brought her to face separation from her husband, since she truly felt for him the immense love and respect which the Victorian convention demanded that a wife should not only feel but also express.

This father and mother must be clearly seen if their son is to be understood. But we need not go much beyond them in the family tree. It was for long a tradition for the biographer to bar his readers' approach to his subject with a stiff genealogical hurdle. Today, when the advance of science might have been regarded as offering more help in relating the effects of breeding upon the character of persons, the length of the ancestral preliminaries has been much curtailed. We

3

may therefore, be allowed, surely with gratitude, to assume that a family group which includes father and mother and their parents provides a sufficient introduction to a study of the eminent. For Lugard hardly this much can be brought clearly into the picture since his grandparents, though moderately distinguished, are indistinct figures. The generations beyond them are difficult to discern at all.

The mother, both by inheritance and influence the larger contributor to the making of Lugard, must come first. She was no ordinary wife of her period. She had been Mary Jane Howard, daughter of a Cambridge-bred clergyman of the north country, the Reverend John Garton Howard. His was an old Yorkshire family which can be traced back through landed gentry and yeoman farmers to the seventeenth century in a genealogy linked with other well-established local families, Greames, Yarburghs, Lloyds, Broadleys, and Gorhams. The Howards claimed to have once held all the land between Hull and Beverley. But by the early nineteenth century, in the rhythm of rise and decline which is the record of so many families of sufficient status to have a record at all, the Howards had become poor. We know little more of Mary Jane's life at home than that there was not much sympathy between her and her mother, and that it was towards divine rather than human love that at an early age she turned her intense nature. She decided to be a missionary and, in a period when such a vocation for a young single woman needed a spirit of great independence—did not Jane Eyre shrink from such a calling even with the resolute partnership of St. John Rivers?—she took service under the Church Missionary Society and went to India. She had worked and over-worked for many years when human love and then marriage came to her late and unexpectedly. At thirty-six, an almost reprehensible age then for matrimony, she married a clergyman who was, like her, working in southern India.

Frederick Grueber Lugard was the son of a soldier. His father, Captain John Lugard (1761-1843), had been an officer in the 6th Inniskilling Dragoons and had served under the Duke of York in the Netherlands campaign of 1793-5. Then, as a prisoner of war, he had passed two years on parole in the park of the Duke of Orleans' chateau at Vilvorde. His royal commander did not forget him and in 1804 gave him the comfortable post of adjutant and secretary of his Royal Military Asylum, Chelsea, which he had founded three years before for the children of soldiers. The conception of the retiring age lay far in the future and Captain John Lugard settled down to forty years' tenure of his office which he held until his death in 1843, in his eighty-second year. In the year before this appointment he married Jane Llewellin Trewman, daughter of the founder of the Exeter Flying Post. There is no more to be learned of her than that she was remembered by one of her descendants, in a somewhat ambiguous phrase, as " a very great madam." Dying in 1861, she left behind her a large family, among them four boys. Little is known of her husband, but that little is to his credit. He left behind him the memory of a charming and gentle nature and, remembering what schools, and especially charitable schools, could be in those days, the 850 boys and 400 girls under his care must be accounted to have been very fortunate. The tablet in the chapel of the Royal Military School at Guston, near Dover, into which the Asylum later developed, stresses his Christianity rather than his martial qualities and describes him as " a sincere and humble Christian, full of faith in the merits of that Redeemer whose Gospel was his rule of life."

If a tablet engraved in 1843 can be trusted, it may have been the religious influence of his father which inclined his second son to become a clergyman. His three brothers were all soldiers, but he succeeded in combining in himself the ministry, service overseas and even military rank by becoming a chaplain in the Madras establishment of the East India Company, and ending his work there with the rank of lieutenant-colonel. He was born in 1808, and as a child of seven was deeply impressed by the distress of his father at the heavy losses of his old regiment at the battle of Waterloo. The boy was given the fullest advantages of education. He was sent to St. Paul's School; from there he passed as a scholar to Trinity College, Cambridge, and took his B.A. in 1831. He was ordained in the same year and it was after holding two curacies in England that he went to India as an army chaplain in 1837, the year in which Queen Victoria ascended the throne.

In contrast with his wife, whose life must be sketched with so few lines, there is a considerable amount of evidence about the Reverend Frederick Lugard, including the recollections of his surviving children. Yet it is not easy to trace his lineaments. He seems to have been a very devout Christian of markedly evangelical stamp, devoted and self-sacrificing in his work, and a frequent contributor to the local Christian paper, the *Madras Observer*. It must have needed great professional resolution, as well as physical strength, to work and to survive for twenty-seven years in the damp heat of Madras in the unhygienic conditions of the mid-nineteenth century. Fortunately he was strong, and had distinguished himself as an athlete at the university, rowing in his college boat when it was head of the river and showing other prowess in sport. Without a heritage of physical strength his son could not have achieved his almost incredible feats of endurance as explorer and pioneer in Africa. It was recorded of the father that he always volunteered for the posts with the worst reputation for mortality. He ended his Indian career as senior chaplain of the Madras Presidency and when he finally left it was with general commendation for his work, and especially for his preaching and his interest in missions.[1] His likeness is preserved in a stone bas-relief in Madras cathedral which commemorates his friend Bishop Dealtry—whose name he took for his second son—and in which he appears as the Bishop's chaplain.

In contrast with his professional life, his private affairs were marked with difficulty and unhappiness, financial and matrimonial. This was due in part to blows of fate, but his own inability to master his pecuniary affairs and a certain helplessness he showed in later life suggest that, for all his kindliness and steady Christian devotion, his character must have had its weak fibres. He was a most unfortunate husband. At the age of twenty-six he married a beautiful young woman. A few years later, soon after he went to India, he heard that she had deserted him for another man. He was left with three small children on his hands, his meagre resources reduced by the expense of a divorce, which left round his neck a load of debts which weighed him down and troubled his children for the rest of his long life. His work brought him much in contact with the missionaries and in 1848 he married one of the women working in Madras under the Church Missionary Society. Three years later she was dead, a victim of cholera, leaving two daughters, Lucy and Emma, to his care. An impecunious widower in India, with five children on his hands, must indeed have been in an anxious situation, all the more as he was a most affectionate and conscientious father. It is not surprising, therefore, that after three

---

[1] F. Penny, *The Church in Madras* (1922), vol. iii, p. 329.

years he found a third wife in the same mission from which he had taken the second.

If the young Lugard inherited strength of body from his father it was from his mother, as so often in the records of distinguished men, that he must have drawn strength of mind. From letters written to her husband in the last part of her married life it is possible to know her intimately and to recognize a character of power and, for those who are not prejudiced by its contemporary framework of evangelical piety, it must appear one of great beauty. In her Mr. Lugard, after all his troubles, found a few years of the deepest happiness. Their children were born from a union of love as well as of Christian partnership. The chaplain's first family had now grown up but Mary Jane took his second family, her step-daughters Lucy and Emma, under her kindly discipline and then, every year of their married life in India, she bore the annual child of the good Victorian wife. In 1856 there was Agnes; in 1857 Ellen Christiana was born and shortly afterwards died; in 1858 came a son christened Frederick John Dealtry; in 1859 came another son, stillborn; in 1860 Charlotte Sophia was born.

Often, to escape the dust and heat of Madras or of Fort St. George, where Mr. Lugard was posted in 1859, the mother took the young family into the hills. When they were separated each child received a loving letter from the father every fortnight exhorting him or her to goodness but showing, too, much feeling for the nature of children. His letters to young Frederick are lost but some of them to his sisters remain written in neat angular writing upon little four-sided sheets of blue paper. In them we can see him gently pressing the little characters into the shape of religious duty and service.

" My dearest Agnes, I am glad to hear you have such nice flowers in your garden. I suppose you are able now to read a chapter in the Bible. Is Freddy learning his letters yet? . . . . I hope the poor Coolie who fell down is well again. The wet weather must be very bad for the poor natives and we ought to be sorry for them and be kind to them. They are not so well able to bear the cold as we are. I think when you have got some money it would be a nice plan for you to buy some flannel and give a bit to each of the poor native women about the house. Ask Mamma how much it would cost and I will give you some money to help. I am, My dearest Aggie,

Your very affecte. Papa, F. G. Lugard."

7

Mary Jane Lugard, after many years of work in India, was by no means strong when she married. The five years of child-bearing and the care of a family of five children made matters much worse. Therefore, in 1863, the very serious decision was taken to send her alone with the children to England. Mr. Lugard, who had only taken two years leave in his twenty-seven years of service, had to stay behind. It was a dreadful separation. Mr. Lugard woke her in the morning as she lay on her narrow little bed by kissing her and murmuring tenderly in her ear "many and great troubles hast Thou shewed me, nevertheless Thou didst turn again and comfort me." Very literally in her view was this text fulfilled: great troubles did come for which she could find no other help than in her religion. She turned back often to this moment and to this text and wondered whether, had she seen all that lay before her, she could have found the courage to set out alone.

The family embarked on March 5th. Since at that date the Suez Canal had not yet been opened, their wretched little ship had to sail to England round the Cape. To live that voyage again with the young Lugard family is an antidote to too romantic a conception of the good old days and of the beauty of sailing ships. The old ship was packed with invalided troops; sickness and mortality were hard at work among them. There were many burials at sea; once a maddened soldier threw himself overboard; one night others broke into a beer barrel and, since beer was then an intoxicant, raged drunkenly round the decks.

We have seen that Mary Jane had a family of six on her hands. Broken down in health herself, she suffered single-handed all the anxieties of a mother in nightmare proportions and to meet them rallied that astonishing strength in weakness, upon which—sometimes alas! in the tradition of the fabled pelican—the good mother draws in order to achieve the impossible. She had the six children with her in a small cabin. The soldier's wife who had been engaged to help her proved of little use. The two babies, who were both delicate and in process of teething, were constantly crying. The mother shivered when rough men sleeping on the deck outside cursed the wailing babies in horrible terms and threatened to string them up to the mainmast. Even when, as rarely happened, all six at once slept peacefully, her nights were broken by her own sickness or anxiety or by the many noises and groanings of the ship. The cabin was overrun with red ants which bit

Water colour of Lugard's mother, 1847

the children in their bunks; it was alive with cockroaches which also found their way into the puddings; the old woodwork was a paradise for bugs, and lice invaded the children's hair. Clouds of mosquitoes were bred in the water-butts and covered the children with bites. The poop steps, which were very difficult and steep, especially when carrying a baby in lively weather, had constantly to be climbed. On deck a small area had been set aside for all the children on the ship. Here she had to be ceaselessly on the watch. The other children were of all ages: fretful and bored, the big ones were noisy and bullying; the little ones screamed their woes. Mary Jane struggled to preserve her little flock from the corruption of bad examples and was complimented upon their remarkable goodness. Most days the sun struck vertically down upon the unshaded deck, yet the cabin was too hot and airless to provide any relief. Food and water were short and the children were often hungry and crying with thirst. Some of the other children fell down the hatch and broke their limbs. There was certainly not much human help to be had; rather were there battles to be fought on her children's behalf, resulting from the intrigues and jealousies amongst parents. The ship's doctor was heard by Mary Jane to say that he wished a wave would wash her sick baby into the sea. Officers—she would not call them gentlemen—were very bad indeed, lying on the decks at night with some girls and giving them drink: she trembled for the soul of Lucy when they paid attention to the child and when they caught hold of Emma and tried to kiss her.

Frederick, as became the one male in the party, was the only one who found some satisfaction in the voyage. In the first recorded incident of his life, after watching with interest the processes that followed the cry of "Man overboard!" he announced his intention, Mary Jane told her husband, of undressing and jumping in. "He should not be drowned. They would send the boat for him. I hope, however, that my representation of the dangers of the sharks and his not being able to swim as the man today did "—(Mary Jane evidently believed in the appeal to reason even with a child of five)—" will deter him from the adventure." A few days later: " They have caught a shark—Freddy is in ecstacies." And later, as their miseries mounted up: " Freddy somewhat enjoys himself. The others hate the ship as much as I do myself." But, towards the end: " I fear Freddy is getting very quarrelsome and sometimes begins the attack. He is not nearly

9

so good as when he came on board. I trust, however, he will recover his good behaviour when we get on shore." In defence of Freddy it must be emphasized that Mary Jane's standards were very high.

All these troubles and events were, we may suppose, the normal accompaniments of a voyage by sail in 1863. But now a series of abnormal troubles fell upon the ship. First they ran into exceptional calms. Day after day they lay motionless under the tropical sun. This experience was as no more than a happy memory to young Lugard: he never forgot the small boats pushing out from the ship to fish in the placid waters and the little sea-snakes they brought back with them. But to his mother these airless, motionless days were almost intolerable. For the first time her Christian resignation has almost a touch of reproach in it. " I have prayed and prayed for a wind. But it comes not. Yet the hairs of our heads are all numbered. He knows we want it. He doth not willingly afflict. It must be for some good purpose."

A second trouble increased the danger of the calm. It was discovered that no less than 100 of the 150 casks in which the water was stored were defective and had lost all their contents. The small water ration was cut still further, hardly any could be allowed for washing, and the children were always crying with thirst. Had the ship been longer becalmed the position would have been terrible. Fortunately the wind rose at last and the captain decided to alter course for Mauritius in order to get water, though he had no charts for the difficult approach to the island.

Calm was followed by storm. A great gale, the worst the captain had known in twenty-three years' service, broke upon the ship. She was blown back forty-five miles: five times she passed and repassed Cape Agulhas in her struggle. A huge tree was lashed to the mainmast to strengthen it. The ship was full of noises, crashes and shouting. There were many injuries and the children were thrown about the cabin. " I have not been afraid—sweet texts have filled my mind. ' When thou passest through the waters, I will be with thee.' . . . ' Thou shalt keep him in perfect peace, whose mind is stayed on Thee.' [sic] " She was ill herself and so was Agnes but " Freddy is quite well and hearty."

The gale, like the calm, came to an end. But even this was not the last of their troubles. Infection began to run through the crowded, insanitary ship. It was now June. " I am almost overwhelmed. Four of the children have chicken-pox and three whooping-cough which tears them to pieces. Freddie and Minnie have both together " . . . . " Our darling Freddy coughed for an hour together without ceasing— He was very patient—a loving kiss and a ' Thank you, darling mamma ' when it was over and he was able to take the dots " (tiny homeopathic pills) " and blackcurrant jelly that I gave him. Not a word of complaint." But this was nearly the end at least of this set of troubles. Early in July the ship reached home having been four months on the way.

The story has been told not so much because it was young Lugard's first adventure, one in which on the whole he acquitted himself well, but because of the light it throws upon the mother's quality. The picture of her is not complete, however, unless it is realized that in this hard experience she drew light and comfort both from her religion and from her love. Her letters written almost every day to her husband are filled with both: they run continuously like two bright threads through the dismal pattern of her story. We have seen something of her religious sense, though a brief quotation can do it little justice. It was closely bound up with her affection for her husband. In her letters she imagines him at different hours of the day thinking of them; she recalls happy incidents of the past; she keeps his memory always before the children. " Oh my husband, how much are you loved! Little Lottie is always sighing about ' Papa dear ' and Freddy prays every night that God would make you come to us soon and expects to find you in the cuddy in the morning in answer to his prayer. As for myself I cannot *talk* of you—I hardly dare think of you except in the dark alone when people cannot see the tears that will come when I think of you." And again, " I fancy you at your solitary dinner and then in your chair and oh! how I long to be with you again. I look at all your kind presents and all your loving attempts to make us comfortable and remember your constant unwearying tender fondness . . . . Oh my Frederick, how I long, long, long, for you."

Mary Jane had a high respect for anniversaries, which she passed on to her sons, and while she was upon the voyage the most important of all came round. " This is our wedding day, that happy day eight years ago that made us one. Oh, how fondly have I been thinking of you, my own darling—And doubtless you have also of me . . . . May God bless my own precious good kind husband, soul and body may

He bless you abundantly. May He bring us together in twelve months or less in some quiet nook in England, loving and serving Him and each other . . . . Is it not a happy day, my love? Do you ever regret it? . . . . May I be a better and better wife to you every year! You cannot be a better husband to me. You were *best* from the beginning." And then she ventures on the nearest thing to a reproach in all her letters, " I have only one thing that I ever wished different—And that is that I have sometimes thought that you were unwilling to confess all your griefs and sorrows to me. Ah, my darling, they would be lighter if they were shared by me . . . . " Her next paragraph suggests that she was thinking here especially of those money matters which so shadowed his life.

These letters reveal the source from which by inheritance and nurture Frederick Lugard drew both the strength of his character and his immense capacity for affection. It may well be that he derived also his tireless, practical ability, since we learn that on this dreadful voyage, besides all those cares for the children which perhaps only a mother can fully estimate, she herself did all the washing and mending, made flannel nightgowns for all the children, made Freddy a pair of black cloth trousers out of his father's old ones, knitted a bed-cover, five pairs of socks and stockings, two pairs of gloves and a pair of slippers for her husband, " rather gayer than I should have made them had I had the choice of wool—purple and gold." They were at least good ecclesiastical colours.

Arrived in England, Mary Jane took her little troop to York, where her mother was living. It was not a wholly happy reunion. It is often part of the price paid by those who serve overseas to find themselves, upon their return home, half-forgotten by their friends and families, and themselves, for a time, ill-adjusted to the conditions of their own country. The returned daughter was soon reflecting sadly that " absence makes the heart grow colder." Mrs. Howard, who was now seventy-seven years old, was not inclined to re-arrange drastically her own comfortable life as an independent widow in order to accommodate a penurious daughter who had chosen to go away as a missionary and return ailing with five children. Out of a fairly spacious house she offered one room to Mary Jane and her three children, who had to sleep upon the floor, and she refused to consider having the two step-children at all even in the holidays and even if they were ill. She shut her eyes to the poverty of the family and showed no signs of being willing to mitigate it from her own more comfortable resources. Mary Jane acted with quick decision. Her attitude to her two step-daughters was faultless: she was not even for a moment tempted to sacrifice their well-being for the sake of her own children. She found a small house in York; rented it at £30 a year; furnished it throughout for £60, and three weeks from the day of her arrival in England had installed herself and her family there. With a young governess at an annual salary of £30, a little nursemaid of twelve years old and one servant she reckoned, she told her husband, that she could manage better on her £200 to £240 a year than by living with her mother and sending the children to school—" for I am a good manager, you know." She could thus escape the matri-archal interference and, above all, she could keep the family together. Small wonder that, after all these decisions and physical efforts, she was unable to send her husband a promised photograph of herself knowing that he would be alarmed to see how thin and worn she looked. It should be noted to the credit, perhaps, of both mother and daughter that, in spite of all this, they remained good friends and Mrs. Howard, even though she retained her ungiving attitude, found a great deal of happiness in her grandchildren, all the more, perhaps, because they lived at a suitable distance.

A caller at 31 Saint Paul's Square, York, during 1863-4 would have found a crowded little household in which, thanks to the courage and efficiency of the mother, there was a great deal more light than shadow. Outside was a tiny garden, divided into five minute plots, each carefully tended and planted with wild flowers uprooted from a neighbouring field. Inside, the six rooms were furnished with the severest economy. The stair carpet had cost only one shilling a yard; the wood nailed round some of the family packages to protect them during the voyage had been trimmed and stained to make shelves and trays; gas, at a cost of 13/-, had been installed in two rooms and on the stairs; in the sitting-room was a hard-worked piano bought, after much serious consideration, for £15.

Everyone in the house, with the exception of Mary Jane herself, was happy. In the schoolroom the five children sat working at their lessons with Miss Liley, the governess. She was herself a mere girl of seventeen: she had dreaded going out as a governess—not without reason in the eighteen-sixties—but had soon found herself treated as the eldest daughter, and was utterly happy with her mistress and her eager, well-behaved pupils. The children were all dressed in clothes made by the mother, the girls, Lucy, Emma, Agnes and Lottie, in plaid frocks with frilled white collars and cuffs; the one little boy of five in a loose belted tunic, decorated with a collar and large buttons, with short trousers just below his knees. In the kitchen Mary Jane and Jane the servant might be found dealing with the formidable washing. There had been some trouble over this. Jane had refused to undertake such a task: her mistress, rising above the usual attitude of her time to servants, quietly set about doing it all herself. Certainly for weeks after " that horrid *Trafalgar* " it had been a highly unpleasant task, as the blankets and bedding were infested with bugs which also got into the house and had to be hunted down one by one. There was always one exciting day in the week when the postman brought the mail in with a grin saying " From India " and all the children came in a clattering rush to the door shouting " A letter from Papa. A letter from dear darling Papa!"

Mary Jane had drawn up the time-table for the day which was closely followed. " Rise at 7. Prayers. Breakfast at 8. School 9 to 12. Walk 12 to 2. Dinner 2. School 3 to 5. Tea at 6. Work and reading aloud till 9. Prayers and bed at 9. For the five hours of school: Scripture $\frac{1}{2}$ hour. English exercise $1\frac{1}{2}$ hours. French 1 hour, Reading aloud 1 hour. The English exercises are Geography, English History, Ancient History, Themes, Parsing, Arithmetic. The little ones, of course, have not so much." Sunday is even more fully described to the father; the nineteenth century Sunday, which, as the writer can attest, lingered on long enough to have played its part in forming many of the middle-aged of today.

" You will like to know our arrangement for Sunday. We all rise about 7. (The mornings are now dark and cold.) Jane lights the kitchen and dining-room fires and lays the breakfast table. Clara dresses the children, and despatches them one by one as they are finished to me to say their prayers, and at least half of Aggy's and Freddy's prayers are about *you*. We meet in the dining-room at 8 for prayers, all dressed in clean linen and our Sunday best. We read a chapter, verse about, in which all join except Lotty, but she also joins in the Lord's Prayer. For breakfast we have coffee (which I go down a little beforehand to make ready) and the children have an enormous plate of bread and treacle and Miss Liley and myself bread and butter and an egg. Breakfast over we repair to the drawing room to the piano and Miss Liley plays hymns and all the children sing. Freddy has a peculiarly sweet voice ... This lasts for half an hour. Then the children all come to my room and repeat to me the hymns and scripture they have learned during the week. This occupies till Church time which is half past ten." (They go off, eight of them, walking two and two). "We have now got a whole pew assigned to us which just holds us all. I shall have to pay £5 5. 0. for it .... As soon as we come home we have dinner. To-day it was a leg of mutton, roast potatoes and a rolly polly pudding .... After dinner the children and Clara have Sunday School with Miss Liley. Jane goes to see her mother .... and I retire to my own room to read and rest or write to my darling. After tea the little ones go to bed and the rest of us .... go to Church. At 9 we have prayers and go to bed." (25 October 1863).

Comment could do nothing to heighten the effect of this picture! Yet Mary Jane called Sunday "my day of love and leisure."

The religion in which the children were brought up was of the evangelical school, though free from its most extreme manifestations. God was brought into daily life as the immediate ruler of all its affairs. Mary Jane looked to Him to help her to find the right house and the right servant: for each success He was thanked, while each trial was a test or a chastisement. Freddy was taught to pray for a fine day and for a party, and he thanked God for helping him to keep still while being photographed. Fortunately this creed produced neither lethargy nor a false resignation since the practical Mary Jane believed that "Our God works by our means and wills that we should exert ourselves." Yet death and the other world played a great part in her thoughts and her main purpose was so to bring up her children and conduct herself that they might not only be blessed in this life but should remain together in the next. Perhaps, she thought, sharing the expectation of St. Paul, they would not have to wait for death. "Do you think He will come soon, dearest Frederick?" she asked her husband. "Do you think He will come in our life-time? I wish He might. Then we should have no further separation but all be caught up together." There was, of course, a puritan strain in her teaching. She condemns sensational novels; she comments sadly upon a profusion of jewellery worn by an acquaintance. As for crinolines, she disapproves strongly—but she conforms: "It would look so extraordinarily singular to be without, but I *detest* the fashion. It is indecent; it is cold; it is inconvenient in the extreme. One upsets chairs and tables and almost one's own children. Yet servants, babies and even Quakers wear them." "The most exquisite pleasure to us both" to which she can look forward is to attend the series of great meetings, the famous May meetings of this period, when the religious, and especially the missionary, conferences were held in London. She comments frequently upon religious matters. She sends her husband notes of good sermons she has heard and though she recalls his " nice sermons on Hezekiah " she suggests—dare one suspect an element of criticism in this?—that these notes may help him to bring variety into his sermons while she praises one minister for preaching only twenty minutes. " But every word tells. There is no tautology." She often wonders wistfully whether she could ever return to her beloved missionary work. Yet, according to her interpretation, her sacrifice in leaving all and following Him had already been rewarded. " I left my parents for the sake of the Gospel and that promise in Mark X, 29–30 has been abundantly verified to me and I trust will be to the end. Had I not left my country I should never have known you, my own sweet husband and you more than compensate for all else." It is interesting to read in one letter her horror when she learns that a certain American religious writer upholds slavery: it is more than possible that in her constant talks with the children, or in helping Miss Liley with the lessons, her small son heard her views upon this question.

The father, writing week by week, seconded Mary Jane's religious teaching with all his great, if remote, authority. Every letter, intimately personal to each child, is mainly concerned with their spiritual welfare. His letters to his elder son have been lost but many of the others survive to show the kind of influence, then and later, he brought to bear upon his son. To Emma, then twelve, he writes, in words which illustrate the contemporary sense of the related religious and economic superiority of his nation:

" You will see in the state of England what Christianity does for a people—the order, the industry, the wealth, and prosperity. It is a profitable lesson. What a contrast to this poor land of idols, where the people are half-clad, and half-fed and where there is no domestic happiness, no truth, no love, no virtue .... You know how the people tell

Lugard aged about sixteen

The Lugard family, 1864
(*Behind*) Emma, the Rev. F. G. Lugard,
Lucy (*In Front*) Frederick, Mrs. Lugard
and Lottie, Agnes

lies as if it was natural to them. Oh, I hope if you have ever fallen into such a habit in the land of Satan, you will utterly break it off now and cast it from you as hateful to Christ." (16 June 1863).

And to Agnes, aged seven:

" How we shall all rejoice together when God unites us again! Then I hope we shall continue together for the rest of life. But after all, how short and uncertain a thing is human life. We ought to have our hopes chiefly fixed on the eternal Kingdom of Jesus, the King of Saints and the Prince of Peace . . . . As little Lottie grows up you must teach her to believe in Jesus and to love him. I hope you do so and Freddy also. I am sure he loves you." (27 February 1864).

And in another letter:

" You know that sweet verse in the 8th chapter of Proverbs. ' I love them that love me; and those that seek me early shall find me.' . . . . How happy I should be if I were quite sure that all my children loved God. I should then feel sure that we shall spend a blessed eternity together in His Kingdom and never part any more after we are assembled there." (17 March 1864).

Upon this point his wife could reassure him. " I feel a delightful persuasion that each of these five children is a child of God." Indeed the effect upon those young minds of these all-pervasive religious influences wielded by parents, and especially by a mother so generous with her love and daily care, was profound. Freddy, above all, perhaps, responded with all the strength of a sensitive and ardent nature. He became, indeed, the model child of the Victorian story book. Everyone—it is, of course, the mother's account—was impressed by his beautiful expression, his wonderful manners, his intense affection for his mother and his sister Agnes. Indeed, Mary Jane suddenly began to fear lest she had been *too* successful, and in her alarm she wrote a complete account of him as he was at that age of six at which human characters are said to be formed in their essentials. For this reason, and for the light it throws upon the mother, the account is worth giving in full.

" It is our darling Freddy who is just now manifesting most decided marks of divine grace, so much so that, while it makes me very happy and thankful, it also makes me think that possibly (though now in perfect health) our Father may be about to remove him to the heavenly garner.

B

For a long time his strict adherence to truth, and his desire in all things to do right, 'to please God,' and his gratitude to God for 'his kindness to him,' and his gentle and grateful and affectionate behaviour to every one about him, have been very observable, but for the last few months there has been added to this a great delight in the Bible as 'the Word of God.' On observing this in November last, though he could hardly read, I made him a present of a Bible, and this has been his constant companion and delight ever since. He pores over it, and spells out from time to time 'beautiful texts,' which he henceforth delights in, and keeps continually in his mind. Latterly his sins have been much on his heart. On the morning of his birthday he was found to be crying silently in his bed. . . . . Miss Liley hearing his quiet sobs went to him. He told her he had been thinking of the text he had just learnt, 'Prepare to meet thy God,' and perhaps he might die tonight, and he did not know if he was ready, if his sins were all forgiven. He wanted to talk to Mama. Miss Liley endeavoured to comfort him, and told him it would take my breath away to come upstairs, and left him. Presently I went up and found him still crying.

" He told me that he thought he should perhaps die tonight, that he had been dreaming that an angel was come for him, and that there were 5 sins he could remember to-day, besides a great many sins that he knew he had done that he could not remember. The 5 sins were such things as letting his Bible fall by accident, jumping about for a few minutes on the sabbath, forgetting that it was Sunday, and hesitating to lend his sister a book which she asked him for. I repeated to him the text 'the blood of Jesus Christ cleanseth &c.' which seemed to satisfy him. And also his favourite text, 'Fear not, little flock; it is your Father's good pleasure to give you the kingdom,' [sic] telling him that if he should die tonight, it would only be that Jesus the good Shepherd would come and carry him safely in his arms to heaven and lay him gently in his bosom there. His sweet smile shewed how happy the thought made him. 'But are you sure,' he said, 'that I am one of Jesus' lambs? ' 'Yes,' I said, ' I am quite sure you are.' 'Well, I think so too. I love the Word of God very much indeed, because it tells me about Jesus and about Heaven, and how my sins may be forgiven; and I love Jesus, too, very much. Oh how kind he is to me. But I was sorry when I thought I should die tonight, because I knew darling Papa and you would be so sorry. I wish we might all die together and then there would be no parting and sorrow.' . . . . He said he should think of those two texts, 'Fear not, little flock,' and ' the blood of Jesus Christ &c.,' and then he thought he could go to sleep. I believe he fell asleep directly after." (3 February 1864).

A week or two later she sent a further report upon the child's spiritual state.

" I promised to give you a specimen of Freddy's prayers. They are something to this effect—' O Lord make me think of my prayers.' This is repeated again and again very emphatically. ' Forgive me all my sins— all I have done today and all the days before. Make me keep thy commandments. *Don't let me get drunken, nor smoke, nor drink blood, nor covet, nor say bad words of my father and mother.*' These are things he has conceived a horror of partly from what he has seen and heard in the streets, and partly from what he has found in his Bible. ' Bless my dear darling Papa. Make him come home soon, and bring him home quite safely, and don't let him ever get hurt or sick and if he is sick make him well again, and bless my darling Mama and make her well, and don't let her be sick any more, and bless all my sisters and my brother, and take us all to heaven when we die, and let us all die together and bless the whole world, and make them all love Jesus and bless the poor heathens and teach them about Jesus and make me be a good clergyman when I am a man, and make me grow to be a man soon. And make my dear Papa rich, and let us all be rich, and make me a holy boy and like Jesus, and create in me a clean heart O God,' and so he goes on for a considerable time varying his petitions from time to time—interspersing a text or a verse of a hymn occasionally, and sometimes saying a little in a whisper which is to be between God and himself alone, and not for me to hear. He is a sweet little fellow, and I trust he may one of these days ' be a good clergyman ' as he so often prays."

Nor did Freddy neglect his father's injunctions to attend to the morals of the only member of the family junior to him. An incident occurred one day that calls the word Jellyby to mind though the spirit of number 31 Saint Paul's Square was a world away from that of the household satirized by Dickens. Freddy, armed with an official box, was an indefatigable collector for the Pastoral Aid Society, a cause, had he been able to understand it, he might have connected with getting rather than giving. One day after the family distribution of rewards for the marks they had gained at lessons, he caught the baby Lottie, as she was about to totter round to the shop nearby and get some sweets or a gingerbread. Lottie's allocation was a halfpenny but she was fully aware of the value of the money. But Freddy stood in her way with his box.

" You know, Lottie," he said seriously, " If you put your halfpenny in here it will help some little child to go to Heaven and then when you go to Heaven you will see that little child there."

But here, Mary Jane, who had observed this, intervened.

"No Freddy, Charlotte is too young. She cannot understand it yet. If she puts her halfpenny in the box she will want it out again."

" Never mind Mamma," said Freddy, " if she does want it out again, I'll pay it for her."

Freddy was growing not only in grace. The milestones were passed one by one. There came the day when he wrote his first letter to his father; the one when he was able to read his verse in turn at prayers; then he got his first pair of real man's trousers " with braces like Papa's and was very proud of them and delighted with the large side pockets"; another day came when he won the family prize for the best general improvement. Then, quite suddenly—at five—he realized and stated that he was the only man of the family and had a commission from his father to protect his mother. He was not, however, such a heavenly child as to be wholly above the claims of the flesh. He shocked Agnes one day when Mary Jane had indulged in an apple-tart to celebrate their father's birthday, by saying that he could do with a hundred and that he hoped there would be apple-pie in Heaven. He showed ingenuity also when, having been told that it was bad manners to ask for more, he remarked, in an interval of conversation, " Can anyone see anything on my plate? " Nor can he have been kept so deeply in cottonwool as to muffle his observation of the world as seen in the streets of York since, when his mother was interviewing an applicant for domestic service, and was unable to make out her peculiar behaviour, it was Freddy, aged five, who coolly pointed out that she was drunk. But nothing so vividly shows the man-to-be than his first complaint—at the same age—that the days were too short since he can find no time to do any little jobs for himself, such as tidying his cupboard.

It must not be thought for a moment that the religious atmosphere of the house made for gloom. " As for the children, their cup of happiness and health is brimful," Mary Jane reported. And again: " Children, servants and governess are all so young and merry. The house rings with laughter and fun all day long from the nursery to the kitchen." But—and here we come to the shadow which has already appeared in some of the quotations—for her " it is endurance vile." Day after day, as the house resounded with all this youth, she shut herself up in her room to write her continuous letter to her much loved husband and confessed to him the losing struggle with her health. She grieved to think that all her married life he had never seen her well. The years of her work in southern India, the strain of bearing and rearing children there, the anxieties of the *Trafalgar* and now the ceaseless work and responsibility of her life were wearing her down. She suffered from asthma and general debility. First she blamed York, and longed for the Nilgiri mountains where once she had felt well; then she realized that she was little better elsewhere; she hopefully tried one doctor and one medicine after another. She leaned especially upon an homeopath who had the advantage that a consultation, plus a tooth-extraction, cost only 2/6d. She was given fatal advice—which she took—to wear wash-leather, and to exclude every breath of air from her room, even pasting over the cracks of the windows and door. Sickly in India, except when in the hills, she yet had strong words for the English climate, especially in the winter.

While she longed for her husband's return, she dreaded another confinement. And she had her anxiety for him. To get him home— and in her great love for him she longed increasingly for his return— she must find him a living or he must get sick leave. Armed with a clergy list and *The Record*, in which advertisements were put, she wrote to patron after patron, meeting with a long succession of disappointments. As she read lists of the sudden deaths of clergymen she was torn between the satisfaction of knowing that, as clergy, they must have been ready, without a long illness to prepare them, to meet their God and the distress she felt for their widows. " God grant such a trial as this may never fall on me! " " At all events I have made known your want of an incumbency and your merits pretty generally all over England . . . . I tell them all that your views are Evangelical, that you are an acceptable preacher and a hard-working clergyman." Again: " I have a bit of energy left and I am determined to leave no stone unturned till I get you home into my arms and in a suitable position for you, if it may be, my darling." She wrote and interviewed his distinguished military brother, Sir Edward Lugard, but with no result. She even considered a living in Oxford—" I had some hesitation as to a living in the diocese of Oxford, but I thought if God put you there it would be all right so I sent the letter." Did she fear it might be a rather difficult region for an Evangelical? But her courage failed her in face of a living of £670. "I have not brass enough to ask for so much!" Yet, learning how livings on crown lands were allocated, she announced, "I think I shall try my hand at the Lord Chancellor." She tilted gallantly at him and failed.

Her ambitions were not high. "If we should get a country living, with a field for a donkey or a black pony to graze in, that would be the thing! Then there must be a cow and a pig and a garden for potatoes. Oh, how happy we should be!" In another letter she wrote: "We have been fated to have but little play time together but plenty of hard working days together. Perhaps we may get some play time yet." And, later—"I wonder if I shall ever be really well again; if we shall ever have real enjoyment of life together in this world. You would not know me when I am well—such spirits and activity as I used to have—such a contrast to the poor, sick, faded thing you have always known as Mary Jane. Well, God's will be done. There is a better world where the voice of joy and health is always heard, and where youth is renewed like an eagle."

At last, early in 1864, Mr. Lugard did return. Mary Jane went to meet him among the spring flowers of Switzerland. We can imagine, though there are no letters now to tell us, the joy of the meeting and the celebration of the home-coming. The joy was short-lived. As the year went on Mary Jane's fears were realized, and she became rapidly weaker. After a temporary curacy her husband obtained the long-desired living and moved into the rectory of St. Clement's, Worcester. But the dreaded separation was near. She was ordered to Malvern in the hope that this famous health resort might save her. But on June 12th, 1865, three months after the birth of her second son, Edward, she died.

CHAPTER II

YOUTH

1865-1878 : Aet. 7-20

LUGARD WAS seven years old when his mother died. According to most views of psychology and education, his character was now, in all essentials, formed and this, as we have seen, in an atmosphere of religion and love as complete and intense as can be conceived. The tenderness, humour and commonsense of the mother and the natural gaiety of young family life must very largely have counteracted what may have been over-repressive or unwise in the religious teaching. His creed might later be lost to him, but he had learned habits of order and industry, and a deep sense of duty; in the close and economical family community ruled by his mother, a perfect "lady" of her generation, he had developed attitudes of self-restraint and courtesy. His deep capacity for affection had been encouraged and developed by all he had been shown and been able himself to express. We need not try to answer the still answerable question as to the proportions in which his mother influenced him through heredity and through seven years of training, though we may assume that he inherited from her his great tenacity of will. His upbringing differed very much from that given to most modern children, and many contemporary educationists, and still more psychologists, might condemn it. But the purposes of a Christian education are not in every point the same as an education directed to purely humanist or civic ends. Those, moreover, who are inclined to condemn might find much in the life that follows to give them pause, especially if they, like the writer, could have visited Lugard's Surrey home and seen, eighty years after Mary Jane Lugard's death, the survivors of her family living in close neighbourhood and in a relationship of deep mutual affection and courtesy, which was a direct reflection of that founded long ago by their mother.

23

The shock of her loss was great. Lugard's sister, at the age of ninety, could vividly remember the sudden sense of unbearable difference when the embrace of the mother's unceasing care, which had surrounded them every moment of their lives, was removed. She remembered, too—for she had never seen a man cry before—the long, passionate sobbing of her father. Mr. Lugard, indeed, was so broken with grief that he suddenly seemed to become much more than his fifty-seven years. He appears from this time to have retreated behind a defence of silence and reserve. His parish work and his studies absorbed his energies, and he ceased to take that very close and affectionate interest in all his children which his earlier letters had promised. Agnes became his special friend, and though he remained an affectionate if somewhat unbusinesslike father, Fred at least had lost something which Mr. Lugard could do little to replace.

There followed some rather difficult years for the young family. Mr. Lugard had, unfortunately, been given a rectorship without a rectory with the unhappy result that he had to resort for a period to a series of lodgings while later, through his financial incompetence, he involved his inadequate personal funds in the expense of building the new rectory. This burden, added to a debt he had chivalrously incurred over the unhappy event of his first marriage and the expenses of his third wife's final illness, landed him in chronic financial difficulties. The ceaseless nagging worry about money soon spread to the whole family and though they bore well a trouble which is of a kind which often demoralizes and disrupts a family, they had to carry, as children, and for long afterwards, a burden which their father's temperament made inescapable.

For a time an aged and ailing aunt of Lucy and Emma came to preside over the family, but this expedient was not a success. Upon Lucy, the eldest child of the second marriage, fell at sixteen the main responsibility for the household. She had caused her stepmother some anxiety upon the notorious *Trafalgar*, but she had been reported as thoroughly reformed by a period of quiet and discipline. It was a severe test for a young girl and it is not perhaps surprising that she appeared somewhat cold and harsh to the younger ones, and she never became so popular with them as her sister Emma, to whom Fred, as he grew older, became very much attached. The little nursemaid, Clara, stayed with the family and prolonged the mother's influence by reminding the children that she had wished only one thing, that they should be good. Emma and even Agnes repeated this advice to the little ones and Fred still clung to the bible his mother had given him as his greatest treasure, and became increasingly versed in its contents.

In spite of all their difficulties and anxieties and the absence of nearly all the treats and little luxuries that enliven childhood, it was not likely that a young family with a large rectory garden to play in were in a state of constant gloom. Fred, as the favourite, tended to suffer less, perhaps, than some of the others. Lucy was indulgent to him, so was Clara, while the servant Jane, from whom little Agnes sometimes thought it necessary to defend the baby, Ned, also favoured the older boy. Yet Fred tended to draw in a little upon himself. Though he was never naughty, he became less docile; he found employments of his own outside the house. A few recollections of his brother and sisters about the growing child may be worth recording. He was very keen upon his little garden, and he insisted upon Agnes, being still his special companion, getting up at five in the morning to work there with him. He arranged that they should tie up their big toes with string in order to wake themselves up and if Agnes were late he would reproach her for not having used this device. He would stay out as long as possible in the garden saying, " Don't let's go in. If we do, they will only make some new rule and we shan't like to break it, you know." He showed a great interest in natural history, and especially in butterflies and birds. One of their early lodgings had been over a furniture shop, and Fred would spend long periods watching the cabinet-makers. This observation and perhaps the building of the rectory inspired him to use his hands, and at the age of fifteen he made an immense aviary for his birds. He kept guinea-pigs, among other pets, and when he found one of them choking from having attempted to swallow a whole carrot he extracted it very neatly with a corkscrew.

Mr. Lugard was unable in his state of mind, and with his lack of money, to arrange a first-class education for his son. The child went first to a dame's school at Worcester kept by two old ladies named Newton, and here he spent a year. At the age of ten he was sent away to a preparatory school kept by some Moravian brothers at Fairfield near Manchester. The Moravians have, in their history, some fine traditions, but these were not evident at this school which was probably selected mainly on account of its cheapness. Here Fred had a most unhappy time. The headmaster, who had made some reputation for the school, was now senile and the strongest impression left on Lugard by the school was the bullying brutality not of the boys but of the German masters. The memory of their arbitrary thrashings marked his mind deeply. Some of their punishments were merely stupid. For only slight offences a boy would be told that he was "in quod," and would be sent for all his recreation period to pace up and down along a track keeping his eyes on the ground. If he raised them a watching master would extend his "quod" indefinitely until all his playtime for days on end might have to be thus spent. If another boy spoke to him he had to join him in this senseless expiation. In the classroom the culprits had to copy the preface to an arithmetic book on to a slate and each time the slate was full it was smudged out and the process repeated. Worse still, vigorous boxing on the ears was a usual punishment, and it seems that this left Lugard with a permanent weakness and partial deafness in these delicate organs. He had to endure two and a half years of this school and he left it in poor health and carrying with him his first experience of injustice and tyranny.

The next move was a very definite advance. In 1871, at thirteen, he was sent to Rossall and stayed there until 1877. He needed all that a good school could give him, and was certainly ready to accept it. If there is something a little negative and disappointing about this important stage of his life, the fault probably lay more with the school than with the boy. Rossall had been founded on a bleak stretch of the Lancashire coast near Fleetwood in 1844, as a northern school for boys of the Church of England. The governing body was at first largely clerical and presumably Mr. Lugard was able to obtain a considerable reduction of fees for his son. The nucleus of the school was Rossall Hall, the home of the founder, Sir Hesketh Fleetwood, whose financial embarrassments had led him to a scheme of development for his estates of which the school was an important part. Under the twenty years' rule of the second headmaster, Osborne, who had introduced the main elements of the contemporary revolution in the conduct of public schools, Rossall grew substantially in reputation and in the number of boys. Osborne, it seems, was a scholar and organizer, but he was a builder in bricks and mortar rather than in the human structure of his school. The school contracted debts which were met partly by economies in the boys' food; bullying was rife, and towards the end of the headmaster's regime a murderous attempt was made by an Irish boy upon the life of a master. This clouded the last period of his headship, which was marked by a drop in the numbers.[1]

When Lugard arrived, the Reverend Robert Henniker had been headmaster for a year, and he presided over four out of Lugard's six years there. The reminiscences about him, recorded by boys and by masters, are somewhat contradictory, but at least it appears that he was almost the opposite of his predecessor, being a kindly and humane person, with a paternal attitude to his boys. According to some accounts he introduced a much more free and genial atmosphere into the school, and it is comforting, when we consider the temperament and age of young Lugard, to hear that it became " a paradise for small boys ". A brilliant scholar, both as classicist and scientist, he knew how to teach boys to think but did not believe in forcing them to work. There must have been some advantages for the boys from this relaxed tension, but these did not include educational distinctions, and in general repute and in numbers, the school went down steadily, though not catastrophically. As to the numbers, it is only fair to remark that his regime coincided with an economic crisis in the nation that was likely to hit the northern middle-class very hard.

Rossall is always a place of cold and high winds, and in 1871 it was also a place of hard living. It was on a bitter September evening that Lugard arrived there to see the school buildings standing on a barren shore, half surrounded by the sea and with its few trees bent to leeward by the prevailing wind. He had developed a bad abscess on his neck at the Moravian Academy, where it had been first neglected and then roughly lanced. He was suffering acutely from this and during the freezing four-mile drive on the outside of a horse-bus the abscess burst. Evidently Mr. Henniker's influence was not yet wholly effective, for he had no sooner arrived than some of the boys warned him that a gang of bullies, who were pledged to give new boys on the first night " something to remember ", might visit him. He lay ill and shivering in his cubicle. The gang arrived, visiting one bed after another. His turn came. He was asked his name, replied " Lugard " and received a blow in the face. " Listen to his cheek " said the leading

---

[1] W. Furness, *The Centenary History of Rossall School* (1945). I am indebted to chapters 2, 3 and 4 of this book for most of the facts about Rossall in this chapter.

bully, " I ask his name and he tells me to ' look out '." Finally a basin of cold water was poured over him in his bed. Next morning he had to be taken to the sanatorium. The doctor emitted an emphatic " Good God " when he examined his condition and heard of his treatment at his last school. It was long before the abscess healed and it left a deep and lasting scar.

Lugard settled down to his life at school. It was not luxurious. The bracing air induced large appetites; the food was " awful " and he had little pocket-money with which to supplement it. He did not remain the phenomenon of goodness that he had been as a young child; his letters to Agnes show—though their tone suggests that they may exaggerate—his indulgences in natural schoolboy naughtiness. In his second year at school he was sufficiently normal to lead a party of boys at midnight under the roofs of the school, a heinous offence, especially with a candle. He gives a dramatic account of crawling over loose planks with the French master—" the Frog " of course— and the school sergeant in pursuit, and concludes his letter in true story style: " Like tales which leave off in the most interesting part I must say ' To be continued ' and in a further letter I hope to tell you today's row." And, the boy foreshadowing the man, he attached to the letter an elaborate plan of the dormitory to illustrate various points in the story.

Among other letters which have survived is one which Lugard wrote from Rossall a year later to his step-sister Emma, at the age of fourteen. It gives us a sudden insight into the character of the boy, his nature still glowing with affection and religious faith, yet suffering those moods of black despair into which children fall, spiritual growing pains which are most severe for those whose spirits are to grow to considerable heights. Here are parts of this long letter, with the spelling and punctuation unchanged.

Rossall,
August 20th, 1873.

" My own darling Emma,

Thank you *so* much for your loving letter. I must confess I was quite un-manned while reading it, and it gave me great pleasure. Emma—I will say for myself that I don't like doing things by halves (in theory anyway if not in practice) and I have (after treasuring my thoughts deep down in my heart for years—for I have felt somehow as I described to you though perhaps not quite so bad for upwards of three years—) I have, I say, made you my confidant and 'my sister' in my own acceptance of the word. Well then (to take up the thread of the sentence) seeing that I've done so partly, why not do so altogether? I intended to have for ever kept my thoughts to myself, since I had no mother; but when I was talking to you in the drawing room, I betrayed my resolution; and now I think I will tell you all my feelings—trusting to your word to keep them to yourself.

First, dearest Emma, we will speak of your mode of comforting and its effect and defects. Yes, defects in one sense though not in another. I wonder whether I should not be alive were it not that some of those texts which you so lovingly and aptly quoted had been my consolation. God knows and he alone, how at seasons such as the one in which I wrote to you—when you feel the *agony of bitterness,* and if I may so speak drain the dregs of a cup which you have long been drinking—what it would be for a mortal if he had *no* spiritual comfort added to his lack of earthly comfort. I am glad you have confided to me a little of your own feelings, though I am extremely surprised that they should be so like my own. I cannot but wonder what reason *you* should have for such misery . . . But it just shows how very little one mortal can read the heart of another, for instance sometimes when I am most wretched I seem in higher spirits than usual . . . . "

The comic note follows tragic. Lugard showed that allied with his intense power to feel and to suffer was a practical strain, resolute and far-sighted. " Secondly " he went on,

" while I *have* space I will speak of something which I meant to have spoken of before but had *not* space, namely of the Dog I want to get. I have thoroughly matured my plans but having often failed in others I submit these to your approval and correction. Well this is the way I intend to proceed. I think it best to let the matter rest until the Private Tuition Scholarship is settled. Now I'll tell you privately that I think my papers won't be *bad.* . . . Now if I do well Henniker will be pleased and therefore will be more accessible. Well then supposing this to have come off and I to have done a moderate paper, I will then go and ask when I can have my prize. He will be in a good humour and answer something trifling. I will then say that I had intended bringing to school a dog which would be *good sized.* He will not comprehend that I mean a *monster* and will most probably give his consent. I will then ask if by paying a little more I may have some scraps from dinner for it, and get him to sign an order for the same. He will most probably give them to me."

The dog, it appeared, was to be a St. Bernard, and more cunning plans were elaborated.

" I would not give more than £5 for which I saw one exactly what I want advertised last week. I would breed these dogs and I think I could gain pretty considerably on them. I need not keep her husband myself. Also with regard to food, I would get 1 cwt. of rice which is *very* cheap, ½ cwt. of cheapest dog biscuits, and 1 cwt. of oatmeal which is dirt cheap. I would make porridge of the oatmeal and boil the rice which, with the scraps (of which I would get a large supply) would form a substantial diet with Dog biscuits as an occasional change. In the Christmas holidays I might let her breed, and with care may rear all pups, these would sell for an average of at least £4. 10s. or £5, thus the first litter would cover all expenses of food, and the cost of the mother . . . "

" . . . This brings me back to the point from whence I started. I spoke of the dog for this reason. Dearest Emma, as I said I know not what I should do were it not that I am a *Christian*; that is I hope a ' follower of Christ.' You did not altogether understand me when I spoke of praying. I did not say I thought it *no use* to pray, certainly not, God grant I never may ! I meant that the relief found in praying and telling all (though to an unseen friend) through constant repetition had lost part of its efficacy. Now though I have the ' Elder Brother ' this ' unseen friend ' there is a (not unaccountable) yearning in my heart all through the long absence from those I love. Can't you understand it Emma darling? Fancy yourself away for months with nothing to call out the best feelings implanted by God in the heart of man, but thousands of incidents every day, fitted to stir up his worst passions and cultivate hatred, and malice. Do not you think it possible even for ' a schoolboy ' to long for something *present* to love, something which may return his love though it be but dumb . . . I may lean ever so on my Elder Brother. I'm afraid I've expressed my argument very vaguely, but I simply mean this, ' I am here, alone, longing for something to love', if you wish to know my feelings read my last letter again . . . "

He then went on to meet those objections that had been raised against the dogs—Killing sheep?

" . . . As to killing it is absurd; I have a pair of legs, which in such a predicament would carry me over ground almost as fast as his, ergo if the impossible were to occur and he were to chase it, by the time he caught it, I would be up with him, and if he tried to kill it (quod est absurdum) I would not answer for all his bones being sound to say nothing of his skin. If, however, (I hope before long there'll be no ' if ') I keep her, I'll teach her such manners that to *look* at a sheep would be high treason."

Secondly, there was the problem of space.

" There is as far as I can see, all England free if it wanted it, don't imagine for a moment that I intend never taking it out, I would do so every day and all day, and it [would] be an unutterable delight every minute to do so. Then there is the garden (at present) I would teach her to keep to the paths (which is easily done)."

Lugard never achieved his St. Bernard, and his black periods often recurred. He knew his school career was not going as well as it should and that he was disappointing his father. He often contemplated—or thought he contemplated—committing suicide. Everything seemed to go wrong. He was constantly late for morning chapel, and as a punishment he had to do endless " drills," a punishment not much more constructive than that of his last school as it meant walking up and down the quadrangle alone and in silence for an hour at a time. At night he toiled late at his " lines " until he became so stupid that he could not do his proper lessons. All interest in his work had gone. He was threatened with a caning. " Fancy the disgrace to be thrashed like a dog! " Even in his favourite game of fives he failed at this time to distinguish himself. He would give his life to please those he loved yet " everything I touch seems to fail . . . . I thought of Papa. I thought how he hopes that I will one day turn out a credit to him and I almost wished he might die before he realizes the sad contrast." At one moment he was inclined to see himself the victim of the masters' injustice; at others his saner self took charge. "I want no answer to my questions. God knows I know the answers but too well. It lies in myself. I have myself to thank for all this misery, and would to Heaven I had never been born." To admit there was some attitudinizing and much adolescence in his unhappiness is not, unfortunately for the young, to say that such sufferings are not real; his cut deep and left a lasting mark in a tendency to moods of black gloom.

That he was not wholly without the sympathy and faith in himself that he needed is shown by the comment that Emma, now twenty-two years old, wrote across one of his letters, " And you will succeed, Fred dear, I am persuaded, and all the better for your bitter experiences now. Work on with that highest motive" (of pleasing God) "and that other motive that you spoke of too, that of pleasing dear papa, and God will bless you." To him she wrote, "Fred, I want your life to be a *noble* life, such as dear mamma would have been proud of, noble because all your actions are done on *principle*." His father, however, was seriously worried about him and made the customary paternal remarks. "He said," Emma wrote, "You were quite ready for any gardening or carpentering and were very persevering in it, which he was glad of but that he would rather see you show more interest in your studies."

In these severe trials of his youth Lugard had the solace at school of a great friendship. He shared his study with James Greenway who took him to his home one Easter holidays, where he was deeply impressed by the happiness of the home-life which he had the brief pleasure to share. Greenway was a gentle and affectionate boy and, like Lugard, a very devout Christian. But he was delicate, and the hard life and the cold, which braced the strong, undermined his weakness. He died, in Lugard's words, "from cold and exposure"; there was an inquest and much perturbation in the school. Lugard was deeply shocked at this new revelation of the fact of death and the first of his verses which survive express his loss and his bewilderment that his friend should be taken and he left. "You have won your way to my heart", wrote the bereaved father, "in your kindness to good and dear James, and I am now going very briefly to ask you a favour . . . . that you will act as an older brother to my two sons Charles and Dady."

Such an experience was maturing as well as saddening. Certain it is that by the end of the next school year, 1875, Lugard could report better success to Emma. There was no one from his home at the prize-giving so, excusing himself in the words of Demosthenes for conditions in which he had to praise himself, he reports that he secured a prize for Divinity—in which, it is not surprising to learn, he was always outstanding at school, winning a row of prizes—and for modern history. He was top of his form in this subject, and third in classics. But the greatest honour was a special mention in Mr. Henniker's official speech of "a remarkable essay written by Lugard" which was held up as a model. "The 22nd of June was a Red Letter Day for me!"

This prize-giving was, incidentally, Mr. Henniker's swan-song. When the boys reassembled in the autumn and went into chapel they saw in the headmaster's seat a small dark man, with long black hair and beard, kneeling absorbed in prayer and oblivious of the rustling entrance of the choir. This was Dr. James, the distinguished Welshman who came to them from a mastership at Marlborough and a Fellowship at St. John's College, Oxford, and who was to go on, after eleven years at Rossall, to be headmaster of Cheltenham and Rugby and finally back to St. John's as President.

His first sermon to the school was an event. He had a most remarkable appearance and a deep resounding voice of great beauty. He had emotions and was not afraid to show them. " A man need not be afraid to wear his heart on his sleeve," he told the boys, " it is only daws that will pick at it." In this first sermon he said to them that Rossall was a city and they were watchmen guarding it. But the enemies were not without, but half-friends within. All were responsible, according to their different gifts, from the youngest boy just fresh from home to the oldest and most prominent. He did not hesitate to speak of his mother who had recently died and of all she had meant to him in his life. Many of the boys never forgot this sermon. On Lugard, then seventeen, the effect was great. He remembered it all his life and sixty-nine years later he could still quote it.[1]

He also said, looking back, " The advent of Dr. James was a revolution." The new head renewed the staff which was very mixed in character, though containing several brilliant men; he brought from Marlborough the full gospel of the public school system; he established a complete and competitive house system; he stimulated the games, playing in them with the boys; he cleared the school debts, and he poured out his scholarship and personality upon his sixth form, especially upon those preparing for the university. Lugard, because he was not among these, missed the full flavour of the new headmaster's influence, and was never quite so deeply impressed by this dramatic and lovable personality as were many of the boys. Yet he did work for him and in a faded essay book, in the writing that changed so little from then until the end of his life, can be read his compositions, written in 1876, with Dr. James' uniform α and $\alpha+$

[1] This was later published in the collection of Dr. James' sermons preached at Rossall, *School Ideals* (1887).

33

at the end of each. The essays are individual enough to reveal the furniture of Lugard's mind at this age as he writes on " Enthusiasm ", " The Scope of Legislation " and " The Œdipus Tyrannus." But the only one which, in view of what was to come, deserves quotation is that " On the various kinds of Courage." " The sources of physical courage ", he writes, " are (1), vigour of constitution, (2) an active or energetic temperament and (3) a sanguine temperament." . . . . " As patriotic is the highest so fanatical valour is the lowest form of physical courage " (Dr. James has a query here!). Lugard goes on to write of those imagined Muslims he was to meet in the flesh in battle through twenty-five years in five different countries. "Around the tombs of the savage Mahometans who fall in endeavouring to spread by the sword and with ruthless cruelty the religion of the prophet, no glory lingers, no lustre shines." At the end he selects his own example of the highest courage. The choice is significant. " We may select as an example of the different beauties of courage combined, England's missionary explorer, Livingstone. Proud as England is of her warriors and statesmen, her inventors and her martyrs, of none is she so justly proud as of the humble missionary who faced the dangers of plague, of wild beasts and wilder men for the sake of the truth he wished to spread and the science he wished to advance, whose moral courage never failed in spite of countless obstacles and comparative neglect, whose spirit seemed to swell as each new danger loomed before him and who died as he had lived for the sake of his God and his country. Justly we may regard him as a pattern of British courage and we shall not disparage England's other heroes by selecting him as the greatest among them." Dr. James, missing the final spelling mistakes, writes " α good " in a quick hand and it is not difficult for us, reading the schoolboy's prose with retrospective thoughts in our minds, to echo the judgment.

All this education was a preparation for life. But for what sort of life? This was a question that must very early face a boy so unprosperously fathered as this. As an infant he had prayed to be a good clergyman, but he had not been long at Rossall before it appeared that this ambition no longer held the future. The Indian Civil Service became somewhat vaguely accepted at home as the goal and it was part of his father's and Emma's reproach, during the time when his school days seemed to be so unprogressive, that the I.C.S. was becoming unattainable. "What then?" Lugard asked in the bitterness of his disappointment with himself. Emma replied that if he failed—and she did not believe that with manful determination he need fail—he might be suited to be a doctor "which would be very nice and just suited to your tastes." But none of them seemed to have a very clear idea as to what this training would cost. Meanwhile, by the time he was seventeen, Lugard was feeling desperately the lack of pocket money. He could only scrape together a few shillings each term and was worried by little debts he contracted. "Expenses fall upon me as I grow older and I find I *must* have a certain amount of money in my pocket . . . . Most fellows of my age have a fixed allowance, some more, some less. I have been told again and again that I am 20, 22 and 25 both in my looks and in my ways." When, therefore, there came an offer, sent on to him by his father from his eldest half-sister Mary and her husband Charles Minchin, to go into his business, Lugard was inclined to take it very seriously. He was worried that his father gave no opinion of his own upon the subject. He argued out the pros and cons; if he went into business now, his younger brother Ned could replace him at Rossall and he would save his father all the expenses of his keep. "I grow more expensive", he confesses sadly to Emma,

"without any intention to do so on my part. My clothes cost more, I eat more and (alas!) I spend more. If I had a salary of my own all this would be taken off Papa's shoulders and I might even aid him a little. On the other hand if I go in for this I have to throw overboard the I.C.S. which if I passed it would be an infinitely better thing besides being a thoroughly gentlemanly occupation and, look at it how I may, I can't bring myself to think that an Assistant in a Sugar Factory is such. Of course 'a gentleman is a gentleman wherever he is,' but still the Lugards have been in the Army and in the Church, good servants of *God* or the *Queen*, but few if any have been tradesmen . . . I think it is an open question and to your sisterly affection I would wish to commit it."

Then, with unusual honesty for one seeking advice, he adds,

"Though I should not perhaps abide by your opinion it would have a stronger weight than any other with me."   (15 June 1875).

Shortly after this, his successes at the end of the school-year led some at school to advise him to think of going to Oxford. This was not seriously considered but the definite decision was taken to go forward for the I.C.S. examination. Dr. James and the staff were chiefly interested in the boys going to the universities and they seemed to pay much less attention to those entering for the services at home and abroad. Lugard was put in the army class where he worked for the I.C.S. with one other boy. His masters seemed to know little about the examination. The two Rossall boys had no chance against the products of the two famous London " crammers " who had brought preparation for the examination to a very fine art, and both of them failed. In order to take the examination Lugard, now nineteen, made his first visit to London, his uncle, Sir Edward Lugard, taking rooms for him in Bury Street and treating him to his first theatre and to dinner at his club.

This uncle was the important man of the family and this visit to him was a great event for his nephew who regarded him with admiration and awe and was much stimulated by his high example. Indeed, Sir Edward came to mean much to the young man in his early career and to the end of his life the white marble busts of his uncle and that of his wife were striking features in his home at Abinger.

General the Right Honourable Sir Edward Lugard, P.C., G.C.B., to give him his full title, was younger than his clerical brother. Entering the army he had greatly distinguished himself in the Sikh wars and the Indian Mutiny. From 1861–71 he held the position of Permanent Under-Secretary of State for War under Sidney Herbert and Edward Cardwell during their great army reforms, and was president of the commission for the abolition of army purchase. He had the rare distinction of receiving the thanks of both Houses of Parliament for his distinguished services to his country. The Lugards are a long-lived family and he was eighty-eight when he died. The younger brother, Lieutenant-Colonel Henry Lugard, also distinguished himself, though not quite so brilliantly, in the Royal Engineers, dying in 1857 at the early age of forty-four as a result of over-work in very bad climatic conditions in the preparation for the attack upon Canton. Both his sons went into the army.

With these traditions and connections young Lugard's second choice for a career was obvious. It is surprising that it was not his first choice, as it had been that of his half-brother, Henry. He now decided to take the army examinations at the end of 1877. He seems to have had the worst help and advice in all these enterprises for he worked very hard for the preliminary examination only to learn that his having already gained the Oxford and Cambridge certificate with distinction exempted him from everything but geometrical drawing. He was thus left with very little time in which to work for the Further Examination, a competitive test for which there were nearly a thousand candidates. The list came out with the names given in order of merit. He began, with little hope, to look for his name, working up from the bottom. The further up he got, the lower sank his hopes. He did not even trouble to look beyond a certain point at the names in the higher section of the lists and he sadly announced to his father that he had failed again. He was now in a state of desperation, wondering what, at the age of nearly twenty, without resources or qualifications, he could do with his life. Two days passed in this state of mind, before he met a chance acquaintance who congratulated him upon his success. He replied that he did not regard his failure as any joking matter. The other then informed him that, among the thousand, his name was sixth on the list.

CHAPTER III

SOLDIERING

1878-1887 : Aet. 20-29

AT THE age of twenty Lugard began his career as a soldier. He left behind him the double rhythm of home and school life with the special trials and joys that belonged to each, and threw off also the subjection and frustration that the emerging adult begins to feel as school life approaches its end. Lugard was now an attractive-looking youth, small and lightly built, but very strong and well-knit. He had inherited his father's good features, his eyes were exceptionally bright with a lively expression in them that was at times almost fierce; there was a fine, thoroughbred cut about his nostrils that suggested an ardent and sensitive nature. In repose his expression was serious, almost sad. He was strenuously ambitious. In addition to the influences of his own temperament and education, he felt the negative spur of poverty and the positive call of a family tradition of service which had reached an impressive height in the career of his uncle, Sir Edward Lugard. Physical strength, an ardent nature, experience as an elder son and a school prefect, all these combined to give him a measure of self-reliance, but he had very little knowledge of the world and, apart from the genuine courtesy which resulted from his training and character, he lacked the social arts with which many of his new companions were equipped.

Lugard went to Sandhurst in February 1878. At once the current of world events which had hardly been felt at the rectory and at Rossall not only reached him but caught him in their strong movements and began to carry him hither and thither about the world. He was now in the service of his country, one which, after the constructive but unexciting period of Gladstone's great reform ministry, was now under the spell of Lord Beaconsfield, who had set himself to make her both feel and exercise her power. It will not be possible in this biography to do much more than refer to that wide historical tapestry into a corner of which, year by year, Lugard wove his own activities, least of all in these early years when, as a subaltern, his contribution to the pattern was so indistinguishably small and so involuntary in design.

As the year 1878 opened, Russian armies were marching rapidly into Turkey and Lord Beaconsfield was stirring a divided Cabinet to act before the bear, that sinister figure which had been built up by British cartoonists, dipped his paws into the Mediterranean and began to reach out towards that new short-cut to the Far East which Beaconsfield himself had helped to open up for Britain. On February 10th, the day upon which Lugard arrived at Sandhurst, the Prime Minister was writing long notes trying to convince his very belligerent sovereign that it was enough at the moment to order the fleet to the sea of Marmara. In March he demanded that Russia should submit the Treaty of San Stefano, which she had forced upon Turkey, to the judgment of a European congress and, when Russia refused, he called out the Reserve and ordered an Indian contingent to Malta. To defend his policy on April 8th Beaconsfield caught up and expressed the pride of the hour by painting a dazzling picture of the greatness and variety of the Empire and its peoples bound by ties of liberty and blood to the metropolis. But also—and the cadets at Sandhurst must have read their part in these words—" There are millions who are bound to us by our military sway, and they bow to that sway because they know that they are indebted to it for order and justice. All these communities agree in recognizing the commanding spirit of these islands that has formed and fashioned in such a manner so great a portion of the globe. My Lords, that Empire is no mean heritage, but it is not an heritage that can only be enjoyed; it must be . . . . maintained by the same qualities that created it—by courage, by discipline, by patience, by determination and by a reverence for public law and respect for national rights."[1]

The words were grandiose but the military sway of which he spoke was based upon forces meagre in size and questionable in efficiency. Soon after this speech, and only eight weeks after Lugard had started his year's course at Sandhurst, all the cadets were ordered away from the College and hastily given their commissions. Sixty years later, Colonel George Wemyss, one of Lugard's fellow cadets, writing to

[1] G. E. Buckle, *The Life of Lord Beaconsfield*, vol. vi (1920), p. 284.

congratulate him upon his eightieth birthday asked him " Do you remember the remark in an American paper when we were turned out of
Sandhurst before our time: ' England has let loose one hundred war
pups from Sandhurst! Let Russia tremble!' I fancy there are very few
' war pups ' left."

The Czar thus represented one more adverse influence upon Lugard's
education. This extremely raw cadet was now given a commission in
the 9th Regiment, the East Norfolk, now called the Royal Norfolk
Regiment. He joined the 1st Battalion at The Curragh. " The officers
are the best set of fellows I ever met," he wrote, " and I am only sorry
I shall have to leave them." (23 July 1878). For an impecunious subaltern could not then live upon his pay in England and it was necessary
to get himself transferred to the 2nd Battalion which was stationed at
Peshawar in the North West Frontier Province of India. In September,
therefore, Beaconsfield having returned from the Congress of Berlin
earlier in the summer bringing " peace with honour ", the troopship
H.M.S. *Euphrates* was able to steam peacefully through the Mediterranean to the Suez Canal with no other hostilities than those caused
by eighty subalterns challenging the captains and majors on the upper
deck to a ferocious round of bolster-fights. At Malta, when the ship
put in, the people, who at that time, *pace* Beaconsfield, hated their
British rulers, gave no welcome to the passing soldiers and Lugard
had a serious fracas with a boatman. He arrived in India towards the
end of the year.

As the railway then terminated at Jhelum in the Punjab, there was
a trek of 150 miles to be done before the draft of the Norfolks
could reach its destination. At Jhelum, therefore, Lugard bought his
first pony and began the process of turning himself into a first-class
horseman, starting in the proper way with a nasty spill. At Peshawar
he settled down for the winter of 1878–9 to military life at an Indian
frontier station. Everything was strange and exciting to him. It was
a life full of contrasts. There was the beauty of the place with acres
of peach, plum, orange and pomegranate and a garden full of roses
filling the air with scent, all flowering against the snow on the Hima-
layan ranges that stood north-east of the station. Yet there was disease
among all this beauty: Peshawar ranked with other imperial outposts
as " a white man's grave " because of its own special deadly fever,
and Lugard soon had his first experience of that silent warfare which

nature wages against the white intruder in the tropics and which was then far more effective and continuous than anything their human inhabitants could contrive. Hard work on the drill-ground alternated with hard play at polo and with racing, with its tearing over the rough ground on his ponies Stamp and Snowball and surviving many falls. There was the contrast between the imported British social life and its Indian setting which was being observed at this very time by another young man, and which was soon to be dramatized to the world in the persons of Mrs. Hauksbee and the " fishing fleet " on the one side and of Kim and Mowgli on the other. But there is no evidence that either side of this contrasting background meant very much to the young subaltern; he was too busy expressing himself physically and professionally in the first flush of adult freedom. On the social side he was not much interested in the gay life of the club or of the drawing-rooms where the regimental ladies passed the intense social hours of their artificial day. On the Indian side there was little in the atmosphere of a British mess, twenty years after the Mutiny, to help a young English officer to break down the barriers from behind which his caste ruled the country and to look deeply into the realities of India. To Lugard, in these first years of soldiering, the people of the country must have appeared mainly as servants or soldiers or villagers beating up the game. The young man accepted without question attitudes of mind that, in spite of the lead given in this matter by the Prince of Wales, the Prime Minister and the Viceroy, only the most thoughtful of his day and generation condemned.

Lugard had not only ponies: he had been able to fulfil another youthful ambition by acquiring a dog. Far from being a " monster "—his life did not allow of that—she was a little fox terrier. Nettle, as he called her, met something of that need to love which he had poured out to Emma. " She always sleeps in my bed with her head and paws on my shoulder and my arm round her." Later he took her on active service and reported " she is my constant friend and companion, never ten yards from me day or night." " You only know half of *me* unless you know my little bitch, Nettle." In April, Peshawar became unbearably hot and he complains of severe heat rash. " I live in a constant state of irritation as though I were the central object in a nest of fleas." He made a brief escape 7,000 feet up into the Murree Hills upon his first attempt after big game, but failed to get his bear. In

May 1879, the regiment was ordered thirty miles away to Nowshera and here cholera broke out. It was necessary to start a process of " cholera dodging " by moving camp perpetually along the banks of the Indus. It was the duty of the junior subaltern to superintend the funerals and, as the British soldiers disliked the idea of their dead being " covered " by Indians, Lugard, to satisfy them, often helped to fill the graves himself and this sometimes at 120° in the shade.

Across all these new and exciting experiences there now broke what was to the young soldier the most desired excitement of all. He was ordered off to hunt that other kind of bear which was thought to be drawing the Amir of Afghanistan into its dangerous embrace. The Russians had been expanding to Tashkent and Samarkand, and only Afghanistan lay between them and the Indian empire. Just before the Treaty of Berlin the Russians, attempting a remote riposte to British pressure nearer home, had sent a mission to Kabul. The Amir, Shere Ali, who had for long tried and failed to obtain a British alliance could not, as " the earthen pipkin between two iron pots ", resist the pressure of the nearer pot. But assertion and expansion were now the keynotes of British policy and Beaconsfield was quick to supply counter pressure. He found in Lord Lytton a Viceroy who more than represented his own romantic and adventurous mind. They determined to send a British mission to Afghanistan and, when this was halted at the frontier, three armies were sent across in November 1878 and occupied the country with little resistance. The Amir fled and died but his son signed a treaty and accepted a British Resident at Kabul in the person of Major Cavignari. The country, however, was seething with disorder and xenophobia and on September 3rd 1879, in a riot caused by a mob of unpaid soldiery, the Resident was murdered at Kabul. The country rose against their subservient Amir and the British took the field again.

There was another school to that of Beaconsfield and Lytton, one which supported Gladstone, now at the height of his antagonism towards Beaconsfield. It believed that it was better policy to halt the northern frontier on the hills and not engage in military adventures in the wild country beyond that could never be held except at vast cost of money and military energy. But Gladstone also revived the humanitarian strain in British policy. " Remember " he exclaimed, " that the sanctity of life in the hill villages of Afghanistan, among the winter snows, is as inviolable in the eyes of Almighty God as can be your own."[1]

Thus when, in the autumn of 1879, young Lugard marched with Gough's brigade through the Khyber Pass to Gundamuk, it was as the agent of an imperialism that an important section of his nation bitterly condemned. There is no evidence from his letters that these great issues of policy interested him: he was mainly concerned with the conflict between his eager will to experience battle and the wretched weakness of a body still suffering from Peshawar fever. " You have pains in your limbs," he writes to Emma, now married to the Rev. Robert Brayne, " a rattling headache, no appetite . . . . but the worst is that though quite empty you are continually vomiting . . . . I got so weak with not eating for a fortnight that I could not stand!—a sensation I never felt before." (L. to Emma Brayne, 26 October 1879). He was not too ill, however, to be thoroughly bellicose. " We are to go route marching all round this country and tread on the natives' toes and see if they mean fighting at all. We did the first the other day and went past . . . . a lot of cultivation and extremely pretty country (for when you do come to a cultivated valley in the midst of the desert of sand and stones which extends uninterruptedly from the Khyber to here it is very pretty and the vines festooning the trees give it a very picturesque appearance). We all have our swords sharpened— at least *I* have only got the point and about a foot of the blade of mine done but it will be enough to poke it through anyone . . . . We were greatly disappointed at the wretched curs treating us thus with silent contempt as we quite expected a scrimmage."

His health became so much worse that he was ordered to go sick. He demurred, dreading lest he should be invalided back to India. His commanding officer, Colonel Daunt, had to speak to him very seriously, pointing out the folly of throwing away his life. He assured him there would be no forward move during the winter and he faithfully promised that he would telegraph to him if there came orders for an advance. Lugard, therefore, allowed himself to be carried back in a litter to Peshawar hospital. He had not been there two weeks when the news came that the Afghans had risen and surrounded General (afterwards Lord) Roberts' column and that Gough's brigade was marching to his relief. Lugard tried to get up and go but the

---

[1] J. Morley, *The Life of William Ewart Gladstone* (1908), vol. ii, p. 152.

doctor warned him that if he did he would never return alive. When he did get away it was December and the fighting was over. He found his regiment quartered in the Amir's palace at Kabul and he passed a pleasant winter with them in the flat irrigated valley of the Kabul river between the mountains. There was much work building roads and cantonments, there was also duck-shooting and skating over the frozen floods of the plain, and hunting the pariah dogs which gorged themselves on the dead and wounded. He stayed there until August 1880 when the regiment marched out through the Jugdulluk pass which was so narrow in places that he could touch both sides of it with the colour which he was carrying. It was surprising that the regiment escaped an epidemic as all along the march they endured the stench from the carcases of dead mules and camels—the war cost the Punjab 80,000 of the latter—with their myriads of attendant flies.

The campaign, which was Lugard's first experience of war, was neither militarily efficient, morally creditable, nor politically successful. The finances of the war, which cost Britain eighteen instead of the estimated six million pounds, were mismanaged; the medical services and the commissariat were bungled and the army itself, except for Roberts' brilliant leadership, caused the Prime Minister acute anxiety. " What alarms me," Beaconsfield told Lord Salisbury, " is the state of the Indian army as revealed in a letter from Lytton written to Cranbrook . . . . "[1] On the moral side it must be repeated that the British authorities treated the Afghans as rebels and resorted to severe reprisals and executions until Roberts himself admitted that " the less the Afghans see of us the less they will dislike us."[2] The war was politically abortive because in the end we had to march out of the country without establishing a Resident or acquiring Beaconsfield's " scientific frontier," and leaving on the throne a candidate from the Russian sphere whose moderate policy, rather than the effect of British intervention, ensured a period of stability for the country. The one material gain, Kandahar, was given up by Gladstone, who won the election of April 1880 largely upon his denunciation of his rival's aggressive imperialism. Beaconsfield had claimed that the character of England " is more calculated to create empires than to give them up." How far Gladstone would go in acting upon the

[1] Buckle, *op cit.* vol. vi, p. 480.
[2] E. J. Thompson and G. T. Garratt, *Rise and Fulfilment of British rule in India* (1934), p. 524. See also on this campaign *The second Afghan war, 1878–80* (1908), the abridged official account.

opposite estimate of his country's character was still not yet certain though the time was not far off when his decision would mean much to Lugard.

At his present level of ideas and ambitions, however, the campaign had been by no means wholly disappointing to the young soldier. True, he had been bitterly chagrined that he had seen no serious action and he had suffered severely, but with no permanent damage, in health. On the other hand he had seen strange new lands and gained much campaigning experience, while in January he was promoted to be a full lieutenant. A medical board in September 1880 found in rather vague terms that he was suffering from " ague which recurs at frequent intervals which has left him in a very debilitated condition." He was therefore invalided to England and spent a year there, returning to India at the end of 1881.

He now settled down to three years of peace-time soldiering, which were perhaps the most carefree of his life. This does not mean that he had no anxieties, still less that he took life easily. He had the ever-present worry about money. It was impossible at that time, even in India, for a subaltern to live on his pay. He had managed it during his first period because he had been on active service and had also had the help of a small legacy. But during his leave in England he was able to estimate the full problem of his father's financial position. No help could ever be expected from that quarter: on the contrary he must help his father and the family as soon as he could. He wrote to Emma in 1883, thanking her for her husband's help to " the dear old Father . . . . [which] has kept off that anxiety of mind which was *killing* him. How I wish that *I* too could help him in his difficulties but alas, it is almost more than I can do to keep my own head above water." One course was to transfer to the Indian army but he had developed a great devotion to his regiment and did not want to leave it. He therefore decided to qualify for an appointment as musketry instructor which carried extra pay. He was fully conscious of the inadequacies of a military education which had lasted for only eight weeks and while on leave in England he had taken the Hythe course in musketry. In the hope of obtaining the coveted post he now worked hard on the ranges as an assistant instructor. But the bad luck that so often attended his efforts in these early years continued: the post no sooner fell vacant than the Government decided to abolish it.

The problem of cash thus remained acute. He decided to try for the interpretership of the regiment, another post carrying a little extra pay. He therefore entered for the Higher Standard examination in Hindustani and Urdu. He worked for this at the same time as he joined the garrison class for a course which was necessary for promotion but which was all new work to a man whose training at Sandhurst had been so brief. He had to work every day at the class from 10 a.m. to 2 p.m. and the only time he could get for his languages was an hour before dinner and during the night. " I sat up almost every night until 1 and 2 a.m. and even later. I then got up early and worked with the Moonshi (native teacher) from 7.30 to 9 a.m." It was probably from this time that he began the habit of working far into the night. He was warned by his instructor that in taking both together he was attempting the impossible. He passed both, a remarkable achievement, only to learn that the interpretership had been abolished, and thus, for all his efforts, he was as badly off in 1884 as he had been in 1881. Quite undaunted, however, he applied for leave to take a transport course in addition to his ordinary work. He worked under Captain Willcocks[1] and thus began a life friendship. When Willcocks was sent to Assam, Lugard acted as transport officer in his place for a time. He also carried out with marked success the transfer of his regiment to a new station and the reception of another regiment at a time when foot and mouth disease had broken out. He was warmly recommended by Willcocks for a permanent transport appointment.

If he worked hard during this period, he also played hard. He greatly enjoyed being at Umballa, a big civil station which provided the scene for many of Kipling's stories. He flung himself into all the activities of the regiment: he was mess and canteen president, and secretary or committee-man for all the manifold sporting events. There were race-meetings, polo matches and gymkhanas with long programmes of events, serious and comic. There were many practical jokes. There was whist at the club in the evening at which he became, fortunately for his slender purse, a proficient player. In other words,

1 Willcocks, (later General Sir) James, G.C.B., G.C.M.G., K.C.S.I., D.S.O., 1857-1926; served in India and the Sudan; 1898 joined Lugard in West Africa (see chapter 29); 1899 colonel-commandant of the West African Frontier Force; 1900 commanded Ashanti campaign; 1902 joined field force in South Africa; 1906 returned to India, active in North-West Frontier Campaigns; 1914 commanded Indian Army Corps in Europe in First World War; September 1915 resigned; 1917-22 Governor of Bermuda.

he lived to the full the ordinary life of a subaltern of his day in India, one which, as he afterwards confessed with deep regret, would have been hardly judged by the strict religious standards of his mother and father. Where he differed most from the average man was in his capacity to work very hard without sacrificing his pleasures and also in his lack of interest in that large area of social life dominated by the mem-sahibs. He was at this time a man's man. In all the many relics he kept of his life in India, consisting mostly of gymkhana programmes and race-tickets, there is not one single dance programme, pressed ballroom flower or similar romantic memento.

One reason for this may have been his whole-hearted devotion to sport. At Umballa he bought Delusion, a grey mare to which he became much attached and which he schooled for jumping and racing with excellent results. There was a strain of recklessness in his sport and after an exceptionally wild tandem race he was seriously warned by his colonel and the doctor that if he repeated this performance, it would probably cost him his life. He gained, perhaps, an even deeper thrill from hunting big game. Taking his leaves early, for he did not care for the fashionable leave period at Simla, he joined his half-brother Henry who was now in the Indian Civil Service, near Nagpur. They had never met until he got out of his train and a stout man of forty-five strolled up to him and said " I suppose you are Fred." With him, in the spring of 1882, he shot his first tiger and some black buck. Incidentally, this was one of his first contacts with the civil side of imperial administration. " Harry, being Deputy Commissioner, is simply king of all this part . . . . So he turned out every male of a village or two and started them into the jungle to 'honk' or 'beat'."

But the sport in which he found that extreme measure of danger and excitement which he craved was pig-sticking. Late in 1882, the regiment was sent to Morar in Rajputana, where pig were numerous. But it was most perilous country, full of blind ravines. His light weight, his daring and the skill and speed of his beloved Delusion, won him many trophies. He delighted in telling his schoolboy brother Ned, for whom he had developed, mainly through the medium of letters, a great affection, of the thrills of this sport.

" We heard from the villagers that an enormous boar described with oriental exaggeration as being as big as a buffalo with tusks as large as an elephant's was somewhere in the neighbourhood. We at once resolved

47

' to fight neither with small nor great, save only against the King of Israel ' [sic] as represented by this prodigy. At last, after much beating, it was yelled abroad that *he* had broken: looking up to the flag-wallahs in the trees they waved frantically for the open country. We galloped hard forward but could see nothing for an old boar is the cunningest of brutes and hates to run. He steers for every scrap of cover . . . . Just as we were turning back I caught sight of him wilily steering for some scrub. ' Gone away ' I yelled and lost ground for my pains for Muirhead happened to be in front of me. An old boar will not run far but when pressed at once shows fight, so I thought of nothing but a breakneck pace, besides the prize was so great! . . . . I dashed at him and *of course* he was too quick . . . . I could not turn for some distance and as I had headed the pig and turned him right back into Muirhead, I never dreamt but what I had lost my chance but it would not have been fair not to have headed him then as he was going straight for a ' bind.' Turning I found that he had dodged Muirhead too . . . . and was fairly turned to bay with his back to a big thornscrub determined to *fight*. I came up to face him at a very gentle canter knowing it was no child's play and he would charge straight. He came at full tilt. I spurred my horse for a gallop past, but there was a shock and then a mutual melee!! He had somehow thrown off or dodged my spear and was straight at me. I tried my utmost to keep him from under my horse (which he would with a toss of his head have ripped open) . . . . I managed to drive him a blow close behind the shoulder which sent my spear above the iron and straight for his heart and then it broke short! . . . . he gored my horse just a *very* little . . . . and falling over the boar we came a mucker into a thorn-bush. Had I fallen off, Ned, it would have devolved on you to pay my debts, my boy . . . . Luckily we righted ourselves without parting company and the boar started off in a different direction. Each few yards he turned and faced us looking such a devil that I was fairly afraid of another rush . . . . But my spear was killing him and turning into a thorn-bush he reeled and fell dead . . . . He was about 36½ inches at the shoulder . . . . bigger than any the Nagpur hunt have bagged and they will be riled at his falling to an outsider."

(L. to E. J. L. undated).

On January 22nd, 1885, having finished his transport work under Willcocks, he rejoined his regiment at Sitapur. Four days later, the relieving column being just too late, General Gordon, standing unresisting outside his palace at Khartoum, was cut to pieces by the Mahdists. England heard the news with bitter sorrow and with a shame that turned all eyes upon Gladstone. Gordon had been sent to

Officers of the 2nd Battalion the Norfolk Regiment, Afghanistan, 1880
Lugard is seated on the extreme right

evacuate the Sudan but bitterness and anger are not rational and the country demanded an expedition that could now relieve little but the national emotion. The British in India were interested to hear that, following Beaconsfield's precedent, an Indian contingent was to go to Suakin. Lugard was playing bridge at the club when he was handed a telegram to tell him that he was appointed transport officer for this contingent. "How the devil did you get it?" cried his envious partner. "By hard work" was the reply he might have given.

He reached Suakin in March 1885 under the command of Sir J. Hodson. The old port, since superseded by Port Sudan, lies in the sandy wastes of the Red Sea coastal desert, which is broken by the jagged hills inland. It had lately been the scene of much desperate fighting. The previous year General Baker, who had been hurriedly sent there with a scratch Egyptian force to relieve the neighbouring garrison of Tokar from the Mahdist hordes, saw his force of 3,700 men utterly routed and two-thirds destroyed by a much smaller force of Sudanese under the famous slave-trader, Osman Digna.

The British then took over the defence of Suakin from the Egyptian government and sent Sir Gerald Graham, V.C., with 4,000 British troops. Tokar was lost and, though Graham won some successes in the field, these could have little result since, in these unhappy months of delay and divided counsels, the main objective of these operations, the opening of a route from the Red Sea to Berber for the relief of Khartoum, was abandoned. Graham's forces were withdrawn and only a minimum force to hold Suakin itself was retained. However, while the sudden flare of indignation at Gordon's death lasted, it was decided to send a column up the Nile to take Berber, and Sir Gerald Graham was sent back to Suakin to crush Osman Digna and to open the Suakin-Berber route to the Nile. He was to begin by building a railway to Ariab, half-way to the Nile.[1] It was thus hoped to master those formidable transport difficulties which, far more than the enemy, had defeated all the attempts to relieve Gordon either up the Nile or across the torrid and inhospitable Red Sea wilderness. From this the handsome Beja tribes, descendants of the notorious Blemmyes of ancient history, had scourged the frontier of the civilized world from the days of the Pharaohs, the Ptolemies and the Caesars. It will be

[1] For an account of this abortive project see Sir R. Hill, 'The Suakin-Berber Railway, 1885,' in *Sudan Notes & Records*, vol. XX, 1937.

C

clear that the transport officer was thus the key-man in the projected operations.

The force which Lugard joined in March numbered 13,000 men drawn from Britain, India and Australia. The conditions which they found were almost intolerable. The dervishes, with many thousand men, mostly of the local Hadendowa group of the Beja, held the country up to the very walls of Suakin. These men, Kipling's "Fuzzies," were full of confidence as a result of the recent defeats and withdrawals of their enemies, and were inspired to the highest point with that religious fanaticism of which Lugard had written in his essay at school. The first need was to obtain some breathing space in the immediate neighbourhood of Suakin.[1] The nearest places to be retaken, lying only a few miles from the port, were Hashim, Handub and Tamai. It was decided to begin on March 20th with an attack on Hashim. Lugard was much excited at the idea of action. The senior officer, however, came into his tent to say that the general had forbidden him to leave the camp as he was a departmental officer and he could not take the risk of losing him in action. " I went to bed feeling utterly down on my luck and now they are apparently having a big fight and there will be a clasp to be won . . . . " It was all the worse because the action was so close. " Horse after horse comes galloping riderless into camp, yet here I am writing letters like a damned old woman . . . . I wouldn't have come on this blasted campaign had I dreamt of such folly as calling a transport officer a non-combatant— I never heard of such rot in my life and I mean to have it out with the General on the next occasion. You may as well tell the old Father that his precious boy is as safe as if he was attending Divine Service in Norton Church." (L. to E. J. L. 20 March 1885).

The next day he did have it out with the general and extorted permission to join in the advance upon Tamai, where 7,000 dervishes were waiting. The first objective was a place called Tofrik where the commanding officer, Sir John McNeill, on March 22nd began to make a stockaded camp. Whilst many of the troops were dispersed collecting brushwood, there was a sudden attack by 5,000 dervishes. There followed twenty minutes of desperate and confused fighting. The enemy penetrated right into the half-made defences. They were

[1] See Lord Cromer, *Modern Egypt* (1908), vol. ii, p. 24 ff. and F. R. Wingate, *Mahdism and the Egyptian Sudan* (1891), p. 244 ff.

forced back with the loss of 1,500 men but the British casualties, fifteen officers and three hundred men, were heavy in relation to their total numbers and five hundred camels were killed or missing.

Lugard had now had his heart's desire in a very desperate piece of fighting. It had certainly sobered him.

" Do not tell the Father " he wrote to his brother " that I was in the fight on March 23rd, of which you will have seen accounts in the papers . . . . They fight like demons, even *women*! (two or three were found among the dead the day before yesterday) . . . . Worst of it is that my shoulder is so bad that I only feel half myself and in a hand to hand encounter I could not slew my sword about . . . . I feel much handicapped but our Fate lies with a higher power and so it must befall. It's real desperate work though. Don't let the Father know as he is old and worries about things now."   (L. to E. J. L. 25 March 1885).

" To-day the usual convoy has gone to take water and stack provisions in the Zeriba where we had the fight. Each time they have had some fighting and to-day we can see that they are going at it hard. I confess I am hardly so keen as I was after seeing all I saw that day! But I do hope to get into the battle of Tamai . . . . It is getting stinking hot here and the place is simply fetid with latrines, stale horse standings, and dead animals of all sorts . . . . I believe that if they hang on to that Zeriba cholera will break out, for the stench when we left of *hundreds* of human corpses plus *hundreds* of camels and mules was suffocating. If this business lasts long enough I may pay off some of my debts and if I can clear myself I shall try and have a look at old England before I return to India—by gad, I should like to see London again! "   (L. to E. J. L. 26 March 1885).

He was to be denied his battle at Tamai. Osman Digna had been sufficiently mauled to allow Graham to occupy it without resistance. This Sudan campaign was as meagre in its results as that in Afghanistan. Gladstone had allowed his judgment to be overborne in sanctioning the two expeditions at all and, as the strength of popular feeling died down, cold reason, which the future Lord Cromer had never ceased to preach from Cairo, reasserted itself. Gladstone once declared that it was harder to justify our having done so much to rescue Gordon than our not having done more, and it was harder still, at a time when there was no question of Britain being ready to undertake the major operations needed to reconquer the whole Sudan, to justify expeditions with limited or, worse, political objectives. The Suakin campaign had not even succeeded in drawing off the pressure from the garrison cut off at Kassala. Lord Wolseley had been the main advocate of this forward policy. But, as Gladstone's biographer points out, the Prime Minister was inclined to solve the difficult problem of how much responsibility for the administration of an Empire should be allowed to distant agents by keeping them on a tight rein.[1] There were other reasons for withdrawal. On April 10th the Russians defeated the Afghans in an attack upon Penjdeh and once more the possibility of war with Russia was on everyone's lips. On April 15th the construction of the railway from Suakin was countermanded and on the 21st it was announced in both Houses of Parliament that no further offensive operations would be undertaken in the Sudan. Although, in the oscillation of the public mood, a general sense of impatience and even of shame with regard to Gladstone's imperial policy contributed to his fall a few months later, his successor, Lord Salisbury, retained this part of his policy.

All the troops were withdrawn from the Suakin region except the Indian contingent which was kept to hold the port itself. Lugard was thus left behind with no work but the care of his surviving transport animals, impatient for news about the possible war with Russia. "I detest the present life I am leading" he wrote on April 28th. "I have nothing whatever to do and being of an energetic temperament it is not to my taste. However the whole force is the same. We are loafing about asking each other for news and longing for a settled plan of action." In August he was allowed sixty days of leave in England, which will be recognized as a merciful reprieve by anyone who has been in the Suakin region at this time of year. Soon after his return in October the Indian contingent left Suakin for India. Those who had fought there had the satisfaction of knowing that, if everything else in the Sudan was lost, this port at least was retained though the Mahdist tide flowed back to its very walls. Lord Salisbury justified its retention with a minimum force on the grounds that it was necessary as a check upon the slave-trade across the Red Sea.

When Lugard returned to India it was as a man who had proved himself in the arduous speciality of transport. Sir Robert Lowe offered him the charge of a transport circle, the technical term for a large transport area, but his C.O. ordered him back to the regiment at Benares. In the cold weather of 1885-6 he was able to break the

1 Morley, *Life of Gladstone*, vol. ii, pp. 314-15.

monotony of regimental life by carrying out a very important reconnaissance survey over the Azimghur district. This taught him a great deal about the civil administration of India and he found the lesson so interesting that his report was selected for special commendation by the Commander-in-Chief. When, in March 1886, Sir Robert Lowe again offered him the command of a transport circle, this time at Lucknow, he was allowed to accept. In this post he was more or less of a free lance and he flung himself into the work with his usual energy, reorganizing the whole system in his circle. He had, among other transport units under his care, some sixty elephants. He proposed, in order to save fodder, to graze them in the forest. The Commander of his division, Sir Martin Dillon, objected to this project as too risky and told Lugard he must take the entire responsibility. The scheme was completely successful and Lugard received the thanks of the government of India for the saving he had thus made in public funds. Thus, piece by piece, he built up his education and practical experience.

In October 1886 Lugard was offered the appointment of transport officer with the field force in Upper Burma. Britain had annexed all the coastal regions of this country in the first and second Burma wars of 1824 and 1852, leaving an inland state to the king who had his capital at Mandalay. In 1876 the government of India objected to their Resident having to kneel unshod before the king and withdrew him from the court. In 1878 the king died, leaving forty-eight sons, and his successor, young Thibaw, to avoid disputes about his position, clubbed to death eighty leading members of his family and followed it up with other massacres of princes. The British, partly as a humanitarian protest, partly in fear for his life, withdrew their Resident altogether. In 1885 Thibaw threatened to impose a heavy fine on a big British timber company and at the same time entered into relations with the French who were trying to forestall us in Upper Burma.

For these two reasons Lord Dufferin, the Viceroy, ordered an invasion by a flotilla up the Irrawaddy. There was little organized resistance, and in two weeks the war was at an end. Thibaw was deported and the country annexed on January 1st, 1886.

The formal ending of the war, however, was by no means the end of hostilities. Thibaw had so effectually cleared the country of rivals that no responsible successor could be found to accept and support the annexation, while the Burmese people, stiffened by the disbanded army, showed a tenacious and diffused resistance of a kind that had seldom been known in India. It was ten months after the annexation that Lugard was ordered to Burma. He now spent nine very strenuous and unhealthy months mostly in the triangle formed about the upper Irrawaddy valley between Mandalay, Mogok and Wunthu. He began by bringing up the river two steamers full of transport men and animals. During this voyage cholera broke out and the doctor died. From a base at Kynetyat he had to organize transport for the march into the Ruby Mines district through two hundred miles of foodless country, in much of which a way had to be hacked through the jungle. As the task of occupation proved increasingly formidable, General Stewart and Colonel Neville Chamberlain were sent to command the Ruby Mines expedition. The transport side of the work was obviously of the greatest importance and was so arduous that there were days when Lugard spent almost the whole of the twenty-four hours in the saddle. To reach Mogok, a name familiar to a later generation of soldiers, it was necessary to climb from the steamy depths of the Irrawaddy up to a height of 3,000 feet, and this against the opposition of the Shan tribesmen. Lugard once more gained permission to join the fighting line. Roberts, now Commander-in-Chief in India, came over and visited the Ruby Mines, and rode down from Mogok to Kynetyat, sixty miles of heavy going in two days, leaving the transport officer in a state of exhaustion.

Lugard was next ordered to organize the transport on the western side of the Irrawaddy, over ranges of mountains to Wunthu. He did this difficult job so well that his chief, Colonel Cather, took him in as staff officer at his headquarters in Mandalay where, owing to his chief's constant absence and ill-health, he was very often in sole charge. The work was very hard and Lugard found himself less and less able to recover from the effects of the very lowering type of Burma fever. There had been some moments of beauty in the campaign, the rich almost oppressive beauty of Burma, and in after years memories would come to him of rubies, and orchids, and massive green jungles, of the wonderfully rich carving upon temples which soldiers hacked down to burn in their camp-fires—a small Buddha picked up on this campaign radiates calm from the writer's mantelpiece—and of lying in the green sward of a mountainside near Mogok discussing Buddhism with one Adams, a V.C. padre. But most of the long hot days were spent inspecting pack-animals and training their drivers; making indents to India for loading ropes and for warm coats for his bullock drivers as they went higher into the mountains; reporting the number of muleteers without shoes or the heavy casualties from sickness among the men. The stub containing the neatly written weekly statements telegraphed to headquarters about his transport strength still exists: " 10 elephants," he writes, "1 jemadar, 10 mahouts Hindustani, 54 duffadars, 385 drivers, 697 mules, 149 ponies, 370 bullocks."

This episode, however, was almost ended. Towards the middle of this year 1887 he received from India a private telegram, the contents of which will, in the next chapter, be given the explanation they require. Its effect was to make him apply to General Sir George White, who was commanding in Burma, for immediate leave. White had become so accustomed to relying upon Colonel Cather and he, in turn, to delegating his work to his assistant, that Lugard was frankly told that he was too valuable and that he would be the last man allowed to go. In addition to the effect of the telegram, Lugard was really ill and the two evils, reinforcing each other, reduced him to desperation. He decided to resign his commission, but before he did this, he wrote to Colonel Neville Chamberlain, who put the whole case before General Lord Roberts. The General sent orders for his relief on the plea of " Urgent private affairs." He left Burma on July 27th and sailed to India.

PART TWO

Lake Nyasa 1887-1889

CHAPTER IV

DIVERSION TO AFRICA

1887-1888 : Aet. 29-30

IN JULY 1887, when he received the telegram mentioned at the end of the last chapter, Lugard, after an apprenticeship of ten years which had included three campaigns, was well on the way to becoming a successful soldier. Six months later, his military career had ended and he was an almost hopeless and penniless adventurer, sailing as a deck-passenger to an unknown destination and on the verge of committing suicide. This astonishing change cannot be explained, nor can the man be understood, without reference to an event in his private life. He himself wrote when an old man, " The real key to the story of a life lies in a knowledge of the emotions and passions which have some-times disfigured, sometimes built up character, and in every case influenced the actions recorded. Of these the sexual instinct is recog-nized as the most potent for good or ill and it has certainly been so in my life."

Between campaigns he had been stationed more than once at large and fashionable centres. It has already been said that he had no interest in the social round of official and military India and never attempted to taste the delights of the Simla season. Parties which were graced by ladies were an ordeal he tried to avoid. He was very conscious of this and perhaps a little inclined to make a virtue of it, for though out-wardly he may have appeared no more than the sporting young subaltern caring for nothing but fighting, pig-sticking, shooting and horses, he hid a reflective nature and in the secrecy of his own tent or barrack-room, he often put his thoughts into verse. In the twenties—and Lugard was in worldly sophistication younger than his age—verse is often a means for striking those attitudes upon which men secretly pride themselves but which they cannot or dare not exhibit in public. Lugard's attitude, as revealed in his verses, was that of a

59

man who, while no anchorite, enjoyed a life in which women of his own social world played little part. He writes in praise of sport, of whisky, of smoking and of his own long-armed Indian chair. Lying there, so his rhymes record, he can even forget his debts, and with detached contentment can watch the couples going, pair by pair, to flirt in the dark plantations. The only joys *he* finds worth lyricizing are his horse, his dog and his pipe. Even when he writes of his friends in the regiment, he breaks off to ask how far their friendship goes when a man ceases to be a jolly companion, ready for sport and ragging, and falls into some trouble. But his cynicism, as he watches the moves of the social game which he will not play, is reserved mostly for women, a subject to which he returns again and again.

When, in the years following adolescence, the temperamental young seek relief for their feelings in verse, this seldom bears quotation and, though Lugard's was probably better than many, the interest lies more in the ideas than in the words. The lightness and inconstancy of " the Sex " is with him a recurrent theme. In one production he writes at length, burlesquing the full, honeyed sentimentality of the eighties, rhapsodizing about the love-light in the blue eyes of a woman in which a man sees his own image and reads of a love that will endure until death. Then, suddenly breaking off into a short jarring metre and harsh words, he asserts that there is not much love of that sort to be seen in Morar or anywhere in this damned country where love is either of the promiscuous sort or to be bought for annas and pice. This note of cynicism about love, and especially about woman's capacity for keeping faith, is constantly struck, not with the deep tones of experience but, as it turned out, with a strange prescience. It was not only that he felt himself at a disadvantage in drawing-rooms but that he had decided that he could not afford to marry, since, as he tells his half-sister, Emma, when he writes to congratulate her upon her rapidly growing family, " I wish my own chance of having little ones were not among the impossibles."

There was indeed, at this time, in his letters and verses a suggestion that he was restless and unfulfilled. Yet this did not arise from any doubt about his profession. Writing to his brother Edward, to stamp on the preposterous idea of his emigrating, he says:

" Give up the Emigration scheme. Now I'll give you my reasons. Of course there are many which are more or less sentiment, i.e. I would sooner see you in the first profession in the world serving your Queen and country than a clerk, a grocer or—an emigrant. It is the profession of your family *par excellence*. But to turn to more practical reasons. An officer's life is the best, bar none, in the world. If one has to face a bad climate or find oneself in a hole for coin, so you will probably in any other profession at starting. *I* have so far knocked along, why shouldn't you? The whole system of Mess life, especially in India, is a grand one. You get your racquets, polo, pig-sticking, riding,—*chacun à son goût*— to the extent he can afford etc. I wouldn't chuck the Service for the most lucrative profession. Again, as the father had given us an education at a public school at a great sacrifice to himself, it is a poor return to chuck it thus. So much for the Army."   (L. to E. J. L. 3 December 1882).

As proof of the sincerity of his advice he was throwing himself whole-heartedly into every activity of his profession, bringing to it not only his youthful energy and enthusiasm but also that capacity for painstaking, detailed and tenacious work which he owed to his mother. Yet he was unsatisfied. The very persistence of his search for danger in reckless tiger-shooting and pig-sticking seemed to testify to a spirit in which there was an inner conflict. Was it because he had proved that even this life, crowded with work and sport, was not using his immense vitality? It was a vitality which could find outlet either in the passion of a great love or in the passion of some great work, or, if he were fortunate, in both at once. But up to this time neither opportunity had presented itself.

In 1886, as we have seen, Lugard was given charge of the transport circle at Lucknow, a large and famous station, full of dramatic memories of the Mutiny with a numerous British community. Among these was a woman, a re-married divorcée, who was famous, not only for her great beauty, the subject of many portraits, but for her intelligence—she published articles and verses—and her fearless skill in breaking horses and in show jumping. Her name is of no importance now: she may be referred to as Celia. She had made, in contemporary language, many conquests: she was attracted by the promising young officer and challenged by his reputed insensibility to women. His interest may have just been caught by a woman who shared his love of horses and his taste for danger.

Their meeting changed the course of Lugard's life. He knew for a brief period an intensity of happiness and fulfilment which he could never experience again though he was to know a calmer and truer love in later life. He drew now upon all the reserves of his rich nature, and shared them—or thought he shared them—to the fullest extent that is conceivable between two persons. They rode together; they discussed all things under the sun; they read verse together and wrote it for and to each other; they watched the splendid settings of the tropical sun with an emotion that seemed to fuse their two identities. Above all, his deeply affectionate and generous nature found at last an opportunity to give and this meant more to him than to accept. Behind all the rather naive and self-conscious mockery of his verses about women there had been, as we should expect from the influences of his childhood, an ideal conception of woman and of love and of this ideal he now believed that in this woman he had found the reality. He kept nothing back, and with the rest he gave an unmeasured faith.

The news that came to him when he was strained with fever and overwork in Burma was about Celia. She had driven a coach and four through Lucknow and, turning too abruptly, or at too high speed, into the gateway of an officers' mess, had landed the whole equipage and herself in disaster. Now she called for him at a moment when he believed she might be dying. He went nearly mad with anxiety and it was his determination to go to her at all costs that led him to threaten to resign his commission if he could not obtain leave. He hurried to India and found that Celia, far from being in a dying condition, had already sailed for England. He hurried after her, finding the long voyage—though not so long as when he had taken it in childhood—unbearably slow. Upon landing he went straight to her address in London. He found a different woman, at that very moment engaged in bestowing her affections elsewhere. She was quite recovered and had already established herself in a pleasure-seeking circle utterly uncongenial to him. It was the strength of Lugard's nature which made the shock of this loss and disillusionment so destructive. At first he refused to accept it, but as the full realization of it came he felt that his reason was in danger. It must be remembered that he was suffering from persistent and neglected attacks of a type of fever contracted in Burma that was known to turn at its worst into melancholia and which had already resulted in several suicides among the military.

Lugard now passed through a period from which his friends and family might well wonder whether he would ever emerge with his sanity. For two months after landing he did not go to his home. Looking for distraction and danger he applied to Captain Shaw, the officer of the newly organized Fire Brigade. It was to him that the song in the contemporary opera *Iolanthe* was addressed and the tragi-comic refrain about the quenching of a great love in fierce cascade may seem to fit Lugard's case very aptly. But the situation was all tragedy, long and deep, to him. Shaw was at first inclined to reject this unknown volunteer but relented. " Your profession " he wrote " was an introduction in itself and your letter so frank and manly. I have no hesitation in promising to help you." So, night after night, Lugard flung himself into the fight against London fires, sometimes returning in the small hours, black with smoke. He kept this secret from his family, but his distinguished uncle, Sir Edward Lugard, found him out. He wrote to Edward, now in India,

" Fred turned up last evening looking better than when he first came home but I thought rather *wild*! . . . . I wanted him to stay and dine but he said he had an engagement and at last out it came that he had joined the Fire Brigade and went out every night (when they were called out) to fires etc. on the engine!! I was rather astonished and questioned him as to his motive etc: he said it was for the *excitement*, he could not rest without excitement so he went to the Hd. Qrs. of the Brigade at Southwark every evening and remained all night, sleeping there in his clothes . . . . In truth, I am rather, indeed very, anxious about him and the risks he runs: he has been out almost every night at great London fires and he is so fearless and daring I dread his coming to grief."

Lugard, thanks to the good offices of Colonel Chamberlain with Roberts, had not resigned from the army. He was, therefore, not a free agent. On December 15th he was obliged, though he loathed the prospect, to join the 1st Battalion of his regiment at Aldershot, preparatory to its sailing for Gibraltar. The change of scene, the garrison routine, even the award of the D.S.O. for his Burma achievements, produced no mental improvement. Rather he became more desperate in his revulsion from all that reminded him of his old life and more resolute to turn his back upon it and to seek for excitement and danger and, if possible, death, in some distant place and among strangers who knew nothing about him. An understanding colonel recommended him for sick leave and he was free. But free for what?

It was in vain that his uncle, Sir Edward, to whom he looked for help and guidance much more than to his father, sent him a last reproachful appeal.

" I had hoped, my dear Fred, that 'ere this you would have had sufficient resolution to conquer yourself and throw off that morbid affliction which seems, if encouraged, not only to blight your own prospects but to bring grief and sorrow to your poor father and all your own family and relations; you too who have given all such cause to feel pride in the name of Lugard, whose career has been so prosperous and distinguished, to end like the stick of the previously brilliant rocket which everyone had admired . . . . I cannot understand it! Nor can I scarcely believe it! . . . . I have the same affection for you as if you were my own son, but to carry out such wild projects as you name, I cannot be a party in the matter."

(Sir E. Lugard to L. 28 January 1888).

Lugard was deaf to this appeal. His one idea now was to cut himself adrift from his home and profession. Where was he to go? All the world might seem to be open yet in reality many ways were closed. England, because it contained Celia, he regarded as barred to him, as he would always be feverishly trying to see her or fighting with himself to keep away from her. He was in no mood to wander about Europe, a continent which, in any case, appeared to offer little of the desperate kind of adventure he sought. India was obviously impossible. But there was another continent which had the two main qualifications—it was unknown and dangerous. It was also close at hand and the journey there would be cheap. Moreover he had not forgotten Livingstone and he had an idea, not perhaps yet very clearly defined, that, even if he did mean to end his life, he might at least do this in some useful way and what could be at once more dangerous and more valuable than some service against the slave-trade? He had heard something of Sir John Kirk[1], and how he had followed up Livingstone's work against the Arab slave-trade and he knew he had done this as consul at Zanzibar. He therefore wrote a letter to the great man, now in England, looked up Zanzibar on the map and resolved to start out in that direction.[2]

[1] Kirk, Sir John, K.C.M.G., F.R.S., M.D., 1832–1922; 1858–63 with Livingstone on second Zambezi expedition; 1866 Vice-Consul Zanzibar; 1873 Consul-General; 1889–90 plenipotentiary at Brussels Slave Trade Conference; 1895 mission to Niger.

[2] From this date until February 1893, the reader, like the writer, can make use of Lugard's own two volume book, *The Rise of Our East African Empire*, which was published in 1893. To avoid crowding the pages with references these have not been used except where verbatim

The idea, however, upon which he first acted in his feverish and uninstructed state of mind was not, from any point of view, a very good one. It was, while waiting for further information about anti-slavery work, to offer his services to the Italian army, then preparing to invade Ethiopia from the vantage point which Italy had recently secured at Massawa. He therefore packed his total wealth of forty-eight sovereigns into his belt, collected the minimum of kit, and with no credentials but his medals and a not very helpful letter from the Italian acting-consul in Gibraltar, he boarded the first ship that happened to be passing for Italy.

Once aboard and alone, he had time to consider the madness of what he had done and to look steadily into the face of his own misery. He reflected that, in the event of his half-pay for sick leave not being granted, this £48 would have to last him for two years or so. His objectives remained unsettled. One moment he wanted only adventure and if possible an end; at another he wished " to join a great and good work such as that being carried on by Emin Pasha[1] or in any work in the suppression of slavery." By chance he found on his ship Rider Haggard's recently published novel *The Witch's Head* in which the hero, crossed in love, also goes to central Africa, and he reflected bitterly upon all the happy chances, including a rich friend and the Zulu war, which befell that favoured character.

At Naples he disembarked, went up to Rome, and found his way into the presence of an official at the British embassy who told him his plan was hopeless, that the Italians had refused similar requests even when they came from Lord Salisbury, and that the only Englishman who had got out to the African front was *The Times* correspondent. He was warned that, if he tried to reach the fighting, he would certainly be treated as a spy. Utterly downcast and feeling very lonely, but still resolved, he returned to Naples, re-embarked and sailed on to Suez.

----

[1] See below p. 166.

quotations have been made, when the two volumes of the book will be referred to as Lugard I and II. This book gives a more detailed description of the main events of the years 1887–92 and a much fuller account of Lugard's own views about current African questions than can be given in the present biography and it should be read by all interested in the subject. This and the succeeding chapters have been supplemented from many other sources, including Lugard's own reports, correspondence, and his intimate pencilled diary written from day to day between 8 February 1888 and March 1889. This, naturally, is even fuller and more outspoken than the account which Lugard published so soon after the events.

At this port, seriously alarmed at the speed with which his sovereigns were oozing away, he wandered around picking up the cheapest meals he could find. Suez was no place in which a respectable English officer could live on the poverty line, but his guardian angel must have been in charge for he fell in with an old German stationer in whose house he fed for the first time on tripe—and Suez tripe sounds especially unattractive—for two francs. He joined the fervent family prayers round the harmonium and met a young German who was going out— significant portent—under the German East African Colonization Scheme. He found a cheap bed with a little Greek restaurant-keeper and confessed to him that he was an English officer who was in trouble. His guardian angel was still active. " He begged me to trust in God and *pray* and quoted the story of Jacob's wrestling in prayer—little he thought that story had formed a keynote in my life of late and in all my progress since I have learned to pray . . . . I asked him what I should pay and pressed him very hard. He replied that *if* I could easily afford it, 3/-; if not, *nothing*. With *great* difficulty I got him to take the 3/-. He was very loathe and when I replied ' If they were the last three shillings I had in the world you should have them,' he said simply ' It is the character of a *gentleman* ' and he couldn't have thanked me better."

An Italian ship, the *Pandora* bound for Zanzibar, came in, and hearing that the first class was £30, and the second £20, Lugard chose to go as a deck-passenger for £3 10. 0. He could not even afford the extra £1 for a cabin of sorts to be shared with the cook and so slept on the open deck among Arab coolies and Italian labourers. As no food was supplied he had to make a bargain with the cook for two meals a day at two shillings, and was obliged to hang about in the hot, fetid galley and take what greasy remains were handed out to him. Washing had to be done in public in half a bucket of water. The young German emigrant, dressed in " a long black coat, black trousers, made-up tie and nondescript billycock hat " was his closest companion and took turns with him at watching over the kit. They could only converse with the help of a little German-French dictionary and by making signs. The deck was so filthy that Lugard, who had no bed but only a rug, had to lie on an iron ledge, which had nuts in it and two pipes sticking out, so that he only had four feet on which to lie with his legs hanging down. Moreover, some hot pipes passed underneath the iron, so that sometimes it was too hot as well as too hard to lie upon. With this he must make do, though the very coolies on board had some kind of mat to sleep upon. In the morning he had to be alert to escape a swilling from the filthy water swabbed over the deck. The ship was alive with fleas and he must sometimes have compared this voyage with his early experience on the sailing ship *Trafalgar*. The contrast would have been to the advantage of the sailing ship for there at least he had the best of company and of care while now he so longed to speak a word of his own language that he hung about near the second class partition trying to catch the attention of some Dutch Roman Catholic priests bound for India, who were busy learning English. He hoped that he might have discussed with them some of the religious difficulties that had now come to add their weight to his trouble. But the priests, with one honourable exception, were too grand to speak to a rather dubious character travelling among the natives on deck.

It would indeed be difficult to find words to express the depths of physical and still more of mental misery into which Lugard had sunk. He had not the facility for finding relief in forgetting, and still less in hating, the cause of his unhappiness. On the contrary, his own feelings had not changed and he regarded the greatness of the past love between himself and Celia as an enduring claim upon his loyalty and service, should he live. This claim, if we may for a moment look ahead, was to be answered in fullest measure, in care, in friendship and material help until the day of her death and this at great cost to himself in every sense. Lugard was not the first man, nor will he be the last, to make such a mistake or to seek an antidote to unhappy love in dangerous adventure. Where he was exceptional was in his great capacity for suffering and his inability to find relief from it either in hatred or in forgetfulness. If the whole of this story could be written it would testify to a loyalty far above the ordinary human level.

In these weeks on board he often feared he was going mad. His belief in his religion, though not his memory of the Bible, deserted him. He could not believe that it would be right, as he assumed his religion would decree, to destroy his hopeless affection. Even his faith in the ties which bound him to his family and friends sometimes failed him except with regard to his young brother. To read the many terrible passages he wrote at these times in his diary, when he struggled with the longing for self-destruction, is to realize to the full the meaning of Milton's words that the human mind can be its own hell.

At the end of February the ship reached Massawa. Lugard, as far as his filthy and public environment allowed, cleaned himself up for the occasion and went ashore determined, in spite of his failure in Rome, to force his way into any fighting that was going. Picking up a Hindustani-speaking Somali, and confronting protesting officials with bland apologies in that language, he boarded a train. The railway had been built as far as Dogali through the foothills that lead up from the sea to the high plateau. From there he made his way to the front at Saati. He walked through the Italian lines at night, in great danger of being shot by a sentry, keeping up the spirits of his servant and of a little boy who had been recruited as a guide, by recounting wonderful stories of his former prowess which the trembling Somali translated to the even more frightened boy. He was given quite a civil reception by *The Times* correspondent and the Italian General Baldisera and also got some valuable free meals out of them. But, for all his pleadings, whether for dangerous scouting work with the soldiers or help even in a menial capacity to the correspondent, both warned him away from the front. And, indeed, no fighting was in sight as a British peace mission to King John of Ethiopia under Mr. Gerald Portal,[1] of whom we shall hear again, had held up the fighting until the season was too late for it to begin. "'English officers,' the Italians courteously said, 'we welcome and love, but English diplomacy we detest.'"[2]

Lugard, with nothing but months of inaction offering if he stayed, had to turn and hurry back to catch his boat. As he went he remarked the excellence of the soldiers' work in building the railway, the roads and the fortifications. He compared this with the incapacity of British troops in Afghanistan and the Sudan to tackle this kind of work, and the necessity in the latter country to import highly paid navvies to work on the railway. He did not analyse very deeply the ethics or even the politics of the war he had sought to join, though he did mark the graves of soldiers of Lord Napier's expedition which, having

[1] Portal, (later Sir) Gerald, K.C.M.G., 1858–94; 1879 entered Diplomatic Service; third Secretary in Rome and Cairo; 1887 sent on mission to Ethiopia; 1888–9 Acting Consul-General at Zanzibar; 1891 Consul-General at Zanzibar; 1892 mission to Uganda.
[2] Lugard I, p. 7.

accomplished its mission of freeing King Theodore's British captives some twenty years before, had marched away leaving this ancient kingdom free, a restraint for which at that date, it is interesting to remember, Disraeli had prided himself. Lugard knew that Ethiopia was a land of slavery and might have assumed, as most others of his generation would have done, that her conquest by a European power was an inevitable and desirable stage in her civilization. His attitude to the adventure, however, arose not from reason but from his state of mind. " My *heart* was never in that venture," he decided a week or two later looking back. " I'd said to myself, that, spite of both the English and the Italian refusal, I'd carry my object through and I did so. But I had no sympathy with the Italians any more (if so much) as I had for the other side, and fighting with absolutely no object in view is to my mind pretty nearly as much suicide as getting another man to cut your throat for you would be . . . . "

So he went on southwards seeking a nobler cause, as a distraction and, if possible, an end. In this mood he came to Aden. Here the hopelessness of his position became clearer to him. He had no introductions to anyone in East Africa; he had no skill to offer, no knowledge of Africa. " If only I had some money . . . . One can be such a hero with money in one's pocket." He was as well versed in Shakespeare as in the Bible, and bitter words from Hamlet came into his head alongside the story of the disinherited Esau. But he refused either to accept or to curse his fate. " Vile word, which causes more harm in the world than any other! " And after all, " young, strong men don't starve as a rule—and what does it matter? " He bargained for cheap terms at a bug-ridden " hotel " under an assumed name and thought himself lucky to win the favour of the Hindustani-speaking Somali butler. He ran into a Scottish trader who treated him to drinks and then offered to help him. Indeed, he marvelled at the kindness shown to him on nearly all sides by those he met on his new low level. The rough Italian boatswain of his ship, the *Pandora*, himself one of life's unfortunates, told him his own story and " he surprised me one evening by suddenly saying, with a fervid imprecation ' I do *anything* for you. You want shirt, I give you my own shirt off my back ' (seizing it in his hand) ' because you have good heart '." [1]

[1] Lugard I, p. 4.

At Aden he picked up a little more knowledge about the continent lying opposite but was still quite undecided whether to go as a white hunter to Somaliland; to ask for a job in a new company then, so he was told, just taking shape, to develop the British sphere of East Africa; or to make his way to Emin Pasha, cut off by the Mahdists, on the Upper Nile. A ship was sailing for Zanzibar and hearing that the consul—successor to Sir John Kirk—was to be upon it and also other Europeans, he decided to go in the hope of making some contact with them. He was horrified to learn, however, that the British India Steam Navigation Company would not allow Europeans to travel as deck-passengers and that the journey, second class, would cost him £13 10. 0. For though he learned at Aden that his half-pay had been granted it amounted to only £10 a month.

On board, however, he did not have much success at first with the consul, Colonel Euan-Smith.[1] There was a great gulf fixed between the first and second class passengers and a British officer travelling penuriously and apparently aimlessly down the coast was fair game for the suspicion of those who had not eyes to penetrate the real man. The consul did agree to put his name forward for employment by the new East Africa Company but, not unnaturally suspicious, suggested that he should ask his Colonel in India to write and state the reasons why he had left his regiment. Lugard, however, needed immediate employment. He now began to pick up news of Africa further south than any point where his imagination had yet played. He heard of the work of an African Lakes Company on Lake Nyasa and that they were willing to engage hunters to shoot elephant and obtain ivory for them, supplying them with heavy guns and equipment and then buying the ivory from them at a reduced rate. He decided to ask the consul to put his name forward for a post under the East Africa Company and, in the meantime, to sail on to Mozambique and try to find temporary employment under the African Lakes Company. The consul, becoming more courteous the more he studied his man, went so far as to give him a letter of introduction to his colleague in this Portuguese town and he also asked Lugard to write to him about the position he found in Nyasaland. And again at Zanzibar, he met kindness and hospitality from some of the British and this helped to

---

[1] Euan-Smith, Colonel (later Sir) Charles, K.C.B., C.S.I., 1842–1910; 1859 Madras Infantry; 1876 Asst. Resident at Hyderabad; 1879 Consul at Muscat; 1887 Consul-General at Zanzibar; 1891–3 British Envoy in Morocco.

restore the sense of identity and status which, in his unbalanced state of mind, he had deliberately thrown away.

Calling in at the little East African ports, where the green verdure and rich red earth come down to the water's edge, Lugard's ship edged down to Mozambique. He liked the look of the port. Whatever criticisms the British may bring against other European powers in Africa on grounds of policy, they must at least admit their aesthetic superiority, and Lugard at once remarked the beautiful avenues of gold *mohur* trees and the houses tinted in pale colours that rested and charmed the eye. In strange contrast with the savagery and slaving in the surrounding country, the place was even furnished with a pier and a bandstand.

Lugard went straight to the British consul, Henry O'Neill, wondering as he went what manner of man he would be and how he would receive a stranger so poorly accredited as himself. He was promptly asked in for a long talk and offered dinner.

The two men studied each other intently as they talked. Lugard, quick and generally sure in his judgments, found himself drawn towards his host. " A man," he thought, " of few words, and of quiet concentrated speech; a man who impresses you that he has a reserve of force." In O'Neill he had found a man very like himself in character and ideas, an ex-naval officer who had served in anti-slavery patrols and was now consul with a brief to report upon Portuguese connivance at the slave-trade. No mean geographer and explorer, he had followed up Livingstone's discovery of Lake Nyasa with detailed survey work round the lake. For all his reserve, he was a man capable of enthusiasm and of daring courage. He had not long returned from a visit to the north end of the lake when he had led the few Europeans and their native allies in a desperate five-day defence of a trading post called Karonga against Arab slave-raiders and in an even more desperate counter-attack on the Arab stockade. In his desk was a copy of an impassioned communication he had sent only the month before to an unresponsive Foreign Office, imploring his masters to let him go inland to fight again and to face the dangerous crisis which was developing in the Nyasa region as a result of Arab aggressions accompanied " by brutal and callous massacres .... and by a wholesale slave-trade which had exterminated whole tribes of natives .... Never, since my arrival in East Africa have there arisen dangers so menacing to British interests in the territories contiguous to Mozambique, or which so imperatively call for the union of all Englishmen resident here to do their utmost to check." [1]

Lugard told him all he could of himself and of his desire to get into Africa, perhaps to shoot elephants for the African Lakes Company. He, in return, told Lugard of his experiences and of the danger threatening the Scottish missionaries and the Company and the plans for another expedition against the Arabs. As he talked the consul summed up the wiry little man before him, and observed the strange combination of strength and of recklessness, of the professional soldier with the wandering adventurer. Even if he could not know the other man's mind or morals, here at least was strength, courage, and military experience, and the need of these up-country was too great for him to ask for other credentials. Suddenly he said " You would be a God-send to them! " Though there was much still to be discussed and arranged, those were really the words which decided the question. To Lugard this remote and dangerous adventure came like the answer to prayer—here indeed might be a useful and worthy cause in which to find an end. But, for all his other renunciations, he had by no means parted with his conscience and he now insisted that he must be absolutely assured that the cause was all it appeared to be. So, keeping his excitement in leash, " I asked a number of questions regarding the *right* of the war, by *whom* prosecuted and under whose authority. Then declared myself ready to engage in it with the greatest alacrity."

" Alacrity "—the word strikes a new note. Had the turning point been reached in his inner struggle and was the will to live asserting itself? We, with the record of his life before us, know that it had but he did not, and a long period of mental anguish with suicidal temptations and a still longer period of desolate unhappiness lay before him. But at least, in the company of O'Neill and his gentle wife, he confessed that for the first time since his return to England from India, " I was as comfortable and as happy as my state of mind would permit." And many others besides O'Neill had contributed to this condition, the obscure people he had met all along the coast, many of them more truly outcast and unfortunate than himself. He was almost exasperated to find that, just as he wanted to abjure his kind, everyone seemed to like him and to want to help him, offering

[1] O'Neill to Salisbury, 3 February 1888, F.O. 84/1901.

service, food, shelter, sympathy, without any hope of return or even of ever seeing him again. Some were men whom, he confessed, he was small-minded enough to think he could never introduce into his London club: " Damn it," he groaned to himself, " *everyone* is kind to me! "

Before Lugard left Mozambique, O'Neill made one suggestion from which much was to result. In the consul's strong desire to win British sympathy and support for his endangered countrymen on Lake Nyasa, he urged Lugard to write about the country and he would see to it that the material somehow reached the British press.

Lugard left Mozambique on March 31st on board the British India ship *Dunkeld*, armed with a letter from O'Neill to the African Lakes Company. On April 5th he arrived at the small Portuguese port of Quilimane. He was now almost penniless but the local agent of the Lakes Company agreed to pay for his transport up to Lake Nyasa and on to Blantyre, a mission station south of the lake. Here he could decide, at the advanced headquarters of the Company, what kind of service he would take up and upon what terms. So two days later Lugard spent almost his last few shillings on the minimum of necessaries for the journey, embarked in a native canoe and set off up a river leading into the interior.

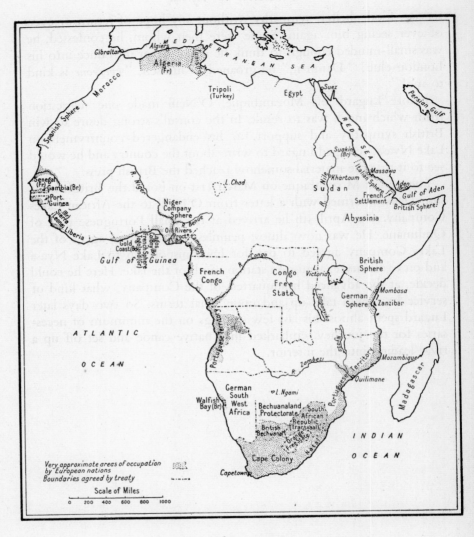

Africa 1888

CHAPTER V

TROPICAL AFRICA IN 1888

1888 : Aet. 30

WHEN LUGARD made his obscure entry into Africa up the river Kwakwa—characteristic African name!—he was almost entirely ignorant of the continent to which, with one brief interval, he was going to devote the whole of the remaining fifty-seven years of his life. He possessed only the fragments of information and observation he had collected during his unhappy voyage down the coast. But if we are to understand the full significance of his work, especially during the next six eventful years amongst the great equatorial lakes, we must pause in our narrative for a few pages in order to take that wide view of the continent which was then only dimly visible to him.[1]

He was entering an Africa, or at least a tropical Africa, still largely unexplored, unadministered and unannexed at a moment that probably marked its lowest depth of disorder and misery. If there is one master-key to the understanding of negro Africa it is the lateness of its discovery and penetration by the outside world. Most of Africa's many problems have been created by the sudden and powerful impact of an advanced, industrial civilization upon tribal peoples who for the most part were more primitive, because they were more isolated than any other large population annexed by Europeans. They were certainly more retarded and untouched than were the tribes in Britain when the Romans occupied this country. The northern strip of Africa had seen the birth of one of the earliest civilizations but, cut off by the desert and other physical barriers from its own continental hinterland, it became the southern fringe of Europe rather than the northern part

[1] There is much contemporary literature upon this subject for East Africa. The most important recent scholarly studies in English are R. Coupland, *East Africa and its Invaders* (1938) and *The Exploitation of East Africa 1856–90* (1939) which will be referred to as Coupland I and II; and R. Oliver, *The Missionary Factor in East Africa* (1953). These have good bibliographies and documentary references. I am also indebted to Dr. A. J. Hanna for allowing me to make full use of his forthcoming book, *The Beginnings of Nyasaland and North Eastern Rhodesia*.

75

of Africa. Most of the rest of the continent had to wait for very nearly the whole five thousand years of historical time while this civilization found its way through Greece and Rome to western Europe until, in the fifteenth century, the Portuguese navigators began to grope their way, year by year, down the West African coast. Even then, the newcomers stayed at the coast: even Dutch colonization of the temperate southern Cape left the wide tropical mass between this point and the Sahara unentered. The early nineteenth century saw a few, brave, dotted lines pricked out by explorers on the great blank space of middle Africa, but Europe had to wait until the fourth decade of that century to learn even approximately where the great Niger river ran, while it was in the lifetime of old men who are still alive as this is written, and only fifteen years before Lugard followed in his footsteps, that Livingstone was still vainly trying to find the source of the Nile and dying in the attempt. Only a very few years earlier, in Lugard's childhood, and centuries after the remote Americas had been mapped and colonized, the first white men set eyes on the vast lakes, those inland seas which had remained hidden from the closely neighbouring civilized world for all the millenia of its migrations and adventuring.

Why did Africa remain closed to the world and why and how was it penetrated during the last hundred years? These questions open up a large subject about which some thousands of books have been written in a dozen languages. We can do no more than pause for a few minutes before this immense prospect, as the small figure of Lugard begins to cross it, and pick out one or two of its general features which will help us to follow his course.

The debate, scientific and popular—for this is a subject charged with interests and emotions—still goes on as to why Africa remained closed and especially why, since the closure was never absolutely complete, her people remained, as it seems, unresponsive to such influences as did play upon the outermost fringes of middle Africa and even seeped down, though slowly and weakly, from the north into the heart of negroland. This is too large a question for a quick answer here. Yet there are some who believe that the dark races of Africa are lacking by nature in some qualities that foster human development and the first observers to force their way into the savagery of the continent had still better reason to think so, especially those who had no religious beliefs nor humanitarian hopes to nourish the opposite view. Yet those first travellers could also experience to the full, as this story will often show, the deadening effect of the physical conditions upon human progress and also the barriers nature had set both to contacts from outside and to movement within. The list is long: surf-beaten shores, rarely broken by natural harbours; thick forests; swamps; deserts and rivers of variable flow, broken into falls as they run off that " inverted soup plate " of our school geography books. Some of these barriers confronted voyagers sailing past the coast or probing it here and there. There was little enough to tempt them to probe very far or to linger—no cities; no gathered wealth for seizure or for trade as in the East and in Peru and Mexico; no tempting natural conditions to invite settlement. If, in spite of all this inhospitality at the threshold, the travellers were brave enough to try to force an entrance, they would be met by intense heat; depressing and fatal diseases; hostile animal, reptile and insect life, and naked black men who, even if they did not always greet strangers with a shower of poisoned arrows—by no means so common a reception as was popularly believed—yet appeared to be neither intelligible, attractive, nor useful.

One use, however, western Europe did find it could make of the African negro and this, in itself, was the most convincing evidence of the intractability and poverty of the continent. Tropical Africa might produce little or nothing in which Europe could trade but at least it bred men and these could be picked up easily on the coast without the trouble of penetrating and annexing their repellent and unhealthy hinterland. An apparently endless supply of these strong creatures was available just as the European discoverers of the western new world, having found that its sparse population was fragile and unserviceable, needed human animals to work it. Thus, through the slave-trade, the negro of tropical Africa was an all too familiar figure to the western world centuries before anything very much was known of the lands where he had been born.

This commerce had become so essential a part of the British system of trade by the eighteenth century, and so necessary to the economy of the Caribbean and the Americas, that it cost the humanitarians some half-century of struggle to bring to an end first the British trade and then slavery itself as a recognized British system. The task of the first great anti-slavery leaders, Wilberforce and Buxton, was carried on by strong societies which were pioneers in the arts of political pressure and publicity, and which, with the support of the churches, could evoke in time an almost automatic reaction from public opinion upon the issue of slavery. After the abolition of slavery in the British Empire in 1833, the humanitarians transferred their attentions to the slave-trade still carried on by foreign nations, a task which necessitated embarrassing diplomatic and costly naval work. But the deep anti-slavery sentiment was also extended to acts of oppression along British colonial frontiers that seemed to partake of the nature of slavery.

It would not be true to say that in the nineteenth century the whole nation was devoted for the whole time to the anti-slavery and cognate humanitarian movements. Though the work of the societies and the churches never ceased, there were years when the intensity of public humanitarian interest declined, when apparently competing causes, such as white emigration to South Africa or New Zealand, clashed against it or when it was discredited by some striking practical failure, such as that of Buxton's Niger expedition of 1841 with its terrible loss of European life. The great achievement of Livingstone was to rekindle the British humanitarian sentiment towards the coloured man and to concentrate it upon the interior of tropical Africa.

There were three sides to his work. As a scientific explorer, with a courage and endurance that would in themselves be sufficient to put him amongst the great men in history—though he shared those qualities with men of coarser grain, such as Stanley—he revealed step by step to the fascinated and horrified gaze of his countrymen the unknown secrets of the heart of Africa. The very fact that in his first and last journeys he travelled alone but for his African attendants, made a powerful appeal to the imagination of his contemporaries, and the direct, modest narrative which enabled them to follow almost day by day the weary, dangerous and yet enthralling course he had taken, deepened his impact, and that of the lands and people he was uncovering, upon their minds.

The second aspect of his work was its Christian character. It may have been difficult for the London Missionary Society to accommodate this wandering moral giant within their organization but there was no doubt that what he represented was Christianity, expressed in dramatic action, courageous and merciful. So impelling is the effect of such rare and complete dedication and self-sacrifice, that Christian missions soon followed Livingstone into the countries he opened.

These results of Livingstone's work are closely related to our subject but it is in its third aspect that the link is closest. Livingstone revealed to a nation, which was concentrating upon what was left of the European slave-trade mainly along the west coast of Africa, the terrible fact that an Arab slave-trade was even then piercing deeply into the heart of the continent from the east and, it could be said without hyperbole, draining it of its life's blood. Thus it was not the normal primitive Africa of all the unrecorded past ages which the traveller found, but one lately entered and ravaged by a wholly new kind of intrusion. Muslim Arabs had for centuries been established at isolated points along the East African coast and islands. A sultan, whose line had come from Muscat, had since 1861 established an independent but, by European standards, not very effective sovereignty from Zanzibar over these scattered settlements and his Arab subjects carried this light allegiance with them as far as they could reach into the interior upon their slave-trading expeditions. It was only in the mid-nineteenth century, with the acquisition of fire-arms and the support of capital from the many Indians in Zanzibar, that the Arabs, with their attendant Swahili, the mixed Muslim coastal people, had been able to penetrate deeply inland and at last reach the heavily populated regions of the Great Lakes. Livingstone sometimes just preceded but generally just followed upon the Arabs as they thrust further and further inland, raiding for themselves but more often arming the warlike African tribes with guns to attack their more helpless neighbours in their scattered villages.

The inland process by which the European slave ships had been supplied on the west coast had been conveniently hidden, but now it was possible for Livingstone, at the cost of his long and lonely wanderings, to record every horrifying part of this eastern operation. First came the surprise raid, often before dawn, on a virgin village; the massacre of the fighting men; the destruction of the huts and granaries; the long march to the coast of the survivors and the women and children, tied together or secured with the heavy slave-sticks; the rough castrating, with heavy mortality, of youths destined as eunuchs for Eastern harems; the callous casual killing or abandonment of the weakly; the indignities of the Zanzibar slave-market and, for many, the miseries of the voyage by dhow to Arabia, the Persian Gulf or even India. The final fate might be to be thrown overboard to the sharks at the sight of a British naval patrol or because of a decline of commercial value through weakness or disease. It is impossible to calculate the numbers of slaves exported annually in any given year from the East African ports. It is estimated, however, that as early as 1840 40,000 to 45,000 slaves passed through the Zanzibar market annually, of whom half were exported, and with the slavers' improving weapons and wider penetration the number must have risen steadily.[1] For each one of the slaves who reached the markets alive, some five or six others—some observers, including Livingstone, put it as high as ten—must have died in the raid, from the resulting loss of food and shelter, or on the march down. A little later than Livingstone's discoveries, Sir Samuel Baker and others began to show that another thrust of this terrible trade was piercing deep into the equatorial regions of the Upper Nile as the Egyptian government, if such it could be called, opened up these hidden regions from the north.

To us looking back, marking the horror with which this news was received in Britain, and knowing the relative ease with which these countries could have been, as eventually they were, annexed and put in order by Europe, it may seem strange that this obvious remedy for Africa's wasting disease was not applied earlier, above all by Britain. Here, especially, if we are to understand the part Lugard was to play in the annexation of Africa, we must remember the attitudes of mind which explain this long delay. These can be understood better if we distinguish the five main motives for colonial annexation and see what happened to them in this period. They are trade, strategy, colonization (in the sense of emigration), philanthropy and the less definable political impulse of nations bent upon asserting their power and energy, and scoring off their rivals, which might be called prestige. Of these motives, at least in the pre-totalitarian world, only strategy and prestige *necessarily* demanded official state initiative. The other three, trade, colonization and philanthropy, were, especially in British history, the spheres where private enterprise was often left to make the first moves. The state would come in from time to time in an auxiliary capacity as the occasion seemed to require and in so far

---

[1] Coupland I, p. 500.

as public opinion, generally represented by vigorous groups of those most active in the matter, could be stirred to demand official action.

It so happened that in the mid-nineteenth century the five motives for expansion were either dormant or only intermittently active in Britain. It was—with one exception—a period in which she was free from any major war, with a consequent relative lack of interest in strategic strongholds: with her superior sea-power Britain reached her summit of power and influence, a delusive height, as we can now see, due to the weakness or distraction of potentially much stronger nations. Even more important, in view of the great part the commercial motive had played in the first empire, the pioneer industrial development of Britain had given her an economic primacy which needed no support from state action, protective or offensive, and in which, with nearly all the world eager for her goods, the acquisition of new lands merely meant, for a nation of shopkeepers, putting the cost of their annexation and administration upon the debit side of the ledger. Even in dangerous and backward areas British merchants, often at first and for long alone, were able to pick up what trade there was without any demand to their government for support or occupation. The philanthropists, as represented mainly by the missionaries, were ready and eager to adventure alone among the peoples most ready to welcome them in the Pacific and in Africa, and for a long time, as we shall see, they were prepared to wield, free from the control of government, the great influence their arrival as the first white men often gave them. As for emigration, even that was often initiated by private groups, though it generally entailed reluctant annexation in the end. But in tropical Africa white settlement was not yet even envisaged.

These are the reasons why Britain, when suddenly confronted in the sixties and seventies with the first revelations of the immense and masterless interior of Africa, made no motion to claim nor occupy it, even though her people became increasingly determined to try to stop the trade that was shown to be gnawing into the body of Africa like leprosy. If it is asked how this policy of restraint can be squared with the forward moves promoted by Disraeli, which, as we have seen, had carried Lugard out to Afghanistan and Burma, the answer is that Disraeli's interest had been very selective. Though it had certainly represented the beginning of a reaction against Gladstone's pacific mood, it had been directed mainly to eastern Europe and to the Indian empire and its border lands. In colonial policy, and certainly as regards tropical Africa, which had hardly claimed Disraeli's attention, the tide of imperialism had not yet turned in full flood. While it was still at the slack it was left to private groups, and even to individuals, to respond to the dangerous but romantic opportunities for exploration, evangelization and trade which middle Africa seemed to offer. From Britain there came one man after another to write his name across the central blank—Livingstone in the largest and noblest characters, and after him, Speke, Burton, Baker, Gordon, Stanley, Johnston, Kirk, Goldie, Rhodes and Lugard. Other names might be added but these, as men who either opened up the continent or moulded British action and policy, or did both, would be uncontested. Eight of these worked in Africa independently of the government while Lugard himself did so until 1898. In the later eighties it was through Chartered Companies that determined men found a means to act while governments, still in the state " of the old cat in the adage ", gave them an ambiguous authorization. This is a matter which will recur often in these pages.

We must, however, narrow our view down to the part of Africa into which Lugard was now entering.

The Portuguese had here been first in the field. They had occupied positions along the eastern, as upon the western, coast of Africa as early as the late fifteenth century and consolidated them during the sixteenth. But after their great burst of exploring and conquering energy, a weakness at the heart led to a paralysis of the too widely spread limbs and by the end of the seventeenth century Portugal had lost every station north of Mozambique to the reviving Arabs. She remained clinging to the southern stretch of this coast, as to the opposite western coast but, not only had she never linked the two, she had hardly penetrated any distance up the Zambezi into the interior. It was Livingstone who, striking up northwards from the furthest station held by the London Missionary Society in Bechuanaland, and having discovered Lake Ngami, found his way alone into the very middle of south-central Africa and then, turning first to the west coast and then right back again to the east, made the first crossing of the continent.[1] The Portuguese were considerably startled by this.

[1] D. Livingstone, *Missionary Travels and Researches in South Africa* (1857).

But worse was to come. It was upon this journey that Livingstone discovered the Arab slave-trade at work and told the world that the Portuguese were not only not attempting to stop it but that some of their officials were even involved in it. He therefore revived the policy of Buxton, who had come to the conclusion by 1840 that treaties and naval patrols along the coast could never by themselves stop the slave-trade.[1] Only the economic alternative of " legitimate trade " could do this, since the root cause of the slave-trade was economic and it would persist so long as the only saleable products of the country were ivory and men and, in the absence of any system of vehicular communications, the one was needed to transport the other.

But the horrifying loss of life—41 out of 193 white men—on the Niger expedition of 1841, on which Buxton had staked all his hopes, and which gained government backing, caused a set-back to this idea. Now Livingstone, after his telling appeal to public opinion, once more gained official support for the policy of opening up communications and the Zambezi expedition of 1858–63 was the result.[2] Its achievements were ambiguous. On the credit side Livingstone found the Shire river leading northwards out of the Zambezi, and he now added the lakes Shirwa and the vast Nyasa to his list of major discoveries. On the other hand the explorers proved, from all too intimate a contact, the difficulties of using the wide but intermittent and cataract-broken waters of the Zambezi for navigation. They also aroused the alarm of the Portuguese at being by-passed into the interior. They felt the cruelty of the physical conditions which killed two members of the party. One was Bishop Mackenzie who, answering Livingstone's call for Christian evangelists, had come out to found the Universities Mission to Central Africa; the other was Livingstone's beloved and long-suffering wife whom he buried under a tree on the banks of the river.

Another piece of knowledge gained was the embarrassments that must beset unofficial philanthropists in the midst of the bloody turmoil of slave-trading and native wars, with the hunted or the escaping turning to them for protection. Livingstone himself learned a further lesson. Although he was accompanied, among others, by his own

[1] T. F. Buxton, *The African Slave Trade and its Remedy* (1840).
[2] R. Coupland, *Kirk on the Zambesi* (1928); D. Livingstone, *Narrative of an Expedition to the Zambesi and its tributaries* (1865).

brother, by the sterling young Scottish doctor and botanist, John Kirk, and by the eager, humanitarian priest, Horace Waller[1] (the two latter to be fellow workers with Lugard), he realized that he was not the man to be a leader even of such a small band of carefully chosen associates. He preferred to walk alone along the perilous and fever-haunted bush-tracks of unknown Africa. Upon his next expedition, therefore, he did walk alone for nearly seven years, covering thousands of miles between 1866 and 1873, and discovering new rivers and lakes and new evidence of the rapidly extending slave-trade, and dying alone, except for his faithful African servants, in 1873.

This magnificent death, the almost incredible courage and loyalty of his servants in embalming his body and bringing it with his diary back to the coast, and his funeral in Westminster Abbey, with the publication by his friend Waller of his diary written almost to the day of his death[2], engraved still more deeply into the mind of Britain the old impression made by the anti-slavery movement. Nowhere was the impression deeper than in Livingstone's Scotland. Since the Universities Mission decided to retire to Zanzibar and to work out-wards from that headquarters, the Church of Scotland and the Free Church, within three years of Livingstone's death, sent out missions which followed in his footsteps to Lake Nyasa. The first, under one of the greatest of missionaries, Dr. Laws, started on the south-west corner of the still unexplored lake and called their settlement Livingstonia, while the other chose a position in the hills just to the south of the point where the river Shire flows out of the lake and named their station Blantyre.

It may be imagined how embarrassing to the Arab slavers was the sudden appearance of two settlements of white men in the very heart of their sphere of operations. The obvious response, it might have seemed, would have been to wipe these weak and pacific intruders out of existence. But the whole position was much too complicated for such a simple remedy even if the Arabs had wished it, and, to do them justice, they showed quite extraordinary restraint in dealing with Livingstone and such other white men as ventured for many years after his time into their preserves. The complication, for the Arabs,

---

[1] Waller, the Rev. Horace, 1833–96; 1861–2 accompanied Livingstone's Zambesi—Nyasa expedition; 1870 onwards member of Anti-Slavery Society Committee; held benefices in Essex (1870) and Northamptonshire (1874–95).

[2] H. Waller, *The Last Journals of David Livingstone* (1874).

was the strange situation which had developed round their acknowledged if distant ruler, the sultan of Zanzibar.

A few words must be given to this in order to round out our sketch
of Africa in the year of Lugard's arrival. The British were at first
interested in Zanzibar only indirectly because of the number of their
Indian subjects there, and also because of their connection with Muscat
on the Persian Gulf, which had supplied the dynasty which ruled the
Arabs of the islands and coastline of East Africa.[1] Trade, too, was
developing, though this was not yet very large. Britain's command of
the sea gave her potential control over the island headquarters of the
sultan's extensive but rather indeterminate and insubstantial " empire."
During the nineteenth century Britain built up a very strong position
at Zanzibar which rested largely upon the personal relations which
two able consuls, Hamerton and Rigby, established with the sultan
and also upon the honesty of Britain's policy in supporting the dynasty,
in refraining from any suggestion of annexation and in protecting the
sultan from all other dangers, whether from local conspirators or
from France. In 1862, following a British arbitration which finally
divided the Muscat and Zanzibar kingdoms, Britain induced France
to sign a treaty committing both nations to respect the independence
of Zanzibar.

But the sultans, for all their affection for the British consuls and
gratitude for British protection, had to endure one very damaging
demand from their powerful friends. This was their gentle but
inexorable pressure against the slave-trade which, with the con-
solidation of the sultans' power in Zanzibar and the increase in fire-
arms, was rapidly building up the prosperity and power of the state.
In 1845 Sultan Said was obliged to consent to the prohibition of the
trade outside his African dominions. And in 1866 Dr. John Kirk, at
Livingstone's suggestion, was appointed to Zanzibar where he shortly
became consul and, by establishing a great personal ascendancy over
the Zanzibar rulers, carried on through patient diplomacy the anti-
slavery cause he had inherited from his chief.

It was, indeed, a most astonishing thing that the nation which was
trying to destroy the main source of the power and revenue of the
sultans, and that for reasons quite incomprehensible to them, should
have been able to maintain the moral ascendancy over them which

[1] See Coupland I for a detailed history of the period.

was exercised and increased by Kirk. Gradually the control tightened. In 1871 a House of Commons Committee sat upon the East African slave-trade, and discovered that a patrol of some half-dozen British naval ships, trying to prevent smuggling along 4,000 miles of coast, only caught some 2,600 out of an estimate of nearly 40,000 slaves who were shipped overseas in the years 1867-9. Restriction of the trade had clearly failed and only abolition remained.[1] A treaty arranging for the prohibition of any trade in slaves by sea was obtained by Kirk from Sultan Barghash, but this time only under threat of a blockade. In 1873 the suppression of slavery itself in the main ports was obtained and in 1876 the complete prohibition of the trade by land was enacted.

This was the result for East Africa of the continuous pressure of the British anti-slavery sentiment, as rekindled by Livingstone and directed at the African end by Kirk. But while legal abolition was an all-important stage in the struggle it was not the end.[2] Sultan Barghash did his best to honour his promises but he was attempting to impose a prohibition which was against the interests and principles of all his subjects over a vast area, in most of which his authority was merely nominal. The southern region of the slave-trade was the hardest for him to control. Here the slavers, by the early eighties, had built up a very large trade. Kilwa, on the coast, was the collecting station for sale and export; the regions round Lake Nyasa were the hunting-grounds and some of the warlike tribes were the slavers' agents and raiders. As the missions established their positions in the heart of this area and as the nearer hunting-grounds got more exhausted, the Arabs pushed their operations further west. Since the missions were most active on the Great Lakes, upon which they had launched little steamers brought up in parts with incredible difficulty from the coast, the slavers began to use a more inconspicuous route between Lakes Tanganyika and Nyasa. From about 1884 onwards a great increase in the southern slave-trade was reported by missionaries and consuls in this area.

The years 1884-8 are of great importance in the history of tropical Africa. They mark the first energetic and deliberate attempt of European nations to take hold of the unappropriated space in the middle of the continent. Up to this time, though in such a large and dispersed movement no generalization can be without some exceptions, the

[1] Coupland II, pp. 164-5.
[2] Professor Coupland seems to have been rather too optimistic in summing up the results of Kirk's achievement in obtaining these treaties.

European powers had been standing as it were upon the edge of the huge primitive central area, watching the explorers as they traced ways into the interior and reported the discovery of great lakes and mountains; watching too, the missionaries who, at first in twos and threes, followed hard upon them to establish their widely-scattered and precarious posts about the interior. Among those standing round the central vacuum Britain had the best vantage points and the strongest claims to enter. She had by now taken up peripheral positions on the west coast, drawn first by the slave-trade and later by anti-slavery motives; in South Africa, attracted first by strategy and then by colonization; in the north-east, past which ran her main imperial route, as the guardian of a collapsing Egypt; while on the east coast, as we have seen, with the destruction of the slave-trade as her main purpose, she had an established influence in Zanzibar. Yet here as else-where—the acquisition of Lagos as an anti-slavery measure was almost the one exception in this period—Britain deliberately and repeatedly refused one temptation after another to take the land and power that were lying at her feet.

In 1884–5, however, it suddenly became clear that other powers would not be so restrained, but were going to push forward, shoulder-ing Britain out of the way, to take what they could. The acquisitive ambitions of Leopold of the Belgians began to appear through their disguise of an international scientific association. Portugal had suddenly awoken from her long colonial sleep and was trying to make good her neglected claims to the interior before other powers could jump them. France, from her old base in Senegal, was pushing along the Upper Niger in the west and establishing her power alongside Britain on the Somali coast in the east.

But these were, for the moment, small ripples in the African pool; it was Germany who made the big splash. Hitherto, though some able German travellers had been at work and German trade was growing in Zanzibar, Bismarck had resisted the first pressures, exercised largely from Hamburg, to take up the colonial question. But now, in 1884, partly, perhaps, for the European reason that he suddenly saw how useful the colonial question could be to distract France from brooding over 1870, and to embarrass Britain, he took it up. As decisive and ruthless overseas as in Europe, Germany, though a tyro in the colonial sphere, annexed most of her empire in some twelve months. In those regions where Britain already had a position, New Guinea, west Africa and south-west Africa, she suddenly took colonies. Gladstone's government, still adhering to the Little England tradition, readily stood aside. In the same year Carl Peters, an especially ruthless German traveller, slipped over into the sultan's most closely cherished regions just opposite Zanzibar and began to make treaties with chiefs who were persuaded to abjure the sultan's power. Other Germans were establishing their influence over Lamu and Witu, little Arab sultanates north of Mombasa. Bismarck then took the initiative with France of arranging an international African conference at Berlin, to which Britain, though the main power on the continent, was invited as a guest. This conference drew up regulations for the freedom of navigation and trade in the Niger and Congo basins; reaffirmed resolutions against the slave-trade, and laid down, in a clause which is very relevant to much of Lugard's work, that occupations of the coast of Africa must be notified to other powers and must be accompanied by the establishment of effective authority.[1] Immediately following the conference, Leopold of the Belgians proclaimed himself sovereign of the Congo, while Germany recognized Carl Peters' treaties, and on March 1st 1885 declared a protectorate over the sultan's regions which Peters purported to have acquired.

This sudden application of German methods to tropical Africa finally shattered Britain's illusion that she could continue freely to exercise her humanitarian and commercial interests there, with the native rulers gradually acquiring civilization, and without, as Lord Salisbury said in a revealing phrase, " the inconvenience of protectorates." [2] Especially did German action tear to pieces the elaborate web of protective diplomacy and influence which Kirk had been spinning round the sultan of Zanzibar and his dominions.

For a brief period some members of Gladstone's Cabinet, and especially the young, more forward minded Dilke and Chamberlain, aghast at the suddenness and ruthlessness of Germany's actions, were for standing up for the sultan's rights and warning Germany off this obvious sphere of British influence. They thought they might use

---

[1] *Protocols and General Acts of the West African Conference.* Africa No. 4 (1885), C.4361; given in Sir E. Hertslet, *The Map of Africa by Treaty* (3rd edition 1909), vol. ii, p. 468 ff. See also S. E. Crowe, *The Berlin West African Conference 1884-5* (1942) and A. J. P. Taylor, *Germany's First Bid for Colonies* (1938).

[2] Lady Gwendolin Cecil, *Life of Robert, Marquis of Salisbury* (1932), vol. iv, p. 225.

some private treaties which a young English explorer, Harry Johnston,[1] had been making round Mount Kilimanjaro, to ward off German claims. But Gladstone was unshakeable. He was, he said, terribly " puzzled and perplexed " to find out that " a group of the soberest men among us have concocted a scheme . . . . touching the mountain country behind Zanzibar with an unrememberable name." (There seems a prophetic ring about the use of such words as a prelude to abandoning the endangered ally.) Gladstone, still undisputed master of his Cabinet, put a prompt stop to this scheme and orders which almost broke Kirk's heart were sent out to him to reverse his policy and advise the sultan to recognize Germany's seizure of the very heart of his mainland empire.[2] Kirk was all but censured for trying to keep Britain's promises to the sultan and Gladstone declared in parliament " If Germany becomes a colonizing power, all I can say is ' God speed her '."[3] Germany did not, however, depend either upon God or upon British support. Five warships were sent to Zanzibar: they ran their guns out for action and gave the sultan four hours in which to accept the German annexation. Kirk told him he must accept the inevitable.

Before the German fleet reached Zanzibar, Gladstone had fallen from power, mainly because the long list of imperial surrenders had found an agonizing climax in the death of Gordon as a result, so it seemed to the public, of the government's weakness and muddle over the evacuation of the Sudan. The end of delusions about Britain's position in Africa was only part of a much wider disillusionment in which, as European nations built up their unity and their huge conscript armies, Britain suddenly found that her mid-nineteenth century primacy had been founded less upon her own absolute strength than upon the relative weakness of others. It should also be remembered that at this time Britain, partly as a negative result of her antagonism with France, and partly from a positive sense of cultural kinship with a " Nordic " Protestant power, was still inclined towards friendship with Germany. But in the diplomatic quadrille in which the main powers of Europe were engaged, nations advanced and retreated, set to partners and then reversed, or at least threatened to do so, as the

[1] Johnston, (later Sir) Harry Hamilton, G.C.M.G., K.C.B., 1858–1927; 1889 Consul-General to Portuguese East Africa; 1890–6 High Commissioner of Nyasaland Protectorate; 1897–9 Consul-General in Tunis; 1899–1901 Special Commissioner in Uganda.

[2] S. Gwynn and G. M. Tuckwell, *Life of Sir Charles Dilke* (1917), vol. ii, pp. 83–4, quoted in Coupland II, p. 392.

[3] Coupland II, p. 435.

shifting balance of power all over the world dictated. Britain had now to dread a sudden combination of powers against her. For the thing that might most readily unite those powers which had suddenly taken to colonial annexation was to find Britain barring their advance in every part of the world, and above all in Africa. This was the consideration which restrained Salisbury, as doctrine and economy restrained Gladstone. For caution was not the only motive for restraint or surrender. There were still many in Britain, not confined to the Liberal party, who not only hated war, but also the greed, the assertions, the imperial expansion, and the armament that led to war, and who believed that other powers had their right to a place in the tropical sun.

When, therefore, Lord Salisbury succeeded Gladstone as Prime Minister in June 1885, he showed no immediate disposition to reverse the Liberal policy in East Africa, which, as Foreign Secretary, he kept under his own office. In September he wrote on one of Kirk's dispatches, overriding his own Under-Secretary, " .... I do not quite see our interest in this Zanzibar quarrel. Keeping every other nation out on the bare chance that some day or other our traders will pluck up heart to go in is a poor policy." Kirk's bitter comment was that Salisbury could ignore the rights of 6,000 British Indian traders, with nine-tenths of the trade, because they had no representation in parliament.[1] In the first half of 1886 a Delimitation Commission of three representatives of Britain, Germany and France (Kitchener acting for Britain) toured the coast to discover the true extent of the sultan's authority. Even while it was on tour, German agents were hurrying about the mainland trying to upset the sultan's authority with the native chiefs and get more treaties. In the end, rather than quarrel with Germany, Lord Rosebery—for Gladstone had returned to office for a few months (February–July 1886)—ordered Kitchener to sign a shamefully untrue and unjust report, which recognized the sultan's rights only to the islands of Zanzibar, Pemba and Mafia; to the main ports and towns between the Rovuma river in the south and Mogadishu in the north, and to a narrow strip of coast.[2]

The sultan's wide claims having been shrunk to this, the next step for the two powers was to partition his empire by annexing the

[1] Coupland II, p. 433.
[2] For the whole story, based on F.O. papers, of Britain's acceptance of Bismarck's high-handed trickery, see Coupland II, chapter 19. See also Hertslet, *op. cit.* vol. iii, pp. 874–6 for the report of the Delimitation Commission.

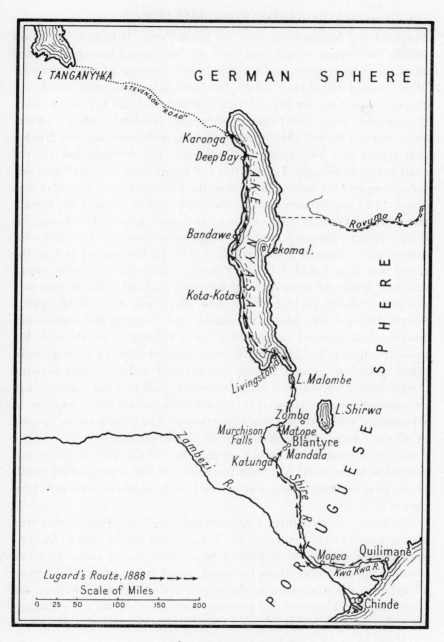

GERMAN SPHERE

L TANGANYIKA

STEVENSON "ROAD"

Karonga

Deep Bay

LAKE NYASA

Bandawe

Lekoma I.

Rovuma R.

Kota-Kota

Livingstonia

L. Malombe

Zomba

L. Shirwa

Murchison
Falls

Matope

Blantyre

Mandala

Katunga

Zambezi R.

Shire R.

P O R T U G U E S E   S P H E R E

Mopea

Quilimane

Kwa Kwa R.

Chinde

Lugard's Route, 1888 ➤ ➤ ➤
Scale of Miles

0   25   50   100   150   200

Lake Nyasa Region

91

mainland and leasing from him the coastal strip. If Britain had stood out the only result would have been that she would have been ousted from the entire region, and the whole of it, instead of the larger part of it, would have been taken by Germany. The sultan had still enough respect left for his old friend Britain to desire her to take over the northern part. The British government resolutely refused annexation, but in October 1886 it came to terms with Germany and divided East Africa into two spheres of influence, the dividing line on the coast being at Wanga. The sultan's full rights over a coastal strip 600 miles long and 10 miles wide and to the four main islands was recognized.[1] The unfortunate Sultan Barghash was persuaded by Britain not to resist German annexation of the main part of his dominions lying opposite Zanzibar, and the Germans prepared to take this over immediately through a German East African Company. Before the treaty was signed Kirk had left Zanzibar, saddened by recent events that had destroyed most of his policy and glad only that Britain was not to be wholly excluded from East Africa but had still an opportunity, if she cared to take it, to continue the civilizing and anti-slavery aims he had pursued so patiently for seventeen years. It may be, however, that in his last two or three years, following a long-established policy in which British interest and influence had become closely bound up with the sultan's position, and in a last vain attempt to warn off foreign powers, he tried to give an excessive support to a potentate under whose flag the tribes of East Africa were, in spite of all the treaties, being destroyed by the slave-trade.[2]

We must return later to take up the story of this British sphere and turn back to see what had been happening in the region to the south of the new German sphere just before Lugard made his obscure entry into it.

We have seen that three Christian missions from Britain answered Livingstone's call by entering the Lake Nyasa region: the U.M.C.A. which, after the death of Bishop Mackenzie, had decided to work towards the east shore from the coast; the Church of Scotland from Blantyre in the mountains to the south; and the Free Church on the western shore. Their isolated positions were soon shown to be dangerous. The missions created a great problem for themselves throughout

[1] Hertslet, *op. cit.* vol. iii, pp. 882–6.
[2] See H. Waller, 'The two ends of the slave-stick', *The Contemporary Review*, vol. LV, April 1889, pp. 528–38; also Oliver, *The Missionary Factor*, pp. 84–5, 102.

eastern Africa because they felt it to be their duty to penetrate immediately far into the interior since the bulk of the population was to be found there on the higher and more fertile land, and because it was here that the slavers were naturally finding their most productive areas. The handful of Scots who went up in 1875–6 to Nyasa found themselves jostled and threatened not only by the tribal wars going on around them, which were stimulated by the slave-trade for which tribal war was a necessity, but also by the northward movement of one of the many offshoots of the Zulu tribe, the Ngoni, who were raiding their weaker neighbours.

Their other danger was of course from the Arab and Swahili slave-traders. It has been remarked that, partly because of Kirk's influence upon the sultan, these had shown themselves surprisingly tolerant towards white intruders. But from about 1884 onwards their attitude changed.[1] Many reasons may account for this. It was partly due to the events that have been described. All round the slavers' preserve European nations were beginning to make their pressures felt. From the north Egypt, represented by Gordon and his assistants, had been reaching down in the middle seventies towards Lake Victoria by land and down the east African coast by sea and this disturbing attempt had been followed by the news, especially exciting to the Arab slave-traders, of the Mahdist rising and the death of Gordon. An increasing number of travellers were coming in from the coast, and among them some of the Germans, and above all, Carl Peters, showed a very aggressive spirit and made no secret of their acquisitive aims. The sultan, his authority eroded from all sides, was beginning to lose both the power and the will to control his widely dispersed Arab subjects; and as these thrust further into the interior to open up new slaving grounds, they tended to escape what was left of his far-flung sovereignty. There was a further cause. The first Arab traders had been men who were based upon Zanzibar and who, after making several journeys, would return there or to other coastal towns.[2] But they had been accompanied by a probably increasing number of half-breed Arabs merging into the Swahili, the mixed race of the coast. These men were likely to be more attracted by the idea of carving out permanent sovereignties in the interior, all the more if they thought

[1] See Oliver, *op. cit.* pp. 98–103 for a discussion of this.
[2] Johnston to Salisbury, 17 March 1890, F.O. 84/2051; quoted by Oliver, *op. cit.* p. 98.

that other intruders were likely to interfere with this migrant trading. These men were less accessible to the sultan's authority. This new phenomenon was especially marked west of Lake Tanganyika and in the Nyasa area, partly because Zanzibar was no longer a safe port for the export of slaves while Portuguese authority connived at the trade.

The Portuguese, too, were becoming increasingly aware that peoples of other nations were working into their hinterland. Both Britain and Germany were now threatening to push right up from the south into the unappropriated middle region discovered by Livingstone and so cut any possibility of the Portuguese linking together their Angola and Mozambique coasts. And now, just north of the Zambezi, were these British missionaries building up settlements along the shores of Lake Nyasa.

Missionaries were bad enough but they had now been joined by traders. The teaching of Buxton and Livingstone about the need for legitimate trade had been given point and urgency by the great practical difficulties of the missionaries in supporting themselves and entering into effective economic relations with the tribes at vast distances inland. It must be remembered that in the heart of savagery white men could not wander about preaching and living in native huts. They were forced, if they were to live and work effectively in tropical Africa, to make clearings in the bush; to build houses, churches, schools and stores; to buy and to grow food; to hire labour and to bring up from the distant coast all the equipment they needed for this and the cloth and other trade goods which were the bulky currency of the interior. All this was made the more difficult by the lack of roads or fully navigable rivers. In many places there was no other form of transport except the expensive and inefficient use of native porters carrying loads on their heads along winding bush tracks. The Nyasa missions could make partial use of water transport, but the course of the rivers was broken by cataracts and their flow was seasonal. Nor did they want to spend the energies of their little bands, overwhelmed as they were by new and difficult tasks, and often incapacitated by sickness, upon these tasks of trade and transport. It was this which led the philanthropic Scottish businessmen who supported the missions to try to unite in practical form Livingstone's " Commerce and Christianity."

They therefore set up an African Lakes Company to handle all the economic tasks needed to serve the missions and to introduce the idea of civilized methods of trade to the Africans. The Company was staffed by men chosen for their good character and education and who shared the missionary call: that they must be young men of courage with a sense of adventure went without saying. The first two managers were John and Fred Moir, the two well-educated sons of a respected Edinburgh doctor. The Company was founded in 1878, with the modest capital of £20,000, mainly by James Stevenson, a Glasgow merchant who was passionately interested in African exploration and mission work. He paid £4,000 to construct a road for the missionaries and the Company. This reached for forty-six miles from the north end of Lake Nyasa, crossing difficult country to a point from which there was easier access to the southern tip of Lake Tanganyika, upon which the London Missionary Society had started work.

One of the main duties of the Company was to attend to the difficult line of communications between the lake and the sea. The Portuguese, who held the coast, were perfectly placed for obstruction. They soon used their power, especially as regards the import of guns and ammunition which were needed for self-defence and also for shooting elephants for ivory, which soon proved the main product for trade. In summarizing this very mixed business of the carving up of tropical Africa into national slices it is presumptuous to throw out in passing quick moral judgments upon every act, especially those of foreign and competing nations. It was quite natural, according to the international ethics of the day, for Portugal to resent intruders building up a position in the rear of her own and for her to make the most, in her weakness, of her chief strength, the control of their communications with the outside world. The arms trade, moreover, was one which for practical as well as moral reasons she could claim to restrict. But with the growth of hostility by the well-armed slave-traders and their native allies, so desperate was the need of the Lakes Company for arms, that the Portuguese, by their control of this traffic, wielded powers of life and death over them. This was all the more true because, as the consuls which Britain had placed in Mozambique, Quilimane and at Blantyre reported, the Portuguese freely sold and even gave arms and ammunition to the Arabs for their own use and to exchange for slaves.

Lake Nyasa 1887-1889

The real crisis began on 4th November 1887, when Arab slavers suddenly attacked the little advanced post the Company had built at Karonga at the north-west corner of the lake. This was a very important place for communications both to the lake and past it, and it was the starting-point of the Stevenson road. It was also in a very fertile area, populated by the numerous, peaceable Nkonde tribe, living dispersed in their excellent villages. A half-breed Arab slave-trader, Mlozi, descried in this spot the focal point for a small principality, and a slave-trade centre. He was frustrated by the presence at Karonga of the Company post, at once a rival in the ivory trade and also a refuge to which threatened chiefs and hunted slaves could turn for protection. It was at this time under the command of a very brave agent of the Company, Monteith-Fotheringham. Mlozi first built three villages with strong stockaded forts a few miles from Karonga and on each side of the Stevenson road.

What happened next is worth telling, for it is one illustration of events which must have been going on all over east-central Africa in their unrecorded thousands. As the Nkonde chiefs and people showed a spirit of resistance to Mlozi's plans, he killed two chiefs and attacked the tribal villages one by one. Monteith-Fotheringham vainly tried to keep the peace. The Arabs then, using his name, induced the natives, who had moved away to the north, to come to Karonga for a conference. They came and camped along the edge of the lake. The Arabs were waiting in ambush and set fire to the masses of tall dry reeds that fringed the lake. The tribesmen, armed only with spears, rushed out in confusion to be mowed down by Arab marksmen who, with Mlozi, were sitting in a number of tall trees. The terrified Africans, men, women and children, rushed to and fro, having to choose between falling to the Arab guns, being burned to death in the flaming reeds or trying to plunge beyond them into the crocodile-infested shallows.[1]

Monteith-Fotheringham and his assistant, Nicoll, who were alone at Karonga, were now themselves threatened by Mlozi. News of the situation, however, went down the lake, and a few weeks later, on 4th November 1887, the little mission steamer, *Ilala*, arrived and, with it, Consul O'Neill from Mozambique who happened to be

[1] In Lugard I, opposite p. 54, there is a drawing which gives a rather crude reconstruction of the scene.

96

touring up-country. With him was a visiting hunter, Mr. Alfred Sharpe[1] and a few other white men. The consul, whose exploit has already been mentioned, correctly waited for the Arabs to attack, which they did with 500 gunmen and hosts of spearmen. For several days on end the Arabs pushed the attack home with vigour and only the arrival of very large numbers of Nkonde from the north drove off the Arabs. The British party attempted to counter-attack the Arab stronghold but failed, and John Moir was badly wounded.

This was the news which, arriving, of course, many weeks later, appeared in full and moving detail in the English and, even more important, in the Scottish papers early in 1888. It created a great stir in the numerous religious and philanthropic circles, especially those connected with the three missionary societies, and with the African Lakes Company. Meetings were held; questions were asked in parliament; representations were made to ministers. For the event was a further disillusionment, following upon that supplied by the German actions, to the hopes of a gradual and peaceful spread of civilization in East Africa without annexation. The dilemma was urgent and painful. Here were these little groups of brave men, some of them with their wives, who had gone into these remote and exposed places with the support and prayers of their fellow-countrymen to fight slavery with the gospel and fair trade. And now, not only was the slave-trade increasing—the *Anti-Slavery Reporter* for 1888 and 1889 was full of evidence about this from many sources and so were the reports of the consuls—but the very lives of the white pioneers seemed to be in danger. What was to be done?

We have already discussed the reasons why what seems to us, looking back, the obvious course of annexing this masterless country to Britain simply did not arise. The supporters of the missions themselves hardly knew what to do or what course to press upon the government. At a great meeting called in London by the several churches concerned, even the enthusiasts, on the advice of supporters who were also members of parliament, deleted from their original resolution a proposal to declare Nyasaland " a sphere of British influence " and merely asked that the government should secure free and favourable transit for British

1 Sharpe, (later Sir) Alfred, K.C.M.G., C.B., 1853–1935; 1891 Vice-Consul in Nyasaland; 1894–5 and 1896–7 acting Commissioner and Consul-General for British Central Africa; 1897 Commissioner and Commander-in-Chief for British Central Africa Protectorate; 1907–10 Governor of Nyasaland.

goods, and check the increasing slave-trade.[1] In parliament the answers of ministers showed a studied detachment: they had, they said, no treaty enabling them to put pressure upon Portugal; it was an internal Portuguese question and they could do nothing. They were not in a position to protect British property so far inland, nor were they prepared to grant administrative powers to the Lakes Company.[2] They were not even ready to make their consul mobile by providing him with a steamer: they were not impressed by evidence about the increase of the slave-trade nor the restlessness and hostility of the tribes corrupted by the slavers. Hawes, consul at Blantyre, was ordered to keep clear of " unnecessary complications " with natives[3] and Salisbury warned him to use only " moral influence " against the slave-traders as no material support would be sent.[4] The Foreign Office under Lord Salisbury damped down the energetic Consul O'Neill at Mozambique. It was at this moment of suspended animation, with Britain's imperial tide showing no clear sign of turning after the long ebb of the nineteenth century, and the British missionary and trading enterprise on Lake Nyasa threatened with extinction, that Lugard started up the Kwakwa river.

[1] *Anti-Slavery Reporter*, series IV, vol. viii, March and April 1888, p. 37.
[2] *Parliamentary Debates*, 12 May 1887, series III, vol. 314, col. 1666; 28 February 1888, III. 322. 1648-9.
[3] *Correspondence Relative to the Slave Trade, 1887*. Slave Trade No. 1 (1888), C.5428, p. 10.
[4] *Ibid.* p. 11.

CHAPTER VI

INITIATION INTO AFRICA

1888 : Aet. 30

LUGARD LEFT Quilimane on April 7th and arrived at Blantyre on May 16th. During this period and the few succeeding weeks he received his first impressions of equatorial Africa. He had met frontier campaigning in the East, but he had been, not a lone adventurer but an agent, however humble of a Britain militant, holding or advancing her position with the whole weight of her strength and policy behind the military force in which he was serving. He had also met wild and unhealthy conditions but nothing so primitive and formless, so unintelligible, as the region which was his present destination.

The first lesson he now learned about Africa was the difficulty of entering it. The delta of the great Zambezi was some sixty miles south of Quilimane but most of its wide mouths were barred to steamers and the narrower but navigable Chinde mouth was not discovered until about a year later. This was an important fact, as up to 1889 it meant that the British must reach Nyasa through Portuguese territory, via Quilimane and from there up the Kwakwa river which came down from near the Zambezi. Unfortunately the Kwakwa was so shallow that steamers could not ascend it and travellers into the interior had to use the long native canoes with a team of boatmen alternately punting and paddling. Five days of this primitive transport, with nights spent on the banks, brought the traveller to Mopea which, except at the flood-season when the two rivers mingled their waters, was separated by some three miles of Portuguese territory from the Zambezi. All the traveller's goods had to be carried across this and put upon other canoes or upon the little steamer which the Lakes Company had managed to transport in parts and launch upon this stretch of the Zambezi. This steamer went up the Zambezi, turned half right and northwards up the Shire river until it came to Katunga, the place where the Shire broke into a long series of cataracts. The traveller had, therefore, to leave the river and walk with his loads thirty steep miles up into the hills to Blantyre. From here he must descend another thirty-five miles to Matope on the Shire, above the cataracts, where he could get the little mission steamer *Ilala* and so sail up into the lake. Yet, slow and difficult though all this sounds, these several waters gave an easier access to the interior than was to be found in most parts of equatorial Africa.

As Lugard followed this route he was overwhelmed with the strangeness and beauty through which he passed. The Kwakwa river ran through high wooded banks, and he watched the trees as his native crew propelled the boat laboriously upstream. He saw " great-limbed acacias with feathery foliage and sweet-scented blossoms, large fig trees festooned with giant creepers." River and forest were alive with butterflies and with birds—he saw kingfishers, highly coloured reed-sparrows, bitterns, storks, and cormorants, while that magnificent bird the great black, white-headed fish-eagle watching, high on a dead branch, would utter his weird cry which had so impressed Livingstone on his last journey and which Lugard soon felt to be even more expressive of Africa than the midnight roar of the lion.

Later the banks grew lower; the forest thinned and the junction of the Shire and the wide Zambezi was a great waste of waters. As he went on up the Shire the river fringed out into marshes filled with elephants and other game which tunnelled their way through grass eight foot or more high.

To the European one of the most troubling things about Africa is the mingling in nature of beauty and malice. The pioneers, of course, felt this malice to the full. Lugard on his way up had to cower from the burning sun in a little shelter made of sticks and grass. By day he was attacked by the giant hippo fly which, as the writer well knows, bites through the clothes and stabs the skin like a skewer, setting the blood flowing. At night the mosquitoes came out in their millions like a thick mist and Lugard either had to swelter with his candle inside a net drawn round his little shelter in the boat, or else on the bank must almost blind himself with fires of green wood in the attempt to ward them off. The river had other injuries to inflict. At first there was noisome mud or mangrove swamps; then islands of matted growth would come swirling down the current; there were bull hippopotami which might charge the boat; in the water were hosts of crocodiles ready to seize a man in their jaws and drag him below the surface; on the banks were poisonous snakes and scorpions, and hyenas whose habit was to slink up to a sleeping man and bite half his face off. And to the traveller sleeping in the open, even if his fire is well-tended, the roar or the deep grunt of a lion always conveys a disturbing message of strength and menace, even though reason argues that he is unlikely to be the aggressor.

But worst of all the many dangers and discomforts was malarial fever. For the first European intruders, this, and not the African, nor the wild animal, was the killer. It has been estimated that of some three hundred missionaries who penetrated east and central Africa before 1884 only six were killed by Africans and for each of these deaths there was some clear explanation, if not justification, from the African point of view.[1] But every mission already had its graveyard for the men and women dead in their prime from fever. Lugard was soon a victim to the prostration that was so especially dangerous for Europeans travelling singly, who needed all their powers to master their dangers, to acquire food—always a difficult problem—and to keep their native attendants in ordered progress. He treated it in the resolute way he attacked any enemy: piling on at once every blanket and garment he could find and not putting out so much as a hand while he induced a terrific sweat which, however weak it left him, washed out the fever, so he believed, in the quickest time. These were a few of the dangers and discomforts which met Lugard and all other travellers of his day. It evokes the question as to what charm the continent could hold to draw men back to it and keep them there. Was it indeed any quality inherent in Africa and not rather the very challenge of its dangers and the unique freedom of opportunity it gave for the expression of their own personalities, whether they were fixed upon power or service?

So much for the physical Africa, as it struck upon Lugard's senses on this first journey. What of human Africa upon his introduction to it? His first study was of his eight naked black boatmen to whose care, though he was unable to speak with them, he had been handed over by the Lakes Company. He observed their physique, their skill and energy in finding their way up the varying bed of the river; the

[1] Oliver, *The Missionary Factor*, pp. 115–16.

ceaseless song with which they kept their rhythm and enlivened their work. He appreciated their good humour and the automatic communism with which they shared everything he gave them, even the chicken bones which they crunched up with their teeth. Round the Zambezi and the lower Shire he saw all the signs of oppression, of the sale of arms and of spirits and, of course, of slavery. If Lugard wanted to learn more about the natives, there were many quite ready to give him advice; some of it that of rough men who had found quick ways of making natives carry out their incomprehensible demands, and of establishing a relationship of fear where respect and understanding were too difficult to create. Lugard's first teacher was a wandering South African gold prospector. " On the first signs of insolence " he told Lugard " or even of familiarity, kick them under the jaw (when sitting) or in the stomach. In worse cases shoot, and shoot straight, *at once*." Lugard was not impressed. " . . . . more pernicious advice than his given to an intending traveller . . . I cannot conceive."[1] Yet Lugard then, and always, believed in strict discipline, for himself and for all others, according to their work and status. These were the principles of his age and they were intensified for him in the training he had received at home, at school and in the army. As one result of this, on his journey inland he had to nurse a finger which he had broken in striking an Indian trader who had been grossly insulting to the overworked British captain of the ship on which he sailed to Quilimane. When the captain said that he could not face the complications of a row in a Portuguese town, Lugard asked the Indian if he was prepared to speak to *him* in that way. He was, with results that were unfortunate to his chastiser as well as to himself.

Lugard met some Portuguese who impressed him by their good manners but he also heard much of the terrible cruelties of the Portuguese half-castes who engaged in slave-trading, or had carved out estates upon which they fleeced the wretched inhabitants. He found a surprising number of European informants as he went on up the Zambezi, as many foreigners had settled under Portuguese administration. There was an Englishman growing opium. There was also a young Dutchman who had a *prazo* (estate) which he claimed was twice as large as the Netherlands. For this he paid £2,000 a year rent to the government, while he aimed at collecting double that from

[1] Lugard I, p. 20.

the wretched inhabitants whom he hunted into marsh and forest in pursuit of his tax. He also met two charming and high-spirited Polish exiles and travelled up the Shire river towards Nyasa with one of them as his host. Everyone was kind to him but everyone warned him that he was upon a very desperate venture.

His main enquiry was about slavery and upon this his new friends were very ready to educate him. He had already had two experiences of his own. On the *Baghdad,* coming down towards Mozambique, a Portuguese soldier brought a long string of men tied together whom he called " prisoners ". The captain insisted upon their being untied while on board, as, if a British man-of-war found them, the ship would be treated as a slaver. " Thus," Lugard remarked, " our British ships actually become the medium of carrying slaves for the Portuguese." In his diary, his practical administrative mind beginning to bite upon this great problem, he went on to write his first serious words about it. He recognized, however, the justice of the view he picked up along the coast that to free slaves at the ports or at sea was of little use to them as they could never get back to their homes and their disposal at the coast was a most difficult problem. " We must go to the root of the evil and crush the traders." While the hampering of the trade at the coast was not wholly wasted, " the *best* work will be the operations inland, *where they are captured.*"[1] A little later, on the Kwakwa, he met an Indian employee of the Portuguese government, with whom Lugard could talk in Hindustani. He was bringing down a barge full of Africans whom he confessed were slaves. The Portuguese, indeed, sometimes admitted British accusations. Their Governor-General confessed his countrymen's participation in the trade that " is a disgrace and it discredits us in the eyes of foreigners, chiefly English." He did, it seems, his ineffective best to reduce it.[2]

There was one important mistake that Lugard did not make. While he hated the Arab slave-trade and meant to fight it with all his strength, he did not assume an attitude of superior racial or national morality towards the Arabs. It is well, on reading of their atrocities, to remember as he did that less than a century before this date Englishmen, who professed a creed enjoining the highest degree of love and service to humanity, were perpetrating similar horrors in the heart of Africa,

[1] Lugard I, p. 17.
[2] O'Neill to Salisbury, 30 May 1888, F.O. 84/1901.

mostly by proxy but often in the direct, cold-blooded ill-treatment and degradation of their slaves on the ships and in the West Indies. Lugard believed that " our horror-stricken outcries in Europe against the unspeakable atrocities of the ' Arab ' slave-raider ill become us when we look back at the history of the past, and recall the fact that for two and a half centuries we ourselves stained our hands with this traffic, and pocketed the gold which was the price of human blood. We have thus a duty of expiation to perform towards the African." [1]

It should also be remarked here that although we must use the current language of the time and refer to the slavers as the Arabs, a decreasing number of these were pure " white " Arabs from Muscat or Zanzibar and many were half-breeds or even dark Swahili who, from their creed, clothes, arms and profession as slave-traders, were classified as Arabs.

But now, up the Zambezi, Lugard, like many others who have gone to Africa with moral principles and purposes learned at home, had to face the withering realism of the " man on the spot." He was told that the facts about slavery were very different from what was believed in Britain; that the native chiefs themselves were in the business and did not want it stopped; that slaves were not badly treated once they reached their destination and so on. But Lugard was not so easily swayed, not even when he was faced by that familiar type, a Mr. Henderson, " who has been here for ten years and knows everything about everything." Nor did he lack moral courage. " I urged that killing all the men and the driving off women and children *could* not be tolerated by Englishmen." Even if some bunkum were talked in England and much money wasted " yet every bit of well-directed effort tells and a good man on the spot is worth more than a dozen committees at home." To his brother, closest confidant, he gave several more of his reasons for wanting to fight the Arab slavers. " I can think of no juster cause in which a soldier can draw his sword. My chief idea in coming out here was to do my little to aid in stopping the Slave Trade and *this* would be a blow at its very roots."

The mixed Zambezi planters—at one party they sang songs in ten languages—not only tried to undermine his faith in the anti-slavery cause but in the Company in whose employment he was to pursue it. On all hands he heard criticisms of the Company. Its meanness, it

[1] Lugard I, p. 27.

was said, came near to swindling; there was much criticism of the Moir
. brothers who managed it and by the time Lugard left the Shire for
Blantyre he was half-determined to try to escape from his engagement
to them. For this reason he refused to go on in their steamer and went
by canoe with his Polish friends.

This part of his journey up the Shire had plenty of incident. He shot
his first antelope. He plunged into the thick grass, well above his head,
in pursuit of four angry lions disturbed over their kill, in the hope
that this would be the end. But, alone in the blinding grass, the instinct
for self-preservation struggled with his resolve; so did the practical
consideration that the lions might merely crunch up an arm or leg
and leave him incapacitated for life. After this he had a very heavy
and enfeebling attack of malaria. He met the Makololo men Livingstone had brought up from the south and who had become a ruling
caste, and heard them speak of their old chief with great animation
and affection. He saw his first drumming, jingling and rather improper
African dance. Then, at last, the monotony of the marshlands ended;
the banks rose again carrying noble trees. Presently, as terrace upon
terrace of the wooded Shire hills came into view standing up against
the brilliant sky, with even higher mountains in the distance, the words
of the hundred and fourth psalm—much of it so gloriously appropriate
to Africa—flashed into his mind with some slight emendations of his
own. " Oh Lord, how *beautiful* are all Thy works—in wisdom had
Thou made them all—the earth is *full* of Thy goodness."

The magnificent sunrise and sunset over the wide waters of the
Zambezi and the Shire were always to be times of sharp sadness for
Lugard. It was all part of the price he had to pay for those two wonderful years at Lucknow. There every faculty that could appreciate beauty
had grown into new life because it could be shared, so that always
afterwards that side of his nature must be fused with loneliness and
sorrow. These were also times of prayer, but prayer of a despairing
kind, as day by day his faith in God died away into a disbelief which
was in conflict with his early training and his religious nature. It was
thus, still in a pathological mental state, that Lugard reached the scene
of his first African adventure.

CHAPTER VII

THE FIGHT WITH THE ARABS

1888 : Aet. 30

ON MAY 9th Lugard's boat arrived at Katunga and he climbed the steep track to Blantyre, up gradients which the local Scottish highlanders found trifles. He slept one night under a tree, and arrived the next day. An unexpected sight met him. In this wilderness, amongst the uncontrolled excesses of tropical nature, river, swamp, jungle and mountain, tenanted by warring tribes, he came upon something like a little piece of England, or rather of Scotland. There was a neat rectangle of houses, built of sun-dried brick. They stood round a pretty garden laid out with irrigation channels. On one side stood the manse and near it a magnificent brick church, built with its west front, towers, lancet windows and pillared nave, on the lines of a miniature cathedral. It had been designed by the Rev. David Clement Scott, the head of the Church of Scotland mission, and built by local labour from local materials. Crowds of neatly dressed schoolchildren could be seen in the quadrangle, while in Mr. Scott's house Mrs. Scott dispensed tea from a silver tea-set over a snow-white table-cloth. Across a river, a mile away, was Mandala, the headquarters of the African Lakes Company, where the Moir brothers had their house and offices.

Lugard found that he was eagerly awaited by the little community, and John Moir at once pressed him to accept the command of the expedition which was at that moment being planned. But before he could do this Lugard had to assess the whole position, geographical, human and military. He found it both complex and discouraging. A brief reference was given in the last chapter to the events on Lake Nyasa, but in order to follow Lugard's first African adventure we must now look more closely at the situation he found.

First, the geography. Lake Nyasa, with the Shire river, is a section of eastern Africa's great Rift Valley. It is almost surrounded by mountains, some of them rising to over 10,000 feet. The lake, the third largest in Africa, is 360 miles long and from 20 to 50 miles wide, with very deep, clear water. But this is often windswept and turbulent, and there are few natural harbours. This superb natural scene, even before the Arabs reached it, was no black arcadia for the several tribes round the lake did not live in amity. Among the most dominant and warlike were the Ngoni, relatively recent arrivals of Zulu origin, who, with their aggressive regimental system, had driven the weaker Tonga from the high grassy plateau west of the lake to live in fear, strung out along its shores, which here are less precipitous than elsewhere. It was the habit of the Ngoni war-parties to go out with their great shields, stabbing spears, and fierce crested head-dresses and steal before dawn into a sleeping village, each brave taking his stand at the door of a hut. Then, with their dreaded war-cries, they would awaken the people, call the sleepers to come out of each hut, and as they crawled through the narrow entrance, stab every man and seize every woman and child, to enslave them for their own use or to sell them to the Arabs.

West and north of the Tonga was another warrior tribe, that of the Bemba. Round the north end of the lake lived earlier settled and more peaceful people, the Nkonde, of whose sufferings something has already been said. In the south round Blantyre another strong tribe, the Yao, had moved in to raid the weaker groups not many years before this date, and there they had met the raiding Ngoni who penetrated to the area round the mission-station. About the mid-nineteenth century, before the Yao had appeared, the Arab and Swahili slavers had arrived in force to exploit existing conflicts, to make the strong even stronger with firearms and to start the systematic export of the weak, broken by their raids, to Kilwa and other ports on the coast. Arabs on Lake Tanganyika, and in the Senga country west of the Ngoni, collected the slaves and ivory sent from still further west and passed them along north and south of the lake. One ferry service passed right across the middle from Kota-Kota, where a line of Swahili slave-traders had made themselves into chiefs; another crossed at Deep Bay. One such slaving chief, Mponda, had his headquarters at the south where the Shire left the lake, and actually commanded its exit with his guns. And now this newcomer, Mlozi (" the sorcerer ") was calling himself " Sultan of Nkonde," and trying to build up a little empire of his own at the northern end of the lake, crush the Lakes Company, who threatened his trade, and also command the Stevenson road, which led not only to the missions on Lake Tanganyika but also to the new slaving grounds in the west. Like a great spider, Mlozi was gradually sucking the life out of the peaceful and prosperous Nkonde people amongst whom he had settled.

Into the middle of this bloody turmoil the missions had come and made their settlements. The Africans, astonished and fascinated by the many wonderful things they did and the marvellous objects they possessed, were inclined to tolerate and respect them, and even to be jealous of the tribes amongst which they settled. When Dr. Laws moved up from the unhealthy south of the lake to Bandawe, more than half the way up on the western side, and settled amongst the beaten Tonga, the fierce Ngoni threatened to raid them. Dr. Laws walked almost alone up the hills to the local headquarters of this dreaded tribe and so impressed its chief by his courage and his bearing that he swore his people should never injure the white men or the people living immediately around them, and even asked for a school. The slave-trading chief, Mponda, himself came to some sort of terms with them. It almost seemed as though, given time and patience, these few Christians would conquer the Nyasa region by moral influence.[1]

Mlozi's attack on Karonga and the fierce fighting that had followed it had therefore created a new situation. Two attempts to destroy his stronghold in counter-attacks had been made and, just before Lugard arrived, Fred Moir had led another attack and had been so badly wounded that he had been sent back to Scotland where, however, he carried on the struggle by different means. A promise had been given to the Company men left at the north end that another force would be sent, and a number of men who had hired themselves for this distant and desperate service had just arrived.

Lugard soon found, however, that the situation was not so simple as it seemed. There were, of course, personal difficulties, since the kind of behaviour that wrecks a village club can flourish equally vigorously on a dangerous frontier. The Moirs, a remarkable pair in many ways

---

[1] The story of the Livingstonia mission under its great founder is one not only of heroism but of amazing practical achievement. It is fully told in W. P. Livingstone, *Laws of Livingstonia* (1921), and not so well, partly because of his modesty, by Robert Laws himself in *Reminiscences of Livingstonia* (1934); see also Oliver, *The Missionary Factor*, Hanna, *The Beginnings of Nyasaland* and F. Moir, *After Livingstone* (1923).

and especially in courage and self-sacrifice, were yet too impulsive to be effective in co-operation. John Moir was a man who, according to Lugard, " lacked the sense of personal fear and was unable to realize the existence of danger." Hardy and unselfish, he yet caused Lugard and all the little band the utmost embarrassment by his impulsiveness and unreliability, especially with regard to his promises, a very serious trait in one who had the control of the boats and stores. Alfred Sharpe, whom Lugard judged the most reliable man and marksman of the party, had refused to serve under Fred Moir. The two consuls, O'Neill of Mozambique, and Hawes, whose post was at the lake, had both fought at Karonga, but they disagreed with each other about policy, Hawes being unwilling to see O'Neill come inland again and fight. Though neither was now present at Blantyre—Hawes being on leave and O'Neill tied impatiently to Mozambique—their disagreement affected the issue since the acting-consul on the lake, John Buchanan, an ex-artisan of the mission who had become a settler, could hardly take a line in opposition to his absent chief, Hawes. He was, moreover, deeply offended because he had only just been told about the proposed expedition.

The divisions were due to more than the local human factor. They reflected the peculiar and uncertain position in which this handful of men were placed as they sat in conference. Everything was uncertain— their status; their military chances; the policy and the attitude of their country. They had gone outside the civilized world to a place where there was no law and no government. They were not even in that diplomatic cloudland, a " sphere of influence ". The consuls were themselves in an ambiguous position, since O'Neill was accredited to a Portuguese colonial government which connived at the slave-trade, and Hawes to the chiefs round the lake. There was little duty they could perform, except to report dangers and disasters, and the ever-growing slave-trade. Hawes and O'Neill were both brave men, and if they differed it was because Hawes was more determined to respect his masters' negative orders, and himself judged that neither the numbers nor the arms nor the political prospects justified another expedition. He therefore advocated that policy in relation to the enemy which is now called co-existence. O'Neill, on the other hand, a more ardent nature, was willing to take a gamble and to use Lugard for his stake when that soldier happened along. We have seen that, just before Lugard came, O'Neill had sent a dispatch to the Foreign Office imploring permission for an expedition against the Arabs, with a dozen urgent reasons, an appeal which had left that department quite unmoved.[1] And now Hawes had gone on leave and left behind instructions forbidding Buchanan to sanction any offensive.

Hawes had good reason. The root ambiguity from which all others sprang was in the mind of Salisbury, and that in turn reflected the ambiguity of the international situation. When the important meeting of philanthropists, described earlier, sent a deputation to Lord Salisbury on April 27th, he replied that, though the government would not assent to Portugal annexing the region, and would try to obtain free importation of ammunition, it would neither send an armed expedition to Nyasa, nor annex it, nor declare it British territory.[2] And very soon after the Blantyre conference, Lord Salisbury reiterated to Buchanan, via O'Neill, " Avoid any participation in warlike proceedings against Arabs."[3] Upon O'Neill's next desperate plea for action to check the ever-increasing slave-trade, above all by a gunboat on Lake Nyasa—an often-repeated request from the mission's supporters—the Foreign Office minute was " The administration would not put one there unless it were a British protectorate, which it is not. We cannot begin a crusade in the interior."[4] When the government was asked in the Commons—not surprisingly by Dr. Cameron of Glasgow—whether, since the government would do nothing, the Lakes Company could be allowed to send a gunboat, the reply was that, not knowing how much the Company would or could protect lives and property, the government were "not in a position to confer administrative power over a district which is not under their control."[5] Certainly the Foreign Office had good reason to doubt whether the directors of the African Lakes Company had either the assets or the resolution to make them a good political investment for the government. Ministers had always to consider both public opinion at home and the isolated position of their country in Europe before supporting speculative adventures, especially those in the heart of a still very little known continent. It was the problem of

[1] O'Neill to Salisbury, 3 February 1888, F.O. 84/1901.
[2] W. P. Livingstone, *op. cit.* pp. 244–5.
[3] Salisbury to Buchanan, 26 May 1888, referred to in O'Neill to Salisbury, 27 May 1888, F. O. 84/1901.
[4] O'Neill to Salisbury, 30 May 1888, F.O. 84/1901.
[5] *Parliamentary Debates*, 28 February 1888, III. 322. 1648–9.

the hen and the egg. The government could not help the British on Nyasa because these pioneers were not strong enough to merit help. Yet they could not, in the circumstances, become stronger without government help. In the history of colonial expansion, where the government is unwilling or unable to take hold of the opportunities that arise, the gap is generally bridged by men of exceptional daring who are prepared to take both the physical and the political risks. Lugard decided to take them. He accepted the command of the expedition.

His own personal doubt at first was whether the expedition of the Lakes Company was a sufficiently moral venture to pass the tests which he had set for himself. His conscience was cleared for him by Mr. Scott, the uncrowned king of southern Nyasaland. These missionaries had their own political problems. The only civilized men in the only civilized centres in the region, they were, willy-nilly, the focus of power and influence to which tribes and individuals turned for help, justice and advice. These practical Scottish divines, members of a fighting race, were no pacifists. They knew that they were probably in their moment of greatest danger. They believed that if Mlozi were able to defy the white men with impunity and establish his reign of slavery and terror at the north end of the lake, all the other Arabs who hitherto had not joined him might do so; the chiefs and the tribes would swing with them, and the fierce Ngoni might come down from the hills and, as Mlozi threatened, sweep the Europeans and all the native groups which had helped them, into the lake. But if another unsuccessful attack were made on the Arabs, this result might be even more certain. Yet neither Mr. Scott nor Dr. Laws, of the Free Church, in his far more exposed position up the lake, hesitated. "I find," Lugard noted, "they cordially support the cause, which they now look on as a crusade, and not only quite justifiable but necessary probably to the very existence of the missions, and the lives of the missionaries along the lake and even *here*. Also Scott thinks that if we do not beat the Arabs they will open a huge slave route along north of lake and British influence will be lost for good." (Diary, Blantyre, 12 May 1888).

British influence! They were not ready yet to ask for more. Yet clearly the missionaries were coming to realize that their little unsupported theocracies in the middle of equatorial Africa must fall either under the Muslim slavers or else under Portugal or Germany. If they must lean on the arm of temporal power, which could they desire but that of their own nation? Those who condemn the missions for thus wanting the flag to follow the Bible should assess the alternatives that faced them in the Africa of the eighties and nineties. Lugard, impressed by their great and now endangered achievements, and by their calm assurance, and impelled by his faith in his own nation, accepted eagerly the conviction that this quarrel was just. Only the representative of the U.M.C.A. refused to co-operate. But his mission, on Lekoma island in the lake and on the eastern shore, was a little less immediately implicated.

But how to deal with Buchanan? He was obliged to represent, on the spot, the neutrality of the distant imperial government. So, when Lugard wrote to Buchanan a formal letter saying that, having been satisfied on all grounds that the expedition was justified, he had agreed to take command, and now asked his sanction, the answer came quickly by runner from Zomba, some twenty miles away. " I much regret I cannot ask you to take command of the expedition; this war policy [is] being carried on independent of the government and in direct opposition to Consul Hawes' wishes . . . . Arab and coast influence in Lake Nyasa is of by far too great magnitude to be even checked by a handful of Europeans . . . . the British government are dead opposed to involving themselves in complications in Nyasaland, and I quite expect there will be a terrible row at the Foreign Office over what has already happened." (Buchanan to L. 14 May 1888).

It was a serious blow for Lugard. " I was aghast ", he said. For a regular soldier to embark upon fighting while on sick leave, under any conditions, was a highly questionable step, but to do so in defiance of a letter in these terms from the only representative of the Queen would have been beyond forgiveness. However, he was not going to yield without a struggle. Buchanan was invited over to Blantyre; Mr. Scott asked him to dinner, and he and Lugard had a long talk. " He is a very shrewd man of great decision," was Lugard's judgment. It is easy to reconstruct their encounter from Lugard's diary.

" I was most delighted," Buchanan said, " to hear of your coming, and that you thought of commanding the expedition. But officially I am *bound* to tell you that the government gives no sanction or support to it. I am bound to follow Hawes' instructions, which were most emphatic, to do *nothing* until instructions come from England. My sole fear is that I may involve Hawes."

" But," objected Lugard, " Hawes cannot direct Nyasa affairs while in England. This is a crisis, and you *must* act upon your own responsibility."

Then Buchanan showed that he was sore at the way Moir had ignored him until he needed his sanction in order to make use of Lugard.

" I disclaim Moir's actions entirely," Lugard argued. " The African Lakes Company are nothing to me. My grounds for going are because I think the cause so great and good a one. But see the risk you make me incur if you compel me to go without your authorization."

" In point of fact," retorted Buchanan, " the whole responsibility must rest on your shoulders or on mine, and you are trying to transfer it to mine."

" I think as Consul," Lugard replied, " you ought to accept it in so far as giving your support goes. Even so I shall have a great responsibility to face. I ought not to be in this part of Africa: I am expressly forbidden to fight while on half-pay. I do not ask you to *call* on me to fight, only to support me. But I must ask you to suppress those distinct expressions about the government not supporting a war policy."

Buchanan was moved, and wavered. Yet he knew his masters and the rules of the hunt-the-slipper departmental game of fixing responsibility. Lugard felt he had won, but so as not to press his victory, he proposed an adjournment for dinner at the Scotts' hospitable table.

" If," said Buchanan at last, " the community will come forward and call upon me to strengthen your hands by my support I will at least tone down my letter."

The whole of the little community, including representatives of the Company and of both Scottish missions, came together and agreed to this step on the grounds that Lugard's leadership would have the effect " of lifting the whole expedition into the sympathy and moral support of the whole community."[1] The letter was signed among others by Mr. Scott, head of the Blantyre Mission, who, as Lugard's host, had had plenty of opportunity of studying his character. Buchanan thereupon wrote a new letter in which, though he said " It is my duty to inform you that Her Majesty's Government will not be held

[1] Lugard I, pp. 48–9.

responsible for this expedition," he yet expressed his personal approval, in view of the wishes of the community, and always provided that the expedition was directed defensively and only against the three main offending Arabs, Mlozi and his two lieutenants.[1]

" I was most proud," Lugard wrote in his diary, " of thus having succeeded in uniting all parties, and lifting the expedition from an enterprise by a trading company into a crusade in which both the political and religious sections equally approved and supported, and which had the earnest wishes for success from the one, and the prayers of the other." (18 May 1888).

Yet he was still taking a large risk. He was, indeed, for the first of many occasions, in very much the position of those sea-captains of Queen Elizabeth, who had to fight the Spaniards knowing that if they failed, or if the diplomatic situation should demand it, even though they had the secret approval of the Queen, they would be disavowed and, perhaps, disgraced. How closely the Elizabethan analogy fitted was shown by a very revealing letter received by Lugard six months later from his cousin, Colonel H. T. Lugard, who managed, with the help of Sir Edward Lugard, to learn something of the inside view at the Foreign Office.

" The Foreign Office learnt from the Consuls near you that you were knocking about in East Africa and they wrote to the War Office asking who you were and what you were doing? The W.O. replied that you were on half-pay on recommendation of a Medical Board and suffering from debility and great mental depression. F.O. then wrote asking if some communication relative to your state of health should not be made to the African Lakes Company . . . you must understand that . . . the War Office is not prepared to *officially* countenance your acts or to send you instructions at present. It is a case in which the Government are evidently not able to do anything or to say anything which might in any way fix any of the responsibility for what is being done on them— but nevertheless I gather that they would not be displeased (quite the contrary) if your efforts to oust the slave-traders prove successful."

(H. T. Lugard to L. 20 September 1888).

It must be remembered that even this very conditional kind of approval reached Lugard months after he had taken his risk and fought his little war.

[1] Lugard I, p. 49.

The Fight with the Arabs

On May 18th Lugard set out down the Shire hills to rejoin the river at Matope, where navigation again becomes possible after the long break of the Murchison Falls. He had with him John Moir and the Livingstonia Mission doctor, Cross, who had, with both moral and physical courage, volunteered to accompany the little force as a non-combatant. At the river they found fourteen white men waiting for them. Some were pious Scottish Company men, but seven of them had been recruited in Natal for this wild adventure, roving men who had knocked about in the South African goldfields and native wars. Some of these, it may well be imagined, were not likely to be very easy to discipline or to make congenial companions for missionaries or for Company men who had been selected for much the same Scottish Christian qualities as the missionaries themselves, and who abjured drinking, swearing and Sabbath-breaking. At the head of the Company men was John Moir. The eighteenth man was Mr. Sharpe, whose character and judgment Lugard most respected and who, upon his side, was delighted at Lugard taking charge. It was certainly no easy band to lead, especially as many of them could not have any personal interest in the cause for which they were asked to face hardship and danger, while Lugard's authority over them was of a very irregular kind, with no possible sanction but what he could create by the force of his own character. He had to set to work from the first to study the personalities of each of these diverse men, and his diary is full of observations about their histories and behaviour. He had the further difficulty that he was a stranger commanding men some of whom had been for years in the country and knew its conditions and the language of the local tribes.

The party boarded the tiny mission steamer, the *Ilala*, the first ever to be launched on a tropical African lake. She had been brought up by the mission and transferred to the Company. She had a carrying capacity of only three tons and quite inadequate cubic space to hold so many passengers. Her funnel belched sparks and smoke which warned the inhabitants of the lake-sides of her coming far in advance, and she had to stop at frequent intervals to collect wood for fuel. They steamed slowly up the river through water full of hippopotamus and crocodile, past banks crowded with game, through the Lake Malombe, past the station of the slaver, Mponda, and so into the clear blue waters of the great lake itself, which broke upon Lugard with its overwhelming beauty and grandeur. They paused at the first site of the Free Church Mission, the old Livingstonia, and there picked up two more of the Natal men. They also took in tow a steel boat belonging to that mission which had been given by the boys of Harrow school. The Sunday came while they were on board, and Dr. Cross held a service. Almost all the men came, " hats off, pipes out and demeanour most reverent."

From Livingstonia they went on to the new site of the Free Church Mission, Bandawe. Here Dr. Laws welcomed them and Lugard, as his guest, had the great advantage of talking to a man who had a deep knowledge of the country and the people and of enjoying the atmosphere of his well-filled library. Dr. Laws, with his industrial schools and commonsense, seemed to Lugard the " most practical and ideal missionary . . . . Though I do *not* indiscriminately admire all missionaries, I am free to say that among such of the Scottish missionaries as I met in Nyasaland there was not a single one whom I did not esteem. I have nothing but praise both of their methods and their work."[1] Dr. Laws, on his side, assayed Lugard's metal. " He is a brave man whom I like very much."[2] Laws should certainly have been a judge of courage. He stayed on, quietly doing his multifarious tasks, healing, teaching—already there were over a thousand children in his schools—building, preaching, studying native languages, confronting hostile tribes, chiefs and Arab slave-traders, writing innumerable letters to England, and generally administering and providing for an ever-growing oasis of civilization seven weeks of difficult journeying inland from the sea. One after another his young colleagues died. Already there were many graves at Livingstonia, and the cemetery at Bandawe had begun to fill.

Is it right, asked Professor Drummond, a geologist with a vivid pen, who visited the region for the Company in 1883 and saw the graves, to go on in missionary work when there is plainly " a barrier of Nature " against men living there at all? Dr. Laws'[3] reply was that the graves were milestones of Christianity, marking its advance into the interior.

There was much to discuss at Bandawe. Native levies had to be raised. Should they be the fierce Ngoni, who terrorized the whole

[1] Lugard I, pp. 68, 70.
[2] W. P. Livingstone, *op. cit.* p. 245.
[3] H. Drummond, *Tropical Africa* (1888), p. 45.

116

region with their night raids and ghastly butcheries and were certainly
the best fighters, or the Tonga, the tribe round the mission who looked
to it for protection? The decision was for the latter, as Dr. Laws was
unwilling that these cruel enemies of his Tonga should be used, and
Sharpe, reluctantly detached from his hunting, was persuaded to go up
the lake by land, a difficult and dangerous job, running the gauntlet
of the Ngoni, to recruit these auxiliaries and to train them in the use
of guns on the way. Except for the doctor, Sharpe was for Lugard
the one kindred spirit in the party, as he had the qualities Lugard
valued most highly: integrity and reliability. But Lugard had great
difficulty in preventing him from breaking away to go after ivory.
Sharpe, little dreaming then of the respectable responsibilities that lay
ahead of him as Sir Alfred Sharpe, Imperial Commissioner for British
Central Africa, dissociated himself from the ideals which moved
Lugard in taking up the anti-slavery cause. He must have enjoyed
greatly twitting his idealistic commander, for he laughed as he told
him " These high objects have not the same weight with me. I have
sunk so low that money and profit come before everything." Only
for Lugard's sake did he remain; yet not only did he stay but he carried
out some of the most arduous and dangerous duties.

Dr. Laws repeated for Lugard the confirmation of the expedition
as a crusade which the Blantyre mission had given him. He allowed
Dr. Cross to go, as a non-combatant, but no other missionary. In
many ways he gave advice and help. Public opinion in Britain was
not ready for a British protectorate, yet this is clearly what Laws had
begun to recognize as the best hope for the future, and he rightly
foresaw that every action which kept a British Company's flag flying
would help to that end.[1]

From Bandawe the little party went on towards Karonga. There
was now hardly standing-room on the deck, crowded with its ill-
assorted passengers, and when the men tried to lie down at night the
problem of space was critical. Yet, as Lugard watched the wildly
beautiful prospect over the lake, with its forested banks, its ramparts
of hills, and little islands feathered with trees, the waves falling on the
golden shores, the open glades with all sorts of beautiful antelopes
grazing and decorated with unknown flowers—a scenic heaven of
which man had made a hell—he was able to abstract himself completely

[1] W. P. Livingstone, *op. cit.* pp. 242–3.

from his associates and from the whole desperate atmosphere of the enterprise. The strands of action and reflection were both strong in his nature, and no poet could have been more deeply moved, and indeed disturbed, than he by natural beauties. Each night he watched the sun set over the mountains on the western shores of the lake, firing the immense stretch of water with intense colours and outlining each rocky little island. His thoughts at such moments were always sad; his great trouble and his unbalanced state of mind still made him long to find death in the coming action. Yet his diary shows that the enterprise was calling up his energies from their dreary trance and that the days gave him less and less time for thinking of his own unhappiness.

Karonga lay twenty-seven hours' steaming north of Bandawe. The little ship made her slow and smoky way up along the surf-beaten western shore. The party landed once, and Lugard, Moir and a few others made a reckless attack on an Arab encampment, drove them out, burnt their huts and took their stocks of rice. On May 28th they arrived at the now notorious, much disputed Karonga. Lugard saw a stockade of poles, open on the lake side, in which, to the disgust of his orderly mind, he saw filthy, thatched native huts, valuable stocks of cloth, leaking kegs of powder, open cooking fires, all muddled up together. At the stockade were six employees of the Company, led by a stocky, bearded man, the real hero of the place, Monteith-Fotheringham. He had come out as a missionary, and was a man of the highest courage and tenacity, who had never broken his word, and had never deserted his dangerous post at the north end of the lake since he had come there six years before. It is a tribute to such a man, as also to Moir, that with their status and knowledge of the country and of the local language, they yet accepted the command of a complete stranger and newcomer. It is also, of course, a tribute to Lugard that he could be offered and could hold the position.

Lugard set to work at once to re-order the whole post, which he condemned as insanitary and vulnerable. He drew up a new plan, dividing the native and white compounds, building stockades and walls, a fire-proof magazine, a stand for arms, a medical store and surgery, a baggage store, a dining-table under shade and many other improvements. In all these activities his love of order and his care for detail found full scope. So did his physical energy, for he undertook some of the roughest work himself to set an example. On the fourth night, having put on his medal ribbons, with their evidence of three campaigns, he made a little speech to the white men in which he gave the four main objects of the expedition as, firstly, the suppression of the slave-trade; secondly, saving the Nkonde, who had helped the white man; thirdly, the saving of the lives of the missionaries; and fourthly, the vindication of British honour. He reminded them of the support of the community, and appealed to them for cordial co-operation and no grumbling, as they could not afford to quarrel. His own position was held entirely on sufferance, and he asked for loyal obedience, as it was in each man's power to make his position an agreeable or an impossible one. He had a hearty response, and he then read out the roster of guard duties.

The two Arab posts which most closely threatened Karonga were seven miles away beside the Stevenson road, now overgrown with high elephant grass, and were known by the names of two of Mlozi's henchmen, Msalema and Kopakopa. They stood about 400 yards apart. Mlozi's own stockade was seven miles further on. On June 1st Lugard decided that he must reconnoitre these posts himself. Taking only Fotheringham and five picked Tonga, he set off in tennis shoes on a cloudy night, struggling through the tall grass and thorns along the Stevenson road. At last they came to a clearing, and on a high ridge could dimly make out the two stockades. Lugard now went on alone into the open, though the moon had suddenly come up, and he could not, of course, see if there were sentries on guard behind the wooden palisades. At such moments, too, his partial deafness was a great handicap, as he would not hear the rustle of an enemy's approach from behind or a low call that would have told him the defenders were alert. He forced himself to go out of cover, right up to Msalema's which, built to the edge of the steep ridge, towered above him. Even at such a moment, Lugard could play spectator to his own danger. " It is curious," he thought, " how our animal instincts rebel against risk to our lives! Here was I in a trembling funk of the unseen danger, with every nerve strained to tension, taking as great care as though I had so much to lose as I thought I had in Burma." He went, step by step, up to the stockade, probed for defensive ditch or pits, tried to gauge the height of the platform inside, and marked the position of the look-out tower. The silence was broken by a loud shout from within the fort. Lugard slunk back into cover, but after the shouting and singing had died down he went out again and made a thorough examination of the neighbouring and much larger stockade of Kopakopa. He could hear a sentry singing a song about the Mzungu (the white man), doubtless about how he would deal with such a one. Suddenly they were observed: both stockades woke up, and a great party streamed out and began to fire at them. Fotheringham said he refused to run from an Arab: the five Tonga instinctively began a war-dance and yelled derisively at their enemies. Bullets whistled round them, until Lugard planted a well-aimed shot in the middle of the enemy party, after which he and his companions were able to slip back into the bush and walk the seven miles back to Karonga, which they reached very eager for their breakfast.

The day following this reconnaissance was Sunday, and Lugard found that in this country, where Scottish missionaries ruled, all took it as a day of complete rest. The Arabs, however, kept a different Sabbath and marked the day by a counter-reconnaissance which led to shooting and the manning of alarm posts. The following day Lugard examined the ammunition and discovered this was of almost every possible type and bore and that there was an even greater variety of guns. Bullets were rapidly cast in the stockade, and hand-grenades manufactured from tins rammed with mud from ant-hills, and odd bits of iron and shingle. On the 6th, Sharpe arrived from his recruiting march along the lake shore. He had been alone and had suffered badly from fever all the way, but he had managed to raise 190 Tonga. He had also attacked one of Mlozi's caravans and had managed to free three women slaves who were being sent to another Arab post as currency to be exchanged for some gunpowder. One boy, held in a gori-stick, a heavy forked branch fitted round the necks of the more recalcitrant slaves on the march to prevent their running away, was wounded in the *mêlée*. Some ivory and other loot was taken, and also an Arab, Muntu Mwema (the good man!), a relative of Kopakopa. All clamoured for his immediate execution, but Lugard refused, keeping him a prisoner and well-fed, though chained. The three young women, standing naked, an exceptionally good-looking trio, in the middle of the camp, were a problem; but as they were of the Nkonde Lugard was fortunately able to hand them back to their own people.

Lugard was now anxious to make his attack before his very mixed group of black and white men wearied, quarrelled, or fell sick *en masse*. So serious was the position with regard to health that at any one time between two-thirds and three-quarters of the twenty-five white men were always either ill or convalescent. Lugard and one other man were the only members of the party who had not been ill. The death of one of the Natal men from the constant fever, accompanied with vomiting, from which they all suffered, threw a gloom over the camp. As he was a Roman Catholic, Lugard confined himself to reading over his grave two penitential psalms and the Lord's Prayer, followed by a hymn.

Lugard was determined, in spite of the ruthless cruelty of the enemy and the primitive character of his auxiliaries, to impose civilized methods of warfare upon his own side. He forbade the use of explosive bullets, but he was worried about the question of loot and of women, the great prizes of savage warfare. Those most experienced in the country warned him that it was useless to interfere, " it was absurd to try and check in three or four days the custom of ages . . . . we could not touch tar without soiling our hands." Lugard was not, however, moved by these arguments, and on June 7th he called a meeting of the leaders of the native levies, with Sharpe and Fotheringham beside him.

These levies consisted now of 220 Tonga, 50 from another tribe south of the lake, and 50 wild Mambwe from the Tanganyika plateau, fine, naked fighting men, who wore a halo of pig-bristles round their heads. All along the shore the wretched Nkonde refugees from the slavers' raids were encamped among the reeds, many having built huts on stilts far out in the waters. Their beautiful valley nearby was marked by the burnt relics of their villages, round which the quick growth of grass and jungle was pushing up amongst the banana groves; the half-choked, self-sown grain on last year's cultivations was all they had for food. If these Nkonde, so bitterly wronged, should get loose among the Arabs, or if their stolen wives should be seized by the Tonga levies, dreadful atrocities and disorders would ensue. Apart from humanity, if they abandoned all in the struggle for loot, the attack might end in disaster, as, indeed, had happened in one of the earlier attacks.

To the assembled Africans Lugard made his speech through an interpreter. He pointed out that the Tonga were now paid levies, not free-lances; that if they stopped to loot they would be treated as enemies; that all loot taken would be equitably divided by the Company's agents. He put forward every argument of practical common-sense, pointing out their danger from the local Nkonde, the need of discipline, and of proving their fighting qualities before the menacing Ngoni. Lastly, he said, that to steal women was against the white man's customs and wishes. Even at such exciting moments, Lugard's diary shows that he could be audience as well as actor.

" With such arguments we carried the day and finding out their war-cry I said that when I shouted that they must charge side by side with the white man. They again went half mad with excitement, shouting, grunting, gesticulating, and a strange sight it must have been . . . . the conference by the light of a solitary candle and the strange sounds of their cries, the strange surroundings, and the ceaseless roll of the surf on the beach, and the steadfast hills around the lake, looking down with the stars on the excitement and passions of war and death, of us ephemeral beings who to-day are and to-morrow are gone and forgotten and replaced by new-comers whose aims and passions carry them to war and death . . . . Yet I think there was something fine in the sight of the Englishmen standing up for the right and trying to conquer by their force of superiority the rooted custom of centuries, saying they would have no carrying off of slaves and women and urging the wild passions of these savages to seek a nobler channel." (Diary, 7 June 1888).

The last preparations for attack were now made. The Nkonde chiefs were harangued and ordered to keep out of the fray. The Tonga were divided into companies, each under a trusted chief who himself was under a white man who knew the language, with two other whites attached to him. The Africans had been drilled to fire and to point, if not to aim, a gun, and instructed, against all their habits, to avoid close formation. On the night of June 15th Lugard issued to each man a strip of bright coloured cloth to tie round his head as the nearest approach to a uniform.

At 10 p.m. the companies began to set out successively on their seven-mile march to the Arab stockades. Each leader had detailed instructions and a plan of the enemy position. It was arranged that Dr. Cross and another white man were to form their " hospital " under a certain big tree 1,000 yards away from the scene of action. The Arab prisoner, well fed and clothed, was taken along as a guide. The hospital tree was reached at 1 a.m. on the morning of June 16th. From this point each section advanced noiselessly in the darkness over the rough ground towards its point of attack. When they were some fifty yards from the stockade Lugard raised a British "Hurrah!" and all broke into a charge. The Arabs, though surprised, must have been sleeping by their guns, for just as the attackers reached the fourteen foot high stockade flashes of flame burst through the loopholes as the defenders received them with a fusillade. Lugard's plan was to blow up the stockade, but he now found that the men with the axes and explosives had failed to come up with the rest. Lugard felt that the only thing left to do was to go straight at the stockade and clamber up and over it. So, shouting the order, he led the way. But as he pulled himself up to the top by an extending branch he was shot at close range and fell in a heap at the foot of the stockade. " I thought I was hit through the stomach and of course mortally wounded." To Sharpe, who was near him, he said "'I have got it .... I am no more use here . . . . I am off to the rear to the doctor. *You take command.*' I begged him to see it through and not to give in if possible." (Diary, 15 June 1888).

Lugard staggered back through the thick bush. His arms were hanging uselessly, so he could not brush the branches and giant spear-grass away from his face, and with the loss of blood a parching thirst set in. But he realized, as he stumbled along, that if he could use his legs in this way he could not be wounded in the stomach. His servant found him, and they wandered about for two hours in the dim light, unable to find the hospital tree, the doctor, or any water. At last they struck the track to Karonga, and he was trying to make his own way back, now hatless in the blazing morning sun and bleeding heavily, when the doctor found him, and he was carried the rest of the way, reaching Karonga at 3 p.m., some fourteen hours after he had been wounded.

Meanwhile the attackers had failed to take the fort and, disheartened by the loss of their leader, they drew away from the stockades in good order and returned to Karonga. Considering the fierceness of the attack and the defence, casualties on the British side were few. One of the Natal men was shot through the head and died a week later; another had a very severe head-wound, but recovered. Five of the Africans were killed and nine badly wounded.

It was not until the next morning that Lugard himself was laid on the table and, his blood-soaked clothes having been cut off, was examined by Dr. Cross. He was found to have sustained a most extraordinary wound. The discharge must have been fired a few inches from his body, as his right arm was blackened and filled with coarse grains of powder, while two big lumps of wadding had to be extracted from it. The bullet had gone through the elbow joint. Without fracturing this, it had then pushed the artery aside without cutting it, and had entered the chest. Deflected by a rib, it had just missed the heart and emerged above the breast pocket, making a long tearing wound as it did so. It had then struck the left wrist, pulverizing the main bone, cutting a minor artery and carrying into the wrist pieces of the letters that were in the breast pocket. Five years later this wound was still open and fragments of bone were coming out of it. It was amazing evidence of his strength of will and body that he had been able to keep going so long in such a condition. Dr. Cross had to decide whether to amputate or not; the patient was in a bad way from loss of blood and from six suppurating bullet-holes which, under conditions in the compound, it was difficult to sterilize. Lugard, who had expected to lose one if not both his arms, had a wonderful moment when he came round from the chloroform and found that both were still there.

The position, however, was one of perplexity and danger. The Arabs might counter-attack. Lugard could not lie down or dress, and spent his time in a chair, wrapped in a blanket, unable to raise a hand to wipe off the flies that clustered about him, or at night to kick aside the rats that crowded the compound and ran all over him, or the snakes that came in hunting the rats. However, the day after the attack he managed to speak to his little force, congratulating them upon their courage, and urging them not to lose heart because the stockade had proved impregnable to a direct charge. He ordered their own stockade to be strengthened, and gave instructions for a guerilla warfare to be carried on against the Arabs, harrying their communications and sources of supply.

The situation of the little group was, however, very unpleasant. Of the twenty-five white men, one was dead and two seriously wounded; Sharpe had resumed his elephant shooting; two of the Company men had resigned. Moir and one Natal man agreed to go to South Africa and try to obtain a cannon. Then, one after another, the rest went sick. The doctor became very ill, and lay delirious, so Lugard's wounds had to be dressed by the one man who had once been to an ambulance class and who washed them out with Condy's fluid every day. Then *he* went sick, and Fotheringham was given command under Lugard; but for all his great bravery and high principle, he was a quick-tempered man, and the atmosphere in the compound became so stormy that Lugard had to resume command. When the *Ilala* arrived on July 1st, almost everyone clamoured to go away in her. Some of the Natal men threatened to go off in a raft if they were prevented from boarding the steamer. It was quite clear that the one man above all others who should have gone was Lugard, since the doctor was too ill to attend to him and there was serious danger, that, without immediate expert treatment, his still rigid arms might settle into life-long inflexibility. But it was also clear that if he left at that moment the whole enterprise would break up. He had a severe struggle with himself, for in his physical weakness he longed to escape, as much from the horrible discomforts as from the dangers of his position. He decided to stay.

There is no need to detail all the many minor events of the next few months: the sufferings of the leader; the kindness and loyalty of some of his remaining men; the intransigence of others, leading in one instance to an attempted duel with revolvers; the varying fortunes of the war with the slavers. All this can be read in Lugard's own book. In the war an important event was the seizure of an island south of Karonga at Deep Bay, one of the main points from which the Arabs shipped their slaves across the lake. Attacks upon dispersed parties of Arabs led to a number of slaves being found, but Lugard gave strict injunctions against any needless shedding of blood, and refused to kill even a spy caught redhanded in the camp. By August 5th, when the *Ilala* returned to Karonga, it was clear that there was no possibility of Lugard recovering under the conditions there, above all with the ceaseless responsibilities and quarrels with which he had to deal. His wounds refused to heal, and lumps of paper were still embedded in his shattered wrist. The doctor, who was so bad himself that he had to leave, used all his medical authority to order him away if only for a period. He at last agreed, and after being nearly drowned trying to reach the steamer in a little boat which was swamped by heavy waves—

for he could not swim a stroke with his useless arms—he reached Bandawe and spent three civilized weeks as an invalid with Dr. Laws and his wife. Here he could have his wounds dressed daily, gently and hygienically. He made a wonderful recovery, though his left arm never wholly regained its strength.

Among the missionaries Lugard met with an appreciation which, coming from men of their courage and judgment, must have been as healing to his sick mind as was their medical care to his body. " Dr. Laws," writes his biographer, " was much impressed by his courage and his character. ' He has suffered a great deal without a murmur,' said the missionary, 'and he has the good of his country at heart '."[1] Lugard, for his part, wrote of the almost embarrassing kindness and generous hospitality he received from a man whom he admired without reservation and from his wife.

When he was well enough to travel further he went on down the lake and up the hills to Blantyre to recuperate further in the care of Mr. Scott, his wife and Dr. Bowie. From Scott, as from Laws, Lugard won the golden opinion which in his self-exiled state was his only wealth. " He is such a fine, straightforward, disinterested man," wrote Scott in a letter, " and has really done good work at the north end against the Arabs; work willingly undertaken because it seemed to need his presence and help." (Scott to Emma Brayne, 19 October 1888).

Small wonder that Lugard could confess to his diary that this period of convalescence represented " the most peaceful and pleasantest days I have known since I left Burma." Was it, perhaps, the nearness he had been to death that made life begin to seem good again?

---

[1] W. P. Livingstone, *Laws of Livingstonia*, p. 245.

CHAPTER VIII

STALEMATE

1888-1889 : Aet. 30-31

AT BLANTYRE Lugard had an interval in which he could review both the war against Mlozi and also his own future. Was it possible with so few men and such inadequate arms to dislodge the slavers from their key point at the north of the lake? And was it his duty to continue in the command? This could only be settled when he had entered into conference with the leading Europeans in the region—Buchanan, Scott, Dr. Bowie, Moir, and Warner, a representative of the U.M.C.A. whose advice at least could be gained. At the same time, with these men, Lugard was able to study the newspapers and all the other available information and see his little war upon something like a world background. This could be done without any self-conceit for the scramble for Africa was now a major world interest and Nyasa was one of its focal points.

The newspapers and letters assured them that they could count upon the steady and eager support of all the humanitarians interested in anti-slavery and mission work. These were using all the pressures at their command. On May 18th, soon after Lugard's arrival at the lake, they had called a great conference in Manchester, attended by representatives from the three Churches concerned and also from the Lakes Company, and the Manchester and Scottish Geographical Societies. But, once again, the meeting stopped short of asking for the government's physical support for the struggle, still less for annexation. If, as one of the clergy said, the government " should think they wanted them to put their hands into the pockets of the ratepayers and take upon themselves the burden of a war in Africa, they were sure to be defeated." The meeting therefore asked only for free access up the Zambezi and measures to check the slave-trade. At a big public meeting in the city the same evening, the Rev. Horace

Waller, in a proposal which strikingly illustrated the dilemma of the philanthropists, said the great necessity, as Livingstone himself had suggested, was for a man like Rajah Brooke of Sarawak to settle there, put himself at the head of a tribe and build up a city of refuge round which an immense population would gather.[1] In August the practical Scots, since the Churches and missionary societies could not directly buy and export arms, set up a Nyasa Anti-Slavery and Defence Fund with the merchants, among whom was James Stevenson who gave £1,000, well to the fore. The object was to raise a fund of £10,000 to support the efforts of the " distinguished officer " Captain Lugard and his associates, since the Lakes Company could not afford military expenditure.[2] It is interesting to notice that of the first twenty-two subscribers all but four were Scottish.

This growing and insistent public opinion was naturally reflected in parliament. The report had just reached Blantyre of a very important debate in the House of Lords on July 6th. In this Lord Salisbury was pressed by Lord Harrowby as to whether the government's giving way to Germany and Portugal meant that Britain was going to retreat from Central Africa. Harrowby asked openly that the Shire and Lake Nyasa region should be declared a British sphere of influence. Lord Salisbury decisively rejected this last proposal saying it would imply " vast military action." He referred, in terms which, to a man of his precision of speech, must have been studiously vague, to " interests of an undefined though very interesting character with respect to those splendid monuments of British energy and enthusiasm shown on Lake Nyasa."[3] This was appreciation which must have seemed rather bitterly ironic to Lugard and Moir in Blantyre. The rest of his speech, when it is remembered that Salisbury well knew what Germany and Portugal were doing and planning at that moment, is a deeply interesting revelation of Salisbury's mind and method. The Nyasaland enterprise was one of those splendid British undertakings " which our race has formed and will sustain rather by the action of the individuals of whom the State is composed than by the political machinery of the State . . . . All that the government can do on the sea coast, all that we can do

[1] *A.S.R.*, IV. viii. May and June 1888, pp. 65–9.

[2] The prospectus, in the Lugard Papers, has no date but must have been issued in August, 1888. It carries the names of the Duke of Portland, the Earl of Aberdeen, Lord Aberdare and many other public men.

[3] *Parliamentary Debates*, 6 July 1888, III. 328. 548.

diplomatically, within the sphere of political efforts in this country, we will do." They would only injure the cause by making a war; they would be fighting " a collection of all the scum of humanity . . . . who combine the grossest cruelty with a species of fanaticism. We must leave the dispersal of this terrible army of wickedness to the gradual advance of civilization and Christianity . . . . And we may be convinced . . . . that this country will not abandon the task to which she has once put her hand, but that she will carry it through successfully and to a triumphant issue by the proper action and the enthusiasm of her individual citizens."[1]

To the " individual citizens " reading this at Blantyre Salisbury's robust confidence in their prospects must have sounded rather heart-breaking. At the very time Lugard read it he was being told by Buchanan, who had so reluctantly approved his expedition, that it was useless, and even dangerous to the other scattered Europeans to attack while " we are the weaker power in Nyasa." Buchanan, indeed, as acting-consul, had been obliged, without any reaction from the government, to suffer a humiliating outrage when the formidable chief Makanjira, upon whom he was calling, seized him, stripped him naked, flogged and imprisoned him. And when at last Salisbury did induce the Portuguese to relax for a time their refusal to permit some arms to come up to the British, they allowed the Arabs to import even more freely so that the British advantage was negatived. All hope was now centred upon getting up a single small cannon, but the Portuguese government, jealous of the intervention of the Lakes Company in what they regarded as their own sphere, and afraid of its own press, which was now getting almost hysterical, refused to hear of importing " artillery ". There is a hint that the Foreign Office was driven to ask—was it a secret hope?—whether the Company were thinking of " running " the gun through. It is evidence of Lord Salisbury's sense of the weakness of his position that he minuted that this possibility, used as a threat, might bring the Portuguese to reason.[2]

It is only fair to say that from the first the Prime Minister did not waver upon certain fundamental points. He refused to allow that Portugal had any historical claim to possess the Shire-Nyasa region and, in a letter to the Queen, stated his firm rejection of that country's

[1] *Ibid.* 6 July 1888, III. 328. 549–50.
[2] Minute by Salisbury on memorandum of Villiers Lister, 13 September 1888, F.O. 84/1900.

" archaeological arguments ".[1] He wished to be firm about the freedom of the Zambezi but, the more he heard about that unsatisfactory river, the less certain was his attitude. " My hopes about the Zambezi," he told the Colonial Secretary in his pithy style, " are breaking down. It is of no use declaring a river to be a highway of nations when there is only one fathom of water in it—and not always that."[2]

But the Nyasa affair could no longer be treated as an isolated incident in the middle of the blank map of Africa, to be settled bilaterally by Anglo-Portuguese diplomacy. The map was filling up rapidly and a new environment was developing all round the region. Following the Anglo-German Agreement of 1886,[3] the East Africa Companies of both powers had been taking shape. The Germans, first to act, but wholly inexperienced, sent in untrained and brutal types and, just as Lugard came down to Blantyre, the Arabs along the east coast broke into revolt and killed the German intruders wherever they could get at them. Sultan Barghash had died in April and his almost imbecile successor could not have controlled the rebels even if he had wished to do so. Bismarck, admitting privately the mistakes of the Company, was yet determined to suppress the rebellion with a heavy Prussian hand, and asked Britain to join with Germany in a blockade of the coast and so put a final end both to the Arab revolt and, a convenient and by no meani baseless plea, to the slave-trade. Salisbury, though he had no illusions as to the " unamiable " national characteristics of the Germans[4] was afraid that, if they were allowed to act alone, they might be utterly unrestrained in their revenge and even seize upon Zanzibar itself. He therefore agreed to joint action.

The coastal rebellion and its repression put the isolated British in the interior into great peril. Consul O'Neill wrote to Lugard to warn him and the others at Blantyre that it was more than ever important to bring the " North End " war to a close as there was a danger that, before the Germans could assert their control, especially in the interior, there might develop an " inter-racial antagonism " that would draw in all the hitherto friendly or neutral Arabs against the British round the lake. " Our quarrel is with Mlozi and his fellow robbers and

---

1 *Letters of Queen Victoria*, series III, vol. i, p. 543; quoted in Cecil, *Life of Salisbury*, vol. iv, p. 263.
2 Salisbury to Lord Knutsford, 12 October 1888, quoted in Cecil, *op. cit.* p. 241.
3 See above p. 92.
4 Cecil, *op. cit.* p. 246.

slave-hunters at the N. End, *not with Arabs in general or with Islam.*"
(O'Neill to L. 10 November 1888). The situation in the interior of
Africa seemed so serious that the consul-general at Zanzibar reported
that the British Indians were fleeing from the mainland, and warned,
when speaking of Uganda, that "the lives of all defenceless missionaries and Europeans in the interior will be placed in considerable
danger." They should therefore be told to leave their posts and make
their way to the coast. This they refused to do.[1] When, later, the story
was told in England, the Archbishop of Canterbury and other religious leaders commended their courage but Salisbury, dreading lest
the blood of these martyrs should lead to military action and so to
trouble with the Treasury, said that they were noble but misguided,
and that they ought to be discreet not valorous.[2]

This was not the only trouble spreading up to Nyasa. There were
signs that Portugal meant to assert herself more actively north of
the Zambezi and her agents were feeling their way amongst the chiefs
and were soon to come into the open. The chiefs had reason to waver.
The British condemned and, as far as they could, discouraged the
things they most desired—the slave-trade, drink and arms: they
could hope to get all these from the Portuguese. Moreover, the
British were manifestly weak. It is yet striking evidence of the character of the missionaries, and of the responsiveness of these primitive
people to this character, that the missionaries were able to maintain
a considerable influence with many of the tribes, and did not suffer
the massacre their weakness invited. Even the great majority of the
Arabs refused to follow their friends on the coast and attack the
Europeans inland.

The central African plot thickened now with the appearance of a
new character on the scene. Well ahead of the imperial government,
beginning to stride northwards on seven-league boots, Cecil Rhodes
was coming up from the Cape to grasp as part of the British empire,
the territories now known as British Bechuanaland, Bechuanaland
Protectorate, and Matabeleland, the still unoccupied regions between
the Transvaal and the new German settlement, and between Portugal's
two coastal colonies. While Lugard was recuperating at Blantyre,
Rhodes' agents were getting that concession from the Matabele chief,

[1] *Further correspondence respecting Germany and Zanzibar.* Africa No. 10 (1888), C.5603,
p. 8 ff.
[2] *Parliamentary Debates,* 28 May 1889, III. 336. 1224-40.

Lo Bengula, that may be regarded as the birth certificate of Southern Rhodesia. But Rhodes' grasp was unlimited—it stretched even beyond this far northern horizon of Matabeleland to Mashonaland, Barotseland and Manicaland. This brought his view to the Zambezi and so to the Shire and Nyasaland. That region, he decided, *must* be secured! And if the Germans barred him immediately north of that, he had, after all, only to cut in quickly and get a corridor up Tanganyika and so, perhaps, into the deep hinterland of the British East African sphere which *might* reach as far west as Uganda. Then, with Britain in Egypt, there was only the Mahdi to be dealt with—he believed that he could " square " even the Mahdi—and the long red axis of British power would run from end to end of Africa, from Cape-to-Cairo, in fact. With unrestricted vision, and a purpose beyond the immediate one of grab, with the solid base of his political power in South Africa and the £1,000,000 a year its gold and diamonds brought him, Rhodes at this moment felt fully able to by-pass the timid and penurious imperial government and daub central Africa red from his own paintbox. All he wanted from the government was a charter to give its veneer of international legitimacy to the company he meant to create and direct.

Lord Salisbury, though it was not realized at this time, had other ideas. Ministers might be driven by national uncertainty or economy to give, by means of charters, an indeterminate measure of authority over an undefined area of territory to these masterful men who forced their hands. But they did not altogether like what they had to do and relations between governments and chartered companies were no easier in the nineteenth than they had been in earlier centuries. For reasons of foreign policy, or because, for all his apparent detachment, he liked to keep power in his own hands, Salisbury, in this same summer with which we are dealing, said that he meant to establish imperial control *before* the commercial advance: he would bring all he could salvage in central Africa from other powers under direct imperial authority. But he had to consider the strict Treasury control of his period and also the fact that he was dependent for his parliamentary majority upon Liberal Unionist support. And behind these lay public opinion, which still needed education. This, at least, was the impression of Harry Johnston.[1] This young man—he was Lugard's

---

[1] See above p. 89.

age—witty, travelled, ambitious, versatile, embarking on a career that was to run close alongside Lugard's in Africa, was already *persona grata* at the Foreign Office. He received Salisbury's views in conversation at Hatfield,[1] the august hospitality of which he had been invited to share.

We may seem to have travelled a long way from Blantyre. But in truth all these strands of action, planning and thinking were being woven round the still unannexed Nyasaland. Some of them were known, others unknown, to the handful of anxious British there. More than that, many strands in the local pattern ran on to make the larger design of British policy in Africa in which Lugard was to be involved and these will recur again and again in this story. And this talk between the ruling Cecil and the versatile young explorer turned consul, has a very close relevance to Lugard's career. It was at this interview that the Prime Minister, with his eye upon Portugal, saw in Johnston the ideal special agent of his policy in central Africa. Salisbury could be a good chief, intelligent, imaginative, witty and generous with trust. But he knew what he wanted. Johnston won his trust: it was Lugard who was made to feel superfluous. His little Arab war was regarded as a very unnecessary, indeed indiscreet affair, and the first impression his name made upon Salisbury's mind was thus an unfortunate one.

Why, we may ask, when Salisbury commended those " splendid individual citizens " on Lake Nyasa, and seemed to encourage them to go on and assert themselves further, when he was already beginning to contemplate stronger action, did he deal with them behind the scenes in so discouraging a way? The answer is not difficult. It was because he knew the question must be settled, when the occasion should prove favourable, by diplomacy supported by gunboats, rather than by heroic deeds in a remote corner of the region in question. In the interval the consuls, as his liasion with these same " splendid individual citizens ", were in an impossibly difficult, weak and often dangerous position. They were like men learning to walk a tightrope while their trainer not only forbade them from swaying a hairsbreadth out of line but also jerked the string painfully from time to time. Buchanan accepted the position. In a letter to Lugard he did

---

[1] For a discussion of this conversation, which Johnston recounted in his *The story of my life* (1923), p. 221, see Cecil, *Life of Salisbury*, vol. iv, pp. 242-3.

not even complain at getting no redress for the outrage he had endured from Makanjira. O'Neill, on the contrary, chafed against the control and suffered the more.

When Lugard suddenly appeared on the scene, the relations of these consuls with him became a test of their correctitude, as was shown by their correspondence with the Foreign Office while Lugard was recuperating. Buchanan was wary but O'Neill made a false step. Lord Salisbury could tell the Portuguese government, with regard to the arms embargo, that the deaths of the fighters on Lake Nyasa " will be held by the English people to be due to the action of the Portuguese government."[1] But at the same time, upon reading a letter from Lugard to Buchanan, he could infer from it that O'Neill had encouraged Lugard to go to Lake Nyasa and assist the Company's expedition. " I am to remind you," was the official rebuke, " that the organizing or encouraging of warlike operations forms no part of the duties of H.M.'s Consuls."[2] O'Neill answered back, not, perhaps, in entire conformity with Lugard's account of the affair, but at least in a generous spirit. He denied that he thought it a warlike expedition.

" Captain Lugard was thinking of visiting the Lake to shoot elephants, and I freely admit that I encouraged him to go. Captain Lugard is a brave, capable and upright man, already distinguished for his services to his country in other parts of the globe, and I felt that the more such men visited and moved about the Lake district the better chance would H.M.G. and the public have of learning the general condition of affairs in that country. And if, contrary to my expectations, further hostility necessitated further hostile measures, then I felt that no better man could be found to command and control than Captain Lugard."[3]

This was not enough for the Foreign Office, which refused to let the matter drop and wrote again, quoting some of Lugard's words and telling O'Neill that he should order Lugard to withdraw the statement he had made.[4] Lord Salisbury did not, of course, personally read every letter that bears his name, especially those addressed to consuls. We do know, however, that through the official at the head of the African section of the Foreign Office, he took a very close personal interest in all African affairs and did in fact draft some of the documents.

1 Salisbury to Bonham, 6 September 1888, F.O. 84/1901.
2 Salisbury to O'Neill, 9 August 1888, F.O. 84/1901.
3 O'Neill to Salisbury, 14 September 1888, F.O. 84/1901.
4 Salisbury to O'Neill, 30 October 1888, F.O. 84/1901.

Africa was playing a rapidly growing part in foreign policy, and Johnston records how Salisbury followed every move and was fully in touch with the geography of the continent, maps of which hung in his rooms at the Foreign Office and at Hatfield. Moreover, Lugard's name was being served up to Salisbury in the press as a brave man, who had committed his life to the forward movement in Africa.[1]

Salisbury, naturally, hated to have his hand forced and he had already, from past experience, developed an attitude of mind towards what he must have regarded as Lugard's type. To him they were " men of energy and strong will, but probably not distinguished by any great restraint over their feelings . . . . trying to establish by means which must constantly degenerate into violence the supremacy of that nation for which they were passionately contending."[2]

Long before this, in 1879, he had written of an incident in West Africa,

" Governor R. has had no better occupation for his spare time than to annex some place with an unrememberable name . . . . Really these pro- consuls are insupportable . . . . I have implored the Colonial Office to recall Governor R." [3]

All this was unknown to Lugard, who was, of course, a soldier and not an official, but it indicated an attitude of mind at the highest level of authority which promised badly for his future career.

The pause in the action which has allowed us to review it in its wider perspective was coming to an end with the summer of 1888. Lugard had had many consultations, written many letters and much material meant for publication, and he had drawn up a complete and detailed scheme for the suppression of the local slave-trade. Now, in October, he was getting restless again. There was much to tempt him to leave the Nyasa struggle, with its endless complications, delays and difficulties. He received a letter from the Imperial British East Africa Company, now just being formed, asking him if he would like to undertake the task of leading a caravan into the interior. He was much tempted but he felt his duty still lay with the little war against the slavers. Towards the end of October, he therefore went up to the

[1] *The Times*, 4 September 1888, letter from the Rev. H. Waller; and see, for example, extracts from the diary of J. W. Moir communicated to *The Times* by his brother F. Moir, 7 September 1888.

[2] *Parliamentary Debates*, 10 July 1890, III. 346. 1270.

[3] Cecil, *op. cit.* p. 251.

far north end of the lake above Karonga. Here he gained a new insight into the character of African life when he saw along that part of the shore the stretch of Nkonde villages which had still not been reached and ravaged by the slavers. He noted the happiness of these naked savages, their fine herds of cattle, the cleanliness of their villages nestling among the banana groves, their fowls and goats, their fields of grain, and their beautifully constructed and ornamented huts. He marked the friendliness of the people to the white man, whom they welcomed with dancing and singing and playing on musical pipes. All this was threatened with fire and massacre. Only Karonga stood between them and this fate, and Karonga was no more than a handful of white men, weary and sick and ill-supplied, and some half-trained native auxiliaries. If Karonga went, the Arab would master the whole region; the Ngoni might then rise and the Bandawe mission station be wiped out. Lugard felt the strain of an almost impossible responsibility.

" God, who defends the right, prevent this! Yet what can *I* do . . . . with half a dozen white men and those *all* sick and disheartened and wanting to go—natives we can't rely on and discontented to boot—bad guns, bad ammunition, no bayonets, no entrenching tools, and so vast an area to guard and so powerful an enemy! It is indeed an uphill task . . . . who am *I* to undertake so great and terrible a responsibility? "

He pondered some strangely severe words from his father who had suddenly turned very Roman, and had sent him a letter upbraiding him—of all defects!—for cowardice. Stranger still, Lugard admitted the charge.

" Yes, I fear that the last year or two of my life has knocked the manliness and courage out of me and left me but a wreck . . . . I resented my father's harsh letter . . . . but reading my own heart can I truly say it was untrue? "

A strange delusion this seems to us who look back upon the story!

Lugard wrote this on December 27th while encamped on a little island in the lake south of Karonga, alone but for some twenty-five Tonga tribesmen to whom he could not speak. He was trying to guard the ferry point at Deep Bay from the slavers who came across from the east side of the lake which they now dominated. On Christmas Eve a strange dhow had come quietly up in broken moonlight and had begun to unload a cargo of arms. Lugard and his Tonga, in a sudden bellicose impulse, had thrown themselves into the water and waded out to it, firing in water waist deep. Thwarted by an unexpected deep channel, they had returned for their canoes and attacked again. They failed to seize the dhow, but they drove her off, riddled with holes and with many dead and wounded. His depression was perhaps the recoil from this fierce action and the utter loneliness, for there is nothing more lonely than to be encamped in some remote stretch of Africa among primitive men with whom there is no mental communion. At such a moment the whole prospect of his life looked utterly dreary. Around him was the African wilderness. He had ruined his military career and alienated his friends. As for going home, what home was there where he could find any real welcome or understanding? He thought of his father's vicarage at Worcester with its acute money worries and its continuing severities which even drove him to the kitchen to smoke his pipe. This was not home to him. As for his great trouble, there had been less time to think of that lately, but it still seemed to him to stand in the way of any future happiness.

He found some solace in shooting. How many beautiful African creatures must have been offered up in sacrifice to appease the broken hearts of white men! Day after day, stippled zebra; tall, solid eland; lovely grey water-buck; graceful kudu; thickset buffalo, fell to Lugard's rifle, and though he felt some stabs of conscience when, as so often happened in the deep verdure of the lake shore, wounded creatures got away, yet he continued shooting. There was always one good reason—the need to fill the pot for himself and his men.

On January 4th he returned to Karonga. Thanks to the efforts of consul-general Euan-Smith at Zanzibar, the sultan had sent up an envoy to try and patch up a peace between Mlozi and the British. The Arabs received his envoy and duly kissed the sultan's letter. But the embassy was not very promising. The agent was a very dark Swahili, who would have little standing with the half "white" Arab leaders; moreover he soon showed himself shifty and vacillating. The negotiations dragged on beyond the last day Lugard had fixed for a settlement. On January 16th the *Ilala* steamed up carrying the long-awaited gun. Lugard began to hack out a clear path along which to take the gun to a position from which the Arab stockades could be shelled. He also kept his eye on the calendar, waiting for the moment when the moon would be full shortly before dawn.

Before launching a new attack he consulted his companions. The enthusiasm for fighting had waned. The little company, now composed of Lugard, Dr. Cross, Sharpe, the faithful Fotheringham, and six other Company and Natal men, was in a bad way. Nearly all were sick; Fotheringham was covered with ulcers. The heavy rains which had broken had a more than physically damping effect on the exposed encampment. The three tribal groups of native auxiliaries were at odds with each other. Discipline over all Lugard's force depended upon consent rather than command. The downward pull on European morale of prolonged isolation in Africa was showing its results. Even Lugard betrayed a certain failure of his iron self-control when he nearly killed one of the local chiefs serving in his camp when he found him brutally ill-treating a woman.

When Lugard put the issue to the vote those for and against fighting were equal. Lugard gave the casting vote for war and drew up plans for attack for the night of February 20th-21st. A track having been already laboriously cut through the bush, the gun was dragged at night the seven miles to a knoll overlooking the Arab stockades, while various parties were put into position to attack the slavers, if they came into the open. The results of the action were not highly successful. Some of the several parties of attackers lost their way in the bush; it was difficult for Lugard at the gun to distinguish friend from foe and the native allies again failed to do their allotted parts. Much of the ammunition for the gun was faulty; the shells were of such high velocity that, meeting nothing stronger than the wood of the palisades, they simply drilled holes in this and burst beyond. The Arabs went to ground and stayed there.

Lugard still hoped very much to make peace and had thought that the arrival of the gun would bring the Arabs to terms. So it might have done. But, unfortunately, at this critical moment news reached Mlozi that the British had joined with the Germans in blockading the coast. It was this, Lugard believed, that put an end to all hopes of peace, and which opened up an indefinite continuance of hostilities. The little democracy at Karonga went into council and decided that Lugard ought to go. The air was full of rumours of new dangers and new diplomatic possibilities: it was said the Lakes Company might be going bankrupt; someone was needed to galvanize its local head-quarters into more active and efficient support, to ensure the dispatch of the proper ammunition for the gun, and, beyond all this, to go back and appeal to public opinion in England. Euan-Smith, now seemingly Lugard's admirer, and other correspondents, sent news of what was happening in and beyond Europe: the anti-slavery crusade launched by Cardinal Lavigerie[1]; General Boulanger returned as a deputy for Paris; a German expedition in Samoa cut up by islanders; the suicide of the Austrian Emperor's only son; the case of Parnell versus *The Times;* Balfour's reforming administration in Ireland.

To this wider world Lugard decided that he must now return. He resolved to make one more attack upon the Arab stockades with the little gun on March 13th. This he did with much the same limited effect as before, leaving the position at stalemate. The night before this his little army gave him a farewell party and a sing-song. All divisions and difficulties were for the moment forgotten. Dr. Cross made a speech on behalf of the Company, speaking of Lugard in terms which he never forgot, for he always looked back to that evening as one of the most valued memories in his life. Fotheringham, who deserves to be well remembered for his long endurance at this un-healthy and dangerous post, spoke next. He said Lugard's rule had been to do what was right regardless of the consequences. He then presented him with a sword and a pair of binoculars. Lugard was deeply touched.

" All were poor men—they were facing constant fever and exposing their lives for a miserable pittance; yet every one of them gave a large subscription."

These two gifts, as the writer was to observe, remained for the rest of his life among the most treasured of his many mementoes of action. Upon the sword the inscription runs:

" From the members of the Karonga Expedition to Captain F. D. Lugard, D.S.O., Norfolk Regt., Commanding the Expedition, as a token of their esteem.

Karonga, Lake Nyasa, Central Africa, March 13th, 1889." [2]

[1] Lavigerie, Charles-Martial Allemand, 1825–92; 1863 Bishop of Nancy; 1867 Archbishop of Algeria; 1873 founded *Societé des missions africaines* (the White Fathers); 1882 created Cardinal; 1888 founded *Societé anti-esclavagiste.*
[2] Lugard I, p. 153.

Lugard then left the Nyasa region by the same route by which he had come, down the Kwakwa river by canoe and so to Quilimane, arriving at Zanzibar on May 3rd. Here he found both Hawes, on his way back to relieve Buchanan, and Portal,[1] who was temporarily relieving Euan-Smith. Portal demands some further introduction. He was one of the able Foreign Office young men who were used by Lord Salisbury in administering his new African empire. At this time he was thirty-one years old, high-spirited, with a fine rather martial appearance. He was confident, perhaps a little too confident, and impetuous, but Lord Salisbury enjoyed riding a thoroughbred. His apprenticeship had been with Sir Evelyn Baring (later Lord Cromer) in Egypt, and he was now just mounting the next flight of steps leading to a promising career. Cromer subsequently described him as " one of the best specimens of that class of Englishmen . . . . who issue forth, year by year, from our public schools . . . . He may be said to have passed through his short but honourable career singing *Floreat Etona.*"[2]

The meeting was a battle of minds and a very unequal one. Lugard, with all the deep feeling his experience on the lake had left in him, urged that the British government should take some responsibility for the tragic situation created by the Arab slavers. Could not the government at least induce the African Lakes Company, about whose competence Lugard had no illusions, to take those decided measures needed to establish their authority? Could not the consul at Nyasa take a strong hand in negotiations with the Arabs? Could not the sultan be induced to send up another and better envoy? Both officials negatived decisively all Lugard's suggestions which were, in truth, not very promising. The matter, Portal told him, was entirely between the Lakes Company and the local people. The blame was upon the Company's local agents, Hawes said, in provoking and carrying on " this filibustering war." Lugard admitted the rashness and unreliability of the Moir brothers but he urged that the government could not entirely wash their hands of the whole affair. Surely the very fact that they had allowed him to fight the Arabs, while on leave, implicated them. This was doubtfully true and an argument likely to embarrass his future career. " These theories," Hawes reported coldly to the

1 See above p. 68.

2 Introduction by Lord Cromer to Sir Gerald Portal, *The British Mission to Uganda in 1893,* ed. by Rennell Rodd (1894), p. xiii.

Foreign Office, " somewhat resemble the gasps of a dying man."
Hawes' main concern was to clear his colleague Buchanan from any
responsibility for Lugard's expedition. All that Portal would say was
that Lugard had better go home and address his arguments to the
Lakes Company.

This was Lugard's first experience of throwing himself against the
rock-like impassivity of a government determined, for reasons which,
whether good or bad, lay beyond the knowledge of the suppliant, to
take no responsibility. In his mind were pictures of the massacre of
the Nkonde, of the agonies of the slaves and the perils of the missionaries. Something *must* be done, but what could it be, in the face of the
cool consular officials, bound by their instructions, who could even
blame the pioneers for their " provocative " behaviour which had
brought on this trouble.[1] There was only one thing and that was to
appeal to the British public. There, at least, he could find a heart and
a Christian conscience even if, as he felt in his impatience, such things
were out of place in the Zanzibar consulate or in Whitehall. A telegram
arrived from the Lakes Company asking him to come home at once
and he left on May 7th, after his three days of useless pleading.

Both officials hastened to report to the Foreign Office. Portal's
dispatch had reached England, and the Foreign Office officials' minutes
had been written upon it by June 1st, four days before Lugard landed.
The head of the African department was Sir Percy Anderson, the
official who presided over the process of accumulating a new Foreign
Office empire in Africa and therefore a man with whom Lugard was to
have much to do.[2] Anderson thought the letters worth careful reading,
particularly one from Lugard which had been enclosed in an earlier
dispatch from Zanzibar.[3] Lugard " writes pluckily and sensibly,"
Anderson minuted, but " shows what the chances are of this ill-
considered campaign." His gun was clearly useless in such country
and " he cannot beat the Arabs with a handful of half-hearted and sick
whites and a rabble of natives certain to bolt." On Portal's dispatch
of May 4th he commented, " the Company and Captain Lugard are

[1] Portal to Salisbury, 4 May 1889, and a private letter from Hawes to Anderson, 7 May 1889,
F.O. 84/1978.
[2] Anderson, Sir Henry Percy, K.C.B., K.C.M.G., 1831–96; 1852 entered F.O.; 1884
British delegate to West Africa Conference in Berlin; 1890 in Berlin to negotiate Anglo-German
agreement; 1894 Assistant Under-Secretary for foreign affairs.
[3] Lugard to Euan-Smith, 8 January 1889, enclosed in Hawes to Salisbury, 8 April 1889,
F.O 84/1978.

at their wits' end how to get out of the scrape they have got into."
His own recommendation was that the Lakes Company should be
informed at once " that H.M.G. have no responsibility for the acts
of Capt. Lugard." Salisbury's initial showing his agreement appeared
to round off this epitaph upon a seemingly hopeless adventure. Yet
was it really so hopeless? In Nyasaland, where the Lakes Company was
so weak, there was, it seemed, no half-way house for the government
between a complete rejection of responsibility and a complete annexation. But the journey from the one position to the other lay through
public opinion, and this in turn depended in large measure upon the
appeal made to it by the acts of their countrymen round Lake Nyasa.
This appeal Lugard now decided to make himself.

CHAPTER IX

THE STRUGGLE IN ENGLAND

1889 : Aet. 31

LUGARD GOT back to England on June 5th. His mind was full of the men he had left behind who were resolved to hold their post of danger on the lake and whose cause he had come to plead. In London he found there was still confusion and uncertainty as to what Britain should do in Central Africa. In a full-dress debate in the Commons in March all parties had re-dedicated themselves to the anti-slavery cause and Salisbury had given strong proof of his own devotion to it by initiating an international conference to meet at Brussels in 1890.[1] But there was widespread disgust at the country being committed by Salisbury to act with Germany in the East African blockade and the Prime Minister, who liked the German government as little as his countrymen did and had fuller knowledge than they for entertaining this dislike, was thrown upon the defensive, a position which, however, he maintained quite firmly.[2]

He was equally firm in reiterating his negative policy with regard to Nyasaland,[3] though, as so often with Salisbury, he was being less negative in secret action than in public word. In March 1889 he rather suddenly sent Johnston on a mission to Portugal to see what negotiation could do. Johnston was at this time fired with the Cape-to-Cairo dream, which he claims to have been the first to put into Rhodes' mind. Moreover, not knowing Nyasaland, he could not visualize what the missionaries had achieved there. He therefore fell in readily with an idea which the British minister, Mr. G. Petre, had already put up to Salisbury, that Britain should abandon the eastern and southern shores of the lake to Portugal. Petre had added that of course " the missionaries would protest loudly ", but they could transfer

[1] *Parliamentary Debates*, 26 March 1889, III. 334. 886-927.
[2] *Ibid.* 28 May 1889, III. 336. 1234-9
[3] *Ibid.* 25 March 1889, III. 334. 680-3.

themselves to the north.[1] This scheme satisfied Johnston as it cleared the way to the all-red route further west between Rhodes' new domain and Lake Tanganyika. Salisbury appears to have deliberately used this proposal to stir up the Scottish churches to an indignation of which he could make diplomatic use, evoking a memorial of 11,000 names in protest.[2]

Lugard, of course, knew nothing of this. He found himself apparently faced with a deadlock. Mlozi could not be crushed without more men and arms. The government would not provide these and the Company could not or, at least, would not supply them in adequate numbers. The directors wrote to him to confess that the appeal for £10,000 for this purpose had only raised £3,000 and James Stevenson declared that, faced with all their non-commercial expenses, the Company had never yet paid a dividend.[3] And even if the Company did provide the arms the Portuguese would not let them through. While Lugard was in England they even arrested Ross, the vice-consul at Quilimane—who, awkwardly, was also the Company's agent— for trying to send up another small piece of artillery for use at Karonga.

Lugard was thus faced, so it seemed, with a struggle as hopeless in England as it had been at Karonga, with Salisbury's position as invulnerable as Mlozi's. Looking for allies, he found his way at once into religious and anti-slavery circles which he had, of course, never met before. He spoke in Manchester to the Geographical Society, at the British Association and elsewhere, and wrote articles.[4] He went to stay with Sir John Kirk and initiated what was to be a great friendship and partnership against slavery. He stayed also with O'Neill. He worked most closely with the priest, Horace Waller, already noted as Livingstone's former companion, one of those secondary figures in the list of British humanitarians who have played an invaluable part speaking, preaching, pamphleteering, lobbying politicians, convening meetings, and writing innumerable letters.[5] He had already, shortly before Lugard's arrival and probably through O'Neill's agency,

---

[1] Petre to Salisbury, 3 November 1888, S.P. vol. 81 (Misc. 1, 1887–92).

[2] Oliver, *The Missionary Factor*, p. 126.

[3] J. Stevenson, 'The Arabs in Central Africa', *Manchester Geographical Society Journal*, vol. IV, 1888, p. 72.

[4] 'Lake Nyassa and Central Africa', *Manchester Geographical Society Journal*, vol. V, 1889; 'Nyassa-land and its Commercial Possibilities, *Proceedings of the British Association*, forty-second meeting, section E, 1889; 'A Glimpse of Lake Nyassa', *Blackwoods Magazine*, vol. CXLVII, January 1890.

[5] See above, p. 84.

Sir John Kirk after his retirement. From R. Coupland,
The Exploitation of East Africa, 1856-1890, 1939

brought out an article publicizing Lugard's adventures on the lake and giving the substance of his plan for dealing with the Nyasa problem.[1]

Waller, who knew how to write vivid propaganda of a kind Lugard could never achieve, lashed out at the complacent British public. " Our ivory-handled knives clatter no less merrily on our plates because British Indians and Arabs between them are tearing Africa to pieces for elephants' teeth ", and " cloves will smell as sweet though a year's cultivation of the Pemba clove-gardens has soaked up the blood of 50,000 human beings far away inland." He then went on to give verbatim Lugard's plan for placing two small steamers on Lake Nyasa, not to act alone as the ineffective coastal patrols had done, but in co-operation with a mobile military force of 1,000 trained Africans with about eight British officers, and a small detachment of Gurkhas, Sikhs or Pathans. Lugard astonished Waller by the detail and economy with which he worked out his scheme, down to the cost per annum of oil for the steamers' engines. He thus reached the conclusion that for £7,000 down for the two steamers and for £6,300 a year, the Nyasa region could be delivered from the slavers, and the work of the Scottish missions and traders safe-guarded.

In his own articles, his first essays in propaganda, Lugard described the scenery and peoples of the Nyasa region and the struggle with the slavers and then gave the reasons why the British there should be supported by their country. It is interesting to list the arguments he thought proper to use in the year 1889 in order to stimulate the slowly reviving appetite of his country for new colonies. First, naturally, came the slave-trade; then followed the need to safeguard the missions; to retain a country discovered by Livingstone; to protect the British traders already there; to open up new lands which promised to be rich in mineral, animal and vegetable products; to replace tribal warfare with law and order; to retain positions for which British men had sacrificed their lives or their health; to prevent these lands falling to rival powers who had no valid claim upon them. There was also the emotional appeal to the old adventurous spirit of Elizabethan days. Most strange to us today, perhaps, was the proposal that Nyasaland should be used as an outlet for the surplus population of India.[2]

[1] H. Waller, ' The two ends of the slave-stick', *The Contemporary Review*, vol. LV, April 1889, pp. 528–38.
[2] F. Lugard, ' The Fight against Slave-Traders', *The Contemporary Review*, vol. LVI, September 1889.

Lugard's estimate of £6,000 a year for securing Nyasaland seems, looking back, a modest sum. But it was more than Salisbury in 1889 could ask from parliament or even from his own Cabinet when Mr. Goschen, or more probably his officials at the Treasury, were reported to be resolutely set against any expenditure upon African adventures.[1] Thus arose the position that in 1889, for the lack of £6,000, Mlozi's wooden stockade stood in the path of British advance and the suppression of slave-raiding in Central Africa.

This situation was not accepted without protest. Only a month before Lugard landed in England there was a debate at the House of Commons, in which his own position was raised. The government showed the same passive sympathy for the " zeal and courage of individual Englishmen " which they had professed for so long. This time, however, a clear impatience with this attitude was shown by both the adherents and the critics of the Scottish pioneers. " To all appearances," said one of the latter, " a private company is carrying on a war in the region of Lake Nyasa and we use diplomatic influence to get arms passed to them through Portuguese territory, while an officer on the active list of Her Majesty's army is in command of the aggressive forces." Why were we fighting the Arabs at all? Why were they attacked ten days after the sultan had sent an envoy to negotiate? Why, on the other hand, asked a Scottish member, did the government practically incite the missions to fight and then do nothing to help them? Let there be an end of the government's " dangerous, futile, almost imbecile course on Lake Nyasa." It was also suggested that the Lakes Company should be given a charter to legalize their position.[2] Commenting upon this debate the explorer, Commander Lovett Cameron,[3] wrote to *The Times* a few days later defending Lugard. He offered to go himself to relieve him. " By the memories of Livingstone and Gordon, I appeal to the British nation not to abandon Lugard, not to wait until it is too late." The analogies were overstrained. Karonga was a dangerous place but it was neither isolated nor besieged: men went there and stayed there of their own

[1] See Oliver, *op. cit.* p. 124 and also Alex Johnston, *The Life and Letters of Sir Harry Johnston* (1929), pp. 142-3.

[2] *Parliamentary Debates,* 2 May 1889, III. 335. 1049-73.

[3] Cameron, Commander Verney Lovett, C.B., 1844-94; 1873 leader of expedition to carry aid to Livingstone; 1878 travelled in the Middle East; 1882 with Sir R. Burton in West Africa; was recognized as a student of African political questions; 1894 claimed to be the originator of the project for a railway from the Cape to Cairo.

will to challenge Mlozi. And Lugard was well out of danger when Cameron's letter was printed.[1]

A few days later Lord Salisbury had to receive another deputation of those concerned about this question and he again gave an answer which in the view of the Scottish press would not " be very cheerful reading for our countrymen at the lakes."[2] The Prime Minister rather rashly scouted the idea of the Portuguese invading the Shire highlands. They were just as likely, he said, to attack Table Bay! He maintained unshaken his oft-reiterated " *non possumus* " with regard to helping the British missions. But he threw out the hint that, although cut off by Portugal from the east, civilization might come to them from the north or from the south. " The north " must mean Germany. But what could be meant by " the south "?

The answer was soon given. At the end of March, into all this wavering and controversy, there suddenly appeared in London the bronzed face and slouching figure of Cecil Rhodes. He had come to get the Royal Charter which he needed to give official cover to what he was doing and meaning to do in central Africa with his new company.

Rhodes was in a hurry. He could only spare some three months of that summer for the London end of his activities. While he was there things happened. Where other people had hopes he had intentions; while they played with ideas he put his will behind them and used the instrument of money to carry them out with immediacy. Kruger's Boers were trying to forestall him in the north but he had outtrekked the trekkers and got his concession. The Portuguese were disputing Manicaland: he was ready to push them out by diplomacy or, if necessary, by force. A host of rival concessionaires were asserting their claims: he set to work to buy them out. Nyasaland must be secured so he must find means to galvanize the British government. In all his recent achievements he had been helped by the support of Sir Hercules Robinson[3] who, on a large scale, held the official position of the Nyasa consuls but who took the risk they refused and lost his job as a result. It is not easy and it is not necessary to follow all Rhodes did

[1] *The Times*, 11 May 1889.
[2] *The Scotsman*, 18 May 1889.
[3] Robinson, Hercules George Robert, 1st Baron Rosmead, P.C., G.C.M.G., 1824–97; Lieutenant 87th Royal Irish Fusiliers; 1846–7 engaged on Irish famine relief work; 1859–79 Governor successively of Hong Kong, Ceylon, New South Wales, New Zealand; 1880–9 Governor of Cape and High Commissioner for South Africa; 1895–7 Governor and Commander-in-Chief of Cape Colony.

in London that summer, but much of it indirectly affects our story and some of it does so directly. And Rhodes offers us one more example of the contrasting minds and methods of the men of the last generation who put together the pieces of the British empire in Africa.

We get one account of Rhodes' most effective appearance at the London end of African affairs from Harry Johnston. He met Rhodes at a dinner party and from that moment all else faded out and the two men found themselves still talking in their evening clothes at Rhodes' hotel when the daylight came the next morning. Then Johnston changed his clothes and went straight on to the Foreign Office with a cheque for £2,000 in his pocket as an instalment of £10,000 a year which Rhodes said he was prepared to pay for the securing of Nyasaland and the regions further west towards Tanganyika. No one in England then knew much about Rhodes. When Johnston arrived with his cheque and Rothschild's guarantee for the rest, Sir Percy Anderson rang up Rothschild and found that Rhodes was good for a million or more; and when Johnston saw Salisbury the same afternoon and told his story the Prime Minister's query was " Rather a pro-Boer M.P. in South Africa, I fancy? " [1] Johnston and Anderson could not believe their good fortune. " A man had come forward offering virtually to let us take over any degree of Central Africa between the Zambezi and the White Nile and find the money to run it, at least until the British public should awaken to its value." [2] Johnston may have rearranged the limelight a little in his account but the facts were astonishingly true.

Rhodes, with his usual practice of buying rivals up or off, got into touch with the directors of the African Lakes Company and offered to subsidize them by forming a new company in association with his own. This seemed an equally providential intervention to them. Rhodes went up to Scotland and the plan was settled on James Stevenson's steam-yacht, *Fire-Fay*, on the Clyde on June 26th, with Fred Moir in attendance.

Rhodes, indeed, took public opinion by storm. His Chartered Company seemed the perfect escape from the dilemma which faced a people which was beginning to desire acquisition as an end but not sufficiently to make them ready to provide the means. It was

[1] Johnston, *The story of my life*, p. 235 ff.
[2] *Ibid.* p. 238.

possible to become enthusiastic about the ends, with their exciting glint of gold and other mineral wealth, now that the prospect of getting them at bargain price suddenly appeared. *The Times*, which as late as 1884 had urged that in southern Africa Britain should not be tempted to "increase the area of our engagement" and remained cold until 1886, suddenly swung round and on May 29th led a chorus of national self-congratulation at the proposed acquisition of "a vast country, one of the richest regions in Central Africa." [1] The article, "from a correspondent", paid tribute to the work of the "disinterested company of Scottish merchants", the Lakes Company. But these had come to a critical stage in their career. "Either they must retire" and the region where they have laboured for 30 years "be resigned to barbarism and the Arab . . . . or the hands of the Company must be strengthened." Now this was to be done. The device of the chartered company which had gained India for Britain and which was being used on the Niger and in East Africa, was to be applied in Central Africa. Leading financiers of England and the Cape would support it and "a certain philanthropic element is not wanting in the proposed board of directors." (There was even to be a flavour of royalty through the Duke of Fife becoming a director). But the prime advantages were that "no additional burdens would be laid on this country; no support of a military force required; no additions to our fleet demanded . . . . the chartered company would be responsible in all directions, counting only on that protection which is the right of every British subject in any part of the world." The leading article of the same day warmly commended the scheme since "The truth is we must either advance or recede." The *Pall Mall Gazette* under a leader entitled "Painting the African Map Red" declared it "one of the greatest schemes that ever startled the somewhat sluggish imagination of John Bull"; cried "Chartered Adventurers, go ahead!"; and told the government "not to fool around any longer indecisively." There was very little discord in the pæan of approval from the public and the press. The president of the Royal Geographical Society, General Strachey, blessed the plan and the Anti-Slavery Society welcomed it. [2] There were a very few warning notes: the London Chamber of Commerce disapproved, fearing monopolies; Joseph Chamberlain was

---

[1] *The History of 'The Times'* (1947), vol. iii, pp. 159-61; also *The Times*, 29 May 1889.
[2] *A.S.R.*, IV. ix. May and June 1889, pp. 120-1.

doubtful; some well-informed missionary circles were in opposition. *The Spectator* remembered the crimes of the East India Company and with prophetic vision said of the new company " the nation had no right to lend them the irresistible strength of its civilization and then declare itself irresponsible for their use of power."[1]

Thus the nation, or the interested section of it, rejoiced—and this was as true of the Niger and East African regions—at the idea of extending the empire while evading the cost not only in cash, but in administrative embarrassment and in moral responsibility. This cheerful evasion was mainly the result of ignorance. Before very long it would be realized that, in tropical Africa at least, there were charges, material and moral, from which the nation could not escape.

And what of Lugard who was reading these items in his morning papers in London and who was to be caught up and swept into Africa for the next ten years on the tide of this new idea? He, too, thought he had reason to rejoice: surely his big chance had come at last! On July 2nd, a few days after the meeting with Rhodes on the Clyde, John Stephen of the Lakes Company wrote to him: " We will amalgamate with his [Rhodes'] Company, should a Royal Charter be got . . . . " The Foreign Office was being slow about this but " we hope you will see your way clear to lead an expedition to finally dispose of Mlozi and his friends, and help to establish a settled government in Nyasaland." But a few days later a very ambiguous letter followed, in which Stephen said Rhodes had done nothing further and suggested that Lugard, whom the Company had treated very meanly, should himself set about collecting the necessary £10,000 which " would not be a great task . . . . with your knowledge of the work . . . . and explaining the urgency of the case. . . . . I hope " Stephen went on " you will soon be back in Central Africa fighting the battles of the downtrodden and neglected against their murderers. God has promised a special blessing to those who do this work." The postscript, however, was more cheerful. News had just come that Rhodes *was* forming his Company and wanted an exact estimate of what was wanted to deal with the position at the north end of the lake. (J. Stephen to L. 12 July 1889).

Lugard, it seems, went to see Rhodes and put all his plans and figures before him. Rhodes, going better than Lugard's characteristically

[1] *The Spectator,* 1 June 1889.

economical estimate, asked him if he would undertake to put his own plan into operation at a cost of £20,000 down and £9,000 a year. Lugard, who had had enough of the Lakes Company, said " yes " but asked to be allowed to choose his own officers and be directly responsible to the board of the South Africa Company. A few days later he had a discouraging letter from Waller, who had a way of possessing accurate inside information, prophesying that the fuss about Rhodes would merely lull public anxiety about Nyasa and produce no quick assistance. He also said that he had heard that the authorities would not allow Lugard leave from the army to go on the expedition and that he was not surprised at this. " Lord Salisbury must see that there is just that species of combustible [material] mixed up with these German and Portuguese difficulties in Africa that might all go wrong with a spark, and he dreads it." (H. Waller to L. 29 July 1889). Clearly Lugard was thought at the Foreign Office to be just the sort of man to supply sparks. His attack on the dhow at Deep Bay had been noted there with disapproval as over-hasty, though the officials had been forced to admit that they could not pretend at that distance to control his proceedings.[1] Euan-Smith, who had appeared to Lugard to be his friend and admirer, had written to Salisbury a little earlier to report that he had persuaded Rhodes to employ Lugard and two other explorers, Cameron and Thomson[2], in different regions and had described them, in terms presumably pleasing to his master, as a " trio of *agents-provocateurs* of a considerable amount of mischievous and ignorant agitation concerning African affairs."[3] The agent Salisbury chose to send out to make a reconnaissance for him in Central Africa was, as we have seen, his favourite Harry Johnston whom he appointed as consul at Mozambique, and he left England to take this up just as Lugard returned.

The next thing was a letter from one of Rhodes' supporters, Albert (later Lord) Grey to tell Lugard that the Company would not send anyone out from England. When Lugard called to see Rhodes he found he had just sailed for South Africa without a word. Lugard was aghast. Rhodes had made use of his scheme, offered him a command

[1] Minute of Anderson on Buchanan to Salisbury, 8 February 1889, enclosing Lugard to Buchanan, 18 January 1889, F.O. 84/1942.

[2] Thomson, Joseph, 1858–94, geologist and explorer; 1879 expedition Dar-es-Salaam to Lakes Nyasa and Tanganyika; 1881 in Rovuma region; 1883 travelled across Masai country from Mombasa; 1885 Sokoto (Nigeria) expedition; 1890 in Central Africa.

[3] Euan-Smith to Salisbury, 15 June 1889, S.P. vol. 79 (Zanzibar 1888–9).

and then thrown him over. He was equally disgusted with the Lakes Company, which he accused of having exhausted Rhodes' patience by their procrastination.[1] For himself, after all his services and his wound, they had done nothing more than offer him £100 which was insufficient even to repay him for his steamer fares and which, for all his poverty, he refused to touch himself but had it paid to a member of his family. He felt that not only had *he* been betrayed but also the men whose cause he had come to plead, and he published a bitter article displaying his sense of injury.

" They looked to myself to help them and my mouth has been shut, and my efforts paralysed, by illusory visions of great undertakings and specious suggestions by men who now announce . . . that they ' mean to send out no one from England'. In this sole phrase they summarize the result of their large intentions and their acknowledgments to myself . . . There was a few months ago a widely spread interest in this struggle with the slave-dealers. Men have waited by common consent to see what would come of all this tall talking about charters. ' *Parturiunt montes, nascetur ridiculus mus* '."

He ended with unconcealed bitterness aimed at the wealthy heads of the Lakes Company.

" Meanwhile the season has been a gay one in London, the delights of yachting are seductive, grouse shooting has begun—there is no time for Nyasa botherations . . . It is no longer a question of dividends . . . It is a question of a heavy and unavoidable responsibility already incurred, which *must* be faced." He would even forgive the garrison if they deserted their thankless post. " A responsibility lies on me. These men trusted me to let their case be known." [2]

In October Lugard went to see Cawston, Rhodes' agent in London, to complain bluntly about the treatment he had received and about the delay in acting in Nyasaland. When told that they were awaiting news of Johnston's proceedings, Lugard urged immediate action and said that although he had now accepted some temporary work for the East Africa Company his heart was really in Nyasaland and he would still go there if asked. To his consternation the secretary of the Lakes Company, Ewing, came in. He did not conceal his indignation

---

1 Lugard I, pp. 158–9.
2 In the article in *The Contemporary Review*, see above p. 145, n. 2.

at Lugard's recent article and especially the barb about yachting. " It was ungenerous." Stevenson had been eager to reply to it but he had advised him to ignore it. Had the directors not worked and thought night and day about Nyasaland and subscribed large sums? Lugard was unmoved. He replied that a remark about the London season could hardly apply to Scotsmen. As for the rest, " Since they *had* chosen to give it pointed meaning, I think it was thoroughly deserved." The chairman had been yachting at the height of the Nyasa crisis and nothing had been done. Horace Waller chided his angry friend about this, saying that he had trodden hard on James Stevenson's toes, but that he was now " a hypochondriac, one day all enthusiasm, the next fathoms down in low spirits and misery, poor old fellow." (H. Waller to L. 26 October 1889).

The latin tag Lugard had used in his article was appropriate only as concerned Nyasaland and only then in relation to the immediate future. In this certainly both Lugard and his friends on the lake appeared to have been utterly let down. Rhodes had rushed back to South Africa to get his pioneer column started for the north; the plans for Nyasaland could wait. The real reason was probably that Lord Salisbury was not ready to agree to the setting up of an administration. He had his own conception of the proper sequence of events. He had first to clear up the diplomatic tangle by dealing with Portugal, especially as regards the southern half of the country, and with Germany who claimed the northern part, including Karonga. The Scottish missions, moreover, could have no wish to come under Rhodes' Company, Nyasaland was thus, in Salisbury's plan, to come under direct British authority and Rhodes' plan was unacceptable, both in form and in time.[1]

Had Lugard known this he would have been saved much of his bitterness. As it was he had to writhe with frustrated anger and sympathy as he read gloomy letters from Laws and Scott while Fotheringham, still at Karonga with the brave Dr. Cross, wrote to him of fighting, disease, death and a sordid war of attrition, each side cutting off the other's stragglers while the wretched Nkonde suffered and the slave-trade continued uninterruptedly. Lugard was also quarrelling with Hawes over a letter Lugard had published in *The Times* accusing the consuls of doing less even than Salisbury had

---

[1] I am indebted for this suggestion to Dr. Hanna.

promised since, by letting the Arabs know that the Company's and Lugard's efforts were strictly unofficial, they had encouraged their opposition. " Surely this is not ' consular protection ' and ' diplomatic effort '! I had rather the Arab forces had been doubled than this misleading statement had been made by the Consul."[1] In his bitterness he was critical not only of the Lakes Company but of Johnston. " It is now an open secret," he said in another fiery article, " that someone has been sent to make peace at any price," and later, in his book, he dealt severely with some aspects of Johnston's proceedings.[2]

There was, however, nothing more he could do and in this mood he gave in to Kirk's suggestion that he should now accept the long-offered employment under the Imperial British East Africa Company, He did so, still hoping to return to Nyasaland, a hope that was not to be fulfilled.

We cannot, however, after having followed the early history of Nyasaland so far, leave its future at this moment of suspense, or neglect to review the sequel to Lugard's adventure. The little band of missionaries and traders had long to wait before the large promises made in the summer of 1889 found any fulfilment for them. Johnston made history in July 1889 by sailing comfortably into the Zambezi by the newly discovered Chinde mouth in a naval gunboat, H.M.S. *Stork*, thus by-passing the Portuguese. But when he reached the Shire river he found—Salisbury, for once, being wrong—a large, armed Portuguese expedition under Major Serpa Pinto preparing to occupy the highlands. He could do no more than protest and hurry on. But he evidently brought in his pocket from Salisbury instructions which allowed him in these circumstances to ask John Buchanan to declare, in August, a British protectorate over the Shire highlands, the first positive act performed by the government in this region since the Nyasa issue began, and one that it must have given the consul-planter great satisfaction to carry out. This did not prevent the Portuguese from attacking the Makololo, and the issue became so grave that the two nations were brought to the edge of war; the conceit of the Portuguese, Salisbury's representative in Madrid told him, being only equalled by their delusions.[3] But the rough thrust of the spearhead of

---

1 *The Times*, 18 April 1889, dated 15 January from Karonga.
2 Lugard, ' A Glimpse of Lake Nyassa ', *Blackwoods Magazine*, vol. CXLVII, January 1890; and Lugard I, p. 159 ff.
3 Petre to Salisbury, 3 November 1888, S.P. vol. 81 (Misc. 1, 1887–92).

Rhodes' pioneering column south of the Zambezi began to tell. Salisbury, believing, as he lay upon a bed of illness, that Portugal was "presuming upon her weakness", dispatched an ultimatum, and followed it with gunboats to Mozambique. The Portuguese wavered: they were increasingly alarmed by the proceedings of Rhodes' Company.[1] Pinto was recalled and there were anti-British riots in Lisbon. In 1890 a convention was drawn up. In Rhodes' view its demarcation was inadequate but, fortunately for him, the Portuguese Cortes refused to ratify, so he was able to continue pushing his very " effective occupation " further and further north. At last in the summer of 1891 the Portuguese bowed to the inevitable and saw much of their inland empire, one even more insubstantial than that of the sultan of Zanzibar, taken by those with the will to develop it, and themselves confined to the territories which they had some claim to have occupied.[2] " Poor Portugal! " was Salisbury's very characteristic comment after his firm but always judicial control of these turbulent transactions. " But people are not reasonable, either at Lisbon or Cape Town."[3]

All this did little to give immediate help to the Nyasa British in their relations with Arab slavers and the militant African chiefs allied to them. But among Johnston's first acts was a tour round the lake making treaties, one of them with Mlozi. Lugard, with something of the uncompromising mentality of the emigré, bitterly condemned this as weakly giving away most of what he and his companions had fought for.[4] In May 1891, after the settling of frontiers with Germany and Portugal, a British Protectorate was proclaimed over Nyasaland. But internally in Nyasaland this was the beginning rather than the end of trouble. One after another the chiefs, Arab and African, rebelled, and it took Johnston, who was sent to administer this unruly little protectorate, seven years to reduce it to order, and this was only achieved very much as Lugard had foreseen, with the employment of a number of British officers, 200 professional Sikh soldiers imported from India, trained Zanzibaris and local native companies, artillery and two naval gunboats on the lake. Even so, there were some serious reverses. In the end, in 1895, Johnston had to deal with Mlozi, who was said

---

[1] Petre to Salisbury, 31 December 1890, S.P. vol. 81 (Misc. 1, 1887-92).

[2] *Treaty between Her Majesty and His Majesty the King of Portugal defining their respective spheres of influence in Africa.* Portugal No. 1 (1891), C.6375; given in Hertslet, *Map of Africa*, vol. iii, p. 1016 ff.

[3] Cecil, *Life of Salisbury*, vol. iv, p. 275.

[4] Lugard I, p. 161.

to be at the back of all the opposition and who was justifying Lugard's prophecies by continuing his murderous raids for slaves upon the surrounding tribes. He refused even to see Johnston remarking " The British have closed my route to the coast: very well, I will close their road to Tanganyika." In the end it took a surprise attack, a dozen European officers, 100 Sikhs, 300 trained African soldiers, artillery, and two days of desperate fighting before his stockaded village could be stormed, facts which are an interesting comment upon the attempts by Lugard and the others to reduce these Arab strongholds. Mlozi was found hiding in an underground cell and, as he had butchered forty-five African hostages during the fighting, Johnston and the Nkonde chiefs, whose people he had harried for years, condemned him to be hanged on the spot. He refused to make any defence. " What is the good? These people are resolved that I shall die. My hour is come." So this reverend-looking figure with his long white beard and long white robes, after killing or leaving his scars upon many white men, including Lugard, and massacring or enslaving uncounted thousands of Africans, having shown amazing courage and tenacity in his long defiance of all British efforts to crush or tame him, at last met his end.[1]

Johnston was assisted in his efforts by the £10,000 which was paid annually by Rhodes towards the expense of policing Nyasaland and the region lying just to the west which was directly under his Company. The arrangement was, however, of a kind that almost inevitably led to recriminations between them. Rhodes' remark, when it finally came to an end, was not unfair. It was that " we are proud to think admhave yearly paid into Her Majesty's Treasury a sum for the we inistration of one of our own provinces because Governments were unable to face the House of Commons to ask them to contribute to their obligations."[2] We may also record here that the agreement between Rhodes' Company and the African Lakes Company was not completed until 1893.[3]

Peace and security thus came to Nyasaland, though it came with agonizing slowness. Yet, if Salisbury's pronouncements and actions are carefully pieced together over the years—and Lugard's work was bound up with the ideas and actions of the ministers in charge of

[1] Sir H. Johnston, *British Central Africa* (1897), pp. 135–43.
[2] ' Vindex', *Cecil Rhodes, His Political Life and Speeches* (1900), p. 419.
[3] Moir, *After Livingstone*, pp. 176–7.

African affairs—it will be seen that he was better than his word. After reiterating year after year the formula of non-intervention, non-annexation and no military adventures, in the end he not only vigorously warded off Portugal, which he had always promised to do, but also took over the territory and finally sent naval and military forces to subdue it and his chosen agent, Johnston, to administer it. When did he change his mind? Was it, as reported by the French ambassador, to whom he had asserted in October 1888 that he would lend himself to no expeditions into the interior,[1] that he was overborne by the sudden awakening of Britain's colonial ambitions, especially on the part of the business interests?[2] Doubtless these influences played their part. But, if Johnston's rather egocentric revelations are to be accepted, Salisbury's mind had turned in favour of annexation long before he felt able to act. Following a long talk in the summer of 1888, during which the Prime Minister had shown an amazing knowledge of African geography and a special grasp of the Nyasa region, Johnston had been walking with him in the magnificent grounds of Hatfield when Salisbury suddenly turned to him and said " What a pity it is no one could put the whole African question lucidly before the public: in some newspaper article, I mean." The young man took this as an order. That night he jotted down the points in their talk and on August 22nd there appeared in *The Times* three columns of " Great Britain's Policy in Africa " (By an African Explorer). If the story of its genesis is true, it is a highly interesting production. It called upon Britain to cast aside her " magnificent inactivity " and start, almost too late, to annex as much as possible of the Africa she had long had within her hands, if she had only cared to close them. Outright annexation was still not advocated but very large protectorates to warn off rivals and to gain commercial advantages, " without at the same time charging ourselves with the internal administration of the country and being compelled on that account to incur considerable initial expense and greatly increased responsibility." The article still anticipated no more than an empire on the cheap but it was frankly empire, and that was still a controversial objective to Salisbury's nation.[3] Salisbury cannot have agreed with all

[1] Waddington to Goblet, 31 October 1888, Archives des affaires étrangères (A.A.E.), vol. 834, f. 235.
[2] Waddington to Spuller, 30 November 1889, A.A.E., 844, f. 265.
[3] Johnston, *The story of my life*, pp. 221-2.

Johnston's views, yet there is much in this article that seems to reflect his mind.

The Prime Minister showed his concern for the Nyasa region in two other ways. We have seen that when Johnston was sent to Lisbon, the young agent was ready to bargain away part of the Shire highlands with their mission stations and that it was Salisbury who intervened to prevent this.[1] And when, the next summer, Rhodes was sweeping all before him, it was no doubt in accordance with Salisbury's wishes that, despite the assistance of that providential £10,000 a year, Nyasaland was kept outside Rhodes' wide kingdom and retained directly under the Foreign Office. For there were two kinds of British imperialism developing in Africa, one which was ready to see the initiative pass wholly into the hands of local colonies and of companies, and one which meant the British government—which Rhodes derisively called " grandmama "—to retain control. Yet, such caution did Salisbury think it necessary to show that, even after he had sent Johnston to Lake Nyasa, Lugard found, when he called at the Foreign Office late in October 1889, that Sir Percy Anderson and Sir Villiers Lister refused to admit to him that Johnston was the accredited agent of government. He was travelling, " being an excellent traveller ", just to see his consular district, and his relationship even with Buchanan seemed to be vague.

This slow, measured advance, in the dangerous conditions of Africa, had its immediate victims, and, as we have seen, thousands, perhaps even millions of Africans died or were enslaved in the interval between Britain's unofficial and her official intervention, while white men suffered death, or wounds, or an almost unendurable strain. Lugard burned with a sense of humiliation at the rejection of his eager services, and from watching Johnston take over the work he longed to do. The two men, so similar in their work, were an absolute contrast in character. Johnston was a travelled cosmopolitan who had already worked in the consular service; master of nearly a dozen languages, European and African; artist; novelist; wit; versifier; naturalist; explorer; Elizabethan in his range of gifts and in the combination of the aesthetic with the adventurous and of an almost *fin de siècle* refinement with the hardness he brought to bear upon the often bloody business of taming a still wild Africa. He was strongly ambitious and perhaps,

---

[1] Johnston, *The story of my life*, p. 233.

with his lack of presence, due to his large head, weak high voice and short stature (Lugard, himself not a giant, always called him "little Johnston"), he needed an extra measure of self-assertiveness to compensate. In spite of his proclaimed agnosticism and his witty, rather risky verses lampooning the leading figures in the Foreign Office, he was well regarded there and married the step-daughter of the all-important Sir Percy Anderson.

Lugard, with his broken record, his impetuous exploits and his passionate advocacies, had no chance at this time of gaining an official appointment above such a man. He had little hope of winning Salisbury's confidence sufficiently for him to be favoured for any important unofficial post. He might well think that in this Nyasa affair he had been given the bitter rind while Johnston appropriated the fruit. On the lake he had attempted the impossible and failed, bringing away a severe wound, and in England he had failed again either to win speedy relief for his comrades or the right to return, either for government or one of the companies, with the authority and equipment to finish the task. It would indeed be easy, especially in view of the long and spirited record of his adventures which he left behind in his book, to exaggerate the importance of the part he had played. In his own natural desire to assert and justify himself at a still difficult phase of his career, he tended to stress and to dramatize his own contribution and there was often a tone almost of self-advertisement and self-justification in his writings at this time. But if there was drama at Karonga, the chief heroes in it were Fotheringham and Dr. Cross and Lugard did not fail to point this out.[1] Yet his part need not be minimized. He thwarted and weakened Mlozi at a time of great peril on the lake. More important, his writings and other activities in Britain all went to swell the increasing volume of public knowledge and feeling upon the subject. He acted, moreover, at the very moment when, as we have seen, British colonial policy was approaching a turning-point, but when private effort and advocacy had still to fill the gap between the nation's opportunity and its will.

What did he gain for himself from this experience? More, perhaps, than he could realize. He committed himself to Africa. He went into the continent with a mind not far from derangement and if the obsession of his loss had not lifted when he came out, at least he now had

[1] In the article in *Blackwoods Magazine*, see above p. 144, n. 4.

the will to live and work in spite of it. He had gone there an all but nameless wanderer and had, in the most testing of experiences, won the good opinion of almost every one of the widely varied men he had met. He had learned much of Africa and especially of its curse, the slave-trade, and he had also begun to assess the play of ministerial minds and public opinion in Britain upon the remotest actions in Africa. From that knowledge came the realization that it was not enough to be the man of action only: he must take a hand in making as well as in executing policy. All this represented no small achievement for an African apprenticeship of twelve months.

PART THREE

Uganda 1889-1894

CHAPTER X

EAST AFRICAN OPPORTUNITY

1889-1890 : Aet. 31-32

IT MIGHT have been thought that after working for one company that was attempting the impossible in Africa, Lugard would not have risked repeating the same experience upon a larger scale with another. But in 1889 the new Imperial British East Africa Company (which in the next few chapters will be referred to simply as the Company) seemed, at least to the public, to be a reasonably promising undertaking and in the sudden enthusiasm for the expedient of chartered companies there was little desire to scrutinize the relation between its ends and its means. Its position, moreover, was wholly unlike that of the African Lakes Company. It was being set up with the open support of the government: the sultan of Zanzibar had granted it a formal concession, and on September 3rd 1888 it received a Royal Charter giving it, on the model of the Niger Company Charter issued two years before, full administrative powers with the right to acquire territory and to levy taxation.[1] The Charter recognized the Company's right to the large concession granted by the sultan of Zanzibar and to a number of treaties already made by Company agents with tribal chiefs near the coast.

It seemed that Britain, through the agency of this Company, was at last able and willing to occupy a part at least of East Africa. The whole of it had been hers for the taking during the greater part of the century, ever since her attention had been drawn to it by her anti-slavery policy and by the interests and activities of her Indian subjects and their Arab neighbours in the Persian Gulf. As early as 1824 Captain William FitzWilliam Owen of the Royal Navy, a man of energy and large views, had acceded to the wishes of the people of

---

[1] *Papers relating to the Mombasa Railway Survey and Uganda.* Africa No. 4 (1892), C.6555, pp. 6–11.

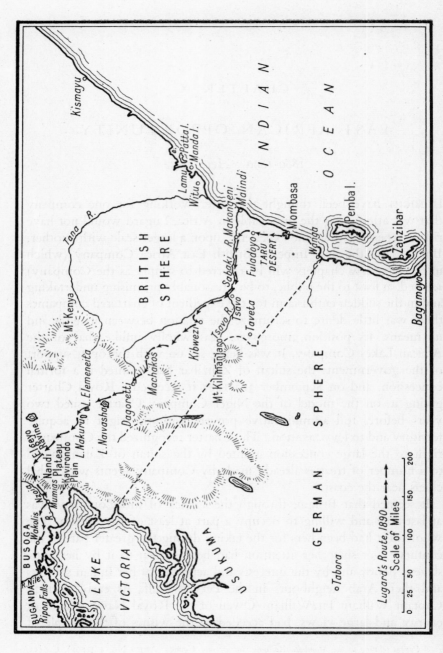

Kismayu

Lamu ○Patta I.
Witu ○ ○Manda I.
Malindi

Tana R.

BRITISH
SPHERE

Mombasa

Pemba I.

INDIAN

OCEAN

Mt Kenya

Sabaki R.
Makongeni

Wanga

Zanzibar

Tsavo R.
Fuladoyo
TARU
DESERT
Kibwezi
Tsavo

Bagamoyo

Machakos
○Taveta

Mt Kilimanjaro

Dagoretti

L. Elemeneita
L. Nakuru
L. Naivasha

El Geyo
Ravine
Njoro
Nandi Plateau
Mumias Plain
Kavirondo

Wakoli's R.

GERMAN
SPHERE

USUKUMA

BUSOGA
BUGANDA
Nile
Ripon Falls

LAKE
VICTORIA

○Tabora

Lugard's Route, 1890 →
Scale of Miles

0 25 50 100 150 200

East Africa

164

Mombasa, then at odds with the sultan of Zanzibar, and annexed the place to Britain.[1] He argued, as Lugard and others were to do, that this was the surest and cheapest way of stopping the slave-trade since naval patrols were expensive and ineffective. He pointed out that Britain could take the whole of East Africa and in a stirring dispatch to the Admiralty declared " It is to me as clear as the sun that God has prepared the dominion of East Africa for the only nation on the earth which has public virtue enough to govern it for its own benefit."[2] The Union Jack flew for two years over Mombasa before the British government's refusal to support Owen's action led to its being hauled down.

It was left to a later British generation to try to make good Owen's high boast. It was commerce plus philanthropy, both struggling with official indifference, which continued to urge annexation. In 1838 Buxton had vainly pressed this course upon Palmerston. In 1875–6 it was once more recommended by witnesses to a parliamentary committee on slavery and again rejected.[3] In 1876 General Gordon, pushing up the Nile to the Great Lakes in the service of Egypt, realized that by far the best access to this region was from the East African coast. Upon his advice the Khedive Ismail sent a fleet to Kismayu. This aroused the opposition of Kirk in defence of his sultan while the British missionaries, who distrusted Gordon's employers as much as they admired him, joined Kirk in urging official discouragement.[4] Finally, in 1877, Sultan Barghash, alarmed by Gordon's attempt and fearing even more dangerous intrusions, is said to have taken the initiative in inviting Britain, the power he knew and trusted most, to occupy and open up the whole of his mainland. William Mackinnon took up the proposal. He was an Argyll man who had built up the British India Steam Navigation Company, and had begun sending his ships to Zanzibar in 1875. The proposal was carried a long way in discussions with Barghash and the Foreign Office: the concessions document was actually drawn up but there followed delays and the scheme fell through. It would have given Britain the whole of East Africa with the sultan's goodwill and without any trouble ·

---

1 Coupland I, pp. 235–70.
2 Ibid. pp. 237–8.
3 Coupland II, pp. 222–4.
4 Ibid. and also Sir John Gray, ' Sir John Kirk and Mutesa', *Uganda Journal*, vol. XV, March 1951.

at that time with European competitors, and it would have saved some ten or twelve years of the worst of the slave-trade. The exact reason for the failure of the plan is not clear.[1] The Company blamed the Foreign Office but the circumstantial evidence of Mackinnon's character seems to accuse him of being at least partly to blame. Kirk, who was best placed to judge, thought it was due to " the little Scotsman's half-heartedness." He was " never hot enough on it." Ten years later, when Mackinnon took the idea up again, in much more difficult international conditions, and got his charter, Kitchener wrote to Kirk " I hope you will now take up the East Africa Company strongly and get rid of Mackinnon. Otherwise I greatly fear that our future work in Africa will become the laughing stock of Europe."[2] Salisbury, too, said later that the great difficulty about the East African question was the character of Mackinnon. " He has none of the qualities for pushing an enterprise which depends on decision and smartness . . . . He has no energy for anything except quarrelling with Germans."[3]

One more chance of taking over East Africa was presented to the British government. When Gordon was killed in Khartoum, one of his provincial governors, that very remarkable character Eduard Schnitzer, an Austrian doctor of Jewish extraction, who assumed the name of Emin Pasha,[4] was left cut off in the equatorial south of the Sudan with his garrison of Sudanese troops. His one very circuitous and precarious contact with the civilized world was southward to Uganda where he got into touch with the famous C.M.S. missionary Alexander Mackay. In 1886 he told Mackay he was willing to make his province a British protectorate. Mackay regarded this offer as coming through the providence of God and sent it to the British government via Kirk. But Salisbury, writing from Balmoral, rejected

1 See Coupland II, pp. 300–18 and Oliver, *The Missionary Factor*, p. 90. I am indebted to Miss de Kiewiet for information on this point. In her work on the history of the Imperial British East Africa Company, she has found evidence that suggests that Salisbury, who took over the Foreign Office while negotiations were in progress, was responsible for their failure: the Arabic interpreter, Badger, reported privately to Salisbury that he had conveyed to the sultan the Foreign Secretary's disapproval of the concession. (Badger to Salisbury, 3 July 1878, F.O. 84/1528.) She has also informed me that she has not found evidence of an " invitation " from Barghash, but only a letter from him to Lord Derby, written at Kirk's advice, asserting " my desire to help them all I can." (13 December 1876, F.O. 84/1454.)

2 Coupland II, p. 469.

3 Salisbury to Goschen, 10 April 1890; quoted in Cecil, *Life of Salisbury*, vol. iv. p. 281.

4 Emin Pasha (Eduard Schnitzer), ?1830–92; travelled in Turkey and Egypt; 1877–8 Governor of Equatorial Province, Sudan; 1888–9 " rescued " by Emin Relief Expedition under Stanley; 1890 entered German service; 1891 explored around Ruwenzori and into Congo forests; October 1892 murdered by " Arab " slave-raiders.

the idea firmly as demanding an armed expedition and said the Germans should be informed: " It is really their business if Emin is a German."[1] There could be no more striking evidence of the indifference of the government at that time to expansion in East Africa, even near the headwaters of the Nile.

Opportunity, thus officially renounced, came back to private enterprise as represented by Mackinnon. It was an alarmingly speculative opportunity and the Scottish steamship owner who, like Stevenson of the Lakes Company, combined with his business interests a very genuine philanthropic devotion to Africa, proved to be less efficient on land than on the sea. Admittedly, the territorial enterprise was much more formidable than the marine. To direct a company that was to penetrate, tame, administer, and develop a vast slice of primitive Africa, in the face of the rivalry of foreign nations and the ambiguous detachment of its own government, needed the highest powers of leadership and an unbreakable determination. It is enough just to place a portrait of the gentle, benignly-smiling face of the religious Mackinnon beside those of Rhodes and Goldie—and we shall see much of Goldie in this story[2]—to draw some conclusions about the prospects of the East Africa Company even before its record is studied. Capital was as necessary as character, yet to the £1,000,000 of the South Africa Company and the £300,000 already effectively invested in a flourishing trade by the Niger Company before it was chartered, the East Africa Company started with £240,000. And East Africa presented the harder and more speculative task. There was no ready-made trade as in Nigeria with the riverways to carry it; there was no colonizing surge as in south-central Africa to sweep the enterprise forward through difficulties and failure to achievement. And from the first the East Africa Company was burdened with the payment of some £10,000 per annum rent to the sultan for the lease of a ten-mile coastal strip over which the sultan retained his sovereignty, and also had to pay him a large proportion of the scanty customs revenue. Its power to tax was frustrated by the privileges granted by the sultan to foreign merchants; and its freedom to impose customs dues by the area being placed in the international Free Zone. The Company suffered much more than the others from

---

1 Oliver, *op. cit.* p. 132.
2 See below p. 482 ff.

the divided aims of administration and commerce inherent in these institutions, while some of their directors, notably Sir Fowell Buxton, were more interested in a third aim, that of philanthropy. In the first two years they had to meet the antagonism of a very tough foreign rival and they were given far less support from the government than they had counted upon.

Lugard seems to have reckoned little with such clouds as were already gathering over the East African scene. He felt hurt and humiliated by the casual treatment he had received from Rhodes and also from the Lakes Company, ascribing the attitude of the latter to what he impatiently called the " dilatory and money-grubbing spirit " of its directors. He knew he could expect no interesting official African appointment from Salisbury's government. He found some compensation in the friendship and appreciation of Livingstone's moral successors, Sir John Kirk and the Rev. Horace Waller. Both these men were deeply interested in the new Company and wanted, if possible, to get Lugard upon its strength. Kirk, who now sought to follow by private action the policy he had failed to secure as a government official, was one of the original seven directors and his long and authoritative experience in East Africa made him a power on the board. But the Company could not afford a large staff: Lugard was not an easy man to place and, as late as October 1889, Kirk confessed to Waller that he had failed to find any suitable appointment for him. It happened that George Mackenzie,[1] the most virile organizer among the directors, was just returning to East Africa to resume for a short time the post of Administrator in Mombasa. Waller and Kirk suggested that Lugard might go out with him, for the few months left of his army leave before his regiment returned from India, in order to have a look at East Africa and to see if he could be useful in any way. Mackenzie at first demurred from taking a man on such a loose tether—in any case he liked to be surrounded by Scotsmen—but, after meeting him, he changed his mind. Kirk tried to define Lugard's vague assignment as follows: " You are free till February and have a liking for African life and work. The Company gives you a passage and you will have free quarters and if you can help with advice, good

1 Mackenzie, (later Sir) George Sutherland, K.C.M.G., C.B., 1844–1910; 1866–78 engaged in commerce and exploration in region of Persian Gulf; 1888–95 Director of I.B.E.A. Company. As a partner of the firm of Gray Dawes and Company he was closely connected with the management of the British India Steam Navigation Company and of Smith Mackenzie and Company.

and well . . . . " (Kirk to L. 16 October 1889). Unfortunately for the Company, at this all-important moment Kirk had to go as one of Britain's representatives to the Brussels Conference.

It was a clear sign of Lugard's determination to get back to Africa that he took this ill-defined appointment rather than return to his military duties, which appeared increasingly uncongenial. " I am going to inspect men's tunics and cuffs," he had gloomily told his brother when this occupation was in prospect, " smell round barracks for nuisances and be told to ' as you were! ' by my colour sergeant." The War Office, however, remembering his Nyasa adventures, laid down very restrictive conditions. This time he was not to overstay his leave; he was not to engage in any military employment or serve with foreign troops. This sentence was scored with double red lines. Lugard laughed to see this. " This child is going to do just as he pleases and the War Office may be damned! " (L. to E. J. L. 30 September and 10 October 1889).

On November 5th he embarked in the ship which carried not only Mr. George Mackenzie but also Colonel Euan-Smith, who was still consul-general at Zanzibar. He was now, or at least appeared to be, Lugard's firm supporter and admirer and the two men must have smiled to remember their last voyage together on the *Baghdad* when a rather suspicious character in the second class had angled for an interview with the great man. On board much talk went on between the three. Mackenzie became increasingly drawn to Lugard—a certainty upon which Kirk and Waller must have counted—and he began to discuss possibilities of finding more important and more permanent work for him in East Africa. The word " Uganda " came often into their discussions. "Colonel Euan-Smith and Mr. Mackenzie were both strongly of opinion that an effort should be made to establish the Company's administration there; and Mr. Mackenzie at this early date (Nov. 1889), sounded me as to my willingness to command an expedition to Uganda."[1] In fact, the directors, having sent a first exploratory caravan into the interior to try to make contact with Emin, were divided about sending another to Uganda.[2] Mackenzie, however, was always for vigour and action. With every day of the voyage Lugard was coming nearer to the important decision that if he should be

[1] Lugard I, p. 219.
[2] Kemball to Mackinnon, 2 December 1889, and Pelly to Mackinnon, 29 January 1890, M.P.

forced to make a choice between Africa and the army, it was the army that he would give up. But he did not reach this position easily. He reflected that he had not a farthing and there were those dependent upon him. He also felt the tug of responsibility to that other African territory further south, where the issue still hung in doubt. But for the moment at least the way back there was barred: "little Johnston" had taken over that adventure. And—" after all, the reclamation of Uganda is just as great a task and one into which I can *thoroughly* enter." The kind of service that offered here had every allurement to a man of his temperament. But, even at this early and uncertain stage of his career, he had laid down in conversations with Mackenzie that he must have a completely independent command and be allowed to select his assistants. Mackenzie, it seems, agreed, though only verbally. The final word lay with the court of directors in London.

The ship reached Mombasa on December 6th, 1889. The rebellion in the German sphere was still being stamped out; there was tension but there had been very little trouble in the British concession except for a spurt of Arab violence in Mombasa during October. But this had been aimed more at the local Christian missions for harbouring runaway slaves than at the new Company which was very audibly and rather tactlessly congratulating itself upon having managed the coastal Arabs with far more skill and humanity than the Germans.

Mombasa was still little more than a small Arab town on an island dominated by the fine Portuguese Fort Jesus. Something of its old atmosphere can, both in sight and smell, be recreated by a visit to the old harbour where the Arab captains still direct the loading of their dhows from which a forest of masts rises below the steep cliff of the shore. But though the Arabs had been there since the eleventh century, the neighbouring Africans, enclosed within their pagan and primitive tribalism, had provided arguments for the detractors of their race by remaining almost untouched by this long influence. Not until the late forties had Europeans, the Germans Krapf and Rebmann, employed by the Church Missionary Society, gone inland from Mombasa to be the first white men to see the great snow-topped mountains of Kilimanjaro and Kenya. They got little further, for the fierce pastoral Masai, a people organized regimentally like the Zulus for war, barred the way. When other white men, Speke, Burton, Stanley, and the missionaries who followed them, pushed into the interior it was by

way of Bagamoyo, along the more southerly routes long used by the
Arabs to their focal point at Tabora. From here caravan routes forked
west to Lake Tanganyika, and north to Lake Victoria and Uganda.
Egypt's European agents found their way into this region southwards
down the Nile from the Sudan. The direct route inland from Mombasa
to Lake Victoria remained practically closed. It was only six years
before Lugard's arrival that Joseph Thomson,[1] commissioned by the
Royal Geographical Society to find if there were any " practicable
direct route for European travellers " from the coast to Lake Victoria,
had got through the country of the arrogant warrior tribe of the Masai
via Kilimanjaro and reached the shores of Lake Victoria. But he did
not get as far as Uganda.

Germany had taken most of what those British who were interested
in East Africa believed should have been the lion's share, and with it
the regular routes inland; they were now believed to be threatening
further large annexations. It therefore seemed urgent for the Company
to pioneer its own more direct route inland from Mombasa to Lake
Victoria in order to secure the hinterland. Although a few Swahili-led
caravans were getting through, the best route had still to be found and
marked out through an almost trackless wilderness, through tribes
whose possible reactions were still little known, and in physical
conditions which for the most part had not yet been seen, far less
surveyed.

Why, it may be asked, did a poorly financed company, faced with
such an immense task, not begin modestly, and only gradually push its
road inland from the coast, consolidating its positions step by step as
it went, instead of aiming almost immediately at a goal distant from
Mombasa by nearly a thousand miles of arduous trekking? The
answer is " Uganda."[2]

Geographically, Uganda stood on the north-west curve of the shores
of Africa's greatest lake, which Stanley had circumnavigated in 1875.
Here was the source of the Nile, or at least the White Nile, from which

---

1 See above p. 151.

2 Terminology is here confusing. The Bantu root is -ganda. Baganda means the Ganda tribe;
Muganda a single member of it; Luganda their language. Buganda is the correct name for their
country. Explorers from the coast, using the Swahili prefix, called the country Uganda. This
name was later used to cover the much larger area embraced by the Protectorate. (See H. B.
Thomas and R. R. Scott, *Uganda,* [1935], p. vi). For the record of the Company, see P. L. McDermott, *British East Africa or IBEA,* 2nd edition (1895), p. 108. This book by the acting-Secretary
of the Company and based upon their records, which so far have not been traced, is a very
valuable, though naturally a somewhat partisan, authority for the early history of East Africa.

the great river drew its most constant supply. It was believed that in some way yet to be discovered control of these " headwaters of the Nile " would give control over Egypt with all that meant politically and strategically. Here, too, was the " lost " province of Emin Pasha, which was actually self-supporting from its wealth of ivory. Might not Emin be persuaded to put himself and his province under the Company? In addition, Mackinnon wanted to get the land between Lakes Tanganyika and Victoria, as one more section of the Cape-to-Cairo route, and though Salisbury, often caustic about his countrymen's acquisitive enthusiasms, called it " a curious idea which has lately become prevalent " and for which he could find no historical foundation—" I cannot imagine a more inconvenient possession "—it was yet a strong lure for the forward party.[1]

The commercial reason is obvious. In Uganda there was a large and advanced population believed to be eager for European goods, a fertile soil, a developed agriculture, and a rich supply of ivory, the one product that could stand the cost of the journey. But the most urgent attraction of Uganda arose, as so often in the record of British expansion, from fear of a rival claim. If Uganda was, as Stanley said, " the pearl of Africa," it was, at the moment when Mackenzie and Lugard disembarked at Mombasa, not only a very inaccessible but also an endangered jewel. For the agreement of 1886 with Germany drew no western boundaries. The point of division on the coast was Wanga, and Germany had managed to run her frontier inland from there in a slanting line towards Lake Victoria, neatly looping in the great massif of Kilimanjaro, which Harry Johnston claimed to have won for Britain by his treaties,[2] because, Stanley taunted, " the German Emperor said he would like to study the flora and fauna." So, just as the British missionaries on Lake Nyasa had been, and still were, threatened by Portuguese annexation, so those on Lake Victoria were threatened by that of Germany.

The Germans were in a very strong position as against the British Company. After the scandal of the Arab rebellion of 1888–9, the German government, admitting that the outbreak was due largely to the inexperience of their agents, took command of the situation by the appointment of an imperial commissioner, and the German Company,

1 Cecil, *Life of Salisbury*, vol. iv, pp. 322–3.
2 *A.S.R.*, IV. x, May and June 1890, p. 90; also Sir H. Johnston, *The Colonization of Africa* (1899), p. 238.

as their impoverished British rival frequently and bitterly pointed out, was able to draw freely upon the military and financial resources of the state. "For every rupee which the British Company spend in Zanzibar the Germans spend at least two thousand," Euan-Smith told Salisbury.[1] The consul had communicated to the Foreign Office his own low opinion of the Company's prospects of succeeding in its enormous task and had seen its only asset in the vigorous ability of George Mackenzie.[2] Being thus ready for rapid and strong expansion, the German authorities were in no mood to smile at the prospect of a British Cape-to-Cairo corridor running behind their new territory. In 1887 they had agreed with Britain not to encourage " annexations in their respective spheres of interest."[3] They then had to watch Johnston's activities in Nyasaland, with Rhodes pushing up from the south and Mackinnon's Company planning to work in from the east coast. Now came a third threat. There was great emotional determination in Britain for the rescue of Emin Pasha lest he should suffer the same fate as Gordon, and Mackinnon and his friends, interested in the "lost" province as well as its "lost" governor, put up over £10,000, while the Egyptian government, then under British control, ultimately provided a further £14,000 to finance an expedition under Stanley for this purpose. The Germans warned Stanley off the obvious east African route. The Belgian king, on the contrary, encouraged a further exploring venture by the great Stanley through his territory. The Germans were, therefore, very disturbed when, after being lost to civilization for the best part of two years, Stanley emerged from the terrible Congo forests, with "hair as white as Snowdon in winter". During most of 1889 he was in the region of Lake Albert trying to "rescue" an Emin almost as unwilling to accept his heroic services as Livingstone had been. In the middle of 1889 Stanley marched along the western slopes of Ruwenzori through Ankole and to the south of Lake Victoria making treaties which he presented to the British Company.[4]

1 Euan-Smith to Salisbury, 31 March 1890, S.P. vol. 80 (Zanzibar 1890–2).
2 Euan-Smith to Salisbury, 3 February 1889, S.P. vol. 79 (Zanzibar 1889), and 22 May 1890, F. O. 84/2061.
3 H. M. Stanley, *In Darkest Africa* (1890), vol. ii, p. 461; see also Hertslet, *Map of Africa*, vol. iii, pp. 888–90. The German ambassador told Salisbury that it was rumoured that Mackinnon, in furnishing large sums for the Emin Relief Expedition, " was not alone actuated by purely philanthropic aims." Salisbury agreed " to discourage British annexations in the rear of the German sphere of influence." But this " rear " was, of course, not yet defined.
4 See below p. 259.

Germany could be expected to act, and Mackinnon heard rumours that Wissmann, the new German Commissioner, meant to set off himself for Lake Victoria. Germany also threatened the Company by holding Witu, a petty so-called sultanate some 150 miles north of Mombasa, which German agents had supported in its renunciation of the authority of Zanzibar. The Foreign Office recognized the German claim and in February 1890 forced the Company to withdraw from some small nearby islands. According to her own theory about hinterlands this would enable Germany to draw a long line inland from Witu. If, this time, it were a straight line, or even if it were drawn to meet the point where her other frontier reached the shore of Lake Victoria, the British Company would be left enclosed within a relatively small triangle of country behind Mombasa and all the region round Lake Victoria would fall to Germany. This was not merely an unpleasant possibility. While rumours about Wissmann's proposed activities south and west of the lake were reaching the Company, the ruthless German explorer, Carl Peters, evading British warships, had already reached Witu and in July 1889 set off for Lake Victoria on a lightly-manned courageous treaty-making expedition, staining his route by violence against the natives. No reliable news of Stanley's emergence from the Congo had then reached the |coast, so Peters could claim to have Emin's rescue as his object and he also claimed the official, if unwritten, support of the German government.[1]

When the Company asked for Foreign Office support against this aggression, the answer from Berlin was that the German government renounced all responsibility for the expedition, while *The Times*, inveighing against German behaviour, yet told the Company it must fight its own battle.[2] What had the Company to show to offset all these rival acts and threats which were forcing upon it tasks it had never expected to shoulder? In anticipation of the incorporation of the Company, headquarters had been established in Mombasa in 1887, use for a while being made of the firm of Smith Mackenzie and Company which represented the B.I. Steam Navigation Company on the east African coast.[3] The Company had attempted to buy off the local Arabs' antagonism against the missionaries for harbouring runaway slaves by an expensive policy of compensation for

1 Carl Peters, *New Light on Dark Africa*, tr. H. W. Dulcken (1891), pp. 14–16.
2 McDermott, *IBEA*, p. 90 ff.
3 N. J. Robinson, *The History of Smith Mackenzie & Co. Ltd.* (privately printed 1938).

slave-liberation. It had sent out some twenty British agents—" raw and inexperienced Scotch lads " Euan-Smith called them[1]—to conduct expeditions in the immediate hinterland and to make treaties. Some sixty of these had been made by the end of 1889.[2] The Company had also established an isolated post at Machakos, 350 miles inland.[3] A steamer was working along the east African coast and some material for a light railway across the coastal belt had been collected, but it was much too light for such rough country and was finally used as a tramway on Mombasa island. The Company had also sent out Frederick Jackson,[4] like Sharpe a gentleman-hunter, and like him destined later to govern the wild places through which he had been chasing elephants. With another young Company servant, Ernest Gedge, they were to lead some 500 men upon the first Company caravan sent towards Lake Victoria, with orders, however, *not* to enter Uganda. This kingdom was regarded as too tough a proposition and eyes were still fixed on Emin's province further north. Jackson, who (in his posthumously published reminiscences) gives a dismal picture of the perhaps unavoidable inefficiency of the Company's first efforts at Mombasa, left Machakos for the interior on August 6th, 1889.[5]

It was at this very early and very critical moment for the future of the Company that Lugard reached Mombasa. Ever since Jackson had been sent off into the interior, where he was now completely out of contact, it had become clear, in view of the German threat and of civil wars now reported in Uganda, that an attempt should be made as soon as possible to reach that kingdom. But it was very important that the Company should make sure that it had found the best route into the interior before it spent money in developing it. And the first step was to find the best point of entry into that great block of country, the future Kenya, which was then regarded almost with exasperation as an immense obstacle between Mombasa and Lake Victoria and which the Foreign Office referred to as that " sterile region ".

1 Euan-Smith to Salisbury, 31 March 1890, S.P. vol. 80 (Zanzibar 1890–2).
2 C.6555 (1892), p. 11 ff.
3 Report of the court of directors to the founders of the company, dated 1 June 1889, submitted at the first general meeting of the I.B.E.A. Company on 6 June 1889 (L.P.). There is a copy in the Royal Empire Society Library.
4 Jackson, (later Sir) Frederick John, K.C.M.G., C.B., 1860–1929; 1889 commanded I.B.E.A. Co. expedition to Uganda; 1894 1st class assistant, Uganda; 1895 Vice-Consul; 1896 Deputy Commissioner, Uganda Protectorate; 1897–8, 1901–2 Acting Commissioner; 1902 Deputy-Commissioner, East African Protectorate; 1907–11 Lieut.-Governor, E.A.P.; 1911–17 Governor and Commander-in-Chief, Uganda.
5 Sir F. Jackson, *Early Days in East Africa* (1930), p. 141 ff.

The first bit was the worst. Immediately behind Mombasa lay the Taru " desert," a hot and usually waterless belt of sixty miles which tried caravans severely, causing Europeans to go sick and driving porters to desert, even though as a result they sometimes met death from thirst or from lions. By contrast, at the little Arab town of Malindi, seventy miles north of Mombasa, now fast becoming the Bognor of Kenya, the Sabaki river reached the sea and Mackenzie thought that this might give a quicker and better route inland to Machakos. But this had yet to be proved. So, while the possibility of Lugard being chosen to lead the first big caravan to Uganda was still being discussed, Mackenzie decided to ask him to survey this Sabaki route to Machakos and to build a series of small stockaded forts on the way. This offer, made on December 11th, 1889, was accepted by Lugard on the same day in terms which showed that his acceptance was linked with the verbal promise of further and more important service on his own terms.

A few days before this had been settled, the long-expected, long-despaired of, world figure of Stanley appeared on the east African coast, bringing down with him that enigmatic man, half-scholar, half-adventurer, Emin Pasha, who had been induced to come, leaving many of his half-mutinous Sudanese troops north of Uganda. He arrived, Euan-Smith reported, " looking dreadfully fragile and delicate, a very small, thin, half-blind man, with a voice in proportion to his size ",[1] and in a state of mind " timorously bitter " against his rumbustious rescuer.[2] Stanley who, as we saw, had come down by way of the west of Lake Victoria, arrived at Bagamoyo on December 4th. Here Emin, in the course of a German dinner party of welcome, fell from a balcony and sustained a head injury. To this is usually attributed a seemingly sudden change of attitude to Britain, which made him refuse Euan-Smith's suggestion that he should take service with the Company. He implied that if he did the German government threatened to take away his German citizenship.[3] Another explanation is probably his aversion from the prospect of future service under the over-bearing Stanley of whom he had now nearly a year's experience as a companion of travel. Emin had long been a romantic hero in the Britain which had sent the relief expedition; and the news that he had

---

1 Euan-Smith to Salisbury, 5 March 1890, S.P. vol. 80 (Zanzibar 1890-2).
2 Euan-Smith to Salisbury, 25 March 1890, S.P. vol. 80 (Zanzibar 1890-2).
3 Ibid.

Sir Francis de Winton, from a portrait about 1880

joined the German service was learned with dismay for it was suspected that he might be planning to return to the region of his long exile and thus intrude into what the Company intended should be its own sphere. Hopes of getting Emin's province for the Company being damped, interest switched to Uganda from which encouraging news had come.

Mackenzie met Stanley in Zanzibar and wrote in confidence to Lugard a letter which at once showed the relative status of the great African adventurer and the eager neophyte. It seemed that Stanley himself might consent to take over the Uganda enterprise which he now advocated. " Of course with his support of the scheme at home the thing will be done and there will be no lack of money, and of course the directors at home would be only too pleased to give him the Chief Command of any Expedition he would care to take in hand." (Mackenzie to L. 17 December 1889). Mackenzie thought it only fair to warn Lugard about this before he broke off his army career, though there would still be work for him in the year or eighteen months before Stanley would be ready for the new enterprise. Mackenzie said that Stanley was anxious to meet Lugard as he passed Mombasa. But the anxiety was not reciprocated. There may have been a strain of personal disappointment in his attitude, but we know enough of Stanley now[1] to credit the reason Lugard gave to his half-sister Emma: " between ourselves I did not care greatly about meeting Stanley. Letters of his that I had seen (not published) had made me disinclined to fall down and worship him, so I went up country again . . . . and did not wait for him." (L. to E. Brayne, 30 June 1890). Stanley, however, went on to Egypt to write his book[2] and then returned to England there to be greeted with a national ovation. His advice to the Company was that while it was highly desirable that a treaty should be obtained from Buganda as soon as possible, the occupation of the kingdom would be a formidable undertaking, demanding 500 Englishmen, 2,000 porters and costing £100,000. He thought such an enterprise should await the coming of the railway.[3]

While Lugard was still at Mombasa another issue was raised between him and Mackenzie. In accepting the latter's commission he had

[1] See especially the picture of Stanley given in R. Coupland, *Livingstone's Last Journey* (1945); also Jackson, *op. cit.* p. 142.
[2] H. M. Stanley, *In Darkest Africa* (1890).
[3] Stanley to Mackinnon, 6 February 1890, M.P.

agreed in general terms not to communicate to the newspapers with regard to the Company's affairs. Late in January Mackenzie, having returned from Zanzibar to Mombasa, sent him a longer, formal undertaking, which had been drawn up in England, enjoining secrecy in the strongest terms both during and after the period of employment. Similar obligations had been enforced upon all the officials of the Royal Niger Company, one reason which has made it difficult for historians to write its history. Certainly what is known of the records of both companies suggests that the East Africa Company had less to hide than its western opposite number. We have seen that Lugard had already realized that at least half the struggle for the annexation of Africa had to be waged in Britain and he recoiled from this restriction. " I detest these solemn undertakings, to keep one's mouth closed for ever ", he told his brother, and wrote refusing this agreement and offering rather to serve without pay. Mackenzie, however, would not accept gratuitous services for the Company—a like offer by Jackson had already been refused—and Lugard had to give way.

The Sabaki trek was a useful trial run for the main event which was to follow. Lugard left Mombasa on December 20th, 1889 and returned on May 11th, 1890, a period of some five months. He set off N.N.W. from Mombasa, striking almost at once, except for the two runaway slave centres of Fuladoyo and Makongeni, into untouched Africa. Here the timid Giriama tribe lived deep in the forest in their carefully hidden and fenced huts, in fear of raiding Masai, who sometimes came right down to the coast. Lugard had 120 Swahili porters with him and was using mules, camels and donkeys. This was an important experiment in transport but, with the men's inexperience in handling the animals, the lack of proper harness and medicines, and the uncertain distribution of fodder, it does not seem, in spite of Lugard's enthusiastic optimism, to have been a great success. Mackenzie had also imported some Persians who accompanied the caravan in order to teach better farming methods, but this also proved one more of the hundreds of ingenious but unfruitful experiments the white man has tried in Africa.

Lugard built his first stockade at Makongeni on the Sabaki and then turned inland and westwards upstream. Here, as can still be seen along this still untamed river, the water bred magnificent trees towering above the scrub bush of the region. Lugard had plenty of incidents of the kind which were common to the trekker in nineteenth-century

Africa. He fell into a native game-pit; he encountered almost every kind of wild animal and reptile as he went shooting for sport and for the pot; he bathed with a crocodile which managed to tear his hand with its sharp teeth before he escaped; he lacerated himself on the great dagger-like thorns of aloe and acacia; he crossed Masai war-paths used by warriors pledged to kill every human being they might meet in order to ensure the secrecy of their raids; he bought crushed grain from native villages at four pounds weight for a foot-long string of beads.

On March 29th he turned back from Machakos after spending two weeks there making a stockade and entering into blood-brotherhood with the Kamba chief of that area. On April 19th he reached Kibwezi and there found two very urgent letters from Mackenzie, dated March 12th and 22nd, which had come up by runner. These letters light up the whole situation. They told him that there was still no word from or about Jackson, but that there was very important news from Uganda which had come by the southern route. The King, Mwanga, who had been expelled by the Muslims, had been reinstated by the two Christian parties with the help of a British trader, Charles Stokes. Mackenzie pointed out that now was the moment to get a treaty from Mwanga, when he had just regained his power with European help. But, a shadow from coming events, he warned Lugard " the influence of the French Priests is very great in Uganda, and their animosity towards the English Missionaries is so strong that it is not improbable but that they would rather favour the supremacy of German rule in Uganda in preference to that of the English." And—here lay the great urgency—German annexation was now a serious possibility. It was believed that " the Germans have very considerably augmented their European and Native forces " and it was now rumoured strongly that it was the intention of the new German Imperial Commissioner, Wissmann, to lead an expedition to the south end of Lake Victoria, and if opportunity offered, to make a dash towards Uganda with a view to annexing it permanently to the German sphere. This would be " a very serious blow to the future of this Company " and " as we are not always sure of a firm backing from our Foreign Office, it would be well to be beforehand and get there first." " Bear always in mind that our great idea is to make treaties and secure supremacy for the Company in Uganda and also " (it is interesting to observe the large hopes on Cape-to-Cairo lines still cherished by Mackenzie)

" from the south of Victoria Nyanza to a point on Tanganyika where the 4° intersects it so as to secure access to and free communication with Nyasa. Whoever succeeds in doing this will deserve great things of his country and have done much for Africa; you, I believe, are the man *destined* to manage it! " Mackenzie had decided that the waterless southern road via Taveta was impossible and he wanted Lugard to push on so fast along a new route through the Company's sphere that he would beat the Germans, and Stokes, with the new Anglican Bishop Tucker of Uganda in his company, who were all using the old route through German territory. If he met Jackson he was to take command, make full use of his caravan and push on to Uganda, taking any line of march he wished. But if he went in westwards over the Nile, let him remember Mwanga's superstitious dread of any stranger coming in that way and how he had murdered Bishop Hannington there less than five years before.

These letters must have made good reading to Lugard. Mackenzie knew his man and his phrases must have rung like martial music in Lugard's mind. " The Uganda Caravan is to be placed under your control; .... I have telegraphed to London informing them that I believe you to be the right man to undertake such a work, and, if given a free hand, that I had no doubt that you could do it in a shorter time than probably anyone else that could be sent there .... I cannot do better than, after stating the facts, to give you a perfectly free hand if you are prepared to undertake the job." It would be a race to get to Uganda first and in concluding his second letter Mackenzie indicated the prize. " If you succeed you will, as a work of lasting and practical good, put Stanley's late work quite in the shade. It is a glorious opportunity of establishing your name and adding to your fame. Wishing you all luck and with the assurance of my hearty support both here and at home. Yours very sincerely, George Mackenzie." (Mackenzie to L. 12 and 22 March 1890).

Mackenzie was not speaking without official support. The consul-general was fully, indeed urgently behind him, a fact to be remembered against the day when there would be angry controversy about the responsibility for this plan. Euan-Smith had for long been urging Mackinnon to push inland.[1] By March 1890 he thought the Chairman was now fully alive to the absolute necessity for the Company to

---

1 Euan-Smith to Salisbury, 15 February 1890, S.P. vol. 80 (Zanzibar 1890-2).

secure Uganda before the Germans got there. " Wissmann ", Euan-Smith told Salisbury, " is now preparing a very large expedition to the interior, and I have urged Mackenzie to hurry forward at all costs a large caravan under Captain Lugard, which is already half-way to the lake." A larger caravan might follow but " Lugard might meanwhile make the necessary treaties with the King."[1] A few days later Euan-Smith was writing, with even greater urgency, and talking about the need for a railway and calling up that financial genie, Mr. Rhodes. " You cannot ask Parliament for money and send a Major Wissmann out," was the response at the Foreign Office. " It looks however as if the Germans would obtain the control of the East coast and the country up to the Lakes."[2] Salisbury remarked that " Colonel Euan-Smith's belief in the German projects is very liberal."[3] He had his own good reason, which was shortly to appear, for not permitting his consul-general to disturb him. But he allowed his ambassador in Berlin to remind the Germans of past treaties[4] and also Euan-Smith's gadfly advice to be passed on to what the latter called the insouciant and sleepy Company,[5] and Sir Phiilp Currie[6] even went so far as to authorize Portal, due shortly to replace Euan-Smith, to attend a Company meeting and " advise them to send up another caravan as quickly as possible to reinforce those which have already gone."[7] Sir Percy Anderson reiterated the government view: " When we gave a Charter to the E. Africa Co. we understood that its main idea was to push up to Uganda."[8]

Lugard was, of course, ignorant of the battle that was going on behind the Foreign Office and Company doors to decide policy and evade responsibility, an issue which will subsequently show the importance of these quotations. He was well content with Mackenzie's urgent and exciting letters, and they would have been more urgent still if Mackenzie had known what was even then happening up-country, in the region cut off from communication, between Jackson and Carl Peters. This mystery, half-revealed, made Mackenzie's next

[1] Euan-Smith to Salisbury, 25 March 1890, S.P. vol. 80 (Zanzibar 1890–2).
[2] Minute on telegram of Euan-Smith to Salisbury, 1 April 1890, S.P. vol. 80 (Zanzibar 1890–2).
[3] Minute by Salisbury on telegram from Euan-Smith, 14 March 1890, F.O. 84/2069.
[4] Minute by Salisbury on telegram from Euan-Smith, 1 April 1890, F.O. 84/2069.
[5] Euan-Smith to Salisbury, 21 April 1890, S.P. vol. 80 (Zanzibar 1890–2).
[6] See below p. 340.
[7] Minute on telegram from Euan-Smith, 1 April 1890, F.O. 84/2069.
[8] Minute on telegram from Euan-Smith, 31 March 1890, F.O. 84/2069.

letter, dated April 8th, even more impelling. Mackenzie had now heard that Peters, with only forty men, had fought his way through the Masai and reached Kavirondo country near the lake; also that Jackson had been invited to Uganda and might have gone, but was apparently reputed to have hung about and done nothing. To tempt Mwanga to make the treaty Lugard was to give him a Maxim gun and war rockets: the same powerful kind of persuasion that had been used by Rhodes to charm the concession out of Lo Bengula. Even the would-be idealistic Lakes Company had stooped to trade in gunpowder. The reason was, of course, that arms were the one item of trade for which every ambitious African chief hungered, for arms represented power, and if these companies were to trade it was difficult to begin by refusing the goods most in request. Mackenzie warned Lugard that if the Germans reached Uganda even a week before he did, all the cost of the caravan would be thrown away.

Lugard, however, continued his march back to the coast. There were reasons: the trouble in his old wound; the desire to get the War Office extension for his leave; the need to re-man and re-stock his caravan; promises of return made to his men. Ambition and inexperience together might have urged him on to what might easily have been a very unsuccessful effort: his return certainly showed that he was an older and wiser man than when he had flung himself into the Nyasa adventure. As if to illustrate the problems and dangers of the attempt, the reinforcement Mackenzie dispatched to strengthen him, cutting the corner by the southern route, broke to pieces on the way, the white leader collapsing and his porters deserting with their loads at the prospect of the dreaded Taru. As he marched back, Lugard met another letter from Mackenzie enclosing a telegram from Company headquarters dated April 20th: " Have messenger dispatched immediately Lugard continue journey . . . . assurance to Mwanga our protection powerful assistance . . . . Germans their aim is Koki between Buddu Ankori [Ankole] . . . . Jackson under your command . . . . utmost importance must arrive at Uganda before Germans. Telegraph latest news of Lugard."

Lugard, thus marching back in the face of all these orders to go forward, reached Mombasa on May 11th. He was in a very bad state. After trying to walk barefoot on the last stages, with his old wound a festering sore and his left arm useless, he had to submit for two or three days of the trek, for the only time in his African life, to the indignity of being carried in a hammock. He had no sooner reached Mombasa than the whole Uganda caravan question ran into a crisis of muddle and clashing personalities of a kind to which wholly new organizations are often liable, and which looked like putting an end to Lugard's connection with Africa, as well as leaving a perfectly clear run to the Germans if they wanted it. The Company had managed to arrange with the War Office for the extension of Lugard's leave, and Mackenzie was about to sail home, when there was a change of plan at headquarters, and Mackenzie found himself involved during the second half of May in playing a telegraphic game of battledore and shuttlecock with them over the exact position Lugard should occupy. London wanted him to push Lugard ahead immediately but only to prepare the way for another figure now entering the story. This was the new Administrator, Sir Francis de Winton, a man already distinguished in the world of affairs and in Africa.[1] He was coming out to replace the vigorous Mackenzie who was wanted back in London. Colonel Euan-Smith, having heard of both Peters' expedition and of an official German caravan with Emin Pasha starting from the coast, strongly urged that Lugard should set off at once and backed his claim against de Winton. (Euan-Smith to L. 22 June 1890). But it had been decided, perhaps because the Uganda adventure now looked like being so much larger an affair than had been expected, and because public opinion was pressing the Company to act, that de Winton was to follow up Lugard, with a larger expedition and overtake and supersede him. Mackenzie telegraphed repeatedly in defence of the sole command for Lugard who " is thoroughly trustworthy energetic has had considerable [experience] handling caravans." (Mackenzie to Mackinnon, 20 May 1890). He also pointed out the difficulty, in view of the shortage of stores and porters, of equipping two large caravans at once, and of using Jackson's tired porters as soon as they returned. Lugard stood grimly by, working on his Sabaki report and map and steadily refusing to serve under the new plan. So grave were the risks of delay that Mackenzie was even driven to commission that

[1] De Winton, Major-General Sir Francis, G.C.M.G., C.B., 1835–1901; 1854 R.A. Crimean War; 1861 A.D.C. to Sir W. Fenwick Williams, and 1870–5 went with him to Canada and Gibraltar; 1877–8 military attaché at Constantinople; 1878–83 secretary to the Marquis of Lorne, Governor-General of Canada; 1885 Administrator of Congo; 1887 secretary of Emin Pasha Relief Expedition; 1889 Commissioner in Swaziland; 1890–1 Administrator of Imperial British East Africa Company's territories; 1892 Controller of the household of the Duke of Clarence.

remarkable character, Stokes—the C.M.S. missionary who, having married a native wife, had turned caravan-leader and trader, and was now employed by the Germans and wearing a German uniform—to hurry on and try to make the treaty with Mwanga. More than this: he asked Stokes to apologize to the King for Jackson's failure to respond to his appeal and also commissioned this person of somewhat ambiguous status to censure Jackson by telling him " how disappointed we were at his want of decision."[1] Such were the shifts which crisis forced upon the Company in its weakness.

When Mackenzie left Mombasa at the end of May, Lugard thought that between them they had won the day, and induced the Company to change its orders. Lugard therefore worked hard preparing his caravan. But when de Winton arrived in the second week of June Lugard was told that he was wrong. The new Administrator had quite clearly set his heart upon this dramatic mission and told Lugard that his orders were unchanged. He had engaged three military officers, all senior to Lugard, to serve under him and had allocated their duties; one of them, Captain Mackay, had been promised the post of Resident in Uganda. Now occurred a battle of wills. The first meeting on June 12th was difficult indeed. " I can't say ", Lugard remarked dryly to his brother, " that I much liked my interview." De Winton, a man of great charm, fresh from experience in the Congo and in helping the Emin Relief Expedition, a K.C.M.G. and C.B., found this young captain standing obstinately in the way of himself and all his staff. De Winton began by reproaching Lugard for not having already started ahead to blaze the trail for them. Lugard's response was to ask to return to England at once.

His future seemed to be in the melting-pot again. But he was determined not to give in without a struggle. He believed that not only Euan-Smith in Zanzibar, but also Kirk, Mackenzie and Waller in England, were all on his side and, though he had some qualms as to whether this was a strictly honourable course, he at once wrote to each of them and then sat down to await the result of his letters.[2] De Winton

[1] Euan-Smith to Salisbury, 21 May 1890, enclosing Mackenzie to Stokes, 21 May 1890, F.O. 84/2061.

[2] It may be of interest to note, as a comment upon the problems of writing history, that the writer, puzzled and disturbed by the whole story, was inclined to share these qualms. It was only upon the verge of going into print and thanks to the kindness of Miss de Kiewiet, who had obtained access to the Mackinnon Papers, that new light was thrown upon the episode which adjusted the moral scales in favour of Lugard.

tried all ways to move him. There were long and difficult interviews almost daily from June 12th to 24th, with Lugard insisting upon repeating the gist of them in letters or making long memoranda. The situation was the more painful because Lugard could not help admiring de Winton's amazing courtesy and patience in dealing with his insubordination though he chafed against his bringing in moral considerations. Using the actual words but abbreviating the voluminous documentation of this conflict, the exchanges may be presented as follows:

DE WINTON. I do not blame you so much as Mackenzie for the delay which has arisen. The Court sends orders and expects to see them carried out. I have come to see that this is done.

LUGARD. I was pledged to my men to bring them back.

DE WINTON. The Company comes first.

LUGARD. I do not assent to this. And I must also point out the impossibility of starting with the men and material I had.

DE WINTON. Peters went with fifty men only.

This was a shrewd thrust but Lugard, had he known all we know of Peters' march, would have replied that Peters, admittedly a marvellous traveller, was also a man without conscience or pity whether dealing with his own men or those he met on the route. By June 22nd, after these almost daily tussles, de Winton at last said he must know the next day whether Lugard would obey orders to go ahead and this without any promise of being even second-in-command since army, not Company, seniority must count. Lugard said he would not go.

DE WINTON. You are giving up your duty for personal pique—you do not trust me: you are keeping something back. I like you personally but I find you impossible to deal with and I fear that those under you will find the same.

Lugard formally in writing again refused to go. He had, he said, only obtained his secondment from the army for the sake of " work a man could feel such pride in doing for its own sake." Upon such work he was willing to serve for nothing. But he also warned de Winton of the enormous expense to the Company of equipping two caravans.

De Winton would not give in. He sent for Lugard and instead of showing anger was so understanding and persuasive that Lugard could hardly withstand him.

LUGARD. Your kindness to me today was such as I have rarely experienced in my life and, I do assure you from my heart, I shall *never* forget it. It only makes my present task harder for I would have longed for an opportunity of showing you by my loyal work how grateful I was for it. You misunderstand me, too, I know, and think I have been undecided and prompted by pique. My life has been a strange one and made me older than my years and I feel I have talents and capacities and, above all, a constitution of iron which can be employed in good work whereas . . . .

and here he repeated his view that he would be wasted as an underling in Uganda. He begged for some other work, any work, even if unpaid, where he could fight slavery. Otherwise he would go back to England.

This was on June 23rd. The older man had, however, one last penetrating shot in his locker and he used it the next day.

DE WINTON. I cannot agree with you in the interpretation you place on the fact of you and I being in Uganda together that your " utility would be sacrificed and your services not required ", in fact I entirely disagree and I speak frankly when I say that you have taken a somewhat morbid view of your position. I maintain your usefulness would be enhanced, and that far from it being sacrificed it would be employed in the best manner possible as regards the Company, and in the noblest enterprise as regards the cause of Africa. No, I cannot agree that there is any sacrifice except that you are sacrificing a chance, which does not often come to a man, for an idea. As for any other work, you must remember that I must think of those who are willing to bear the heat and burden of the day. You, and I say it in no offensive manner— " are turning back when harnessed for the day of battle " and I must consider them first. Well, you have had an entirely free choice, and if you are suffering from disappointment you yourself are alone the cause of that suffering. I think this should be clearly understood because you knew from the date of the first telegram that the Court had decided upon my going to Uganda.

The shot went home.

LUGARD. I cannot bear to be accused of " turning back when harnessed for the day of battle ", or of wishing for an appointment without having borne the burden and heat of the day, to obtain it. You say in your letter that my "usefulness would be enhanced—in the noblest enterprise as regards the cause of Africa", and that I would have an opportunity of working together with you and you would (you are kind enough to say) listen to such plans, and results of experience as I have. In conversation you told me that by giving me command of the advance caravan &c., you were practically placing me next to yourself,—and though it is of infinitely less importance to me what position I occupy in the caravan than that I have opportunities in Uganda itself, I am naturally unwilling to be subordinate to others in the event of your returning after having had the entire command given me. I had strong reasons from my own point of view, which possibly was wrong for deciding as I did, but it shall never be said of me that I turned back when there was work to be done. Those at least were not my reasons, and sooner that it should so appear I will with your permission cancel my decision. At any rate you will see that I am not turning back if you want me and that since my conduct bears that appearance I am ready to offer myself at once. [He went on half in defence and half in apology.] Indeed I recognize the fault in my own character most strongly, and know that an independent spirit, and a desire for unfettered action are not traits which will advance my own interests. It is due to the events of the last four years. These positions of constant responsibility, with men far older than myself serving under me—together with a heavy private trouble which sent me adrift, and made me reckless of my Army career and of either money or ambition, fostered in me that spirit of independence, which I know will not be to the advancement of my interests.

DE WINTON. Of course I am very glad if you will come. I shall have plenty for you to do, and I feel sure, now you have decided, you will serve the Company loyally and faithfully and I do not think you will have cause to regret it.

Truly I think you will be happier now your mind is made up, as if you had gone to England you would all the time have been wishing to be with me.

(From letters between de Winton and L. 24 June 1890).

So it was decided. What Lugard did not know, though he must have wondered if something of the sort were not happening, was that four days after this, on June 28th, the Company telegraphed to de Winton to say that the directors were much pleased with Lugard's Sabaki report; "encourage him to proceed without delay Uganda. Give him pretty free hand settlement there, instruct him to on return journey locate stations between Victoria Nyanza Machakos, confirm his present confidential position subject to your orders only."[1]

De Winton—and here lay his fault—kept this telegram to himself. He telegraphed back some weeks later that Lugard was "decidedly eccentric", and that there were officers more senior and better qualified than he who could not be expected to serve under him. He would therefore follow Lugard in a month's time, send Captains Mackay and Williams on to Uganda and send Lugard to Witu and to Tana on the coast.[2]

There can be little doubt both that de Winton thought that he was doing right and that he had the right to do it. He was, after all, Administrator-General, and a man of standing and experience. Was he a bad judge of men? Time was to prove that he had been mistaken about Lugard. But he was also hampered by the inexperience of the directors to whom he was responsible. They showed their distrust and sent contradictory orders. Euan-Smith, watching at close quarters, pitied him when de Winton told him that his directors thwarted him at every turn, "for never was there a man more anxious to do his utmost." But, the consul-general believed, he was unfitted for the job, too old (he was fifty-five), too soft, too credulous, too kind to wield powers to which it would be hard to find a parallel since the days of the Great Mogul. For these reasons, and because there was need for a capable man at the coast, Euan-Smith strongly advised him not to go to Uganda himself, and not to recall Lugard.[3]

On August 6th, Lugard set out gloomily under orders to proceed by the shortest possible route to Lake Victoria, there, after making two stations between Machakos and the lake, to await the Administrator.[4] De Winton did not approve of his starting by the Sabaki route because it was longer, but decided not to have another conflict with his difficult subordinate. He entrusted him with his son, Fenwick, to work under him. At the very end, de Winton's kindness having got under his guard, Lugard confessed to him the nature of the trouble that had, so he believed, warped his nature, and this unlocked all de Winton's compassion and religious feeling.

---

[1] Company to de Winton, 28 June 1890, M.P.
[2] De Winton to Company, 1 August 1890, M.P.
[3] Euan-Smith to Salisbury, 23 June, 18 August, 2, 16 September and 2 December 1890, S.P. vol. 80 (Zanzibar 1890-2).
[4] C.6555 (1892), p. 87.

East African Opportunity

DE WINTON. And now I am going to take a very great liberty and you must forgive it. But there is a duty common to all our humanity and that is to try and alleviate pain and suffering. Now my friend you are in pain and you suffer, forgive this allusion to your trouble but there is a remedy dear lad, within the reach of us all. Take it to Him, leave it with Him, ask Him to bear it for you, and your burden will pass away. I speak from experience, from the experience of a very hotheaded and passionate youth, from the experience of a strong self-willed middle age, which even now presses sorely in its vanity and vaingloriousness in all I strive to do. And so I venture to send you this book.[1] I only read it for the first time last year, but it contains oil and wine—and it has been a great help to me. It is a copy given me by my dear wife, so I will ask you if you don't care to read it to give it to Fen to take care of, and to forgive me my apparent impertinence. As to your doing your duty in the work before you I have no fear but that you will do your best, and while I may appear somewhat cold-hearted as compared with George Mackenzie's warm and kind words, it is not because I have less confidence in you than he has, but because I have been brought up in a different school—a school in which you yourself are a scholar and a student. [As for his son] . . . . He is a good lad with strong desires to do his duty, so bear with him for my sake, and now goodbye. You see, as dear Paul said, what a long letter I have written you with my own hand.

(De Winton to L. 5 August 1890).

He ended " affectionately yours ", words not often used in those more formal days, especially between men and in official life.

Lugard kept the little book which de Winton had given him and the writer found it among his papers. It was a strange episode and one that tells much of the strength of Lugard's will, self-confidence and ambition. He trekked away from Mombasa perplexed and divided in himself, for while his heart had responded to the man whom another Company agent called " one of the most lovable personalities who ever worked in Africa ",[2] his will was unbroken. And while de Winton wished the party God speed, thinking that he had won, Lugard very well knew that his letters would be working in his own favour in London. To his brother he confessed his perplexity. De

[1] *The Greatest Thing in the World.* This little book by an anonymous author is a presentation and anthology of the New Testament teaching about love. It had run by 1891 into several editions in several languages. Upon the title page de Winton has written, with obvious relevance, " Motto for 1892, ' In all thy ways acknowledge Him and He shall direct thy paths.' Proverbs. III. 6."

[2] C. W. Hobley, *Kenya from Chartered Company to Crown Colony* (1929), p. 72.

Winton " even told me that he had been praying for guidance how to deal with me,—and in truth I *was* a difficult man to deal with in that matter! What can one do in such circumstances, and with such a man? I don't know what to do,—his methods and ways are not mine!" (L. to E. J. L. 25 July 1890).

Lugard won the last round. Kemball, one of the directors, told Mackinnon that de Winton had not acted in the spirit of his instructions and had revised the decision taken in London to send Lugard.[1] The problem was " whether Lugard is to be sacrificed or de Winton. It is pretty clear that the two cannot work together as far as Uganda is concerned."[2] Sir John Kirk, too, who had never approved of de Winton's appointment, took Lugard's side. Mackenzie instructed Waller to send on to Lugard his opinion that " he was the best man out there ", that he had " unbounded confidence " in him and that he had " lost no time in instilling this belief into the minds of the Board " and that Mackinnon himself had been won to this view and used " the highest terms of satisfaction and praise." (Waller to L. 8 July 1890). The result was that de Winton found himself overruled. Lugard was to command the expedition; his chief was to stay on the coast as Administrator.

In November the directors sent another telegram repeating their instruction of June 28th about Lugard going to Uganda. This time, remarking that there had been no mention of the former one having been communicated to Lugard, they instructed de Winton to show him this one, a wounding mark of distrust.[3] De Winton replied that he did not admit the charge of disobedience; he had doubted Lugard's fitness " not for want of capacity, but on account of certain peculiarities of character and disposition."[4] A few days later he complained that his views were not considered by the directors while " the opinion of a subordinate receives prompt and entire endorsement."[5]

Lugard's own conclusion of the story is found in a letter to Emma.

" All is settled now, and as usual I have got my own way entirely like an obstinate and self-willed man as I fear I am. You must remember that Sir Francis was in a *most* difficult position. He came out to command this.

---

1 Kemball to Mackinnon, 19 August 1890, M.P.
2 Kemball to Mackinnon, ? August 1890, M.P.
3 Company to de Winton, 4 November 1890, M.P.
4 De Winton to Company, 8 December 1890, M.P.
5 De Winton to Company, 16 December 1890, M.P.

His whole heart was in it . . . . He was made to look a fool before everyone, deprived of the command &c., Capt. Mackay resigned. Capt. Williams elected to serve under me, tho' a little senior to me in the Service. Capt. Smith being much senior declined to serve under me. Mackay had to forego the appointment of Resident in Uganda already promised him definitely . . . . Difficulties arose, and I think both of us made mistakes. I at first resigned, but was jostled into staying and then I got worried and out of health, and *wrote angrily and perhaps intemperately to my friends,* being of opinion that Sir F. was not dealing frankly with me, and that he would only make a mess of the business . . . "

(L. to E. Brayne, undated).

Lugard had struggled for his opportunity and won it. It remained to be seen what use he would make of it, and whether he could justify the astonishing confidence he had shown in his own powers.

Before continuing the narrative, however, there is one further point about this period of Lugard's life in East Africa which should be mentioned in passing. In Mombasa Lugard was brought into very practical contact with the question of slavery. This problem in Zanzibar and in the coastal strip, after Britain took over their protectorate, is far too complex for any full treatment here. But it was one which deeply interested Lugard and for many years he and his teacher upon the subject, Kirk, were bitterly critical of the negligent and dilatory handling of the matter by the British government, which was afraid of provoking trouble amongst the Arabs. At the time of which we are now thinking, the main difficulty, one which Lugard had already encountered in Nyasaland, arose from the almost irresistible temptation for missionaries to " harbour " runaway slaves. This problem illustrated the complications of a subject which seemed so simple to philanthropists at home. Slavery, an institution deeply embedded in the social and economic life of a people, could not without injury to both master and slave be abolished by the wave of a hand, especially a foreign hand. Yet, until it was so legally abolished, there was bound to be a difficult period when humane and Christian European residents had to stand aside and tolerate what they had now come to regard as an abominable wrong. The Company, true to the profession of its motto " Light and Liberty ", had redeemed a number of slaves at considerable expense and had made an agreement with the Arabs to redeem fugitives at so much a head. Meanwhile the Church

Missionary Society promised not to harbour unredeemed fugitives at their mission station of Rabai, near Mombasa.

Lugard found in 1890 that both sides were breaking their agreement. He therefore drew up a scheme that the fugitive slaves should work to earn money with which to buy their freedom.[1] This was acceptable to the mission and the Arabs and was a good education for the slaves whose danger, upon emancipation, was the demoralization brought on by sudden freedom in a strange country.[2] This incident, though Lugard's policy was not effectively followed up in East Africa, represented the second phase in the story of his dealings with the problem of slavery.[3]

[1] A copy, in Lugard's writing, was sent to the Foreign Office by Euan-Smith, 14 June 1890, F.O. 84/2062.

[2] Lugard I, p. 292 ff.

[3] I thought it would be interesting to ask Miss de Kiewiet to give me her impression of Lugard as he appeared from her study of the Mackinnon Papers and she supplied this note. "Even before he went to Uganda, Lugard distinguished himself as by far the most able of the men in the Company's employ. He appears to have been quite unaffected by the confusion and disorganization which dominated the Company. His Sabaki stations and his Fuladoyo slave experiments stand out in striking and refreshing contrast to the rather slipshod work done by Company agents elsewhere."

CHAPTER XI

THE TREK INTO THE INTERIOR

August–December 1890 : Aet. 32

LUGARD LEFT Mombasa on August 6th 1890, starting by the Sabaki route.[1] He had with him George Wilson, whom he greatly liked, but who was not at the time really strong enough for the trek, and two young men new to East Africa, Fenwick de Winton, the son of his chief, and William Grant. He had also a very remarkable Somali, Dualla, who had been with both Stanley and with the Hungarian explorer, Count Teleki, on their travels, and had lived in England and Aden. This man, whom Lugard, writing in 1893, described as " the most energetic, valuable native I have ever met, thoroughly trustworthy and very conscientious and willing,"[2] spoke English, Arabic and Swahili as well as his own language. It is, indeed, a striking fact, as the writer can testify from personal knowledge, that this people imprisoned in their sterile country, have great latent intelligence which can seldom be known except when they move outside its borders. Lugard had another well-known African with him, the Sudanese officer, Shukri Aga, who had been with Emin Pasha when Stanley reached him and had travelled with him to the coast and to Egypt when the other leading officer, Selim Bey, failed to join the relieving force.

A great deal of Lugard's life for the next sixteen years was to be spent on trek in Africa. Neither space nor the interest of the reader would allow of too frequent references to the daily circumstances of

[1] As with Nyasaland the story of Lugard's expedition to Uganda is very fully told in his own book. I have borne this in mind in these chapters and have tried to avoid unnecessary repetition. I have made use of his diary (which fills nine large books and was naturally fuller and less discreet than his later published work) and also of the large volume of official reports, letters and other material bearing on the incident. I have not thought it necessary to load the pages with footnotes giving the references to Lugard's book but have done so where there has been literal quotation or where readers might be well advised to read of an important matter in greater detail. The full official report of the march will be found in C.6555 (1892), pp. 87–99.
[2] Lugard I, p. 300.

the march so it may be well to speak of them now at the moment when he was setting out upon his first pioneering journey. For the trek itself, apart from the success of its ultimate objectives, was a comprehensive test of a man's powers, physical, administrative and moral, especially where routes had to be found through unmapped and unknown country. Lugard's generation fully realized this, for they were reading eagerly, one by one, the detailed, dramatically illustrated records of the explorers and pioneers as they came out hard upon the conclusion of each exciting and competitive journey in "Darkest Africa".

The African caravan was based upon human porterage. An African porter could carry a load of seventy pounds' weight balanced upon his head as he walked up to twenty miles a day along the rough, narrow, meandering path made by wild men or wild animals; the men, like the animals, having found it easier to wander round almost every obstacle rather than remove it. The main contents of the loads were firstly the equipment of the white man, tent, clothes, bedding, bath and the rest; secondly food for master and for men; thirdly trade goods; fourthly arms and ammunition. Coming back to the coast, ivory might make a fifth category. The second and third of these need some comment. It is not generally realized how large a problem food presented to early African travellers. They were mainly dependent for this upon what the inhabitants of the region could or would supply. Few agricultural tribes in primitive conditions, although there were some striking exceptions, grew any large amount of surplus food which could be available for passing strangers, while pastoral tribes would rarely part with their animals. In any case there were generally long stretches of unpopulated or desolated land over which food had to be carried. A European who was a skilled hunter could add a valuable meat ration to the daily fare of maize flour, and such a man was a very popular employer. But game, though at this time astonishingly abundant in parts of the country, did not always conveniently present itself for the pot. Lugard was a passionately keen hunter, but shooting could be an arduous extra task, and was difficult to combine with survey work. Not only food but water could be gravely lacking in the dry season and to carry any considerable supply was almost impossible.

The third category of loads, the trade goods, composed mainly of beads and cloth, were the bulky currency with which alone food or service or ivory could be bought. Here much depended upon knowledge and forethought in stocking the caravan. The tribesmen, even in an almost virgin country such as that penetrated by Lugard, were by no means ready to take any goods that were offered. Swahili caravans, as we have seen, had just begun to pass through and already some of the tribes had their views about beads, being highly selective as to colour and size. The only cheerful factor was that, as the coast receded, the price of food decreased. But there were the heavy tasks of ordering and invoicing the goods; distributing them into equal loads; packing them securely—beads were awkward objects to transport—and checking them on the route against damage or theft. So high was the cost of paying and feeding porters on the long trek inland between Mombasa and Lake Victoria that it was reckoned to cost between £250 and £300 to transport each ton from Mombasa to Uganda. The sound economic reasons for enslaving men and seizing food must have become painfully clear at No. 2 Pall Mall, the headquarters of the East Africa Company, when the cost of caravans was worked out in the ledgers.

There remained the difficult art of conducting the caravan. For porterage the inland tribes were still quite unsuitable and unwilling. It was the usual custom, therefore, to recruit so-called Swahili from the melting-pot of Zanzibar. This name was used to cover men of inland tribes who had long been accustomed, often as slaves, freed slaves, or freemen, to do caravan work with the Arabs. Many of these were Wanyamwezi from the region of the old Arab centre of Tabora. Good Zanzibar porters under a good master could be prodigies of endurance, cheerfulness and adaptability. There was nearly always one among a group who, captured in youth from up-country, could talk the local language or something near to it. But there were many who had become almost professional malingerers or deserters. The latter made a habit of disappearing, often with their loads, rifle and advance pay, during the early part of the journey: if they left it too late they were forced, for self-preservation, to stay with the caravan. De Winton pointed out to Lugard that he suffered a very high proportion of deserters when he set out for Uganda and he put this down to the Sabaki route, of which he disapproved, because of the prolonged opportunities it gave, as compared with the Taru desert, for easy escape during the first marches. A caravan going on Lugard's long and hazardous trek was obliged to take some so-called soldiers and so great was the value of a breech-loading gun that there was a high premium upon desertion or theft. As soldiers, the Company recruited Sudanese from Egypt since these men were more disciplined and, being strangers, less likely to desert or join the porters in making trouble.

Once the caravan had passed out of reach of the last contact with civilization, its efficiency and safety depended entirely upon its European leader. It was Stokes' success in conducting caravans up the German route to Lake Victoria which made him so indispensable and so politically important. For the work was perilous and arduous. Within the caravan, order and discipline were essential but the leader had no recognized legal means of enforcing these: he could rely upon moral suasion, impressing the men with his resolution, justice and also with an indefinable quality, a common touch, which can win the allegiance of primitive men and of which humour is no small part. In so far as he lacked, or scorned to use, these qualities, the commander must lean more or less heavily upon force, applied as a rule with the rhino-hide whip, with the bullet always ready for emergencies. The imagination can suggest how easy it was for white men, away from all the restraints of their own society, ignorant of local language and custom, pushing a mass of uncomprehending black men through strange country, to lower their standards to their surroundings. There were such numerous moments when it seemed so much more speedy and effective to kick than to argue, to flog than to reprimand, to push on faster than the more weak of the loaded men could stand, to abandon the sickly when hands could hardly be spared to carry them as well as their fallen loads. Easy, too, to be slack, not to look carefully after the health and food of the men; not to allocate loads fairly or to settle quarrels patiently.

If this were true of relations within that little moving society of the caravan, how many more temptations there were to harshness and violence outside it! Why wait, when bullets were so convenient and effective, to see if the warriors peering through the bushes were friendly? Why endure palaver over *hongo*, the levy some tribes would ask of passing strangers? Why barter at length with unintelligible savages whose grain or cattle were needed and needed quickly? Add to this the strain of tropical life, with its fever, danger, and loneliness, and the bursts of almost ungovernable rage that could master even the best of men when faced with what seemed the inexplicable stupidity or malice of Africans. Even missionaries sometimes failed to live up to the standards of their religion. There had been at one time scandals about harsh methods used in the early days of the Blantyre mission: the great missionary to Uganda, Mackay, once fired at a deserting porter.[1] Stanley almost seemed to relish the many occasions when, as he saw it, it was necessary to shoot his way through Africa; Carl Peters gloated over the effects upon the Masai of his bullets " employed in emphatic relations to their own bodies." He could savour the dramatic contrast between the carnage and destruction he was inflicting with the Advent bells then ringing in Germany and could proceed to cut off the heads of the fallen Masai.[2] Lieutenant Höhnel who went with Count Teleki in 1887 across Lugard's route to discover Lake Rudolf, sneered at the gentle methods of " some roving philanthropist " and declared that " In districts where might makes right .... to employ force is the only means of producing the necessary impression."[3] Livingstone had acted upon a very different assumption. But then he had not been in a hurry, nor had he been responsible for the safety of a large body of men. Yet Joseph Thomson, on his great and urgent journeys, preserved his sense of humanity and justice, and Jackson had, on a first hazardous encounter, succeeded in creating excellent relations with the Masai.

How did Lugard come out of this severe test? He had not Livingstone's Christian dedication to help him though he had the lasting habits of his Christian training. These merged with his more conscious standards which were those, he claimed, of an English gentleman, derived immediately from family, public school and army training, and ultimately, perhaps, from the code of the medieval Christian knight. It was a double sense of caste in that he felt himself to belong to a class within his nation and to a nation within Africa, both of which, he believed, held the code of *noblesse oblige*. It would have been difficult

[1] Oliver, *The Missionary Factor*, p. 83.

[2] Peters, *New Light on Dark Africa*, pp. 222, 231–44. Peters became so notorious in Europe that his own government dropped him, and it was left to the Nazis to make him a hero and the patron of the revived colonial movement in Germany. Ch.-A. Julien, *Les Techniciens de la Colonization* (Paris 1947), pp. 32–3.

[3] L. von Höhnel, *Discovery of Lakes Rudolf and Stefanie* (London 1894), quoted in Coupland II, p. 354.

for an Englishman of the nineties, entering Africa and seeing the nakedness, ignorance, cruelty and superstition of the people, not to believe that his race was superior and therefore justified in imposing its dominion. Early travellers differed from each other as to whether the inferiority of the African was something permanent, decreed by nature or by God, or due to remediable circumstance of environment, and already admitting of exceptions. The difference may sound rarified and doubtless many white pioneers were unconscious as to which view they held; none the less their dealings with black men were directly affected by their beliefs.

Considerations such as these might help us to analyse the whole range of Lugard's dealings with Africans. But at the moment we are seeing him only as a caravan leader setting out on his first independent expedition into the continent. Here his most evident quality was his love of order. To attain this in caravan life required disciplined obedience. Yet flogging which, short of death, was the major sanction where imprisonment and fining were impracticable, was to be inflicted on his men only as the very last resort. He records with pride that he ordered only two such punishments on this first march and one was for an offence against a Kamba woman. Early in the march, seeing Dualla, who had been brought up in the very different caravan traditions of Stanley and Teleki, strike a porter, he reprimanded the proud Somali in front of all the men and never had to repeat the lesson. After a little experience of his Swahili porters, he rejected indignantly the damning things that had been said against them as a class. " I know " he said " no such typical raw material in the world: you can mould them as you will. Some of them have the making of heroes in them, as many instances vivid in my memory attest; . . . . most of them are singularly easily trained to be willing workers, most patient of hardships, plucky and ready to expose their lives, adaptable to routine and discipline however novel and unwelcome."[1] Yet, as we shall see, Lugard never shrank, if he considered it necessary for the safety and success of the expedition, from flogging and flogging severely, and it must be admitted that for offences especially hateful to himself such as brutality to the weak or treachery he could award the sentence with moral satisfaction; though physically the sight of flogging induced in him a powerful sense of nausea.

[1] Lugard I, p. 238.

Lugard was happy as he went forward. It seems that the great majority of men shrink from responsibility and many then and since have gone to Africa in order to escape from it into the anonymity of the bush. But he could never have enough of it and without doubt, the chief charm of Africa to him lay in the absolutely unrestricted opportunity it offered " to rely solely on one's own resources, and that success or failure depend on one's self."[1] With such an approach it was natural that he should relish almost every aspect of life on the march, even the hardships.

To enter into his experience we will abbreviate his own account of the day's march.[2] " Daybreak brings a stir among the sleeping forms . . . . You tumble out of your last unfinished dream and your camp-cot, and substitute the realities of a heavy pair of boots, leggings, knee-breeches and karki [sic] jacket, with a pith ' solar ' hat . . . . You buckle around you the belt which contains your hunting-knife and rounds of Winchester ammunition: you fill your haversack with the paraphernalia which only long experience has taught you to select . . . . understandable only ' by the trade.' The man you call your gun-bearer presents himself and you proceed to dress him up like an (African) Christmas tree . . . . The dawn has hardly broken when we emerge from our tents to give the order to the caravan headman ' to take up loads.' These, during the night, have been stacked under guard in front of the tents . . . . the caravan *askari* . . . . have laid them out one by one in long rows . . . . At the word there is a rush from all parts of the camp; every porter seizes his own load, and he seems to have a dread lest it should be appropriated by another, however heavy and unwieldy it be . . . . Just as the sun appears above the horizon, I lead the way followed by a few *askari*. Every porter shoulders his load, the Wanyamwezi strike up their strange but musical chant, and in two minutes the camp, but now a scene of animated life, is deserted, the smouldering fires die out with the rising sun. . . . Giant beetles come from every quarter to roll up into balls and carry away the bits of offal about the camp." The hyenas and the vultures come in to scavenge. " Meanwhile we are on the march, following a narrow path, and pushing our way through bushes and thorns . . . . Before the sun is well up we are wet up to the waist . . . . If the caravan is proceeding

1 Lugard I, p. 243.
2 Ibid. pp. 243–53.

199

along game tracks . . . . I select such as bear in the direction I wish to go by my pocket compass. Each path that branches away is ' closed ' by the men who follow me " with twigs or grass. After some two hours there is a halt. " By this time the caravan has opened out," the sick or lazy have lagged behind. The halt gives a rest and a chance to close up. " Arrived in camp, the site for the tents is indicated by me with small flags." In half an hour the tents are pitched, the stockade of branches is in place, the inevitable cup of tea is made. " Each little coterie of men select the small site for their bivouac: one goes off to collect material to build the huts, another to draw water, another for firewood, and stones on which to place the cook-pot." The men, tired though they should have been, would go off long distances fishing or trapping small game.

Lugard would, perhaps, go shooting for meat, or would adjudicate over disputes or offences. There were his diary to write, and his notes to make on the route, the soil, the tribes; there were his mapping and road-chart to keep up. " Sharp at six the sun sets. The headman blows his whistle and asks if all are present, a lusty chorus replies for every little fraternity of messmates." Then at last, these men who had carried heavy loads on their heads through the hot day, would lie down in the open or, if it was raining, under little shelters of branches or squares of cotton cloth and go to sleep.

Such was one of many hundreds of days and nights of trekking upon which Lugard now embarked, mostly making tracks where no white man had walked before. Those who, in much later and more peaceful days, but before the motor-car became universal, have trekked on foot or with transport animal—camel, horse or mule—can understand the intense charm of such travel, and round out his picture. There are the hushed, sleepy voices at the dawn start; the precious dewy coolness before the sun reaches its height and begins to hurt; the sudden halt over the fresh spoor or dung of big game on the track; the glorious nights when limbs relax round a huge resinous burning log whose flames, a protection from prowling carnivores, shoot up towards a sky of stars of a number and brightness unknown in our dull north.

Lugard's first instructions were to find the best road to Uganda and to make treaties with the tribes along it. There was still no certain news of Jackson's caravan so he had little or nothing to go upon except

such information as there was about the route followed by the few
Swahili slavers and traders who had gone through. He was still marching along the Tsavo river which flows into the Sabaki when he ran
into such a caravan and had an opportunity of fulfilling the main
motive which had brought him to Africa and which was to make him,
in the changing circumstances of his time, the true successor of Kirk
as Kirk in turn had succeeded Livingstone. Here, Lugard had again,
as in Nyasaland, as direct a contact with the evil as Livingstone himself.
The slavers scattered into the thick bush but he was able to capture
some of them, and sent them back to Mombasa for trial. He found
himself with some emaciated children on his hands and took them
along with him. He gave them a meal of chicken to begin with; had
little white coats made to replace their filthy rags and tucked them up
at night under a blanket " as snug as dormice ".

On September 20th he arrived at Machakos, the one post the
Company held in the interior. Here he found only 80 loads had arrived
by the direct Taru route instead of the 500 he had been promised.
Machakos was in the region of the Kamba, a large group, though not
one that had any centralized government. This was the first important
East African tribe Lugard had encountered. A rather poignant interest
lies in all early contacts with peoples who had been cut off from any
relationship with the civilized world. One of the most dramatic and,
in retrospect, tragic human encounters in history was that between
Columbus and the first natives of the New World he met. It is worth
remarking that in East Africa—to generalize no more widely—it was
exceptional for the first white men to be received with hostility.
The Kamba had, of course, by now seen several white men and this
was Lugard's second visit to Machakos. But it served to show how
difficult it was to avoid those misunderstandings which, once begun,
almost automatically widened until suspicion and dislike clouded the
friendly atmosphere of the first encounters.

On his first visit to Machakos Lugard had made friends with the
local chief N'sibu, a fine old man who brought his strapping sons and
even his wife and daughter to see him, so that " they might hear all
his words to me, and fulfil them when he was gone, and that never
between his family and ourselves should there be aught but peace . . . .
And in return we pretended to offer him ' protection '." Even at this
" station " the Company could do nothing to save the chief from Masai

raids or stop the ceaseless inter-tribal warfare. "I would not make a treaty on such terms, but I gave him a flag as an emblem of friendship and alliance."[1]

Now, on his second visit, Lugard found that the white Company agent left at the post was about to punish a local tribesman accused of firing an arrow at one of the Company men. Yet Lugard at a glance found that the offending missile did not match the type in the man's quiver. Then he was told of a hostile village the agent wanted to "hammer." He sent Dualla to the place, where he met with nothing but friendship. Lugard then called a meeting of local chiefs and they brought their complaints: these were of women violated—it was here that Lugard flogged one of his own men for this offence—of food stolen and so on. Lugard himself they accused of bringing up "coast Masai" (Sudanese) and openly challenging them to war. He found they referred to the daily bayonet exercise he imposed on the Sudanese to keep them occupied. Lugard set all to rights and sealed the agreement with some of the chiefs by entering into blood-brotherhood. By this each man cut his own arm, mingled his blood with that of his "brother" and then consumed some of the other's on a piece of meat.[2] At Machakos Wilson nearly died and was saved only by Lugard's devoted nursing during days and nights.

From Machakos he marched on into the edge of the Kikuyu country where, screened by a fringe of forest, this tribe took the brunt of the Masai raids and retaliated in kind. Even by the time Lugard's book was produced in 1893, the Kikuyu had acquired, he says, a reputation for inveterate hostility and treachery. Since then, while it is admitted that they have proved one of the ablest and most progressive groups in Africa, they are in many quarters condemned as dour, assertive and politically minded, and as these words are written there is a crisis in Kenya over the so-called Mau Mau movement among the Kikuyu. It is interesting, therefore, to read Lugard's testimony after living among them for more than a month, that he "was more favourably impressed by them than by any other tribe I had as yet met in Africa . . . . I had no hesitation in trusting myself almost alone among them, even at considerable distances from camp . . . . I found them honest and straightforward."[3]

[1] Lugard I, p. 284.
[2] Ibid. pp. 318-19.
[3] Ibid. p. 327.

He was impressed, too, by the high standard of cultivation and by its immense extent, and also by the system of irrigation. He was easily able to buy no less than 20,000 lb. of grain and beans for his men. More scrupulous than most European official agents of this period of " the scramble ", he felt unable to use the treaty forms with which he had been provided because he considered that he could not fairly ask the chiefs to give up all rights of rule in their country nor pledge the Company to protect them. Instead he entered into blood-brotherhood with some of the chiefs, and made very special friends with Eiyeki[1] (or Waiyaki) and Miroo who were " extremely intelligent, good mannered and *most* friendly." They helped him to choose a site where he built a strong stockade. This place was called Dagoretti and here he left in charge the well-disposed Wilson, who had quite broken down, thus giving him a chance to recuperate in the bracing air of this high land with its charming almost English-looking scenery of green hills, forests, glades, streams, bracken and springy velvet turf. The site of this post can still be traced. Here one can stand on a ridge with the rolling wooded Kikuyu hills to the north while to the south the dry Masai steppe stretches away into blue distance: a meeting place of contrasting scenes and peoples. It was close to this station that the future capital, Nairobi, was to develop and already Lugard noted that the conditions here made it possible " in the far future " that it might prove suitable for white colonization. In later days he was to look back with very mixed feelings upon the rapid realization of this possibility. He was also to regret bitterly that it was by the mishandling of the Kikuyu in the next two years, that the happy relations possible with this most friendly tribe, were turned into hostility and bloodshed, so that " the people became estranged . . . . [and] hopelessly disaffected."[2]

It was here on October 18th that Lugard received the definitive order that he had so much desired: that he was to go on independently to Uganda; de Winton was to remain at the coast. He heard other

[1] Unhappily Eiyeki (or Waiyaki) later turned against the British. Shortly after Lugard left East Africa, the Company officer at Kikuyu, while shaving in his tent, is said to have seen the reflection of Eiyeki preparing to spear him. The chief was wounded and arrested and died on his way down to the coast. J. R. L. Macdonald, *Soldiering and Surveying in British East Africa* (1897), pp. 120-1. When the writer tried to meet his son at a wayside store the report caused a stir and the man, mistaking the reason why he was " wanted ", disappeared. But this was after the Mau Mau trouble had broken out.

[2] Lugard II, pp. 535-6. It should be noted that Portal made the same point a little later. Portal to Mathews, 6 February 1892, Rodd Papers.

news which largely altered the situation within which he had been working. He must have heard of the Anglo-German treaty of June 1890 before he left the coast but now his mail-bag would bring the full story. Lord Salisbury, amid a growing chorus of disapproval about his weakness over Africa, and especially over Uganda, to which the newly returned Stanley had been adding his loud and authoritative voice, had been personally and quietly conducting negotiations with Germany, where the young Kaiser was taking over the helm from the pilot he had dropped. On May 22nd, at a Merchant Taylors' dinner, the day after Stanley had bitterly attacked the government about its feebleness in not supporting the Company's claim in the interior, Salisbury replied in words that Lugard would have done well to ponder, for they revealed the attitude of one of the two or three minds which then and for some years would govern his actions. After dryly remarking that it was evidently now the proper thing for distinguished men in their after-dinner speeches to talk of Africa, he denied that he had surrendered anything, or had yet made any agreement. But—and this was the passage that most concerns our subject—" whether we enter into close relationship of possession and responsibility with all this magnificent territory which Mr. Stanley has revealed to the world is a subject on which the public opinion of England and Parliament ought to be consulted." They must look on such propositions " as bargains are looked at in this great city, from the point of view of prudence as well as from that of boldness. The extension of the British Empire, so long as it is a question of maritime territory, is a matter that need alarm no Briton. We have a fleet . . . . but when invited to take possession of countries only accessible to the sea after three months' travel, of course an entirely different set of considerations come into view. I do not wish to rub up old sores; but of course it is within the memory of those present that we did wish to relieve a town called Khartoum, not nearly so far from the sea as many places we have heard of lately, and the results were not precisely of the most brilliant character. (Laughter)."[1]

Yet, in the secrecy of diplomatic negotiations, in which Salisbury had pitted Stanley's public appeal in Britain against that of Carl Peters in Germany, he was, even as he said this, nearing success, and by paying over the counter the barren little island of Heligoland, useless

1 *The Times,* 23 May 1890.

to Britain but deeply desired by Germany, he was able, once more going better than his word, to gain from Germany a reasonable northern frontier for Rhodesia and Nyasaland including the famous Stevenson road. A British protectorate over Zanzibar and Pemba, so long foreshadowed and so late achieved, was readily accepted by the harassed sultan, and recognized by Germany, who also abandoned her threatening outpost at Witu with the islands Manda and Patta. This, on the hinterland principle, cleared the Company's claim to the northern half of Lake Victoria and up to the Congo border if—and this was still a very large pre-supposition—the claim could be made good. But what of Stanley's treaties and the land between Lakes Victoria and Tanganyika which Lugard was to annex? That was more than Salisbury, not much moved, as we have seen, by the Cape-to-Cairo vision, was able to get from the German Foreign Office, all the more as the validity of the treaties was assailable.[1] " The question " he told the Cabinet " practically, to which Aye or No must be replied is, whether Sir William Mackinnon and Mr. Stanley are to be overruled or not."[2] Overruled they were, and the southern shores of Africa's greatest lake went to Germany though thirty years later the decision was reversed by the judgment of war. But by this loss to one Chartered Company Salisbury was able to make a gain for another, and present Rhodes with a good frontier along the Stevenson road and on to Lake Tanganyika. We may note that the British ambassador in Berlin, Sir Edward Malet, was enthusiastic about the part Sir Percy Anderson's amazingly detailed knowledge of Africa had played in Berlin, where he had been sent during the negotiations.[3] It must be emphasized that this agreement, signed on July 1st, was for a British sphere of influence, *not* a protectorate over Uganda. It is also important to remember, in view of future events, that France was not a signatory to this treaty.[4]

It was well, indeed, that Salisbury's agreement with Germany had been so favourable, otherwise the protracted delays in starting the expedition, for which Lugard's personal difficulties had been partly responsible, would have given an opportunity to Germany,

1 See below p. 259, n. 1.
2 Cecil, *Life of Salisbury*, vol. iv, p. 285. See also pp. 277–302 for a lively account of the negotiations, based on the Salisbury papers.
3 Malet to Salisbury, 1 July and 9 August 1890, S.P. vol. 63 (Germany 1890–2).
4 *Correspondence respecting the Anglo-German agreement relative to Africa and Heligoland.* Africa No. 6 (1890), C.6046. See Hertslet, *Map of Africa*, vol. iii, pp. 899–906.

a nation of quick and decisive action, to annex Uganda. Even so, occupation within the sphere of influence had still to be made effective.

De Winton sent Lugard further instructions and advice about Uganda, based upon the information brought down by Jackson, who had arrived back at the coast on September 4th, having missed Lugard on the way. These instructions seemed to read well on paper, but in view of the uncertainty of the position in Uganda, they could only be of a most general nature.[1] It is interesting to notice that de Winton, who thought he knew Lugard's characteristics and had suffered from them, in his next letter warned him " to keep a watch on a too great exhibition of self-confidence. Cool, quiet judgment and plain common-sense will be your best companions: self-confidence is an unruly, uncertain jade, and cannot be relied upon." (17 September 1890). In spite of all that happened, de Winton bore no grudge, and he made it clear that Lugard could count upon his full understanding and support, a most valued pledge for a man launched hundreds of miles into the heart of Africa to deal with an altogether incalculable situation. Lugard was also ordered to hurry in order to outpace the trader, Stokes, coming up the German route with his dangerous supply of arms and so save Uganda from the ever-present threat of further civil war.

On November 1st Lugard left Dagoretti. His caravan now numbered 3 Europeans, 66 Sudanese and Somalis, 285 Swahili (porters, *askari* and servants), each man carrying eight days' food in addition to his load. He had with him the rather battered Maxim gun which Stanley had dragged across Africa. With no guide, but using his compass, he plunged into the wide grasslands on the way to Lake Naivasha, where he could not hope to get food and where the Masai were dominant. He ran into only one party of these warriors who came out in their war dress, with their huge-bladed spears and gaily painted five-foot shields. He marked " their extremely arrogant indolent air ", their well-built naked bodies and intelligent faces. This fighting tribe, so striking in their attitude of proud self-containment, were strangely tolerant of peaceful European intrusion into the wide lands under their mastery. So now, when Lugard refused either to halt or pay *hongo*, they let him pass. Lugard went on past Lake Elementeita and the flamingo-clouded lake of Nakuru, up a stream-bed in the almost sheer, forested

1 A copy of these instructions was sent to the Foreign Office in November 1892, F.O. 84/2264.

sides of the beautiful Elgeyo ravine and across the Nandi plateau to the edge of the Kavirondo plain where the land drops suddenly from some seven thousand feet to about four thousand, the whole route one of astonishing grandeur. On this last part of the journey they saw no human life, only the scattered carcases of buffaloes, killed by that great rinderpest that swept all through the continent at this time, killing wild and domestic herds, as it must often have swept through Africa before the Europeans brought their science for its control.

The party climbed down the steep scarp on to the great plain that curves about Lake Victoria, not a load being lost in the descent, and marched through thick grass to the headquarters of the chief Mumia, which had become a kind of halting place for Swahili caravans just outside Uganda and near the great ivory-producing regions. This same chief, old and infirm, was still there to recall Lugard's coming when, forty years later, the writer visited his place, and he survived until as recently as 1949. After three days, Lugard's party forded the Nzoia river, waist deep, and leaving behind the friendly, but naked and very primitive Kavirondo, entered Busoga, the tribal area next to the kingdom of Buganda and to some extent tributary to it. At once a heightening of the scale of civilization was observed. After halting two days at the village of Wakoli, one of the leading Basoga chiefs, to re-provision and to hear news of Buganda, Lugard pressed on towards this kingdom. Every effort was made to delay him. All canoes had been removed to the opposite side of the Nile which here pours its great waters out of Lake Victoria, and trips over the low shelf of the Ripon Falls to begin its 2,500 mile run to the Mediterranean. But Lugard was determined not to be kept out by the distrustful King. He found, forgotten in the jungle which bordered the lake, a tiny cockleshell of a canoe and, well aware of the risk, went across in it himself. As he neared the opposite bank two men with rifles rose from behind a boulder and walked off. The little canoe went back and forth until the local chief, not daring to repeat the murder of Bishop Hannington of five years before on the eastern side of the Nile, allowed the use of two or three larger canoes and soon the whole caravan stood within the borders of the kingdom that was the goal of their long journey. But Lugard learned afterwards that more than one man, by King Mwanga's orders, paid with his life for allowing him to get thus unopposed across the Nile and enter Buganda.

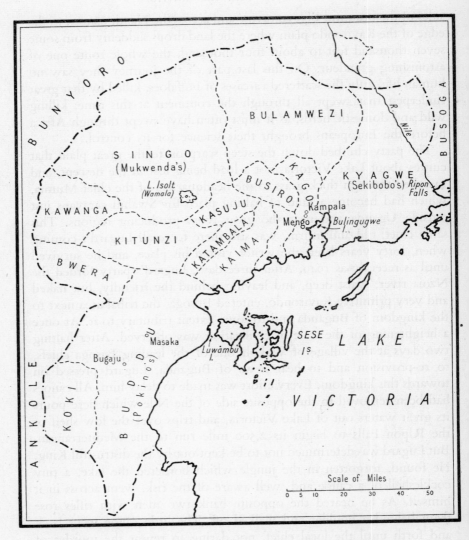

Buganda, 1890. Taken from Ravenstein's map which was based on Lugard's explorations and published in F. D. Lugard, *The Rise of Our East African Empire*, 1893

CHAPTER XII

KAMPALA

December 1890 : Aet. 32

It was on December 13th 1890 that Lugard crossed the Nile and camped upon its western bank just within the kingdom of Buganda. He did not linger there. As he had told de Winton, he had long thought out exactly what he would do upon arrival. He believed that he should combine courtesy and impartiality with a display of will-power and thus show the King from the first moment that he would not be tricked nor coerced. It was for this reason that he had so resolutely and quickly crossed the Nile and he now marched straight on, undeterred by a series of messages from the King proposing stopping places at short distances from his capital. Polite letters also reached him from both the French and British missionaries. As he entered the kingdom he was amazed, after all he had seen of emptiness and of primitive humanity on his march, at the degree of civilization in this remote place. He marked the roads, the tall, regular fences, the people's long garments of russet barkcloth or spotless imported cotton, and their dignity and respectful manners. He marched westwards parallel with the lake, through Buganda's alternation of low, grassy, flat-topped hills and its forested lowlands, descending at intervals into swamps of black mud matted with beautiful plumed papyrus and water-lilies. Round each hut were the dark cloisters of the banana groves which supplied the staple food of the people. An envoy from the King met him with the royal band of flutes, drums and many kinds of gaily decorated stringed instruments and at each halt the musicians turned dancers to the entertainment of the visitors.

In this way Lugard, with his caravan more than three hundred strong, approached Mengo. This name belongs to the hill which was the site of the King's palace, one of several closely neighbouring small hills; another, Rubaga, held the Roman Catholic mission, and yet another, Namirembe, the Anglican. The King sent a messenger instructing Lugard to camp in " a wet and dirty hollow ". He declined and looking round, saw " a low gravelly knoll " of untenanted land, just over a mile away from the royal hill, and, in spite of message after message from the palace to deter him, he led his men up there and made his camp. Upon enquiry he was told that the name of this hill was Kampala. This name was later extended to the whole capital city which, with its corrugated iron roofs tinted with red dust, sprawls ever more extensively around the whole group of hills. But the grassy site of the camp, now surrounded by the growing suburb known as Old Kampala, remains much as it was. On one side is a plaque with the inscription—" On this spot the flag of the Imperial British East Africa (Chartered) Company was first flown by Captain F. J. D. Lugard on behalf of the British government on the 18th December 1890." It is easy to walk about on its almost flat but very restricted summit, to identify general lines of Lugard's camp and to look out at the three surrounding hills crowned with the Kabaka's palace and the striking architectural contrasts of the Anglican and Roman Catholic cathedrals.

This day when Lugard set up his modest headquarters and looked across at these three neighbouring hills, which represented the chief factors of his problem, was to represent a turning-point in the history of the country and is a good occasion for us to review the history and the situation of Uganda which Lugard was now anxiously trying to assess, and to collect together such scattered references as have been made to its affairs.[1]

1 Uganda has a considerable literature even for the period before 1892. This falls into several categories. There are the accounts of the early explorers and especially J. H. Speke, *Journal of the Discovery of the Source of the Nile* (1863); Sir S. W. Baker, *The Albert N'yanza* (1866) and *Ismailia* (1874); H. M. Stanley, *Through the Dark Continent* (1878) and *In Darkest Africa* (1890). Then there are the official Blue Books between 1892 and 1895, the more relevant of which will be found in the list of references. The next category is that of the books written mainly by the British and French missionaries and by soldiers and administrators: references to the more important will be found. The most valuable recent books are those already cited by R. Coupland and R. Oliver. The *Uganda Journal* contains much information and some scholarly articles on the history of this period by H. B. Thomas, Sir John Gray, R. Oliver and others. The hand-book *Uganda* by H. B. Thomas and R. Scott (1935) is an outstanding volume of its kind and contains, with much other material, an authoritative historical summary and an excellent select bibliographical list, including a list of official publications. The writer has also been able to use the large amount of material in the Lugard Papers, which includes the six substantial volumes of Lugard's diaries, a number of confidential official papers and a large collection of Lugard's correspondence, especially with the local missionaries and with the Company officials in Africa and London. A study has also been made of such material as exists in the Secretariat archives at Entebbe and of the Foreign Office papers in the Public Record Office; the Gladstone Papers in the British Museum; the Portal Papers and the Anti-Slavery Society Papers in the Bodleian

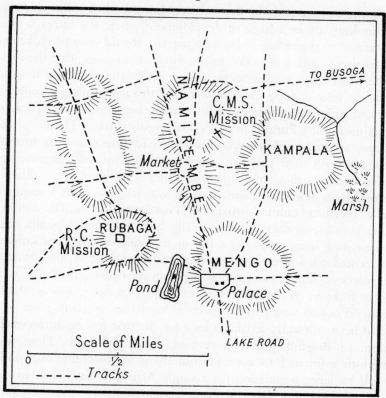

Mengo and Environs 1890. Based on a sketch map by the
Rev. R. H. Walker. Published in F. D. Lugard, *The Rise
of Our East African Empire,* 1893

The kingdom of Buganda was, and is, something exceptional in
Bantu Africa. It was at that time the most important of a group of
interesting small kingdoms. We cannot reach back here into the
legendary origins of these kingdoms nor even assess the evidence of

(Rhodes House), and .he Church Missionary Society Papers. It was not possible to visit Zanzibar to see the archives there but much of this material is to be found also in the Foreign Office
and in the Portal Papers and I have been given invaluable evidence from their contents by Sir
John Gray and Mr. Anthony Low. On the French side, use has been made of the unpublished
archives of the Ministère des Affaires Étrangères at the Quai d'Orsay; of the published *Documents
Diplomatiques Français*; and of the reports of proceedings in the Sénat and Chambre des Députés
contained in the appropriate *Journaux Officiels.* Enquiries made in Uganda about obtaining access
to such material as might be possessed by the Roman Catholic Fathers were not profitable.
See Oliver, *The Missionary Factor,* p. x for a discussion of the material available from mission
archives.

the anthropologists upon this subject. Indeed, their ideas and their terminology are in a stage of development where the attempt of the uninitiated to generalize upon such matters would only provoke their chastisement. Suffice it to say, in the simplest language, that the region of the Great Lakes was the scene of one of the latest waves of what had probably been a long succession of southward-moving peoples, of different racial composition from the main negro stock of Africa, and sometimes called Eurafrican or by the linguistic name Hamitic. These groups, at once mobile and masterful, had imposed their lordship, entwined with their peculiar systems of kingship and religion, upon the sedentary tribes. In some parts they still lived their different, pastoral lives alongside them. Lugard was later to meet a somewhat similar racial and cultural situation in Northern Nigeria. The dominant Hima peoples, as they have generally been called in Uganda, were, in their pure state, non-negro, but in Buganda, where their kingdom had existed for some centuries, they had been largely absorbed, and the rulers no longer maintained the pastoral rituals which the writer saw in Bukoba, to the south-west of Lake Victoria. It appears that the fusing of contrasting peoples of these kinds has in many parts of the world been culturally fertile, at least for the first few centuries of their union. In Buganda this had certainly been the result. Here was a kingdom estimated to contain something approaching one million people,[1] a large population for a single African polity, with an autocratic monarch, an elaborate court ritual, ministers, courtiers, pages. It possessed also, apparently alone in Africa, something very like a mobile civil service holding provincial offices of several grades which were attached to landed estates rather than the feudal reverse of this system, where baronial dynasties held hereditary lands and offices. There were, in what was to become the Uganda Protectorate, three other adjoining but much less substantial Hima kingdoms. In the north was Bunyoro, whose vigorous and warlike king, Kabarega, was at that time trying, with some success, to win back the much greater power his kingdom had once possessed. He was pressing hard upon the two much smaller states of Ankole and Toro to the west of Buganda. Any power which interfered with this process was bound to incur his formidable resentment.

1 It is impossible to say exactly what the population of Buganda was then. The present figure for Buganda Province is given as 1,323,627, *Uganda Annual Report, 1953* (H.M.S.O. 1954), p. 121.

Kampala

Buganda had entered history in 1863 when Speke and Grant returned to Europe after discovering the kingdom, then under its strong and stern King Mutesa, in a great journey from the coast at Bagamoyo to the west of Lake Victoria and back up the Nile to Egypt.[1] On their way they met Baker and his wife, coming down from the north into Bunyoro to discover Lake Albert. There was no sequel to this discovery for some ten years though an occasional Arab reached Mutesa's court from Zanzibar and a few Baganda made the return journey to and from the coast. It was an open question, as the scramble for Africa began, which power would try to grasp Uganda and from which direction. In the early seventies it seemed as though Egypt, through the energy of the British governors, first Baker and then Gordon, whom the Khedive employed, would secure the prize. They pushed down into Bunyoro, and their European subordinates reached even further. It would have been ironic indeed if these men, pledged to suppress the highly destructive slave-trade of the Egyptians and northern Sudanese, should in effect have opened up this practically virgin country to its depredations.[2]

Now came a dramatic diversion. In 1875 Stanley, exploring from Zanzibar, arrived in Buganda from the south of Lake Victoria. In his bluff, journalistic way he records how he told King Mutesa—a slender man over six foot high, " large-lustrous-eyed "—" about Europe and Heaven "; gave him his own version of Christian theology and, moved by the King's eager questions, promised to send him Christian teachers from England. Having written a letter containing a challenge to Christendom to send teachers to Mutesa, Stanley proceeded on his immense journey which was to bring him out at the Atlantic coast nearly two years later. At Mutesa's court he had met Gordon's assistant, Linant de Bellefonds, who carried Stanley's letter down the Nile to Gordon. Gordon sent it on to England where, bearing the date April 14th, it was published in the *Daily Telegraph* on November 15th 1875. Neither Stanley nor the *Daily Telegraph* of that period seemed the most likely agencies of evangelization. But the Church Missionary Society received a cheque for £5,000 from an unknown donor and a few days later decided to act. It was a bold as well as a quick decision. Uganda was still little more than a name and it was dangerously and

[1] Speke, *op. cit.* p. 261 ff.
[2] Coupland II, especially pp. 271–99; Sir John Gray, ' Sir John Kirk and Mutesa', *Uganda Journal*, vol. XV, March 1951.

expensively remote. The safe plan was always to move gradually inland. But, remembering St. Paul's immediate response to the call from Macedonia, the Society took this leap into the dark and distance of equatorial Africa. A long train of political consequences for Britain and Uganda was to follow from this decision. Offers of men and money poured in, and seven men, one of them the Scottish engineer Mackay, were sent out. Two of these reached Mutesa's court in July 1877. By the end of the year two of the party had died and two had been murdered by islanders when travelling over Lake Victoria, while one was left alone for many months until Mackay, who had fallen sick on the journey up, was able to join him in November 1878.

Their Christian teaching was well received at the court. In 1879, however, two French Catholic priests arrived. They were " White Fathers" of the *Société des Missionaires d'Afrique*, which had been founded in Algiers by Cardinal Lavigerie and which, looking for new fields to conquer with its rapidly growing numbers, found them in the interior of the continent. Hearing of the plan to send priests to Mutesa's court, Dr. Cust of the C.M.S. travelled to Algiers in the vain attempt to beg the Cardinal not to send these missionaries, with such vast stretches of pagan Africa still untouched, to work in the very place where the C.M.S. had begun.[1] This early history of the missions is all too relevant to Lugard's work in Uganda. There is no need to emphasize the depth of bitterness aroused in the hearts of those already there by the arrival of the new missionaries who made claims to higher authority and truth, nor the bewilderment and disunity created amongst the Baganda by the tragic division of Christendom.

In a kingdom like Buganda there was no possibility, as Dr. Oliver has pointed out,[2] of the two missions developing large stations of their own, such as Blantyre and Livingstonia, where each could have pursued its evangelization in considerable isolation from the other. Such a policy of separation and self-containment was possible only amongst weaker and smaller tribes. Here, as in the old kingdoms of Kent and Northumbria, the missionaries naturally tried to convert the ruler and his court and they had to build up their new societies under his powerful and suspicious gaze. The evils of Christian disunity

1 E. Stock, *History of the Church Missionary Society* (1899), vol. iii, p. 105. The authoritative story of the Uganda Mission will be found in chapters 74, 90 and 91 of this volume; see also R. F. Clarke, *Cardinal Lavigerie and the African Slave Trade* (1889), p. 126 ff.

2 Oliver, *The Missionary Factor*, pp. 73-4.

were thus seen at their maximum, as both tended to compete for the support of the King and the ruling class. Both denominations met with a genuine response from the high-spirited and intelligent Baganda, especially among the official classes concentrated at the capital. Nor was Christianity the only new creed to attract the Baganda from their pagan religion: the Arab and Swahili traders from the coast had built up Muslim influence during the reign of Mutesa. This King, a strong man and alert enough to be aware that he might need foreign aid against foreign dangers, was relatively tolerant. Upon his death in 1884, however, he was succeeded by one of his sons, the eighteen year old Mwanga, who had almost every serious fault a ruler can have, at least in a situation crowded with new and imponderable dangers. All Europeans—seldom, of course, quite disinterested observers—loaded him with depreciatory adjectives. He was said to be cowardly, cruel, treacherous, vacillating and a slave to his own unnatural sensuality. To such a man had descended the absolute power of the Buganda kingship, with its right instantly to condemn any man or woman in the country to death in the most atrocious forms for any cause or passing caprice.[1]

But it would have needed a very strong or wise ruler if he were not to be demoralized by the situation which Mwanga inherited. The introduction of the new religions in the court and the capital, with their novel ideas and rituals, had deeply disturbed the whole of Buganda society and challenged the paganism in which the autocratic monarchical system was embedded. The unfortunate Mwanga felt his power threatened on all sides. The Arabs brought him news of growing German intrusions on the coast; rumours reached him of Thomson's travels east of Lake Victoria in lands as yet untrodden by any white man. The Arabs, making their last bid for power, played on his fears of white men and their revolutionary religion. In January 1885, he first mutilated and then killed three young C.M.S. adherents,[2] and when, later in the same year, the mission sent up to Buganda a Bishop of Eastern Equatorial Africa, James Hannington, the first white man to try to enter the kingdom from the east across the Nile, Mwanga ordered him and his fifty African followers to be murdered in cold blood. A smoker of the drug *bhang*, which is said to provoke

[1] Sir Apolo Kagwa, *The Customs of the Baganda*, tr. E. E. Kalibala (New York 1934), pp. 82–3. Five of the chief office-holders only were exempt.
[2] J. P. Thoonen, *Black Martyrs* (1941), p. 93.

fits of rage, and addicted to the practice of sodomy which he is supposed to have learned from the Arabs, he became frantic when some of his pages, who had become " learners " under the Christian missionaries, refused to submit to his vice. In May 1886 he asked all those of his pages who had accepted this Christian status to confess themselves. Immediately thirty youths came forward, both Anglicans and Roman Catholics. Mwanga gave them the choice of submission to his will or of being burnt alive. All chose martyrdom. They were trussed and thrown into a slow fire, yet not one saved himself by submission.[1] It may be imagined how deep an impression this news made upon a church-going generation when some months later it reached England and Scotland, where Livingstone's countrymen were now watching the work in Uganda of the great missionary, Mackay. What latent powers, men asked, must such a people possess, whose sons not only embraced so exacting a faith but were ready for its sake to face death in its most terrible form! The diary of Bishop Hannington, written up to the moment when, imprisoned in a dark hut, he was taken out to die, was also published.[2] The blood of martyrs not only nourished the seed of Christianity in Uganda but cried to Europe for further support and sacrifice.

In Uganda the Christians now began to organize themselves in readiness for a trial of strength with the Arab-led Muslim party. There was a counting of heads and, much more important, of guns, for upon these, with the ammunition to fire them, the issue would depend. But Mwanga, in his desperation, suddenly turned to the pagan majority for support and planned to entice the leaders of all the three parties of the " new " religions to meet him on an island in the lake, meaning to leave them cut off there to starve. The plot was revealed and the three parties combined to depose Mwanga and enthrone his younger brother Kiwewa. There followed an agreement between them to share out the state offices and lands and to establish religious toleration. This brittle alliance could not last. In October 1888 the Muslim party made a treacherous attack upon the Christian leaders; drove them away from the court; imprisoned the missionaries; shipped them off to the south of the lake, where Mwanga also had fled, and set about forcibly converting and circumcising the Baganda.

1 Thoonen, *op. cit.* pp. 242-9.
2 *The Last Journals of Bishop Hannington*, ed. E. C. Dawson (1888).

This was no isolated event: it was part of that Arab reaction to the increasing threat from Europe to their power and their trade, the more southern manifestations of which have been related.[1] How far it was a concerted movement with a clear objective it is hard to say. Certainly it was at this time that Lugard was struggling against the Arab threat to Karonga and the Nyasa missions, and that the Bushiri rebellion against the Germans broke out. Mackay believed that the whole movement was secretly stimulated by the sultan of Zanzibar, a policy for which, in view of European, and especially German, aggression, he could hardly be blamed. But the Arabs had sufficient reason for a simultaneous and spontaneous reaction against the new pressures.[2]

Mwanga now presented himself as a penitent suppliant at the Roman Catholic mission station at the south of the lake. Soon after this, Stokes arrived with a supply of guns and ammunition and with these the scattered Christian parties took up the war again. They were only partially successful against the Arabs. These had replaced the insufficiently docile Kiwewa (whom they proceeded to starve and torture) by his brother Kalema who now collected some thirty members of the royal family, men and women, and put them to death with obscene cruelty. A deadlock ensued. The Christians were not strong enough to oust the Muslims but they had command of the lake and the fertile Sese islands which lie off Buganda, and whose inhabitants possessed a great fleet of the excellent canoes of the region. Mwanga himself was able, with Stokes' help, to establish himself on a small island close to Mengo, Bulingugwe, a place that was to become notorious in Lugard's day.

Meanwhile Stokes went back to the coast: but before he left, rumours had reached him that Jackson's caravan was coming up from Mombasa, and he and Mwanga wrote letters, to await Jackson in Kavirondo, imploring his help. Later, in early October, the Christians drove Kalema and the Muslims out of Mengo with great slaughter, nearly all the Arabs being killed, and they regained the ruined corpse-strewn and vulture-infested capital and mission stations. The two parties of Christians divided the chieftainships between themselves while Stokes received his reward, £2,400 worth of ivory, as an instalment of his

[1] See above pp. 93, 130–1.
[2] See Oliver, *op. cit.* p. 108, for his arguments upon this question, also H. B. Thomas's review of this book in *Uganda Journal*, vol. XVII, March 1953, p. 74.

claim for £20,000. Following this success, letters from the English missionary Gordon and the chiefs went to Jackson telling him that though Mwanga had returned to his capital he was still anxious for help.

Jackson found all these letters awaiting him when he reached Mumia's early in November.[1] But his orders directed him towards Emin's province. He had been told not to go to Uganda and he was too weak in numbers, trade-goods and arms for any large adventure. He replied at once: his help, he said, did not now seem to be essential; and if he were to come Mwanga must make it worth the Company's while and accept its very sweeping demands; he would wait a month for a reply. To this Mwanga, under the guidance of Père Lourdel, one of the White Fathers, replied in terms which Jackson found " somewhat ambiguous." Gordon wrote at the same time to warn Jackson that Père Lourdel, who was now the keeper of the King's conscience, would dissuade the King from putting himself under the Company's influence: " he advises the King to invite persons of all nationalities and not to give an advantage to anyone in particular." There was still a danger, Gordon said, of the Muslims staging a " come-back " and even joining forces with the Muslim army in Wadelai.[2]

Jackson found Mwanga's letter unconvincing. He sent him a flag as a sign of the Company's protection until he could get instructions from the coast, and forthwith set out with Gedge exploring and seeking ivory towards Mount Elgon. But, hard on the dispatch of Mwanga's " ambiguous " reply, the Muslims returned to Mengo and Mwanga was once more an imperilled fugitive on Bulingugwe island. New and urgent requests were now sent off to Jackson agreeing to all his conditions, Lourdel on Mwanga's behalf offering ivory worth £2,000, free rations, a monopoly of trade and acceptance of the Company's flag.

These letters were lying unopened in Jackson's base camp at Mumia's when, on February 2nd 1890, Carl Peters arrived, read them, and browsed upon Jackson's past correspondence with Uganda.[3] How he must have laughed and gloated over Lourdel's letter! Here was his

1 Jackson, *Early Days in East Africa*, p. 221 ff. There is reason to believe that the sequence of events as here related is confused; doubtless because Sir Frederick had died before he could finalize his book for the press.
2 The Rev. E. C. Gordon to F. Jackson, 23 November 1889, L.P. It has not been necessary here to give all the details of this correspondence, copies of which are in the Lugard Papers.
3 Peters, *New Light on Dark Africa*, p. 318.

perfect chance not only to thwart Britain but to get the prize himself. Within two days he hurried on to Buganda, where he found Mwanga again victorious, thanks to a consignment of guns and powder received as a ransom for some captured Arabs, and the Muslim army again beaten back to Bunyoro. It is worth noting for future reference that Peters believed that there was great danger of another civil war.[1] Peters was cordially supported by Lourdel, and he made, in no very onerous terms, a treaty of friendship with Mwanga and the Roman Catholic party, with the Anglicans reluctantly agreeing, and slipped away before Jackson, who now felt he must follow him up to Buganda, arrived to demand *his* treaty, one in more exacting form than Peters'. This was refused; so was his request to fly the Company's flag. According to one account—and these points are all relevant to Lugard's later actions—when Mwanga heard the Company's terms " he lifted up his voice and declared he would not do this." He said " If I do this the country is no longer mine." The Anglican party pressed for acceptance and threatened to leave the country in a body if this was not done.[2] It was agreed that two important Buganda envoys should go to the coast to verify Jackson's claim that Uganda was within Britain's sphere. Jackson thereupon started back for Mombasa, leaving his assistant Gedge with a few men to keep watch on the situation. To the original and abiding religious difference between the two Christian parties this episode had added another: the French Roman Catholic priests could accuse the British Company of having failed to respond to Mwanga's call for help while the Anglicans could accuse the French of being against the Company and of having encouraged German influence.

Such was the recent history of the country which Lugard contemplated from his camp on the little hill in December 1890. Buganda's isolation had been suddenly broken down; new and strong influences had penetrated it; new weapons had been presented to it; a distant world of which its people knew nothing was taking hold of its affairs. It had just experienced six years of persecution, of weak tyranny and of bloody civil wars in the name of religion. Faction and violence had become almost habitual. To claim, as the French priests afterwards claimed, " that all had been peace until the arrival of Captain Lugard

[1] *Ibid.* pp. 396–7.
[2] Letter to Euan-Smith by Samwiri Mukasa Muwemba, one of the Baganda envoys to the coast. Zanzibar Archives (kindly supplied by Sir John Gray).

with his Maxim gun " is hardly a fair comment upon the story that has been told. It was denied by their own Bishop Monsignor Livinhac who, leaving Uganda at this time and passing through Zanzibar, told Euan-Smith that the country had been devastated by the ceaseless fighting, and that such was the enmity between the Anglicans and the Roman Catholics that it would become too great for the missionaries to control.[1]

The year 1890 was a year of great international importance for east and, indeed, for the whole of Africa. There were British treaties with France and with Portugal; in July the far-reaching Anglo-German agreement was signed. The next month saw the signing of the Brussels Act, fruit of the Conference in the calling of which Salisbury had played so large a part. This dealt at length with the suppression of the slave-trade, a question in which Kirk had been able to provide his great expert knowledge. The Act gave precise philanthropic justification for annexation in the obligations it laid upon the powers in abolishing this evil. Especially relevant to the problems of East Africa were the clauses prohibiting the import of fire-arms and commending the construction of roads, fortified stations in the interior, and railways, and also the introduction of steamboats on lakes and rivers.[2] All these were to be regarded as measures aimed at the slave-trade. To Lugard, equally zealous to extend British power and to suppress the hated evil, such obligations played a dominant part in directing and justifying his actions.

Lugard realized the intense difficulties and dangers of his position from the first but it was only by degrees that he learned to measure their exact nature.

The wars in Uganda were called religious and the parties were given religious names, and the most enduring division did, of course, derive from the existence of two missions sent by the different branches of the Christian Church. For this reason, and because the two denominations as they exist in Uganda today carry deeply the imprint of these early tragic events and of the settlements which followed them, anyone who writes of these events should do so with a sense of their sadly controversial character. It would, however, be misleading to pretend that what follows has been written from the high summit of complete

1 Euan-Smith to Salisbury, 30 July 1890, F.O. 84/2062.
2 Hertslet, *Map of Africa*, vol. ii, p. 488 ff.

impartiality: for that it would be necessary for the writer to have no personal association with either Christian denomination nor, perhaps, with Christianity itself.

We have nearly two thousand years of history to present the truth that no divisions reach down so deeply into men's natures as those between different Christian sects, and the rift may be deepened by a conscious or unconscious sense of guilt because the Founder of the faith had so solemnly enjoined unity upon His followers. Between the Anglicans of the C.M.S., an organization which emphasized, especially at that time, the Puritan and Protestant element in their Church, and the French White Fathers, stood the Reformation and all that had happened since of armed conflict and doctrinal controversy. It was natural, therefore, that each side should most ardently desire to win this fine, responsive nation of Buganda for its own Church and should feel a bitter regret, that could easily pass into resentment, that their potential converts were being won to what they must regard as a less pure version of their faith. How hard for men holding such a belief to respond to political appeals to show trust, toleration, or a spirit of co-operation towards the other side or to enjoin such an attitude upon their equally ardent but more excitable and factious followers!

These followers themselves demand some analysis if the terms applied to this conflict are not to mislead. There were, without doubt, in each party a number of genuine and devout converts to the new faith. The leading men in the nation, holders of the great offices and of the wide estates that went with them, were divided, almost equally it seems, between the two missions. Captain Williams,[1] who joined Lugard later as his second-in-command and who had a longer and closer association with the Baganda even than Lugard, disagreed with Lugard's opinion that the majority had no genuine religion. He told Lugard that " nearly all the Chiefs, and certainly everyone of note, is outwardly a most enthusiastic professor of the religion to which he belongs . . . . Nearly every Chief has evening prayers for all his people about, and does his best to teach his slaves etc."[2] Bishop Tucker who arrived in Uganda a few days after Lugard—a second Bishop, Parker, had died just before reaching Buganda—was amazed at the hunger of the people for Christianity. Thousands crowded in and

[1] Williams, Colonel William Hugh, C.M.G., J.P., 1857–1938; 1876 entered army and served in South Africa, Uganda, Sudan; 1895–7 Vice-Consul in Asia Minor.
[2] C.6555 (1892), p. 128.

around his church; hundreds had arrived at dawn to listen for hours to Christian teaching before the service began. And when he told them he had brought with him seven loads of New Testaments, partly in Swahili, cries of joy burst from the assembled people.[1] This, however, applied to what may be called the ruling class and their followers who had been in contact with the few missionaries who were established in the capital. Even allowing for the spreading of the new faith through wars and dispersions, it cannot be applied to the great masses who, following their official or territorial leaders, ranged themselves upon one side or the other. It is therefore a misnomer to talk of Christian, Roman Catholic or Protestant armies.

The purely denominational division was deepened by the national one. One set of missionaries was English (or Scottish) the other was predominantly French. There was, therefore, a cultural and linguistic as well as a confessional division between the two parties. Hence the names of Wa-Ingleza and Wa-Fransa came into use (Wa meaning people or tribe) and, little though the African who used them on the shores of Lake Victoria could understand of their meaning, these terms seem less inappropriate than the religious ones.

This conflict in a remote African tribe had, of course, a wider setting. In East Africa itself, as Lugard pondered his position, he had to think of the Muslim Baganda army, quartered to the north on the frontier of the native state which was Buganda's enemy, Bunyoro. Further north was still that isolated body of Egyptian and Sudanese soldiers left by Emin which might unite with them or even, to look still further northward, bring their fellow-Muslims, the Mahdists, down upon the weak, divided, fertile and highly desirable Buganda. To the south was the German sphere. Since the signing of the Anglo-German Agreement of July 1890, it no longer held an immediate threat. But the German territory possessed the safest and most frequented route to the coast: it contained also stations of both missions, their nearest bases and refuges, whenever Buganda became dangerous. And it must also be noted that the Anglo-German Agreement allowed only that the Uganda region was a British " sphere of influence ". This was an extremely ambiguous term and the British government was still renouncing any intention of annexing it. If, therefore, the Company failed to make its claim effective, and anarchy should ensue,

[1] A. R. Tucker, *Eighteen Years in Uganda and East Africa* (1908), vol. i, pp. 108-10.

the Germans were exactly placed to fill the ensuing vacuum. At that very moment Emin Pasha, enigmatic to the last, had entered the British sphere and was engaged upon some mysterious enterprise, drawn back towards his old province, from which Stanley had so lately " rescued " him. But perhaps Lugard's greatest external danger was Stokes, the bearded ex-missionary in the long Muslim robes, who, by running in a supply of guns and powder could initiate and sustain destructive warfare and, by his handling of his trade, could present one side or the other with the means of victory.

Stokes, indeed, had the power to make Lugard's dangerous position almost impossible. For, in his survey of his position, the factor that Lugard could most certainly assess was his own physical weakness. He had marched in with 270 porters, some of them " brave good fellows " but wholly undisciplined and very excitable. He reckoned a third as good reliable men, a third as indifferent, and the remaining third as useless. He had about fifty Sudanese and Somalis, who had been given some training as soldiers, but with whom he could not communicate except through Dualla. He had little confidence in his veteran Maxim gun. He was very low in ammunition, much of his stock having perished on the long march: his total reserve was eleven rounds per man. Moreover, as cartridges had a very high value in Buganda, and his men were short of food, even this small reserve tended to drain away. It was therefore a recurring nightmare to Lugard that Stokes or some of the Arab or Swahili traders would bring in large supplies of arms which would allow one or other party to shoot his little company out of existence. For Stokes was reported to have little love for the missions, while the coming of Lugard superseded the position he had developed as a general plenipotentiary with the King of Buganda, and the Company threatened the monopoly he had established over the trade, such as it was, with the country.

The shortage of food was another very serious danger. Lugard was obliged to detach a party of his small force and send it to Busoga where food was more plentiful than round Kampala, but Mwanga blocked their return at the Nile crossing. Bananas were a novel diet to his men: they were also bulky to transport and perishable for keeping. But hard grain was difficult to get and to send men foraging was to deplete his force while, as strangers, they were likely to provoke or to encounter enmity.

In such a situation a soldier's thoughts are never far from his communications. Lugard knew only too well what these were—leading back through a wilderness which took three months of difficult marching to cross. And at the end of that? Here he could find some slight reassurance, thanks in the main to the character of de Winton. The chief Lugard had replaced as commander of the expedition might sometimes treat the younger man with disingenuity or proffer advice which went painfully near the mark; he might be at odds with his directors but Lugard could be sure that as far as it lay within de Winton's power, he would not fail him. And he knew that his other friends in London were well-placed to support him.

But support was far away and in the meantime his position was isolated and weak. His tiny camp with some 100 men capable of fighting, and these with inadequate armament, was surrounded by a large population and by three armed parties, each holding some two to three thousand guns, one certainly and another probably hostile in their attitude. His instructions from de Winton, (16 September 1890), were to obtain a treaty to regularize the position of the Company, to prevent the import of breech loading arms and ammunition, " to obtain the control of all White affairs," (an ambiguous precept); " to endeavour to be perfectly impartial"; " to consolidate the Protestant Party . . . . conciliate the Roman Catholics . . . . point out . . . . the scandal which their differences present to the cause of Christianity." While being absolutely impartial, he was yet " to be very careful of the Priests " and to put all transactions with them into writing. As for Stokes, he was to be prohibited from selling arms. As for Mwanga, " you should . . . . impress him with a sense of the power of the Company." " What power? " Lugard must have asked himself bitterly. He could now have questioned each item of these instructions which even singly would have been hard to attain, and together were impossible.

One important key to the position would have been in Lugard's hand if he could have understood exactly what the priests really wanted. It may be questioned whether they were very clear about this themselves. The uncertainty of the situation explained and, indeed, excused their actions much more than Lugard, who from the first was quite certain what *he* meant to do, was willing to recognize. As Frenchmen they naturally had a loyalty towards France and felt they could, if necessary, claim the diplomatic support of her government as well as the ecclesiastical support of Rome. But Cardinal Lavigerie had tried and failed to persuade the French government to accept from Mutesa a privileged position in Buganda. That was in 1879. At the Brussels Conference it appears that the Cardinal tried to secure the declaration that Buganda was an independent and neutral state and had again failed.[1] Germany seemed a more likely successor than France if the Company should fail to establish itself, as seemed highly probable. But in Africa of " the scramble " almost anything could happen and Salisbury was at this very time showing by his negotiations with Portugal over Nyasaland that, if the missionaries of a nation firmly planted the Cross, that nation might overcome its first unwillingness to plant the flag beside it. There was no reason, now the power of Mwanga seemed to be secure, why the White Fathers should favour the Company. On the contrary, it was natural that they should be alarmed at the prospect, as they would foresee it, in the conditions of Uganda, that their Anglican British rivals should have the support of a British Company, behind which, they supposed, must stand an Anglican British government. It was not surprising that Mwanga, at this time very much in their hands, should have accepted from Peters a German treaty and refused one to Britain.[2]

The situation was, therefore, full of obscurities. While the priests were not sure of the status or of the power of the Company, their policy must be to play for time. In the meanwhile they had one great advantage, their hold upon the King who, even though his vices prevented his baptism, was still their adherent, with nephews they could hope to bring up in their church. The seventeenth-century principle of *cujus regio, ejus religio* was not fully operative in Buganda in 1890, but the King's claim on his people's loyalty still pulled the pagan majority and the waverers towards him. And he still wielded some of the power of an autocratic king even if his personal prestige was much tarnished. He had, for example, control over ivory, the one export that could bear long transport to the coast and he was still Stokes' best customer, with all that implied. It will thus be seen that Mwanga was a valuable, if not a very respectable, ally for the French priests

---

[1] A. Nicq, *Le Père Siméon Lourdel* (1895), pp. 153–5.

[2] McDermott, *IBEA*, pp. 128–9; *Church Missionary Intelligencer*, vol. XLIII, July 1892, pp. 519–21; *Morning Post*, 16 and 29 May 1890. I am indebted to Sir John Gray and Mr. H. B. Thomas for information upon this question.

and yet, if they were to cling to him, it would be almost impossible for them, any more than for their missionary rivals, to avoid being involved in politics. They were, however, very careful and correct in their dealings with Lugard and his complaint in his diary is that he could not detach their interest from what seemed to him small matters, about their own rights with regard to customs dues, transport and travel, in order to arouse their interest in the large questions of government which had to be settled.

Lugard's dangerous situation was not even static: it began to worsen from the moment that he arrived. There had been a brief time after the Muslim victory when the two Christian parties had been thrown together. Sailing back across the lake towards Buganda, as the C.M.S. missionary, Cyril Gordon, told Euan-Smith, they had camped together at night on the shores " for each other's comfort and safety." (E. C. Gordon to Euan-Smith, 20 October 1889). And, in their precarious and crowded camp on Bulingugwe island, they had worked hard to reconcile their flocks whose antagonism in the crisis jeopardized all hopes of victory and even of survival. Early in 1890 the native leaders had themselves been so alarmed at the growing split that, in an attempt to bind their own revengeful natures, that they have taken an oath together that " we shall not betray and shall never kill our friends of the opposite religion, and furthermore, if we are stronger than them, we shall not kill them. Any person who breaks these words and kills his friends, will be answerable for it in the final day of judgment."[1]

That was in February 1890 and it was now December and the atmosphere was changed. Mwanga, especially, was estranged from the British by Jackson's treaty terms and by his bringing a flag, an object of the deepest suspicion to the King, who was convinced that the British were only waiting their chance to avenge themselves upon him for his murder of Bishop Hannington. Whether or not the priests or their clerical rivals had encouraged the belief, the Company was now identified with the Anglican mission and the Ingleza party. The unhappy Gedge, whom Jackson had left behind, after a time made wretched by Mwanga's neglect and insults, had gone off to Usukuma, the German south end of the lake, and only returned in December, in such a state of nervous frustration that Lugard sent him back to the

[1] Sir John Gray, ' The Year of the Three Kings of Buganda ', *Uganda Journal*, vol. XIV, March 1950, p. 48.

coast at the first opportunity. " Poor fellow," was Lugard's thought, " the strain has been too much for him—after a year in Nyasa I got the same . . . . Day and night anxiety, and exposure to danger, and very heavy responsibility laying on you . . . . Now *I* take up the burden from his shoulders and *more*. I have to push onwards and settle things; he had but to remain passive. It is indeed desperately anxious work." (Diary, 23 December 1890). Their official relationship was so vaguely worded that it was well that Gedge *was* unfit to dispute control with his resolute successor.

So imminent seemed the prospect of war between the two factions that the Ingleza, as the weaker party, had been planning, should it break out, to depart *en bloc* with Gedge into Busoga. Lugard could not agree to a plan that was not only one of despair but would bring war and oppression upon Buganda's innocent neighbours. The one thing that still checked the resort to arms was the common fear of the Muslims, waiting and watching upon their northern frontier.

Intractable though the problem appeared, Lugard had to attempt its solution and to do so at once. His actions show that he felt he must make up for his only too patent lack of physical power by sheer force of personality, in the hope that, by making a large and impartial display of both firmness and courtesy and by a steady application of justice, he might win so much confidence in himself that he would not have to fall back upon force. He therefore approached both missions with the utmost cordiality. Towards the French priests, in spite of much that he had been told, he was determined to keep an open mind, and he was, in the words used in his official report, " excessively polite", and the copies of his letters, made by his industrious assistant, Grant, fully bear this out.[1] The French Bishop, Monsignor Hirth, had sent a polite letter to meet him on the road promising co-operation from the Fathers and from their converts *if*—Lugard little knew how difficult that condition would be to define!—their rights were preserved and justice done to them. Lugard called upon both missions, on their respective hills; explained his plans; asked their advice and urged them to give their full co-operation to the new authority which he represented.

On December 19th, the day after his arrival, deliberately choosing his own day and time, Lugard went the long mile across the valley

[1] C. 6555 (1892), p. 100. The letters are in the Lugard Papers.

and up to Mengo to have his first meeting with the King. During his trek he had torn to rags the few clothes he had brought with him on what was to have been a short trip. He could not, therefore, hope to look impressive. " I, however, had a pair of comparatively sound Melton cords, which for ten years had accompanied my travels; and a jacket of a sleeping suit, fitted with brass buttons, ensured at least respectability."[1] He took a dozen Sudanese with him and their " present arms! " and bugle flourish made some counter-show to the band of drums and other instruments which struck up as he approached. The King was in the durbar hut. These large huts, of which Mutesa's tomb near Kampala is one of the very few specimens remaining today, had high roofs supported on a small forest of tree trunks and floors thick with dried grass and were, by African standards, quite impressive. Lugard found the place stifling, packed as it was to the limit with Baganda in their long robes of white cotton. He cut through any possible ceremonial difficulties by bringing his own chair and sitting on it. Then he shook hands frankly with the King. In one glance he read the face of the man whose character would be of so much importance to him. His features " are negroid, but show traces of Wahuma [Hima] blood; his face betokens irresolution, a weak character and a good deal of sensuality."[2] His habits of giggling and of caressing his courtiers were especially, perhaps unreasonably, offensive to the Englishman.

Lugard read the letters he had brought in English; Dualla put them into Swahili and the King's interpreter into Luganda. The crowd was mainly made up of Roman Catholics, anxious to learn if he were hostile to their cause. Lugard made a short speech, saying he had come to bring peace and had power to make treaties and to settle disputes. There was great relief that he made no mention of a flag, a symbol of which they had developed a nervous dread. Then Lugard, carefully keeping the initiative, rose and left, saying this was merely a pre-liminary meeting. He sat up most of the night writing out two long letters for the two missions, explaining just what he hoped to do. He now showed what were those long cogitated " plans and thoughts " of which he had told de Winton. His twelve-page letter to the Roman priests, in addition to an earnest plea for understanding and support, put forward a plan for ordering the country.

1 Lugard II, p. 23.
2 Ibid. p. 24.

The main points of this plan can be briefly summarized. Firstly, the supply of arms was to be strictly controlled as laid down in the recent General Act of the Brussels Conference: they were to be gradually called in and registered so that in time only regular soldiers and licensed holders would possess them. Secondly, there should be a British Resident at the King's court who should hold the same position as Residents at the courts of Indian Princes and who should have control of all white men. Thirdly, the revenue was to be collected under control of a board of the principal state officials of Buganda with the Resident as chairman, and used in part to defray the cost of the occupation. Fourthly, there was to be absolute freedom of religion. All disputes between the missions were to be settled by the Resident with appeal to the Company in Britain.

Lugard made a strong plea to Monsignor Hirth, the head of the White Fathers, for the loyal acceptance of the Company's authority and their full co-operation.

> "It is not therefore, Sirs, only with a view of asking your opinions and advice, however much these will and have already assisted me, but in order to ensure your cordial and hearty support and the weight of your influence with one party in the state, that I appeal to you to deal openly and frankly with me, and, having once given your approval to the views I set forth, to use your whole influence to impress upon your followers the advantage of their fully acquiescing in them."

The end of the letter, however, contained a warning, one which he was hardly in a position to give.

> "In conclusion, Reverend Father, I would remind you that the support given to your mission and the cordiality with which its extension is viewed will, as in every country and Government throughout the world, depend on the loyal manner in which you and the other Reverend Fathers associated with you support the authority of the Administration."
>
> (L. to Mgr. Hirth, 17 December 1890).

Lugard also wrote to Stokes forbidding him to import arms; with the arrival of the Company this lucrative trade now became smuggling. Then, calling the chiefs to his camp, especially those of the Fransa party, he carefully explained the terms of his proposed treaty. On December 24th he went across to the King's hill and presented the treaty in full durbar. Searching and intelligent questions were asked and answered and Lugard was much impressed by the ability of the chiefs. The questions concerned the registration of guns, the collection of taxes, and whether Buganda's vassal states were to be made to pay tribute. " I scowled and looked as fierce as I could and insisted on reading the treaty through [saying] that discussion should come afterwards." His own account shows, indeed, that even he, in his weak position, found it difficult to be just in his opinions or in his methods. " After some discussion I asked if the King were ready to sign . . . . He shuffled and I got more determined and rapped the table and told him to sign if he wanted peace. But he cares for nothing except his own comforts. He begged for a little delay to think it over, I said No. His chiefs knew all about it and had agreed all must sign, this evening, or I would go away with all my men to Unyoro (his enemy Kabarega). The King got very excited, and was trembling visibly." Realizing that many of the chiefs were ready to sign, Lugard insisted upon the King's signature. Mwanga " said he would sign, and then a clamour began of the crowd at the entrance. They said their country was being sold, and that they would shoot the first man who signed and the White-men." There was a breathless moment. Guns were raised by the group of the King's boon companions crowded round the door, for, contrary to custom, all had come to the meeting with their fire-arms. " De Winton says he twice heard a man cock his gun, and all say they began putting in cartridges." (Diary, 24 December 1890). " Had one rowdy let off his gun, there would have been a terrible mêlée in the little hut."[1] But Lugard did not at the moment realize the extent of his danger. One rifle was actually aimed at him when an Ingleza chief, Zachariah, knocked down the barrel.[2] It was hardly the moment to press matters. Mwanga was obviously in a state of great excitement, even terror. So Lugard arranged to come for a final answer two days later, and he and young de Winton, who was with him, rose and walked out of the durbar hut, glad to be still alive.[3]

Mengo and the neighbouring hills were full of anxious discussion all that next day, which was Christmas. The British had a dinner party at their camp, which was attended by one of the most friendly of the French priests, Père Brard (whose constant advice in Swahili

1 Lugard II, p. 35.
2 The Rev. R. P. Ashe, *Chronicles of Uganda* (1894), p. 154.
3 The account of this important interview in the diary is only partly used by Lugard in his book, Lugard II, p. 33 ff.

was "*Pole-pole*" i.e. go gently or slowly); the Protestant missionaries; Gedge; a visitor, Dr. Stuhlmann, the assistant of Emin Pasha who, now in German employ, was stationed at Bukoba, on the west of Lake Victoria. Lugard, however, was restless. He knew that until he got his treaty he had no foundation for his position, and his shortage of men and arms, of ammunition and of food to supply them, weighed constantly on his mind. No one else, he felt, understood the danger of the situation. Therefore, having sent a letter bringing separate and special greetings to his guests in case he should be unable to come himself,[1] he slipped away in the darkness and with only Dualla and four or five men went across to see the King alone. It was a typical act, one which pushed courage beyond discretion. As he entered the palace the drums sounded and men with guns appeared on all sides. Realizing that there could be no chance of a quiet, confidential talk he turned back, amid half-suppressed jeers and chuckling from the crowd at the palace, and dropped in to the end of the dinner party.

Next day, after another durbar, the chiefs, unarmed, came streaming up Lugard's hill and said they would sign the treaty but only subject to their delegates now at the coast confirming what Lugard had said about the British position in Uganda. According to the C.M.S. missionary Ashe, Lugard had not only failed to realize the full danger he had been through in the durbar hut but also the reason for the sudden change in the situation. " He need not have been astonished, for the explanation of the great change is simple enough. The French fathers bade their faction sign the treaty, an order which was immediately obeyed."[2] Had he fully understood this, Lugard would have been divided between gratitude for their action, anxiety at the strength of their influence, and mystification about their motives.

Lugard and de Winton therefore set off across the valley to Mengo to get the King's signature. Mwanga, faced by the unknown, not unnaturally followed his usual wriggling tactics to the last. First he tried to stop the two men from coming by warning them they would be murdered by some bad men if they came. Then he asked for his present. Lugard said he was waiting for canoes from the King to fetch it from the south of the lake. " Then the King told someone to sign for him. I would not have this and insisted upon his making a mark. He did it

[1] Lugard to Gedge, 25 December 1890, Gedge Papers.
[2] Ashe, *op. cit.* p. 155.

with a bad grace, just dashing the pen at the paper and making a blot; but I made him go at it again and on the second copy he behaved himself and made a proper mark. Then one of the Fransa chiefs, who could write, wrote Mwanga's name opposite the mark and several of the head chiefs also signed, but they took very long struggling with the letters of their names."[1]

There is no need to expound in detail the terms of the treaty since few of them could be carried out and another treaty later superseded it. Its main value to Lugard was that it legalized, or, at least, formalized in the view of the European powers signatory to the several agreements about Africa, the position of the Company, as offering " protection " to, and being granted " suzerainty " by, the Kabaka of Buganda.[2] It established the position of the Resident to control external and European affairs and the sale of arms and to preside over a finance and revenue committee. Freedom of trade and freedom of religion were guaranteed and slave-trading was forbidden. An interesting clause was added by the King and chiefs providing that " if another white man, greater than this one, shall come up afterwards " the treaty would be null. It was also agreed that final ratification would depend upon the two envoys to the coast returning with confirmation that Uganda really had been allotted to the British sphere.

Both the missions made their private but well-informed comments upon this event. R. H. Walker of the C.M.S., while he characterized Lugard as " a quiet gentlemanly man " regretted that he had been unable to sweeten the acquisition of the treaty with the expected gifts, but came " as a poor man ". Mwanga, he said, hated the English. " The English have come," said the King, " they have built a fort; they eat my land, and yet they have given me nothing at all. They have made me sign a treaty, they curtail my power and I get nothing from them in return." Walker prophesied that if there *were* war Lugard would have to go, if only because he would have no food.[3] The comment from the side of the French priests in charge of Mwanga's political conscience was, of course, even more authoritative. " Cet acte qui le faisait descendre au rang de vassal, le roi ne l'avait pas signé sans une grande répugnance . . . . Quelle humiliation pour l'orgueilleux Mwanga de mettre ses milliers de sujets et de tributaires sous le

1 Lugard II, pp. 39–40.
2 C.6555 (1892), pp. 16–18.
3 R. H. Walker to C. H. W., 1 and 2 February 1891, C.M.S. Papers (Unofficial Papers).

protectorat d'une simple Compagnie commerciale! "[1] Lugard, though he had a capacity for imaginative insight in favourable conditions, was in no state of mind to share the priest's sympathy with Buganda's King. His view of the bloodshed and confusion which had reigned in the country for seven years, his estimate of the King's character and his confidence in the benefits he meant to bring the people, all combined to make him regard the treaty he had won as a supreme and unquestionable good. Armed with this confidence he was able, without apology, to admit in his book, after his action had been questioned in parliament: " The treaty was certainly obtained against his will—I have never said the contrary." But this was only another way of saying that its signature meant not the end but the beginning of his troubles.[2]

[1] G. Leblond, *Le Père Auguste Achte* (Maison Carrée, Alger 1912), p. 125. [Translation: " This document which reduced him to the rank of a vassal, had not been signed by the King without great repugnance . . . What a humiliation for the proud Mwanga to put his thousands of subjects and of tributaries under the protection of a simple commercial Company! "]

[2] Lugard II, p. 41.

CHAPTER XIII

THE FIGHT WITH THE MUSLIMS

December 1890-May 1891 : Aet. 32-33

THE SIGNING of the treaty did no more than mark the end of the first round. Lugard may have felt some satisfaction at this formal regularization of his position, but it neither added to his physical power nor did anything to reconcile the dangerously opposed forces in the country. Two days after the ceremony of signing, there was an alarm at night, which, though only one of many, is worth describing because it illustrates the interwoven obscurity and tension within which Lugard was now caught as in a net. For if the people who now surrounded him were sophisticated and full of great potentialities, they were also subtle and factious. Two leading Fransa chiefs sent a note in the evening which was translated to mean that the Ingleza were so enraged because Lugard had not given their party the full support they had expected that they had asked the Fransa to join them in an attack upon him. During the day three local women who came to the camp brought to Lugard's men warnings that an attack *was* intended. As darkness fell there was a great outburst of drumming and of noisy excitement from the nearby hills. Lugard handed out ammunition and got his men on the alert. The peasants living near his camp began to desert their houses and some who were caught said they were running away because war was coming. Lugard, quite uncertain as to the quarter from which an attack might come, sent out Somali scouts, who were, of course, quite ignorant of the country. Then a messenger he had sent to the C.M.S. mission returned to say the translation of the note had been quite wrong: it said the Fransa feared they were going to be attacked by the Ingleza. But the scouts now ran in and gave a vague alarm. So the whole company was roused and stood to arms.

In the moonlight (an advantage upon which Lugard had calculated in arranging the date of his arrival) this very mixed crowd of men, all strangers from distant lands, Zanzibar, Somaliland and the Sudan, most of them mere porters, fell into lines on the little hill. " I turned to my men—the porters for whom Professor Drummond can find no words bad enough—and asked if they were ready to fight. With one voice the reply came back in chorus ' *Eh-walla, Eh-walla. Tayari* ' (Yes, yes. Ready). ' Where you die we shall be killed first.' I was deeply touched by their loyalty; and that scene, as we stood in the moonlight awaiting an attack from overwhelming numbers, every man struggling to be in the front rank, is as vivid to my mind's eye as though it had occurred but yesterday."[1] No attack came and towards morning Lugard lay down and slept on the ground, and was there found when a leading Fransa chief, the Kimbugwe (later well-known as the Regent Stanislaus Mugwanya), called on him early the next day. The visitor was usefully impressed by the signs of the prepared-ness and was also treated to a description of the powers of the Maxim gun. Later, there followed much recrimination between the two parties as to which had actually prepared an attack and who had sent warnings.

Such alarms, by night and day, were numerous. Bishop Tucker, arriving on December 27th from the south, having come by the German route, had no doubt about the state of affairs and he relied, of course, upon the opinion of Gordon and Walker, the experienced missionaries who received him, which accorded to that given by the departing Livinhac. " Uganda in December 1890 ", the Bishop said, " was like a volcano on the verge of an eruption." A few days after his arrival his large congregation, at the sound of an accidental shot, seized the guns they had brought with them into the church and rushed outside.[2] The whole atmosphere, indeed, was one of alarm, of confusing and contradictory rumours. Lugard, of course, as the missionaries of both sides were not slow to point out whenever they disagreed with him, knew little or nothing of the country, its language and customs. Bishop Tucker recognized at once the impossibility of his position. " With miserably inadequate resources it was almost impossible for him to take an independent line." The Bishop thought, in view of his ignorance of the country, he should rely upon the advice of the missionaries, upon whose counsel the native leaders

[1] Lugard II, p. 43. Even the professional illustrator seems to have caught something of the spirit of the scene.
[2] Tucker, *Eighteen Years in Uganda*, vol. i, pp. 100-1.

235

themselves relied.[1] The question was, of course, *which* missionaries? Lugard was, indeed, obliged to turn for advice, information and linguistic interpretation to both groups. The difficulty here was that both were biased in their own interests, full of grievances and deeply suspicious of each other and of him. His days were spent in endless talks with them, with the King, or with chiefs of both parties who constantly came to see him. But for the short walks through the banana groves down his little hill and up the nearby ones of Mengo to see the King, or of Rubaga or Namirembe to visit the missions, he was practically a prisoner in his own little fort.

He tried in interminable discussion to convince all sides of his impartiality and goodwill and to instruct them in his conceptions of order, justice and tolerance. He seems to have succeeded in this according to the C.M.S. side. Walker reported that he was " a quiet patient man " and that " confidence in him is felt by both parties ",[2] while another, G. K. Baskerville, wrote that " the Company's men have done all they can to help us in our work."[3]

But Lugard gave most time to the Fransa chiefs. He made friends especially with the Kimbugwe and Cyprien, the Kauta (King's chief cook and a very high official). The chief minister, the Katikiro, Apolo Kagwa, was an Anglican, a fiery personality, destined to be one of the most famous of the Baganda, and he saw much of him. But his closest friend was a man whose character deeply impressed him, Zachariah Kizito, the chief who had acted in his defence at the critical moment in the durbar hut, one of the few men who was trusted by both sides and who later came and lived by the Fort to act as Lugard's adviser and assistant. But Lugard was deeply impressed by the high spirit and intelligence of many of these leading Baganda; they were mostly young men but dignified and commanding. There was, however, a group of Fransa, close to the King, led by Gabriel the Mujasi, commander of the armies, whose trust he could not win and who remained wary and hostile.

Lugard's life was thus one of ceaseless anxiety. What the country could do to Europeans he could learn from the condition of Gedge with his " shattered health and broken nerves, longing for rest and

[1] Tucker, *op. cit.* pp. 125–6.
[2] Walker to C.M.S., 27 February 1891, C.M.S. Papers, Eastern Equatorial Africa Mission, 1891, letter 66.
[3] Baskerville to C.M.S., 1 June 1891, ibid. letter 303.

peace, yet tortured by the fear that he was deserting his post," and also from the experiences of the Anglican bishops of Uganda. Bishop Parker, who had followed the murdered Hannington, died very shortly after his arrival in Usukuma. Of Tucker's party, three were dead and four of the five who reached Uganda were too ill to walk from the lake shore to the mission. The Bishop himself, who was to spend eighteen years in Uganda, was soon ill and returned almost immediately to the coast. The roll of death and invaliding amongst the little groups of Europeans who penetrated and occupied Africa tells only half the tale; it must be remembered that those who stayed did much of their work while in a feverish condition—malaria is mentally as well as physically depressing—ill-nourished or half-poisoned from bad food, without adequate medicines or reliable servants, seldom daring to relax and rest whatever their condition, yet always aware that overstrain was a quick way to the death which was striking down their white companions. William Grant, a modest, sensitive, industrious man, had to be helped through deep fits of depression, and Lugard, at thirty-two, could be thankful that he could help his companions because "my varied life and feelings make me able to sympathize with the most opposite of men . . . . I seem to have lived the lives of many men." (Diary, 17 January 1891).

Lugard's upbringing certainly helped him to take the strain. It had given him a strong taste for order. He knew that disciplined exertion could be a double defence against disease. He worked off his depression and fear in his diary at night and in the morning was round the camp briskly striving for perfection. As he had cleaned up Karonga, so he now dealt with Kampala Fort.

It was no easy task. His 100 or more men[1] were cramped at close quarters in a strange and hostile country, living in something like siege conditions. At first their camp site was only fifty-six yards square though later the King granted more land. There was the inevitable problem of women coming into the camp, spying and causing trouble. There were conflicts between his Sudanese and his Swahili. Men lost or sold cartridges, cloth from their loads and even guns. Most of them were grain-eaters who did not relish the eternal banana of Buganda. Lugard had to dominate them by a mixture of humanity,

[1] The numbers were continually changing as a result of deaths, desertions and the detachment of parties seeking food. Fifty men had to be sent to accompany Gedge to the coast.

justice and firmness. For all the good spirit he had evoked, he felt himself obliged to resort at times to severe public floggings, and hard labour in chains. He felt this to be justified because the lives of the whole company depended upon discipline and proper behaviour to the surrounding people. One of his most valuable projects was to pick out the best of the porters and train them as soldiers whom he called the Zanzibari levy.

His diary is full of the accounts of the plans of the fort, the wooden stockade and embankments, the layout of the camp, the large storehouse to shield the loads and food from Buganda's torrential rains, the *baraza* hut for his incessant interviews, and the deep underground cellar, protected from fire and theft, which he had made for the powder and arms. In them lay his main hope of holding his position, and imposing peace, not so much, so he hoped, by using them, as by being in control of the main supply. For this reason he was very stern with Stokes when, early in February, that trader arrived from the south. Much to the King's anger, Lugard forbade him to sell any of his dangerous goods, but offered to store them. Stokes complained that he could make £250 a head-load on gunpowder in Uganda. He denied that he had any guns but later he admitted their possession and offered to sell them. Lugard refused to buy at his exorbitant price but proposed that he should store them. Stokes agreed, but when he got back to German territory he changed his mind. Lugard wrote to Emin Pasha at Bukoba warning him to keep an eye on Stokes and prevent him trading in arms.

On January 31st reinforcements under Captain Williams arrived, having come up by the Company's route from Mombasa. He brought with him Dr. Macpherson, seventy-five Sudanese soldiers and one hundred Swahili porters. The meeting could have been embarrassing. Williams was a regular soldier who had come out on the promise of commanding the troops directly under de Winton, the Administrator-General. He now had to accept as his chief a man who was his junior in army seniority and had thrown up his military career to go adventuring in Africa. De Winton had laid down that army seniority was to count but Lugard, inflexibly determined to command, had appealed to higher authority and obtained a ruling that seniority was to be according to length of service with the Company. It might have been all the more difficult because Williams was a brilliant officer, full of energy and ambition. But he was also a man of good sense and he accepted the situation, only laying down that as he had recruited and trained his own Sudanese, he should be in command of all the fighting men of this race. Happily, Lugard from the first liked and respected Williams who measured up to his highly exacting standards, and though there was, almost inevitably, to be a little trouble between them, the presence of a partner upon whose resolution and efficiency he could absolutely rely, not to speak of the seventy-five additional soldiers he brought with him, was an immense relief to him.

He needed this reinforcement. The situation in Buganda continued to be obscure and baffling. Lugard's diary reveals his almost regular oscillations between confidence and anxiety. One day he feels he has at last won the full confidence of the Fransa chiefs: he has induced them to come to terms with the Ingleza; he has had a *baraza* with the King and chiefs and they have been impressed, he believes, by his lectures on toleration and justice and agreed to some reasonable compromise; the French priests are friendly; the Anglican missionaries reasonable. The next week, or the next day, everything has changed. War drums are heard; conflicts between the parties are reported; the King is suddenly truculent and wants to invite a visit from Emin Pasha. The missionaries of both parties are writing difficult letters and seem mainly interested in extending their activities to Busoga where Lugard cannot guarantee to protect them and where he fears they will spread the conflicts now tearing Buganda to pieces. The priests are complaining that the Ingleza snatch the crucifixes from the necks of their converts. The Rev. Walker is warning him that even though the big chiefs want peace, the lesser fry round Mengo are longing for war with its prospects of excitement and loot. (Walker to L. 3 February 1891).

In February the two parties were more than once just about to attack each other when Lugard struck in to divide them. On the 19th, for example, Lugard looked out to see both the King's hill and the Fransa hill covered with men, and huge masses of their opponents running from the Ingleza hill. " I marched down," runs Lugard's diary, " with Williams and a company of Blacks, and steered for the top of the King's hill where the Catholics had assembled. On the way I met the Kauta . . . . and the Sekibobo [chief of the large Kyagwe

province, both leading Fransa chiefs] and told them to send on men
to disperse their people. This they did, for the chiefs themselves (most
especially these two) are very great friends with me now, and have
long since ceased to wish for war, or for a quarrel with us." The
crowds dispersed a little but remained on the hills. " So I formed up
the Blacks in extended line, bayonets fixed, and down on the knee,
and sent for the Maxim which was brought very quickly. I also got
angry with the chiefs and spoke strongly and roughly till they
redoubled their efforts to disperse the mob. I said I would open fire
with the Maxim in a few minutes. The sight of the gun made them
tail off a bit. Then I went to the King and told him things were quiet
and the people dispersing. He was very grateful and sent a messenger
later to thank me. We returned to camp and to breakfast." (Diary,
19 February 1891).

Thus Lugard, by a mixture of rational argument, personal friendship, and disciplined strength, tried to dominate the faction-ridden
capital and country. But his personal influence could not affect more
than a handful of chiefs who had the character to appreciate him and
his policy; they could not extend their convictions to their excited and
resentful followers. If Lugard and the King, the two ruling powers,
could have worked together, all would have been well. For Lugard,
largely from necessity but partly from predilection, was already revealing what was to be his basic principle in dealing with Africans, which
was afterwards known as indirect rule, by his efforts to do everything
with and *through* instead of apart from the constituted authorities. Thus
he did all he could to persuade the bewildered King to act firmly, to
arbitrate justly between the factions in full council. He urged the
missionaries not to come to him with grievances but to try to get the
King or the proper chiefs to deal with each matter. He even tried to
organize a Baganda police force, drawn from both parties, to patrol
the streets at night. But he was dealing with a political system that was
staggering weakly under the impact of the external forces which he
himself represented. Though there were moments when the weak,
corrupted, but not unintelligent young King seemed to feel the impress
of the Englishman's strong mind and good-will, he was fundamentally
opposed to Lugard. As an autocratic ruler he quite naturally hated to
acknowledge a new and incomprehensible master and could still hope
to throw him off; he was also the leader of the superior Fransa party,

226 shelter. While waiting I ran out the heads of the Sea by hut mwanga, & it has formed the basis & reference of all I have done since. In fact roughly as I run it out in pencil in my road book I have adopted it almost verbatim, - So the time was well employed.

Dec. 18th) I started ahead of the Safari today, taking with me the Soudanese in their very best turn out, - & after all they did not look so bad in their blue jerseys, & (more or less) white pants. It & mile up & down hill I arrived at Mengo. Here all the country is one mass of cultivation & bananas, & people. They swarm here like the bees inside a hive, & I was smothered up with the crowd of sight seers I was shewn a miserably low & dirty spot to camp in, but after my demurring they said there was a better beyond. This too turned out to be a hollow between two hills, - on the further of which was the king's Palace &c. It was all on a slope, full of rank grass, & damp. So I went on the top of the hill, & found it feasible to camp there tho' it was stoney, & rough, & rather narrow. I got message after message from the king saying it was a bad place, - too much rain, - & he wanted to give me a better one &c but I replied I had already camped & would look at the other site tomorrow. I afterwards got a letter to same effect from him thro' the missionaries. I have since heard that it is not etiquette to camp on the top of a hill; - only the king does that. Whether this is true or not I don't know, but I am glad if it is, for I want to shew them that I have not come here to trifle & fool, & mean to go thro' with my work spite of mwanga. My action at the hill was quite a scare to them. Of course (as I knew) it is the etiquette to wait there, & get my permission & honour & then to come on by easy stages, with Royal permission for each march & so on. But my own idea is that it is better to shew, mwanga that we do not now intend to be fooled, & that we come like men who are not afraid. - I had to wait a terribly long time for the Safari, & a thunder storm began but fortunately it did not come down heavily till we had our tents & everything up. In the afternoon the 2 English missionaries, Rev. Walker & Gordon came over, & I found them extremely nice men, - most cordial &c. Neither are men of very marked character & decision - I mean neither are men to lead men, or likely to come to the front & guide the ship in a storm. They run in double harness almost ludicrously. - Each entirely which was opposed to Ingleza-cum-British authority. Lugard, for his side, honestly desired to be impartial, yet knew, in his weak position, that if the worst should happen, he would have to rely upon the Ingleza party which openly accepted his authority and whose inferior strength he could, he hoped, level up into equality with his own force. Yet, in carrying out his instructions to be impartial and in making his bid for peace and unity, he felt obliged to do all he could to conciliate the Fransa party, and to avoid showing special favour to the Ingleza, a policy in which he was running the risk of alienating the latter who had counted upon his support and were bitterly disappointed by his attitude. Yet, except for a few leaders, he was unlikely to win support from the Fransa.

There seemed such a wide choice of unpleasant possibilities that it was difficult to know what to do to guard against them. The most likely was war between the two main parties. But it was also conceivable that they might join hands against him and in one massive wave sweep over his force on its little hill and leave nothing behind. Again, the Ingleza often threatened to migrate in a body. This would leave him exposed to the Fransa, or else the Muslims might come down and attack the weakened Fransa Christians and himself along with them. Or, even more unpleasant, the Fransa might make a temporary alliance with the Muslims and attack him or the Ingleza or both. There was also a gang of young roughs, the King's boon-companions, who were so much out of hand that the King himself more than once warned Lugard not to come over to his palace lest he should be murdered. They were the men who, Lugard feared, might touch off the explosion of all the wealth of combustible material with which he was surrounded.

The irreconcilability of the two parties came to a head over a long-standing question in which Lugard had to intervene with quite inadequate knowledge and power. This was the so-called division of the country. This device of dealing with irreconcilability by means of physical partition, which has been resorted to upon such a large scale in the nineteen-forties, was the first solution attempted by the Baganda. After Mwanga's deposition in 1888 the three monotheistic parties had made a division of the chieftainships. Then the conquering Muslims had redistributed these in their own favour. There had been another redistribution after the victory of the Christian parties, and this treaty had been confirmed again after Lugard's arrival. The division was at once complex and unstable. The great offices of state, which carried special titles, were linked with the main regions or provinces of the kingdom. These were shared equally between the two parties. But underneath each of them was a graded hierarchy of officials, each with his own official estate. According to the agreement, these were divided *alternately* between the two parties. Thus the Sekibobo, the Fransa chief of the large northern province of Kyagwe, had an Ingleza under him and he, in turn, a Fransa and, so on.

Three difficulties soon developed. As both parties expected war and were trying to strengthen their position, chiefs of one party tried to evict those of the other party which then struggled to restore the balance by similar evictions. The second problem was the unwillingness of subordinates or peasants to render their customary services to masters of the opposite sect. Day after day incidents occurred in the provinces and litigants or messengers hurried into Mengo with their grievances which they retailed, of course with exaggeration, to the leaders of their party who in turn rushed to Lugard or to the King with a story weighted with still more swollen figures.

A third and even more insoluble problem arose over changes of religion. It had been agreed, in order to retain the balance between the parties, that if a chief changed his religion, he should forfeit his office and with it, of course, his official estates. The purpose is obvious and, so long as there was a high degree of stability between the parties, the system caused little trouble. But with the position of Mwanga, the King, as the head of one faction, there was a growing temptation for men, and especially the nominal Christians or even pagans who supported the Ingleza party, to swing over to the royal side, and it looked as though in time the Fransa might in this way win the whole kingdom. The Ingleza therefore stood by what was, in effect, a standstill arrangement. This seemed to put them against freedom of religion but Lugard could hardly agree to the upsetting of what was really a balance of political power upon which his own position, if not his safety, might at any moment depend. A fierce controversy developed over this during March, with Lugard endeavouring to find some compromise both sides would accept along the lines of fixing the major chieftainships while allowing freedom to the lesser chiefs to change without forfeiting their offices and estates. The French priests, who saw the growing predominance they expected thus checked, were naturally much incensed and were able to take their stand on the principle of religious liberty which Lugard had promised to observe. In the end the best he could achieve was an agreement to freeze the *status quo* for two years. It is interesting evidence of the depth and persistence of the Uganda religious problems that to this day it is a rigid convention that some of the chief offices should be held by Anglicans and others by Roman Catholics, according to the original allocation.

Another controversy arose over the Sese islands, which lay in the north-western corner of Lake Victoria, close to Buddu, and which, as the King claimed them as his special province and even as a tributary state, had not been divided with the rest. The C.M.S. missionaries, urged on by their converts, now pressed for this further partition. The King refused. To show how difficult it was to separate religious, political and military considerations, Lugard took up the Ingleza case because the islands were not only agriculturally very rich but also because the fleets of canoes possessed by the islanders commanded the lake and the essential communications of Buganda with the south. In the end Mwanga reluctantly agreed to this division which deeply angered the French priests.

While Lugard, living in what he called "this hornets' nest of Uganda", was thus being stung almost night and day from every quarter, he was always haunted by the thought of his communications. On March 11th there arrived from the coast some mails, coming on ahead of a Company caravan which reached Kampala on March 31st under James Martin. He was a famous character in East Africa, a Maltese ex-sailor who had turned professional caravan-leader.[1] He might, as Lugard admitted, be a "charming little man," respectful and generous, but his caravan was "a deplorable and hopeless spectacle." Lugard saw young boys and weakly men, unarmed, nearly starved and naked, all skin and bone, with stragglers dragging in after them. He wondered how many had been left dead on the trek. As Martin was illiterate, there was no roll either of men or of loads and the new Company employee, Stephen Bagge,[2] (a young gentleman

---

[1] Jackson, *Early Days in East Africa*, pp. 66–7; also J. M. Gray, 'Mutesa of Buganda', *Uganda Journal*, vol. I, January 1934, p. 145.

[2] Bagge, Stephen Salisbury, C.M.G., 1859–1950; 1890–3 served with I.B.E.A. Co.; 1894–1902 district officer, Uganda; 1902–10 provincial commisioner, East Africa Protectorate; 1916–17 served in operations against German East Africa; referred to as "the last of Captain Lugard's expedition to Uganda", *The Times*, 12 October 1950.

with a distinguished future, and, as it happens, a friend of the writer's family), was carried in with ulcerated legs in a state of physical collapse and acute mental depression.

But, whatever the situation in Buganda and on the way up to it, at least at the far end of the line in Mombasa and, even more, in London, Lugard still felt he could rely upon support. De Winton had splendidly kept his word, and this in spite of further humiliations, when, as we have seen, headquarters showed clear signs of greater confidence in Lugard than in himself. The first sign of this was a telegram, which, this time, de Winton sent on. It was a further instruction from the Company (dated, it should be remarked, November 18th 1890 in London and received by Lugard on March 11th 1891), which ran: " Captain Lugard inform him directors request will not return before important object Uganda mission complete." With this Mackenzie sent Lugard a letter, dated July 18th 1890, of emphatic approval and support from the directors who " appreciate the work you have done so well " and " have the fullest confidence in your zeal and judgment." Lugard's position and seniority had been several times discussed at the council board which decided in his favour. Mackenzie's letter was sent " open " through de Winton so that he could read it. But de Winton had already, in forwarding an earlier mail, nobly written that it gave him a great deal of pleasure to read such letters and that " In George Mackenzie you have a warm and sincere friend, and while he is one of the Court of directors you need not fear that your interests will be forgotten." (De Winton to L. 5 August 1890). And now de Winton had sent up Williams and his batch of Sudanese, expensive men to recruit, to arm and to pay. Certainly there was a worrying comment on this from de Winton. " By last minute mail it has been intimated to me that I have done wrong in supporting you with Williams and the Soudanese, but I cannot agree with such an idea. When it was determined that I was not to go to the interior but remain upon the coast, I felt that you should be supported as far as lay in my power and be made as strong as possible." How else, without a brave show, could he impress Mwanga? " I have written back and have no doubt they will see the necessity of it . . . . though you may have sometimes mistrusted me, I have endeavoured to do my duty, 1st towards the Company, then towards all the employees under me." (De Winton to L. ? October 1890).

There was further evidence of de Winton's generous and reconciling quality. Though there is other testimony to the high quality and charm of the young man's character, Lugard has very little to say of the son his chief had entrusted to him: their relations seem to have been correct rather than warm. One of Fenwick de Winton's letters to his mother was sent on by her to Lord Lorne, a director of the Company and, as he had heard there was " some friction ", he sent the letter on to Mackenzie giving, as his reason, that in it Fenwick spoke of Lugard " in the warmest and most admiring terms." He added that " de Winton himself has used most kindly expressions in speaking of Lugard." Mackenzie, though critical of de Winton senior, entered into the plot and sent the letter on to Lugard, to complete its circle, with renewed expressions of the directors' confidence in him, but taking the opportunity to give him a little lecture. " I know your good points and appreciate them but that does not make me blind to your weaknesses, and if you will not take it amiss, for I mean it kindly, I think you a ' wee bit ' *over* sensitive and the feeling is apt to be intensified by the many privations and worries of an African life." (Mackenzie to L. 9 November 1890). De Winton made a characteristic comment upon this correspondence, which was sent " open " through him. " It appears they have got it into their heads that you and I do not agree. That such want of agreement does not exist in my mind I need hardly tell you, and I don't think it exists in yours. So you and I need not trouble our heads about it so long as we do our duty to the best of our ability . . . . I have written to assure them on this point." (De Winton to L. 6 January 1891).

While hardness and danger were beating the metal of Lugard's character into shape, his friends were thus doing their best to refine it with example and precept. His influential humanitarian friend Horace Waller, as might have been expected, struck a still higher note. In a letter which began with further assurance of Lugard's high credit with his chiefs and of his own great respect and affection for his friend, he wrote:

" . . . . I can only say their opinion of you and your work was expressed to me in the highest terms of satisfaction and praise—I use the plural, for I was with Sir W. Mackinnon directly after I left Mackenzie."

He continued, in a passage which shows, in its conclusion, that he was aware of Lugard's great personal sorrow.

"And so if all goes well you are going to take your part in shaping the future of a very wonderful people. These Uganda natives have had reproduced in them and in this 19th Century that marvellous spirit of devotion to the teaching of Christianity which marked the first 3 centuries of Christ's Church . . . . You are not the first man whom God our Father has taken out into the wilderness to talk to where no man shall overhear or overlook . . . . Examine and see whether sorrow and misery are in any way to be traced back to cravings against which iron bars of God's own forging and setting are placed about and around as forbidden ground."

Lugard cannot have found it easy to answer these letters. It was especially difficult to reply to de Winton. To him, he wrote ". . . . it is not for me to discuss such contingencies as ' friction ' with my Chief. At the same time your *most* kind letter is in itself a mark of confidence which I fully appreciate . . . . And I have not only to thank you for your kind *expressions* but for your action in supporting me with reinforcements etc. I shall be able to prove to the directors *most* conclusively, the absolute necessity of your action—their questioning its advisability seems to me madness." (L. to de Winton, 29 April 1891).

Definitions of lunacy in Kampala and in 2 Pall Mall East were likely to differ, especially from a Company which was now beginning to be appalled by the discrepancy between its resources and the cost of its undertaking. Lugard's very first report, dated January 7th 1891, must have caused some raising and wrinkling of brows at headquarters. He asked for a Resident for Buganda with four or five capable assistants and clerks, while others would be required for Busoga and outlying districts. There should be at least 500 trained soldiers, with a British officer in command; a supply of specie to inaugurate a money economy; and a steel boat. Yet in the next paragraph Lugard coolly remarked that " the value of Uganda to the Company . . . . *per se*, has been much overrated." It had no exports, he said, except ivory, and with transport to the coast at such a high figure " there can be no trade."[1] Lugard evidently had unbounded faith in the pure philanthropy and patriotism of his employers. Yet the Company itself was torn between ambition and economy. De Winton's letter told him that the directors were planning to send a steamer up to the Lake in sections which, so the dismayed de Winton reported,

[1] C.6555 (1892), p. 87.

would require porters to the unattainable number of 2,000. Yet, before the caravan had left, a later letter told him the plan had been abandoned.

Lugard had too many physical dangers close at hand to be able to give much thought to financial ones which seemed so remote. As March went on he turned his mind more and more to thoughts of action. The close confinement in the fort near Mengo, with its stifling and uncertain climate, both physical and political, were beginning to tell upon his active character. Very early in the enterprise he had been turning his eyes northwards, and cherishing highly speculative hopes of reaching up towards the Mahdists, whose movements in the southern Sudan were now quite obscure from the world. Somewhere near Lake Albert, under their Sudanese commander Selim Bey, was still, as we have seen, the remnant of the Egyptian garrison which, arriving late at the rendezvous at Kavalli, on the southern shore of Lake Albert, had not been " rescued " with Emin and Stanley. Lugard believed that Emin himself was feeling his way back to his old province, with all his prestige, knowledge and utter unaccountability. If Lugard could get there first, what an asset these trained and relatively inexpensive soldiers would be! But between him and them lay Bunyoro, and on its borders stood the Muslim party, whom the King and the Baganda were keen to attack. This expedition would, at least for the moment, bring unity between the factions, so Lugard was at least acting upon one of the commonest causes for making war. News of Muslims raiding for women in northern Uganda made an occasion. " Putting ambition on one side," Lugard argued to himself, " this, I think, is the most solid work for the Company." A military diversion seemed the more essential because the land question, already outlined, was greatly embittering the parties and the missionaries upon both sides constantly warned Lugard that this time civil war was really coming. Monsignor Hirth, who returned from German territory with some new priests on February 21st, told Lugard that if war did come, it was expected that the Germans would march north and help the Fransa, a remark which Lugard regarded as close to intimidation, and a slur on the German authorities which, as the event finally showed, was undeserved. Hirth and his party continually spoke as though all the wrong was on one side, whereas Lugard was convinced that the Ingleza, as the weaker party, were suffering much more.

Martin's caravan brought back the envoys, one of whom, Samwiri Mukasa Muwemba, was able in his old but vigorous age to give the writer in 1953 an account of his experience. To Lugard's dismay, the letters they carried back from British authorities on the coast made no mention of his mission, for Euan-Smith was following orders to avoid official responsibility for the Company, though, he reported, the envoys could not yet understand " the difference between the British Company and the British Government."[1] Yet the letters did confirm to the Baganda, for what they could make of the information, that the European Powers had placed Uganda in the British sphere. The decision to march was therefore taken. But of what party was the general to be? Lugard tried to solve this poser by going to the King and telling him he should take command himself. " He was ' knocked into a cocked hat ' by this. He said he was an old man. I said I was older than he." In the end the King appointed Apolo Kagwa the vigorous Anglican Katikiro. Kabarega, the King of Bunyoro, sent taunting messages to Mwanga telling him he had lost and ruined his country by admitting Arabs and white men; for himself, he would fight to the utmost rather than allow a white man into his country. Lugard now had again the sudden horrible thought that Mwanga might, as he did at a later time, join forces with Kabarega and the Muslims in the attempt to wipe out the Ingleza and the British force by sheer numbers of men and guns. " The possibility is too gruesome to contemplate." (Diary, 23 March 1891).

There was, however, no overt sign of such a *volte-face*, though it might, of course, take place on the battlefield itself. All went forward for the war. Lugard gave a ceremonial present to Mwanga, a large mixed collection brought up by Martin's caravan. It was produced article by article and made a huge sensation as it piled up. It included shot-guns and cloth and enabled Lugard to make the remark, which would shock some modern aesthetes and anthropologists, that " the barkcloth hangings of his house must now be replaced by chintzes etc." (Diary, 8 April 1891).

Lugard read out to the King and his Lukiko the letters from the coast. There was one from de Winton enclosing a letter from the sultan of Zanzibar, dated September 22nd 1890, telling Mwanga to treat the English well as " they are our very best friends, and we have

[1] Euan-Smith to Salisbury, 14 September 1890, F.O. 84/2069.

all confidence in them . . . . and whatever kindness you show them is as if you have done the same to us." De Winton also enclosed a letter from the consul-general to Mwanga in which he wrote of the greatness of Queen Victoria " who does not desire your land "— a misleading truth—and lectured him on his people's sectarian enmities. In another letter the Katikiro was asked " Are these then two Gods that you worship? . . . . Is there not rather one God over all? " They must strive to live at peace and the missionaries would help them to this end. Then, as if to make sure that this would be impossible, he said, " Listen to all that the English Bishop says when he arrives." Lugard shivered as this was read out. " This to the Catholics," he wrote in the margin. " Enough to set the whole thing ablaze! Why the Bishop, and not the Resident? " (Euan-Smith to Kagwa, 27 September 1890).

To make matters still worse, the consul referred to the Company's flag, an object which was the centre of controversy and which the Roman Catholics regarded as a Protestant symbol. The consul's letters did not refer at all to Lugard who had anxiously awaited their confirmation to strengthen his weak position. " Fortunately Sir Francis spoke nicely of me in his letter," otherwise he might have appeared to be an unauthorized impostor.

The two Baganda envoys then testified that it was true that Buganda had been placed in the British sphere. After this there was nothing to delay the march against the Muslims. The ceremony of beating the sacred war drums was therefore held outside the King's house. Lugard watched and within five minutes masses of armed men began to come pouring in from all sides, shouting, dancing and waving their guns. He thought to himself how often he had expected such a wild mobilization against himself. But now it was " No longer Christian against Christian, and we against both, but all of us on the same side, about to become comrades in war against the common enemy." (Diary, 8 April 1891). The general, the Katikiro, was ceremonially presented to the army on April 1st and he marched away northwards with the advance guard. Lugard reluctantly lent some guns to the Baganda and sold some kegs of powder in return for ivory. He stayed behind a few days himself to write his letters and reports. He strongly censured Martin, who was to take them to the coast, for the gross inhumanity with which he had conducted his caravan, though the fault lay largely

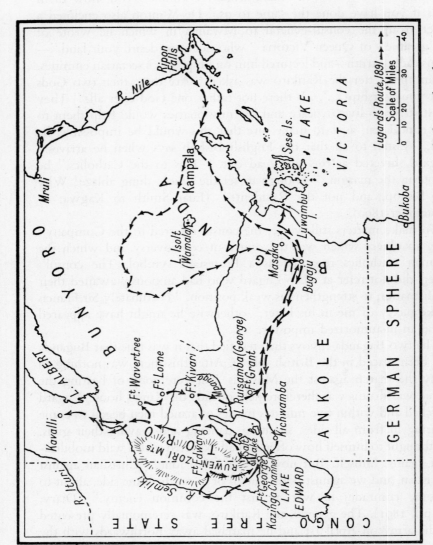

The March to the West, 1891. Taken from Ravenstein's map which was based on Lugard's explorations and published in F. D. Lugard, *The Rise of Our East African Empire*, 1893

with the Company agents who had sent him off with too many loads, too few porters, and too little food. On April 8th, he set out for the " front " with Williams, Grant, the doctor, 150 Sudanese, 160 " Zanzibari levy ", and 300 porters carrying pounded grain, a party in all of some 600 men.

Lugard should have been glad that he had at long last escaped from his fort and had now a chance to see the country he had come to win. But it was an unpleasant march. The solid rain of Uganda's wet belt poured down upon them as they walked or camped. The ill-drained valleys between the low grassy hills were soggy with inky-black, stagnant water. The country, which showed signs of having been heavily populated, had been destroyed by the last few years of civil war; huts were falling into ruin and there was no food to be had. No game, not even birds, could be seen. Thousands more Baganda were joining the army. Spearmen and riflemen were in the proportion of about four to one, the great majority of the guns being muzzle-loaders. Lugard was so persecuted for ammunition that he had hard work to keep the watchword he had set himself for Buganda, "eternal patience and a never-ending courtesy." The line of march lay north-west through Singo and the chief of this ravaged northern province of Buganda, the Mukwenda, an Ingleza chief whom Lugard warmly approved, came to meet them. About April 21st the country suddenly changed. Grassy hills gave way to abrupt bosses of granite, so char-acteristic of many parts of tropical Africa; the tall, stark borassus palm began to appear. It bears an orange-coloured fruit beloved of elephants, which here abounded and killed one of Lugard's men. Bananas gave way to grain though there was little of either to be had in this frontier land.

As the army marched daily during April the rain poured down upon it every day, sometimes with hail as big as peas. All were soaked day and night; the loads of food were saturated; the white men went sick; even Lugard had a severe and painful chest cold. His men kept going amazingly well though the soldiers were Muslims called on to fight their fellow-believers in a quarrel not their own. Lugard was anxious about the military prospects as they reached enemy country at the beginning of May. They were surrounded now by dense crowds of men which Lugard estimated at 25,000. The tactics of the Baganda were to rush in *en masse* where they saw a chance of victory. But no one knew just how many guns the enemy had. Was it 2,300 and had Kabarega joined them with 1,300 more? Lugard's little force, for all its discipline and its Maxim, would have little chance to decide the issue. Either the Baganda would rush wildly ahead and win the day, or they would break back in panic, overrunning Lugard's force and leaving them to join in flight or take the brunt of a pursuing, victorious army. He felt they were advancing blindly as he could not persuade the Katikiro to send out scouts or spies: he was given the simple answer that men were afraid to undertake such dangerous service. Lugard, however, induced one captured woman to go back and so made contact with the enemy. He then sent Dualla, a keen Muslim and most anxious for peace, to offer his terms. But in spite of promises of honourable treatment for their king, Mbogo, and land for themselves, the Muslims in the end refused to give up their leader. The parleys were broken off, and the clash seemed unavoidable. The Baganda chiefs had, indeed, done their best to bring the parleys to this result.

There is something disturbing in the picture of civilized men making use of tribal armies or joining forces with them. On this occasion Lugard could say to himself, in the soldier's conventional terms, " It is in God's hands, and our cause seems the right one " (Diary, 4 May 1891); he felt he had done his best to make peace and must now save the desolated province from the enemy. Yet he was unhappy. It was not gloom about the issue, though he made an elaborate will in the body of his diary, carefully disposing of all his few possessions. It was rather that, with the battle upon them, the two chief men in the army, were, unknown to their soldiers, quarrelling in their tent in much the same irrational way as two other commanders had quarrelled on the eve of the battle of Philippi.

It has been said that Lugard liked and admired Williams. So he did and so he continued to do. Yet their relations grew strained. Lugard found it hard to see the entire handling of the Sudanese, the main body of soldiers, completely in the control of Williams who also appropriated his " Zanzibari levy ". Williams, on his side, could not forget that he had come out to command the troops directly under the Administrator. Now he found that he, a regular, an artillery officer of great promise, who had never served under less than a colonel, had to play second to a captain in a marching regiment.

The Fight with the Muslims

Lugard was still soldier enough to understand exactly how he felt. He also saw that Williams' was so stiff with military tradition that he could hardly unbend: he took every comment of Lugard's as a command or a censure whereas, said Lugard, analysing the situation " I like to work much more in the family party way, I think, and have as little ' superior officer ' business as possible." (Diary, 4 May 1891). At last, one night, Williams came out with the whole grievance. After this he felt much better but, as so often happens, when one man has thus unloaded his grievance, it is the other's turn to take up the burden of resentment. Yet Lugard, sitting in his tent, his eyes swimming with tears from the smoke of a thousand camp-fires of wet green wood, wrote pages in his diary to show how strenuously he grappled with his own faults and how much he had taken to heart the precepts of his recent correspondents. " I thought that the bitter lesson of my life had taken away most of that contrariness, self-conceit, jealousy and opinionatedness, which I well know to be absolutely intolerable in a travelling companion and which I well know is one of my miserable characteristics. As he [Williams] says, I am a very difficult man to serve with. He struck true and I had nothing to say, except that I had tried hard to study his feelings, and since we should probably have to fight together presently, we must try and make the best of each other." Lugard flagellated himself further with Williams' virtues. He was " absolutely invaluable . . . he manages the Sudanese a thousand times better than I could . . ." (Diary, 22 April 1891). "It has always been my pride and boast that everyone got on well with me and I was *most* easy to serve with. I think the matter partly is that Williams is every inch a soldier and I am more like a civilian . . . but I think I am at least man enough to take a lesson even though the dose may be disagreeable." (Diary, 4 May 1891). Lugard's generous humility seems to have been successful. Williams in a letter a little earlier had written, " Lugard is a good man and we are more like brothers than first and second so that the omelette won't be spoilt by the frying pan slipping."[1]

This was not Lugard's only subject for deep introspection as he marched towards Bunyoro. The reader has probably begun to suspect that the domination of Celia over his mind was passing. He had hardly realized it himself until the lack of any letter from her, or even

[1] Williams to G. Cawston, 4 April 1891, Cawston Papers, MSS. Afr. s. 76.

news, when Martin's caravan came up, suddenly revealed the change in himself. Like many another at such a moment, he looked at himself with surprise, almost with shame. Was it not those who feel such injuries most deeply, he asked himself, who " view with dismay in the course of years that the wound is healing and only a scar remains? " He looked back incredulously on the self he had been only three years before " leaving Aden for Africa, maddened with grief, reckless, almost insane, with a broken career behind me . . . an adventurer— possibly to find only navvies work with a bare subsistence." The ordeal had changed all his life. " I was then a different man entirely . . . only five years between that old life and *this*! . . . Am I once more beginning to see with healthy eyes? " (Diary, 15 April 1891). Yet he did not then or later forget, for what he counted as forgetfulness was, in truth, a great measure of constancy. So when, trekking on a line that no white man had traced before, he suddenly discovered a small and beautiful lake set with islands, which the Baganda called Wamala, he rechristened it, in a spirit of pain and loss, remembering lovers' shared joy in a great love-story, by a name which only he would understand, Lake Isoldt. So it was marked on his maps— forgetting the " d "—and reported to the Company but the native name was not displaced and, rightly, perhaps, from all points of view, the romantic name he gave it has been forgotten.

Lugard's not very ample periods for meditation during the march were not all spent upon past memories or upon humble self-examination about his relations with his second-in-command. The very act of marching set his mind upon the destination and beyond, and his ambition began to vault over an astonishing number of obstacles. What lay beyond the blue hills of Bunyoro, now coming into view to the north? On April 25th he looked out of his little tent at a full moon. " I wonder what this moon and the next will bring us! Of course ambitious ' castles in the air ' float in my mind during idle hours on the march. Supposing we defeat the Mahommedans—and that *should* be probable enough—it seems as though the conquest of Bunyoro *must* follow." What would this mean—garrisons at Kaba-rega's capital—at Mruli—along the Nile? " Then, if it is true that the Mahdists are *not* in Emin's old province, and that Selim and his men are loyal and will come to us as Shukri asserts (and none should know better) we may have quite a small army." They would take Emin's old steamer on Lake Albert. " Then, (*if* it all comes off) what is to stop us from marching on Wadelai? " And if Wadelai, could he not raise a Sudanese force there and take over Emin's old province. " That is a stake worth trying for. *If so* (again and again, of course, an ' if ') we might even be able to clear the way up to Gondokoro." Then he would write for more forces from the War Office and " make a simultaneous advance from Gondokoro by boat to Khartoum, while the British advance from Assouan." These were " if's " indeed, and such, on this occasion, they were to remain. But it was men who were led on by such almost limitless dreams who opened up the new continents.

It would seem that if Lugard had given more of his mind to an assessment of the position of the Company which was employing him he might have abstained from such hopes and even held back from the next instalment of adventure upon which he shortly set out. There should have been enough in de Winton's very frank letters to warn him. It is not clear when he received those of December 5th and 25th 1890 but they were not obscure. The directors were seriously perturbed, they told him, about the expenses de Winton was incurring, " being of opinion that the measures I have taken to support you in Uganda are on too large a scale for the object in view." For these measures de Winton said that he was responsible, as he had believed that an envoy like Lugard should have a force sufficient to impress Mwanga if he were to get a treaty out of him and arbitrate between the conflicting interests, as his instructions laid down. This official letter was accompanied by an unofficial one in which de Winton was even more frank. He said " I send an official [letter] as the Court are becoming frightened at present expenditure, but it will I fear add somewhat to the present difficulties of your position. You may however depend upon me to back you up by all means in my power." He gave him an absolutely free hand as to how he should act but suggested, rather unrealistically, that he might have to take " forcible possession of the country as the only way of restoring peace and order." He did not scruple to show his opinion of the inefficiency of the Company which was employing them. " I only wish they had some more defined policy and instead of sending out expensive steamers and ordering impracticable things to be carried out, they would adopt a policy of concentration and do one thing at a time."

(De Winton to L. 25 December 1890). Lugard was not very sympathetic at this picture of his chief in risking his own position to support his difficult subordinate. He had given his trust so completely to Mackenzie and Kirk, and had, it seems, been so alienated from de Winton in their passage of arms, that he was inclined to put all the blame on the latter for rusting railway gear and lighters at the coast, unsuitable steamers and for £200,000 "*thrown away*", as he wrote, with little result, though much of it had, in fact, been spent upon his own expedition. He was mainly anxious lest Mackenzie should have to take the blame. (Diary, 12 February 1891).

We must return to the campaign. The army was now coming up to a river which divided Bunyoro from Buganda and fighting was imminent. The "Christian" army was, as may be expected, very far from being united. The Katikiro and the Ingleza chiefs, strongly pro-Company, had begged Lugard to give them the Company flag to take into action. He reluctantly agreed. But the Mujasi, who had led his detachment in sulky isolation from the rest, and the other Fransa chiefs, refused it, so it was, to Lugard's chagrin, now publicly flown as the flag of a faction, and not, as he claimed, of a government.

Upon reaching the river on May 5th, Lugard had a council of war with all the chiefs. The enemy were well-armed and in a strong position on the granite hills, the lower slopes of which were matted with verdure. Lugard's tactical possibilities seemed limited by the refusal of the Baganda to divide forces. Yet to attempt to cross the swampy river before them *en masse* in the face of the enemy was to invite defeat. Lugard at last persuaded the Katikiro to lead an advance guard by night downstream to a better and more open crossing and to hold it. Lugard followed at earliest dawn after having first deceived the enemy by giving the signal on the drums for a day's halt. Thus the whole force got across the river without losing one man. This, apart from moral support, was his only important contribution to the battle which followed. The Baganda, once over the river, having indulged in some war-dancing, immediately rushed up a steep hill with a speed and *élan* which astonished Lugard, and, after one setback, reached the top. Here, using their guns, according to the method of the country, more as improved close-range than as long-range weapons, they discharged them when a few yards from the enemy. There was little left for Lugard's force to do but to direct some fire upon the retreating foe, who appear to have lost some hundreds of men to a few score of their attackers.

What was to follow victory? Lugard wanted to march straight on to Kabarega's capital. But, like many a leader of tribal levies before him, he found his army had very different ideas. He was told that there were impassable swamps and rivers between him and his objective, that food was scarce and that the war-bands, after ravaging such Banyoro villages as they could find, would break up and go home with their loot.

Lugard, however, was not inclined to give up all his dreams of further adventure. He therefore decided to march in a great circuit, first going south to the rich Buddu province, ruled by an important Ingleza official, the Pokino, in order to collect and prepare a large stock of food for his march. From there he would go through the kingdom of Ankole, the king of which, Ntale, had helped the fugitive Christians in the civil war. Then he would march on to the next kingdom, Toro; restore the royal line ousted by Kabarega; and perhaps attack that hostile king or, at any rate, threaten his western flank. But, as he was going into practically unexplored country and unknown conditions, his actions would have to be decided by opportunity. His expedition would at the least open up a route from Buddu to Ankole and Toro and perhaps northwards to Wadelai, and so allow him at once to reach the rich deposits of salt reported to exist there; to divert the north-south trade from German territory into Uganda; and also to stop the trade in arms and powder from the south into Buganda and Bunyoro. But perhaps his most important object was to reach the Sudanese "garrison". If he could persuade these Sudanese to follow him, he would command some hundreds of soldiers, who could be cheaply engaged, and with whom he could dominate Buganda and so be relieved from the sense of powerlessness so hateful to his masterful nature.

He had no idea as he took this decision that it was to open him to severe criticisms on the grounds that he turned away from the dangerous situation in Mengo and left Williams with quite inadequate forces at Kampala to deal with it. He took with him the bulk of the Company's men—110 Sudanese soldiers, 138 of the "Zanzibari levy" and 185 porters. With him were Grant and Dr. Macpherson, de Winton staying with Williams. This made 438 in all with one of the two

Maxim guns. Williams took back less than a dozen soldiers to re-inforce the Kampala garrison which would consist of 220 men, and these the worst. Williams does not appear then, nor for the next few months, to have made any protest; on the contrary he continued to hope that things round Kampala would remain sufficiently quiet for him to join Lugard upon his adventure. As far as dangers of violence or disease were concerned, there was little to choose between the two tasks and we may note that Lugard's party went badly provided with the necessities for Europeans in such conditions, adequate clothes, tinned food, tea, soups, spirits and, above all, medicines, including quinine. These had given out one by one and Lugard frequently complained bitterly against the incompetence of Company officials in England and at the coast which endangered the lives of their hard-pressed agents in the interior.

It is very difficult to discover whether in taking this journey to the west Lugard was acting upon any instructions. When Mackenzie first asked him to go up country straight from the Sabaki trek, it was in order to get the land between Lakes Victoria and Tanganyika, later allocated by the 1890 Agreement to Germany. When he finally set out from Mombasa he was merely going forward as an advance guard for de Winton, and had no orders as to what to do when he reached the lake.[1] After he was put in sole command he had a number of letters from de Winton giving instructions or forwarding them. But all of these which survive are concerned with his dealings with Buganda and the making of the treaty. De Winton, sending on the telegram, dated in London November 18th 1890, from the directors which said that Lugard was "not [to] return before important object Uganda Mission completed", confessed to "a feeling of vagueness as to what was intended by their message." This was followed by urgent advice from London about strict economy and the sending of as much ivory as possible to pay expenses. (De Winton to L. 25 December 1890). In his report on his journey Lugard referred, as a reason for taking it, to "my original instructions (vide telegram from the directors, dated about March 1890)" to make a treaty with Ntale, but, as the Company's records appear to have been lost or destroyed, this cannot now be verified. It is clear that the government were not satisfied as to the validity of the treaties Stanley had made on his

[1] C.6555 (1892), p. 87.

hurried journey through this region, though it was upon these, within the sphere left to them, that the Company's claim rested.[1] Lugard was probably instructed to make new ones in proper form. The writer was told when in Ankole of the belief that Stanley's ceremony of blood-brotherhood was not done in the correct way which Lugard had later followed. To secure valid treaties within the British sphere was still necessary and also to make the first motions towards " effective occupation " by which alone Britain could substantiate her claim against her rival " scramblers ". Whether these reasons were adequate to justify this distant and perilous march was to remain a very contentious question.

But, even though Lugard could not anticipate the criticism that was to follow, he was certainly a little uneasy, and did at least give up his first intention to take Williams with him, though the trek he planned would be a great strain upon the leader. Grant, of whom Lugard always spoke well for his courage, industry and reliability, was not a soldier and was not regarded by him as a true second-in-command, while the doctor was not, of course, in the running for such distinction and was far from being the " all-purpose " man such an enterprise demanded. There were two Sudanese native officers who had been with Stanley and Emin, Shukri Aga and Suroor Adam, but these men, in the eyes of the exacting Lugard, had serious faults. Dualla, the Somali, was his closest native assistant and his interpreter, brave and sensitive, but almost hysterically excitable especially when fighting was in progress. Lugard, therefore, again pointed out to his employers the urgent need for more European assistants of the highest standard.[2] Williams was given orders to follow him if things were quiet in Buganda, leaving young de Winton in charge, but—here is a hint of doubt—only if he could honourably leave Buganda " for after all this is our *first* duty, and the one for which we came." It is significant that he made a note upon the pages in his diary in which he gave the reasons for his decision to march west, that Williams had read them. (Diary, 8 May 1891).

---

[1] Sir John Gray, 'Early Treaties in Uganda, 1888–1891', *Uganda Journal*, vol. XII, March 1948; and H. B. Thomas, 'More Early Treaties in Uganda, 1891–96', *Ibid.* vol. XIII, September 1949. Stanley admitted that he had made only verbal treaties (Stanley to Mackinnon, 6 February 1890, M. P.), so that the copies in the Foreign Office cannot be genuine (F. O. 84/2081).
[2] C.6555 (1892), p. 117.

CHAPTER XIV

THE MARCH TO THE WEST

May-December 1891 : Aet. 33

THE TWO men parted on May 14th. Williams swung round to return to Kampala. Lugard marched almost due south towards Buddu, the Buganda province lying on the west of Lake Victoria. The Pokino, the Ingleza chief of this region, hurried ahead to collect food for the expedition, as this was only to be obtained in this grainless country by laboriously drying bananas and making flour of them. Food was, indeed, once more Lugard's ceaseless preoccupation. The rinderpest had wiped out the cattle of the pastoral Ankole people and he would therefore march through a land of scarcity, almost of famine. Four hundred marching men need a lot of food. It was at once Lugard's care and joy to shoot game but he needed seven or eight large antelope a day to feed them: their pursuit took time and energy and Lugard sadly records a trail of wounded animals whose blood tracks he could not stay to follow.

From the map on page 250, which will greatly help an understanding of this chapter, can be traced Lugard's route from the dry, rocky Bunyoro country, later annexed to Buganda, to the green hills and swamps of central Buganda. Lugard marked the changing scene, rapidly mapping and recording all these vast, virgin African lands with their lakes, rivers, plains and forests which he was taking over for his masters in Pall Mall. Making a standing camp at Bugaju, about a day's journey inland from Lake Victoria, he went on a circuit with a small party to the lake-shore, seeking to survey the narrows between the mainland and Luwambu, one of the Sese islands. From here, he believed, the canoe traffic could be controlled and perhaps, if steel boats and steamers could be obtained, a terminal point established for trade and communications across Lake Victoria and inland to Lakes Albert and Edward. He was checked, however, by the hostility of the

Fransa who were strong in Buddu. Wherever he found himself in a Fransa neighbourhood, even though his ally, the Pokino, was lord of Buddu, the people refused to give him food and they hid the canoes which would have allowed him to examine the islands and the narrows. His friend Zachariah, who, bringing a party of Baganda, had volunteered to journey all the way with him, told him that they would not have dared to do this without the express orders of the King. And the King, Lugard must tell himself, was under the sway of the French priests. By contrast, when he passed through Ingleza villages, the people greeted him with joy and pressed food upon him. Even so far away from Mengo, Buganda was thus divided into a chequerboard of factions called after European nations and Christian denominations.

Lugard was tempted to punish the hostile villages but, in his anxiety not to add to the bitterness in the country, he restrained himself. He returned to Bugaju and there collected his men and all the food that was ready. A young man named Kasagama, who claimed to be the rightful ruler of Toro, and whose kingdom had some years before been overrun by Kabarega, had joined Lugard, who resolved to restore him to his father's throne.[1] Lugard now marched off westwards and crossed the borders of Buganda into the kingdom of Ankole. Here were the dry, grassy plains of these Hima people, but there were now neither cattle, buffalo nor eland. Zachariah went ahead to tell the king, Ntale, that Lugard was coming in peace but also in authority, to make a treaty with him. For Lugard meant to beat the bounds of the region allotted to Britain as her sphere, showing the Company flag where frontiers were yet undefined, and carrying it along the Semliki river which, according to Stanley, King Leopold and Mackinnon had agreed upon as a dividing line. In Ankole he noted the tall, slender figures, aquiline noses and piercing eyes of the handsome ruling class and these, in their turn, showed much interest in the Somali Dualla, who seemed so much closer to their race than the more negroid Baganda.

The king sent friendly messages to Lugard but refused to come himself to see him. He pleaded his poverty, the royal herd having

---

[1] Mr. H. B. Thomas pointed out to the writer that Toro had been part of the Bunyoro "empire" but Kasagama's grandfather, a son of the then Mukama (king) of Bunyoro, had asserted his independence. Kabarega had, thus, some justification for trying to re-conquer the country.

been reduced from 7,000 to 300. It was here that Lugard first saw survivors of the breed of Hima or Ankole cattle, with their monstrous horns—domestic animals today considered strange enough to merit exhibition among the wild creatures at Whipsnade. Lugard believed that Ntale had a superstitious fear of meeting the white man. Perhaps, from his divinations of a fowl's entrails, a method of enquiry which so much of Africa shared with the ancient world, he had seen unfavourable omens. If so, time was to show that they lied. He sent his son,[1] however, a handsome boy, who made blood-brotherhood with Lugard at a solemn ceremony and signed a treaty giving Lugard all that he asked, the acceptance of the Company's flag as a symbol of British protection and sovereignty and the promise to stop the trade across his country in arms and powder. Lugard sent the King in return a load of cloth. This, as Lugard noted, was certainly getting kingdoms at bargain prices. But the Company's main payment was still to be made: it was the protection of Ankole against Kabarega, and the more distant menace of the Sudanese garrison. And this was only to be accomplished at the cost of European and African effort, sweat and life, and long and deep controversy in Britain. It may have been, as Dr. Oliver has pointed out to the writer, that Lugard, first seeing Bunyoro from the standpoint of Buganda, too readily assumed the role of knight-errant against the wicked aggressor Kabarega, and that if he had happened to enter the country by the north he might have found himself the ally of that ruler against the three other kingdoms. Certainly Bunyoro suffered much from this historical accident. But, by whichever route he had come, Lugard must have tried, weak though his forces were, to make alliances and protect his allies as the first instalment of the ultimate *pax Britannica*. Meanwhile, with this much reservation, we are bound to follow events as Lugard saw and described them.

The westward march went on. Day by day, almost hour by hour, Lugard entered its events in his diary; 265 pages of foolscap, closely and evenly written to cover the paper to the last quarter-inch, describe the first half of the march: the changing scene; the attempts, generally successful, to make friendly contacts with the local peoples; the

---

[1] Sir John Gray questions Lugard's accuracy about this relationship. ' Early treaties in Uganda, 1888–1891', *Uganda Journal*, vol. XII, March 1948, p. 37. The writer, in discussing the events of this period with aged men in this region, was informed that the treaty was made with the uncle of Ntale.

flogging of his men for their ineradicable habit of looting food; self-satisfaction with the meticulous order and arrangement of his camps; days of sickness and strain; eager hopes and plans for the future; memories aroused by past anniversaries; little character-sketches of his companions, brown and white. As he approached Lake Edward his mind was working anxiously on the chances of making contact with Selim Bey and his soldiers, cut off in a waste of barbarism somewhere far away to the north, and there was much talk with Selim's two brother officers of the chances of success.

Another anxiety now troubled Lugard. Rumours, increasingly distinct, suggested that Emin Pasha, after leaving his German post at Bukoba, where static subordination did not suit his temperament, had entered the British sphere ahead of him. Lugard had conducted some correspondence with him from Buganda. Emin had refused King Mwanga's invitation to visit Mengo; he had agreed to co-operate with Lugard in checking the trade in arms, and on March 8th he had written a characteristically obscure letter which had reached Lugard on April 15th. In this he referred gratefully to an offer of help Lugard had made to him in 1888. " Perhaps ", Emin wrote in English, " some day or other, I, the eternal wanderer, shall cross your path again and be allowed to express to you personally my feelings . . . . Shall I wish you joy to (sic) the great numbers of Europeans presently in Uganda? . . . . Look out! Uganda becomes a powerful neighbour and I feel quite overwhelmed. Well, let me wish you every success! Uganda and its northern countries are worth having and your task is a very important one—so greater the honour for you."[1] Now, it appeared, this remarkable man was indeed crossing his path. Was he challenging Lugard's claim to these same northern countries? Was he trying to forestall Lugard by calling upon the services of his old troops and their officers?

This last was what Lugard especially feared. And on July 23rd he was indignant when he encountered a party of five ruffianly Swahili, armed and carrying a German flag, on their way from the German sphere to look for Emin, carrying letters and looting food as they passed. Lugard did not follow Carl Peters' example by opening this correspondence but he arrested the men and wrote Emin a stiff letter

[1] Reproduced in facsimile in Lugard II, p. 122.

expressing surprise at these armed incursions, demanding an explanation of his entry and asking whether he was acting under the orders of his government. (L. to Emin Pasha, 3 August 1892).

About two months after leaving Williams, Lugard approached the large lake which had been discovered by Stanley only just two years before. Stanley had passed this way along the western shore of the lake and had called it Albert Edward Nyanza. Lugard was fortunate in having a number of men who had been with Stanley but they were, of course, quite ignorant of geography, and Lugard had no map to help him upon what was as much a march of exploration as one initiating administration. Stanley's book with its map, though so quickly published, had not reached Lugard who, for the most part, took his own uncharted road. The only map he had was Bartholomew's political and still very provisional one of the whole continent upon which the entire region where his work lay could be covered by a five-shilling piece.

Lugard was now coming to a region where Africa excels herself by the lavishness and variety of her giant beauties. In 1953 the writer, armed with the requisite documents and maps, followed, as closely as modern communications admit, the course of Lugard's western journey. Pausing, as he did, on the Kichwamba ridge, with its beautiful trees and dark crater lakes, one can see a view of almost terrible beauty. Far below lies a great valley running from north to south, its flat plains and marshes visibly crowded with elephant and buffalo. The valley holds two beautiful lakes, linked by the narrow Kazinga channel, through which the water flows strongly. Neither Stanley nor Lugard reproduced this strange formation very exactly upon their maps though Lugard made the better attempt. Beyond the southern lake can be seen mountains, now part of the Belgian Congo, which rise as the eye runs northwards to the seventeen thousand foot grandeur of the Ruwenzori range, the Mountains of the Moon. Upon these, first seen by European eyes only during Stanley's north-south expedition, barely twenty-four months before Lugard came upon them from the west, Stanley had gazed for three days " spell-bound and wondering ".[1] The great jagged spine of snow-covered peaks is generally hidden by cloud, and only their vast forested base can be seen. There

[1] D. Stanley, *Autobiography of Henry M. Stanley* (1909), p. 371. The full story is in Stanley, *In Darkest Africa*, vol. ii, p. 260 ff.

are few greater natural exhibitions in Africa than when these too-modest mountains, perhaps after days when nothing but the base has been visible, suddenly reveal shapes so high and so white that it is almost impossible at first to believe that they are not clouds. The lonely Emin, on one of his rounds far to the north, could have seen them, but shrouded as they were, and short-sighted as he was, he failed to make this great discovery. As Stanley remarked, it was striking evidence of the difference between the minds of primitive and civilized men, that none of his native followers had thought it worth while to point them out to him. Beyond the mountains the wide Semliki river curves round towards the Albert lake.

Lugard descended the escarpment and brushed aside a hostile party of Banyoro who controlled the narrow Kazinga channel. He crossed the connecting water in frail but large canoes made of grass by the local natives with whom, as almost everywhere along his route, he made friends. Then he went on to take the valuable Salt Lake at Katwe which the Banyoro had controlled. Lugard, too busy and anxious with the manifold cares which his standards of African trekking imposed upon him to stand and stare, was not, perhaps, so sensitive as other travellers to the beauties of Africa, some of which he was the first to uncover for the civilized world. But now and again he stopped in wonder, as now, when he found the Salt Lake, its waters a deep claret colour, its fringe of salt white as ice, while southward the waters of the great lake now known as Edward, clear, blue and set with green islands, stretched to an unbounded horizon. Because this area is a game reserve, elephant, buffalo and hippopotamus still frequent its shores and white fleets of pelicans in tight formation move over its waves.

To Lugard Ruwenzori was above all the mountain-mass that lay between him and the still distant Sudanese, of whom runners, sent far ahead, could find no trace. In a highly defensible position commanding the narrow ridge between the Salt Lake and Lake Edward, Lugard now built a stockaded fort, the levelled site of which is still clearly traceable. No more imaginative than Stanley, he gave this wonderful place the name of Fort George. He was thinking of his trek companion, George Wilson, and also of George Mackenzie. The fort not only dominated the Salt Lake but was a base from which the narrow Kazinga channel between Lake Edward and the northern lake could be controlled. The latter Lugard calls Ruisamba on his map but it was later named George.[1] Thus, Uganda's four lakes, with their wild tropical beauty and their uncouth amphibious monsters, were made to carry the four prosaic names of the Hanoverian dynasty, George, Edward, Albert and Victoria.

Lugard, like most other grown-up children, enjoyed designing and building, and he was happy in the making of his fort, even though timber was almost unobtainable, the ground too rocky to take the posts, and tools almost wholly lacking. He now commanded the salt supply and used it as currency to buy provisions, while the discovery of a great cache of food-loads left by the fleeing Banyoro enabled him to build up a reserve of 14,000 lbs. He wrote exultantly of this, delighted to have achieved the economical standards which both his nature and his necessities demanded. His standards of honourable conduct were also satisfied because, having as we have seen accepted the Banyoro as his enemies, it was permissible, even meritorious, to loot them. Indeed, in African exploration at this time, native enmity was almost an advantage, its ineffective injuries being generally outweighed by the gain of sanctioned plundering.

Lugard was delighted by what he regarded as the key-position of his fort in this almost unknown land, and was tempted to linger perfecting its structure, writing his diary and reports and mapping this undiscovered country. But his main object, the Sudanese garrison, still beckoned to him. So, on July 27th, he set off with the bulk of his men, leaving the doctor rather unhappily in charge of a small garrison, with many local native allies camped around. He marched westwards through the southern foothills of the Ruwenzori range and down still lower into the floor of the great rift valley to the deep rushing Semliki river.

Following up rumours of both Emin and the Sudanese being ahead of him, Lugard ran into a camp of Manyuema raiders from the Congo Free State, and realized that these men had been confused in native reports with the Sudanese. They were a phenomenon worth some study. They were in the service of a notorious leader, based upon the Belgian sphere, one Kilonga-Longa, who figures much in Stanley's pages, and whose headquarters were on the Ituri river not a hundred miles to the north-west. Men of a large cannibal tribe whose home

[1] The names of the lakes were officially gazetted as Edward and George in 1908.

lay west of Lake Tanganyika, they had become the assistants and imitators of the Zanzibar Arab slavers who had established their deadly power in this region about the time Livingstone had reached it. He had found himself, on his last journey, a helpless spectator, and indeed a guest, of these pitiless men. These Manyuema recruits, with their initiative and energy, had now spread out in bands far away from their original home, and had built small settlements from which, with their guns, they preyed upon the local tribes, enslaving them and levying tribute of ivory, moving on to virgin areas when they had ruined those surrounding them. Yet these men, representing with their Arab mentors a new disease which must have depopulated Africa if new and more civilized masters had not arrived to sweep them away, were individually men not only of noble physique but, on the evidence of both Livingstone and Stanley, who had seen the worst they could do, of impressive carriage, bearing and intelligence. Even Lugard could not withhold his admiration for this band of some twenty-five to thirty men, armed only with old muzzle-loaders, who could terrorize a large population which detested them. To his astonishment he found himself confessing that he found them " excessively hospitable, most respectful, quiet, self-possessed men, very much more civilized than the savages and indeed a really nice lot of fellows to whom I took a fancy." Thus, in the conditions of an Africa suddenly stirred by new ideas and ambitions, the ablest tribes became the most injurious and took the obvious course which their neighbours' poverty and helplessness suggested and which their new weapons allowed. The temptations to such action proved irresistible, not only to black men and Arabs, but sometimes, where there were no strong principles of humanity or of far-sighted self-interest to restrain them, to Europeans who succeeded them as masters. For it must be admitted that in the Congo region, under Leopold II, the destruction of African life for hasty commercial ends still continued for some years.

Lugard heard that Emin had passed their way and the Manyuema story added to the insoluble puzzle of his character. He had, they said, seized by force some cloth they had bought from his men in return for slaves but had not returned the slaves. Yet he had asked them to catch some pygmies for him, which they had done and they now embarrassed Lugard by taking a pair of these tiny dwarfs, three foot high, and handing them over to him as if they were animals. Lugard felt obliged to take them to save them from a worse fate, and they presently became the pets of the camp, always merry and laughing.

Going on, he was able to see the abandoned huts Emin, accompanied by Stuhlmann, had built on the slopes of a hill. He could also see, in dramatic contrast with the region devastated by the Manyuema, a still unviolated stretch of Africa such as he had seen north of Lake Nyasa and in Kikuyu country. This was an Africa as it must have been in all its more fertile regions, when innocent of all major human evils except the old spear-and-arrow tribal conflicts, so much less injurious than the new fierce unresting greed, made irresistible by bullets, for white ivory or black, as slaves were called. Here, at the foot of Ruwenzori, was rich soil. " I have never seen anything like the cultivation. As far as the eye can see, endless acres of plantation extend, all looking most luxuriant—bananas, grain, and beans . . . . The people go about the fields unarmed—a rare thing in Africa—with only sticks in their hands . . . . The fields are wonderfully well kept, not a weed to be seen."[1]

But where he followed Emin's path he found the people distrustful and inclined to flee from him. They told him Emin's party had seized food by force without payment. With personal and patriotic complacency, Lugard explained to such chiefs as he could approach that *he* belonged to a different nation, one that had taken over the country but would neither loot nor hurt the people in any way, but would pay for produce in goods or in salt—the salt of the lake he had taken from the Banyoro. Lugard had still not found the Sudanese but he had proved Emin's trespass, opened up and mapped new country as far as the unsurveyed border with the Congo State, and shot his first elephant. Excited by his first pursuit of this new, huge and dangerous quarry, and by the valuable tusks they carried and for which they were now being followed with guns into the most secret parts of Africa, Lugard seemed on this occasion to lose all his humane scruples. He would fire and fire into a herd, until sometimes half a dozen wounded beasts were plunging off into the forest, most of them to die a lingering death with their wealth unrecovered. His frank confessions of this in his diary must offend the more humane standards of today and perhaps, at an even deeper level, they induce a sense of shame for a race which, even in the centuries when better things might

[1] Lugard II, pp. 179–80.

have been expected, has fallen with such greedy wastefulness upon each new natural treasure brought within its reach. But Lugard, at least, differed from most contemporary sportsmen in that he repented almost nightly in his diary.

Lugard, aged thirty-three in 1891, was happy in the immense effort and achievement of his expedition. At night he could sit outside his tent and rejoice as, with the sunset, the clouds that blanketed the legendary Mountains of the Moon melted away and a level blade of the setting sun struck through to the summits white with the snow that is so strange and exciting when seen from plains and valleys of equatorial heat.

Having failed to locate the Sudanese, Lugard now turned round on his tracks, and got back to Fort George on August 6th, noting that he had now walked exactly 1,500 miles from Mombasa. The next day, leaving a hundred men at the fort, he marched northwards for Toro, east of Ruwenzori and west of Lake George, through country where no white man had been before, for Stanley, on his last trek with Emin, had gone west of the mountains. In spite of all his efforts the caravan began to stretch out over miles. Lugard, though stopping at ridges to take angles and write up his road book, was well to the front. The sun was fierce, the track rough and the men heavily loaded. Suddenly the scouts in front shouted that the enemy was before them. To his dismay Lugard saw that this must be one of Kabarega's main armies, sent to attack him and armed with many guns. With the help of an aged Muganda who had migrated here on the heels of Lugard's expedition, the writer was able to locate the site and to see that the opposing army had chosen a perfect position. Here the foothills of Ruwenzori slope down towards Lake George, and the enemy stood in the narrow space between lake and mountain, upon the slope of a hill, with a river in front of them and a dense acacia wood between them and Lugard. Taking his binoculars, Lugard saw that the low hills were literally black with men, swarming like ants.

The position was grave. Lugard had only about forty men with him, and the rest were trailing along wearily, many of them still some miles behind. It was 3 p.m. and there was to be no moon. "My heart misgave me that we had tried too big a game. It seemed impossible that we could beat these hordes with 450 men and there was no retreat anywhere. Defeat meant annihilation." (Diary, 9 August 1891).

Men of all races and nations in his motley advanced company were now put to the test. For himself, he waited with apparent calm until about 100 of his men with guns had come up with him. Then he drew them out in line. The Somali scouts, chosen for their dash and pluck for this dangerous work, which most men refused, now fell back on to the line. The Maxim was brought up. Lugard had, as we know, little skill and no faith where this clumsy prototype of the machine-gun was concerned. Moreover the box of reserve ammunition was not there and Dualla was beside him, maddening him with his hysterical clamour. At 4 o'clock he advanced with his little group, holding fire as long as he dared until he saw some of the enemy hordes outflanking him along the hills to the left. He therefore fired the Maxim at a dense mass of the enemy. To his relief the machine responded and mowed down a group of men. This effect, at the novel range of some 800 yards and with the equally novel noise of the gun, really won the day. The handful of Sudanese, weary though they were, rushed on the enemy and completed the rout. Perhaps the bravest action was that of Zachariah whom Lugard had not long before severely censured for wasting precious ammunition. Zachariah now led his little party of Baganda into a charge, withholding fire so long that in the end they chased the enemy away without ever firing a shot, an action which deeply impressed Lugard. The whole army of southern Bunyoro now fled, leaving their camp and food to the exhausted victors upon whom, as soon as they reached it, the heavens unkindly poured a deluge of rain.

The little battle had shown once more what discipline plus one machine-gun could achieve even against vast numbers, some 500 of them armed with guns. Later, in his own book, Lugard was able to write of this encounter with a superior smile, referring to Stanley's prophecy in his book that after him no one would be able to enter Toro without a large army. Certainly not, Lugard agreed, with pardonable self-righteousness, by Stanley's methods, since he made enemies of even friendly tribes by his harshness. As regarded this area, however, Lugard was unjust since, as it happened, Stanley's march past Ruwenzori had been unusually pacific.

Lugard went on northwards parallel with the lake shore. Finding what seemed a perfect site between the hills and a deep river gulley commanding the way south to the Salt Lake and to Fort George, he built another stockade which he called Fort Edward after his distinguished uncle, Sir Edward Lugard. He cursed the Company for its mean equipment as he forced his men to cut trees without axes and implant poles in hard ground with four broken spades. He was now coming into Kasagama's own country, and he called in the people, terrorized by Kabarega, and presented to them their young chief, returned to take up his ancestral position. Rejoicing, yet fearful still, the tribesmen gathered warily about him and heard Lugard's promises of protection and just and humane dealing. He drew up a treaty in which Kasagama ceded sovereign rights to the Company and promised to suppress the traffic in arms, while Lugard, mindful of the Company's expenses, laid down the hard condition that all ivory was to be their property. It seems a heavy tax where no other trade existed, but then Lugard meant Company rule to bring about in return a new era of peace, production and prosperity. Guns were to be brought in and registered. Slave-raiding was forbidden. It seems Kasagama was glad to regain his throne on these terms. Though it was to be long before the Company was able to afford him much protection, he was yet to rule an enlarged and peaceful kingdom of Toro until 1928, to die peacefully having been awarded the M.B.E., and to be succeeded by his son.

From Fort Edward the indefatigable Lugard sent back to Kampala a heavy consignment of reports; letters to all his friends, relatives and official colleagues; full instructions for Williams; maps; indents for goods; fair copies of treaties; records of trials and punishments and many other documents. His official report to the Company was even gloomier reading for its directors than the last. He sketched out a series of routes and stations, asked for at least twelve Europeans to man them, with 500 trained soldiers, and gave the most minute details about the proper strength, conduct, pay, food and timing etc. of caravans to and from the coast.[1] All these documents were dispatched on August 17th in charge of a small picked party of men. This period of writing and building was one which yet allowed Lugard for the only time on the trek to rest and read a little after midday. His choice of literature was *Pickwick Papers*.

On August 26th the party, diminished by another small garrison left behind under a Sudanese sergeant, set off again. Another large

---

[1] C.6555 (1892), pp. 106–27.

Bunyoro army came to meet them armed, it was said, with 2,000 guns. But when Lugard, with 150 soldiers, each with a reserve of only twenty rounds, walked steadily towards them they broke and fled before he could fire a shot, leaving him happy to have won a bloodless victory. The track led them lower and lower into the deep hollow of the Rift across the southern tip of Bunyoro. Even though it was hostile country Lugard, anxious to show even his enemies the justice and restraint of the British, struggled to stop his mixed and predatory followers from looting. All prisoners were lectured and released; all stock seized was set free; no huts were destroyed. But it was a ceaseless struggle. The Baganda especially, who looted even allies, simply could not understand the idea of not robbing and destroying the enemy as part of war.

When they again met the Semliki river it flowed before them, deep, one hundred feet wide and quite impassable. The villages were deserted and all the canoes were on the other side. Some of the Zanzibaris bravely swam the river, which contained many crocodiles, and brought back three canoes. Lugard went over and gradually all the party crossed and were pushed and pulled up the steep bank, not excepting the aged milk-cow which Lugard had brought all the way from Busoga. The baffled Banyoro enemy now came to the bank where it seems they had hoped to attack the party at night. Marching parallel with them, the Banyoro fired at them from the opposite side of the river with guns which, Lugard remarked, included Sniders and Winchesters, but which never succeeded in hitting their target.

This part of the journey was perhaps the fiercest physical test of the men and of Lugard's hold over them. One night we find Lugard writing in his diary about the experience, many times endured, of getting across one of the numerous swamps of the country. " No one who has not tried what it is to force a path through matted vegetation in a swamp can conceive the labour. First, you push the wall of green stuff down before you; then clamber out of the depth you are in on to this—down you sink (there is no bottom, all is springy vegetation) and so you go on. The grass has an edge like a fret-saw and occasionally an edge catches your face or hands and cuts a deep gash. The stalks are clothed with spines and if you touch them your hand is covered with the almost invisible white thorns and causes great irritation. Presently you find the wet slippery mud has changed to quagmire

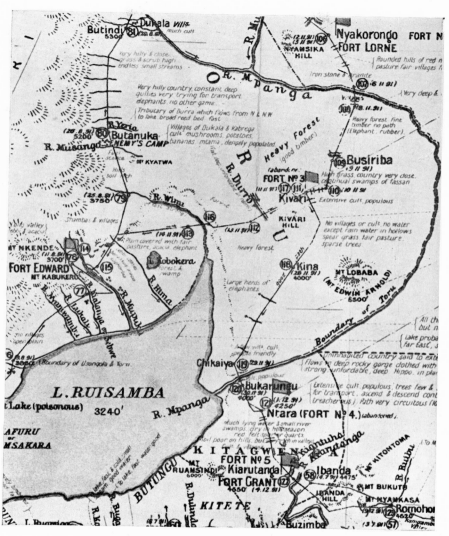

Small section of Lugard's chart made on his journey to the
west of Buganda with his notes on soil, products, vegetation,
etc. From F. D. Lugard, *The Rise of Our East
African Empire*, 1893

and you sink deep into it at every step. After the leading man or two has passed and broken the path through the reeds (here generally 12 ft. high) the track is a deep pool of water, and so on and on up to one's thighs. More than once the programme was diversified by running into a swamp-wasps' nest and then the frantic efforts of the men to get rid of the stinging insects gave a ludicrous touch to monotony." (Diary, 1 September 1891).

Tests of endurance were at least diversified. A day or two later, Lugard, faced with a choice between thick forest in the valley and steep rocky hills above it, chose the latter and led his men up almost perpendicular faces of granite, each move being up or down six foot or more of sheer smooth rock. In the end they found they had progressed two and a half miles for a day of desperate climbing and Lugard simply could not imagine how the loaded porters had achieved this and also pushed the old cow up and down with them. When Lugard, unimpeded, had reached a summit utterly winded, these porters, carrying, in addition to their guns and personal belongings, loads of sixty-five pounds, often made heavier by soaking rain, would reach the top singing and shouting merrily. And finally when, after marching perhaps from 7.15 a.m. to 6 p.m. through such conditions, they would make camp only to be sluiced with torrents of rain, there was never a moan. No wonder Stanley fetched Zanzibari porters all the way round Africa to the Congo mouth for his great Emin relief expedition! And many of these men with Lugard had quite lately been through that march of nearly three long years with Stanley, and seen more than half their number meet terrible and lingering deaths by disease, starvation, or poisoned arrows and skewers set in the path. Yet in the mornings, when Lugard started the caravan off, the men would sing and shout "Mwaka—Mwaka!"—"Years! Years!" meaning they were ready to go on with him for years. These were the unremembered men, who, whether as villains when in the service of the Arab slavers, or as heroes when marching with the white explorer, alone made possible the penetration of innermost Africa in the last forty years of the nineteenth century.

Was it, perhaps, the seemingly endless and exciting variety of the march that drew both the white man and his dark companions to the interior? Rocky hill and swamp were succeeded, all in a few days, by forests filled with sweet-smelling flowering trees alive with beautiful

K

birds. Then came undulating grassy plains. On and on they went. They had left the borders of Bunyoro where the Batoro still cowered in fear lest their oppressors should return. They had left, too, the white ramparts of Ruwenzori, and had crossed the hot valley of the Semliki, the lowest level, at some 2,000 feet, which Lugard had struck since Mombasa. Now they rounded a low hill and shortly after leaving suddenly filling its vast basin up to the sheer cliffs of rock, there broke upon their view the blue waters of the immense Lake Albert. And if nature showed a bewildering variety, so also did man. The cowed Batoro and the militant Banyoro were left behind and they were suddenly amongst a new tribe " the most affable savages I had ever met," Lugard calls them; intelligent, naked people who greeted and entertained them with the utmost friendliness and begged Lugard to build a station among them. The true explanation for their welcome was, as so often happened in Africa, not so much friendship for the strangers as fear of an enemy, here the terrible Kabarega who had already despoiled them, so that, with their cattle killed by rinderpest and not daring to sow for others to reap, they lived by drying and selling salt.

Lugard now began to climb up the slopes that lay on the other side of the Semliki. On September 6th, camped on peaceful, green foothills, he heard shots and hurried out to investigate. Now at last he saw the Sudanese whom he had come so far to find. They reported that their camp was at Kavalli on the shore of Lake Albert. Three native officers and a number of men came into the camp. There followed a scene of the wildest delight, with old comrades meeting, talking, kissing and congratulating each other and " everyone temporarily became a fool and jabbered as is right and proper on such an occasion." (Diary, 6 September 1891).

This goodwill was delusive. Lugard was to learn, like Stanley, that in Africa " rescues " are not so easily consummated. Since Stanley's book had been translated at once into ten languages, most of the civilized world—though not as we have seen Lugard himself—had read the story, written in Stanley's exciting sledge-hammer style, of his rescue of Emin and of his having left behind the greater part of the Pasha's equatorial garrison. But no one knew what had happened since to these troops, or whether to credit Stanley's story of the mutinies, the repeated vacillations and delays in concentrating the men and their dependants for the march, which had at last led Stanley to leave so many of them behind. Climbing the 2,000 foot scarp up to Kavalli, the place to which Selim Bey had brought down his troops from the north to join a vanished Stanley, and where he had remained ever since, Lugard soon saw that he would meet with a difficult situation. Nor was it without danger. One of the commanders of the Egyptian force, Fadl-el-Mula Bey, had seized and imprisoned his governor, Emin, while Stanley was waiting, and Lugard had yet to learn what manner of man was this Selim Bey who commanded forces twice as powerful as his own, and what was the true reason for his failing to obey and to follow Emin. He had only the assurances of Selim's brother officer, Shukri Aga, whom Lugard by no means regarded as a wholly admirable character, that Selim had always been loyal and had made ready to go only just too late for the impatient Stanley. What, moreover, had passed between Emin and his former officer, Selim, before the elusive Pasha had moved out northwards twenty-nine days before Lugard's arrival?

When Lugard arrived at Kavalli on September 7th, his behaviour, in its quiet resolution, was like that neither of the gentle, indecisive Emin nor of the ebullient Stanley. Selim first sent to ask that his old fellow soldier, Shukri, should be sent over to see him. Lugard records his reply. "'Certainly not, I am the British representative and I have most urgent matters to speak to you about.' . . . . I therefore desired him . . . . to come with all speed to see me. I knew of no custom by which an inferior officer went to communicate before the principals had met." (Diary, 7 September 1891). While waiting, Lugard set to work to build one of his perfect camps, with every line straight and measured, a durbar hut for himself, symmetrically spaced huts for his officers and for each category of his men, an arms rack, latrines, a tall flagstaff and a home-made Union Jack. He worked all day and nearly all night supervising this, mending and oiling the guns, making up his reports and arranging the eternal collection of food. He would have done all this in any case but he was well aware that it would impress a mob of soldiery which was trying to cling, with uncertain success, to their long-ago standards of military order.

Day after day passed and still Selim did not appear. Lugard became increasingly anxious, the more so as he was now very unwell and quite unfit for arduous negotiation. Then, early on September 11th, Selim sent a message to say that he was ready. Lugard, determined not to appear in a hurry, assigned 4 p.m. as the time, the place to be in his own quarters. " On occasions like this," was his thought, " I am a little more punctilious and tenacious of dignity than is my wont." Stanley had described Selim in prose very different from Lugard's style.

" He is six feet high, large of girth, about fifty years old, black as coal: I am rather inclined to like him. The malignant and deadly conspirator is always lean. I read in this man's face, indolence, a tendency to pet his animalism. He is a man to be led, not to conspire. Feed him with good things to eat, and plenty to drink, Selim Bey would be faithful. Ah, the sleepy eye of the full-stomached man! This is a man to eat, and sleep, and snore, and play the sluggard in bed, to dawdle slipshod in the bed-chamber, to call for coffee fifty times a day, and native beer by the gallon; to sip and sip and smile and then to sleep again; and so and so to his grave . . ."[1]

Lugard, ignorant of this delineation, made a somewhat different estimate of the huge black officer—" a Sudanese with no other blood in him "—who now came into his audience hut. " He is no fool, however, and I saw that in the first five minutes, and that I had met a man who was shrewd and suspicious and strong-willed." Moreover, he was sufficiently an autocrat in his wild province to come and negotiate alone with the white leader. Selim now poured out his version of the events of the past few years. He passionately denied that he had ever been disloyal and insisted on blaming Emin and Stanley for not waiting a little longer for him to join them. He went over all that happened since April 1883 when they had been cut off by the Mahdists from Khartoum and indeed, from the world. Fadl-el-Mula had been the rebel and, after Stanley left, he and Selim had come into conflict and had separated, Selim bringing all those loyal to him down to Kavalli while Fadl-el-Mula stayed at Wadelai and flirted with the Mahdists. Selim's party had suffered greatly from hunger and native attacks and he had been obliged, by the food problem, to scatter his men in small detachments to prey upon the neighbouring country-side.

What most impressed Lugard, and was, indeed, strange almost beyond understanding, was Selim's unbreakable loyalty to the Khedive. This black Sudanese had been cut off from all contact with Khartoum,

[1] Stanley, *In Darkest Africa*, vol. ii, p. 138.

let alone Egypt, for nearly ten years. During the whole of this time he and his men had drawn no pay, their distant sovereign had been defeated and had utterly neglected his province and his soldiers for years even before that. Yet they still clung to this one-sided allegiance. It was pathetic to see how in all these years of utter isolation, while committing every crime upon the native inhabitants, Selim and his officers, scorning to rebel like Fadl-el-Mula, or to accept the offers of the Mahdists, had clung to the Egyptian flag and to all they could retain of military discipline and propriety. When their uniforms perished, they grew cotton and wove coarse cloth to make new ones, at least for the officers. It was true that they had permitted themselves a lavish excess of promotions: in one detachment of forty, which Lugard later inspected, he found two majors, three captains, five lieutenants, three sergeant-majors, five sergeants, seven corporals, one bugler and fourteen privates. Yet they had at least tried to preserve the pride of the officer caste. Lugard, with his code of loyalty and discipline, was much moved when Selim arranged a parade of the 600 men he had so far brought in. They formed a hollow square and then marched past in two companies, with drums and bugles at the head. These were the remnant of a force of 3,000 men; some were grey-headed; nearly all were wounded and scarred; some were dressed in skins and barkcloth. " It was " Lugard felt " a sight to touch a man's heart to see this noble remnant who were fanatical in their loyalty to their flag and their Khedive." (Diary, 17 September 1891).

But this is to anticipate. Before this review Lugard, more ill each day with fever, had to struggle in argument with Selim. When Lugard offered him and his men a release from their exile and employment under the Company, Selim declared that he had grown grey under the Khedive's flag. " Through all dangers and difficulties he had never swerved from his loyalty to it and he would serve it to the death." (Diary, 11 September 1891). Lugard explained that the Khedive was now one with the British; that the Sudan had been abandoned and that they had more than fulfilled their engagements. He told him all that had happened in the world, including the Company's occupation of Uganda. Finally, Selim relented so far as to say that, if shown a written statement from the Khedive absolving him from his allegiance and permitting him to undertake this new service, he would come. But to get this would take a year! Lugard's next effort was to induce him to serve temporarily with him while awaiting his answer. At last Selim agreed and terms were drawn up on these lines. Selim stipulated that he should still fly the Khedive's flag and that all orders to his men should be given only through him.

But when this treaty was written Selim again drew back and there were more days of argument. Perhaps, as with Emin, long isolation bred this tendency to indecision. It might be, for all Lugard could discern, a moment of real peril for his own party. Outnumbered in men and guns, offering valuable loot, he was in a strange country, with Muslim armies within Selim's reach at nearby points of the compass: Baganda to the south-east, the Sudanese rebel garrisons and the Mahdists to the north and the Arabs and Manyuema to the west. It was probably Dualla and Lugard's other men who, by talking with Selim and his followers, convinced them all that Lugard was a good master but not a man to be trifled with. At last Selim gave in. Lugard, slight and fever-ridden, was by then utterly worn out with, as he put it, the exertion of matching the strength of the giant Selim. It was after this final agreement that the parade was held and Lugard spoke to the worn soldiery telling them they would find the British kind and considerate masters but hard upon disobedience. " I said that I thanked God that the news had reached me that they were here and were loyal and deserted and that I had been able to come . . . . before they had undertaken any rash enterprise." To himself he added " And I *do* thank God (as I said in my speech) that it has fallen to my lot to come to their relief as well as that I have been able to secure so fine a body of men for the Company's service." (Diary, 17 September 1891).

Part of Lugard's task was to clear up the mystery of Emin Pasha. Selim's story was that Emin had tried to get him and his men to join the German service. He had, however, admitted that he was no longer governor and that Britain and the Khedive were now one, and Uganda in the British sphere. He had told them they could make their own way east to the coast—which was hardly true—but tried to induce them to go west with him aiming, it seems, to reach the hinterland of the Cameroons, which had lately become German, or the Atlantic coast.[1] In the end, however, he left hurriedly, apparently because he heard the news that Lugard was coming, and went off first to the north and later westwards having, to Selim's anger, bribed some of

---

[1] G. Schweitzer, *Emin Pasha his Life and Work* (1898), vol. ii, p. 155.

his men to go with him. The rest of the story of this strange man, if we look ahead, is tragedy. He did not realize, nor fortunately perhaps did Selim, that the decisive and final struggle was even then beginning to be waged in central Africa between the Europeans—in this case the Belgian and cosmopolitan forces of the Congo State—and the Arabs whose mastery had preceded theirs, a brutal and bloody war of extermination by which one tyranny was succeeded, for some years, by another only a little less destructive. Urged on in Europe by Stanley, who claimed that his expedition had been all but wrecked by the treachery of the Arabs, the Congo State government made a concerted attack upon the Arab Manyuema and the rest, who had established themselves as rulers and traders in ivory in the west of this government's sphere.

This was the last decisive round in the struggle between European and Arab for the control of east and central Africa, which had developed after 1884, in one section of which Lugard had been engaged on Lake Nyasa and which was still being carried on there by Harry Johnston. All vestiges of the old, surprising moderation towards the European pioneers which the slavers and ivory-raiders had from time to time shown was over; now it was a war to the death. Emin, struggling onwards, now without Stuhlmann, disavowed by his own government and rapidly going blind, contracted with some Manyuema adventurers to convey him westwards, and stumbled into the fringe of this ferocious conflict. But the Manyuema and their Arab leaders were out for his blood: they regarded him as a Muslim convert who had perverted, and had helped the Germans to kill fellow Muslims. They therefore took him on October 23rd 1892, as he sat at his camp table, and cut his throat. The Belgians later avenged him by executing the two Arabs who had been most responsible for his death.[1]

While Selim collected his people, Lugard indulged in a brief but strenuous campaign against the elephants in search of ivory and excitement. He got plenty of both, rashly exposing himself in search of the maddened animals he wounded with his inadequate gun. With surprise and shame he analysed his own terror at such moments. In India he had been regarded as utterly fearless in stalking tiger or riding

[1] *Ibid.* vol. ii, pp. 294–304. Part of the story of the final struggle with the Arabs is told by S L. Hinde, *The Fall of the Congo Arab* (1897).

down wild boar. But now, " I fairly funk it. The strain is so great
that I am trembling from head to foot, and my knees even knocking
together! " (Diary, 24 September 1891). Yet he pursued this doubtful
pleasure with passion. In the intervals of the pursuit he had time for
other private thoughts which though the conscious testimony of the
subject in such matters is never conclusive, might be of interest to
psychologists looking for evidence of the motives which draw men
into such a life as he had been leading for many years. The reward
of which he dreamed in this forest, hitherto untrodden by a white
foot, was " A small cottage and grounds (or a lease of one) in Devonshire or Norfolk. Here would be my ' *Home* '—here I could collect
all my sporting trophies, my war trophies from Afghan, Burma,
Soudan, Nyassa and Nyoro; friends could come and stop with me,
and occupy it while I was away earning more money to complete
its purchase and doing good work perhaps again in Africa." Such a
cottage could provide a place of retirement " for my Father's last
days." (There is no woman, it should be noted, in this cottage of his
dreams.) " Well, no matter—enough of castles in the air! " (Diary,
3 October 1891).

Meanwhile at Kavalli, where Lugard was touched to find a great
welcome from his men upon his return from his hunting circuit, that
cumbersome concentration of the scattered soldiers and their dependants which had exhausted Stanley's patience was still going on.
Officers would have fifty to a hundred women, children and slaves,
while every private had his own smaller collection. The total numbers
of soldiers, porters, women, slaves and children which Lugard had
somehow to get across hundreds of miles of wild country, rivers, hills
and swamps, was nearly 9,000. Walking in single file; spaced, when
there was no straggling, at about nine feet apart; it can easily be calculated how many miles the caravan covered. Add to the picture
that large numbers of the " wives " and slaves were naked women,
dressed only with a bunch of leaves fore and aft, that they were trying
to bring with them not only their toddlers, babies and emaciated slaves,
but loads of food and even their heavy grindstones; that many were
sick or starving, while before long small-pox broke out. Lugard's
civilized sense both of order and humanity was stretched to breaking
point by his vain attempt to contain this vast procession of unregulated human appetite and misery. He did what little he could to

restrain the effects upon the countryside of these hungry hordes and, to ease his conscience, led them as far as possible through Banyoro country, though even here he tried to prevent personal violence, enslavement or the destruction of huts. He sent picked men of his own to the rear to collect the exhausted or abandoned children, of whom a dozen or more might be picked up in a day, though some had been thrown aside to drown in the black swamps. His two Europeans and each responsible man in the force were soon saddled with a nursery of little deserted children to keep warm and nourished at night and to guard on the march and Lugard had his own collection. Over rivers Lugard himself, ever conscious of the need of setting an example, might stand up to his waist for hours in cold water with his men, helping to pass stupid and frightened women and children across extempore bridges of felled trees.

There were times when, standing upon some high point and watching the endless file of humanity snaking after him for miles, his conscience wounded him not only with the thought of their misery but of what he was bringing upon the country. With every mile he had realized more and more the terrible cruelty of the Sudanese, with their long ingrained habits of robbing and enslaving by the power of the gun. The women, nearly all from the equatorial tribes, struck Lugard as even more callous than the men. It was a strange experience to look at that great mass of his species and to know that, apart from the three white men, there was in all probability not one among them who had any sense of pity even for their own people and that, though Lugard could force his men, when in his sight, to go through the motions of helping and protecting the weak, they had no glimmering of the meaning of what they did. There were moments when he regretted bringing this "horde of locusts" upon the country. But he realized, as domestic humanitarians have not always done, that refusal to act may be more merciless than action. "There are strange dilemmas in Africa" he thought "of which our critics have no conception!" From one point of view these Sudanese were a brave and loyal body of men; from another "they are as villainous a lot of slave catchers as one could find." Yet there they had been, in territory now presumably in the British sphere, out of sight and out of mind, suffering, deteriorating and preying destructively upon a vast area. Lugard had brought them out, and was in process of harnessing the force they represented

281

to what he believed to be humane and progressive ends. And already he had in some measure restrained looting, imposed discipline, stopped slaving and the killing or ill-treatment of any enemies captured on the way, or the overloading of children and slaves.

Selim, though Lugard had been forced to lecture him most severely, since he had himself been catching young girls and driving them in slave-sticks, was ready to admit that his men had got out of hand and that Lugard's ways of order, justice and kindness were the best, and also that he owed Lugard the deepest gratitude for bringing him out of Equatoria. In so far as there were still cruelties or irregularities, the responsibility, Lugard considered, rested on those who acted on " the principle of expecting one European—and that not always the right man—to do the work of twenty, and of leaving all these vast countries without adequate supervision and administration . . . . "[1] After all, he thought, Gordon, the darling of the British public, had used just such men and such methods on a much larger scale in the southern Sudan. It is certainly interesting to record that Lugard's men who had been with Stanley reported that *his* methods had been very different. Stanley, so they said, would fall in the men, issue so many rounds to each and say " now go off and loot! " Lugard believed enough of what he was told to accept " some startling and ugly facts . . . . re that celebrated and heroic chief." It may now be apparent that Lugard's ceaseless collection and hoarding of food reserves was not something to smile at: it represented the livelihood, and perhaps the lives, of innocent tribesmen, who were thus saved from the casual looting by hungry and ruthless Sudanese soldiers or Swahili porters.

We cannot follow the crowded incidents of this painful exodus by which Lugard led his 9,000 for some 600 miles into the heart of the Company's territory. Both Grant and the doctor were ill—Grant was a mere shadow, and had to be carried—and Lugard had neither medicines nor any European food or comforts left for them. He himself had fever but managed, with his great strength of body and will, to remain in ceaseless and active control. To a man so well-read in the Bible, the obvious analogy must often have been in his mind. But if he were a new Moses, he must have felt that he had to struggle on without the visible help of God, or even of an Aaron, to support

[1] Lugard II, p. 236.

him; his Joshua was far away in Kampala; he had to impose his ten commandments by the single force of his own will; he had no provision of manna; there were no wealthy Egyptians to despoil, nor was he able to kill off the surplus of his own stiffnecked people.

He led the caravan in a south-westerly direction and at chosen points he established stockaded posts, which he called forts, and detailed the most responsible Sudanese officers he could find with a party of soldiers and their dependants to hold the posts against the Banyoro. The local chiefs were at every point called in, blood-brotherhood made, their authority recognized, and their right established of appeal to him against oppressive conduct by the Sudanese. To these the strongest orders and warnings were issued through Selim. After Forts Edward and George, already established, came the most northerly, Wavertree, called after Sir John Kirk's home, and to the south one which young de Winton later called Fort Lorne. At each of these Lugard relieved himself of some 2,000 Sudanese soldiers and dependants. He had to get the remaining thousands across a bridge of trees down steep banks and over the raging torrent of the Mpanga river, acting policeman single-handed to control entry on to the frail structure and to save the weak being trampled or jostled into the river by the strong.

Across the Mpanga, Lugard established a third fort at Kivari, again on the edge of Banyoro country. The neighbouring Toro people came out to ask him whether this new British power had come to stay. They told him that up at Mruli in the north, where the local people had submitted to the Sudanese and these had been withdrawn, Kabarega had taken vengeance upon them in wholesale massacre. Had the British really come to stay or would they, too, desert them and leave them to death or slavery? Lugard's answer should be remembered: it had meaning for the future. " I replied—how could I do otherwise?—that these countries were ceded to the British by the nations of Europe, and that the British flag never went back."[1]

Leaving the greater number of his charges to rest round the new forts, Lugard, suffering from heavy fever, accompanied by Selim and a picked 900 men, marched westwards round Lake George to revisit Fort Edward. Here he found Fenwick de Winton awaiting him, sent by Williams with fifty-six of the best remaining men of

---

[1] Lugard II, pp. 249-50.

his own small and inferior force, a subtraction so generous as to have left his own position dangerously weak.

Williams' blunt, soldierly letters, which Lugard eagerly opened, were eloquent of his unselfishness and his resolute way of handling the impossible state of affairs at the capital. A few phrases from his letters will reveal the man and the situation.

June 16th. " . . . The men here are a sad lot of cripples and after the men leave for you there will be few sound men left . . . I have sent you nearly all the food-purchasing cloth and I am hard put to it to keep the posho going . . . I am awfully sick that I can't come on with you . . . "

September 12th. " . . . We nearly had an outbreak, but I hustled about the streets with a black or two and stopped an actual fight . . . a protestant chief had turned catholic and the Katikiro wanted to turn him out . . . Meanwhile French Bishop had been urging me to have religious freedom, claiming it as a right . . . The Kabaka's drummer beat his war drum in the night and the fat was in the fire. I patrolled Mengo with 3 men for about 4 days . . . I got a resolution from the mission [C.M.S.] to say my·conduct was everything bad, all about the freedom of religion, which I treated as childish nonsense . . . I have divided the Sese islands . . . agreeably to protestant ideas . . . The Germans were awfully civil and want to catch Emin . . . There isn't a bit of quinine in Kampala . . . You need have no anxiety about Uganda. I will keep it, as I said at first, pretty quiet . . . You will, I hope, learn from this scrawl that I have had no bed of roses here . . . but this is a big job and we must all do our part, however disagreeable."

These were letters—there was much more in them than this—to reassure Lugard. In Williams he had a real man to hold the position at Mengo. Yet, to a leader of Lugard's temperament, it was still not easy for him to accept a subordinate as strong as himself. Was Williams, he wondered, not going beyond his brief in settling policy? Was he not, in this matter of "religious freedom", favouring the Fransa as against the Ingleza? In his diary Lugard characterizes Williams' picture of affairs in Mengo as neither wholly good nor wholly bad. In his book, written later when on the defensive, he claimed that the affairs of the kingdom, which had promised peacefully when he left, were described by Williams "in a way which reassured me greatly."

He left de Winton behind in charge of Toro with written instructions, which are faintly prophetic of indirect rule, to work through Kasagama. De Winton's task was all but impossible as he was not allowed in his instructions to give direct orders to the turbulent Sudanese, but must report to Lugard—who would be at Kampala![1] Lugard marched back to Kivari on November 23rd and found more news from Williams. Sir Francis de Winton had gone home—he did not know the full story of discord and resignation[2]—and Mackenzie had come out again to take his place; a Company official and fifty of his men had been massacred on the way up from Mombasa to Uganda by the Sotik tribe. His brother had been wounded and nearly murdered in the Manipur disaster in India. (" Thank God for his escape, the boy is about the dearest thing in the world to me.")

Lugard's adventures were not quite over. One more is worth recording. He had to recross the formidable Mpanga river where it entered Lake George. He was torn between admiration and dismay at the sight of this glorious and apparently impassable obstacle. The river " here flowed in a rocky gorge, some 700 or 800 feet deep, whose precipitous banks were clothed with the densest forest. Here the mists and vapours hung, and the trees dripped with continual moisture. Every class of fern—from the tree-ferns to the moss-ferns—was to be found beneath the moisture-laden trees, whose limbs were clothed with them, and with mosses and long-bearded lichens and orchids. The flowers familiar in our hot-houses grew in these perpetual shades and gorgeous butterflies glanced like meteors through the forest twilight. Below foamed and eddied a seething torrent of water, confined between its rocky walls. No trees grew on its banks which could reach more than a quarter of the way across. I sat down on a rock to think the matter out. Nothing has stopped us hitherto from the coast till now. . . . Behind me were a mass of over 3,000 souls in a foodless country. . . ."[3] He solved the problem and succeeded in getting all his following safely over, including their sheep and goats.

Planting two more forts—one called after the faithful Grant—to guard Toro against Bunyoro, and confirming the King of Ankole in his duty to stop the traffic of slaves and guns through his territory,

[1] See Ashe, *Chronicles of Uganda*, pp. 187–8, for his comment upon this.
[2] Some evidence of this is given in letters from Kemball to Mackinnon, 1 and 11 January 1891, M.P.
[3] Lugard II, pp. 260–1.

Lugard marched on with his much diminished forces across the almost foodless country of the pastoral Banyankole. In mid-December he reached Buddu where he was welcomed by its rugged Protestant chief, the Pokino, and the C.M.S. representative, Mr. Walker, whom he greatly admired and who was now the only experienced Anglican missionary in Uganda. Again he was boycotted by the Fransa villages and received with joy and gifts of food by the Ingleza. Before going on he detached one of his most trusted Sudanese, Ferag, and 150 men to hold a position on the shores of Lake Victoria at the Luwambu narrows where he hoped to develop an embryonic port.

As he turned northwards and neared Kampala he reviewed those results of his western march, which constituted its justification. He had crossed the Nile to enter Uganda almost exactly a year before. Having spent the first six months coming to terms with the King, trying to settle the feud between the Christian factions and going to war with the Muslims, he had spent the second six months upon the western expedition. In the course of this his achievements could, he thought, be listed as follows:

(1) He had secured for the Company, as far as one man could in a preliminary march, the vast regions to the west of Buganda up to the borders of the Belgian sphere.

(2) He had opened up a route for communication and trade across Ankole to the valuable salt lake and the ivory producing area of Toro, and had closed, as far as he could, the destructive traffic in arms from the south to Kabarega.

(3) He had pushed the hostile Banyoro out of Toro, reinstated its ruler and built and garrisoned seven forts to hold back the enemy and protect Toro and Ankole.

(4) He had brought down the Sudanese who in their isolation were at once a menace to the country and also a potential danger to himself, and, after using them to garrison his forts, was able to return to Kampala with an extra hundred good fighting men.

(5) He could congratulate himself that this march of 732 miles had cost the Company nothing as he had paid his way with ivory and salt, had hardly fired any ammunition, and had suffered hardly a single casualty.

Thus, as Lugard set out upon the last lap of his return journey to Kampala, he felt proud of what he had done, and confident of what he could do, for the Company and for its territory. He had received, on the whole, reassuring news from Williams about the situation in Buganda. He calculated that his hardly-expected return, not only alive but successful from this long march, would enhance his authority with the Baganda. This was his state of mind when, on Christmas Day, as he drew near to Kampala, weary, sodden with rain, dressed in rags, with thorns piercing his worn-out boots, he was met by a messenger from Williams bringing him mail from England. In this he found letters written a year ago: letters from his old fellow-campaigners in Nyasaland; letters from his brother Ned in India. But there was also a letter from the directors of the Company in London. It ordered him to evacuate Uganda immediately and to withdraw to the coast.

CHAPTER XV

CIVIL WAR

December 1891-January 1892 : Aet. 33-34

WE HAVE reached a month in Lugard's life when every action he took was given a special significance, firstly because of its bearing upon the future of Buganda and secondly because his conduct became an international issue between France and Britain and a subject of vigorous debate in Britain itself. But in describing the events of January 1892 it will probably be clearer to give a straightforward account based in the main upon his own and Williams' evidence and to take up later the chief points where his accuracy or his conduct was later questioned.[1]

This was Lugard's entry in his diary when he had read the Company's letter ordering immediate evacuation. " This was a thunderbolt indeed. It is the second time now that a long spell of *very* hard work in Africa has been ended by a reverse so complete that all my toil has seemed to be merely waste—and worse. *This* collapse will be *terrible* in its results." (Diary, 25 December 1891). One by one the possibilities —no, certainties—that must follow evacuation passed before his mind

1 The events described in this chapter are based, in addition to those listed on pp. 210–11, on the following primary sources: Lugard's private diary; the official reports in the Blue Book, *Further Papers relating to Uganda.* Africa No. 2 (1893), C.6848, especially pp. 30–52; letters from and to the missionaries, the Company, etc. in the Lugard Papers; and Lugard II, pp. 286–360. Further evidence is contained in the writings of the C.M.S. missionaries, R. P. Ashe, *Chronicles of Uganda* (1894) and C. F. Harford Battersby, *Pilkington of Uganda* (1898). The Roman Catholic version is presented in a publication of the Catholic Union of Great Britain, *Notes on Uganda, or an analysis of the various reports etc. issued on the late war between the I.B.E.A. Co. and the Catholics of that British Dependency* (London 1893), referred to as *Notes on Uganda*; Père J. M., *L'Ouganda, La Mission Catholique et les Agents de la Compagnie Anglaise* (Paris 1893); and G. Leblond, *Le Père Auguste Achte* (Maison-Carrée, Alger 1912). The official Company account is in P. L. McDermott, *British East Africa or IBEA*, 2nd edition (1895).

The material used later for chapters 18 and 19 has of course retrospective value.

Lugard borrowed so heavily from his diary for his book (Lugard II) that much of the two is identical. I have continued, however, to work mostly from the diary as this is fuller and contemporary, but have sometimes used the book. In order to avoid a large mass of footnotes in this section I have not, except for quotations of special importance, entered all the many references to these two sources.

as he sat alone in his tent awake right through the night. The Ingleza party would leave Uganda as they had long threatened to do. The C.M.S. missionaries would be bound to follow them and their work would be ended. The Muslims would swoop down, as they had before, upon the remaining Christian party, who would probably flee to the Sese islands. The solemn assurance he had given Kasagama and his subjects would be falsified almost as soon as spoken and a frightful vengeance from Kabarega would fall upon them for joining the British. The blow to British prestige from this retreat would never be recovered. He might have added that the Sudanese he had planted all over the country would now be able to indulge in their plundering habits without any control.

He turned to the letter again and read it more carefully. Signed by the secretary, McDermott, and dated August 10th 1891 in London, the evacuation order lies before the writer, covering only a sheet and a half of paper, of purple typescript, smudged by the tropics. It made the following points:

(1) "The Court of Directors" have decided "to retire temporarily from Uganda and restrict their operations for the present to the coast . . . . " Lugard was accordingly ordered " to make arrangements with all practicable despatch to withdraw your establishments from Uganda and the lake districts and return to Mombasa."

(2) Though the evacuation was to be made " without avoidable loss of time ", the manner of it and the exact timing was left to his discretion. No word was to be said about it, until he had secured from the King an extension of the treaty for five or ten years or in perpetuity—a questionable instruction, to say the least. If Mwanga desired it, and any officer should volunteer, a British Resident might be left with him, all expenses for this being paid by the King! A gratuity of £1,000 to £2,000 might be paid, in return, to Mwanga.

(3) The Company would wish " to re-occupy the territory about to be evacuated as soon as the financial affairs of the Company permit of their doing so."

(4) It was suggested that Lugard might consider setting up a joint council of delegates from both missionary communities to help to re-establish some day the authority of the Company, but no pecuniary liabilities of any kind must be undertaken for this purpose.

With the official letter had come a personal one from George

Mackenzie. This explained that the Company was in serious financial difficulties. There was a crisis in the city and no one would invest in the Company. The government had allowed the railway project, which might have saved the situation, to be shelved.[1] Uganda was costing £40,000 a year, and bringing in no return. The Company would fall back to the coast with Lugard's station at Dagoretti as its most advanced post. He could bring the missionaries away, if they wished to come: they had gone there before the Company which repudiated any responsibility for them. No blame attached to him whose good work was strongly and widely appreciated.

Looking again at the official instructions, there was not a proposal here, Lugard thought, that would not have been laughable if it had not been so charged with disaster. Resume again—after broken faith and ensuing anarchy! Find a volunteer to carry on in dependence upon Mwanga's bounty! " Would you find a volunteer to go and hang himself? " He could hardly credit the order. " Well, if it is to be done, there is a cruel, cruel wrong to be done. Hundreds—nay, *thousands*—of lives may be sacrificed and the blood must lie at some-one's door . . . . I would accept the responsibility of *not* obeying orders willingly and making a representation first, but I am told that everything, position of missions, everything, has already been con-sidered and the decision is final; the Company *can't* keep up the expense of Uganda. Does it lie with me in such a terrible pass to abandon everything connected with self, and give my life to save these poeple? This is the question I ask myself and I dare hardly reply to it . . . . Am I to plunge into war again when my whole soul yearns for peace and quiet? Am I to *more* than risk my commission? It is a terrible sacrifice. God help me to decide aright! " (Diary, 25 December 1891).

Carrying this crushing secret in his mind and there turning it over and over, he went on towards Kampala. The going was slow: the Sudanese, and especially the women and children, were tired out; the rain poured down; there were swamps to cross. And he had fifty letters and scores of newspapers to read. There was a copy of a very firm letter from Bishop Tucker, then in England, to Sir Thomas Fowell Buxton, in which he declared that the arrival of the Company, with the strong support of the Anglican party, had compromised the position of the latter, which would now be left in great danger.

[1] See below pp. 388–92.

The missionaries could not desert their converts. If, as was probable, they were killed, the responsibility would lie with the Company and with the government which had authorized its activity within Britain's sphere of influence. But the British side of the story will best be told when Lugard returned to England to take part in it. The record of this chapter is of events in Buganda.

Lugard had made up his mind to reach Kampala before the year ended but, with his weary and sodden caravan, he only just managed it. He marched in on December 31st. The Baganda, though not the most strict of African tribes, were scandalized by the nakedness of the long procession Lugard led in. He himself was in rags with broken boots—for such an extensive trekker he seems to have been culpably careless about the provision of footwear—and many of the Sudanese women were naked but for their bunches of leaves. Lugard remembered that when Speke had discovered Karagwe, the king had informed him that his donkey, a creature not seen before, would be objected to as indecent unless he made a pair of trousers for it. True, Lugard himself was escorted into Kampala by masses of Baganda, singing and playing on their varied musical instruments, but he observed gloomily that this jubilation was confined to the Ingleza.

Up the low hill, through the splendid food gardens Williams had now made, into the fort, and at last he was with his second-in-command and could share with him his devastating secret. Under the blow Williams rang true to the fine type he was. "Like myself, he heard the news with utter consternation, and exclaimed that it simply could not be done. He said he would be ashamed to hold up his head in any society of gentlemen if he were involved in so gross a breach of faith." What did Lugard intend to do? Lugard replied that he could not keep their men without payment and he had no money of his own with which to pay them. But Williams had a little money, and he now declared that he would use up every penny he had in the world "sooner than consent to break faith by leaving the country after our pledges of protection." He possessed only £4,000 but he was ready to give it all. Quickly Lugard decided to accept Williams' "grand offer": he would stay and try to hold on while Williams went home "to make a buzz", as he called it, in England and appeal for money. They decided it would be better to hand the country over to Germany *before* they walked out rather than leave it to be taken over by

Germany or some other power *after* the land had flowed with blood. "Such was the upshot of our conference and that is the kind of man which my colleague, Captain Williams, R.A., was!"[1]

Lugard now set himself, with Williams' help, to assess the situation as it had developed in his absence. It certainly appeared as though Williams' letters to Lugard, written by a courageous man anxious not to worry a chief who was himself upon a dangerous mission, had been over-optimistic.

After the defeat of the Muslims in the spring, the White Fathers had launched a great evangelizing campaign. "The fight with the Musselmans was hardly over before it became needful to begin another and far more arduous battle with the Protestants", wrote one of the priests.[2] It was determined to make the Baganda themselves embark upon a well organized crusade in Buddu, where the rivalry was very bitter. The priest would "excite in the hearts of all the Catholic chiefs the sacred fire of zeal which makes an apostle". Even "the crowd of those who pray" were every day "invited to take part in the crusade against heresy". The Father goes on to describe approvingly how one of their young converts, deliberately taking service with an Ingleza chief for the purpose, had secretly "instructed" his household and had brought forty slaves and followers to the writer. The meaning of this in a country where, for most of the people, the religious names merely meant political factions, and that in an African kingdom on the brink of civil war, may easily be appreciated.

Thus the main trouble had been over the question of so-called religious freedom. Upon this Williams had been inclined to accept the view of the Roman Catholic priests who saw in the freezing of the *status quo* the one obstacle to that rapid increase of their adherents which their influence over the King seemed to promise. Williams had, therefore, violently offended the opposite party who stood upon the letter of the stand-still agreement. Some very sharp things had been written by the Anglican missionaries to Williams reproaching him about this and about the delay in dividing Sese, asserting that the Company was dependent upon their support. They also wrote letters to England accusing Williams of ruling Uganda through the French priests, and asserted that he "cares nothing for religion one way or

[1] Lugard II, pp. 291-3.
[2] Père Streicher in *Notes on Uganda*, p. 122 ff.

another ", and spoke of the necessity of having a Christian man in charge.[1] Monsignor Hirth, for his part, had written a letter to Williams which in Lugard's view suggested that the Company should cease to try to protect the Ingleza party and should co-operate with the Fransa, since the existence of two parties must lead to war. He said " the history of all the Missions established during this century prove to me that in all heathen countries where Protestants were to be found in opposition to Catholics the former have never triumphed except through *violence*."[2] (14 July 1891).

In Williams' report to Lugard, the violence which then followed was due to Fransa not Ingleza aggression.[3] There were a number of attacks upon the Ingleza, notably in what were, considering the all-important matter of communications, the key provinces of Buddu to the south-west and Kyagwe to the east. Communications by lake were equally important. The Ingleza chief who was the Gabunga, or " Admiral " in charge of the canoes, had been driven out earlier and reinstated by Williams. The Fransa attacked one of the Ingleza islands. Moreover, the day after the French Bishop wrote his letter, the King, in defiance of Williams' orders, suddenly ran up a huge flag of his own as a way of publicly dissociating himself from the Company's flag.

This was all gloomy enough news. On the credit side, the Ingleza, though greatly outnumbered, had, by their spirited resistance, saved themselves from being overwhelmed. Williams had managed to keep Stokes in order and had taken over a large stock of his dangerous goods to store at the fort. And just before Lugard returned, another large caravan under Martin had arrived from the coast with a substantial supply of arms in time to save the situation in Kyagwe. The French Bishop's own remarks threw some light upon the situation. Referring to the incidents which led to disorder, he wrote on December 27th that in these local conflicts " thanks to their audacity the heretics are generally victorious but it is clear that a general conflict will sooner or later break out."[4]

A few days after this, on the eve of Lugard's return, something of importance took place at Mengo. Accounts given by Williams, Ashe, Pilkington, Leblond and the Catholic Union are contradictory and it.

[1] Walker to T. W., 29 September 1891, C.M.S. Papers (Unofficial Papers).
[2] This letter is given in full in Lugard II, Appendix 11, pp. 660–2.
[3] C.6848 (1893), pp. 26–9.
[4] Leblond, *Auguste Achte*, pp. 156–7.

is therefore extremely difficult to piece together any authoritative story. It appears, however, that there was something like a reassertion of paganism led by a group at court of which no party had any good to say, called the *futabangi*, or bhang-smokers. They were also causing trouble in Kyagwe, where it is said they were weary of the strife and the claims of the two Christian parties. It is possible that this group at court, which encouraged the King's vices, made a bid for his support. The Fransa party seems to have reacted strongly, to have threatened the King to replace him by a young nephew then being brought up by the French mission in Usukuma, and finally to have murdered some of Mwanga's pagan boys.

Mwanga, according to one account, was also influenced by the arrival of the Company caravan, thinking that the Ingleza party had as a result become more powerful than the Fransa.[1] He therefore sent word to the Anglican missionaries that he wanted to join their church. They appear to have behaved very properly in face of what might have been a great temptation. To a message from Mwanga that he wanted to turn Protestant, G. L. Pilkington, in a letter written to the C.M.S. on December 27th and 28th, replied that " in so far as the matter was a political one, it was none of our business." Mwanga should consult Williams. " The King's proposal comes, I suppose, only from political motives. Really we have not much to do with it." The next day, Pilkington went to see Mwanga alone and gave him the uncongenial information " that his soul was of no more value in our sight or in God's than the meanest of his subjects, and that we wanted real, not nominal Protestants . . . . I finally told him to do what he believed God wished him to do."[2] It may be noted that letters written privately at the time and in ignorance of all the public controversy which was to follow have a special value in the record.

The wretched King then turned to Williams, who prided himself upon having won a personal influence over him, and declared his wish to become a Protestant and come over to the Ingleza side. Williams, who was interested only in getting the King's political co-operation, not in his religion though, of course, the two almost inevitably went together, advised that such a serious step should not

[1] Letter from the Rev. G. K. Baskerville, 31 January 1892, *Church Missionary Intelligencer*, vol. XLIII, September 1892, p. 672.

[2] *Ibid.* pp. 670–1.

be taken hurriedly. But if the King was ready to make an agreement with the Company, Williams was prepared, among other terms, to allow him to draw a small number of the guns brought by Martin, which were so eagerly coveted by him. The Fransa chiefs however (according to Williams and Ashe), outbid the other side by offering Mwanga a large amount of ivory while his sister, a Roman Catholic convert, pleaded with him. While the King wavered, so Père Leblond writes, " For three days, at Rubaga " (the priests' headquarters) " there was deep anxiety and prayer upon prayer was addressed to Heaven."[1]

Whatever the reason, the vacillating Mwanga was won back to the Fransa party. Not only that: he actually agreed to go publicly to mass on January 1st, the very day of Lugard's return. " The King comes to mass " wrote the priests in their diary. " The leaders compete among themselves for the honour of carrying him on their shoulders . . . . this is a veritable triumph." On January 4th the entry ran: " Mwanga comes up to Rubaga. The number of catechumens who are coming to catechism has nearly doubled. We have 4,000 to 5,000 people on weekdays."[2]

The picture is obscure but it does light up the dangers and difficulties of the parties, forced to revolve round the cornered King, the prey both of his misfortunes and his weaknesses.

This was the situation which Lugard found upon his return as the new year opened. He himself was more than usually busy. He had his report on his expedition to write; a strong private letter to compose pointing out to the Company the terrible results evacuation would bring to Uganda; his maps and diary to make up; and 140 letters to answer. All these had to catch up Martin's caravan which had already started back to Mombasa. He had to send off a party of some 400 Egyptians and Sudanese who had chosen to go back to Egypt; and Selim and the new Sudanese had to be housed and integrated with the rest of his force. Important as all his writing was, Lugard was perhaps showing a tendency, which was to grow, to give too much time, even when that element was limited and danger threatened, to his activities with the pen. His doing so certainly shows that he did not

---

[1] Leblond, *op. cit.* p. 158. In the bitter spirit which characterizes so much of the missionary writing of the time, the Father writes of Williams rejoicing prematurely in the success of his " perfidious machinations ".

[2] *Ibid.* p. 158.

expect that the catastrophe that had always been just round the corner ever since he first came to Kampala was this time really going to come.

Williams still hoped the King could be won over and he went three nights running to have serious private talks with him. This angered and alarmed the Fransa leaders round the court and they beat the war drums in protest. An army of both Fransa and Ingleza had gone out to ward off a Muslim attack: from this the Fransa returned almost at once, leaving the Ingleza in the field. Another joint army was ready to go to Kyagwe against the *futabangi* under a Fransa chief greatly respected by Lugard, the Sekibobo, Alikesi Sebowa: here, too, the Ingleza portion went off and the Fransa did not start. By these defections, the Ingleza were seriously weakened in the capital. Lugard made a personal appeal to the Sekibobo and at last he went, leaving his favourite child, Malia, a little girl of four or five, in the care of Lugard who was very fond of her.

Lugard thought he could breathe again. But he now found himself assailed upon both sides by the two groups of missionaries, each accusing Williams of the grossest partiality towards the other side during Lugard's absence. Williams' talks with the King led to no result, even though Lugard dropped all reference to the flag because it seemed to frighten Mwanga more than any other topic. In all his actions Lugard felt crippled by his secret knowledge of the evacuation policy, which he had been forbidden to disclose. He suspected that the growing intransigeance of the Fransa party was due to knowledge of this secret having somehow got into their possession, especially when a new party of priests arrived from Europe via the German sphere on January 7th. It was upon this date that a telegram came through to Lugard to tell him that through private liberality, in fact through a great C.M.S. appeal, the Company were enabled to postpone evacuation for one year, until December 31st 1892. (How this development occurred will be seen presently when we consider the British side of the story.)[1] Unless quite unforeseen circumstances should intervene, the evacuation would irrevocably take place on that day and the continuance of the Company in Buganda even for the twelve months would be possible only if the very strictest economy were practised. "I handed the telegram to Williams", Lugard writes, "and we shook hands over it like a couple of schoolboys."

[1] See below pp. 395-6.

The relief from immediate tension was great. But the reprieve was temporary and conditional and Lugard felt that he must take a firmer grip upon the affairs of the country and try to make the Baganda face and solve their own problems. Unfortunately, he could no longer persuade the opposing chiefs to visit him together: they came separately up to the fort and it is extremely doubtful, as the gulf widened further, whether more than a very few of the most thoughtful Christians could grasp his reiterated teaching about the need for an impartial state and freedom of religion. But he was not to be allowed the time necessary to try out the use of reason. On January 22nd a Fransa sub-chief named Mongolobo murdered an Ingleza man. He had had his rifle stolen by an Ingleza and as, in his view, the Katikiro, to whom he rightly appealed, delayed justice, he arranged to compensate himself by seizing some other Ingleza's gun. This he did by getting one of his men to sell beer by the roadside and, when a passing Ingleza stopped to drink, one of them snatched his gun and ran into the neighbouring compound of the sub-chief. The aggrieved party naturally chased him and Mongolobo shot him dead as he entered the compound.

Lugard realized that in the existing tension this killing might lead to riots and riots to general war. It was therefore in the spirit of his European tradition of imposing martial law that he walked over to Mengo to demand swift and exemplary punishment. The Mujasi had always hated him but now even his former friends, the Kimbugwe and the Kauta, met him with frivolous and contradictory excuses about the King being unable to see him, and only after he had been treated, for the first time, with studied discourtesy and kept waiting outside, did Mwanga at last appear. Lugard demanded that the perpetrator of the outrage should be executed at once: if there had been provocation those guilty of it would be flogged. There was much giggling and laughing between the King and his Fransa chiefs and Lugard, not only angry but exhausted by being kept out in the fierce sun, went away and left Dualla to report. The Somali followed later to say that Mongolobo had been brought up and had been acquitted, in spite of Dualla's protests, on the grounds that the murdered man had followed him into his enclosure: Buganda law allowed self-defence in these circumstances.[1]

January 23rd was a day of strain. Lugard wrote to Hirth begging

[1] Dualla's account of the " trial " is printed in C.6848 (1893), pp. 99–102.

him to come over and see him so that together they might try to retrieve the dangerous situation. " Can you, Monsignor, use your influence to save so terrible a blow to the country as must be produced by war—a war which we have now with the utmost difficulty succeeded in averting for over a year? "[1] It was no prejudice against the Roman religion, but the desire for justice that had moved him over this last incident. Finally he begged him, if war should break out, that he and all the Reverend Fathers should come over to the fort and stay with him. The French Bishop refused to come to see him, referring to the insecurity of the roads, his Sunday duties and also, with surprising pettiness, to Lugard's not having seen him when he called, which had been at a time when Lugard had been exhausted and unwell. He defended the King's decision in the case and warned Lugard not to support " the unjust pretentions of the Protestant party, who aim at the attainment of exclusive power in Uganda." Lugard's comment is that Hirth's letter of July 14th to Williams shows that his party had exactly the same ambition. Hirth's letter also contained the significant warning that the public opinion of the whole of Europe was following the struggle step by step and would judge the issue from their correspondence. The Protestants would never dare attack unless Lugard gave the word. " If, however, you think it proper to order the attack, will you be good enough to give us warning " so that they might seek safety.[2]

Lugard was deeply disappointed by this letter. Fearing that, if further insults were offered to himself he would have to take them up officially, he now sent Dualla to the King. The Somali came back to report that he had been treated with derision by the Fransa chiefs who said that if there were war they would capture Kampala and kill all the Europeans. Lugard was astonished at these open threats, the first of their kind, and putting them together with the attitude of the Bishop, believed that news of the evacuation had reached the French mission. Taking all the facts into account, together with the Fransa beating of the war drums, he came to the conclusion that a section at least of the Fransa had determined upon war.

It was upon this conclusion that he now based his actions. Although he knew that the fort could be defended against assault it could not,

[1] Lugard II, p. 332.
[2] *Notes on Uganda*, p. 147.

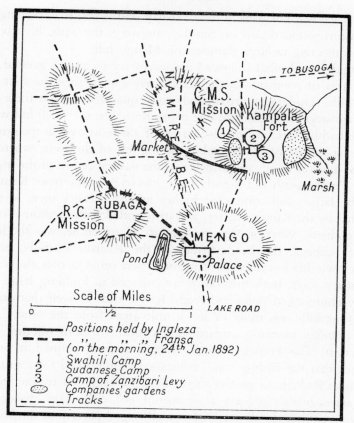

Mengo and Environs 1892. Based on a sketch map by
the Rev. R. H. Walker, published in F. D. Lugard,
The Rise of Our East African Empire, 1893

especially with its newly enlarged numbers and their many dependants,
stand out for long against a siege. In view, therefore, of the inferior
numbers and weapons of the only party which would side with the
fort, and considering that the strength of this party had been further
diminished by the dispatch of many of their armed men on military
duty in the provinces, he resolved to strengthen them by issuing forty
muzzle-loaders and a keg of powder. He did this on the night of the
22nd but spies instantly reported it with exaggeration to the Fransa
chiefs. He assumed that the immediate effect of this action was good

as the peace was not broken the next day. However, that evening the war drums sounded and on Sunday morning, the 24th, he saw the Fransa collecting in large numbers on Mengo hill.

To understand what followed it is necessary to have a general idea of the area of conflict. On the sketch map can be seen the four low green hills, standing, approximately, in a quadrilateral. Of these four hills, two stood to the north, one being Kampala, the small hill where Lugard had his fort, and three-quarters of a mile away was the summit of the larger hill of Namirembe, the highest of the four, where the C.M.S. mission stood, and which was the natural centre of the Ingleza party. To the south and slightly west, just over a mile from Kampala, was the larger and somewhat higher hill of Mengo, then, as now, crowned by the King's quarters and surrounded with the houses of the leading chiefs. West of Mengo, opposite Namirembe, was the lower hill of Rubaga, the headquarters of the Roman Catholic priests. Today two brick cathedrals confront each other across the valley. In January 1892, both missions were engaged in building large temporary churches of poles and reeds. It will thus be seen that each of these four hills was more or less a mile apart from the others.

On Sunday morning Lugard sent to both missions offering them protection. The French Fathers, Lugard reports, refused it on the grounds that the Bishop was "indisposed"; but asked for a guard to be sent to Rubaga to protect them. This was regarded by Lugard as a very unreasonable request as it would not only have divided his scanty forces but the dispatch of a small armed party into the heart of the Fransa stronghold might well have provoked a conflict. It is evidence of the bitterness between the missions that Ashe, who arrived shortly after the fighting, accuses the priests of hoping to embroil the Company with the Ingleza if the latter should attack this focal point when Company men were there.[1] The Anglican mission was not much more reasonable than the Roman. They said they would not leave their goods. As they were somewhat nearer than the priests, and divided from him by no hostile forces, Lugard sent over forty porters to bring them and their loads to the fort.

Believing that conflict was now almost unavoidable, Lugard issued 300 of Stokes' muzzle-loaders and 150 Sniders to the Ingleza. But he continued to send messengers to the King, trying to induce him to

[1] Ashe, *Chronicles of Uganda*, pp. 226–7.

keep the peace and deliver up the "murderer" and he was actually receiving reports promising success when a sudden outbreak of firing from, as he asserts, the Fransa side, at last precipitated the general conflict. Events now happened quickly. The main strength of the Fransa was on Mengo and they attempted to drive a wedge between the position of the Ingleza on Namirembe and the fort, while the Ingleza, on their side, rushed at Rubaga, which lay in front of them. Lugard saw Rubaga going up in flames just as the mass of the Fransa began to rush down Mengo hill. He had no intention of waiting to see if they meant to attack the fort. But he was aiming at a difficult target. The Fransa, as the left the top of the hill, were some 1,400 yards away. The only open space was on the road that ran past the fort and up the hill to Mengo. It was surrounded by dense banana groves which gave perfect cover and in which he could not tell where the Maxim was striking. Lugard gave the order to fire at the one bare spot. Williams' Maxim broke its rivet-pin at the first shot and was out of action. Lugard's jammed every half-dozen shots and sometimes fired only a single shot. But with a mixture of luck and skill he somehow kept it going for a few critical minutes. These minutes decided the action and may have decided the future of the country. For, using the gun at its most extreme range, Lugard got in amongst the Fransa force just where they were in the open. He estimates that very few were killed or wounded—the Kimbugwe and the Kauta received shots in the legs—but the next moment the whole mass had disappeared amongst the bananas. As with the Banyoro, those few shots at that, to them unprecedented, range, really settled the issue and allowed Lugard to claim that the Maxim had saved enormous bloodshed. Before the Fransa could recover, Lugard ordered Williams and a party of Sudanese and Zanzibaris, drawn up on the knee at the ready, to charge. This they did with immense speed and spirit, clearing the Mengo hill of Fransa. Williams caught up with them just in time to save the King's fine palace buildings of timber and reeds from complete destruction.

Acting under Lugard's orders, both Williams and Grant hurried from different directions to Rubaga. The Ingleza had fired all the inflammable thatched buildings and the church, but the Fathers were all unharmed in a brick building, their mud storehouse was safe and only their West African doctor, who appears to have joined in the fighting, had been killed. As the priests still refused to come to the fort, Lugard mounted a pony, which had been brought up by the last caravan, and galloped across himself, to implore them to come over for safety and consultation. " They were most courteous: standing among the blazing ruins of their houses and church, they offered me wine and said I had saved their lives and were greatly delighted that their storehouse had escaped the fire." Lugard mounted the Bishop on his pony and led all eleven priests across to Kampala. " I expressed my bitter sorrow at this day's work and indeed, I felt unmanned at the destruction in twelve hours of a year's hard work and at the devastation I saw around me."

It may be imagined that the fort now became, physically and socially, a very uncomfortable place. It was crammed with refugees and with the wounded of both sides being cared for by Dr. Macpherson and Dr. Gaskoin Wright of the C.M.S. The French Fathers insisted that the crowds of dependants they brought with them should all be accommodated inside the fort and Lugard and his officers had to turn out of their own private quarters and offices in favour of an unruly mass of African women and children. That night, however, in spite of the almost suffocating over-crowding, Lugard managed to have a talk with Bishop Hirth who suggested that the only solution would be to divide the country into two parts, a plan which at first seemed to Lugard too difficult of execution.

The next day Lugard did all he could to reassure the Fransa and to persuade the King, who had bolted to his usual retreat on the little island of Bulingugwe, only six and a half miles from Mengo, to come back. He realized that the dispersal of the Fransa and the burning of part of Mengo and Rubaga by the Ingleza was a barren victory, if such it could be called. The strength of the Fransa in the country as a whole was undiminished. Lugard was not strong enough to impose peace and war was likely to spread all over the country. To check it and restore order it was essential that the King should return. Mwanga, personally of dubious value, was still the most precious asset in the kingdom, the queen-bee, as Lugard put it, and as our own generation has lately had to learn again, without which the Buganda hive could not function. A leading Fransa chief was sent to Mwanga offering him, with the leading Fransa chiefs, an honourable reinstatement. The King replied that he was eager to return. The Bishop now said he wanted to go at once to the King at Bulingugwe. The Ingleza chiefs begged Lugard on no account to allow this. They said that if he went there would be no hope of peace. But Lugard was doubtful whether he could honourably detain the Bishop, who was his guest, against his will. He was, moreover, anxious about Bagge who was on the lake in a boat, unaware of danger. The Bishop made two promises. " He assured me again and again that he would do his utmost to bring back the King " and that he would see that no harm came to Bagge. " With his hand in mine at parting, he protested he would do his utmost to bring back the King." But as soon as he reached the island he sent back a message to say that he had not been able to transmit Lugard's message. This, in Lugard's view, was a grave breach of faith, one which the Roman Catholics seem to admit.[1] The Bishop also asked for the Fathers to be sent to him and said that all messages or letters to the King would only arrive safely if sent through them. It throws light on the complete lack of confidence prevailing between the two sides that Lugard could assume that this directive was given so that the Bishop could control and colour all his communications with the King. He also states that the Bishop did nothing to warn or assist Bagge. When the next day (January 28th) Lugard sent as a " neutral " Stokes' much respected Muslim headman, Mafutaa, to the island to take letters and to report, this man came back to say that the King and his chiefs were most eager to return but that the Bishop was preventing them. The Bishop did not even answer Lugard's letter.

The next night the Fransa took the offensive and attacked and burnt the village of an Ingleza chief on the lake-shore. Lugard therefore decided that the island must be attacked. His own reasons were that he wanted to reinstate Mwanga; that he had tried for six days to make peace; that the Fransa had renewed the fighting; that their forces were massing in Buddu to the south and in Kyagwe to the north, while there was always the possibility that the Muslims or the *futabangi* might join them. Lugard declared that in a state of war " as a soldier I should have been guilty of folly " if he had allowed a hostile force to concentrate close in his rear.

The little island of Bulingugwe lies just about half a mile from the lake-shore. It covers only some 200 acres but rises to the same

[1] Leblond, *Auguste Achte*, p. 167.

height as the hills at the capital. It is now deserted and covered by a dense mass of trees. Williams, whom Lugard sent to the island, was able to reach it easily from the shore with the Maxim while the heavy but wild firing of the Fransa did his men no damage. This incident was later called a massacre. Williams' official report estimated that considerably less than a hundred were killed but an unknown number were drowned on the other side of the hill out of sight and out of range in a panic rush for the canoes. All the Fathers were presumably on the far side as none was hurt and Williams again rescued them from the angry Ingleza and sent them back with the doctor to Kampala. They arrived rain-soaked and exhausted at the fort and Lugard did everything in his power to make them comfortable with his small space, poor equipment and scanty food. He treated them as honoured guests, taking their *parole d'honneur* that they would not again endanger themselves by leaving the fort while hostilities continued. He found them all "courteous, gentlemanly and polite." Unfortunately the Bishop managed to get away with the King in a canoe. Thus Lugard's main purpose had been defeated.

CHAPTER XVI

SETTLEMENT AND DEPARTURE

January-June 1892 : Aet. 34

THE MAXIM had fired twice, each time with locally decisive effect. But Lugard felt no elation. He had hated the necessity, so he stated, of intervening in the struggle and he was under no illusion that these two bursts of fire, and the few deaths and wounds they had inflicted, had opened the way to an immediate settlement. From Kampala, and its surrounding hills, momentarily cleared of the Fransa, he strained his imagination to look out over the country and measure the dangers and difficulties which faced him from every point of the compass. With no intelligence service, he had to live upon rumours or, worse, deliberately falsified news.

The Fransa, as if by a prepared plan, were moving *en masse* southwards down into Buddu while the Ingleza there were fleeing northwards, a confused and dangerous disentanglement which must take weeks or months to complete. Hirth and Mwanga went down to the frontier of Buddu and Hirth was soon reported to be at German Bukoba. Lugard thought the priests and their party had hopes that the Germans might support them, while arms were only too readily procurable in this region. The C.M.S. missionaries, Walker and Ashe, the latter newly returned to Uganda by the German route, were cut off at Masaka in Buddu; so were Ferag and his Sudanese nearby at Luwambu. Bagge was in danger; de Winton was isolated in Toro. The Muslims, still massed and well armed, were waiting to the north-west under the rival claimant to the throne, Mbogo, and had a perfect opportunity, with or without Kabarega, to swoop down and attack the divided Christians. The *bhang*-smokers were a menace in Kyagwe. Across the Nile, endangering the Mombasa route, there was unrest in Busoga. The rightful heir to the throne, since Mwanga had no son, was his nephew and he was being kept by French priests in German territory. Most of the Ingleza chiefs and their followers infuriated Lugard by their inactivity and arrogant claims and their concentration upon dividing the lands and offices of the Fransa chiefs instead of taking the necessary military measures.

During the next two months Lugard, with inadequate knowledge and strength, struggled patiently to manage, even if he could not master, a complicated situation, and, with good luck to reinforce good management, he at last succeeded in avoiding complete disaster. His Sudanese garrisons in the rear of the Baganda Muslims kept these potential enemies, or so he believed, from moving. Ashe and Walker managed to get safely to Namirembe. Ferag fought his way back to Kampala; a German boat picked up Bagge. Williams voyaged to the Sese islands, saving an Ingleza island from the Fransa and so keeping the southward route open. He thus showed the Company flag on the lake, got news and also made contacts at Bukoba with the Germans whose behaviour, in spite of rumours to the contrary and some mysterious actions, was more than correct. A new Company agent in Busoga, Mr. C. S. Reddie, managed to survive the unrest there. The Ingleza chief Mulondo defeated the great Fransa magnate, the Sekibobo, and warded him off Mengo.

Lugard worked doggedly to get back the King who alone, in the eyes of the Baganda, could give to his position the constitutional legitimacy which was being exploited by the French Bishop. It was difficult to get a message through to Mwanga, and protracted negotiations over long distances in a changing situation led to misunderstandings and charges of bad faith. Lugard had to endeavour, with the finesse and daring of a circus rider, to drive the three turbulent parties, controlling the Ingleza through their continued need, as a minority, of his help; playing the Muslims with offers of a favourable settlement, and curbing the Fransa with the threat of putting in a Muslim king if Mwanga were not soon produced. This last questionable expedient showed the true danger of his position. He had not realized the full weakness of the Ingleza until he saw their inability to make use of the opportunity he had helped to make for them. " They are a mere handful compared to the other side and they daren't face the others at all." If the Muslims should attack, the Ingleza, he believed, would never stand up to them. From his knowledge of the New Testament he drew worldly wisdom. " Thus the more I think of it the more the verse recurs to me that it is advisable to compound with the adversary quickly while one has the chance." (Diary, 3 February 1892).

Then, unexpectedly, the possibility of Mwanga's return came as a rift in the clouds. Lugard had carried on negotiations about partitioning the country through Père Achte, but it may have been Lugard's return to Mwanga of four of his wives, charged with verbal messages and full of stories of their good treatment, which at last reassured the King, who was probably becoming weary of exile. He sent the two great Fransa chiefs, the Kimbugwe and the Sekibobo, to Kampala. Both of these Lugard had regarded as friends and they now came to him with honourable and manly bearing. Lugard had practically adopted the Sekibobo's little daughter, Malia, who had been captured at Bulingugwe. He was devoted to her and it happened that, when the Sekibobo arrived unexpectedly, he found Lugard and the child having breakfast together. The two chiefs brought a letter from Hirth demanding half the country and warning Lugard that war would continue if this " justice " were not done.[1] The chiefs, however, were favourably impressed by Lugard and agreed to try to bring back the King and make peace. It is not clear what had led to this change of policy, since Lugard's weakness was quite apparent to the Fransa and their European advisers. The Sekibobo went back to Mwanga, who was on the frontier of Buddu, with the proposals for peace and an insistent message from Lugard that he must return before these could be agreed. According to Ashe, though he was not always a reliable informant, and to the account given later to Lugard by Mwanga, himself not always a pillar of verity, the King had been kept practically as a captive and managed to escape in a canoe from the French priests only by a stratagem[2].

On March 30th news suddenly came that the King was on the way. The scene should be described in words Lugard wrote the same evening in his diary. A messenger came to tell him that:

" The King was trembling with fear and said he was ready to be killed or made a prisoner and came to throw himself on my mercy.... Messenger after messenger came bringing salaams, and I sent Wadi Hamis down to take my salaams. Presently a huge vast crowd in the wildest

[1] Lugard II, pp. 409–10.
[2] Ibid. pp. 421 and 432–3; and Ashe, *Chronicles of Uganda*, pp. 309–12.

excitement appeared on the King's Hill, and surged down into the valley towards Kampala. I rode out to meet the King, and found him being carried on a man's shoulders. The great mass in front on meeting me turned round and followed me, and amid huzzas and great excitement the King and I shook hands over the heads of the crowd . . . . The crowd increasing each moment came on to Kampala, men clearing the road with vigorous blows for my horse and the King. From the main road up to Kampala Gate all available *askaris*, mostly Sudanese and Somalis, were drawn up on each side of the road and presented arms, while my buglers and drummers [executed] a prolonged flourish, and the drums, horns and bugles of the Waganda tried to rival their row. At the Gate I had stationed a guard to keep out the mob . . . . Mwanga in his dirty clothes, like a common peasant, travel-stained, unshaved, dishevelled, and looking utterly played out, was the shadow of his former, sleek self. Dismounting, I led him to the house by the hand; for the poor devil was by this time almost in a state of collapse what between fear, excitement, anxiety and fatigue. He limped painfully along. It was almost dark now. I presented him with somewhere near a bale of cloth and the musical box, saying I knew it was the custom of Uganda to give a guest a small present for welcome. He was immensely pleased, and really I think felt for once in his life *grateful*. He said he had come not knowing what dreadful fate to expect, and he found himself received like a truant child returned. People flocked in to salaam to him. The head Catholics who had come with him embraced the Protestants, and all was a scene of congratulation and joy. The Waganda seemed all bursting with delight. I told Mwanga I had wished him to come to Kampala before going to his own place, because I wanted all Uganda to see at once that we had come to an understanding and were friends . . . . Outside were the French priests and several of the English missionaries who all shook hands with the King." (Diary, 30 March 1892).

This public reception was followed by much private conference between the King and Lugard. The former was quite embarrassing in his declarations of gratitude for the forbearance and justice with which he had been treated and his promises to give Lugard his full confidence in future. Lugard, upon his side, repeated what he had so often said before, that the Company wished for the continuation of the monarchy and the peace of the country. They then entered into long discussions as to how this was to be attained and Lugard was impressed by the shrewdness and knowledge of the King when they began to plan a partition of the country between the rival factions. It seems, indeed, that at this time he revised the estimate at least of Mwanga's ability, which Williams had from the first rated more highly. Lugard tried to leave the whole decision to the King and the big chiefs, but the rift between the factions was still too great to allow of a harmonious agreement between them and all begged Lugard for his adjudication. He therefore drew up a solemn written treaty of peace between the parties which was accepted, after long and sometimes rather heated discussions.

By the terms of the new treaty, signed on April 5th 1892, the large and fertile province of Buddu was set aside for the Fransa. Here all armed men of the party who had fought against the British must reside. To Buddu were added two islands off its coast and a number of estates that would allow Fransa parties going to and from the capital to camp on their own land at night. Outside Buddu, the Fransa would have to register their arms, but there was nothing to prevent the extension of the Roman Catholic missions, with the Resident's permission, anywhere in Buganda. A note at the end declared that there was nothing prejudicial to the Roman Catholic religion in this agreement, which had been made at the express desire of the four leading Roman Catholic chiefs, who wished to have a separate portion of the country for their party and who preferred Buddu to any other province.[1] Yet, as soon as the document was signed, both parties bitterly assailed the division as unjust. The Roman Catholic Fathers argued that Buddu was inadequate while the Anglicans were indignant because Buddu gave their rivals control of what was still the main route out of the country, and of the way to Ankole and Toro; also contact with the German sphere, with all that that might imply.

This agreement between the two Christian parties, accompanied by an intricate re-allocation of titles and estates, did, however, open the way to a broader settlement of the country as a whole. Lugard worked out a new treaty between the Company and the King and the chiefs of both Christian parties which they all signed on April 11th 1892.[2] By this Mwanga confirmed the suzerainty of the Company over Buganda in return for protection, and undertook to fly the Company's flag, to enter into no treaty relations with or grant concessions to other Europeans without the Company's consent. The

---

[1] See Lugard II, pp. 427–9; also C.6848 (1893), pp. 98–9, for the text of the agreement.
[2] Lugard II, pp. 434–6 for full text of the treaty; also C.6848 (1893), pp. 96–7.

consent of the Company's Resident was to be obtained and his counsel taken before any war or other serious acts of state were undertaken, while the Company, upon its side, promised to uphold the power and honour of the King and the display of his court. There was to be absolute freedom of religion and freedom of trade to all comers. Europeans were to be under the jurisdiction of the Company and could not carry arms or obtain land without its consent. All arms were to be licensed; the slave-trade and slave-raiding were prohibited. The cost of the organization of the country and the upkeep of the garrisons was to be defrayed from the revenues of the country.

As Lugard signed this treaty, and as he drew up the last clause which laid down that, unless by mutual agreement, it was to be in perpetuity, he must have remembered—he can never for an hour have forgotten—that, officially, the term of the Company's power was numbered in months. His every action was dictated by his faith, indeed his determination, that this evacuation should never be carried out.

The agreement between the parties and the new treaty with the Company were solid gains but there was still much to do before Lugard could leave for Britain where he had decided to go in order to continue the struggle there. He still had a difficult hand to play, and had to lead from weakness. Williams was away: he had gone to settle Busoga after returning from Bukoba, where he had failed to get Mwanga's nephews away from the French mission. The other white men were frequently ill. Both the Christian parties ceaselessly assailed Lugard's settlement, his competence and his justice, and both sets of missionaries did not hesitate to tell him they were writing letters to blacken his reputation in Europe.

On the Anglican side, while Lugard respected Walker and Pilkington in spite of disagreements, he was almost always at odds with the headstrong and capricious, but in some ways able head of the C.M.S. mission, Ashe, whose book, its margins scrawled with Lugard's angry contradictions, lies on the writer's table. With his complaints, his attempts to control policy, and his nagging claims for compensation for property lost in the disorders, he was Lugard's most constant trial so that he wrote his incessant replies to him in a spirit of " weary despair "; accepting that with the C.M.S. there seemed no relationship possible but one of " understood antagonism."[1] Many of the Ingleza chiefs, encouraged in this way, challenged Lugard's attempt to be impartial and arrogantly reminded him of their power and of his dependence upon it. They now knew that money for the upkeep of the Company was being subscribed in Britain by supporters of the C.M.S. and they therefore assumed that he ought to rule in their interests. On one occasion the Katikiro actually brought him a letter to send to his directors asking them to replace Lugard by some truly " God-fearing man who would rule them well and bring peace to their country." Lugard read this on a day when he was feeling ill and exhausted and for once he was unable to control his anger. He called the Ingleza leaders to the fort and waved the letter in their faces.

" ' Is not this an insult? How dare you write such a letter—read it and tell me—every line is an insult, and this from *you, you* whom I have worked so hard for. *You* who now claim to have been through-out ready to die for me. You who want more than 5/7 of the country after *I* have won it, and saved you from extinction.' Poor devils they had not a word to say. The faithful Kagolo collapsed like a burst bladder, muttering ' This is the first I have heard of it. Let those who wrote it answer! ' " (Diary, 2 April 1892).

There was, however, some excuse for the attitude of the Ingleza chiefs, since Lugard had been obliged at times to lean on their support more heavily than his independent spirit liked to admit. But he was always straining to reach the position of impartiality which his dignity no less than his duty demanded and he now decisively declined to treat the Ingleza as a victorious ruling caste. In explaining this to Ashe, he began the definition of those views of colonial government which were to develop into his well-known system of indirect rule. He explained that " it was not British policy in the many countries I have lived in and seen to rule natives despotically when it was possible to rule them through their own chiefs and customs. Least of all here in Uganda where so elaborate a system of native administration existed ready to hand. But . . . . I meant *all* the chiefs, a fair representation of the population, not a small section (by far the smallest)." If now with the Fransa, Muslims and *futabangi* without a voice and the King

---

[1] Amongst the Anti-Slavery Society Papers are letters written to his family by Walker strongly condemning both Lugard and Williams, and stating that the missionaries were advising the leaders of their converts not to obey " the fort ". The C.M.S. papers throw further light upon the relationship between Lugard and the missionaries.

at least partially discredited, he had to act somewhat despotically, and also give the Ingleza the chief voice, this was only for the moment: in the final settlement *all* parties must have their proper voice in the government. (Diary, 20 April 1892). By May Lugard was able to tell himself that he was at last in control of the kingdom and no longer dependent upon one section of it. " I think (and *know*) that both the King and Protestants have learnt a lasting lesson and know that the power and the actual rule of the country is in my hands. . . . The Protestants learnt it in the recent trial of strength between us . . . . They have I think learnt . . . . that I will not for a moment recognize or tolerate the position they tried to take as rulers of Uganda and legislators for the Catholics or Mohammedans." (Diary, 8 May 1892).

If Lugard found the Anglican missionaries and the Ingleza party difficult, his relations with the other side were no better. He liked some of the Fathers very much: he could appreciate their culture and good manners even though he had to talk with them in Swahili or Latin. But he felt himself unable to rely upon them and above all was he distrustful of the Bishop, whom he regarded as an irreconcilable opponent, and in whose presence the other priests were " like dumb, driven cattle." " I believe him to have played for a big stake and a dangerous one and to have lost. I believe his influence to be thoroughly for bad, viz. for war . . . . Please God I shall play my cards honourably and straightforwardly no matter with what double-dealing he may respond. He has had the worst of the game so far and if he continues as before, probably he will lose it *in toto*." (Diary, 27 March 1892). Hirth had certainly lost the very considerable asset of the King. Mwanga, in the changed situation, began to gravitate towards the Ingleza, bringing over with him the pagan masses and the nominal or wavering Christians. He again raised the possibility of becoming an Anglican. But, as one of the Fathers now confessed, Mwanga would be small credit to any religion. Politically he was all that could be desired, friendly and co-operative towards Lugard and visiting the fort with inconvenient frequency.

So April went by with Lugard still confined in the fort by his work. This consisted of the endless round of interviews; the collecting of news and the dispatch of orders; looking after his own men; improving his quarters; enduring the complaints of the missionaries in the morning and asking them to dinner in the evening. " The Resident of

Two notes from Monsignor Hirth to Lugard, 24th January, 1892

Uganda " he complained " is a mere slave, and penal servitude without anxiety and free from missionaries were a state of comparative bliss— of *otium cum dignitate*! "[1]

News bad and good came in. Early in April he heard of the death of de Winton, far away and alone, after struggling to carry out his almost impossible task in Toro. Lugard, in the midst of other worries, felt the stroke of this news deeply. " Poor boy, it was very sad that he should die alone out there in the Mahommedan camp with no friend near to hear his last wishes. Four men left the coast with me last August year. Of these de Winton and Brown are dead. Wilson was as good as dead . . . . Grant has twice been so ill that we have feared for his life. Such is Africa!" (Diary, 7 April 1892). And a few days later, after a more than usually serious attack from the C.M.S. missionaries and Ingleza chiefs, his spirits fell to zero. " I feel utterly worried to death and most intensely disgusted with the Waganda. I feel just now that if I could only once honourably get out of the country and shake its dust from the soles of my feet, nothing would ever induce me to return." (Diary, 17 April 1892).

The evacuation question was always with him to add to his gloom and his anxiety about the future. The main reason for the retreat was financial and it maddened him, with his own rigid economy, to reckon up the waste of Company money going on outside his control. Martin, for instance, when the civil war broke out, had hung about for sixty-one days with his expensive caravan, waiting for mails instead of going on. (How serious for Lugard were the results of this delay will appear later). Lugard reckoned he could run Uganda on £25,000 a year. He noted Stanley's statement in the press that the Congo Free State cost £170,000 a year and, in spite of its waterways to carry trade, had a revenue of only £25,000. How, he asked himself, could Mackinnon, a friend of the Belgian King and fully aware of this, have imagined he could run the far less promising and accessible East Africa upon " anything but a magnificent yearly deficit." He wondered " what was the object of starting this Company on an apparently impossible basis? " (Diary, 9 May 1892). The whole concern was not only bankrupt, it was dishonourable. He thought of the treatment of porters and other employees on the caravan routes, with men sometimes neglected, or unpaid or kept long beyond their

[1] Lugard, II, p. 469.

313

contracts. " I shall hand in my cheques and have done with a Company which, it seems to me, is not honourable in its dealings with Europeans or natives. Assuredly this is one of the most important reasons which is taking me to the coast and to England, once more the old Nyasa situation over again!" (Diary, 13 May 1892).

Thinking over the future of the Company and of the country, he sketched out a complete plan for its administration, one based, as his later plans for Nigeria were to be, equally upon the need for economy and his appreciation of the political capacity of the people and their effective constitution. He now played some part in helping forward the many judicial cases over lands and titles, by means of which the drastic rearrangements necessitated by the war and its settlement were reduced to order. He was thus able to study the legal ability of the Baganda. He noted their intense conservatism in this sphere and their strong conception of justice. He believed that their ideas should be further educated only very gradually. This was especially true " as long as we can't speak the language, and can only hear a filtered version and a minute percentage of all that goes on in argument " and when " dealing with a people who are excessively shrewd, with the most wonderful perception of justice and legal argument." (Diary, 8 May 1892). It must be admitted, however, that in these last months, because of the weakness of the monarchy and the urgency of a settlement, he departed somewhat from his careful rules of always working through the King and his ministers, and Kampala tended to drain authority across the valley from Mengo.

In all his anxieties for the present and the future there were some moments of relief. Lugard was deeply touched by the growing appreciation of his character and purposes he seemed to detect among many of the Baganda. Zachariah, his friend and trek-companion, appeared to have absorbed his own standards of justice and decency and was distressed to think how little his people had given in return for all Lugard and his colleagues had done and suffered for the country. He even offered, in order to make some return, to go with a volunteer band and shoot elephants and give all the ivory to the Company. And it was not only among the Ingleza that his work found appreciation. His old enemy, the Kimbugwe, wrote to tell him this of his party: " They like you greatly . . . . Now we ourselves place reliance on your integrity . . . . Now all the Catholics wish to become your

children utterly and entirely." (Kimbugwe to L. 16 April 1892). And
Père Achte confirmed this " They have full confidence in you as you
have been able to prove."[1] Even the fierce young Mujasi, his greatest
enemy, whom he wounded with the Maxim in the Mengo battle,
was won over, especially by the care Lugard took to protect his wife
Nalinia, sending her with great difficulty, under escort, to join her
husband in Buddu while the disorder still continued. Offering to come
and make peace, he wrote to Lugard as follows: " I come on your
account alone, for I, the Mujasi, am the enemy of the Protestants. I
trust in your integrity. And I like you because you are unable to tell a
falsehood . . . . You let us speak our words and if you do not like
them, you refuse them . . . . I want very much to see you, Kapelli.
God help you to do your work well. We are completely for peace.
Goodbye. I am your child. Gabriel Mujasi."[2] This was certainly a
letter which did credit both to the sender and the recipient. To those
who know the Baganda as a people among whom it is possible to
have friends in the fullest sense of the term, it is a pleasure to learn how
soon their character could be appreciated.

Lugard also drew no little sense of support from the steady loyalty
of Selim Bey and his other Muslim officers and especially from the
high-spirited and devoted Dualla.

He had some lighter alleviations. The Sekibobo seems to have
left the child Malia under his guardianship so her childish laughter
still alleviated the atmosphere of strain and overwork in his quarters.
And sometimes there were humorous situations. In Buganda it was
the custom, when an overlord restored a man to his estate, to present
him with two daughters or other comely virgins for his enjoyment.
When Lugard arranged such a restitution for the Katikiro, that
eminent man was puzzled as to his proper course of action. Finally
he sent Lugard two cows.

Lugard was torn between his desire to get home in time to fight
evacuation before its date fell due, and his determination not to leave
the country until he could hand it over to Williams in decent order,
with its major problems settled. The greatest of these which remained
unsolved was the position of the Muslims, still collected in their
menacing strength to the north-west. He flattered himself that by a

[1] Lugard II, pp. 465–6.
[2] The letter in full is in Lugard II, pp. 481–2. "Kapelli" was the Baganda corruption of
" Captain ". Lugard was, and still is, known by this name in Buganda.

mixture of strategy—the position of his Sudanese in their rear—and diplomacy—his frequent dispatch of Muslim messengers with friendly assurances—he had prevented them from taking the golden chance of falling upon Buganda when it was helpless in the grip of civil war and confusion. He had even in his extremity been driven, as we have seen, to the questionable course of threatening the Fransa with the succession of Mbogo as king if they did not hasten to make peace. He wondered to himself that he, who had fought the Muslims in Nyasaland, should now be inviting them to come into Buganda. Later, when the return of Mwanga ruled out the possibility of Mbogo's succession, he had to lecture the Christians severely upon the principles of religious toleration to which he was committed, and to which they were always ready to appeal when it suited them. " The Mahommedans say they number as many souls as the R.C.'s and Protestants combined " and the King did not deny it. " Will any Christian fanatic say they are to be exterminated? I reply that is not my view of God's will for his creatures . . . . Meanwhile I am here not as a teacher of religion, not as a Protestant, but as a legislator." His duty to his own conscience was to obey the words: " ' Know, O man, that to know and to do the thing that is right and to follow after justice, *that* shall bring a man peace at the last.' Let me be plain without (God knows) meaning to be irreverent . . . . It is *not* my duty to set myself in God's place and pose as an arbitrator of which religion is right or wrong." (Diary, 7 April 1892).

Lugard's plan, based on these principles, was to go out and meet the Muslims and to bring them out from their sullen isolation on the fringe of Kabarega's kingdom and give them, in exchange for the large northern border province of Singo which they dominated, three small provinces of Kitunzi, Katambala and Kasuju, all within easy reach of Kampala and in the middle of the country between the main areas of the two Christian parties. Here they would be less dangerous and more open to influence from the fort, near which Mbogo must reside. But the only way to win them over seemed to be for Lugard himself to go out and lead them in.

To achieve this he had not only to overcome the hostility of the Christian parties but the deep suspicion of the Muslims, who were unwilling to give up their king and fearful lest their enemies, or even Lugard himself, were drawing them into a trap. The events of the last six or seven years had built a great barrier of hostility and suspicion between them and their countrymen. The possibility had to be faced that, when Lugard went out to meet their large and heavily armed forces, they might fall upon him. Alternatively they might attack the Fransa or even—such was still the incessant and utter uncertainty of the position—they might suddenly enter into at least a temporary alliance with the more irreconcilable of the Fransa and turn jointly upon his little band. The first two weeks of May, when Lugard went out to meet the Muslims, were, therefore, days of great strain. Williams was still away in Busoga so that Kampala was deprived of leadership, while the other Europeans were almost all sick or worn out. He himself was tormented by the unromantic ills of toothache and neuralgia while his old Nyasa wound was having one of its periodic eruptions.

Lugard left Kampala on May 13th with 100 of his own rifles and 350 Baganda and marched north. The vast Muslim host came on to meet him. There were some 10,000 of them apart from the fighting men. The advance party had twice the number of rifles held by Lugard's men. The air buzzed with rumours of plots and treachery as envoys ran between the approaching forces. Lugard relied greatly upon his two Muslim assistants, Selim Bey and Dualla, both of whom showed the most perfect courage and loyalty and did all they could to persuade their fellow-Muslims to confide in Lugard's good faith and justice. On May 22nd the two parties approached. Lugard had a little shelter of poles built in which to receive Mbogo; the latter halted to put on his gold-embroidered robes. In an atmosphere of tension and excitement the armed men of both sides made a circle within which their leaders met. Lugard affected an easy and unconstrained manner, but Mbogo's nerves were clearly at the extreme stretch. Lugard's men, obeying orders, unostentatiously surrounded the meeting place.

For two anxious days the leaders fenced with each other. Mbogo fought every inch of the way. First he wanted delay; then he wanted to stay in the Muslim province with his own people. There were other pleas. Lugard refused to give way upon any point or to delay more than one day longer. Mbogo must leave his people, renounce his crown and come to live in Kampala. At last Mbogo gave in, though it is difficult to understand what arguments could have finally prevailed on him to surrender his strong position. But the crisis was not over. The Muslims had to be removed into the new provinces, and the people there moved out. There was danger still that this might touch off the spark of war, while famine resulting from the general dislocation was another danger. Then Mbogo and his large personal following had to march into Mengo with Lugard, through hostile crowds, and submit to Mbogo's hated nephew, Mwanga.

All went well, though there were many anxious moments. " At his first gate ", runs Lugard's diary, " stood Mwanga to receive us . . . . The meeting was a curious spectacle. They held each other's hands and gave vent to a long-drawn Oh!—Oh! in a guttural, then Ah!— Ah! in a higher note, then long low whistles as they gazed into each other's faces. This went on for a very long time and became extremely ludicrous to a European conception, for at times, while giving vent to this exclamation indicative of intense surprise, their eyes would be roaming round in a very inconsequent manner. Then they fell on each other's necks and embraced and then again began the former ceremony. Then Bambeja (princesses) who had followed Mbogo fell on Mwanga's neck . . . . Meanwhile the same performances were going on between chiefs and chieflets and common people on every side . . . . till the crush became greater and greater and it was hard work to preserve one's dignity or even one's balance . . . ." (Diary, 28 May 1892). There were vehement expressions of joy as men said, " That now at last war had been taken out of the country and that this had been impossible but for us." A few days later, when they had had time for consideration and discussion, the Muslim leaders added their signatures to the treaty between Mwanga and the Company. By this, among other clauses, it should be remarked that they formally agreed to the prohibition of the slave-trade while they were promised freedom for their religion. Mwanga, upon this occasion, made a most excellent speech in which he asserted that he, like Lugard, was now impartial in matters of religion, and that the British would see that the Muslims were treated with justice.

On June 9th Captain J. R. L. Macdonald,[1] R.E., chief of the railway survey party, arrived with an escort of Indian soldiers. He was able to say that he had made a very encouraging report upon the railway

[1] Macdonald, (later Major-General Sir) James Ronald Leslie, K.C.I.E., C.B., 1862-1927; 1882 gazetted in Royal Engineers; 1885-91 in India; 1891 chief engineer on Uganda railway survey; 1893 acting-Commissioner, Uganda Protectorate; 1900 with China expeditionary force; 1903-4 commanded military escort of political mission to Tibet; 1909-12 general officer commanding Mauritius.

project. He brought mails which confirmed what Lugard called " the sentence of death to all our work " in the evacuation of Uganda at the end of the year. Apart from the reputation of his country and the good of Uganda, Lugard felt that by his promises and by his actions, he had pledged his own honour to all the men and the parties who had relied upon his word and accepted his settlement. He was now on fire to start for England. By leaving in June he would barely have time to get to the coast, reach England, launch his campaign and get word of its success all the long way back to Uganda before the fatal date, December 31st 1892. He had hardly been able to endure the weeks he had been obliged to give to the Muslim affair and other aspects of the general settlement. Such were his standards that he could not find the moment at which he could regard *all* the affairs of the country in a state satisfactory enough for him to hand over to Williams who now returned from his long sojourn settling the disorders in Busoga. Most of all, he greatly wanted to go west and inspect and regulate the Sudanese garrisons. He spent much time in writing an immense volume of memoranda for the instruction of Williams, himself a man of bluntness and brevity: they covered some fifty different subjects, explaining each of them fully. He had been writing his diary at enormous length for the last three or four months, not knowing just what case the missionaries might be bringing against him in England, and many of his entries for a single day cover eight or nine foolscap pages of small close writing. At the last moment Williams fell ill and very nearly died and for a time it seemed as though Lugard would have to abandon his plan of going to England. Fortunately Williams recovered just sufficiently to allow him to go upon the date arranged.

Lugard had now to say farewell to Buganda. He valued and, indeed, needed, appreciation and he does not hesitate in his diary and his book to describe the widespread regret and even dismay at the sudden announcement of his going. " I do not believe there was one man who was glad that I was going." There was Mbogo who, trusting his word, had come in and agreed to live near the fort and had given him his magnificent royal war-drum as a symbol of his regard.[1] His own

---

[1] This drum, with its decorations of tassels of hair and bells, stood in the hall of Lugard's house at Abinger almost to the end of his life, and his many guests were summoned to their meals by the deep and rather ominous tones. (It was said to be covered with human skin.) The writer, after a visit to Uganda, told Lugard that its return to the country would be welcomed and to this he willingly agreed. A replica of the drum was made in Uganda and sent to him.

officers, and especially Selim Bey, were much disturbed: Dualla refused to stay without him. The old Pokino showed his grief. Zachariah, though his great affection and understanding taught him that for his own good and that of Buganda Lugard must go, yet told Lugard " my heart cried." Lugard could have said that of himself with regard to Zachariah and also to little Malia who was often at the fort in these last days and, he admitted, played " the deuce " with his work. Her father, the Sekibobo, was again one of his closest Baganda friends. His British colleagues gave him a farewell dinner at which he commended them to Williams with genuine and unstinted praise of his successor. Ashe allowed that he was "a gentlemanly man and very energetic ",[1] and even Père Brard wrote a courteous note of farewell, saying that his presence would have added to the peace of the country and hoping that he would return. Strangest of all the King seemed to regret his departure and sent after him a letter addressed to the Queen and signed by the chiefs as well as by Mwanga, an unusual tribute to a setting sun, which gave Lugard great pleasure and provided a very satisfactory conclusion to his work for the country. This testimonial is worth recording in full.

[*Translation*] UGANDA, MENGO, June 17, 1892

"TO MY FRIEND THE QUEEN, OUR GREAT SOVEREIGN:

" I and all my chiefs send you many greetings. I write this letter to thank you. Thank you exceedingly for sending the representatives of the Company in order to set my country to rights.

" When they reached Uganda, at first I did not like them; I did not think that they could set the country to rights. After we had fought, Captain Lugard wrote me a letter, and invited me, and restored me to my kingdom; then he went and invited the Mohammedans as well, with whom I had been at war, and brought them back, and gave them a part of the country. But now my country is at peace; the agents of the Company have arranged it excellently. Now I earnestly beseech you to help me; do not recall the Company from my country. I and my chiefs are under the English flag, as the people of India are under your flag; we desire very, very much that the English should arrange this country; should

---

[1] Ashe to C.M.S., 12 June 1892, C.M.S. Papers, Eastern Equatorial Africa Mission, 1892, letter 369.

you recall these agents of the Company, my friend, my country is sure to be ruined, war is sure to come.

" Captain Lugard has now brought to terms these three religions; he has returned to England; he will inform you of the state of affairs in Uganda. But I want you to send this same Captain Lugard back again to Uganda, that he may finish his work of arranging the country, for he is a man of very great ability, and all the Waganda like him very much; he is gentle; his judgments are just and true, and so I want you to send him back to Uganda. So, our friend, persevere in helping us, for we are your people.

" May God give you blessing and long life.

(Signed) I, MWANGA, King of Uganda, and my great chiefs. "[1]

---

[1] Lugard II, pp. 518-19.

321

CHAPTER XVII

THE RETURN TO THE COAST

June-September 1892 : Aet. 34

LUGARD'S TREK back to Mombasa was one of the most painful experiences of his life. He had been very worried over the question of withdrawing men and rifles from Kampala for his journey and so weakening the fort just when his own departure, added to the rumours of evacuation, might provoke a crisis. So, in his eagerness not to deprive Williams of a single man or rifle that he needed at the difficult moment, he asked Captain Macdonald, who was returning at once to the coast with his large railway survey party and its escort of Indian soldiers, to allow him to travel down under his protection. Macdonald agreed.

Lugard was taking with him Dualla and some forty Somalis, a number of women and children bound for Egypt, and some time-expired Swahili—200 in all, for the most part unarmed. It was not easy for him to join another man's caravan. Nothing but his double determination not to weaken Williams and also, with the fight for Uganda in prospect, to get home as quickly as possible, without waiting for a Company caravan, had led him to propose this plan. He was therefore deeply chagrined when, before they left, Macdonald wrote him a letter asking him to agree in writing that everyone " European and native " (Lugard being the only European except Macdonald's junior officers) going down with him was " to be entirely under his command ", and Lugard's men were to be informed of this. Lugard had never, of course, intended to interfere with Macdonald's caravan, though he was trebly senior to the other man, in the army, in the Company, and in experience of Africa, where Macdonald was a newcomer. But he had intended to be in charge of his own unarmed people, marching as near Macdonald's party as security and convenience demanded. A very awkward interview ended by both tearing up their letters and leaving the difficult question at issue largely open.

The Return to the Coast

This was only the beginning of trouble. The quarrels of weary Europeans trekking together in Africa in the conditions of the nineties, and for long after, are generally best forgotten. Unfortunately this affair was to have even more significance than Lugard, who took it seriously enough to write down the full story of it in his diary, could know at the moment. It must be remembered that only Lugard's account survives. It has not proved possible to discover any very enlightening evidence giving Macdonald's side of the story,[1] though it does appear that, after transporting their full dress uniforms 800 miles for the very purpose of their royal interview, Macdonald and his assistant, Captain J. W. Pringle, R.E., were asked by Lugard not to wear them when he presented them with their Indian escort to Mwanga.[2] But, according to Lugard's very full diary written night by night on the march, and to a long statement he wrote out a little later, Macdonald's behaviour was outrageous from first to last. This statement Lugard put in a packet and wrote upon it: " Deposited and sealed in the Foreign Office (by permission) to be opened if necessary by me on Captain Macdonald's return." It was entitled " The Case of Captain Macdonald, R.E." and its significance will appear later. It was returned to Lugard unopened in 1895 and it was left to the writer to break the seal some fifty years later.

When considering the evidence in this statement it must be remembered that Lugard was completely in Macdonald's power. The lives of all those in Lugard's charge depended upon his sticking close to Macdonald between Uganda and the first Company post in Kikuyu. Macdonald, according to Lugard, did all he could to humiliate his unwilling companion, and to a man of Lugard's temper and experience the treatment was a torment. Macdonald directed him to be ready for the march at a certain hour and then kept him waiting; he made him always march at the back; he countermanded his orders to his men. Lugard had to watch in silence what, as an experienced trekker, he regarded as his incompetence in conducting the caravan, choosing bad sites, and inflicting the maximum of hardship upon his men and upon Lugard's party of women and children. Macdonald

[1] Macdonald's book *Soldiering and Surveying in British East Africa* (1897) has some slight reference to this march. Elsewhere in it he deals out both praise and blame to Lugard but, in the circumstances, with restraint.
[2] Pringle's diary, 10–15 June 1892, in Makerere College Library. This document contains a few references to " our touchy friend."

ran out of food so that his men were almost starving and yet he repeatedly refused to accept any meat from the game that fell to Lugard's efficient rifle, or the flour Lugard had husbanded so carefully as to have a surplus. To have done so would have been a confession of his own incompetence. He insisted upon Lugard joining him at dinner, dragging him out of his camp through the rain and the dark bush, and then himself read a book. Angry letters went between the two. On one occasion, after an open row in front of their men, Macdonald wrote in official terms, as if to a subaltern, to say that he proposed not to take notice of Lugard's show of temper. Again and again Lugard, by his own account, forced himself to show outward civility to his overbearing companion, and to attempt to establish better relations. He could even admit that, in any other circumstances, Macdonald might have been an attractive personality. We need not imagine that Lugard was an easy companion, yet, even allowing for the state of mind in which he wrote his record, Macdonald's treatment of him seems to have been inexcusable.

They arrived at Kikuyu on August 7th. "At last!" wrote Lugard, with immense relief. "I pitched my camp on the other side of the fort to theirs and at last I am my own master." But he could not thoroughly enjoy his freedom: there was too much news at Kikuyu to anger him. He found that his friend George Wilson, whom he had left at Dagoretti, had been cut off by the Kikuyu: he had been demoted and the post abandoned. A loyal group of the Masai who had befriended Wilson had been attacked and shot down, without warning, by a Company officer who had succeeded him. Ill-chosen agents and a mixture of slackness and of the unregulated foraging or punitive expeditions by Swahilis had alienated the Kikuyu who had looted and murdered in revenge; the harmless and inoffensive Teita tribe had been "taught a lesson", and there was war with the Kamba. How different had been the situation when Lugard had passed through on his way up two years before and patiently made friends with these people! And how especially tragic was it, in view of the future, that the Kikuyu, whom he had found so exceptionally friendly, had already been started along the path of alienation which at the time of writing this chapter has lead them, under evil leadership, to the atrocities of the Mau Mau movement.

Lugard and Macdonald found mails waiting for them at Kikuyu.

But they learned that a very important and urgent sealed dispatch for Macdonald had missed them on the way. From his mail Lugard could read for the first time of the accusations against him by the priests, the protests of the French government, with the first answers given by Lord Salisbury and also the leading articles in *The Times* upon the subject.

He quarrelled with Macdonald to the end, for the engineer's last offences, in Lugard's eyes, were to interfere in Company administration at Kikuyu and to grudge Lugard a few rifles to defend his forced march to Mombasa to which, ahead of the rest, he now hurried. Between Machakos and Mombasa Lugard met the ever-itinerant Martin coming up with a huge, well-stocked caravan for Uganda—intended, presumably, to be the last—and with him was a German journalist, Eugène Wolf, correspondent of the *Berliner Tageblatt*, going up, in view of the great European interest in them, to report upon the recent troubles in Uganda. He seemed an " extremely nice fellow " and, after some talk with Lugard " to be entirely on our side." Indeed, he himself questioned whether, now he had heard Lugard's story, there was any point in his going up, but Lugard urged him to go and make an impartial investigation. A little further on Lugard found that this " nice fellow " had left a sick porter to die on the track, with the probable assistance of the hyenas, and he again inveighed against the brutal way in which caravans were conducted. This was not the last he was to hear of this German.

Lugard reached Mombasa on September 1st. Here he found the new and energetic Company Administrator, Mr. E. J. L. Berkeley, lent to the Company by the Foreign Office. He also found Sir Gerald Portal,[1] newly knighted, now consul-general, who came over from Zanzibar. They met for one day before Lugard's ship sailed. What Portal learned from Lugard and telegraphed to the Foreign Office will find its place in a later chapter.[2] From Portal Lugard learned that the mysterious dispatch which Macdonald had missed on the road was from the British government, sent by special messenger, and contained orders to him to return at once to Uganda and to " draw up a Report for the use of Her Majesty's Government, gathered from reliable sources, which should explain the causes of the outbreak and the

---

[1] See above pp. 68 and 140.
[2] See below p. 405.

action of British officials."[1] Lugard's feelings upon hearing this are not difficult to imagine. If he was not quite overwhelmed by the news, it was because he was so confident of the rightness of his actions, but it was a hard blow to take. To be publicly put on trial, after his arduous and dangerous services and, indeed, because of them, in his absence and upon the evidence of a handful of Europeans, many of whom his position and duty had forced him to offend—these were menacing circumstances enough. In Macdonald, moreover, he was to have as judge a man who was junior in the service both to Lugard and Williams, an engineer who knew little of administration or of Africa, and almost nothing of Buganda and its turgid politics. But, worst of all, this man was now his enemy, setting off to Buganda, still smarting from the wounds he had received from Lugard in their fierce cut and thrust on the journey down to the coast. On the Roman Catholic side, ironically enough, the appointment of Macdonald was later questioned on the grounds that he was likely to be too favourable to Lugard and it was recorded, leaving the reader to draw the conclusion, that the two men had met on the coast, which gave Lugard time to communicate his ideas and his notes to his colleague.[2]

Lugard made his case to Mr. Berkeley, who appealed to Sir Gerald Portal. But nothing could now be done to reverse the decision. On September 14th Lugard sailed for England, knowing that upon his arrival he would have to fight with all the powers he possessed not only for the honour of his nation, involved, as he believed, in the retention of Uganda, but for his own honour and reputation. This was now on public trial not only before his countrymen but if, as seemed likely, the French government should take up the matter, before all western Europe.

---

1 *Papers relating to Uganda.* Africa No. 8 (1892), C.6817, p. 1.
2 J. M., *L'Ouganda*, p. 319.

CHAPTER XVIII

THE ARRAIGNMENT OF LUGARD

1892-1893 : Aet. 34-35

TWO CONTROVERSIES have now to be considered. One concerned Lugard's record in Uganda and especially his alleged atrocities. The other concerned the future of Uganda and whether Britain should annex it or leave it to its fate. These controversies developed simultaneously and were almost to the end closely interwoven. Since Lugard himself played a major part in both it is, therefore, difficult to disentangle them. Yet because they are very different in character and in scale, the one concerning a man and the other a country, and because a biography of Lugard cannot treat the public trial of his competence and humanity as a minor theme in a larger story, it seems best to present them separately and to ask the reader to bear in mind that they were contemporaneous.

We must begin with the more intimate story of Lugard's trial at the bar of national and international opinion. The news of the fighting in Uganda reached Europe in a way that was to prove most unfortunate for Lugard. He was barred by the troubles in Busoga from communicating by his own direct route to Mombasa. Martin, who had left Uganda just before the conflict, hung about for two months waiting for the mail from Lugard to catch him up before he at last continued his trek to the coast, bringing with him nothing but rumours as to what had happened in Uganda. Without command of the lake, Lugard could not by-pass Busoga and get news to Kavirondo that way. Meanwhile, as we have seen, the priests and their Fransa adherents got away south to the islands, to Buddu, and to German territory, where Hirth was able to send off at once, by the established southern route, his own version of the unhappy events.

The news reached France first through the French consul in Zanzibar. On April 8th the French Foreign Minister, M. Ribot, told his ambassador in London, M. Waddington,[1] that he had received news of British atrocities in Uganda. The Roman Catholic Fathers had sent a telegram to Cardinal Lavigerie—news which saddened his deathbed —which spoke of " Missions wiped out by Protestants. Six Fathers prisoners. Bishop and refugees in Bukoba. Catholics killed, dispersed, enslaved . . . . " The ambassador was instructed to make the strongest representations and to point out that the directors of the Company were under an obligation to protect both missions.[2] But Waddington found that the Foreign Office had no news of these events. It was not until April 18th that Portal in Zanzibar, writing to his wife, broke off with a hurried postcript—" I can't go on, my darling, I am too busy and too worried. At this moment I have just received terrible news of awful massacres of Catholics in Uganda."[3] He feared this would be the end of the Company and that British officers were to blame. The telegram he sent that day to Lord Salisbury was startling enough with its report of massacre, burning, sacking, flight and imprisonment. A few days later the Company agent in Mombasa telegraphed that Ashe and de Winton had been killed.[4] The Foreign Office reply to Portal struck a note of scepticism typical of its head. " We desire to know every source of information." Further telegrams from Foreign Office and Company representatives reported that the news came from German sources, which declared that " Lugard caused the outbreak " and was in a critical position.[5]

Meanwhile the news had reached the European press. *Le Temps* of April 30th added to the facts, already sensational enough, that Catholic converts and French missionaries had been fired upon by the British with Maxim guns. The affair was given great publicity in Germany. Ribot now instructed Waddington to demand an immediate inquiry into Lugard's conduct. But neither in answer to the increasingly indignant demands of the French government, nor to pressing questions in parliament, could the perplexed ministers make any other answer but that no information whatever had reached them from Lugard about these reported events.[6] All they could do was to affirm their

---

1 Waddington, William Henry, 1826–94; a French subject of English birth. After a mainly political career he became Ambassador to Britain, July 1883–93.
2 Ribot to Waddington, 8 April 1892, *Documents Diplomatiques Français*, t. IX, p. 398.
3 Portal to Lady Portal, 18 April 1892, Portal Papers, MSS. Afr. s. 113.
4 C.6555 (1892), p. 131.
5 Ibid. p. 132.
6 *Parliamentary Debates*, 28 April 1892, IV. 3. 1570; 2 May, IV. 3. 1768; 26 May, IV. 4. 1911.

Sir Gerald Portal, from a drawing by the
Marchioness of Granby, 1894

belief that this officer could not have behaved with such wanton cruelty. In Paris, Lord Dufferin, the British ambassador, referred M. Ribot to an earlier dispatch from Portal which admitted the disturbed situation in Uganda and said that, as both sides bitterly accused Lugard of partiality, the presumption was that he was impartial.[1]

The arrival of Martin at the coast early in May did little to clear the obscurity. He could tell of events in Uganda before he left, such as the return of Lugard with Selim Bey and the Sudanese, but he could give no account of the fighting because this had drawn a curtain between him and the country he had just left. But he did express doubts whether Lugard would have enough food and ammunition to hold out for long if he were hard pressed, and his general impressions were such as to lead Portal to pronounce the Uganda situation " very serious ". Portal's only comfort lay in his view that Hirth was given to both pessimism and to exaggeration,[2] a faint wisp of comfort upon which the Foreign Office seized eagerly. Martin was sure that the assertion from French sources that Lugard served out rifles to the Ingleza must be false. Salisbury decided, however, that this report was too full of " combustible material ", and too much based on hearsay for him to venture to publish it.[3] " But it is an extraordinary thing," Portal wrote, " that we don't get a word either from Williams himself or from Lugard."[4]

To the opposition in parliament, and above all to the French, it was more than extraordinary: it was unbelievable. Must it not mean that the British government was concealing something? French pressure was maintained during June. Ribot told Dufferin that there was the most lively discontent on this subject in French parliamentary circles. He was supported by news from his ambassador in Berlin that the German Foreign Secretary also had shown his marked disapproval of the Uganda events and of the British attitude towards them.[5] In the British parliament, during June, the Uganda question was raised no less than nine times. The Irish members made the most of this useful stick with which they could beat the hated Tory government and they

[1] C.6847 (1893), p. 5.
[2] Portal to Anderson, 9 and 23 May 1892, P.P. s. 106.
[3] Minute by Salisbury on Portal to Salisbury, 23 May 1892, F.O. 84/2231.
[4] Portal to Anderson, 17 June 1892, P.P. s. 106.
[5] Herbette to Ribot, 2 June 1892, D.D.F. IX. p. 472.

put all their nationalist and sectarian feeling behind the strokes. They probed hard to discover the exact status of the captains, Lugard and Williams, in order to demonstrate the complicity of the government.[1]

It is interesting to see how politicians and public reacted to this attack upon the name of Lugard during the two months in which there was no evidence at all for the defence. Lugard's name was not unknown. It had come into some prominence, as we saw, over the Nyasa affair and he had been by no means silent since then. We have seen how early he realized that, if Africa was the place for action, Britain was the place for decision, and that this decision lay ultimately not with the officials, nor even with ministers, but with their masters. He wrote his long reports to the Company in the determined hope that they would go a good deal further than Pall Mall East: those he had written between his arrival in Uganda and August 1891, though still unpublished, had already, as it happened, found their way into the hands of many members of parliament. They had grumbled at the difficulty of getting hold of them from the Company, and had been suspicious about some excisions.[2] In the debates on the Uganda railway which had taken place upon March 3rd and 4th—and of which more later—there had been many quotations from these dramatic reports and much canvassing of the rights and wrongs of Lugard's vigorous actions and no less vigorous ideas.

It was the purpose of the opposition to prevent any forward move in East Africa by proving, among other points, that Lugard had used harsh and even violent methods to dominate the country. It is remarkable, therefore, that, in attacking the policy and its agents, the opposition, even in the height of parliamentary controversy, felt obliged to confess their admiration of the man. Labouchere, the most whole-hearted and continuous opponent of British dealings with Uganda, and the most unrestrained of critics, declared Lugard to be an independent man of independent judgment " who writes home an honest and full report."[3] Sir William Harcourt, who hated all that Lugard represented as an agent for expansion and annexation, and who read aloud to the House a large part of his report to illustrate this

---

[1] See especially questions by Colonel Nolan, *Parliamentary Debates*, 3 June 1892, IV. 5. 542 and 16 June, IV. 5. 1277.

[2] These reports were officially published in May 1892 in C.6555 (1892).

[3] *Parliamentary Debates*, 4 March 1892, IV. 2. 55.

aversion, ended by saying " I have formed the very highest opinion of his integrity, his intelligence, his industry, and his courage."[1] Gladstone, who had clearly studied the report with great care, took the occasion for a full scale attack upon the government and upon the actions of a man whose character and activities were almost as far apart from his own as was possible for one of the same species. Yet he, too, broke out in terms almost of panegyric. " Captain Lugard's Report makes upon me—and I have no doubt it made on the Right Hon. Gentlemen—the impression that whether these proceedings towards the natives may be juridically justifiable or not, yet, that he is a frank man, a brave man, an able man, and an upright man . . . . His Report bristles with propositions, and throws a most important light on the subject before us."[2] It may be that the success of the opposition in finding in Lugard's report some depreciatory remarks about Uganda's potential wealth, which they could use as arguments against the building of a railway, inclined them to support his veracity. But their tributes were warmer than political tactics demanded. The whole debate, indeed, moved around Lugard's report, which was subjected to almost as respectful a scrutiny as a piece of the Scriptures under the higher criticism, or rather, perhaps, as if sects were trying to prove their case by the quotation of isolated texts.

In the absence of any ammunition from Lugard, the ministers defended him as best as they could although, realizing the difficulties of his position, and knowing his decisive nature, they had their secret qualms which Portal's telegrams did little to soothe. " From the known character and antecedents of that officer ", asserted Mr. Lowther, Under-Secretary for Foreign Affairs, when a parliamentary question credited Lugard with responsibility for the massacre, " it is impossible to believe that he was directly or indirectly a party to it."[3] Lord Salisbury went further. Lord Herries drew his attention to the reports of atrocities and said it seemed strange when " a great part of Europe was ringing with these accusations ", with accounts in all the newspapers, that there was no information from the people who were said to have assisted in these atrocities. A commissioner should be sent out since the honour of England was at stake. Lord Salisbury replied that it would take too long to send a commissioner. Although

1 *Ibid.* IV. 1. 80.
2 *Ibid.* 3 March 1892, IV. 1. 1872.
3 *Ibid.* 26 May 1892, IV. 4. 1911.

he had no personal acquaintance with Lugard, he had read his reports and had formed a high opinion of him. " All his reports breathe a spirit of the utmost impartiality and loyalty . . . . "[1]

It was perhaps Lord Salisbury's defence which gave Lugard most encouragement. He described afterwards how, upon meeting the mail on his way to the coast, he read his letters and newspaper cuttings and learned that he was " stigmatised as a liar and a murderer; we are accused of heartless cruelties and of needless massacre . . . . I find a considerable section of my own fellow-countrymen believing, or pretending to believe, these charges against an absent man who had not been heard in his own defence. I read on, and presently I find the calm judicial reply of England's Prime Minister: . . . . And *The Times* exhibits in the same sense the traditional trait of the national character:—' See fair play ' . . . . Can the reader imagine the effect of such words? No, it is wholly impossible in this busy city of a thousand distractions, with the news of the entire world pouring in from hour to hour, to imagine, still less to realize, what balm those words conveyed in the isolation of Central Africa."[2]

There was plenty of such balm for him in the newspapers. *The Times* now and throughout the long controversy supported him and his policy; reserved judgment on the atrocity issue; maintained full reliance upon his ultimate vindication and gave his reports lavish reproduction.[3] Most other papers, except the few Liberal organs (especially the *Daily News*) and the Roman Catholic papers, supplied an interim defence in the long period of waiting. Their motives were not wholly pure. This was a period in which there was a growing antagonism towards France. The continuance of Britain's occupation of Egypt, alongside her reiterated promises to evacuate, was the central reason. The British, upon their side, were becoming increasingly aware that France had been challenging Britain along the colonial and commercial frontiers of the world. And France was now moving towards an alliance with Russia. Resentment was mingled with a certain measure of contempt because of the political scandals and ministerial instability displayed across the channel. Sectarian prejudice

1 *Parliamentary Debates*, 13 June 1892, IV. 5. 825.
2 F. Lugard, ' British Officials and French Accusations ', *Fortnightly Review*, vol. LVIII, November 1892, p. 689.
3 See, for example, *Weekly Times* of 13 May and *The Times* of 6 June, 13 June and 7 July, 1892.

was another of Lugard's doubtful allies. In a conflict of evidence between Roman Catholic priests and a British officer, a large part of Protestant England felt able to wait with confidence for the reports that would prove who were the liars and aggressors. The White Fathers were even referred to, with obvious intention, as Jesuits.[1] Lord Salisbury, unmoved by the almost weekly frictions with France—though as Foreign Secretary he had to handle them—countered hostile emotions by calm diplomatic gestures and, in this, the last, year of his ministry, tried to create an atmosphere of *détente*.

The French were, however, in earnest on the Uganda issue. In a much divided country, divided even upon the great issue of Church and State, the defence of Frenchmen, even if they were missionaries, would command almost universal favour. And these White Fathers were the followers of Cardinal Lavigerie, who had tried to bridge the domestic rift by advising churchmen to accept the Republic. The current Uganda story, which remained without authoritative denial, was enough to stir men of spirit into indignation. On May 31st, the Prince d'Arenberg, a politician very active in colonial affairs and one who had supported Lavigerie's policy of co-operation with the State, raised the isssue in the Chamber of Deputies. England, he said, amidst applause, would never have borne such treatment of *her* subjects, and it is right " that the English should know that we will never accept this violation of the rights of man and that we shall know as well as they how to protect the lives and the properties of our compatriots." Ribot, in reply, claimed that Britain was responsible for the acts of a Chartered Company and that she had broken the Brussels Act which enjoined upon its signatories the protection of religious freedom. Reparation for the missionaries must be made.[2]

As week after week went by, with the Foreign Office obliged to repeat that it still had no news from Lugard, the patience of both British and French critics was becoming exhausted. If Harcourt could exclaim incredulously about a Company which received no reports for nine months from its agents, French scepticism was forgivable. On the French side the evidence piled up week by week: there were more and more details about the " atrocities "; lists were compiled of the losses of a cathedral, churches, schools, stores, orphanages and

---

[1] Letter from the Rev. C. Sutcliffe, *Manchester Guardian*, 3 June 1892.
[2] Journal Officiel (Chambre), 31 May 1892, p. 686, c.2.

so on, an impressive list to those who did not know that they referred for the most part to what were, with whatever enlargements or adaptations, essentially native huts of poles and thatch.

Lord Salisbury's government was coming to its end in the mid-summer of 1892. His majority had been steadily eroded by by-elections and Gladstone, with weakening body and failing eyes, but with an unexhausted will to make one last attempt to liberate Ireland, was rallying his uncertain supporters for the electoral battle. In his last weeks of office Salisbury took two steps with regard to East Africa. He formally accepted the Company's reiterated policy of evacuating Uganda, and he decided to agree to the French demand for an inquiry into the conduct of Lugard. It may have been the last-moment date of this decision, which was made a few days before the dissolution of parliament on June 28th, or the impossibility of finding any other agent already in the region, that led to the appointment of Captain Macdonald. He was, the telegram to Portal ran—and it may be useful to repeat its wording—to " draw up a Report, . . . gathered from reliable sources, which should explain the causes of the outbreak and the action of British officials." There followed the surprising addition that if he had already been in Uganda it would not be necessary for him to return.[1]

Portal rushed the order by special messenger to Macdonald who was, as we know, on his way down to the coast in unhappy partnership with Lugard. Before it could reach Macdonald the first news received directly from Lugard himself reached England. It was in the form of a hurried letter written on February 11th in which he gave his own version of the recent fighting.[2] This reached the Company headquarters on July 14th, and was published in *The Times* the next day. On the 14th, also when Lugard's full report reached the coast, Portal telegraphed triumphantly to Salisbury that these reports completely disproved the accusations brought forward by the French and accused the French Bishop of inciting the war.[3] Confronted the next day by Lord Salisbury with news of these reports, and also of the commission sent to Macdonald, the French ambassador could only remark the obvious, that the various reports were very contradictory and that it

[1] C.6817 (1892), p. 1.
[2] Ibid. pp. 2-4.
[3] Portal to Salisbury, 14 July 1892, *Further Papers relating to Uganda. Africa No. 1* (1893), C.6847, p. 11.

would be difficult to arrive at the truth.[1] He added that there was no information about Lugard's attack on the island and Salisbury admitted that there were still obscure points and that he reserved his opinion until he should get fuller information.[2]

That fuller information was, however, to be long in coming. Delay, both avoidable and unavoidable, dogged the handling of the Uganda affairs from beginning to end. Martin, returning to Uganda with Portal's urgent messages, met Macdonald at Kibwezi, twelve days' march from the coast. The appointment as Commissioner represented a blow to Macdonald, who had finished his survey of the railway, and had now to turn back on September 10th and to retrace the weary 600 miles to Uganda. But when he got back to Machakos, news of the change of government, considered in conjunction with Lugard's return to the coast, caused him to delay. Macdonald states in his book that at Machakos he received two contradictory telegrams on the same day, one ordering him to go back to Uganda and report, the other ordering him to come to the coast. The Foreign Office records do not support quite this degree of confusion but it is clear that, after confirming Salisbury's instructions of June 24th,[3] Rosebery did actually send a telegram on September 5th[4] to recall Macdonald and another on September 30th[5] to confirm his commission. Having started for the coast, and having marched a hundred miles back, Macdonald then ran into Bishop Tucker of the C.M.S. who told him that the Masai had cut up the messengers with more recent orders directing him to go on to Uganda and report. So the unhappy Royal Engineer faced again the march to Uganda, carefully putting a little distance between his caravan and the Bishop's lest, after six weeks of travelling association, he should arrive in Uganda with an alleged taint of partiality.[6]

Macdonald must for the present be left at this point where he set out upon his laborious and distasteful task, while we return to follow the subject of his investigation who was travelling in the opposite direction. Lugard, so long lost to the world, reached Mombasa on September 1st. It was here, as already recounted, that he heard of

[1] Ibid. p. 11.
[2] Waddington to Ribot, 20 July 1892, A.A.E. vol. 875, f.170.
[3] C.6817 (1892), p. 1.
[4] Rosebery to Portal, 5 September 1892, F.O. 84/2237.
[5] Rosebery to Portal, 30 September 1892, F.O. 84/2235.
[6] Macdonald, *Soldiering and Surveying*, pp. 105–6, 127–8.

Macdonald's commission and entered his protest that a man junior to himself, with little African experience, should report upon a senior officer. And from whom, he asked, could he in Kampala derive his information, especially of the later negotiations, during which even Williams had been away? All the essential documents were with him, and there were no copies in Kampala. " As regards Captain Macdonald himself, I had full faith in his impartiality and honour, but it was unfortunate that the one and only man with whom I had had any personal difference in Africa should be selected as my judge! "[1]

Portal, who arrived opportunely in Mombasa on September 13th, had little to say of this side of his talk with Lugard. He was chiefly interested in the larger issue of the future of Uganda. But it is clear that he was deeply impressed by Lugard and by his views. He had already told Salisbury that among the Company employees only Lugard and Williams were any good. He now reported that Lugard seemed to have acted throughout with great discretion and strongly urged his new chief, Lord Rosebery, to see him upon his return.[2] This letter had a wider importance and we shall need to consider it again.

Lugard's one idea was to hurry back to England. He never seems even to have considered following Macdonald back to present himself in person, as an extremely formidable defendant, in Uganda. Instead, he hastened across the continent from Marseilles and reached England on October 3rd. Though he was himself more concerned from the moment he landed with the evacuation question, then perplexing the whole country from the Cabinet downwards, than with his own indictment, we are following this second theme to its conclusion. For if the French accusations were wholly true, then Lugard would have dishonoured Britain as Carl Peters had dishonoured Germany, and in a country which prided itself upon its humanity his public career was likely to come to an end. And he would have been disqualified as an advocate to the British public on the wider Uganda question.

The Lugard affair had not stood still while the subject was at sea. After the appointment of Macdonald, the British government naturally wished to have a moratorium on the dispute until his report should

1 Lugard II, p. 546.
2 Diary for 13 September 1892, P.P. s. 107, and letter to Rosebery, 14 September 1892, P.P. s. 106.

come to hand. This was far from the mind of the French ministry, even though items of news were at last coming in which contested their case. Above all, Lugard's own reports of the war had come on the same mail-boat as himself. It was now known that he had arranged a general settlement, and that Mwanga had written to the Queen praising his work,[1] while most of the British missionaries had by now confirmed his account of the conflict. But the Quai d'Orsay had kept up its offensive: Waddington was upon Rosebery's doorstep soon after that reluctant minister had been coaxed into taking office in the middle of August. He pressed him on the indemnity question and before the end of the month had sent in a long and gravely-worded dispatch, alluding to the fuller information that had come in, but marshalling the evidence to prove that Lugard had deliberately provoked the war. "Your Lordship will understand the emotion which this cannot fail to produce in France . . . ." The evidence, he wrote, in his gravest sentence, shows " that the European officers took the initiative and the responsibility of deciding on the destruction of the civilizing work of our Fathers, and of condemning in a body a population who had been won over to Christianity."[2]

In September, the ambassador being on holiday, his *chargé d'affaires*, Baron d'Estournelles, who seems to have been a pioneer in psychology, contributed an interesting analysis, which he called an impartial reading, of Lugard's mind, as revealed in reports now available. He decided that Lugard had suffered from an extraordinary mental re-action as a result of the crushing disappointment which evacuation must bring to all his great achievements and hopes.[3] From this " interesting analysis ", as Ribot called it, d'Estournelles went on to study the English scene and reported that, while France was concerned only with the massacre, England was concerned only with the evacuation. Even Lugard, recently returned, did not behave, as he should have done, like a man in the international dock, but seemed interested only in the future, not of himself, but of Uganda. The French representative explained to Rosebery that after nine months they were unable in France to understand " *ce beau calme Britannique* " which they put down to indifference. He presented Rosebery with his psychological analysis of Lugard and then urged the Foreign Minister to agree to an

[1] See above pp. 320–1.
[2] C.6847 (1893), pp. 18–21.
[3] D'Estournelles to Ribot, 9 September 1892, A.A.E. vol. 877, f.87.

M

indemnity. But, though Rosebery listened attentively and did not contradict the Frenchman on any point, he gave him no satisfaction.[1]

Rosebery was, in fact, engaged in a struggle within the Cabinet in which at this point the major and the minor issues about Uganda touched. For the French pressed their claim for an indemnity on the ground that the British government was responsible for the actions of Chartered Companies, the point upon which the whole controversy in the House of Commons turned and one which anticipated in some aspects the later problem of the relations of government with public corporations. Rosebery was pressed to give the French ministry some satisfaction, if only in principle, in order to help them to face another interpellation in the Chamber. Though he doubted whether the French ministry would survive in any case, he sent a draft of his reply to Gladstone that did in fact admit the principle of responsibility, which, as we shall see later, he had his own reasons for wishing to establish. But Gladstone pounced upon this at once, so Rosebery left out that part, and made the usual plea of delay for the Macdonald report and ended, as he described it, with " a tag of agonizing politeness."[2] The Cabinet, though faced with a problem that was essentially political, referred it to the Lord Chancellor, Herschell, for a legal opinion, and the French were informed of this. This gave another excuse for delay.[3] This typical British evasion drew the angriest communication Ribot had yet written in which, with scornful French logic, he tore to pieces the view that Britain could sign a solemn international agreement taking Uganda into her sphere of influence, exercise her sovereignty through a society to which she had delegated her authority, and then disinterest herself in the actions committed there in flagrant violation of the general obligations of civilized nations, hiding " behind the opinion that a Crown Counsel might formulate."[4]

Thus spurred on by his master, Waddington saw Rosebery again and pointed out that Macdonald's position in reporting upon English army officers was very difficult and the French would therefore wish to send their own Commissioner. Rosebery replied that this would only further prolong and complicate matters, and he showed his

1 D'Estournelles to Ribot, 12 October 1892, A.A.E. vol. 877, f.318.
2 Correspondence between Rosebery and Gladstone 13, 18 and 19 October 1892, Gladstone Papers, B.M. Add. MSS. 44290 and 44549. (It appears however that Rosebery sent off his letter on 17 October without waiting for Gladstone's reply. See C.6847 (1893), p. 27.)
3 Waddington to Ribot, 26 October 1892, D.D.F. X. p. 58n.
4 Ribot to Waddington, 29 October 1892, D.D.F. X. pp. 58–9.

irritation at this persistence. He was still more irritated when Waddington left him to see if he would get more satisfaction from other
ministers and called upon Gladstone. The Prime Minister told him
that in his view it had been civil war in Uganda and it was very hard
to say who started anything while, according to Waddington, he tried
to confuse the issue of the responsibility of Chartered Companies by
saying there was no general rule: each one differed from the rest.
But he did deliver an opinion, contrary to that of Rosebery, that
he saw no reason why the French should not make their own
enquiry.[1]

It was only too easy to drive further the wedges splitting this
unhappy Cabinet. Rosebery did not hesitate to show his annoyance
at Gladstone's intervention,[2] while Lord Ripon confessed to Lord
Kimberley his alarm at Rosebery's high-handedness. " If he gets his
way about Uganda, as I suppose he will, he will be very difficult to
manage."[3]

On the liability issue, the French won the round. On November 7th
the British Cabinet, with an eye more upon parliament than upon
France, worked over a series of drafts in which they would admit, in
elaborately guarded terms, their very conditional liability for the
actions of Lugard, as an agent of the Company.[4] This important
letter, as finally composed, was as follows:[5]

The Earl of Rosebery to the Marquis of Dufferin.

Foreign Office, November 8, 1892.

" My Lord, Her Majesty's Government have recently had under their
consideration the complaints made in France as to the conduct of British
officers in Uganda, and the material losses which it is believed in France
have been sustained in consequence by French subjects.

In ordinary cases Her Majesty's Government would await the result
of full and impartial inquiry before taking any action in a matter of this
kind. But circumstances, partly natural and partly accidental, have
delayed, and will yet further delay, the investigation they have ordered,
and they are anxious that no feeling of soreness or injury shall be

---

1 Waddington to Ribot, 2 November 1892, *D.D.F.* X. p. 62.
2 Rosebery to Gladstone, 4 November 1892, B.M. 44290.
3 Ripon to Kimberley, 5 November 1892, B.M. 43536.
4 Notes of Cabinet proceedings, 7 November 1892, B.M. 44648.
5 C.6847 (1893), p. 34.

permitted to grow up in consequence of this postponement. Your Lordship is therefore authorized to give M. Ribot the following assurance:—

That if, after full investigation, a state of facts is revealed which gives rise, according to a just interpretation of the law of nations, to a liability on the part of the British Government to make compensation for material losses sustained by French subjects during the recent conflict in Uganda, and not satisfied by the Company, the British Government will not be backward in discharging its obligations in that respect.

I am, etc.

(*Signed*) ROSEBERY

Lugard, caught now in the mainstream of English political life, which was running for him like a mill-race, and might be carrying him to disaster, was not unaware of how his action on those six days some ten months before were embittering Anglo-French relations and adding one more burden to the already staggering Cabinet. He was absorbed with his Uganda retention campaign, but if his personal vindication was for him, as the French complained, a secondary interest, it yet demanded time and care. Three days after he landed in England, Sir Philip Currie[1] of the Foreign Office wrote to him to say that in view of the " serious representations " made by France against the Company's agents, and in spite of the fact that Macdonald was on his way to Uganda to investigate them there, Lord Rosebery " considers it only fair to yourself and to those recently under your orders that he should be given the earliest opportunity of replying to the charges which were contained in Waddington's letters of May 25th and 29th, and August 30th."[2]

Lugard was quite ready. He had not, until then, seen the ambassador's charges but he had collected from the newspapers and letters which met him on his way to the coast, the main initial accusations made against him by the priests. He had spent much of the voyage writing a reply, and as soon as he reached England he expanded it in order to meet the additional accusations which had accumulated during his voyage. He did not seem distressed, much less overwhelmed, to find

1 Currie, Philip Henry Wodehouse (later 1st Baron Currie), P.C., G.C.B., 1834-1906; 1854 entered Foreign Office; 1884 Assistant under Secretary of State for foreign affairs; 1889 Permanent Under Secretary of State for foreign affairs; 1893-8 Ambassador at Constantinople; 1898-1902 Ambassador at Rome.

2 Those letters are in C.6847 (1893), pp. 7-9, 10-11, and 18-21.

Europe, according to some French opinions, "ringing" with his name, linked with stories of violence and cruelty. This was just one more round in the hard physical and mental struggle for which he seemed to have been made. He could not foresee, however, how long his trial would last. It falls into two main parts. In the first, he was answering the French accusations; in the second he had to face round to the thrust, deeper, more painful and much harder to meet, from his own side. His defence took five successive forms. There was firstly the memorandum which he wrote mainly on his voyage home and issued as a private publication[1]; secondly his answer to the French ambassador which he addressed to the Foreign Office; thirdly his article in the *Fortnightly Review;* fourthly his official answer to the charges in the Macdonald report; and fifthly his book, written, unlike his first official reports upon the events in question, after he knew all the accusations to which they gave rise. Lugard's published *Reply* thus dealt mainly with the long list of alleged injustices and atrocities which appeared one after another in the British and foreign press, after having been sent to Europe by Hirth and the other priests. Lugard's pamphlet covers thirty-one pages, and almost every one of its fifty-five paragraphs deals with one of the numerous counts against him. To select and to summarize briefly the most important charges, he was accused of deliberately provoking the war; of committing or allowing atrocities of all kinds, general and particular, in the course of the fighting; of neglecting to protect the Fathers and then of imprisoning and ill-treating them; of gross partiality in many ways towards the Protestant faction; and of cheating and oppressing the Roman Catholics in the final settlement.

The picture of Lugard which the plaints build up is that of a man without pity or principle. Many of the accusations are wild and vague in wording. Hirth, especially, writes in melodramatic style, mixing up what he asserts *did* happen with what *might* have happened, weaving rumours and hearsay evidence into the story as fact. None of the priests suffered the smallest physical injury, but Hirth builds up his account as if, at the will of the two captains, they were being hunted to death. In an article in *The Tablet* entitled " The Butcheries at

---

[1] *Reply by Captain Lugard to charges of Mgr. Hirth and French Fathers in Uganda.* No date: "submitted October 29th, 1892." L.P. To this he added an appendix containing some of the letters to the French Fathers, and also extracts from the reports and newspaper articles by the priests and other writers. Privately printed. This will be referred to in this chapter as the *Reply.*

Uganda "[1] he writes " . . . . we were bound to be burned alive . . . . It only remained to die." This is a recurring theme. Père Guillermain wrote of the priests who went to the fort after the Bulingugwe episode that they were " treated like the lowest human beings. What a disgrace for France to see her sons kept prisoners in an English fort and reviled like low criminals! "[2] Hirth blamed Lugard equally for wanting to send them away and for trying to keep them. " Their gaolers, who are white men, threaten to convey them to Mombasa: this shows how great a hold religious hatred has on the heart of our persecutors." But as, if they got to Europe, they might expose their captors' misdeeds, " they judge it better to have them in prison to succumb to the fever and the misery which is wearing away their lives."[3] " We regret one thing," wrote Hirth, " not to have been held worthy of the crown of martyrdom; all chance is not yet lost."[4] Hirth even suggests that " the massacre " was carefully planned and was worse than that of St. Bartholomew. " The stain of that may be wiped out; but we have had in Uganda our St. Timothy, and of this the heretics must ever bear the burden and the blame."[5]

The notes of misery and doom, very disproportionate where not contrary to the facts, run through Hirth's letters. " My heart bleeds by day; at night a horrible nightmare oppresses me; I cannot banish from my thoughts the terrible scenes I have witnessed . . . . How sad the fate of our poor Uganda! A very little more and it would have become a Catholic kingdom, and now it has relapsed into error, perhaps even barbarism, for who knows how many centuries to come? " He speaks of " the great nation of the Bagandas, which is doomed to die out."[6] One of the many examples which could be given of the wild statements which exacerbated continental opinion against Lugard was that taken up by Prince d'Arenberg in the Chamber of Deputies. " We can cite one significant fact . . . . that the aggressors [Protestants are meant] were armed with Maxim guns, and it is difficult to believe that these perfected weapons were not procured from British officers."[7] We may smile at this flattering description of Lugard's two veteran guns, only

1 4 June 1892.
2 *Daily News,* 6 March 1892.
3 *The Tablet,* 15 October 1892.
4 *Ibid.* 4 June 1892.
5 *Ibid.* 15 October 1892.
6 *Ibid.*
7 J. O. (Ch.), 31 May 1892, p. 686, c.1.

one of which could be relied upon to fire, and that not very certainly, for two minutes. Neither gun, of course, was ever allowed out of the control of Lugard and Williams. Again, Hirth declares that the British officers frequently uttered threats of death against Mwanga and " kept on writing letters to persuade the Catholics to apostatize," both of which charges Lugard denies, asking for one copy of such a letter to be produced. Speaking of Lugard's engaging of the Sudanese, Hirth said that " One of their chiefs, who would not sell himself to him, disappeared mysteriously." This amounted to a charge of murder.[1]

The priests even pretended to be able to report the thoughts of the two Englishmen. Speaking of Lugard's bringing the Sudanese to Mengo—his 100 soldiers being referred to as 700 to 800—Hirth goes on: " From that time the Captain's plans were laid, although they were kept secret. The Catholics, who from day to day became more numerous, were to be put an end to."[2] Again, speaking of Williams, " Before the eyes of this captain we were plundered and disgracefully treated, whilst he stood behind the gun like a warrior proud of his victory. Truly he might be proud; he had just fired on women and children."[3] Elsewhere the Captains are called " brigands " and men " destitute of all honour."

" Such contemptible trash," is Lugard's comment, " obviously a mere sensational lie, is not worth replying to."[4] All the same he went over each charge, showing, where possible, its patent inaccuracy, or flatly denying its truth, his word against the priests. On the charge of imprisoning and ill-treating the Fathers, he described the difficult conditions in which he had to entertain them in the fort where life was always hard and ill-provided. Upon his general treatment of them and of their religion, he quoted from a number of their own letters written to him at the time thanking him for his kindness and justice; the originals of these are on the writer's table. Lugard was especially zealous to defend Williams. He could not bear to think of his loyal colleague being unable to answer for himself and he knew that his difficult position in charge of Uganda might be weakened by the attacks being made upon him in Europe. For himself he referred people to

1 *Reply*, p. 27.
2 *The Tablet*, 4 June 1892.
3 *Daily News*, 6 March 1892.
4 *Reply*, p. 11.

his full reports, written month by month in ignorance of the indict-
ments that would be made. On the religious issue he concluded: " My
own personal view is that it belongs to God alone to judge in which
form he will be worshipped; to me Catholic, Protestant and Mahommedan have each of them much that is good, and I deplore and detest
the narrowness of view which prevents the full appreciation of this
good. The Fathers have painted me as a rancorous and fanatical
Protestant, though they well know the picture is untrue. The Protestant Missions, as the pigeon-holes of the Church Missionary Society
can show, have written volumes on my complete subservience to the
' fascinating influence of the French Fathers.' "[1]

This is enough to indicate the character of some of the charges
and of Lugard's first reply: it leaves for later discussion some of the
more considered charges made by the Fathers. These were collected
and restated, with an analysis of Lugard's defence, in a small book
published by the Catholic Union of Great Britain in 1893, under a
sub-title almost every word of which was controversial.[2]

Lugard's next act of self-defence was a vigorous article in the
Fortnightly Review.[3] This must have been dashed off very soon after
his arrival and it has an air of haste. It is a piece of hard hitting in which
he carried the fight a long way into the enemies' camp, reaching some
hardly tenable ground in the attack. He accused Hirth of bad faith
and of other offences and states " the Catholic party had been taught
to aim at a political supremacy and a French suzerainty ", a charge
which, as we shall see later, was difficult to sustain. " But ", he concluded the article, " after reading page after page of invective, I can
truthfully say that the feeling uppermost in my mind at the conclusion
was one of pity and sorrow for men whose very bitterness of language
proves the intensity of the interest they had in their work . . . . As I
claim sincerity for my own motives, so am I bound to accord it to
theirs. I accuse them only of mistaken methods, and I think we should
be lenient in our judgment of what they have written in the bitterness
of the discovery that those methods were misjudged, and have led
to disaster instead of to success." The note of pitying superiority which
had gone into this conclusion was not likely to sooth the wounds of

1 *Reply*, p. 30.
2 *Notes on Uganda, or an Analysis of the various reports etc. issued on the late war between the
Imperial British East Africa Company and the Catholics of that British dependency* (London 1893).
3 'British Officials and French Accusations', *Fortnightly Review*, vol. LVIII, November 1892.

his enemies. The article was read by Cabinet ministers with mixed feelings. Harcourt sent it to Gladstone with the remark " It is not likely to facilitate our settlement with the French government."[1] " On the surface ", Gladstone replied, with caution, " Lugard seems to make a case against the R.C.s. I hope he has right on his side."[2]

Having thus published his defence in two forms, Lugard set himself to answer the official charges of the French government. Currie sent them to Lugard on October 6th; his reply in its final form is dated December 6th and the next day it was sent to Paris. The charges against Lugard were (i) discrimination in favour of Protestants and Muslims and against the Roman Catholics in his administration, (ii) massacres and barbarities, (iii) provoking war by his actions and especially by giving arms to the Protestants, (iv) failing to protect the French missionaries, (v) imprisoning them and exposing them to insult by the Africans, (vi) responsibility for heavy material losses and (vii) delay in sending a report on the disturbances.[3]

It appears that Lugard first replied to the charges with the verbal lavishness natural to him. Edward Vicars, of the Foreign Office, was obliged to condense and rearrange his reply and eliminate all that was not relevant to the ambassador's charges. " Please deal gently with it ", Vicars begged, having finished this large task, " as . . . . though it is undoubtedly your child I feel as if it were nearly related to me." (Vicars to L. 30 November 1892). The memorandum, thus arranged, followed so closely the lines of his earlier *Reply*, much of which was repeated verbatim, that we need not consider it here.

As far as French pressure was concerned there was now a short lull while the Quai d'Orsay digested this interim defence and waited, with what patience it could, for the long promised, long-delayed Macdonald report. France was hampered at this time by more changes of government, with Ribot reconstructing the ministry, then failing and giving way to Dupuy for a few months. Her offensive slackened and Gladstone was even able to refer early in 1893 to Anglo-French relations being " most friendly."[4] The day after Lugard delivered his reply, the government, as will be explained later, decided to send Portal as Commissioner to report upon the future of Uganda. Lugard

[1] Harcourt to Gladstone, 8 November 1892, B.M. 44202.
[2] Gladstone to Harcourt, 9 November 1892, B.M. 44549.
[3] C.6847 (1893), pp. 37–50.
[4] *Parliamentary Debates*, 3 February 1893, IV. 8. 479.

therefore called off his whirlwind campaign against evacuation. While one Commissioner was following the other up the long route to Lake Victoria and the two were there together making their reports, he flung himself, seemingly unexhausted by the crowded weeks he had passed, into the writing of his book which he carried through with almost reckless speed.

There was no close season, however, with regard to Uganda affairs in the British parliament. Their main theme was that of evacuation. But both in the course of debates and question-time, Lugard's character and deeds were a frequent subject. Labouchere, who must by now have known Lugard's reports by heart, quoted largely from them in order to demonstrate his harshness and so blacken the whole policy of advance into Africa. He spoke of the " monstrous atrocities " committed under the regime of " this man whom we are all asked to admire."[1] Gladstone took the occasion—the subject was the address on the Queen's Speech—to announce the Liberal government's confirmation, after some hesitation, of Lord Salisbury's appointment of Captain Macdonald to enquire into the justice of the French claims. Were they to assume without any enquiry that, whatever the facts, Britain could disclaim responsibility? It must have been painful for Gladstone to support a view he had contested in the Cabinet. And if there was at least one voice always ready to condemn Lugard's actions in the Commons, there were always several roused not only in his defence but in his praise. Mr. Burdett-Coutts, for example, who called himself " the only representative [of the Company] in this House ",[2] gave a long and highly favourable interpretation of Lugard's conduct. "I do not understand", he said of Labouchere, " the spirit in which he seeks to raise prejudice against an Englishman, situated as Captain Lugard was, in a distant and unexplored country . . . . To my mind it was a noble exhibition of bravery, self-reliance, and good judgment."[3]

The following month, in the Commons, Gladstone had to insist again to Labouchere that he must wait for the Macdonald report into " the sad and lamentable transactions " in Uganda.[4] It was from Chamberlain, whose positive mind was now settling into certainty

1 *Parliamentary Debates,* 3 February 1893, IV. 8. 461, 463.
2 *Ibid.* IV. 8. 572.
3 *Ibid.* 6 February 1893, IV. 8. 579–80.
4 *Ibid.* 20 March 1983, IV. 10. 554.

about imperial policy, that the subject of controversy won the most glowing praise. Chamberlain was indignant that "we do not do justice to our bravest and noblest citizens. Of Captain Lugard I know no more than any Member of the House may know—I know him only through reading his works. He was, I believe, an Indian officer who was sent to Uganda under the orders of the Company. He undertook a work of the highest responsibility and the greatest importance, and I say that anyone who reads his accounts impartially will agree with me to this extent, that he was, at all events, a man of extraordinary power and capacity, tact, discretion and courage. Courage is a common virtue, but he has shown it in no common way, and he has exhibited a modesty which is beyond all praise. I say that it is something for England, for the United Kingdom, to glory in that we can still boast such servants as these."[1] The next day, pressed by an Irish member, who accused Lugard of responsibility for the antagonism that had led to bloodshed, Sir Edward Grey, the Under-Secretary for Foreign Affairs, while he admitted there had been a slaughter of Catholic natives, not only argued that "we are bound in honour to Captain Lugard, and to every party concerned, to wait for Captain Macdonald's Report" but went so far as to give it as his opinion, upon the evidence so far at the government's disposal, that the French party had fired the first shot.[2]

In the House of Lords the Duke of Norfolk now turned upon Lugard the heavy guns he carried as the first noble in England and leader of the Roman Catholics. The Duke had already taken up the matter outside parliament and had had a stiff brush with the Company, which refused to supply him with information, while Rosebery protested his inability to coerce the Company in the matter.[3] Lugard wrote to the Duke a forthright letter offering to come and see him, but the Duke refused an interview, and said that if the Company did not satisfy him he would take action. His action, however, did not prove very effective. It consisted in raising the issue in the House of Lords in May and asking for a discussion on the subject of the Macdonald report. He insisted that there must be the most thorough investigation of "a story on which no Englishman would care to

---

[1] *Ibid.* IV. 10. 598.
[2] *Ibid.* 21 March 1893, IV. 10. 726.
[3] Rosebery to Norfolk, 1 January 1893, and Norfolk to Rosebery, 24 January 1893, F.O. 83/1237.

dwell." But Rosebery said any discussion before the report came would be premature.[1]

In order to maintain the suspense of all action until the Macdonald report should come, Rosebery had to struggle not only against his political opponents and the French government but even against his own colleagues. He wrote a sharp note to Lord Ripon, the Colonial Secretary, on the subject. " . . . . I cannot imagine what can be gained by a preliminary discussion before Macdonald's Report arrives. It would be injudicious and unpatriotic; and I should decline to take part in it."[2] It was nearly another two months after this before the long-awaited, long-delayed report arrived. Macdonald had signed it in Kampala on April 7th and, with a covering letter from Portal, then in Uganda, it reached the Foreign Office on June 27th.

1 *Parliamentary Debates,* 15 May 1893, IV. 12. 885.
2 Rosebery to Ripon, 2 May 1893, B.M. 43537.

CHAPTER XIX

THE MACDONALD REPORT

1893-1894 : Aet. 35-36

WE MUST now consider the long and perplexing secret document which was put before the Cabinet and upon the contents of which the reputation and future career of Lugard might depend. The report is in three parts: the first section upon the causes of the war (2-22), the second upon the charges and counter-charges that had been made (22-33), while the third is an appendix (39-104) containing a great many letters and verbatim reports of evidence to illustrate the first two parts.[1]

Macdonald's method was to list all the charges and counter-charges from newspaper cuttings and to submit them to " the representatives of the respective parties who figured as accusers ", allowing them to add or eliminate charges. Native evidence, some of which was recorded, was not accepted on the grounds that it was so *ex parte* as to be valueless.

The report goes minutely over the events which were described in chapters 12–16. We need consider it only briefly. It records the flat contradictions between the two parties, moved, on the French priests' side, by one of the deepest of human sentiments, religious zeal, mingled in this case with sectarian animosity; while, on the other side, British soldiers were reporting, naturally with the most favourable construction, upon their own military and administrative activities. It must suffice to pick out the four or five main points upon which Lugard's ability, humanity and sense of justice were held in question.

Macdonald's first charge is that Lugard, while pledged under the

---

[1] Macdonald's report was never published and remained in the Foreign Office archives. It is to be found in F.O. 2/60. There is a copy in the Lugard Papers with Lugard's pencilled comments in the margin. The bracketed numbers refer to the pages in the printed F.O. copy. References in this chapter are made to it under the title *Report*.

Company's charter and by international agreements to uphold religious freedom, yet retained the custom by which men lost their office and estates if they changed their religion, or, rather, their Church membership. He states that Lugard treated what was a mere custom as if it had been part of a written agreement between the parties (3–7).

His second charge is that, after gaining some " superficial success " in maintaining confidence and order, after disposing of the Muslim menace which was the main sanction enforcing unity on the Christian parties, he did not return to Kampala but went off to the west for six months taking with him some 90 per cent of the soldiers and 80 per cent of the porters, and leaving Williams with a quite inadequate force with which to maintain peace and order and carry out the promises made in the treaty with Mwanga. This weakness led to a sharp deterioration in the position in Uganda, while Macdonald is at pains to show that the various advantages which Lugard claimed to result from his expedition amounted, in practice, to little or nothing. Especially with regard to the Sudanese soldiers, all Lugard achieved, he said, was to remove their plundering activities rather nearer to Uganda and to strengthen his garrison there by no more than a hundred men. Macdonald uses Lugard's own reports, with, for example, their stress on the necessity for a strong garrison in Kampala, to prove this argument (7–11).

Macdonald's third charge was the gravest of all. " On Captain Lugard's return from Kavalli he does not appear to have realized the changed conditions, and, by adopting a high-handed policy and by injudicious management of the crisis, he precipitated civil war in Uganda " (13). In order to sustain this case Macdonald went minutely over the events leading up to the fighting of January 24th. He censured Lugard for his harsh handling of the " murder " which arose from the gun theft, especially for demanding the " murderer's " execution, although the killing, the report states, constituted legitimate self-defence by Uganda law. Lugard is further censured for sending the Somali, Dualla, to negotiate upon an issue which should have been handled only by a European, and so inviting insult, and for his issues of arms to the Protestants on January 22nd and 24th. This had a provocative effect and allowed the control of events to pass into the hands of savage allies (18–19).

This, the most damning, was not the last of Macdonald's condemnations. Lugard was charged with neglecting to give adequate protection to the priests at the outbreak of hostilities (19–20); of falsely charging them of using their knowledge of the Company's policy of evacuation to injure his position (30–31); and of treating the Roman Catholics unjustly in the allocation of land after the war (35–36). On this point, Macdonald said that, after leading the priests to believe that their party would get a very large share of the country, if not indeed a half, Lugard, under pressure from the Ingleza, after the Fransa had kept their word by returning the King, allocated to them only one province.[1] On the other hand, rather surprisingly—perhaps because Williams, the chief actor there, was at hand to justify the operations—Lugard was defended for ordering the attack upon Bulingugwe island (32–33); for his conciliatory action after this (20–21); and for his treatment of the priests (30–32); and he was absolved from responsibility for African acts of barbarism and enslavement. On the contrary, upon this last count, Macdonald censured the priests " for the grossly exaggerated language they have used with regard to those atrocities which, when examined, prove to have been surprisingly few " (35).

This was the report which, a year and five months after the events it judged, came into the hands of the Cabinet. The first thought of ministers, as politicians, was that it was not the kind of report that could be published or could, indeed, be of very much use to them as a reply to the reiterated protests of the French government. As an

[1] The point with regard to the division of land after the war was very complex as it hinged largely upon a long letter which Lugard wrote to Père Achte in Latin on March 6th 1882, in answer to one in which Achte offered to make peace. Achte wrote, of the Fransa chiefs, " Ils vous demandent de partager le pays en deux parties distinctes. Le capital du Roi serait au milieu." To this Lugard replied that if certain conditions were accepted, and especially the return of the King, " non recusem quas obtulisti conditiones de terra dividenda . . . Sed tu, Pater Achte, *fide Britannica eaque militari fretus,* ne dubites quin, *rege reddito,* pro virili parte nitor pactionem conficere quum Protestantibus tum Catholicos acceptam, conditionibus quas obtulisti congruentem." The official translation is: " . . . I would not object to a division of the country on the conditions you name . . . And you, Father Achte, can trust the word of a British Officer, that when the King has returned I will do my *utmost* to effect a settlement satisfactory to both parties on the lines you indicate." (91). Here there is clearly plenty of material for misunderstanding and matters were made worse by Père Achte interpreting a general remark at the beginning of Lugard's letter. " Crede mihi, te obsecro, illiud unum jamdudum consequor ut pacem obtineam, necnon ut jus aequum utrique parti aequaliter distribuatur." (" To preserve peace here has (I beseech you to believe) been my one aim here, and to see that justice is done equally to both sides.") It should have been clear that Lugard is here speaking generally of his attitude and that it was justice, not land, that he meant to deal out " aequaliter." Yet upon this Hirth made the stinging reproach that Lugard had forfeited his *fide militari* " by a deceit " and that this would be published in Europe (101).

351

official document, lying on the desk of a minister 3,000 miles away from Uganda, it must have been read, once the competence and impartiality of its author were accepted, as condemning Lugard for some important failures in judgment, ability and humanity, and it made him largely responsible for provoking the final hostilities. Thus it put the Company, and so, to a still undecided extent, the British government, in the wrong.

But could the report be divorced from the circumstances in which it had been drawn up? These circumstances were to constitute the chief element in Lugard's defence and we should consider them before we look at his reply to the charges.

Macdonald had, through no fault of his own, conducted a trial in which not only the accused but any counsel for the defence was absent. It appears that after Lugard left there was a revulsion of feeling against him. It is difficult to recapture the reasons. It may have been relief at the removal of the strong hand; it may have been the eager desire of the several parties to pile upon the absent one all the blame for what had happened, rather than each should accept that share which undoubtedly belonged to most of them. Portal, indeed, received evidence of this attitude even before he entered Uganda. He was, in any case, quite in the mood to condemn all the Company agents for he had been sending back to the Foreign Office, as he marched inland, letters strongly criticizing what he regarded as the lethargy and inefficiency in the running of the Company's stations on the way up. He was, perhaps, the more ready to disparage as he hated " this beastly country " and every minute of time he spent there. Before he reached Uganda he was met by letters from some of the British there, showing grave discontent and making accusations against Lugard, especially of breaking his word.[1] When Portal arrived in Kampala he heard from Macdonald of the censures of Lugard which he was writing in his report and he sent them on at once in advance to Rosebery. To his colleague, Rennell Rodd, who was acting for him in Zanzibar, he was still more frank. " I find Williams, Eric Smith " (a Company agent sent up to relieve Williams), " Macdonald and missionaries all sitting in open-mouthed astonishment at Lugard's reports which, I fear, must be read only as vivid works of fiction." Macdonald's long and careful report " will be read with something approaching to consternation

[1] Portal to Lady Portal and to Rosebery, 3 March 1893, P.P. s. 109.

by the public who have been so enthusiastically chanting Lugard's praises. The general impression here is that the man is off his head, and I should not wonder if this were the case. He was quite mad three years ago after his return from Nyasa."[1] It is especially disappointing, after their virile partnership and Lugard's emphatic defence of Williams in Britain, to find that even he, if only momentarily, had turned against his former chief. Portal writes that he is " guarded about Lugard, but evidently sore about him and thinks he has been gravely to blame and war wrongly reported, [and] feels he has been badly treated."[2] What Hirth had to say about Lugard can be imagined, while, to add to the damning chorus, Gedge, whom Lugard had superseded and packed off from Uganda in a state of nervous collapse, had returned to the scene as *The Times* correspondent and was " strong against Lugard's actions .... but has been guarded in letters to *The Times* so far."[3]

This, then, was the atmosphere in which Macdonald concluded his report. But the worst has still to be told. One member of the little group of Europeans on the north-west coast of Lake Victoria needs very special mention, since his antagonism to Lugard was to have considerable effect though it was finally of a boomerang character. It is a strange story, which reflects seriously upon both Portal's and Macdonald's judgment.

It will be remembered that Lugard, on his way back to the coast, met a German newspaper correspondent, Eugène Wolf, on his way up to Uganda and had so satisfied him with his story that Wolf said he wanted to turn back. But he was urged by Lugard to go on and judge for himself.[4] What he did not tell Lugard was that he had been commissioned by Portal to report to him upon the condition and prospects of Uganda, including the " actual history as to the unfortunate events in Uganda .... and as to the causes and origin of all the trouble." But he was not to publish anything himself without first showing it to Mr. Berkeley, the Company Administrator.[5] It was clear that when Wolf reached Kampala with Martin's caravan, a few days after Macdonald, he claimed, and was given, something very much

1 Portal to Rennell Rodd, 31 March 1893, P.P. s. 109.
2 Portal's Diary, 23 March 1893, P.P. s. 111.
3 Ibid. 22 March 1893.
4 See above p. 325.
5 Portal to Wolf, 7 August 1892, P.P. s. 106.

like the position of co-Commissioner. "We intend to make all enquiries together" he wrote to Portal "and then work out our Reports independently of each other." Yet such precautions in favour of impartiality seemed to have been superfluous since he went on: "do not send back those men on whom the blame, as it looks today, must ultimately rest. Today, already, I think I would face Captain Lugard openly and tell him frankly 'you have done much to add, to raise, such a bitter feeling, such an evil spirit, but I will wait yet and decide later on.'"[1]

In the report Wolf's signature is found upon each item of evidence and in one place he even wrote in his opinion of the reliability of a witness.[2] Macdonald's use of Wolf was actually acknowledged in the preamble of his report where he states that Wolf "was present at the enquiry and signed the evidence as witness." Macdonald gave the very inadequate reasons for taking this course that Wolf was debarred (though only for the moment), from sending publications to the press except with Portal's consent. "His presence was of value to me."[3] Certainly Wolf's knowledge of French and German must have helped Macdonald in the interpretation of the evidence of the Roman Catholic missionaries, but he cannot have been an impartial medium. Portal found Wolf "strongly anti-Lugard" and had to persuade him to say and publish nothing until after Macdonald's report got home. There is external evidence of the part Wolf played not only, as we shall see, from Bishop Tucker, who may be accounted a partisan, albeit a moderate one, but by the French priest, Antony Philippe.[4] Gedge's diary, also, confirms the intimate association of Macdonald with Wolf. At Kampala they seem to have messed together regularly; and they were in company for the journey, lasting nearly a month, which was undertaken by Macdonald to the French Fathers' establishments in Buddu.[5] It is also worth recording that Wolf, who continued his attacks upon Lugard after his return to Germany, was acclaimed on the priests' side as "l'homme de la Providence .... Honneur", writes Père Leblond, "à cet homme loyal et courageux."[6] He was made a Chevalier of the Légion d'Honneur by the French government,

1 Wolf to Portal, 12 December 1892, F.O. 2/61.
2 *Report*, p. 61.
3 *Report*, p. 2.
4 A. Philippe, *Au Coeur de l'Afrique* (Paris 1929), p. 114 ff.
5 Gedge Papers.
6 Leblond, *Auguste Achte*, p. 212.

received in audience by the Pope who, at the request of the Superior of the White Fathers, named him, Protestant though he was, a Commander of the Order of Pius IX.[1]

Lugard's critics had some qualms about the possible reactions of their victim. Portal was writing to Rosebery letters which would undermine his faith in Lugard, and warning him that the report would be "severe and disagreeable", but fully proved by the evidence.[2] Yet he wrote to the Foreign Office " I wish it were possible to avoid the publication of Macdonald's big report, but I suppose it must come out. It will make the devil of a row, and Lugard will naturally say that he declines to admit what he would call the charges of a junior officer against his senior . . . . the whole thing is most disagreeable and unfortunate, and has been made worse by Lugard's apparent inability to restrain his pen."[3] Macdonald, for his part, though Portal wished him to remain and take charge, was anxious to get back to England in order to answer Lugard's expected counter-attack.

The scene must shift from Uganda back to London where Rosebery and his colleagues were much troubled by the report, which reached them on June 27th, and by Portal's letters. But at this fateful moment in Lugard's career, the mistakes made in the circumstances of the commission suddenly came to his aid, reinforced, it seems, by some of the Foreign Office staff. The Cabinet decided to appoint a small committee of their own members to study the report, but even in the letter discussing whether a non-parliamentary military expert would be a desirable addition, Gladstone wrote to Rosebery: " Re Captain Lugard and Macdonald. Salisbury seems to have blundered in appointing a personal enemy to report on Lugard's acts. Certainly a difficult situation."[4] On the morrow of this discovery came another even more damaging to the report. Two long articles appeared in the *Berliner Tageblatt* by Wolf in which he gave the gist of the Macdonald report (which the Cabinet were keeping absolutely secret), and claimed to have in his possession duplicates of all the evidence and most of the other documents. Sir Clement Hill, of the Foreign Office, who was asked to write a memorandum on these, pointed out that Wolf used

[1] *Ibid.* p. 213.
[2] Portal to Rosebery, 22 March 1893, P.P. s. 109.
[3] Portal to Villiers, 10 April 1893, P.P. s. 109.
[4] Gladstone to Rosebery, 20 July 1893, B.M. 44549.

" precisely the same headings " as Macdonald, and spoke of " our enquiries." He went out of his way to condemn the behaviour of the Anglican missionaries and to praise Hirth. But his strongest condemnation was for Lugard and his " breach of faith " over the peace terms. " In Germany the person who acted so would have to leave the service at once."[1] This publication was most embarrassing for the government and the telegram they sent to Rodd, the acting consul-general at Zanzibar, was severe. " You should take the first opportunity of expressing to Sir Gerald Portal the amazement felt by Her Majesty's Government that Capt. Macdonald, in making his enquiry, should have associated Herr Wolf with himself."[2] Portal's reply to this, disclaiming responsibility and playing down the part Wolf had played, was a little less than frank.[3]

But, if the Cabinet's faith in the report was shaken by these revelations, it was not destroyed. The main charges were weighty and supported by evidence and argument. The Cabinet committee set up was, therefore, a strong one. It consisted of the Lord Chancellor, Lord Herschell, who had recently reported upon the government's liability for Chartered Companies; secondly, the Chancellor of the Exchequer, Sir William Harcourt, whose deep-seated aversion from all that Lugard had said and done has been illustrated; and thirdly, Mr. Campbell-Bannerman, the Minister for War. This committee called upon Lugard to write a defence to the charges. This defence he sent in on August 18th.[4]

The document was accompanied by a letter in which he protested against judgment having been passed upon him in Uganda not only in his absence but in that of all the documents which would have explained his policy and which he had taken away with him, and he asked if he could now produce these and appear in person before the committee. He claimed that Macdonald was not qualified by six weeks' residence in Uganda to adjudicate upon his general handling of the situation, and he had in any case gone beyond his brief. He offered to show Lord Rosebery the proofs of his book, which would be the best answer—inevitably a long one!—to this charge. Finally he protested strongly against Macdonald's use of Wolf.

[1] Memorandum by Sir C. Hill, 25 July 1893, F.O. 83/1241.
[2] Rosebery to Rodd, 11 August 1893, F.O. 83/1241.
[3] Portal to Rosebery, 23 October 1893, F.O.C.P. 6497: East Africa, Part XXXV, No. 60.
[4] It is to be found in F.O. 83/1242.

Lugard arranged his defence round three main points. These, leaving out certain secondary issues, may be summarized as follows:

1. The march to the west. He was obliged to get more troops because he had learned from Williams that there was no chance of getting more from the Company. Most of his own men were not soldiers, but armed porters, who were time-expired and could not be kept in Uganda against their will. Moreover, Somalis and Sudanese recruited in Egypt were very expensive: the Kavalli Sudanese he obtained cost only one-sixth of their pay. He further justified this trek by showing that it did succeed in the several purposes to gain which he had set out.[1] As for Williams' forces, he had waited for news that all was quiet in Uganda before he finally turned west. He might have added that Williams made no protest at the time and even wanted to accompany him. This item in his defence seems a somewhat brief reply to the long and reasoned charge which Macdonald put forward. The question as to whether Lugard had any definite instructions to go to the west has been discussed above, with his reference to his " original instructions ". He does not appear, after he was accused, to have cited these orders in his defence.

2. The responsibility for hostilities. Here Lugard, in his own defence, pointed to the evacuation order and to the need to make some decisive settlement so as not to leave the onus unfairly upon Williams when he should finally leave him in charge. But it was, he said, the threat that the King might support the British side as a result of his proposed transfer to the Anglican Church—a religious matter in which Lugard was not officially interested—which roused the Fransa to violent courses. Lugard felt that the time for the prolonged balancing policy had passed, and that upon this occasion he must stand firm if there were defiance and provocation. The " murder " was only the *ultima causa* of the outbreak. It was easy for Macdonald to judge its exact character at his leisure a year later, with all the evidence collected; to Lugard at the time it was rather a matter of martial law than of any other law, though he refused to say now whether he would in fact have executed the accused man himself. As for his use of Dualla, he had endured one insult to himself, and it was not wise to court another, which would have demanded an official reaction. Nor was Dualla, intelligent and travelled, an ordinary " native ". But it was the Fransa,

---

[1] See above p. 286.

357

not he, who, having spoken and acted in the sense of making a declaration of war, actually began the fighting. It was not until after the war drums had been beaten that the main distribution of arms took place in order to save the weaker side from extermination. As to Lugard's conduct of the war, he protested against a junior officer, who had seen very little fighting, laying down a fiat as to whether a senior man's military measures were justified.

3. Terms of peace. Lugard pointed out that his main reason for not giving the Roman Catholic party more than Buddu was their then hostile attitude. He definitely said that if events made it advisable further concessions should be made. He might have added that Buddu, which the priests condemned as if it were a plague-stricken desert, was a large and most fertile province. He might also have added that the restriction concerned only the Fransa as a party, with their armed men, not Roman Catholics as such.[1]

It seems as though Lugard had held himself in with difficulty in this relatively temperate defence, and at the end he suddenly released his compressed indignation in a passage that must have been more satisfying to himself than useful for his cause when addressed to, and indeed to some extent, aimed at, his ministerial judges. It is so much in character that it is worth quoting almost in full.

" For my own part I have no sympathy with that species of humanitarianism which appears to consider a war, undertaken against savages armed mainly with spears, a matter of small moment, while an outbreak between two native factions of *soi-disant* ' Christians ', whom for a year, with the utmost labour and difficulty, we had kept apart, is stigmatised as ' an unhappy war '—' a forbidding chapter ' etc. etc., and my policy of letting them as far as possible fight it out together is loudly condemned. I will state frankly my view that the disregard for human life and suffering which has been only too plainly shown in the dealings of many—if not of most—of those who have been in Africa, when contrasted with the sentimentality evinced about this outbreak between two factions of the natives in Uganda—an ordeal by which alone an ultimate peace could be effected—betrays to my mind an unworthy fear of the loud-voiced criticisms of a parcel of missionaries who have done much—as stated in this report—to bring about the ' deplorable ' situation .... As it was, the war was

---

[1] Lugard II, pp. 430–1.

between two factions animated by the meanest and most rancorous jealousy and rivalry and characterised by lying, theft and murder before the event and by atrocities after it, while the teachers of religion are not held inviolate by the investigator. Such being the case, strong and decided measures were the best for the ultimate good."

There can be little doubt that in writing the first part of this conclusion, Lugard was thinking of the inhumanity he had alleged against Macdonald in his dealings with his porters and his joining—gratuitously as Lugard thought—in punitive expeditions against the Kikuyu, which he appears to have done rather lightheartedly and without any official warrant.[1] But the Kikuyu had no one to publicize their losses. This whole passage raises issues which must be faced at the end of this chapter.

The Cabinet committee were not, understandably enough, satisfied with Lugard's reply. The Lord Chancellor wrote a memorandum upon it which showed that both his legal eyes and the political eyes of his colleagues had scrutinized it with care.[2] How was it, it was now asked, that Lugard should have chosen to act so strongly upon one particular deed of lawless violence, when there had been so many upon which he might have taken strong measures, and why did he choose such a dubious case as Mongolobo's "murder"? And how could "Martial Law" be said to exist when no war had yet broken out? It would seem, Herschell went on, that Lugard would have been wiser to allay than to aggravate the excitement. Lugard's own words suggested that he had decided the time had come to precipitate rather than prevent a crisis. As to the issue of arms, he made the first issue (of only forty guns) *before* the war-drums had been beaten, to save the weaker side. It did not save them: Lugard intervened with his strong force which he could have done without having issued the arms. If, however, both factions were what he describes them in such strong terms, why did he place weapons of precision in the hands of one such party, and later employ them in the attack on Bulingugwe island? The committee asked Lugard to reply upon these points.

He found their questions " distinctly hostile—apparently they have accepted Macdonald's views." (L. to E. J. L. 30 November 1893).

---

[1] Macdonald, *Soldiering and Surveying*, p. 111 ff.
[2] F.O.C.P. 6538: East Africa, Part XXXVI, No. 4.

However, he had to answer. He gave a fuller account of the Mongolobo affair, showing that all the evidence he had at the time pointed to the guilt resting with the killers, and that it was an isolated and outstanding act which might have led to war if not firmly dealt with. It should not be forgotten that the Ingleza and their European missionaries were also excited and difficult to placate. He explained that by forcing a crisis he meant not war, but an assertion of authority and strength which would save the situation. " I cannot too strongly say how bitterly grieved I was at the outbreak of war and how keenly and intensely I felt it."

As to control of his Ingleza Baganda allies in the field, that would have been impossible, as Macdonald now knew, as he had recently turned them loose upon the Muslim party, incidentally breaking Lugard's pledges to the latter.[1] In any case, Lugard denied that the Ingleza had committed atrocities: they had behaved with a restraint and humanity quite novel in Uganda. He had *not* waited to intervene in the fight until the Ingleza had been defeated: he had intervened at once and they had *not* been defeated; with the help of their new arms they had been victorious round Mengo. " Yes," he asserted, coming to what was really the heart of the matter, " it was essential in my view that the Protestants should not be annihilated and driven out of the country." The Company could not have maintained itself without their presence. Surrounded by the Fransa, they would have been at their mercy and might have had to choose between starving and cutting their way out of the country. As for the Ingleza, who had welcomed the Company and stood by it, they would have been exiled, enslaved or massacred. In conclusion, Lugard again politely offered to send the committee a copy of his book, which had been published in the interval, since in that they would find the fullest account of the whole story.[2]

The Cabinet committee can hardly have wanted any *more* information. They had all too much: their problem was to judge the conflicting evidence and to satisfy the conflicting parties. The Foreign Office had now been pleading its ignorance and asking all critics to await the forthcoming report for nearly two years after the events in question had occurred and putting off the reiterated demands made by

1 For these events see Macdonald, *op. cit.* p. 242 ff.
2 Lugard's book came out at the end of November. This helps to date this undated document.

the French government and by members of parliament for information and for action. Yet Gladstone's Cabinet still hesitated and having used both the sending of the Macdonald report to a Cabinet committee as one reason for delay, they now pleaded the coming Portal report as a further excuse, though this second document was not supposed to deal with Lugard's conduct.

Not surprisingly, after a slight exercise of patience, French indignation kindled again. Uganda was not the only place where French and British were at odds. Beyond the main causes for alienation in Europe and Egypt, interests were clashing in Siam, China, Newfoundland, Madagascar and, increasingly during 1893 and 1894, along the Niger. Here in 1893, the expedition of Lieutenant Mizon into Niger Company territory had resulted in a long and angry diplomatic conflict. Contacts with France upon colonial questions increased so much during 1892–3 that our embassy in Paris was writing to the Foreign Office for a new press in which to keep the correspondence with the African department—1,200 dispatches exchanged in the last eighteen months.[1] Successive French ministries felt that in the Uganda " atrocities " they had a peculiarly effective weapon to use against a country which prided itself upon its correct and humane behaviour.

French irritation was thus a natural accompaniment of the almost unregulated struggles for expansion and assertion in Asia and Africa, and Britain, when the mood was on her, was ready to retort in kind. The mood of France at this time was peculiarly restless. The shadow of 1870 had not yet lifted: the desire to dispel it by a spirited external policy was frustrated by a creaking constitution and deep political and social divisions at home. The French, Lord Dufferin told his government, are " morbidly longing for sympathy and admiration . . . . They have a feeling that we are always getting the better of them all over the world and crossing their path at the very point where it is about to open on some extraordinary advantage."[2] Rosebery had found it necessary, shortly before this, to speak very severely to M. d'Estournelles about the anti-British violence of the French press.[3]

In the autumn and winter of 1893, the French ambassador, now M. Decrais, who had taken up his duties in July, was ordered to resume the pressure for a Uganda settlement. Rosebery told the ambassador

[1] Phipps to Rosebery, 26 August 1893, F.O. 27/3120.
[2] Dufferin to Rosebery, 3 November 1893, F.O. 27/3121.
[3] D'Estournelles to Develle, 3 July 1893, *D.D.F.* X. p. 413.

that the Macdonald report was not a diplomatic question proper and that he had submitted it to a Cabinet committee. The French ambassador declared himself astonished at the use of this device, hitherto used only for domestic affairs when the Cabinet was divided,[1] and the French Foreign Minister, M. Casimir-Périer,[2] condemned Rosebery for trying to escape from his responsibility and put it upon an anonymous committee.[3] The French embassy, watching affairs closely, had already discovered the enmity between Macdonald and Lugard: "But he [Lugard] has some powerful supporters who will agitate no doubt to diminish at once his responsibilities and the reparations which are due to our missionaries."[4] The publication of Lugard's book was noted with the justifiable comment that, like most English books of the kind, it was "*peu condensé*."[5] In spite of this poor recommendation, the Foreign Minister told the ambassador to buy a copy for the French government.[6]

With the return of Portal to the country, hard on the heels of his report, which he was apparently asked to rewrite upon arrival,[7] the French were cheered by the discovery that Portal was regarded in Britain as " infinitely too favourable to France ". Less cheerful, however, was the news that, in eagerly awaiting this report, the one question of interest, even to Lugard, still seemed to be the future of Uganda, not the grievances of France.[8] It was exasperating news, too, that the Cabinet committee was proceeding to examine its Uganda dossier with " judicious sluggishness and deep mystery ".[9] Questioned about this, Rosebery gave new reasons for delay. One was that two new documents had turned up in the Lugard affair—an item which provoked a vigorous but unintelligible mark in the margin at the Quai d'Orsay—and the British Foreign Secretary went on to plead the frightful overwork of his government. " Je m'acquitte de ce message," wrote the ambassador, " mais sans conviction."[10]

1 Decrais to Casimir-Périer, 20 December 1893, A.A.E. vol. 890, f. 363.
2 Casimir-Périer, Jean, 1847-1907; 1876 first elected Deputy; 1877 Under-Secretary of State for public instruction and later Under-Secretary for war; 1893 Premier and Foreign Minister; 1894 resigned and became President of the Chamber; 27 June 1894 President of the Republic; 15 January 1895 resigned.
3 Casimir-Périer to Decrais, 31 December 1893, *D.D.F.* X. p. 713.
4 D'Estournelles to Develle, 8 September 1893, A.A.E. vol. 888, f. 77.
5 D'Estournelles to Develle, 23 November 1893, A.A.E. vol. 890, f. 143.
6 Develle to D'Estournelles, 29 November 1893, A.A.E. vol. 890, f. 189.
7 For evidence upon this point see below pp. 450-1.
8 Decrais to Casimir-Périer, 29 December 1893, A.A.E. vol. 890, f. 400.
9 Ibid. 6 January 1894, A.A.E. vol. 891, f. 24.
10 Decrais to Casimir-Périer, 11 January 1894, A.A.E. vol. 891, f. 58.

The Macdonald Report

These two new documents to which Decrais referred are ones of importance to our story. Lugard had not only the " powerful supporters " to which the French had referred; he had the fighting spirit to deploy them effectively, even when in battle with a British Cabinet. In a rich torrent of mixed metaphors he reported his defiance to his brother. " It looks as though they wanted to make me a Jonah to lighten the ship for France. They'll find I am a hard nut to crack yet—I've got various irons in the fire." (L. to E. J. L. 13 December 1893). Two of these " irons " were Bishop Tucker and Williams, both now in England. They wrote him letters in answer to his requests and their testimony was of great value to him because of the weight which their character and close knowledge gave them. Williams, who seems to have recovered from his temporary alienation from his colleague, wrote of the violent prejudice against Lugard of Wolf and also that " Macdonald associated Wolf with him in the enquiry." Gedge, who was close to Macdonald, had been equally biased. Williams also stated his opinion that Lugard had been absolutely right to bring in the Sudanese and the Muslim Baganda, both points upon which he was criticized to the Foreign Office by Macdonald and Portal. For himself, Williams complained of the French priests' " atrocious charges against us, none of which they have ever publicly modified or withdrawn." The letter of the Bishop who, like Williams, had been in Kampala during Macdonald's enquiry, was even more valuable to Lugard, though he had failed in his effort to get permission to see the Macdonald report.[1] He now stated the unqualified disapproval with which the English missionaries regarded the whole enquiry, and confirmed all the Cabinet's doubts about the employment of Wolf. In spite of his violent prejudices, Wolf was allowed to sit as " a sort of Joint Commissioner." He was permitted " to examine and cross-examine witnesses, to suggest this and that possible explanation . . . every scrap of evidence passed through his hands. . ." For three or four months his intercourse with Macdonald was incessant. The Bishop also complained that Macdonald refused to hear the evidence either of leading chiefs, or of the representatives of the C.M.S. missionaries, both of whom could have thrown light upon the causes of the war. Any one of these errors would have been enough to vitiate the report: taken together they made it " a parody of justice ".

[1] Anderson to Tucker, 16 December 1893, F.O. 83/1244.

Lugard sent these two documents to the Foreign Office. In his covering letter he remarked that Macdonald's latest reported action, that of making war on the Muslims and expelling them and disarming the Sudanese under the threat of annihilation by the Maxim, are " a very pertinent commentary on much of the criticism he has passed upon myself in his report."

This evidence, and especially the Bishop's letter, gave serious pause to the Cabinet. It was not only what the Bishop *said* but what he *was* which counted with the politicians. He was a man of high character and known moderation, " a very fine fellow ", Euan-Smith had told Salisbury, " a muscular Christian in the best sense of the word, and a man of striking energy and lovable character ".[1] He was also the representative of a great and remarkably tenacious missionary society with very wide support and influence in Britain. Moreover. Portal himself had highly praised his temperate and pacifying influence in Uganda.

" Too late," Sir Percy Anderson minuted when he sent on these two documents to Rosebery. But Rosebery, though he agreed it was a pity they had not arrived before the last meeting of the Cabinet committee, ordered them to be printed and circulated to the whole Cabinet.[2] One result was that Herschell interviewed the Bishop who pressed home his points.[3]

It must have been no small help to Lugard's cause that at this very moment dispatches arrived from Uganda reporting in full the very severe measures Macdonald had taken against the Muslims. In Sir Percy Anderson's note—and its very wording is significant—" he allowed and, indeed, encouraged the Christians to drive them out . . . . He then partitioned their territory among the Christians ", making war inevitable.[4] Moreover, contrary to his own claim, he seemed to have done this without the assent of Portal, who, having handed over the administration to Macdonald, was already on his way to the coast. Portal was unwilling to return in order to relieve Macdonald of responsibility, and, indeed, accused him of alarm and exaggeration and wrote in his diary that he was in a " nervous and worried state,"

---

[1] Euan-Smith to Salisbury, 21 July 1890, S.P. vol. 80 (Zanzibar 1890–2).
[2] L. to Anderson, 3 January 1894, enclosing Williams and Tucker to L. 21 and 23 December 1893, and minutes of Anderson and Rosebery, F.O. 83/1309.
[3] Herschell to Rosebery, 19 February 1894, F.O. 83/1309.
[4] Anderson to Rosebery, 22 February 1894, F.O. 83/1309.

and " all for more swashbuckling policy and direct administration."[1] As Portal, before his sudden and early death, had been in close touch with Rosebery, he may have added to his later doubts as to the complete competence of their Commissioner. Lugard had found Portal very friendly upon his return; and Lugard wrote to his brother that Bishop Tucker told him he thought he had squashed the Macdonald report, " Sir Percy Anderson is now *very* cordial to me and seems to identify himself with my defence! I *think* I shall win." (L. to E. J. L. 27 March 1894). Yet he had some apprehension when he heard that Macdonald was on his way home. " Truly," he told his brother, " the gods have fought on my side to keep him away so long. Please Heaven the Uganda question and his ' Inquiry ' will be finished before he arrives to stir the mud . . . . I wish Macdonald was going straight to India. I hope he won't be able to upset the apple-cart here—I've my hands full without having to fight him, but, by all that's vindictive, if he forces me I'll make things buzz a bit around him, I think . . . . " Then, capable of self-knowledge, for all his fierce self-will, he broke off, " I am tired, old boy, and am writing in a high falutin' and conceited way . . . . " (L. to E. J. L. 7 April 1894).

Lugard had now little to fear from Macdonald. The latter's authority had been successfully shaken and, when he finally returned in the summer of 1894, it was intimated to him that his report was by then a *chose jugée*, which it would be very unwise for him to take up. Gladstone was sinking into his retirement, leaving a government weak with dissensions, in which the Uganda issue had been one of the more important. It was not, therefore, surprising that with a subject which was so thorny with personal, party, religious and international difficulties, the Cabinet should have flinched from decisive action. They came at last to a stumbling political halt in a position of chosen obscurity. Under the mounting fire of French indignation, the new Prime Minister, Rosebery, who wanted to come to a general settlement with France on all outstanding differences, at last authorized a dispatch which contained this passage: " The inquiry by the committee of the Cabinet into treatment of the Roman Catholics by Captain Lugard revealed such great discrepancies of evidence that, while carefully guarding himself against attaching any blame to the British Officers,

[1] Diary, 15 May 1893, P.P. s. III; letters to Lady Portal, 26 June 1893, P.P. s. 113.

Lord Rosebery has expressed to M. Decrais the willingness of Her Majesty's Government to indemnify the Roman Catholic Mission in Uganda."[1] The British government suggested that it was the principle that mattered, not the sum. The French feeling was that the size of the payment was *not* secondary to them.[2] They had originally claimed a million francs: Portal and Macdonald had advised £22,000. Unfortunately for the French case, Monsignor Livinhac, who had been formerly in Uganda, and was now the Superior-General of the White Fathers with headquarters at Algiers, was in London and he, Cardinal Vaughan, and the Duke of Norfolk weakened the French government by being far more interested in securing rights for the future, than compensation for the past. The two governments now found themselves haggling like a couple of market women. The Foreign Office wanted to keep the payment strictly related to the actual material damages, not to any vague compensation for bad treatment or " spiritual damages ". The French said that, after all their missionaries had suffered, they would not accept a mere " charitable offering ".[3] Lord Kimberley, the new Foreign Secretary, started the bidding as low as £5,000.[4] The French Prime Minister noted that Dufferin seemed ashamed to make this offer which certainly was hardly consonant with a proud statement he had made that " when a great country recognized that it was a debtor, it should acquit itself liberally."[5]

So the matter dragged on. Kimberley actually suggested that Britain would pay up if the French would remove Hirth from Uganda, as Macdonald, now much sadder and wiser, had reported upon the impossibility of working with such a man and begged that he might be replaced by someone more moderate.[6] The French replied they would first like to see the money and then they would consider the question.[7] They concluded from Portal's report, published on April 10th, that what he did not say was more important than what he did as far as concerned their affair. He was silent about the missionaries and about Lugard, but his strong condemnation of the Company

1 Rosebery to Decrais, 7 March 1894, F.O. 83/1310.
2 Decrais to Casimir-Périer, 8 March 1894, A.A.E. vol. 892, f. 80.
3 Casimir-Périer's note on interview with Dufferin, 21 March 1894, *D.D.F.* XI. p. 117, n 3.
4 Casimir-Périer to Decrais, 22 March 1894, A.A.E. vol. 892, f. 190.
5 Decrais to Casimir-Périer, 29 March 1894, A.A.E. vol. 892, f. 248.
6 Macdonald to Portal, 10 November 1893, F.O. 83/1310.
7 Decrais to Casimir-Périer and Casimir-Périer to Decrais, 5 April 1895, A.A.E. vol. 893, ff. 32 and 40.

showed, they assumed, what he thought of that officer.[1] A few days later d'Estournelles spilt over to Kimberley the French hatred for Lugard. Not only France but Germany also, he said, considered the whole Uganda affair as bad for the honour of England, crushing for the Company and for Captain Lugard. He listed again the misdeeds of Lugard who had not hesitated to destroy the nascent civilization of Uganda by the most barbarous methods. He took up a remark of Kimberley's about Hirth with the retort " that it was inadmissible and shocking to name in the same breath Captain Lugard and this prelate who had rendered such great services which even the British had recognized."[2]

This was by no means the end of the matter. The deterioration in Anglo-French relations in the next four years, and the entanglement of the Uganda compensation issue with a number of other colonial disputes, prevented its final settlement. We cannot follow its intermittent recurrence on both sides of the Channel in diplomatic and parliamentary proceedings in which the name Lugard continued to fester in this unhealed wound, just when the French felt that he was inflicting new injuries upon them on the other side of Africa. It was not until the general settlement of 1898 that Britain at last settled this controversial payment for the sum of £10,000.[3]

For Lugard the British side of his arraignment was more important than the international side. But he could now afford to wait calmly for the end of the affair. As we shall see still more clearly from the next chapter, his deeds, his book, his resounding campaign for the retention of Uganda had made him a public figure, controversial, indeed, but no obscure and convenient scapegoat to be driven into the wilderness of censure and resignation. True, he was to have no clear, public acquittal from the charges, but two events may be said to have concluded the matter for him. After the government's many evasions and pleas for delay, Sir Edward Grey at last announced in the House of Commons, in reply to a demand for the publication of the Macdonald report, that " it cannot be regarded as disposing finally of the question either of fact or of principle with regard to the only point arising out of this war which is still in dispute—namely, the claim to compensation put forward by the Catholic Missionaries. Her

---

[1] Decrais to Casimir-Périer, 12 April 1894, A.A.E. vol. 893, f. 115.
[2] D'Estournelles to Casimir-Périer, 25 April 1894, A.A.E. vol. 893, f. 232.
[3] F.O. to Treasury, 8 February 1898, F.O. 27/3437.

Majesty's Government are therefore not prepared to present the Report to Parliament."[1]

This was not a statement likely to satisfy Lugard's critics, and Lugard's acts, his Maxim gun and the wrongs suffered by the French priests gained recurrent mention in both Houses, Labouchere and Dilke keeping the question alive in the Commons.[2] It was not until the June debate on Uganda in the Lords that Lord Rosebery rounded off Sir Edward Grey's pronouncement upon the Macdonald report. The Duke of Norfolk was indignant that the report should be " bottled up ", and said he would not undertake not to go on pressing for its publication. How much his cause had been put upon the defensive since it was first set in motion is shown by his plea that non-publication should not be allowed to result in Roman Catholic Missionaries " suffering in any way from any reflection upon their conduct imputed to them in the past."[3] Lord Rosebery insisted that the report was confidential and that it would be against the public interest to present it to parliament, all the more as he was still in communication with the French government about the questions it raised. (We may note in passing that he stated, as if it was very much a fact to be remarked, that the present Commissioner in Uganda was on cordial terms with Hirth). Lord Salisbury, speaking with the responsibility that came from experience and wisdom, accepted the government's reticence. But he was quick to question the propriety of admitting (" even recognizing," he added with a not illegitimate indulgence in his customary sarcasm, " to the utmost the zeal of France for the Roman Catholic Church,") that France had any right to protect Roman Catholics throughout the world. Lord Rosebery took the occasion to make the final official interment of the Macdonald report as far as its British aspect was concerned. Macdonald, he said, had not been appointed as a judicial Commissioner, " he happened to be an engineer officer on the spot " and he was asked " to furnish the government in confidence a *prima facie* relation of the impression produced in his mind by such enquiry as he could conduct in Uganda." He went on with the muffling vagueness with which the government had decided to wrap this awkward document—" The Report in itself was, I will not say

1 *Parliamentary Debates*, 17 April 1894, IV. 23. 620–1.
2 See for example *Parliamentary Debates*, 14 February 1895, IV. 30. 836; 1 April 1895, IV. 32. 605; 27 May 1895, IV. 34. 367.
3 *Parliamentary Debates*, 1 June 1894, IV. 25. 145.

Cartoon of Lugard by Spy (Leslie Ward) autographed by
Lugard and Ward. From *Vanity Fair*, 19th December, 1895

satisfactory, but at any rate by no means conclusive, and the noble Marquis" (Lord Salisbury) " who has had so vast an experience in relation to these matters will be the first to feel that this Report is not a document that should be laid before your Lordships' House as a definite Report on this subject."[1]

The satisfaction that these pronouncements gave to Lugard suggested that he may have been ready for something worse. He asked his brother to observe "that they have thrown over Macdonald's report and condemned it as unworthy to see the light." (L. to E. J. L. 27 June 1894).

The second and more intimate event which concluded the affair for Lugard was an interview at the Foreign Office with Sir Percy Anderson. Lugard pointed out to the uncrowned ruler of Britain's new African territories that he had now been publicly on trial for practically two years; that he had been called upon to write a reply to the charges against him, that he had never had a word of reply even to his offer to come in person armed with the all important documents of the case. " Personally," he concluded, with his usual ringing certainty, " being satisfied in my own mind of the rectitude of my actions, the charges do not in any way distress me, for I have nothing to regret and I would act in a similar manner were I again placed in similar circumstances." Still, the enquiry had been an official affair. He would shortly be leaving England and before doing so he would like to receive an official letter disposing of the imputations upon his character.

Sir Percy Anderson had a difficult task with the resolute man sitting in his office. He had to satisfy him with private words without allowing him to make any public use of what was said. If, he said, Macdonald, who wanted to go back to India, ever tried to open the question he would be told he had better be entirely silent. Lugard was unduly sensitive—a strange charge, indeed, in the circumstances! He should not think there was any accusation of dishonourable conduct against him. He should be contented with Lord Rosebery's statement which made it clear that the government did not think Macdonald's report satisfactory. It was their desire—how truthfully he could say this!—to let the whole matter drop into oblivion. How could the government send him a private letter? They could only send a public document and in that case they would have to publish the Macdonald report and the evidence.

[1] *Ibid.* IV. 25. 153.

This was as far as the Foreign Office would go. Lugard had, it seems from a reading of the archives, been helped by Anderson himself. His department never treated Lugard as if he were under a cloud. He was consulted upon Uganda affairs, and the War Office was twice asked to extend his leave because the Foreign Office desired his services. Anderson sent him on a delicate mission to Paris in March 1894, to discover the plans of the West African explorer Monteil,[1] and highly commended Lugard's tact and ability upon this mission.

Lugard's final defence is to be found in his book, *The Rise of Our East African Empire*, which will be referred to in the next chapter.[2] Here, writing with full knowledge of the accusations, he gave his own account, based upon his diaries, of what had happened. But there were two other powerful factors which had helped to justify him which were not of his designing—one was the impression made by his own character and the other was the trend of events in Uganda after he left.

In the first Lugard was fortunate in the occasion which lifted him at once into the public eye not only as the man accused by the French, but at the same time, as the man who, by his acts, his dramatic dispatches and his speeches in Britain, sought to add a new country to the Empire at a time when the imperial question was among the two or three main public issues of the hour. He was, as we shall see, on the front of the political stage for some twenty-two months and he met nearly all the great men of the land in the lobbies at Westminster, at dinner parties and at the clubs. His confidence, his expert knowledge, his wide imperial view, the impress of his forthright character, his courtesy and charm, were exhibited for all men to see. Even those who were prepared to disapprove of him, must have felt as they marked him—" This man is neither a fool nor a brute. This is not a man to be thrown on one side at the bidding of French politicians or priests. He may have made mistakes but he is essentially sound, a soldier and a gentlemen." We have seen how his reports were quoted in parliament and the tributes paid him there. Soon he was so well known in person that such tributes became superfluous. Men of the stamp of Kirk, Mackenzie, Waller, Tucker and others as worthy were

---

1 See below pp. 466–7.
2 See below pp. 439–42.

his friends. The Queen and the Prince of Wales accepted copies of his book. Most of the Anglican missionaries supported him, forgetting their own earlier grievances now that he was being attacked by their Roman Catholic rivals.

Three examples of the effect Lugard created may be selected. One shows the impression made by him upon a man of the very highest judgment and character, Lord Stanmore,[1] who had been a most excellent and humane governor of Fiji. Before he even met Lugard he paid him a tribute in the House of Lords and urged that he should be sent back to Uganda. Stanmore had been an early experimenter in what was to be called the indirect method of administering tribal people, and had tried to protect the very attractive Fijians from the local settlers. He could already discern in Lugard those ideas which were afterwards to become Lugard's most substantial contribution to his country's work in Africa. Lord Stanmore gave this view in parliament and urged that the government should make use of his services, in words which have a wider interest than their immediate purpose. " I have not ", he said, " the honour of any personal acquaintance with Captain Lugard, even of the very slightest description, but it is impossible to read what Captain Lugard has written, and to know what he has done, without perceiving that he possesses that quality which is the first, the best—and I should not very greatly exaggerate if I even said, the only—essential to the successful government of native races, the power to make them act in their own way under their own leaders and of their own free will in the direction in which he wishes them to go. A man possessing that power, even if in other respects a man of but ordinary average ability, may do almost what he pleases with such a people; he can mould the course of events like wax, while a man far abler in other respects and of more varied talents but without that necessary power will be as unable to deal with natives as he would be to shape with his bare fingers a block of granite. Possibly there may be reasons against the further employment of Captain Lugard. All I would say is that they ought to be very strong ones indeed, for in a great national enterprise the Government cannot afford to throw away or disregard the services of instruments whose fitness has been already proved." Then Stanmore who, for all the status his birth and

---

[1] Stanmore, 1st Baron, Arthur Charles Hamilton Gordon, G.C.M.G., 1829–1912; successively Governor of Trinidad, Mauritius, Fiji, New Zealand and Ceylon.

achievements had given him, knew the bitterness of misunderstanding and ingratitude from his political and official masters, added that Lugard ought not to be rejected because of the displeasure of " a small knot of Members " in the Commons, or the " dissatisfaction of either British or foreign ecclesiastics "; still less because of that " incurable though very natural love of docile mediocrity " on the part of the bureaucrats.[1]

The plea failed but it was inevitable that the two men, the one at the end and the other on the uncertain threshold of a career in colonial government, should meet, drawn together by their common mind. Stanmore wrote to say he was " very anxious to have the honour of being introduced " to Lugard. They met and at once established that constructive intimacy in public matters which is possible when men have not only similar principles but similar temperaments. Lugard coached him for the debate which he raised in the Lords on June 11th. They were soon on the most friendly terms. In one letter, in which Stanmore invited Lugard to dinner to meet Lord George Hamilton and Lord Wantage, he added that the latter was a V.C. " and I think one brave man generally appreciates another." (Stanmore to L. 13 June 1894).

One more incident must be added to this account of their association, because it shows how men of their character regarded the rough process in which they were engaged. " You say ", Stanmore wrote to Lugard, " that I should be ' shocked and distressed ' if I knew ' even a fraction ' of what is done by Europeans in Africa. That is possible; but though shocked, I should not be surprised, for it is impossible to surpass the fiendish conduct I have been cognizant of in Australasia. If we ever meet again, I will tell you some of the lengths in the way of murder, vice and cruelty, ' respectable ' settlers can proceed to (and a great many had not even the outside veneer of ' respectability '), though, on the whole, I think the polite gentleman whom one meets in London or Sydney in dress clothes and with drawing-room manners, but who will torture ' a nigger ' to death without a scruple, is the worse villain of the two, for he knows better . . . . I have a whole mass of sealed-up papers marked ' Incredibilia ' though they are true enough." (Stanmore to L. 11 November 1894).

[1] *Parliamentary Debates*, 1 June 1894, IV. 25. 136–7.

Such words evoke a retrospective shame that such things could mark the extension of empire, but it is fair to note that Britain often exported the antidote with the poison in that men such as Stanmore and Lugard were ready to spend their lives on the frontiers and to bring cruelty and oppression, imported or indigenous, under some measure of control.

A second testimonial to Lugard's conduct and character came from a most unexpected quarter, that of a French explorer, M. Lionel Dècle, a man, admittedly, whose admiration for Britain led him to live much in that country and to apply later for British citizenship.[1] He went to Africa upon an official mission,[2] and found himself treading in Lugard's footsteps both in Nyasaland and in Uganda. As a result he conceived a strong admiration for the Englishman and, after he encountered Hirth and Macdonald, an indignant belief that he was being falsely accused. According to his account, after long conversations with Hirth, he " absolutely proved in writing his deliberate lies." When Hirth swore Lugard had fired on Europeans with his Maxim for half an hour, Dècle retorted " A Maxim fires 600 rounds a minute, viz. 18,000 in half an hour. Captain Lugard hadn't so much ammunition and you are all alive and well. Besides I have been out with this identical Maxim and it is absolutely worthless and with luck you may be able to get it to fire 2 rounds in a minute and yet you give people to believe that it fired 18,000." He told Hirth that though he had never met Lugard he had heard such things of him that it was impossible that he should do a weak or cowardly thing. To this Hirth is said to have replied that the man who dared in Europe to proclaim himself Lugard's friend would proclaim himself a scoundrel. Altogether, according to Lugard, Dècle formed a very adverse opinion of Hirth and it was an opinion about which he made no secret. (L. to E. J. L. 27 June 1894). He not only contradicted him in Uganda, but sent a strong official report to his government highly praising the British for their absolute impartiality, and stating that the French Fathers had deceived the French consul at Zanzibar and that Hirth was an " intriguant de la plus belle eau." The consul, Labosse, in writing to Casimir-Périer, regretted that a Frenchman, on an official mission, should have taken this line, and compared him

[1] See Dècle to Barrington, 2 November 1898, minuted by Salisbury, S.P. vol. 127 (Miscellaneous D–L).

[2] His experiences are recorded in his book, *Three Years in Savage Africa* (1898).

unfavourably with Wolf who was well received by the British, like Dècle, but was not taken in by them.[1]

It was not enough for Dècle to have received this excellent impression of Lugard *in absentia*: he was determined to see him. First, however, he went to France where he " greatly riled them by fearlessly stating the facts." Coming on to England, he told his story to Lord Ripon and Lord Kimberley and then came to see Lugard, suddenly walking in on him. " I *never* had such an interview! " Lugard told his brother. It was now that Dècle gave the account of his experiences which has just been quoted. He praised Lugard for all he had done and said that all subsequent events had proved how right he had been. " ' One thing I'll tell you. Beware of Captain Macdonald.' He added that he had himself seen that Macdonald had got all my reports and had covered them with marginal notes digging up subversive evidence even on the most trivial points." This might well have been evidence of Macdonald's thoroughness. But Dècle believed that " he was working all he knew to smash me." (L. to E. J. L. 27 June 1894).

Perhaps the third volunteer to justify Lugard was even more surprising. He was an English Roman Catholic Bishop, Patterson, the titular Bishop of Emmaeus. Having read the story, this intellectually brave man wrote to Lugard in November 1892, and asked for an interview, and for more information. He then made a minute examination of all the evidence and came to this conclusion: " I must say that the more I read and think over your report, the more evident it is to me that you acted honestly and impartially in the interests not of one party but of all." He based this mainly on Hirth's and the other priests' own statements. " I am, I need not say, quite ready to take your generous and charitable view of their action and to believe that they were very generally not consciously untruthful, though I must also say that this does not cover the *whole* of their position in my judgment." (Bishop Patterson to L. 12 December 1892). In his next letter the Bishop thanked Lugard for his confidence in his goodwill. " Of course, as you truly say, it would be more consonant with my religious convictions *a priori* to believe that our missionaries were accurate and unimpeachable: but I have always noticed that among the many good qualities in the French character, accuracy is not one." He was " convinced that *no good whatever* can come of blinking [at]

---

[1] Labosse to Casimir-Périer, 22 January and 11 May 1894, A.A.E. (Zanzibar), vol. 19.

the truth " and he was ready, pushing his principles to the extreme of practicable application with the persistence of the Good Samaritan, to do all he could to rebut " the wild statements which have been so recklessly scattered, abroad and in England too," though he thought the letters of Lugard's opponents were likely to react generally in his favour (23 December 1892). His next act was to send copies of their correspondence to some English and Irish Roman Catholic Bishops. Then he raised his sights toward Rome where, so a friend had written to him, " the French have had it too much their own way hitherto. It is such folly," the Bishop commented, " for us not to have a duly accredited agent at Rome to give the Pope *authentic* accounts of things all over the British Empire." This was written on January 28th 1893. The next month this energetic champion of what he believed to be the truth, took all the papers to Rome. From here he wrote to Lugard that some of the cardinals had already swallowed the French version and " The worst of it is that some other Englishmen who are coming here are not of my opinion." He and those who believed with him must exert their influence. " The matter has not yet come before his Holiness. His extraordinary acuteness and judgment make one trust that when he has the matter before him he will see how things really are." (8 February 1893).

In England at exactly the same time, Lugard had, by special invitation, had an interview with Cardinal Vaughan and some of his colleagues. " His representations," so the Company secretary reported to the Foreign Office, " were understood by my director to have been satisfactory to his Eminence . . . . "[1]

So much for the measure of vindication Lugard's character gained for him. The other form of vindication was provided by the actual course of events in Uganda. We have seen how both Portal and Macdonald, upon their little acquaintance of that country, condemned their absent predecessor. Portal, able but highly-strung and impressionable—he had not been reporting from Zanzibar very long before Salisbury remarked that its strong sun had got into his head[2]—seems, after his first very favourable opinion of Lugard, to have believed all his detractors: Lugard alone was the villain of the drama. It is interesting to notice how quickly Portal later turned against almost

[1] I.B.E.A. Co. to F.O., 8 February 1893, F.O. 2/57.
[2] Minute by Salisbury on Portal to Barrington, 2 September 1891, S.P. vol. 80 (Zanzibar 1890-2).

everyone in the country from whom he had gained this view. He swings from praise of Macdonald's " cool and clever head "[1] to censure of him as a nervous alarmist, afraid to take responsibility.[2] There was also strong criticism of Gedge, " an incorrigible liar "[3], and of Williams and Hirth. The latter put his views " with more force than courtesy "[4] and " though a gentleman " was " quick-tempered and untruthful ", and wrote " violent letters ". All the missionaries except Bishop Tucker were reported to be reckless in their accusations and the religious parties had made the government of the country under the Company impossible.[5] Threatened by Hirth with the menace of a strong hostile Roman Catholic state in Buddu, and by the further menace of Hirth's prolonged possession of Mwanga's young heirs, kept safely in German territory, Portal found himself obliged to give way and to increase immediately the Fransa share of the country allotted by Lugard,[6] an increase which Lugard himself had meant to make when tension should be relaxed. By the end of his dealings with Hirth, Portal must have developed considerable sympathy for Lugard, all the more as he quickly learned to loathe the whole country and to conclude that " all the Waganda are liars to the last man."[7] It was true that while there he had to suffer the loss of a much-loved brother, and was himself tired and worn. But had not Lugard's much-criticized action taken place at the end of a much more physically and mentally exhausting period in equatorial Africa, lasting for the best part of three years? And he had none of Portal's advantages, including direct imperial authority and the presence of the wise and moderate Bishop Tucker to represent the Anglican mission.

Macdonald also had found himself in almost exactly the same position as Lugard, with the Fransa holding aloof and the Ingleza warmly aiding him in a war against the Muslim parties in which he appears to have been no more, and perhaps less, able than Lugard to control his native allies. Furthermore, the Sudanese, whom Lugard had been so much condemned for bringing into Uganda, although criticized for their brutality when not under control, and later—in

1 Portal to Rosebery, 22 March 1893, P.P. s. 109.
2 Portal to Lady Portal, 26 June and 9 July 1893, P.P. s. 113.
3 Diary, 31 July 1893, P.P. s. 111.
4 C.7109 (1893), p. 15.
5 Portal to Lady Portal, 4 April 1893, P.P. s. 113.
6 C.7109 (1893), p. 14.
7 Portal to his mother, 7 April 1893, P.P. s. 108.

Lugard's view through overwork and mismanagement—becoming mutinous, yet provided the indispensable military strength behind the whole policy of occupation and won the strongest and most authoritative commendation for their loyalty, fighting qualities, and for their cheapness.[1] The latter was a vital point when parliament scrutinized every penny spent on Uganda and when Indians, Somalis or even Sudanese imported from outside were many times more costly. Finally, to complete this story of justification by after events, Sir Edward Grey confirmed that Lugard's successors had found it necessary to re-establish a line of forts to control Bunyoro, a policy which had been widely condemned, not least by Macdonald himself, as useless and oppressive. Now Macdonald had to sign a report stating " The withdrawal from the old forts was considered by Kabarega as a victory."[2] Well might Lugard score a double line beside this sentence in his copy of the Blue Book. As for Mwanga, he did later turn against the British and, as Lugard had once feared, joined with Kabarega in a desperate attempt to expel them. Both kings were finally captured in April 1899 and exiled to the Seychelles, where Mwanga died in 1903.

Still looking ahead, we find that Hirth continued to be a storm centre. He broke his word to Portal about sending back the young princes and after protracted recrimination provoked a severe rebuke from Lord Rosebery himself. It was at last decided, in 1894, that the only way to gain peaceful relations between the Roman missions and the British agents was to rearrange the ecclesiastical organization. The Mill Hill Mission, manned by British or Irish priests, was put in charge of the area north and east of Kampala, the part remaining to the White Fathers being divided into British and German spheres. Hirth controlled the latter, whereas before he had controlled the whole region.[3] Thus from almost every angle, the light thrown backwards upon Lugard's actions helped to explain and excuse if not, indeed, to justify them.

This brings us to the end of this strange story. It concerns something more than one of the many conflicts, large and small, which marked Europe's occupation of Africa, not only because its issues touched so gravely upon Lugard's honour and competence, but because of the wide religious and international ripples set in motion by this disturbance

---

[1] *Parliamentary Debates*, 11 June 1894, IV. 25. 786; also Portal in *Reports relating to Uganda by Sir Gerald Portal*. Africa No. 2 (1894), C.7303, p. 31.
[2] *Papers relating to Uganda*. Africa No. 7 (1895), C.7708, p. 27.
[3] Leblond, *Auguste Achte*, p. 215 ff.

on the shores of Lake Victoria, and because the conflict represented part of the birth pangs of the new British protectorate of Uganda. Up to this point the incident has been described with the minimum of comment, leaving the reader to judge its tangled issues. Some would say the biographer should stop there. But surely it is better for one who has read the evidence, made some study of the country and the scenes of the event, and also discussed it with some of the actual participants, including the chief actor and some aged Baganda, to offer, not indeed a judgment, but an opinion.

Even if we put upon one side the view of Macdonald's character as seen by Lugard, and assume that he went to his work with a desire to judge fairly, it must be admitted that he committed some serious errors. He made far too little allowance for the position—for which he was not, of course, responsible—which led to his judging a man in his absence, and being obliged to rely mainly upon the evidence of witnesses some of whom were bitterly hostile to Lugard and were still struggling to undo his settlement. These circumstances should have led Macdonald to be very careful both in his handling of the investigation and in the presentation of his final opinions. This was the more necessary because much of the report, and even more of the evidence, is concerned with questions not of fact, but of plans and purposes upon which Lugard's testimony was essential. There was, also, much hearsay evidence and in Lugard's copy of the report he has made indignant jottings in the margin where Hirth states what Lugard said upon occasions when Hirth was not present. It is significant that Williams, who seems at most times to have been more hated by both sets of missionaries than Lugard, but who was present to speak for himself, came out of the enquiry very well and this not only where the fact that he was second-in-command was a complete answer to the charges against him. Indeed, Macdonald and Portal went out of their way to see that this complete vindication was entered into his file.[1] A further weakness of the report, which the legal eye of Herschell may have noted, was that none of the witnesses was sworn and that some of the evidence was taken at the Roman Catholic station of Villa Maria where Père Achte, himself a witness, was on this occasion used as interpreter. And these errors were additional to the crowning error of the use made of Wolf, of which sufficient has been said. In

[1] Portal to Williams, 2 April 1893, sent by I.B.E.A. Co. to F.O. 4 August 1893, F.O. 2/59.

all these circumstances Macdonald should at least have framed his charges in less confident terms.

Leaving aside the deep question of the morality of colonial annexation which must underlie the whole incident and, indeed, most of Lugard's activities in this volume, the most serious official charge, and the one which Lugard found it hardest to meet, concerned his actions at the time of the final hostilities. Even allowing for the difficulty of judging long after the fevered event, it still seems as though, if peace at the price of anxiety and uncertainty which he had for so long paid, were still the prime end, Lugard was not blameless. His own defence against this charge is not wholly consistent. At one moment, in writing to the Cabinet committee, he seems to admit, or rather to assert, that he believed the moment for action had come. He certainly did not hesitate a moment, when hostilities broke out, to take this action. In his copy of the missionary Ashe's book, where the writer states that it was only by the Katikiro's stratagem of getting the fort between himself and the Fransa that he involved it in the fight, Lugard has pencilled " Not true, I opened fire the moment after the fight was beyond doubt begun."[1] Thus, as Herschell pointed out, he did not carry out his implied intention of leaving the factions to fight it out. And it is not easy to reconcile his statement as to the necessity for the ordeal by battle, or his view that " strong and decided measures " were best, with the sentence in his second reply where he says he was " bitterly grieved " at the outbreak of war and felt it intensely. Unless, of course, a man may grieve thus bitterly at measures which he yet believes essential.

The explanation can probably be found by trying to understand Lugard's character in relation to the position in which he found himself. He was a soldier and, though he was far more humane than most other European pioneers in Africa, he yet believed there were situations which demanded action and he hated prolonged uncertainty. There can be little doubt that, perhaps half-unconsciously, he had found the long strain of balancing between two opposing forces intolerable before he left for the west and it irked him to find the situation much the same when he returned. As he said, he knew he must soon go; the future of Uganda was uncertain; the party most friendly to the Company was in danger and he longed for some

[1] Ashe, *Chronicles of Uganda*, pp. 230–1.

decision before he went. In such a mood, his mind may have been like powder ready for the spark. The Mongolobo murder supplied it. He may very likely have been mistaken in his own summary verdict upon this, but to him it seemed a test case of his power to impose order and the treatment he received at Mwanga's court immediately after it was an indignity of the sort his spirit could not endure. It may well be that if he had then sent Williams instead of Dualla, the whole story might have been different. But after Dualla's return, with his account of insult and defiance, it was difficult for a man of Lugard's nature to retreat. He determined to act and the first issue of arms to the Protestants was probably an extra precaution following this decision. From the purely military point of view, utterly cut off as he was from any line of retreat or from any outside aid, it was mere military prudence to reinforce the weaker party upon whom alone he believed he could count in the crisis that seemed imminent. It was a difficult calculation to make. The additional armament might not be enough to guarantee success if things went badly, while it might well be enough to tip the scale in favour of war. As soon as he believed war was certain, he made his larger issue of arms. He probably hoped that his firm showing would bring the King and his party to their senses without the need for any, or at least for any prolonged, military action. But it must be remembered that Livinhac, Peters and Tucker, widely different types, had all believed that a revival of civil war—for such a war had been sporadic for years—was almost unavoidable. What would make Lugard most "bitterly grieved" was the general extension of this civil war, passing largely outside his control, which resulted from the King's flight with Hirth. Leonard Woolf, who made a detailed analysis of these actions of Lugard as an agent of "economic imperialism" decided that he worked for "this evil policy" from noble motives because he was "muddle-headed."[1] There is this much truth in the judgment that, as will appear many times, Lugard was so absolutely convinced of the rightness of his purposes that he had little use for logic in deciding his action in a crisis or in defending it afterwards.

The Roman Catholic priests, and especially Hirth, were much to blame for the almost hysterical exaggeration of some of their accusations. Their dramatic stories were winnowed out in the evidence until

[1] L. Woolf, *Empire and Commerce in Africa* (1920), pp. 290-1.

most of them were swept away and but little hard fact remained from all the reported deaths, imprsionment, enslavement, the decapitation of a woman in Sese, the "sucking babes" thrown into the bush and the rest. The pictures given of Lugard deliberately planning the destruction of the Roman Catholics, and of Williams gloating over the victims of his Maxim, were melodrama carried to excess. It is difficult, indeed, not to agree with Bishop Patterson that Hirth was guilty of something worse than exaggeration. The evidence points to his having deceived Lugard when he left Kampala fort, having agreed to try to bring the King back and so restore peace. Mwanga was not a man whose evidence can generally be respected but on this occasion his assertion that Hirth would not let him return either from the island or from their next retreat on the lake, fits in with the rest of the evidence. Hirth's statement that on Bulingugwe, where he stayed for three days, he was not in touch with the King can hardly be taken seriously by anyone who has seen this tiny island. Hirth, by his own admission, tried to undermine the faith of the Fransa in Lugard's offer of peace which he states he regarded as "*un piège*" (a trap or snare). This action Macdonald condemned, surely in very lenient terms, as "very injudicious, and to the detriment of the negotiations."[1] There seems to have been also a streak of cynicism in Hirth. Williams told Lugard that Hirth spoke of the Macdonald report as "*une plaisanterie*" (Williams to L. 23 December 1893), and when taxed by Macdonald with his gross exaggerations, he answered "Que voulez-vous, Monsieur, il fallait intéresser le publique."[2]

Yet Hirth's position must be understood. His conduct at the time and later, when he broke his word about restoring the young princes and gave Lugard's later successor, Colvile, so much trouble, is not difficult to explain. He had no sinister designs against the British agents. Nor was he likely to be working secretly for France. He had only one object, to extend the sway of his church. The obvious weakness of the Company made it perfectly legitimate for him to expect that it might be withdrawn and Uganda fall to some other power or leave him, as Lavigerie had tried to arrange at the Brussels Conference, and as many other missionaries attempted or desired at this period, to be the spiritual head of a theocracy. The key to his rage against Lugard

[1] *Report*, p. 29.
[2] Portal to Lady Portal, 4 April 1893, P.P. s. 113.

can probably be found in the much quoted sentence, " How sad the fate of our poor Uganda! A little more and it would have become a Catholic kingdom . . . . "[1] He was, of course, speaking in terms of religion, and at a moment when the guiding object of his life seemed to have been defeated. The priests claimed with truth that their converts far outnumbered the Anglicans and, with the King on their side, and chief after chief following him and bringing over their adherents, they could hope to overwhelm the Ingleza entirely in no long period. Yet Hirth always spoke as though his followers were the persecuted minority and all the aggressions were upon the other side.

It was Lugard's action in defending what he regarded as the rights of the weaker party which checked the projected Roman advance. And it was the so-called battle of Mengo, with the scattering of the Fransa, and the fickle King's later desertion to the ascendant Ingleza side, which restored the balance between the two churches which has since been largely maintained.

In an issue of this kind, how is it possible for religious partisans of either side to come to a judicial decision as to the rights and wrongs of the conflict? A detached arbitrator could do little better. For the debate about these events was, and still is, confused, because of the difficulty of finding terms to cover a conflict which was in name religious, but was so, in truth, only to a small degree, since both missions were ready—were almost obliged—to employ political forces. It is necessary to insist again that, while the Baganda could breed youths capable of martyrdom, and could number sincere Christians of both churches, the vast majority who called themselves Catholics and Protestants, Fransa and Ingleza, were simply political factions following their King, their chosen leaders or their local chiefs. The European missionaries and Lugard thus found themselves involved in a maze of misunderstanding and inconsistency. Lugard was pledged to give what the Fransa consistently claimed, complete religious toleration. But Lugard might, in the last resort, if the ever-threatening conflict broke out, be dependent upon the side most friendly to him. Could he stand by and watch them being undermined? Thus Lugard was forced into an inconsistent position in which the impartiality he claimed was really beyond his power to maintain. The French priests were thus given a strong count against him. They could also point

1 *The Tablet*, 15 October 1892.

out the weakness of his argument that it was because a rumour of the impending evacuation by the Company had been brought in by the newly-arrived priests that the Fransa had been encouraged towards belligerence. Surely the presumption would have been the very opposite, that they would have bided their time until Lugard and his soldiers and his Maxim gun had disappeared from the scene.

The religious aspect of the event makes sad reading. The action of Hirth and his fellow-priests has figured most in this account because they took the initiative in accusing Lugard, and the Anglican missionaries who had attacked Lugard earlier could afford to stand, for most of the time, in the background and watch this conflict. But their conduct was little less militant. They expected to use the Company to strengthen their position and the degree of independence Lugard tried to maintain appears to have angered some of them. It is not on record that they voiced anything so bad of their rivals as Hirth when he said " the reverend ministers . . . . practised the superstitious ceremonies of a religion as bad or worse than Islamism ",[1] but both Lugard and Portal had severe things to say of their unreasonable attitude, and even Bishop Tucker, himself the peacemaker, admitted to Herschell that commonsense " had perhaps not always characterized the proceedings of the Mission."[2]

It is hard for Christians to be confronted today with the record of this old rivalry but it is only just to Lugard to remember the deep nature of the antagonism in which he found himself entangled. The immediate disputants must not, however, be charged with too great a responsibility for the part they played in a tragic division which stretched back through three hundred and fifty years and which still divides Christendom as deeply, if not so stridently, as it did sixty years ago. Today in Buganda the two branches of the Church live side by side, not indeed in partnership, but in quietness and courtesy, while their African clergy and people, who are only indirectly heirs to the historic division, achieve the virtue of tolerance more easily than their teachers.

With all these considerations in our view, what should be our verdict upon Lugard?[3] As far as contemporary opinion was concerned, we

[1] *The Tablet*, 15 October 1892.
[2] Herschell to Rosebery, 19 February 1894, F.O. 83/1309.
[3] For a recent judgment on this issue see Oliver, *The Missionary Factor*, pp. 140–9, and ' Some Factors in the British Occupation of East Africa, 1884–94', *Uganda Journal*, vol. XV, March 1951.

have seen that the great majority of his fellow-countrymen acquitted him and that the government treated the charges as "not proven". But not only did they not send him back to Uganda, they did not, for the next six years of his prime of life, employ him at all. But this was, no doubt, due less to any considered judgment as to his having been guilty, even if only in part, of some of the charges against him, than to Foreign Office fear of delegating power along controversial frontiers to such a positive, forward-moving and vocal agent. But above all, with Anglo-French relations as perilous as they were becoming in 1894, it would have been a high provocation to France to employ him. We can, however, be more detached than Lugard's contemporaries, and we are certainly better informed. We need not, like Macdonald and Portal, measure his responsibility by considering his position in Uganda in isolation from its wider context and as if it were a normal commission. Insofar as he made mistakes, only a fraction of the blame would lie upon his shoulders. The greater part must certainly be charged to those who sent him out upon an impossible mission, the ill-armed, ill-supported agent of a Company which was even then beginning to sink under the weight of a task far beyond its resources. But the Company in turn could pass on much of its own responsibility to a government, parliament and nation which had delegated to them activities which, for political and financial reasons, they shrank from undertaking directly. Economy in this context was often cruel at once to its agents and to its potential subjects. Lugard, like many others of his day and earlier, had to risk the condemnation, as he had to take the strain, of trying to execute a policy which reached beyond the resources, moral and material, which were needed to support it. What he did achieve in his two and a half years in Uganda was substantial enough. And the name he left behind him in that country was not that of an oppressor: the old men who knew him and his work seem to remember him with a kind of admiring wonder at his strength and uprightness. When, in 1937, Lugard restored the royal drum, Wanga, which Mbogo had given him, the Kabaka, Mwanga's son, said, in his speech of appreciation, that this was " but another illustration of his readiness at all times to sacrifice his personal wishes for the sake of the public good. Lord Lugard's name will always be remembered in the history of Buganda, where his local name Kavere (or Kapelli) is now perpetuated in Buganda as a surname."

This chapter cannot close without a postscript dealing with the fate of the Sudanese whom Lugard, clutching at such strength as he could find, had brought down from Kavalli. We have seen the bargain he struck with Selim Bey, and the way in which he brought these men and their dependants into Uganda. Lugard never forgot his pledges to these people and in all the stress of his fight for his own reputation and for his Uganda policy, they were always upon his mind. His papers and the Foreign Office archives testify to his persistent struggle with uninterested British officials and an indifferent or impotent Khedive, to obtain recognition for the claims of those men, so pathetically loyal to Egypt, to proper status, payment and, where desired, repatriation.[1] It may be imagined with what especially bitter feelings he read of Macdonald's conflict with Selim Bey, who, accused of threatening to assist the Muslim Baganda party—who had also, in Lugard's view, been mishandled—was captured and sent down in disgrace to the coast with Portal, and died on the way.[2] Lugard believed, and Williams agreed with him, that nothing but harsh and injudicious treatment could have shaken Selim's loyalty.

The whole story of these Sudanese must be read with regret. It must be admitted that Lugard had taken upon himself a grave responsibility in bringing these hordes of abandoned soldiers and their dependants into or near Uganda though, as he rightly said, if they had to batten upon Africa it was better they should do so where they could be under some measure of restraint than outside any control. It was, moreover, somewhat hypocritical of Lugard's detractors in Uganda or Britain, to will the end and not the means. " These men," Williams said in his own blunt way, " were our strength . . . . no person is as competent to judge of these people as I am: and my belief in the men was justified in their behaviour." (Williams to L. 23 December 1893). In the end Lugard's successors leaned too heavily on this "strength". The ill-paid, overworked soldiers mutinied and the story ended in the tragic events of 1897.[3]

This record of the Sudanese, from the condemnation of Lugard for his employment of them to this sad end, is only one more illustration of the moral of this whole story. This is that the besetting and perhaps the ineradicable sin of an imperial democracy is the refusal to face facts,

[1] I.B.E.A. Co. to F.O., 22 February and 15 May 1893, F.O. 2/57.
[2] Macdonald, *Soldiering and Surveying*, pp. 267–73; and Portal, *Mission to Uganda*, pp. 256, 266.
[3] Jackson, *Early Days in East Africa*, pp. 304–15.

the habit of willing the respectable end and not the less respectable means. The cost of this discrepancy has to be paid for somewhere by someone or by many. In this instance payment was widely and unevenly distributed between Lugard, the missionaries, the Baganda, the Banyoro and the Sudanese. It was, perhaps, the two last who paid most heavily, though their full story would take us too far outside our proper limits. Certainly Lugard proved to the full, and not for the last time, what a heavy burden, physical, political and moral, had to be taken up by the remote agents of a nation whose policy is the ever changing product of party debate.

The tide of colonial policy had ceased to ebb. We can see now, looking back, that even the period of slack water was over and the tide was turning. But it was the movements caused by the Uganda affair, more than anything else, that showed contemporaries that the flood was now running again towards imperial expansion. This will be still more apparent in the next chapter, when we look at the other side of these events which, for the purposes of our subject, we have somewhat arbitrarily divided.

CHAPTER XX

THE CAMPAIGN FOR RETENTION

1890-1892 : Aet. 32-34

IN CHAPTER XV we saw how the order to evacuate reached Lugard in Uganda, and how he afterwards heard of its temporary postponement. But we have yet to consider what had happened in Britain to produce the order and its countermanding. We must, therefore, go back to the point where we dropped the earlier history of the Imperial British East Africa Company at the date when it launched Lugard into Uganda.

That was in August 1890. It will be remembered that de Winton in his letters to Lugard told him that he was being severely censured for his extravagance in sending up the men and supplies Lugard was demanding. Yet there was still talk of sending up a steamer to the lake and of building a narrow gauge railway sixty miles inland, a project for which the rails were actually sent, to lie idling at Mombasa. When Mackenzie came back to Mombasa to take over from de Winton at the beginning of March 1891, the Scotsman could still write cheerfully to Lugard " I am satisfied with the progress that has been made all round " and urge him to build up his administration even though Mackenzie already doubted whether Uganda could pay its way by trade. (Mackenzie to L. 22 April 1891).

This optimistic tone is surprising in a man fresh from headquarters. Even before the end of 1890 the directors were being obliged to face the clouds gathering over their East African horizon. The agreement with Germany had relieved them from the frictions along the coast with their formidable neighbour, and they had some fifty employees, mostly on or near the coast. But revenue was not increasing to meet their rising expenses. And they were beginning to realize that Lugard, at the other side of some 800 miles of then unprofitable wilderness, with porterage to him at £250 to £300 a ton, was likely to be a costly and highly speculative investment.

It was the main argument of the Company in demanding government support, and later in its fight for compensation, that it had injured its proper commercial policy of a gradual advance in order to respond to the demand of the government that it should rush into the far interior and occupy Uganda before Germany or any other power could get there first. Mention has already been made of the letters of the consul-general urging the immediate dispatch of Lugard's caravan. But these issued from the unofficial impatience of the man on the spot. More official was the advice offered by Portal in London at a Company meeting, and there is a record of a visit by two directors to the Foreign Office, when Currie urged them to push on into the interior before the Germans, with the hint that continuance of their concession depended upon their making it good by means of treaties.[1] This seems to have been the main pressure for the forward movement, and Sir Percy Anderson later almost admitted it.[2] But a study of the Foreign Office papers in the spring of 1890 shows how careful were the officials, closely guided by Lord Salisbury, never to be led into any official commitment, and to draw a clear line, or at least a line that was clear to them if to no one else, between the responsibility of the government and that of the Company. The evidence shows also that at this date the Company were ready enough to make the venture.

On December 17th 1890, Sir William Mackinnon wrote an important letter to Lord Salisbury, in which he put forward the claim of the Company upon the government. He pointed out that his Company had now to compete not with a German company, but with the German imperial government which had superseded it and which, like the Belgian and Italian governments, was providing lavish revenues for the development of its new territory. Mackinnon, however, was not asking for a subsidy but for co-operation in carrying out the obligations the government had assumed under the Brussels Act to put down slavery. The contracting Powers had agreed that, in order to carry out their promises, they should introduce administration, establish stations, roads, telegraph lines and " in particular . . . . railways." Hitherto, the Company, unsupported, had been carrying out these national obligations and had also been forced, by fear of

[1] I am indebted to Miss de Kiewiet for this suggestion and evidence of this interview; Sir Lewis Pelly to Mackinnon, 20 March 1889, M.P.
[2] Memorandum by Anderson, 17 November 1892, F.O. 84/2263.

foreign competition, to embark upon a territorial expansion outside its original plans of gradual advances inland, and quite beyond the resources of its original capital. For every reason a railway was essential and all the Company asked of the government was that it should guarantee the interest on the capital needed to build a railway. This, by encouraging investors, would enable the Company to raise the capital needed to continue its large task.[1]

Three days later Lord Salisbury acted. He was ready to make the first small response to the Company, but he had two hurdles to cross. The first was presented by the Treasury, to which he now took the matter. He put the case for the Company sympathetically. It was not a purely commercial body, he said, for " the majority of, if not all, the subscribers are actuated rather by philanthropic motives " than by the expectation of adequate returns. It had relieved Britain of direct responsibility for carrying out the Brussels Act. It would be " a grave scandal " if, the German government being active next door, the slave-traders concentrated on the British sphere. The railway passed through a " sterile region "—the future Kenya!—and could not pay until the dense populations round Lake Victoria became more civilized. A subsidy, which would save the expensive naval patrols on the coast, seemed therefore justified.[2] Early in February 1891, the Foreign Office wrote again with further arguments in support of a subsidy, especially the success a railway must have in abolishing the slave caravans.[3]

The reply from the Treasury was surprisingly favourable. It admitted that the naval patrols on the east coast cost up to £110,000 a year. But it pointed out that parliamentary sanction would have to be obtained.[4] Here lay the second and more formidable hurdle at which the Prime Minister might well shy. In studying policy there is often a tendency to watch the head and the hands of a minister and not to look down as carefully at his feet to see from what kind of a political stance he is working. And Lord Salisbury in 1891 was standing upon very uncertain ground. His party did not command a majority in the House of Commons and his ministry was dependent upon the support

---

[1] McDermott, *IBEA*, pp. 173–80.
[2] *Papers respecting proposed railway from Mombasa to Lake Victoria Nyanza.* Africa No. 2 (1892), C.6560, pp. 1–2.
[3] *Ibid.* pp. 2–3.
[4] *Ibid.* pp. 3–4.

of the Liberal-Unionists. He was, therefore, in no strong position from which to embark upon colonial adventures.

In spite of the uncertainty of the political prospects, however, Lord Salisbury went cautiously ahead with the Treasury and the Company, and a plan was drawn up for the government to guarantee a 5% return on a paid up capital of £1,250,000. It appears, according to McDermott, who was on the headquarters staff, that the Company would have recalled Lugard from Uganda at this earlier date but for these negotiations. Yet, it was generally believed—and such a belief was bad for a Company looking for capital—that the directors had been rebuffed by the government. Dr. Briggs, a great friend of Lugard, who was reporting to him upon developments at home, wrote in January that Lord Salisbury had sent Mackinnon " empty away ": and " it seems to have been a blow to him and inclined them to be luke-warm in their ' philanthropy ', he told me in the event of their meeting with an unfavourable reply—they intended to contract their operations and reduce expenditure all round. I have heard it said that de Winton will resign! " (W. H. Briggs to L. 23 January 1891). (It is possible that Lugard did not receive this warning letter until a year later, on his return from his western expedition, and met it with the evacuation order.)

Briggs' next letter, for all its joking tone, defined the real difficulty, the lack of prospects they could hold out at a time when the Niger Company could offer a flourishing trade and the British South Africa Company held out the lure of gold. " I take it *you* are the man upon whom their hopes are fixed, and I believe myself, upon your opinion and report the scope of their future proceedings very much hinges . . . . But the question—can you do this, does the country contain the primitive form which hereafter may develop into the gentle *Dividend*. There's magic in that word, and the Chairman would embrace you as a brother . . . . if you could supply the material with which he could smilingly face the next meeting of the shareholders. They have had to take it out in philanthropy so far . . . . Well, my dear boy, have you got a gold-bearing reef about you? " (W. H. Briggs to L. 12 February 1891). Lugard had not, and we can now appreciate more fully the gloom which his frank avowals of the complete immediate unproductivity of Uganda must have cast over Company headquarters. But the government's February proposals gave the directors a brief moment of relief and decided them to hold on in Uganda.[1]

It is clear, however, that in the Foreign Office and in No. 11 Downing Street doubt was beginning to arise. Salisbury saw that his task was even harder than he had expected. In May he made an attempt to educate and to move public opinion in favour of his policy. Speaking at Glasgow about the three Chartered Companies, and praising the East African one as " far more purely philanthropic " than the others, he went on to make a special appeal to Scottish pride in their countryman, Mackinnon. Carefully, by way of the slave-trade, he reached the proposed railway. This would kill the caravan trade for " I do not see that any slave-dealer who presented himself with a body of slaves to be carried on trucks to the coast would be very civilly received." At that point he revealed his own difficulties. As Foreign Secretary he naturally took a great interest in the railway. But his was " a purely Foreign Office point of view." Mackinnon wanted government help, " and I always speak of the Treasury with awe, still more of the Treasury when it is acting, as in this case it necessarily must act, under the guidance of and according to the principles of the House of Commons." He had to confess, with what seems an excess of diffidence in a Foreign Minister who was also Prime Minister, that he did not know if the Treasury would be able " consistently with the sound principles of finance which are always upheld " to give the help or whether the railway " must be deferred to a distant date."[2]

Salisbury's doubts about his own power to push through the proposed guarantee proved to be well founded. The Treasury flinched from bringing it to the House of Commons and fell back on the plan of first asking for a small grant to finance only a preliminary railway survey. This survey was to cost £25,000, of which the Company was to pay £5,000.[3] With this sadly reduced offer the Company had to be content, Mackinnon promising to find the £5,000 himself if necessary. The government had, however, left the vote to the end of the session. As this approached, they promised the opposition that no contentious business would be introduced before the prorogation. On July 17th Sir William Harcourt, for the Liberals, gave notice that he regarded

[1] McDermott, *op. cit.* p. 183.
[2] *Ibid.* pp. 186–90.
[3] C.6560 (1892), pp. 4–7.

this vote " as in the highest degree contentious " and meant to oppose it. Mr. Gladstone was not present but Harcourt stated that he had approved the action. The Chancellor of the Exchequer, Goschen, at once gave way and undertook not to proceed with the vote that session though he declared that the policy was unchanged and the matter ended with a wrangle over the mysteries surrounding the words protectorate, sphere of influence, British territory, and sovereignty, which served to thicken the fog of uncertainty which hung over the whole East African issue.[1]

This check was to prove the beginning of the end for the Company. It was natural for the directors to protest against Harcourt's action as a mere piece of party warfare. Unfortunately for them it was more: principles as well as tactics lay behind it. The government now came back to the Company and suggested that it should advance the whole cost of the survey, until the government could carry the vote through parliament, which they promised to do before the end of the financial year. The unhappy directors agreed, but to them time was all-important and they felt that they had lost the tide that *might* have led on to fortune though, in retrospect, we may conclude that there were African and other circumstances which made success within any commercial time-limit almost unattainable.

We can now see what had led up to the evacuation order which broke upon Lugard with such startling abruptness. The directors, as soon as they learned that the government had substituted a vote for a survey in place of a guarantee for the railway, and that even this vote was going to run into parliamentary obstruction, decided to lighten ship. The court of directors met on July 16th 1891 and with heavy hearts, because they realized, some though not all, that the decision would mean on the shores of Lake Victoria, passed the resolution to evacuate Uganda and to fall back, as the limit of their operations, upon the post Lugard had made at Dagoretti in Kikuyuland.[2] This would allow of a reduction in expenditure of the £40,000 a year which, to the economical Lugard's indignation, was their estimate of what Uganda was costing. On August 10th 1891 they sent the letter ordering evacuation, which reached Lugard on December 25th, and on August 20th the government was informed of the decision.

[1] *Parliamentary Debates*, 20 July 1891, III. 355. 1759-61.
[2] McDermott, *op. cit.* pp. 193-5.

In his personal letter to Lugard which accompanied the official order, Mackenzie said that Britain was "passing through one of the severest financial crises ever known in this country." Baring's had succumbed and other banks were in a critical position. The Stock Exchange and the investing public were chary of parting with their money. It was therefore hopeless for the directors to place further shares on the market in order to raise the capital essential to their operations on the present scale. Had the government, by giving the railway guarantee, identified themselves to this extent with the Company, the public might have come forward. But Sir William Harcourt and the radical opposition had destroyed that hope and what might happen when parliament should meet again was very doubtful. (Mackenzie to L. 10 August 1891).

The Company's retraction, rather surprisingly, did not affect the railway survey. Salisbury had made up his mind upon this and, under his influence, the Cabinet decided to go ahead with the plan, seconding Royal Engineer staff for the purpose. But as parliament had not granted the funds, the Company had to take the risk of advancing the whole £25,000. Salisbury's intentions are not wholly clear, but it seems that he hoped that, in spite of a temporary evacuation, the railway would make an ultimate return to Uganda possible. The views of Lugard and the missionaries about the dangers of evacuation had not yet been received. The project was negotiated during July and August. Salisbury wanted Lugard to be put in charge of the survey and on September 29th he wrote a letter upon this subject to his Chancellor of the Exchequer which reveals his imaginative sense of African realities. Lugard, in command, was to be given the money and his orders, but that was all. Goschen was to "require no guarantees or securities; and challenge no expenditure . . . . In this case I have a great dread of the wisdom of Downing Street. It is rough Colonist's work—to be done by trusting well-chosen men—who will do the job as best they can—by hardihood, resource and a quick eye—but often with irregularities in detail, against which you cannot guard without embarrassing them."[1] Salisbury had shown his capacity to trust in his dealings with Johnston and Portal. If he had been in a position to appoint and support him, Lugard might have won still more of his confidence and would not have had to wait for

[1] Cecil, *Life of Salisbury*, vol. iv, pp. 312-13.

Chamberlain in order to find a master who could extend the essential arm of ministerial support between Whitehall and the African frontier. It was due to Salisbury that in spite of his doubts about the Company's financial and administrative capacity, doubts which his trusted consul-general Portal was increasing with every dispatch he sent from Zanzibar, he did tell Goschen " let the survey go forward, reserving all decision upon its results to a future time." (29 September 1891).[1] So the machinery was set in motion which, since Lugard was clearly unavailable, drew Macdonald from India and set him and his colleagues working inland from the East African coast just before the end of the year.

In Britain the public announcement of the proposed evacuation of Uganda forced the country into the first realization of the issue which had to be decided. That old campaigner for African causes, Horace Waller, in a letter to *The Times*,[2] jabbed the still unhealed wound in Britain's honour by linking the words Uganda and Khartoum, and the pain and anxiety of this association of experience was to be a constant element in the ensuing debate and one with no small influence upon its conclusion.

The two stories were not without some geographical connection. Waller's vivid pen pictures Lugard " a man of consummate tact ", arriving in the middle of glaring factions, breathless after their long struggle. " Looking over the heads of these he could see an exasperated body of mongrel coast Arabs . . . . In the extreme distance the Mahdi's vedettes were quartering the ground." He then described Lugard's brilliant success in imposing peace by " the individual force of his character and presence." But " what will be his surprise when—just as Gordon was told to return from Khartoum and leave the people to their fate—he in turn is bidden to forsake the people whom he has made his own? "

The Times, which seems to have been in close touch with the Company, came out a few days later in wholehearted opposition to evacuation. On the same day there appeared a long article " from a correspondent " giving all the arguments in favour of retention with intimate knowledge of the facts, and also an emphatic leading article which declared that " such a withdrawal would be nothing short of a

[1] Cecil, *Life of Salisbury*, vol. iv, p. 314.
[2] *The Times*, 22 September 1891.

national calamity." All possible arguments were set out: the almost certain massacre of missionaries and their converts; the effect upon the slave-trade; the loss of prestige; the loss of capital; the prospect of a Mahdist invasion; the abandonment of all Lugard had achieved and of the vast possibilities of developing this unknown country. The railway was the urgent and over-riding necessity and the article ended with the true prophecy that, if Harcourt and his friends gained the power they so confidently expected, they would find their " short-sighted and partisan " destruction of the railway-survey vote a very embarrassing achievement.[1] The press chorus was mostly in tune with this, discordance coming from the few Liberal papers.

Bishop Tucker was staying in a country house in the highlands " when to our great delight it was told us that Sir William Mack-innon's yacht was steaming up the loch." Sir William was, however, a gloomy visitor. He was in a state of deep depression about the future of the Company. He " showed us how utterly impossible it was for the Company, in the then condition of its finances, to continue without assistance its hold upon Uganda. . . . . ' Uganda is costing us £40,000 a year,' he said. ' Help us to raise a sum of £30,000 and we will under-take to continue in the country for at least another year. If you will raise fifteen thousand pounds I will myself give £10,000 and will try to raise another £5,000 amongst my friends.' This was our first gleam of hope. Time, we felt, was everything. Public opinion must be aroused. The case for the retention of Uganda, we felt, was over-whelmingly strong. Of the facts and merits of the case the general public knew nothing. Information must be spread abroad. For this, time was everything."[2]

But a grant for such a purpose from mission funds was not possible.[3] A memorial from the Anti-Slavery Society to Lord Salisbury, placed as he was, could not but fail.[4] The attempt to raise the money by means of a special subscription fund was also a failure. But on October 30th a meeting of the C.M.S., called the Gleaners Union Anniversary, was held in that historic forum of philanthropy, Exeter Hall. Bishop Tucker, on the eve of sailing for Uganda, made an appeal for money to prolong the occupation of Uganda, and support the gallant Captain

---

1 *The Times*, 28 September 1891.
2 Tucker, *Eighteen Years in Uganda*, vol. i, p. 144.
3 Stock, *History of the C.M.S.*, vol. iii, p. 439.
4 *A.S.R.*, IV. xi. September–October 1891, pp. 213–14.

Lugard in his difficult position. News, moreover, had just reached England of Lugard's journey to the west and his defeat of Kabarega's forces. A wave of enthusiasm swept over the audience. The regular collection at what was a missionary meeting could not be given to the occupation fund, but the audience were asked to come up to the platform with promises or payments. In half an hour the total or £8,000 was reached.[1] Lugard was told afterwards that people even brought their watches and brooches. Within a few days the required contribution of £15,000 had been easily passed.

Those who, consistently with their doctrines, characterize all colonial expansion as due to an evil force called "economic imperialism", should pause to analyse the motives that moved not only that missionary audience but Mackinnon himself, who at this stage well knew that, in a commercial sense, he was throwing good money after bad. There was then, and all through the controversy, much criticism of the Anglican mission for favouring annexation. The reply of the Bishop was that the mission had gone and had remained for many years alone and unprotected in the heart of Africa and would have been content to do so indefinitely. But the advent of the Company, and the sectarian strife that followed, had inevitably involved the missionaries and their converts, and the sudden withdrawal of the Company *now* would result in their ruin, either by massacre or expulsion. To save this far outpost of their Church, to keep faith with their Baganda fellow-Christians and, before it was too late, to save another brave Englishman from the fate of Gordon—these were the motives, all doubtless mingled with the indefinable sentiment of patriotism, which led the meeting of Victorian churchgoers to subscribe their pounds and shillings.

The friends of the mission now approached the Company directors. These had no material interest in prolonging the occupation but, closely bound up as most of them were with the humanitarian and religious groups, they agreed to postpone their evacuation order for one more year. On November 11th, the requisite sum having been subscribed by that date, the Company made up the total and telegraphed to Mombasa ordering a special messenger to be dispatched with all haste to Lugard with the news.[2] This telegram, as we have

1 *Advertiser*, 3 November 1891; *Northern Chronicle*, 4 November 1891; Stock, *op. cit.* vol. iii, p. 438 ff.
2 McDermott, *IBEA*, Appendix 11, p. 528; and in C.6847 (1893), pp. 1-2.

seen, reached him on January 7th 1892, fourteen days after the arrival of the evacuation order.

Lugard and Williams might shake hands over this telegram like a couple of schoolboys. To men of their will and spirit the postponement meant that the final issue could and *would* be decided the way they wished. But for those most concerned with the affairs behind the scenes at home, the following months were full of anxious consultation.

The year's grace won by private philanthropy in fact gave less than that period to the Company before, in face of the slow contact with Uganda and the dangers and difficulties of evacuation, it must decide the issue. Since it normally took three months to reach Uganda from Mombasa, the telegram of decision must be sent from London by October, 1892. And the problems of the Company were unchanged. Early in the new year Kirk, at once a friend and a director, wrote to warn Lugard of this. The position of the Company, he said, was so critical that within the year it would have either to fall back to the coast or wind up altogether. He blamed not only de Winton's earlier extravagance but Mackinnon's character. " Sir William is one of the most unpractical men I have ever had to do with and with all his success in India, he is ignorant of Africa." He began to wonder whether, under the efficient young Portal, with whom he was in correspondence, Zanzibar might not resume the mainland, a plan that would naturally appeal to a man who had himself been consul-general based upon the island. (Kirk to L. 20 January 1892).

During February more news came in of Lugard's journey to the west. The first reports from Macdonald on the railway were also published. These rejected Lugard's Sabaki river route into the interior but spoke very favourably of the alternative Teita route for the first stage of the railway.[1] On March 3rd 1892 the railway survey vote came again before the Commons, and a vigorous, at times almost passionate, two-day debate took place. Mr. Lowther opened with a very sympa-- thetic plea for the Company, and re-stated Britain's obligations under the Brussels Act. If the vote were refused, Lugard would have to be withdrawn from Uganda. " We stand," he said, " at the parting of the ways."[2] This cliché, which was the underlying theme of the

[1] C.6560 (1892), pp. 9–11.
[2] *Parliamentary Debates,* 3 March 1892, IV. 1. 1836–45.

debate, was truer than he guessed though he could not foresee how long the politicians would stand in unhappy indecision in front of that bifurcation.

To our generation, looking back across a period of confident annexation and of prosperous economic development in the African colonies, it is not easy to understand the motives which made our grandfathers so reluctant to take the road which offered to lead them to a larger empire, though perhaps the recent widespread revulsion from " colonialism " may make it less difficult to appreciate than it would have been some ten or fifteen years ago. Even the Conservatives were half-hearted and apologetic; their leaders assured the House that it was being asked to commit itself to nothing more than " an experimental survey ", the discovery of that very information for which the opposition was clamouring. The grant would allow Lugard to remain whereas his withdrawal would almost certainly lead to a Muslim inrush, the revival of the slave-trade and the destruction of the missionaries.

It is especially interesting to consider the elements that made up the opposition's case for it was upon this question that they were to make their last stand against the new forward movement which they called " jingoism ". In their speeches can be seen the negative forces against which Rhodes, Goldie, Mackinnon, Kirk and in his own at present humbler way, Lugard, were all struggling. It is because Lugard was a propagandist for the new imperialism at home, as well as a practitioner on the frontier, that the arguments used in the debate are so relevant to his biography. The debate, moreover, as we have seen in the other side of this story,[1] was largely concerned with analysing Lugard's first report to the Company.

The Liberal argument was that there was no obligation upon the government to enter upon the proposed responsibility either to help the Company, or to fulfil the mandates of the Brussels Act. Their main reason was that Uganda was under neither British sovereignty nor protection but was merely a sphere of influence; its boundaries had been drawn simply to prevent other nations from advancing into it. It was useless for George Wyndham, in one of the most practical speeches of the debate, to point out that if Britain neglected her sphere, situated as it was between spheres being actively occupied by other

[1] See above pp. 330-1.

powers, it would become a sort of vacuum or even a cesspool.[1] The Liberal leaders, Gladstone, Harcourt and Bryce, were able to sweep away these African realities and satisfy themselves with the juridical contention that Britain had no obligations within such a " sphere ". What laws, asked Gladstone, ruled in a " sphere "; what legitimate authority can be exercised over natives or Europeans?[2] Harcourt carried the argument further in a way that would have made Lugard a criminal. " Every act of force you commit against a native in a sphere of influence is an unlawful assault; every acre of land you take is a robbery; every native you kill is a murder, because you have no right and no authority against these men."[3]

The other arguments of the opposition were founded largely upon a very close examination of Lugard's reports. Quotations were made to show that the slave-trade hardly existed and that the way to Uganda was dangerous and that a railway would have to be imposed and protected by considerable forces—" The report of Captain Lugard ", Harcourt said, " shows that . . . . you must have plate-layers with rifles every 100 yards along the line . . . "[4]—Uganda was commercially unpromising, full of dangers and difficulties. The Company's entry and treaty had been effected by force and coercion. This, as painted by Lugard himself, they asserted, was the true condition of the kind of Arcadia held out by the government. As for protecting the missionaries: " Men like Livingstone did not bring conquering armies and Hotchkiss and Nordenfeldt guns with them," said Harcourt.[5] Labouchere, who was to prove the most uncompromising and consistent opponent of retaining Uganda, asked why the state should have to spend money trying " to prevent these very remarkable Christians from cutting each other's throats " when " the blood of the saints is the seed of the Church."[6]

Upon the matter of procedure Salisbury was castigated by the opposition for allowing the money to be spent before parliament had sanctioned it, and Gladstone used his indignant surprise for his peroration, which, though both sides denied that Uganda was a party issue, was in the hackneyed terms of party cut and thrust. In the

[1] *Parliamentary Debates*, 3 March 1892, IV. 1. 1851.
[2] *Ibid.* IV. 1. 1877.
[3] *Ibid.* 4 March 1892, IV. 2. 71.
[4] *Ibid.* IV. 2. 82.
[5] *Ibid.* IV. 2. 82.
[6] *Ibid.* IV. 2. 57.

absence of proper investigation " I will wash my hands of all responsibility for such proceedings, which I believe to be probably without any parallel in the history of this or perhaps any other Administration."[1]

One of the chief complaints of the opposition was that the government had withheld information. Lugard's reports had been sent to the Company and had only been seen by those members of parliament who had been able to get hold of them. That there had been some expurgations roused deep suspicions, especially the ready ones of Labouchere. Here some injustice was being done to the Company. The original report on the writer's table shows very little red ink and the excisions are critical remarks about the activities of Stanley, complaints against the Company for not sending sufficient arms or other supplies, denials that his Uganda expedition was costing £40,000 a year and, finally, any remarks likely to offend Germany or Belgium. The only excision of the kind suspected by the Liberals, and one natural enough in a Company trying to attract capital, was an opinion that Uganda was very unlikely to offer any minerals.

Before we leave this debate, since the questions of the clash between British humanitarian standards and frontier methods occurred so often in Lugard's life, it is of interest to notice that the Liberals were not entirely doctrinaire or partisan. In Gladstone especially, mixed up with much that we can now see was negative and factious, there are the authentic notes of justice and humanity. And the old statesman, for all his complaints of lack of information, had thoroughly got up what material there was. He lamented Carl Peters' " fruitless slaughter of a large number of the Masai." But how could the government be sure that the British survey would be a " bloodless operation." With insight and foresight, he went on: " We know that the greatest jealousy prevails in that country and must, naturally, among the natives with regard to any attempt to dispossess them of their lands. Is not that exactly the thing we are going to do? " Lugard had shown him all too vividly that " these people who are at variance with one another are agreed in being hostile to the admission of the English."[2]

There was naturally intense curiosity as to how a party holding such views was intending to act when, as seemed imminent at this date, the responsibility should pass to them. Gladstone managed to combine

[1] *Parliamentary Debates*, 3 March 1892, IV. 1. 1880
[2] *Ibid.* IV. 1. 1874-7.

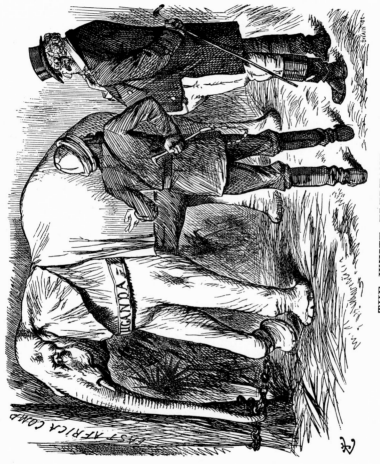

THE WHITE ELEPHANT.

Present Proprietor (*log.*). "SEE HERE, GOVERNOR! HE'S A LIKELY-LOOKING ANIMAL,—BUT *I* CAN'T MANAGE HIM! IF *YOU* WON'T TAKE HIM, I MUST LET HIM GO!!"

his outright denunciation of the survey vote with a piece of intellectual balancing of a kind that marked his later years and one which, not surprisingly, is reported to have provoked cries of " Oh, Oh! " and laughter from the benches opposite. " I wish to state, in the most expressive terms that I can command, that I am determined for one to exempt myself, by the declaration of to-night, from every jot and tittle of responsibility connected with the undertaking; and yet, at the same time, I do not go so far as to deliver a final judgment."[1] It was registered with interest by the press the next day that in the opposition list of 113 which confronted the government's 211, neither Gladstone's name nor that of Harcourt, who had been even more vehement than his leader, were to be found.

The debate was hardly over when the stories of the so-called civil war in Uganda began to come through and diverted interest from the railway survey. It was, as we have seen, the main Uganda theme in the press and parliament during the summer. But these dramatic events made no important difference to the Company's position in Uganda or to the determination of the directors to escape from it. Upon May 5th the Court passed a resolution that in view of the length of time required for communications with Lugard, he should be instructed to retire to the coast by the end of the year. The acting-secretary, Ernest Bentley, wrote to Lugard on May 10th sending him this resolution. The troubles that had broken out merely reinforced the directors' view that the occupation of Uganda was beyond their resources and, while deploring deeply the retreat which was forced upon them, made it clear—for they knew their man—that these instructions gave Lugard no discretionary powers but were imperative. He was to bring his " entire force " back to Dagoretti and return at once to England.[2] Lugard left Uganda five weeks after this letter was written, and long before it could reach him there.

The Company sent a copy of this letter to the Foreign Office and Mackinnon wrote confirming the determination to evacuate. He again impressed upon Lord Salisbury that the Company had occupied Uganda only for imperial interests and that if the government had given them any support, the evacuation would be unnecessary. Mackinnon said the directors " still cling to the hope " that the government

---

[1] *Ibid.* IV. 1. 1872.
[2] C.6847 (1893), pp. 3-4.

would " avoid the very serious danger and national reproach that must accompany the retreat." The only answer was the coolest and curtest reply from Lord Salisbury, mainly concerned to forbid the Company to order Lugard to hand over his surplus ammunition to the chiefs.[1]

Salisbury had reason to be non-committal. Power was about to pass from him for a few years. Following the general election of July, with Ireland as its main issue, and an adverse vote in the Commons in August, he resigned. The aged Gladstone took office. Relying for a majority upon the Irish members, and with a divided England behind him, he prepared to make a hopeless assault upon the solid obstacle of the House of Lords in the cause of Irish Home Rule. His Cabinet, numbering such mature ministers as Harcourt and Morley and such brilliant rising stars as Asquith and Grey, was individually strong but collectively weak. There were several important reasons why Gladstone needed to add the brilliance and aristocratic glamour of the reluctant Lord Rosebery, one among them being his value as a bridge between the Queen and what she called, in her unconstitutional frankness, " this iniquitous government ".[2] Rosebery, with this position in the Cabinet, was to exercise a decisive influence in the Uganda issue.

The period when the Uganda policy hung in the balance was the time when Lugard's life was most closely intertwined with the central events of British politics. These must always consist of the issues which affect the existence of governments, and it is seldom that any colonial question comes so close to the basis of party power as did that of Uganda from 1892 to 1894. It cannot be claimed that in the early nineties, when the political horizon was dominated by the great questions of Britain's relations with Ireland and with a Europe rapidly growing dangerously competitive, Uganda ranked equally with these. Yet events so fell out that for a period, especially when the Liberal government first took office, the destiny of this remote Nilotic region roused intense feeling in the country and nearly broke up the ministry.

In some degree all Cabinets must suffer from the strains caused by their being the place where diverse political ideas, drawn from within and from outside their circle, have to be brought within the grasp of personal unity and co-operation and then carried into executive action. But Gladstone's last government was quite uncommonly

1 C.6847 (1893), pp. 3–5.
2 *Q.V.L.* III, vol. ii, p. 143.

disunited. Under their aged chief who was determined to remain in power even though, as he said himself, he felt " the doors of his senses gradually closing upon him," his colleagues were torn between reverent loyalty and exasperation. They were disheartened by the hopelessness of their main Irish purpose and dismayed by the high and jarring tempers of Harcourt and Rosebery, the two rivals for the succession. These personal difficulties at once expressed and enlarged certain deeper differences of principle affecting the whole range of policy, but especially clear in the Uganda question, which stood like a signpost at the parting of the ways between the old " Little England " radical liberalism, and the new liberal imperialism.

Rosebery, having been coaxed out of his Achilles' tent by Gladstone, the Prince of Wales and other distinguished suppliants, went with dragging steps to the Foreign Office. He had no sooner taken it over on August 20th, when he was immediately confronted, as we have seen, by a complaining French ambassador, talking of Uganda atrocities. But he was also plagued by the same region from another department of the office, with Anderson pushing at him the papers which demanded an immediate decision upon the evacuation question. His patrician instinct was against retreat but he realized that in this he might well be alone against a Cabinet solidly pledged, by its principles and especially by what its members had so recently said on the Uganda question in the House of Commons, to evacuation, or rather to stand by, doing nothing, while the Company carried out its long-threatened retreat.

While Lugard during September was reaching Mombasa, embarking for England and writing at sea his defence against the priests' charges, the conflict which would end either in confirming or destroying all he had done, was raging between the ministers. It proceeded behind a very complete screen of Cabinet secrecy, now partially withdrawn for historians. It would take us too long, and too far from Lugard himself, to recount in all its dramatic detail the clash of ideas and personalities out of which Liberal policy was re-shaped and the future East African dependency born. But some brief account will help to set the scene in Britain before Lugard arrived to play his part.[1]

---

[1] The writer hopes it may be possible to publish a fuller account of this episode at a later date. The account which follows is based upon (in addition to the Lugard Papers) the F.O. papers; the Gladstone Papers; the Portal Papers; A. G. Gardiner, *The Life of Sir William Harcourt* (1923); Lord Crewe, *Lord Rosebery* (1931); Algernon West, *Private Diaries* (1922); the contemporary press and other contributory sources.

On August 24th, Rosebery asked Sir Percy Anderson to draw up a memorandum on the Uganda question that was to be an impartial statement, not a "plaidoyer" for any particular course. But it appears that Rosebery could not sustain this ideal of impartiality. Sir Percy's first draft, of August 25th, which is plastered with revisions and minutes, covers five pages. But as it finally emerged on September 13th from Rosebery's amending hand, and in print for the Cabinet, it covered more than eight, and the additions were all in the direction of strengthening its main plea that Uganda could not be abandoned. It admitted that Kirk, the one man of real African experience, had distrusted the policy of rapid expansion into the interior. But it pointed out the discovery by Anderson, when in Berlin in 1890, of the "active hostility" of the German Colonization Society which [dispatched Peters on a treaty-making expedition into the interior and thus forced the hand of the Company. It was also stated that British interests justified Lugard's moves beyond Buganda, and demanded that they should be followed northwards and the Upper Nile region saved from the Belgian or, even more likely, the French, occupation that was threatened. The authors must have realized how often in our colonial history the final impulse for a long delayed annexation had come from the fear that France would forestall us. We may note that this document, which brought out clearly what Lugard had achieved in Uganda, and quoted his opinions upon the cost and practicability of holding the country, provides the most weighty evidence of the part he had played, with his derisory resources, in making it possible for the retention of this region to become even a possibility for his country. For the memorandum became in the end a strong plea for retention. In its concluding words it quoted Lugard's statement that his Sudanese troops represented "a fine body of men, ready armed, and soldiers by profession," who would be a very cheap force, and that Lugard also suggested that some revenue could be expected from the country.[1]

To support him in his view Rosebery was being presented with a great deal of information and advice, official and unofficial, all tending to show the dangers of evacuation, the difficulties of re-occupation, and the possibility of the Germans taking over. Mackenzie even went so far as to warn the Foreign Office that upon evacuation the French

1 The several versions of Anderson's memorandum are in F.O. 84/2258.

priests might declare the country a French protectorate.[1] And, recently returned from Egyptian army headquarters, Major F. R. Wingate wrote insisting on the importance of Britain maintaining the administration of Uganda.[2] The Cabinet, as Rosebery said, were " scattered over the face of the globe." But he circulated Anderson's memorandum and called for a meeting.[3]

On September 13th, something decisive happened to confirm Rosebery's fears. Portal met Lugard at Mombasa, and on the same day he telegraphed to Rosebery urging the postponement of evacuation[4] and followed it up immediately with the grave warnings Lugard had given him that evacuation " must *inevitably* result in a massacre of Christians such as the history of this century cannot show." Moreover, evacuation would utterly destroy the respect in which the English name was held by the chiefs with whom Lugard had made treaties. " I hope you will see Lugard who is very strong on the subject." There was the utmost urgency since " messengers sent full speed even *now* would be only just in time to stop the withdrawal of troops from Uganda."[5] To a man as highly strung as the new Foreign Secretary, such a thought as Lugard had put in his mind meant that he could not sleep for the haunting fear that, after all these warnings, he and his colleagues might allow the story of Khartoum to be repeated in the case of Uganda.[6] Hearing that Lugard might stop in Egypt to clear up the question of the Sudanese troops, Rosebery ordered that he should come straight home. He rightly foresaw that he would have need of him.

Rosebery's two chief colleagues, Gladstone and Harcourt, entered into the discussion with their minds absolutely made up against any intervention. It was no calm opposition: the emotions of both were as deeply involved as were Rosebery's, and Anderson's memorandum stirred them. " Rosebery has circulated a Memo . . . . by Sir P. Anderson (of the F.O.) in the highest jingo tune advocating the annexation of the whole country up to the Albert Lakes, with a view to the ' reconquest ' of the Sudan via the Albert Lakes."[7] " I hate

[1] Mackenzie to Currie, 9 September 1892, F.O. 84/2258.
[2] Memorandum by Wingate, 21 August 1892, F.O. 84/2258.
[3] Undated note of Rosebery, F.O. 84/2258.
[4] Portal to Rosebery, 13 September 1892 F.O. 84/2237.
[5] Portal to Rosebery, 14 September 1892, P.P. s. 106; Rosebery sent this to Queen Victoria, Q.V.L. III, vol. ii, pp. 163–4.
[6] West, *Private Diaries*, p. 61.
[7] Gardiner, *Life of Harcourt*, vol. ii, p. 192.

Africa and ' spheres of influence ' and all their tribe." This was Harcourt's approach, while Gladstone was " horrified and astonished to find how Rosebery had given way to the jingoism of the Foreign Office " and could not talk to Rosebery about it without getting " very excited ". He would sooner die than submit to a military occupation.[1] Harcourt was even more lavish with his emphasis: he would " die a thousand deaths rather than have anything to do with it."[2] This was unusual language for British ministerial correspondence.

Harcourt wrote to the Prime Minister at length to discredit Lugard's case. " Captain Lugard threatens all sorts of horrors if we do not occupy at once. Bishop Tucker swears he will remain at his post and die— in short every sort of bogey is invoked to involve us in this horrible quagmire, which will be as bad as Khartoum. Captain Lugard declares that as ' an officer holding H.M.'s commission he has pledged his own honour and that of the British nation to remain there for ever.' And in order to facilitate the process he has just annexed two other provinces larger than Uganda . . . . The railway is *projected* but not *built*, and I hope never will be."[3]

Harcourt treated the heretical Rosebery to what their recipient called "typical Harcourtian outbursts". " You ask ", he wrote to him on September 23rd, " if I don't ' fear a great disaster '. Frankly speaking I do not. I can quite see that it is the game of Lugard and Co. to play on our fears in order to force their policy upon us or induce us to give them a subsidy—the worst of all resources. But if there was it is not our fault. *Non haec in foedera veni*. In Gordon's case *the government* sent him to Khartoum . . . . He was *our* plenipotentiary. Lugard had no authority to ' pledge the authority of the British nation ' as he impudently phrases it." Then, as if trying to disarm in advance this dangerous opponent, Harcourt goes on: " There is one thing quite clear to me, that in nothing we decide or do shall we attribute any weight to Lugard's actions or opinions, or entrust him with any authority." Why, if any " religious fanatic or hare-brained *militaire* choose obstinately to place themselves in danger [should] they have the power to commit the nation to untold sacrifices of blood and treasure " and to permanent annexation? The Company went to Uganda from

1 West, *op. cit.* pp. 60–1.
2 Gardiner, *op. cit.* vol. ii, p. 193.
3 *Ibid.* p. 192.

jealousy of foreign power and " earth hunger ". It is the same spirit which inspires the whole of Sir P. Anderson's memorandum and the letters of Lugard. " . . . . It is because I am deeply opposed to the policy of annexation and conquest and international rivalry that I view our committal to the first step with the greatest dread."[1]

Gladstone and Harcourt were, it is clear, concerned not so much to avoid a disaster in Uganda, as to avoid the responsibility for one. Great irritation was expressed at the *damnosa hereditas* bequeathed by Salisbury. But this at least meant that most of the responsibility could be shifted back upon his government and to that end there was much research into the relevant papers. The results allowed Gladstone to come to the comforting conclusion that the policy of standing aside and letting the Company evacuate had been adopted by Salisbury before his dismissal and in that policy, Gladstone concluded drily, " I have every disposition to concur."[2] And the old man, his eyesight strained by poring over the mass of Uganda documents, and especially by Harcourt's hand-writing, opined with relief, " there is no Uganda question, properly speaking, for decision. It has been settled by the Company and the late government . . . . "[3] At the height of the crisis Gladstone—who on one day sent three letters and two telegrams to Rosebery on this question before lunch—told Rosebery he would excuse Harcourt's trenchant tone, " had you gone through, like Harcourt and some of us, the terrible and instructive experience of the Gordon Mission, in which we adopted a unanimous decision under the most seductive appearances."[4]

Rosebery found himself isolated, facing a solid Cabinet, deeply, in some cases passionately, committed to their policy. He proceeded to play, from what seemed his almost hopeless position, a game of extraordinary skill, patience and courage. He had at least one very august sympathizer in whom he could confide. " The Queen," Victoria told Rosebery, " could never support this or anything else which lowers the dignity and power of her Empire, and she trusts to Lord Rosebery *especially* to uphold this . . . . The fate of Gordon is not, and will not be, forgotten in Europe, and we must take great

---

[1] *Ibid.* pp. 194–5.
[2] Gladstone to Harcourt, 21 September 1892, B.M. 44549.
[3] Gardiner, *op. cit.* p. 195.
[4] Gladstone to Rosebery, 21 September 1892, B.M. 44549.

care what we do. The difficulties are great, doubtless, in Uganda, but the dangers of abandoning it are greater."[1]

Rosebery followed three main lines of argument against his colleagues. He denied that Salisbury, who, rather strangely, had gone off after his resignation to the continent without seeing his successor, had intended to do nothing and he quoted a parliamentary answer by Balfour to support his point. Secondly he predicted that "unluckily the public will, roughly, attach the responsibility to the government." Thirdly, playing for time—a device of which he made no secret to the Queen—he urged delay. Was it wise to rush so important a matter? " Lugard will be back next month. Harcourt calls him ' a mischevious lunatic ' and says he does not heed a word that Lugard says. I do not share that view. But, whether that be so or not, would not the Cabinet be taxed, not unjustly, with levity, if, without waiting for the principal witness and authority, it settled evacuation as a policy in full view of the lamentable consequences that all authorities, without exception that I am aware of, predict? "[2]

Gladstone was not convinced: Rosebery had not had his long experience of distant agents trying to lead governments into their worst errors by alarming prophecies. " I admit Lugard to be a witness. I hardly attach much value to his authority. But *if you do* and you think you cannot or should not be responsible for a decision until he comes, I am not certain that you mean things to remain as they are in the interval."[3] Rosebery's silence about this filled Harcourt " with the utmost alarm." He reiterated to his chief that " the overwhelming majority of the Cabinet and still greater majority of our Party " would reject the idea of British annexation. And " The ghosts of 1884 haunt me." And the next day he bade Gladstone pay more attention to Salisbury's correspondence with the Company than to " Sir P. Anderson's Jingo Memorandum or the scrappy and hysterical letter of Lugard."[4] And he went on to remind the Prime Minister, as he was reminding the Foreign Secretary, that the greatest age of the Roman Empire had been during the two centuries of its *non-extension*.[5] " Are we to attempt to create another India in Africa? " he asked Rosebery—a

1 *Q.V.L.* III, vol. ii, p. 158.
2 Rosebery to Gladstone, 22 September 1892, B.M. 44289.
3 Gladstone to Rosebery, 23 September 1892, B.M. 44289.
4 Harcourt to Gladstone, 24 September 1892, B.M. 44202.
5 Harcourt to Gladstone, 26 September 1892, B.M. 44202.

question to which Lugard would have given a quick answer—and then, applying the never very exact organic simile to politics, he went on, " If you give the heart too much work to do by extending the limbs and the frame beyond measure you enfeeble its action, and it succumbs."[1]

The crisis reached its height on September 28th when the time remaining for a decision could be counted in hours. Algernon West,[2] Gladstone's secretary, was running to and fro between the ministers, trying to moderate their views or, at least, the too forcible expression of them. Now, in an attempt at reconciliation, he warned his master that Rosebery " meant mischief." In other words Rosebery was showing himself ready to play his strongest card, the threat of resignation. He had demanded a Cabinet meeting on the subject. At this the rift between the Prime Minister and the Foreign Secretary would be displayed—" The *first* time during a Cabinet experience of 22 or 23 years," Gladstone said, " that I have known the Foreign Minister and the Prime Minister to go before a Cabinet on a present question with diverging views."[3] Rosebery declared " the most heartfelt and bitter regret at our difference of opinion on this point," but he persisted in his lone stand.[4] The tension grew. " The last days have been horrible," Gladstone admitted to Harcourt on the 28th.[5] Gladstone and Rosebery had a heated talk. The next morning West tackled his formidable old master with the warning that if he made no concession to Rosebery, the ministry would be broken up, as Rosebery would resign. Gladstone replied grimly, but not very truly, that it would be worse for Rosebery than the government. But he went on to the Cabinet deeply disturbed by what his secretary had told him. Faced by the certain disaster which Rosebery's resignation would mean to so shaky a government, Harcourt himself led the way to a decision to subsidize the Company so as to postpone the evacuation for another three months after December 31st 1892. But it was insisted that this measure was taken only in order to obviate the dangers that might arise from *immediate* evacuation: the policy of evacuation was

1 Gardiner, *op. cit.* pp. 196–7.
2 West, Rt. Hon. Sir Algernon, P.C., G.C.B., 1832–1921; clerk in the Admiralty; secretary to Sir C. Wood at India Office and to Mr. Gladstone when Prime Minister; Chairman of Board of Inland Revenue; served on prison commission, and vice-chairman of licensing commission.
3 Gladstone to Rosebery, 25 September 1892, B.M. 44289.
4 Rosebery to Gladstone, 27 September 1892, B.M. 44289.
5 Gardiner, *op. cit.* p. 196.

maintained. The government reserved to itself absolute freedom of action with regard to any future measures consequent upon evacuation. Having agreed upon this, with quite different purposes in view, Harcourt and Rosebery went together to the Foreign Office to draft the telegram to Portal which the Cabinet the next day ratified.[1] We may note that it was this Cabinet which also confirmed their predecessors instructions to Macdonald to go up to Uganda and report upon Lugard's conduct.[2]

Perhaps, outside Anderson's little circle in the Foreign Office, only the Queen knew exactly what Rosebery was playing for. After the Cabinet meeting, on the same day, he revealed this to her. " The delay gives time to receive information; to elicit the real feeling of the country, which is, he is certain, against evacuation . . . . From every point of view therefore he thinks that this delay is favourable to his policy, it is not what he would wish but it is more than this morning seemed attainable." The nature of " his policy " was clear to Rosebery's sovereign, as it was the same as her own, but it is small wonder that he concluded by imploring his royal correspondent to keep the letter absolutely secret to herself, even though, he added, he meant to tell the Cabinet tomorrow the spirit in which he was acting.[3]

Time had been won again, but no more than time and very little of it. The Company agreed very reluctantly to continue in Uganda. They consented for public reasons for this course still offered them loss rather than profit. Harcourt was thus right to suspect that—" the Uganda smoke is only scotched. The whole force of Jingoism is at the bellows. I see H. Stanley leads the way—a worse guide no one could have. Lugard, I observe, has come home. I hope however we shall have the firmness to shut out the blast."[4] At Balmoral, however, where he now went to stay, he believed he had succeeded in cooling a little the Queen's ardour for Uganda: it appeared she had " no missionary propensities—on the contrary she thought that they were very troublesome people . . . . "[5] Gladstone, also observing Lugard's return, told Rosebery he gathered he was at loggerheads with the Company[6]

1 Rosebery to Portal, 30 September 1892, F.O. 84/2237.
2 Notes of Cabinet proceedings, 30 September 1892, B.M. 44648.
3 *Q.V.L.* III, vol. ii, pp. 159-60.
4 Harcourt to Gladstone, 3 October 1892, B.M. 44202.
5 Gardiner, *op. cit.* p. 198.
6 See below p. 415.

and that " they [are] probably much afraid of him. But were I in your place, I would see him on his request, not otherwise, or what Vergil called *ultro*."[1]

It was true that Lugard arrived on October 3rd. He had returned upon several occasions to his own country from distant regions of trouble but this time his landing was a public event. His name was now known throughout western Europe, bearing a heavy accusation and providing a cause of dissension between Britain and France, as well as between two branches of Christendom. Most men in his position would probably have given their whole attention to clearing their names and defending their causes. Lugard had his defence, written on board, in his pocket but, as we have seen, he at once threw himself with much greater energy into the larger struggle about the future of Uganda. On trial by the Cabinet, and with every motive to placate them, he threw himself into the campaign which was putting *them* upon trial for their African policy. He was applying the lesson he had learned over Nyasaland, and again in watching from Uganda the handlings of its affairs in Britain, and that was to appeal to public opinion over the heads of a government.

His first task upon arrival was to size up the state of this opinion. He landed only two days after the Cabinet's decision to delay evacuation had been announced and, as he read the daily newspapers of two days before, he could conclude that, with the exception of the two Liberal papers, the *Daily News* and the *Manchester Guardian*, almost the whole of the press had turned or was turning against evacuation. *The Times* frankly regarded the three months' postponement as a period in which " public opinion will have the opportunity of declaring itself in ways more impressive to the tremulous politician than the most convincing argument."[2] The *Pall Mall Gazette* remarked that this announcement was advice to the Company to pervert " Assisted Evacuation " into " Assisted Occupation ". If this should happen " we should not be very much surprised if Lord Rosebery did not greatly mind."[3] Lugard could read of Stanley's agitation and also the long, published letters of Mackenzie,[4] Kemball,[5] Stanley's

1 Gladstone to Rosebery, 3 October 1892, B.M. 44549.
2 *The Times*, 1 October 1892.
3 *Pall Mall Gazette*, 1 October 1892.
4 *Daily Graphic*, 28 September 1892.
5 *The Times*, 29 September 1892.

fellow explorer, Mounteney-Jephson,[1] Horace Waller, Lord Grey,[2] and many others against evacuation. His own name, with quotations from his reports and canvassings of his views, was scattered lavishly through the papers and nearly always with praise. This reached its zenith in a letter from Horace Waller in which Lugard found this passage. " I have never read a series of letters in which the highest attributes of the officer and the gentleman shone forth more nobly than in these which were penned by Captain Lugard on the battlefield and in the camp during the early days of this year."[3] There was also the account in the papers of the C.M.S. deputation of September 23rd to Lord Rosebery, with the minister's very non-committal reply. (Rosebery told Gladstone that " I was so loyal to you all that I left them, I fear, under the impression that I was a strong evacuationist! ")[4] So much for the news he found waiting: on the day after he landed he read of the Company's acceptance of the government's offer.[5]

Lugard plunged immediately into the controversy. Three days after he landed he posted a letter to *The Times*. Modern correspondents to this newspaper would look enviously at its length; it filled two entire columns of the paper and numbered over 2,500 words, and ended with the promise to continue the subject soon in another letter.[6] He divided his subject under three headings, commercial, political and philanthropic. With regard to the first, revising the gloomy estimate which had weakened the Company's position, he insisted upon Uganda's great possibilities for tropical products and mentioned coffee, wheat, cotton and gums. He used the old mercantilist argument Chamberlain was to develop so vigorously, the one that had been used to incite the Elizabethans to occupy savage America, " the necessity of opening fresh markets." Why should not the Company benefit indirectly from this trade? He could bear witness to their high aims and methods, while " their names alone are an unanswerable voucher for their absolute integrity." He could argue this since he had no personal interest in the Company, having merely been a temporary employee.

On the political side he urged the key position of Uganda on the great central line of communication along the Great Lakes to the

1 *The Times*, 30 September 1892.
2 *Ibid.* 24 October, 17 and 22 November 1892.
3 *Ibid.* 29 August 1892.
4 Rosebery to Gladstone, 23 September 1892, B.M. 44289.
5 *The Times*, 4 October 1892.
6 *Ibid.* 8 October 1892.

Nile. If Britain evacuated, it was France, he suggested, which would take over. And the sources of the Nile commanded Egypt: what would happen if they fell into civilized but unfriendly hands? British honour too, was pledged. He had made treaties, and given promises of help in the name of the Company, and—the very point Gladstone and Harcourt contested—the Company represented the nation. On the philanthropic side, he urged the obligation to defend the lives of the missionaries, and to save all parties from the destructive civil wars which must follow evacuation and which would most likely end in Muslim supremacy and the general revival of the slave-trade. While attacking government policy, he was careful not to attack the government too openly. He even elaborated a case that they had not yet really committed themselves and that this need not be a party issue.

It was an able piece of argument, free from self-assertion or self-defence. There was no word about his own position and his only reference to the French priests was a plea that their danger and dependence upon British protection should be remembered. The letter bears the marks of discussion at Company headquarters. Does it also bear the impress of a conversation with Rosebery? For the Foreign Secretary ignored his chief's warning and asked Lugard to dinner very soon after his return. It is not clear whether the meeting preceded the letter; if it did it would explain the obviously well-informed political hints it contained. But these might equally have come through Kirk, who was at once Lugard's friend and adviser and who was also hard at work with Lord Rosebery. (Kirk to L. October 1892). Harcourt snorted at Lugard's letter in his usual style, writing to Gladstone of this Jingoistic letter and of his determination to hold firm despite any outcry. But he took Lugard seriously, noting that neither he nor Stanley had yet put forward any definite proposals as to what the government should do.[1]

Mackenzie, writing to congratulate Lugard on his letter to *The Times*, pointed out that Lugard's first duty was to go up to Scotland and pay his respects to Mackinnon. " It must be remembered he is the prime mover in the whole affair and but for his patriotic and noble exertions there would be no ' Ibea ' today." (Mackenzie to L. 9 October 1892). It was hard for Lugard to go away just as he was entering the fight but he obeyed. The head of the Company was failing in health.

[1] Harcourt to Gladstone, 9 October 1892, B.M. 44202.

The long drawn out anxiety was telling upon him. He had put so much of his hopes and his money into this great venture that its threatened failure and the indifferent and indeed hostile attitude of the government was breaking him down. It was to a man in this state of mind that Lugard went.

Mackinnon had been anxiously coached as to how to treat this returned traveller. For, it appears that it was not only Macdonald and Portal who had anxieties about the return of Lugard: they were shared by his friends. Even Kirk had written earlier to Mackinnon in fear lest certain interested parties would "play upon his morbid sensitiveness and so turn him against us."[1] And now Stanley wrote a letter to Mackinnon which shows the impression Lugard made upon a shrewd and knowledgeable observer. Allowance should, perhaps, be made for some initial prejudice on Stanley's part. And on Lugard's side we know that in following the famous explorer's footsteps he had built up a very critical attitude towards Stanley. Further allowance must be made for the white-hot state of mind in which Lugard had returned in order to defend his cause and himself. With this necessary degree of interpretation, the letter gives us from the outside a picture of a man who, in this book, must mainly be viewed from his own writings.

"Captain Lugard took luncheon here yesterday and afterwards he came up to my room to see me. I have taken a good look at him, and have read him thoroughly. He is one of the most *cranky* men I have seen, and I wonder more than ever that de Winton was so blind as not to see how he should have been managed. And now I have come to the conclusion that I must do you another service by putting *you* on your guard . . . . I know of no man living more likely—unwarned—than you to quarrel with Lugard. He is the strangest mortal in temper, stubbornness, and disposition you will have met for a long time. When you meet pray take care, and let him speak freely his opinion. He will be quite frank—perhaps too frank. He will give you the impression as he speaks that he has his own *fixed* opinions, his own determined views as to his duty, as to what he conceives to be right or wrong, as to how things should, or should not be done . . . . Do not let him guess by any mannerism, any constraint, that it is possible you have any criticism to make on any act.

1 Kirk to Mackinnon, 30 August 1892, M.P.

. . . . He is a vastly clever man, but he can show a mulish temper, and obstinacy such as I have rarely met. I passed a very agreeable time with him, but it was because I allowed him to talk, and express what he liked, and in his own way.

. . . . He can be of great use to you—and us pro-Ugandians. He is willing to give it provided he is not *crossed*. Excepting this extraordinary opiniative and cocksure manner of his he is really a man of singularly good endowments. He is good-looking, self-reliant, brave and sharp. Fancy de Winton opposing himself to Lugard ! ! ! He might as well have tried to drive Gordon to do a thing he had made up his mind not to do."[1]

This letter may help to explain why Lugard so often got his own way! We should note that, in the strenuous partnership of the Uganda campaign, Lugard and Stanley worked together cordially, and there are letters from Mrs. Stanley then and later showing close and friendly if never really intimate relations.

Mackinnon seems to have heeded this emphatic warning for Lugard certainly could not complain of his reception. Mackinnon had from first to last shown the greatest kindness towards his adventurous agent and warm appreciation of his work. He had, indeed, almost from the first been loaded with compliments from Mackinnon personally and from the directors. All this was in great contrast with Lugard's relations with the Scottish directors of the Lakes Company. From the time of his return the Company made full use of his advice and help. Lugard, though still a poor man, resigned from their service the moment he landed in order to be a free agent but he remained in very close touch with the Company's office and especially with Mackenzie. There were a few small differences of opinion and Mackenzie once exclaimed that in his anti-evacuation campaign he was " doing good yeoman work, stirring public opinion up, but he is a cranky, curious fellow to handle."[2] We know Lugard well enough by this point in the story to realize that he was not the easiest of employees or ex-employees, but the directors were men of a kind to know the value of the service he had given and Kirk was always there to understand and interpret. Gladstone's use of the word " loggerheads " to describe his relations with the Company was completely inaccurate.

[1] Stanley to Mackinnon, 8 October 1892, M.P.
[2] Mackenzie to Portal, 2 December 1892, P.P. s. 113.

Lugard hurried back from Scotland to rejoin the opening battle. He found himself very much an African lion in the political and social world. Almost every episode of his Uganda adventures was now known. The accusation of the priests and of the French government made him not only a hotly controversial figure but in most quarters added to his attractions. He had that very moving appeal of a man who suddenly emerges from a life of intense danger and achievement for an interval in the safety and luxury of the capital. His small slim figure and rather haggard, hungry-looking face, with the eyes which really merited the well-worn adjective, piercing, were soon well known. But Lugard was the last man to be affected by consciousness of his own glamour, though he occasionally found it useful to exploit his fame for his main purpose. He preferred to come forward not as a hero of action but as a colonial expert, a political figure challenging the Liberal government with appeals to reason, based on facts and figures, as much as to sentiments of humanity and patriotism. From his rooms in Jermyn Street he could be seen darting out to the Foreign Office; to Company headquarters in Pall Mall East; to fashionable political lunches and dinners. He sat far into the night, sometimes until dawn, writing letters and articles, and composing speeches. He was in constant touch with Rosebery and it is unfortunate, though not perhaps surprising, that he has left no record of what must have been very interesting conversations. He had been in the country only a few days when the Prince of Wales, then struggling against his mother's unwillingness to allow him any initiation into the counsels of government, wrote to him. It is interesting to notice that the letter was written by Lugard's old chief, de Winton, now in Royal employment: theirs must have been a strange and rather sad meeting. The Prince asked him to come for an interview. A few days later the Duke of Cambridge followed suit. Stanley was anxious to co-operate with him, and Lugard's diary shows engagements with the C.M.S. and the Anti-Slavery Society.

On October 17th Lugard's second long letter appeared in *The Times*. To his former arguments he added a new category, " colonial ". Subsequent events give his plea a prophetic significance. He extolled the potential farming value of the highlands on the way to Uganda. In the Mau plateau region " are enormous stretches of absolutely unpopulated lands with a network of streams and with the richest natural pasture, an excellent fodder grass being mixed with white clover, trefoil, etc." East Africa would also, in the region nearer the coast, "offer opportunities for emigration to the congested and over-populated districts of our Indian Empire." Lugard clearly foresaw pos-sibilities that were afterwards in large part realized, but not their attendant difficulties, with the unravelling of which he was to be much concerned. He went on to argue strongly in favour of the railway but also—Lord Rosebery having almost certainly warned him it was beyond immediate possibilities—that East Africa could be held without it. His final paragraph summarized the case he reiterated during the whole campaign.

> "Surely, Sir, in view of the interests involved, the greatness of which I feel, though I am so feeble an exponent of them; the obligations we have incurred by accepting this country as part of our 'sphere of influence', and by taking the initiative in the Brussels Act; in view of the awful anarchy and misery which must follow the repudiation of the pledges made by the company to the natives; of the destruction of mis-sions; the impetus to slave raiding; the abandonment of the political key to Central Africa—in view of all these, and all they each severally mean when closely considered, the moderate paltry sum, which will save the situation, will not be denied by the Government of the 'richest nation in the world'."

Throughout October the struggle among the ministers went on. It was no longer a Cabinet secret that Rosebery was in favour of retention. There were many questions at issue. Should Salisbury's correspondence be published to prove his inaction? Rosebery fought against this method of shelving responsibility, much to Harcourt's anger. In any case, Salisbury made a published statement that his government had always contemplated retaining Uganda.[1] Should the device of handing back the mainland to the sultan of Zanzibar be tried? True, the sultan was now a client king of Britain but at least he would serve to shield the Cabinet from responsibility. This plan was one which would naturally appeal to the consul-general as the power behind the island throne. Kirk and Portal had discussed and approved it. It had already interested Salisbury. Harcourt and Glad-stone liked it because they thought it would not load Britain with "indeterminate responsibilities".[2] Rosebery, to Harcourt's surprise

[1] *Daily News*, 28 October 1892.
[2] Gladstone to Rosebery, 21 October 1892, B.M. 44549.

and satisfaction " embraces this idea very cordially," but it was for the opposite reason that, being in almost daily touch with Portal, he knew that it must, in reality, mean the commitment of Britain.[1] But Portal, energetic new broom though he was, realized that he had not yet sufficiently reformed Zanzibar to enable the island to carry the liability, which East Africa must represent for at least a year, without a British subsidy, and this was more than Rosebery yet dared to demand.[2]

Then there was the King of the Belgians, irreverently called " Nosey" in the Cabinet, making obscure hints that he might run Buganda and Bunyoro on behalf of Britain.[3] Earlier in the month there had been a suggestion from Labouchere that a commission might go out and oversee evacuation. This would at least have relieved the government from the fierce attacks he led, with his Radical and Irish following, upon their Uganda indecision. But Gladstone and most of the Cabinet were still sternly hostile to taking even that degree of responsibility which sending an evacuator implied, above all since the Gordon affair. Indeed, Gladstone recoiled from the idea with horror. " For me to send a Commissioner to superintend evacuation would be doing the most dangerous of all things. . ."[4]

Gladstone might think he could still maintain his original ground without budging. But Rosebery showed, by the contrast between his reception of the Anti-Slavery Society delegation on October 20th and that of the C.M.S. almost exactly a month earlier, how his policy of waiting for public opinion to warm up had succeeded in that it allowed him to show more of his hand in public. The delegation was impressive, and variegated. Among the one hundred and twenty men it contained were twenty members of parliament, many names well-known in the churches, philanthropy and commerce, and drawn from all over the British Isles. In their speeches there was much appreciative reference to Lugard. Rosebery began his answer by remarking significantly that " I am only one member of a Government " but he went on to speak strongly of the importance of Uganda and then, picking up a remark made by Mr. Bosworth Smith, the well-known Harrow master, who played a vigorous part in the retention campaign, he continued " That continuity of moral policy is a moral force by

1 Harcourt to Gladstone, 20 October 1892, B.M. 44202.
2 Portal to Rosebery, 3 October and 3 November 1892, P.P. s. 106.
3 Leopold to Gladstone, 29 September 1892, B.M. 44516.
4 Gladstone to Morley, 17 October 1892, B.M. 44549.

which, in my opinion, this country has to be judged." The anti-slavery policy of Britain was her great moral achievement. " My belief is that, having put our hands to the plough in that great enterprise, we shall not be able, even if we were willing, to look back."[1] This assertion, really superfluous as regards the slave-trade, could be read, in spite of some safe additional remarks, as a hint about East Africa. Two days after this the brilliant pictorial comment by Tenniel, reproduced opposite page 400, appeared in *Punch*.

Suddenly, at the end of the month, Rhodes, appearing in London, intervened in the Uganda transaction, as he had done with regard to Nyasaland. Strangely enough it was to Harcourt he went and, stranger still, Harcourt gave him a very cordial reception. Rhodes, he told Gladstone, opposed evacuation, and also the Mombasa railway. (Rhodes' rejection of the latter shows how far his grandiose acquisitiveness mastered his practical sense: his hopes were still set on the Cape-to-Cairo axis, a line of communication unsuited to the opening up of Africa). He offered to administer Uganda for £25,000 a year, as against the Company's estimate of £40,000. " It is a tempting offer," was Harcourt's surprising comment, which suggests that finance was the chief motive for all his opposition.[2] His son's journal confirms the idea. After spending a Sunday with Rhodes at Lord Rothschild's " W.V.H. is delighted with him, likes his hard sense and knowledge of affairs, and says even Jingoism is tolerable when it is done ' on the cheap '."[3] Rhodes wrote a formal letter to Rosebery (undated but received at the Foreign Office on October 31st) offering, at his own expense, to bring on his telegraph line from Salisbury via Johnston's position on Lake Nyasa to any point in Uganda the government wished. His ultimate object, he said, was to link up with the Egyptian system but he was aware that " under existing circumstances at Khartoum, such an undertaking cannot at present be carried out."[4]

The offer was not accepted. The Cabinet remained in its paralysis of indecision with the natural result that tempers grew even more strained. Morley found Harcourt's high-handed manner intolerable, and reported Rosebery's irritation at " the excessive activity " of

1 *A.S.R.*, IV. xii, September and October 1892, p. 275.
2 Harcourt to Gladstone, 30 October 1892, B.M. 44202.
3 Gardiner, *Life of Harcourt*, vol. ii, p. 199.
4 C.6847 (1893), p. 33.

Gladstone's "next door neighbour."[1] Rosebery was equally angry, as we saw earlier, with Gladstone for going over his head to the French ambassador about Uganda. Lord Ripon, in turn, complained to Lord Kimberley about Rosebery's high-handedness, and Kimberley warned Ripon that Rosebery was "in a very ticklish condition."[2] While everyone found the tension intolerable, Rosebery, playing for time, could still insist to Gladstone "I see no special cause for haste in the Uganda matter."[3] He could say this though the day before he had received a letter from the Company confirming their evacuation policy. The Company had consulted Lugard about the time it would take Williams to concentrate his forces. Lugard advised two months. They were therefore sending Williams immediate orders to begin evacuation.[4]

Rosebery was indeed playing a dangerous game with time. Aware of what was going on in Uganda, with parliament in adjournment, he had to keep one eye on the Cabinet and the other upon the country, impatiently watching the slow but growing movement of public interest in Uganda. The press was becoming increasingly favourable to his cause. But this was not enough. What was wanted was one of those great stirrings of public opinion which can force a government in power to reverse its policy. This is a very rare political event in Britain between elections. In recent days, perhaps the clearest example has been the movement against the Hoare-Laval pact over Ethiopia. In 1892 it was clear by the end of October that some great effort was needed if the too-slowly turning tide of opinion were to be swung rapidly and strongly in favour of the retention of Uganda. Did Rosebery actually encourage Lugard to hasten the movement? It is hardly a matter upon which there can be direct evidence but Lugard, who was the last man to make wild claims, wrote in his own note upon the period, as if he were describing the most natural of occurrences, "Lord Rosebery was glad to utilize me in giving effect to his opposition to the views of his colleagues and I had constant interviews with him."

Whether he was given the hint or not, Lugard needed little prompting to see and to grasp his chance. He sprang into action as a political

---

1 Morley to Gladstone, 31 October 1892, B.M. 44257.
2 Kimberley to Ripon, 6 November 1892, B.M. 43536.
3 Rosebery to Gladstone, 2 November 1892, B.M. 44290.
4 C.6847 (1893), pp. 33-4.

propagandist with the same fierce energy with which he forced his way through the natural and human obstacles of Central Africa. He and Mackenzie plotted out a great campaign of speaking through England and Scotland. As soon as it was known that Lugard was on the oratorical war-path, demands for him, far more than could be accepted, poured into the Company's office, from which the campaign was organized. It was often suggested that Stanley or Jephson should speak in his place.

Lugard's first speech, on November 3rd, which should hardly have been utilized as part of the campaign, was given to the Royal Geographical Society, before which all explorers came to register their discoveries about the great continent which was at last being revealed. It proved a great occasion. "Last night's show," wrote his brother to his fiancée, " was a huge compliment to Fred. I am told 300 to 500 people, Lords and Dukes and all sorts of swells, were turned away at the door for want of standing room! " The Prince of Wales sent a letter of regret that he was unable to be present, the Archbishop of Canterbury and the great Stanley did the same. Lugard was requested to read his paper again at a special meeting of the Society later in the month for the benefit of those unable to attend on this occasion.

It must be admitted that Lugard's paper, which began by deliberately playing down the romantic notions cherished about the dangers and difficulties of African travel, and went on to give strictly geographical and ethnographical accounts of the country, might have had a somewhat deflationary effect upon his distinguished audience had they not been so ready to admire and agree.[1] But suddenly, at the very end, he answered their expectations. He told them how he had pledged his honour to the people of Toro, re-established them and defended them from Kabarega. They had told him that they would hardly have dared to stay and risk destruction if it were possible they should later be deserted. " And I replied, ' Do as you prefer: but these lands are British. We have taken them by agreement with the nations of Europe, and are come to stay.' " So they stayed, escaping from Bunyoro in

[1] It is interesting to note a passage in the diary of Wilfrid Scawen Blunt, the great opponent of Britain's control of Egypt, for November 3. " Dined with Esmé Howard and went afterwards to hear a lecture by Captain Lugard at the Geographical Society. Lugard a little, thin, dark-faced man, not unpleasing, but his lecture terribly dull. The theatre crammed, for the agitation got up for annexing Uganda grows daily." W. S. Blunt, *My Diaries*, Part 1 (1919), p. 100. Lugard's brother, commenting on this page in a letter to the writer, says "I was present and the enthusiasm both during the reading of the paper and at the reception afterwards was tremendous." (25 January 1954).

their thousands, and he sent de Winton out to them. He concluded in a style which—the Chairman himself remarked it—shows the influence his childhood's reading of the Old Testament had left upon him. " And de Winton did as I had told him and went round the country with Kasagama, and appointed Chiefs to districts and helped them to arrange the country in peace. And in this task this brave young officer died."

The President, Sir M. E. Grant Duff, when he rose to thank Lugard, was in a difficult position as he could not indulge in any open advocacy for the retention of Uganda. But he made his meaning clear when he referred to the " almost lapidary brevity and strength " of Lugard's last paragraphs, which " seemed altogether too good for these degenerate days of paper: they should be stamped on bronze or graven on stone."[1]

From Lugard's diary, and the many press reports, we can compile a summary of his tour, with its crowded programme of interviews and public dinners, giving the names of some of his distinguished hosts or chairmen. For those who are interested to see the choice of cities and societies the list is given below.[2]

[1] ' Travels from the East Coast to Uganda, Lake Albert Edward, and Lake Albert', *Proceedings of the Royal Geographical Society*, N.S. vol. XIV, November 1892, p. 817.

[2]

November 5.	London	Chamber of Commerce
November 7.	Manchester	11 a.m. Chamber of Commerce
		3 p.m. Manchester Royal Geograpical Society
		Public Dinner
November 8.	London	Dinner at Colonial Institute
November 10.	London	Kensington Town Hall (Lord Lorne and H.R.H. Princess Louise present)
November 11.	London	11 a.m. Ravenstein
		Dinner with Lord Rosebery
November 12.	London	National Liberal Club
November 15.	Edinburgh	Royal Scottish Geographical Society (Duke of Montrose in the Chair). Lugard awarded the Society's Silver Medal
November 16.	Edinburgh	Chamber of Commerce (Lord Lorne)
November 17.	Glasgow	R.S.G.S. (Sir Rennie Watson)
November 18.	Aberdeen	R.S.G.S. (The Lord Provost)
November 22.	Dundee	Chamber of Commerce (Lord Camperdown)
November 23.	London	Dinner with Fishmongers' Company
November 24.	London	R.G.S.
November 25.	Cambridge	Lunch with the Master of Trinity
	London	Dinner with Bryce
		Meeting at the Guildhall
November 26.	London	Dinner with Stanley
November 28.	Newcastle	Chamber of Commerce (Mayor of Newcastle)
		Newcastle R.G.S.
November 30.	Liverpool	Chamber of Commerce
		Public Dinner (President of Chamber)
December 2.	Birmingham	Meeting in the Town Hall (Other speakers, Mr. Bosworth Smith, the Bishop of Worcester, etc.)

In all the cities he visited Lugard was given a most impressive reception. Bishops, mayors and aldermen, peers, acted as chairmen, supporting speakers, and his hosts for his night's entertainment. Each visit was crowded with public engagements and private interviews. His speeches were reported in the London and provincial press, provoking leaders nearly always favourable to his policy, and subsequent letters from correspondents. At Kensington Town Hall he had to address a large overflow meeting.

It was always the man and his cause, rather than his platform gifts, which roused his audiences. Lugard's method as a propagandist was simple. He approached his main purpose indirectly. In his own words " I gave addresses in almost every case nominally on geographical and commercial aspects of East Africa and Uganda, with only a mere incidental reference to the political aspect, since I thought this line more appropriate for an officer in the regular establishment of the army. I had large audiences in the principal cities of England and Scotland and much enthusiasm was shown for the Retention of Uganda, and that the hopes that I had held out to the people of Toro that Britain would protect them from the tyranny of Kabarega of Unyoro (from which I had freed them) would be implemented."

Many of his audiences must have been puzzled and disappointed. The hero they had come to see turned out to be such a small, quiet man who struck no attitudes, but quietly and conscientiously told them about the nature of Uganda, its problems, peoples, scenery and products. Yet it may be that, with the British public, the contrast between the adventurous achievements of Lugard and his quiet, almost gentle presence and rational speech was not ineffective, especially with those who distrusted flamboyance and jingoism. He could leave the heroics to Stanley, who was also in the campaign and gave a strong speech at Swansea on October 3rd.[1] And always at the conclusion he gave

---

[1] *Western Mail*, 4 October 1892.

December	3.	Birmingham	Public breakfast. Presentation of illuminated address
December	5.	London	Foreign Office
			Dinner with Moberley Bell, manager of *The Times*
December	7.	London	11.30 a.m. Treasury
			3 p.m. Foreign Office
			Evening: Attended Stanley's address to Constitutional Club
December	8.	Cambridge	Dinner at Trinity College
December	12.	Norwich	Meeting (Mayor of Norwich)
December	20.	London	Merchant Taylors' dinner.

his hearers a little of what they had come to hear, a theme his supporters on the platform could be trusted to take up.

He did manage to suit his speeches in some measure to his audience. It was easy, for example, to appeal to the Scots. At Edinburgh he concluded his speech, the subject being " Characteristics of African Travel ", as follows: " In Africa my task has been no easy one. I have come to England to find a still harder one before me, and one for which I have no qualification—the task of publicly explaining our duties and responsibilities in Africa. Scotsmen have been Britain's foremost pioneers in Africa—from Livingstone through successive years to the East Africa Company of today, which is largely, almost entirely, Scottish—its Chairman, Sir William Mackinnon; its Vice-Chairman, the Marquess of Lorne; and most of its directors. Scotsmen have made Nyasaland . . . . Scottish missions, as I can testify, have done a great and good work there; already they are penetrating into East Africa too. Already British lives have been given for East Africa, already large sums of money have been spent without hope |or expectation of return. Shall these lives be wasted, this money be worse —a thousand times worse—than mis-spent? To Scotsmen I can leave the reply with confidence, for Scotsmen have ever shown themselves sensible of British honour and good faith."[1]

There can be no doubt that Lugard's campaign was effective. For this there is the evidence of the press and later references in parliament. " Captain Lugard ", wrote one newspaper, " is doing an all-important service as he passes from city to city and tells about Uganda and its people and productions and the work in which he was then so recently engaged."[2] He, better than anyone, could give his countrymen the information they required in order to make up their minds about Uganda and he gave it in full measure. But, though he led the cause, he was by no means alone. Not only Stanley and Jephson, but Bosworth Smith and others were on tour. Meetings were called all over the country which Lugard could not attend. Bishops and clergy were very active, being careful to disavow any general claim that missionaries required government annexation or protection, but drawing attention to the special circumstances of Uganda, and the dangers or civil war and enslavement hanging over its people.

---

[1] *The Scottish Geographical Magazine*, vol. VIII, December 1892, p. 625.
[2] *Aberdeen Free Press*, 19 November 1892.

The Campaign for Retention

The Church Missionary Society was, of course, the headquarters of this side of the campaign and in a country which still held a church-going people, as at the time of the anti-slavery movement, every priest could be a ready-made propagandist and every pulpit a platform. And it was a case the clergy, from the Archbishop down, could plead with conviction, so strongly did the young Uganda branch of the Church, sanctified by martyrdom, beg for the continuance of the power which could bring Christians protection, maintain peace and foster the beginnings of civilization. The Roman Catholic party, too, and their White Fathers had come to realize that annexation by the British government was better then being left masterless for a period in which the several Muslim forces in the region might combine before some other European power could come in. So strongly did Bishop Tucker feel about the situation that when, in September, Portal was instructed to inform him at Mombasa that if he went back to Uganda he would go entirely at his own risk, he replied in a very strong letter. The Company, he wrote, authorized by the government, had compromised the missionaries, by claiming their support and then threatening to leave them after they had incurred the hatred of the Company's enemies. " A course of action that I dare not at the moment trust myself to characterize . . . . "[1] He formally asked the government if the Germans could be invited to come in and take over Uganda before rather than after it had fallen into civil war and chaos.[2] Bishop Tucker's views and reports were, of course, very influential in church circles in Britain.

The stirring of the mind of Britain upon this question was shown not only by crowded meetings and newspaper articles. Protests and memorials from all over the country began to pour in to the Foreign Office, where these not unwelcome manifestations of democracy in action, all carefully collected, were initialled by Rosebery. They started to come in during the middle of October. They reached their peak in the second half of November and went on coming in up to late December. There were 174 in all. Of these the majority, 101 in number, came from religious bodies of some kind, mainly but not wholly Anglican, or from parish meetings; 24 were submitted by Chambers of Commerce; 13 were officially sealed by Town or Borough Councils

---

[1] Stock, *History of the C.M.S.*, vol. iii, pp. 445–6.
[2] Tucker, *Eighteen Years in Uganda*, vol. i, pp. 191–2.

and there were 34 general meetings.[1] Members of parliament almost certainly received a heavy post from opponents of evacuation.

Some analysis of the reasons given against evacuation should reveal the springs of Britain's colonial policy. It is, however, a characteristic of the democratic party system that, in order to win wide support, the protaganists of a policy tend to throw in every reason which they can imagine will appeal to one or other element in the electorate. It is not always possible, therefore, to be sure which were the reasons which were decisive for national action. If, however, we treat these petitions as a sample of public opinion and classify their reasons, some results emerge, though they can be offered only tentatively. It appears, then, that the following six reasons can be distinguished against the policy of evacuation.

1. The set-back to the suppression of the slave-trade.
2. Possible result in civil war and the massacre of Christians.
3. The loss to Great Britain of potential commercial opportunities.
4. The serious check to the spread of Christian civilization.
5. The damage to British honour and prestige.
6. The material and spiritual injury to the missions.

The first reason appears most often, that is in 80 petitions, but only comes first in 7. The second is given 66 times and comes first in 44. The third occurs 67 times and is put first in 32. Too much importance, however, should not be attached to the order in which reasons were given. The wording of many of the documents shows clearly the influence of Lugard's teaching and also of the missionary case. The part played by the Chambers of Commerce in the main cities was no doubt of some political importance. But, as far as effective economic imperialism went, their interest was rather doctrinaire and there was little sign then or for long afterwards of the business world being prepared to invest in East Africa or for many individual firms to go vigorously pioneering in search of openings. East Africa, unlike the East Indies, and to a lesser extent, West Africa, had to be occupied, administered, and its transport and production laboriously developed,

[1] Mr. Anthony Low and the writer came almost simultaneously upon this file in the Foreign Office, F.O. 84/2192. He has published a most interesting article, based largely upon it—see ' British Public Opinion and the Uganda Question: October-December 1892 ', *Uganda Journal*, vol. XVIII, September 1954. He has presented a much fuller analysis of the material than the one given here: a few slight discrepancies between the two are due to differences of classification.

before it could offer much by way of dividends. The main impetus came from the missionary movement, with the Church of England behind it, and from the strong, continuing anti-slavery tradition. These general sentiments combined with the feeling, which Lugard did much to foster, that Britain's honour was pledged. It is to be remarked that there is no evidence of any anti-retention meeting being called, except for one which broke up in disagreement. The memorials collected in this Foreign Office file are of great interest not only for the subject of Uganda, but as evidence of the working of democracy in Britain at this time. They show an astonishing variety in the size and type of meetings, from great public and civic meetings, presided over by mayors, to little collections of villagers or working men, and other Meetings in which members of different classes, religious denominations and even of political parties joined together to press their opinions upon the government.

The mounting force of public opinion played upon the divided Cabinet. Referring the French case against the autonomy of Chartered Companies to the Lord Chancellor had done nothing to relieve them from the pains of responsibility and decision. But the ministers continued to fight against going the way in which Rosebery and public opinion was driving them. On November 1st Morley said he would resign rather than agree to Britain remaining in Uganda.[1] A Cabinet meeting on November 4th merely allowed the reiteration of clashing opinions, with Rosebery and the Prime Minister " sparring all through the Cabinet."[2] Rosebery seems to have brought up on this occasion the idea of a Commissioner going out to advise upon what should be done.[3] Three days later the Cabinet met again and discussed the liability of the government for the acts of Chartered Companies. Lord Herschell had given it as his opinion that " the first clause of the [Company's] Charter itself renders this country responsible to foreign powers in respect of all acts of the Company's officials in the government and administration of the territory within its sway." Where the government did not use the powers taken in Clause 8 to dissent from the acts of the Company, it became liable for them.[4] This opinion was given with regard to French claims but it also shook the Cabinet's position of

[1] West, *Private Diaries*, p. 70.
[2] *Ibid.* p. 72.
[3] Notes of Cabinet proceedings, 4 November 1892, B.M. 44648.
[4] Memorandum by the Lord Chancellor, 5 November 1892, F.O. 84/2275.

non-liability for Lugard's treaties, with their promises of protection. It was decided at this meeting to send a commissioner to Uganda, the very step from which Gladstone had recoiled in horrified rejection less than a month before.[1] But the commissioner was only to report. As with the decision to prolong the Company, some members of the Cabinet meant this decision to lead to very different results from those steadily pursued by Rosebery.[2]

Before the matter was finally settled another subsidiary crisis blew up. Rosebery suggested making one further request to the Company to carry on for a little longer, presumably to enable the commissioner to make his report at leisure and in safety, which was hardly possible with the evacuation so imminent. Mackinnon called a meeting of the directors and they decided to reply to Rosebery on November 18th that the cost would be £50,000 a year and that it would be impossible, in the unstable and dangerous condition of Uganda, to undertake a further period of less than three years.[3] This prolongation might have saved the Company. It so happened that Stanley was with Mackinnon at the Burlington Hotel when this reply was sent off to Rosebery. Stanley exclaimed at such a figure, " Rosebery wants to stand well with the country and at the same time to pacify Harcourt. At £25,000 he *might* have been able to do both." Stanley was right. The larger figure could never have been got past the Chancellor of the Exchequer. As they were still talking Rosebery's answer arrived. " Mackinnon's hand trembled as he opened it and when he had fully understood its meaning, it was only by a great effort that he was able to suppress his emotions." The letter was a curt refusal to consider such a sum. From that day Stanley observed a change in his friend. The cause for which for many years he had lived had failed and he was now ready to die.[4] Before very long, Anderson was writing to Rodd to say " Poor Mackinnon seems to be breaking up and the crew is taking to the boats." He was with some cynicism explaining how the Company's claims were being " reduced, crushed down till they are tangible . . . . I have no doubt you are right as to the value of the

1 Notes of Cabinet proceedings, 7 November 1892, B.M. 44648.
2 The Cabinet's decision to send Portal was taken, as Mr. Low points out in his article (cited on p. 426), just before the retention public movement had reached its climax, but public opinion changed the result of the commission and enabled Rosebery to take the really decisive step of sending Portal advice as to the character of his report, as described on p. 431.
3 McDermott, *IBEA*, pp. 279 ff.
4 D. Stanley, *Autobiography*, pp. 448-9.

assets. You must remember that the Old Man of the Sea had no particular assets, but it was worth something to Sinbad to get rid of him, and the Co. does deserve consultation. Had no Mackinnon come to the front, and spent the large sums which he and his friends unquestionably did spend there would have been no British sphere at all."[1] This may serve as Mackinnon's official epitaph.

During the negotiations over this question during the middle days of November, Rosebery and Gladstone could hardly speak to each other. Rosebery complained that Gladstone was always violent and unreasonable about Uganda and that he snubbed him over it at Cabinet meetings. But it happened that on November 21st Rosebery received a letter from Portal saying that in time Zanzibar could administer the interior for half the price the Company was paying. West took the letter to Gladstone and Harcourt and read it to them and " both liked the idea! If it had been made in October, they would both have gone out of their senses with rage. What a healer Time is! and Rosebery will get his way."[2]

Rosebery's way? Perhaps even West, though no man had seen so many facets of the Cabinet disagreement over what he called " the accursed thing " as Gladstone's secretary, did not yet realize what " Rosebery's way " meant. Gladstone and Harcourt liked the Zanzibar plan, firstly because it sounded so cheap and secondly, as we have seen, because they could hide from public responsibility behind the flowing robes of the puppet sultan. The conflict of intention was still there and made it difficult to decide upon the instructions to the commissioner or the choice of a man. Over the instructions, Gladstone flinched from a draft by Rosebery which contained the words " liabilities ", " administering " and " administration." The two last " are words with poison in them, as touching to insinuate *a foregone conclusion*— which is, I think, what the Cabinet did not mean to do." He would accept phrasing about the report " dealing with", instead of " administering ",[3] and the Zanzibar plan must be brought in.[4] So it was settled. The Company's evacuation was accepted and the carefully worded instructions to report were drawn up.[5]

---

[1] Anderson to Rodd, 5 April 1893, Rodd Papers.
[2] West, *op. cit.* p. 82.
[3] Gladstone to Harcourt, 18 November 1892, B.M. 44549.
[4] Rosebery to Gladstone, 9 December 1892, B.M. 44290.
[5] C.6847 (1893), p. 50.

But *who* was to go and report? Rosebery wanted a person of " high standing ". He had been set upon appointing a commissioner long before he had brought the Cabinet round to it and had written early in the month to consult Portal. " My private opinion is that either Lugard or Williams would be the best man, but I think I should find great difficulty in obtaining the consent of my colleagues to either of these appointments, as they have been so mixed up with recent events that they would not have the necessary character of impartiality; which does not affect my opinion, however, that they are very fine fellows."[1]

The choice fell upon Portal himself. It seems strange that Rosebery could have persuaded his colleagues to an appointment not much less tendentious than that of Lugard would have been. Gladstone might well tell Rosebery " Much depends upon the question what sort of man is Portal? Clearly a clever and constructive one but I should like to know more—and you will have the means of learning."[2] Rosebery might well have blushed to read this. He did not need to learn; he knew his man, one after his own heart and mind. And the Cabinet should have remembered this, for a revealing letter from Portal had somehow got out into the press. Lugard had been at the back of this for, on the day they had met in Mombasa, Portal had been so deeply impressed by Lugard's warnings of the results of evacuation, that he had written off to a friend in England and finished his letter with the words " Will the government sit quiet and allow this to take place and then be hooted into an immense expedition? I am speaking plainly to them on the subject."[3] Gladstone had written at once to Rosebery about this improper letter and asked for a reprimand[4] and Rosebery telegraphed for explanation of a letter which seemed to him incredible. Portal could send only a reply protesting that he had no recollection of writing such a letter and had certainly never authorized publication.[5]

But the Cabinet, in spite of this knowledge, were tempted to discount it because they were lured on by their anxiety to avoid responsibility. They could claim that Portal had been appointed by Salisbury with a commission that more or less covered his new assignment: this relieved

1 Rosebery to Portal, 4 November 1892. P.P. s. 113.
2 Gladstone to Rosebery, 21 November 1892, B.M. 44549.
3 *The Times*, 10 October 1892.
4 Gladstone to Rosebery, 13 October 1892, B.M. 44549.
5 Rosebery to Gladstone, 14 October 1892, B M. 44290, and Portal's diary, 11 October 1892, P.P. s. 107.

them from having to do anything so embarrassingly decisive as to appoint a wholly new commissioner with new instructions. Had they known what Rosebery was writing privately to Portal, spurring on a man already active and ambitious enough to want to gain this great hinterland and, perhaps, see it added to his coastal domain, they might well have accused their colleague of something worse than being egotistical and high-handed. He told Portal there might be a saving clause in his instructions to cover the possibility that retention might prove insuperably difficult. " But ", he added, " as a rather one-horse Company has been able to administer I suppose the Empire will be equal to it and therefore that saving clause is mainly one of form."[1] The Foreign Secretary was not at all afraid of the word "administer". And a few days later, when the formal instructions had at last been hammered out, Rosebery, to make assurance doubly sure, sent with them a confidential letter to Portal, to say he had little to add. " But I may say this, as my confident though not my official opinion, that public sentiment here will expect and support the maintenance of the British sphere of influence."[2]

As soon as the public announcement was made on November 24th that a commissioner would be sent, Lugard called off his campaign. On December 1st Portal's appointment was announced. Lugard's action was well founded. He knew Portal and he knew Rosebery; he also knew something of the strength of that " public sentiment " to which Rosebery alluded as he had done so much in the last four weeks to strengthen it. Victory was much more than half assured.

[1] Rosebery to Portal, 1 December 1892, P.P. s 113
[2] Rosebery to Portal, 9 December 1892, P.P. s. 113.

CHAPTER XXI

THE DECISION

1893-1894 : Aet. 34-36

LUGARD HAD finished his speechmaking tour but it was not to rest that he now turned; only to another form of advocacy. He set to work immediately to write up his book from his diaries and papers. And his book, both consciously and unconsciously, was an argument in favour of imperial advance, more subjective and dramatic than his platform advocacy.

With Lugard absorbed in the task of writing in great haste his two volume book; with Macdonald in Uganda and Portal on his way up, the government might hope for a pause in the Uganda affair which would allow them to concentrate, without fear of a resignation from the indispensable Rosebery, upon their Home Rule Bill. But they had to reckon with parliament. They had been most fortunate in being able to enjoy, since their accession, a long prorogation from August 18th 1892 to January 31st 1893. But parliament reassembled with an opposition determined to make the most of the shufflings, inconsistencies and internal divisions which marked the government's dealings over Uganda.

The Queen's speech, mentioning the dispatch of Portal to report upon " the best means of dealing with the country," gave the Conservatives an early opportunity to criticize; and Lugard went to the House on February 3rd to hear them. But Labouchere jumped in first to taunt his own Gladstonian party for deserting Gladstonian principles and bowing the knee to King Jingo. Smarting from his failure to acquire either the ministerial office he had hoped for, or the embassy in Washington, he bitterly reproached his leaders. He then plunged, as in former debates, into a detailed attack upon Lugard, quoting long extracts from the first report to prove his inhumanity, going on to condemn him for saying that he had pledged his country

432

to remain in Uganda, when he had no right to pledge more than the Company. " The government had at first accepted evacuation. Then Captain Lugard went about the country "—earlier he had talked of his " careering " about the country—" and the big drum was beaten. He went about saying that we would be disgraced if we did not take over the country. He not only contradicted his own Report but he contradicted in one speech what he said in another . . . . Well, in December, this agitation bore fruit. The Ministry, apparently, did reconsider its decision." He went on to analyse Lugard's inconsistencies further, to comment upon Rosebery's strange position and to protest passionately against the new idea that Britain had a divine mission to annex wherever she could. Making a favourite radical point he said " We have want and misery here." If there was money to be spent, let it be upon the well-being of the masses. He finished by quoting at length Gladstone's very strong speech, made less than a year before, against the Lugard expedition and the railway. He moved an amendment to the address in favour of evacuating Uganda.[1]

Poor Gladstone had a difficult task in answering this well-aimed thrust from his own rear. He tried to obscure his own difficult position in a thick mist of impressive words. He made an oblique reference to Lugard's propagandist campaign as if Lugard had been acting merely as the Company's agent; protested that the Cabinet was still " almost entirely destitute of such information " as would enable it to decide its Uganda policy. Not only had they to wait for Portal, but also for the settlement of the French claims and the Macdonald report. Portal had not gone up to administer and, he added, with what must at this stage of his knowledge of Uganda have been very near ·wilful blindness, his withdrawal " will create no such vacuum." Finally, he insisted that there was no committal to annexation—Portal was absolutely free as to what advice he should give and the government were also quite free as to their decision.[2]

Balfour commented with cool sarcasm upon this speech. Gladstone was " a master of safe phrases " so devised that they " cannot by any ingenuity be brought home to him at any later stage of a controversy . . . ."[3] He asked—and the Conservatives continued to press this difficult question—what provision had been made for the safety

[1] *Parliamentary Debates*, 3 February 1893, IV. 8. 455–78.
[2] *Ibid*. IV. 8. 478–88.
[3] *Ibid*. IV. 8. 488–92.

P

of the country, after the date of the Company's evacuation, between Portal finishing his task and the government receiving his report and deciding upon it. This was an extremely awkward question. It confronted the Cabinet with the hateful African realities they were trying to evade and forced them to the point of having to commit that first definite act which might be putting one foot on to the edge of the Uganda quagmire and being irresistibly sucked down, inch by inch, into the annexation they had so utterly denounced. The opposition enjoyed the sport of pushing ministers into this painful position. They drew from Harcourt an angry speech in which he threw back upon the Tories the taunt of having had themselves no policy to fill the gap, in their case between Company evacuation and the arrival of the railway. Chamberlain, still in his Liberal Unionist detachment from either party, caustically pointed out that this was to condemn the last government for folly as an excuse for being equally foolish.[1]

Rosebery was so angry at the performance of his colleagues in the House of Commons that next day he showed his hand more clearly than ever before in a memorandum to Gladstone. " I cannot understand the difficulty of giving the assurance asked for by Balfour and Chamberlain." Portal was going up with full powers, not " as a mere reporter—to take down something in writing and hurry away bag and baggage, leaving the population to its fate."[2] Gladstone admitted to " some confusion " last night and to having used careless expressions before the resolute attack of Labouchere and the opposition.[3] But he did not circulate Rosebery's memorandum. At this the Foreign Secretary declared he was " broken-hearted ". They *must* give the same answers in both Houses to questions which would be pressed the next day. They hastily looked up Salisbury's original appointment of Portal as " Commissioner and Consul-General in the British sphere " to make sure that they could claim that the last government had given the commissioner adequate powers and thus save themselves from the difficulty of defining new ones.[4]

Uganda still occupied much of the time of the Commons when the debate on the address was resumed on February 6th. But on this day Lugard, perched in the gallery, could listen with more satisfaction.

1 *Parliamentary Debates*, 3 February 1893, IV. 8. 495–6.
2 Rosebery to Gladstone, 4 February 1893, B.M. 44290.
3 Gladstone to Rosebery, 4 February 1893, B.M. 44549.
4 C.6555 (1892), pp. 1–3; and *Parliamentary Debates*, 6 February 1893, IV. 8 554–6.

There was a long and vigorous defence from the Tory and Company side by Mr. Burdett Coutts of Lugard's character and actions, including his absolute disinterestedness in his campaign for retention, and this was echoed by Mr. J. Lowther. Even more satisfactory, Sir Edward Grey, who handled the critical issue of Portal's powers with more firmness than his senior colleagues, explained and defended Lugard's actions in a speech which struck a very different note from that of Gladstone and clearly reflected conversations he had now had with Lugard.[1]

But Lugard had found it difficult on February 3rd to endure in silence Labouchere's long attack upon his actions and speeches in spite of its angry testimonial to the success of his retention campaign. He had hurried home to his rooms to write one of his immense letters to *The Times* to confute Labouchere. He poured scorn on the idea that he had possessed sufficient force to coerce Mwanga into a treaty. Labouchere had enlarged upon the idea of Uganda becoming productive by the labour of slaves for the advantage of the leisured classes. "Does not Mr. Labouchere reap a larger benefit from his own journal" (it was known that the profits were large) "than those who labour through the night to set up the type or make the paper?" Lugard had also been stung by Gladstone's reference to him in the debate as if he had been a mere agent of the Company, so he went on: "From the day on which I arrived in England I ceased to have any connection with the Company, and have drawn no pay from them (nor from anyone else) since then . . . . If the earnest wish to see the work in which I have been engaged in Africa continued and brought to a successful issue has compelled me to undertake a task most distasteful to me and to ' career through the country,' I hope that thereby I shall not have justly merited his (Gladstone's) dispraise or forfeited in his estimation the opinion he formerly expressed of me."

Finally he turned again to the question, always in his mind, of humanity, and protested against Gladstone's use of the term "massacre". It was probable that in all the operations in Uganda (which had partaken of the character of a civil war), less than four hundred people had lost their lives whereas in one engagement on the west coast a Maxim was said to have killed several thousand, yet these operations were officially approved. And how much had the brief operations in Uganda

[1] *Ibid.* IV. 8. 572–91.

gained! This included " the welfare of a large country with great possibilities, and whose inhabitants are a singularly intelligent and withal a very engaging race . . . . That my advocacy of a cause so great", he went on modestly, " has been painfully deficient in ability, that I have made, perhaps, mistakes, I am indeed aware, and it is surely not to be wondered at. But I deplore that through any such deficiencies in myself a cause should be jeopardized which in abler hands might have triumphed, and that the oft-repeated ridicule thrown on my thoughtless remark that the wants of the people were so varied as to include even opera glasses and rat-traps should have power to turn sympathy into laughter, while clever but empty phrases, such as the 'immoral continuity of Jingoism' should weigh in the balance against results achieved by months—nay years—of work, and that such tricks of debate should decide the fate of a nation."[1] Labouchere, unmoved from his position by the arguments or by the character of his opponent, wrote a strong reply on the same day Lugard's letter appeared.[2]

It was natural to Lugard that he should always want to confront his enemies, political or otherwise, in person. We have seen that he tried to see the Duke of Norfolk. He now went to see Labouchere. He later described the interview to the writer. When he gave his name to the servant the man hastily tried to shut the door but Lugard stepped quickly inside. The man ran to warn his master and Lugard followed him. Labouchere jumped up and at once put a table between them. It was quite clear that both master and man thought this dangerous " bushwhacker " had come to avenge the politician's attacks with a horsewhip. When, at last, the two men confronted each other, they could not have been more utterly contrasted. Not that Labouchere was a coward, or a man only of salons and lobbies. He too had had a wandering and adventurous youth. But his clear, atheistic, mocking, gallic mind, capable of analysing but never of entering into the emotions of other men, was utterly alien to the soldier with his intense feelings about personal and national honour and the inextricable association of the two in his own mind.

" Mr. Labouchere," Lugard said, " you have called me a liar and a murderer. You well know that this is untrue and that I am neither."

---

[1] *The Times*, 6 February 1893.
[2] *Ibid.* 7 February 1893.

" Oh yes, yes," Labouchere replied, sizing up the tanned, stringy, taut man across the table and realizing that, if only verbal violence was to be used, he could deal with the situation. " Yes. But it makes good copy. It brings you before the public—you can always deny it."

This, to him, brazen cynicism was not what Lugard was prepared for and it left him speechless. But the meeting opened the way much later to a new and better relationship.

He also desired to meet his other chief opponent, the Chancellor of the Exchequer. He had managed by now to see most of the Cabinet when he found himself actually summoned by Harcourt. He had no knowledge then of the ungoverned temper of the old Liberal minister, who, for all his charm and brilliance, tended to use over-emphatic and even violent language. He came in to confront that huge figure, the formidable countenance wreathed with white hair and side-whiskers, and based upon an immense jowl. It was rather like a meeting between David and Goliath with the giant having all the advantages of moral position in his high office and of physical position behind his vast ministerial desk. " I had hardly taken a seat ", Lugard records,[1] " when he poured forth a torrent of invective against all African explorers, missionaries and, above all, Chartered Companies and their promoters, including Rhodes. I sat silent until he turned upon me and said (in effect) that he supposed that I, like Stanley, had on occasion put men to death, and that I had no legal authority to act as judge and could therefore be held responsible for my action. I replied that I had never put any man to death in Africa, but that occasions might arise in unexplored Africa where strong measures were necessary to maintain discipline and prevent excesses. He took little notice and when he had exhausted his denunciations, I was dismissed."

It had been a galling experience for Lugard. He was therefore astonished to get a letter, in Harcourt's own hand, a few days later. In this he apologized for appearing to cast doubt on the bona fides of Lugard's treaties. He had only wondered whether the " thin veneer of civilization would enable these simple folk to master the Law of Nations." He begged him not to repeat some indiscreet remarks he had made about Rhodes. Most surprising was the conclusion " Permit me to express the pleasure and information which I derived from our conversation and my sense of the good temper and toleration

[1] In a note in the Lugard Papers.

which you showed for opinions which did not altogether agree with your own. I shall hope when I return to London to have another opportunity of discussing with you these interesting questions." (Harcourt to L. 24 December 1892).

In this way Lugard turned the edge of his opponents' weapons and shook them in their confident denunciation not only of what he had done but also of what he stood for. But he could spare little time for political action in the first half of 1893, as, finding for the purpose a refuge with his long-suffering regiment, he was busy writing, and felt he could confidently wait for Portal's report. Labouchere, however, refused to allow him or Uganda any close season from parliamentary attention. On March 20th on the debate on the estimates, he raised the whole matter again by trying to reduce the vote for Portal, and once more wearied the House with a long speech about Lugard's misdeeds and about the certainty that Portal's mission would lead to annexation.[1] He made a bitter attack upon Rosebery who, in a striking speech at the beginning of the month, had openly defended imperial annexations, in a world that was "not elastic", as "pegging out claims for the future."[2] Was this, Labouchere asked, the policy of a Liberal? Gladstone reiterated his unconvincing belief that Portal had a commission to inquire and report and nothing else.[3] This allowed Balfour to remark his astonishment at the government's illimitable passion for information and to enlarge upon the obvious and widening gap between Rosebery's intentions for Uganda and the blind repetitions of his colleagues.[4]

There were other points of interest about this debate. It showed the effects of the education the country had been having in African conditions. Mr. Wyndham raised, at last, the fundamental question as to "what meaning did Her Majesty's Government attach to this sphere of influence?"[5] With subsequent knowledge of the immensely difficult task of bringing order and development to Africa, it is difficult to understand how ministers could refuse to see, what Lugard and others were pointing out so vividly, the results of leaving vast areas of Africa in a state of indefinite and dangerous suspense, with firearms

1 *Parliamentary Debates*, 20 March 1893, IV. 10. 539–49.
2 Rosebery's speech at the Royal Colonial Institute, *The Times*, 2 March 1893.
3 *Parliamentary Debates*, 20 March 1893, IV. 10. 552.
4 *Ibid*. IV. 10. 555–6.
5 *Ibid*. IV. 10. 563.

flooding in, and with the old tribal rule violated and no new system of control to take its place. Finally, Chamberlain wound up the debate with a speech which took up the challenge of those Liberals, who had pitted the welfare of the masses against imperial expansion, by declaring that the two were completely linked through the operations of a trade which, in a protectionist world, must be carried into new lands if forty million people were to be nourished on this island. He advocated annexation and a railway and urged the government to abandon the policy of enquiry, the policy of postponement, and drift, and make a bold stand " because the result will be the same."[1]

It was in this speech that Chamberlain spoke his panegyric of Lugard which has been quoted earlier.[2] Almost the whole debate, indeed, was flattering to Lugard, whose earlier exploits and letters to *The Times* were canvassed, generally with approval. But some of Labouchere's group were tired of these compliments to the chief mover in actions they condemned. " A great deal," said Mr. Picton of Leicester, " has been said in praise of Captain Lugard. I should be the last to avail myself of an opportunity in the House of belittling a brave man; but much as the private and individual qualities of Captain Lugard may be considered admirable, I think his policy is absolutely abominable and most reprehensible. It is policy like that which has brought our country into disgrace all over the world."[3] Lugard could listen to this condemnation unmoved. It was, at least for the time being, a diminishing theme in the national chorus: the new trumpet notes being sounded by Rosebery and Chamberlain were beginning to drown it.

Lugard finished his book by midsummer and it was published in November. Under the provocative title of " The Rise of Our East African Empire " it filled two volumes and contained some 350,000 words, and a large number of charts and maps. These represented some of the most valuable of Lugard's achievements, gained at immense cost of careful labour. They were carried out with the help of the famous geographer, E. V. Ravenstein. Between the four scarlet covers were 130 illustrations, very characteristic of their day, many of them full-page, nearly all artists' impressions from Lugard's description of scenes and events, tangled tropical forests, wide rivers and lakes,

1 *Ibid.* IV. 10. 590–605.
2 See above p. 347.
3 *Parliamentary Debates*, 20 March, 1893, IV. 10. 589.

charging buffalo, and Lugard's encounters with Nyasa slavers, with
Bunyoro armies or with Mwanga at his crowded court. Author and
artist, responding to the mood of their day, have produced an atmosphere of romance which the dramatic, day-to-day narrative, extracted
mainly from Lugard's far more voluminous diaries, fully supports.
Romance and drama needed little forcing: they naturally surrounded
the lonely figures of the men who pushed their way into a resistant
continent and revealed its wild natural magnificence and its strange
tribes and animals.

The personal, and indeed very subjective, account of Lugard's
doings is interrupted, with little feeling for literary effect, by a number
of digressions upon general questions, historical and administrative,
and above all upon Lugard's chief concern, that of slavery, of which
he shows his profound but unsentimental knowledge. Over this
subject he had been in close touch with Kirk and had learned much
from him. The book ends with three chapters devoted mainly to
the Uganda question, in which Lugard was able to marshal again all
his arguments in favour of retention.

It may be that to readers of our age, this book of 1893 often strikes
a discomforting note of egotism. We have in recent years developed
a habit of understatement and, with regard to acts of courage, a
tradition of professional modesty which sometimes borders upon
affection. But we must remember not only the date, but the youth
and ambition of the author, who wrote at a time when he was being
lionized and when he was burning with ardour for a contested cause
in which his adventures and personality could be used as elements in
the struggle. He wrote also in the convention of many travel books
of his day, though he had neither the power nor the wish to equal
the tone of Stanley's journalistic but highly effective style.

One characteristic of Lugard which reviewers or leader writers,
who made large quotations from his book, justly emphasised was his
versatility. He also reveals his almost remorseless thoroughness especially
when he turns to discussing policy and future plans. Whether the
subject is slavery or the future administration of Africa, or the pros
and cons of Chartered Companies, he combines large principles with
the minutest details as to time, place, numbers and costs. He foresees
the destiny of East Africa, the settlement in the highlands, with some
station in the Kikuyu uplands near his Dagoretti—the future site of

Flora Shaw, about 1894
From *The History of "The Times,"* 1947

Nairobi—as the main administrative centre between Kampala and Mombasa. On the future of Uganda he tore the veil of ministerial pretence from the scheme of ruling through the Zanzibar sultan and argued for an outright protectorate and a railway.

On the form of administration, he advocated the recognition of the native institution of chieftainship. There is a humane and liberal commonsense in these passages in which we can read the further germination of the ideas of his future system of indirect rule. In his opinion " the object to be aimed at in the administration of this country is to rule through its own executive government. The people are singularly intelligent, and have a wonderful appreciation of justice and of legal procedure and our aim should be to educate and develop this sense of justice. Not only, I think," he went on with prescience of what was actually to occur, " may we hope in the present that sub-ordinate officials for the administration of Uganda may be supplied by the country itself but in the future we may even draw from thence educated and reliable men to assist in the government of the neigh-bouring countries."[1] No administrator then should attempt any radical change without prior discovery of " the views of highly intelligent chiefs." From that he goes on to the choice and distribution of staff, the treatment of swamps, and the method of establishing a heliograph system of communications, and a dozen other questions.

The book came out at a very important moment for Lugard's main purpose, just as the Uganda question hung in suspense awaiting Portal's report. There can be no doubt that it made a very powerful hit, though at the then heavy price of two guineas at a time of light purses it was not a financial success for his publishers, and later Lugard, with a consideration for them which is rare amongst authors, bought up a large number of copies in order to help their sales! The book was reviewed at a full and thorough standard upon which this age of authors may look back with envy. It was also treated throughout the press as an important contribution to a burning current question, and almost every review, as Lugard had hoped, treated it as such. The collected reviews and articles in the Lugard Papers fill three large volumes containing cuttings, many of them being leading articles covering several columns, the total number being 133. They come from a very wide range of civic, provincial, national daily and weekly

[1] Lugard II, pp. 649-50.

papers and magazines, a number of which have since passed out of existence.

The impression made by the book was highly favourable both to Lugard's achievements and to his cause. Only the two or three Liberal papers cavilled at the second, while joining in the applause for Lugard as a man. There were a very few suggestions that the volumes might have been somewhat pruned and have been better arranged. But, on the whole, the book was praised in every aspect. The daily papers of November 22nd carry long discussions of its contents. His publishers must have found it difficult to choose from the wealth of compliments the selections most suitable for their advertisements. The *Daily Telegraph* called for gratitude due from the empire to such a man, one of the " accomplished and heroic pioneers of its extension who knew, like Cæsar, how to fight with one hand and in the other to hold their faithfully written Commentaries." Lugard was hailed as the " Bayard of African enterprise" (*Pall Mall Gazette*), as "a first-class fighting man " (*The Athenaeum*). On the Liberal side, the *Manchester Guardian* praised Lugard's courage and impartiality while even the *Daily News* lauds his "seriousness of aim "; he writes " not merely as a traveller but as a statesman or, at any rate, as an administrator." The only notes of discord came from the sectarian newspapers, on the Roman Catholic side for obvious reasons, on the Anglican because of Lugard's criticisms of their missionaries.

The book fulfilled other intentions of the writer. An analysis of the reviews and the articles upon it shows that, in so far as this was still needed, it helped to clear Lugard's name from the charge of atrocities just as the Cabinet was reaching its final judgment upon this question. It also carried much further that education of the public about East Africa which had been begun by Speke, Thomson, and Stanley. Above all, it fulfilled its main immediate purpose. It revived in the nation the interest and the ideas which had been generated during the retention campaign and flung one more weight into the scales that were already, thanks in part to Lugard's other efforts, coming steadily down in favour of the retention of Uganda.

A few words, which the reader should store in his mind for future reference, should be said of the most important review, or rather reviewer, of the book. In his impetuous ignorance, Lugard went to see *The Times* reviewer to make sure he got the kind of treatment his cause needed from the leading " daily ". The reviewer turned out to be a handsome woman who was also dealing with all colonial affairs in the paper, and had been partly responsible for the very clear line the newspaper had taken in favour of retaining Uganda. This is not the moment to interrupt the Uganda story with a digression upon the past and future history of Flora Shaw. It can only be recorded now that she gently reproved him for this literary impropriety. She did not however punish him for it. In her review, she called the book the " most important contribution that has yet been made to the history of East Africa " and said that " the imagination will be dull to which the conflict of hostile barbarism and civilization fail to present itself with something of the grandeur of a modern epic."[1]

To Lugard's expressed gratitude for the review she replied modestly that she felt herself " that it did not deal fairly by the immense amount of matter that the volumes contain. If we could stir the country to feel more than it does the importance of dealing in the best way with our African possessions it would be a real gain." To this she added, " I am nearly always at home late in the afternoon. . ." (F. Shaw to L. undated). From then onwards the two naturally had cause for co-operation: they met socially also and *The Times* continued its steady support of Lugard personally and of his forward policy.

The Queen, the Prince of Wales and the King of the Belgians accepted specially bound copies of the book and Lugard sent copies to some of the leading politicians. He was now on the crest of the social wave. He found " piles of cards " left at his club and political hostesses competed for him as a prize for their dinner-parties. His engagement book was crowded with distinguished names. He now at last met Lord Salisbury, who picked him out for a long talk at a dinner at the Stafford Northcotes and invited him to stay at Hatfield. He made friends with Chamberlain and was several times a week-end guest at Highbury. There were even occasions when he was too much engaged to accept invitations to dine with Chamberlain. He also visited Lord and Lady Jersey at Osterley Park where he had a good talk with Balfour. Lord Knutsford, the last Colonial Secretary, told him at a dinner party that it was an honour to meet him and that he had read his reports and his book. There were dinners or long talks

1 *The Times*, 22 November 1893.

with Sir Edward Grey, Lowther, Bryce, Moberley Bell of *The Times*, Sir Percy Anderson and many others. One day at a dinner party, Lugard was pointing out the difficulties for a Commissioner in exercising justice legally in a sphere of influence so as to satisfy "Labby & Co", who might say that he was liable to trial for hanging a man. Yet, he added—and the reader who has followed his travels will know there was no brutal cynicism here—in Africa *practically* there would be no difficulty, there were lots of ways of doing things. Sir James Ferguson, who was in the listening circle, interrupted him. " I have no doubt whatever, Captain Lugard, that *you* would find a way of doing *whatever* you were resolved to do." " He said it very nicely," Lugard told his brother, " and everyone laughed . . . . " (L. to E. J. L. 5 June 1894). So naively pleased was Lugard to chance upon this evidence of the impression he had made!

The picture of Lugard spinning in the social whirl of 1893 and extremely vague about the identity of many of the celebrities he was meeting, has some incongruity in it. Lugard knew this and shows it in his frank, rambling letters to his brother, then back in India. " Dined with Mrs. Chamberlain on the 16th. Met some nice people, a Mr. Sidney Colvin (don't know who the deuce he is) and sat next Duchess of X. Got on a good deal with her . . . . She asked me to supper. I went—and found the *fastest* performance I have ever witnessed. Ladies smoked everywhere, and the talk was not Exeter Hall. Sat next Lady Randolph . . . . She has a son at Sandhurst. Her face is one that has a great fascination to me—she is still very beautiful and you can see that she has lived her life. Mrs. Patrick Campbell (2nd Mrs. Tanqueray) was there—also Colonel Brabazon—'beautiful Brab '— who ' carried on wonderful! '—Dined at Lady Flower's, sat next Miss Paget (daughter of Sir James, M.D.) who flooded me quite in metaphysics—I don't know *when* I've been so bowled out! Met Captain and Mrs. Eardley Wilmot who asked me to call. I have just now come from dining at Marjoribanks (Liberal Whip) and met Lord Tweedmouth—he married the Duke of Marlborough's daughter. His sister Lady (& Lord) Curzon I talked to most of the time. She brought me a note from the Duchess of X asking me to go and stay with her—big house-party ' only nice people are asked and everyone does exactly as they like,' Lady Curzon said. Don't know if I shall go—don't want to meet any more or any of his sort, I don't mind fast *ladies*—but fast *men* are hateful to me. I find myself gasping at their audacity like a fish on a bank. The Chamberlains were there tonight, Lord and Lady Sandhurst—young Ferguson (married Lord Dufferin's daughter), Haldane, Albert Grey (director, S. African Company etc.), Lady Wilton, Mr. Asquith, a Duchess of sorts and lots of others. So you see I've been plunging tremendously, advertising myself and my book everywhere."

He was not so absorbed that he could not step back and see the humour of his position. " I wonder what these people think when they read of the deck passage and my gratitude to my pal the boatswain! I suppose they say he's a *complete* adventurer, started with 50 sovereigns as a decker out of some slum." This was an over dramatization: even if the London society of 1893 had been so incapable of recognizing birth and breeding, they could read the dedication of his book to his distinguished and titled uncle. However, Lugard was not without some of the anxieties of the social upstart, and what follows is the more interesting in view of the pride and deep desire for independence which had made him resign from the Company and which led him to refuse the most tempting offers to lecture for money, though he was entirely without income and had his always impoverished father to care for. " Curious world, old boy—and it's amusing to see the Duchess and diamonds side, after trying the other. However, I can't run to this—I had to buy a new hat today, someone boned my good one at this damned club and left me a *beast* in its place. I have commissioned Willcocks to buy me a cheap second-hand portmanteau and if I meet any more Duchesses I shall have to buy a new overcoat, and goodness knows where it will stop for my dress suit isn't as new as it might be." (L. to E. J. L. 20 December 1893).

Lugard could use those hours at dinner-parties, in ballrooms and at fashionable week-ends, for his main purpose because the social and political life of the nineties was an almost indivisible whole. The serious business of government was interwoven with the gaiety and luxury of the privileged class for which it was still almost a monopoly. Wives of politicians played their part—this was the time when that " wonderful girl "[1] Margot Asquith, was rising to her prime—and in any case there were always those precious post-prandial moments apart from the ladies, when it was possible for him to have twenty

[1] West, *Private Diaries*, p. 101.

or thirty minutes in a corner with Salisbury or Chamberlain, Rosebery, Grey or Bryce.

But Lugard also had on this leave the time, a rare element in his hurried arduous life, to keep up with old friends and make new ones in the almost professional circle of African experts. He was in almost continuous contact with his most revered leader, Kirk, and stayed with him often at Wavertree, his Kent home. He visited his admirer and mentor, Horace Waller. He was able to greet Williams, back after holding so long and so well the position Lugard had created. The two partners-in-arms spoke together on December 12th to a crowded audience at the Royal Colonial Institute and paid each other compliments.[1] He made friends with the well-known scout and hunter, Selous, and the two had a joint exhibition of big game trophies and African curios at Rowland Ward's famous Mecca for hunters in Piccadilly. He also met that most modest and gentle of African explorers, Joseph Thomson[2] and, with less pleasure, the absolutely opposite type, Stanley who, for all his blemishes, was yet a great man. All these men, publicly and privately, praised their young colleague. He was especially delighted to meet his old friend and former chief, Willcocks, and to tell him of all the strange events that had filled his life since they had been conventional soldiers together in India.

Lugard's intense concentration upon the main purpose of his life, in its varying applications, led him to use almost everything that came his way as means to his end. Such a man is not likely to spare much attention for those human interests which are an end in themselves. Yet in the many encounters of those two crowded years in England, the world of art broke in upon his own indifference. There was the actor and dramatist, Brookfield, who became " a friend whom I like *immensely*, a man of very good family .... who is always searching for someone to do a good turn to and who has helped many a poor girl on and off the stage." He "knows everyone in London worth knowing." With Lord Sandhurst, the Under-Secretary for War, he put Lugard up as an honorary member of the select Beefsteak Club. Then, one night at a dinner-party, Lugard found himself greatly attracted by the face and the talk of one of the guests. He asked his name. " Dixie." They left the party together and walked all the way to

1 *Pall Mall Gazette*, 15 December 1893.
2 See above p. 151.

Sloane Square under the gas-light, letting the hansom-cabs go by. It appeared he was an artist. " Surely," said Lugard, " you are not *Dicksee* who painted ' The Viking's Funeral '? " But he was. " I was delighted. We chummed a lot." Frank Dicksee sent him an engraved copy of the famous picture. Another encounter in this class was with James Barrie. He took an intense and sudden liking for Lugard. Called away from an appointment by the illness of his beloved mother, Barrie wrote from Kerriemuir, " Had it not been for this, you would probably have seen me 'ere this, for I hope you will let me say that I had not known you an hour before the feeling came to me ' Here is a man I should like to have for a friend.' And that is how I feel still. I don't know how it is with you, and this is as rare as it is a delightful feeling to me." (Barrie to L. 6 December 1893). Pinned to this letter is another asking Lugard to dine at the Garrick Club with Birrell, Orchardson and a few others.

Lugard, still young and in spite of frequent trouble with his Nyasa wound, full of vitality, enjoyed his experience of London society. But it never, even to the smallest degree, turned his head, certainly not away from gazing at his fixed goal. In the remaining part of his time in Britain, among many lesser tasks in pursuit of his aim, he concentrated mainly upon two. One, of course, was to follow up all he had done in the Uganda retention campaign by seeing the question through to what was for him the only possible conclusion. The other was to take up the wider international aspect of the same issue.

The first task demanded close attention to what was happening in East Africa. Portal, with Rosebery's " unofficial " instructions in his pocket, started up-country on January 1st 1893, accompanied, amongst others, by his brother, Captain Raymond Portal, and the Company Administrator, Mr. Berkeley. We have already referred to those aspects of his expedition which threw light upon the charges against Lugard. We must now briefly consider Portal's doings in relation to their main purpose, the decision about the future of Uganda, and trace their effect upon those in Britain, including Lugard, who were eagerly waiting the results of his mission.

As he went by way of the posts that Lugard and others had established, Portal sent back, in the sweeping terms that were natural to him, his condemnation of the Company's " so-called administration ", and of the way in which its agents, by the violent methods that arise from inefficiency and weakness, had antagonized the tribes. He found Kikuyu in " a state of siege." " The combination of administration and trading is fatal." To his wife he was even less restrained. The Company's reports were " a string of lies." The Company was a " miserable fraud " and " a disgrace to the English name."[1] It must be remembered, in reading these denunciations, which drove a few more nails into the Company's coffin, that the philanthropic directors at home had little or no knowledge of the deficiencies of their agents; that they had attempted an impossible task and that Portal, whose position on the coast had brought him into almost unavoidable friction with the Company, started out in a prejudiced frame of mind. Yet the failure and inhumanity of the Company agents on the way to Uganda, which Lugard himself had condemned on his journeys, only serve to light up by contrast what Lugard had achieved with such poor resources at the terminal point.

Portal spent just over ten weeks in and around Kampala, the nerve-centre of Uganda, from March 17th to May 30th. As some Liberals had feared, and the Conservatives had hoped, he was obliged to fill the vacuum caused by the Company's imminent withdrawal by action of a kind that was a committal to further action. Abandoning Toro, he brought in and enlisted over 450 of the Sudanese soldiers whom Lugard had left in posts west of Uganda[2] and he took the Company's European agents into the government service. On April 1st, when the Company's regime officially ended, Portal, who was camped at Kampala fort, lined up his men on the little grassy summit, hauled down the Company's flag, and ran up the Union Jack. The event is commemorated there upon the same plaque which tells of Lugard's hoisting the Company flag. Major Eric Smith thereupon left Kampala, with all the Company porters and soldiers who had not been taken over by Portal, and was followed by Captain Williams.[3] Portal, having made his revision of Lugard's settlement between the religious parties, then began to write his report on the future of the country.

A historical detective is needed to unravel the mystery about the writing and printing of the report, and to discover what the Foreign

---

1 Portal to Rosebery, 24 January, 4 and 22 February 1893, also to Lady Portal 16, 22, 23 anuary 1893, P.P. s. 109 and 113.
2 C.7109 (1893), pp. 4-5.
3 *Ibid.* p. 11.

Office, and especially Rosebery, did to it and when they did it. According to his diary Portal wrote his report in Kampala in the first half of May: the entry for May 18th reads " finished final report."[1] After he had said his last prayer at the grave of his much loved brother, Raymond, who had died of fever, Portal started for the coast, leaving Macdonald in charge.[2] But when, on June 25th, he was halted by serious news from Macdonald, he sent on Berkeley, " with all speed in charge of my dispatches on the subject of my mission," and full power to supply explanations and supplementary information.[3]

All this time there continued to be questions in parliament and discussion in the press. The government steadily refused to give any information or to make any decision until Portal's report should have been received. By April 1893 Portal's first dispatches were coming in with his severe criticisms of the Company. Gladstone found them " astonishing " and suggested that Portal had better be asked to return to Britain on the heels of his report.[4] Portal had written to Rosebery, ahead of his official report, telling his chief what he hardly needed to be told, that he meant to advise strongly against evacuation.[5] Berkeley arrived back in August with his papers and information. Grey told the Commons on September 4th that " reports " had been received but were under consideration and that no report could be considered final while Portal was still in Uganda; nor was the government bound by it.[6] Clearly there were some things in the report that were not likely to be to the taste of the Cabinet, or, perhaps, to that of Rosebery. If so, Rosebery must have been given some idea of its contents by Anderson, who had read it by August 30th and considered it " admirable,"[7] yet he was almost too emphatically telling the Cabinet that he had refused to look at it. He said that he would not regard it as definite until Portal returned as Portal might well want to modify his first hurried version.[8] It was clearly very necessary for Rosebery's difficult task of coercing the Cabinet that Portal's report should be regarded as a wholly independent document. On September 18th, Grey's

---

[1] P.P. s. 111.
[2] For further information upon the Portal mission see C.7708 (1896), and Sir Gerald Portal, *The British Mission to Uganda in 1893,* ed. Rennell Rodd (1894).
[3] C.7303 (1894), p. 21.
[4] Gladstone to Rosebery, 5 April 1893, B.M. 44549.
[5] Portal to Rosebery, 25 June 1893, P.P. s. 109.
[6] *Parliamentary Debates,* 4 September 1893, IV. 16. 1875.
[7] Anderson to Currie, 30 August 1893, F.O. 83/1242.
[8] Rosebery to Gladstone, 17 September 1893, B.M 44290.

announcement in the Commons, that the island of Witu would in future be administered not by the Company but from Zanzibar, led to angry protests in *The Times* and from the anti-slavery interests on the lines of Lugard's own views which were very critical of the government's soft handling of that slave-owning island. Two months later Rosebery wrote to tell Gladstone that Portal had arrived that morning. He had seen him for a few minutes and Portal was now going to the country for two or three days to mature his report. " Hitherto I have not touched it with the tongs."[1] There now followed, in this matter, so long subject to evasion and delay, another long and, to the public, inexplicable pause. The French, as we have seen, were put off with the excuse that the government were waiting for the final Portal report as they had previously pleaded that they were waiting for the Macdonald report. Chamberlain was told by Gladstone on December 7th that Portal had not yet finished his report though he was " very busily engaged upon bringing it to a final shape," and that no decision was yet possible.[2] On December 18th it was said that the report was now being printed and had not yet been seen by ministers.[3] On December 20th Lugard told his brother that the report had come from the printers and was being read by ministers. (He added that Portal was in great favour everywhere and must " have the deuce of a lot of cousins," since everyone, especially duchesses, claimed this relationship.) On December 27th Gladstone pleaded, when Chamberlain pressed again, that the reason for the further delay was the great importance and complexity of the question, and he could not yet say— in typical Gladstonian language—when it would be in " a state of ripeness " to bring before the House.[4] On the same day Rosebery told Gladstone again that he had considered himself " bound in honour " not to look at the report until it was circulated to the Cabinet so he had only " a very recent acquaintance " with it. He still claimed there was no hurry and would not suggest a Cabinet upon it until it was " otherwise convenient."[5]

What was the reason for this extraordinary delay? Was Rosebery still playing for time and were his colleagues now so far beaten by

1 Rosebery to Gladstone, 27 November 1893, B.M. 44290.
2 *Parliamentary Debates*, 7 December 1893, IV. 19. 651.
3 *Ibid.* 18 December 1893, IV. 19. 1615.
4 *Ibid.* 27 December 1893, IV. 20. 269.
5 Rosebery to Gladstone, 27 December 1893, B.M. 44290.

him and by circumstances as to have given up all hope of defeating him? Had Portal been rewriting his report under Rosebery's influence and did not Rosebery's reiterated denial that he had read it cover the almost certain fact that he must have discussed its contents, at least in general terms, fully with Portal and Anderson? Who else but Rosebery could have instructed him, either directly or indirectly, how to revise it? Was the report, as first drafted, too strongly in favour of administration from Zanzibar, a solution which had by this time become plainly distasteful to public opinion?[1] Lugard's own view was that " Portal did himself no good at all in Uganda—had to write an entirely new report to order on his return . . . . " (L. to E. J. L. 27 March 1894). Lugard was likely to be well informed, but by no means impartial.

No one in England was more impatient than Lugard to see the report. It would not only settle the issue for which he had been struggling so long, but it might directly or indirectly reflect upon his own work in Uganda and so affect the Cabinet's judgment about the charges against him for which he and the French government were still waiting. Fortunately his book came out almost on the day of Portal's return. The two men met early in December. He did not know, of course, that Portal had written in very critical terms about him. He reported to his brother " Portal is *very* friendly—which is significant, but . . . . there's no knowing what he is saying to the F.O. in secret." (L. to E. J. L. 13 December 1893). It need hardly be said that, at the final moment, when the critical decision was being taken, Lugard was not silent. He took the occasion of Williams' paper on Uganda at the Royal Colonial Institute on December 12th to attack what he expected Portal to recommend, the device of attaching Uganda to the Zanzibar sultanate. His bold speech was said to be the important feature of the evening, which finished up with a dramatic episode. While the air was full of speculation about Portal's unpublished report, someone put into the hand of Lord Lorne, the chairman, a copy of the newly arrived *Zanzibar Gazette* from which he read extracts from a speech made by Portal after his return from Uganda at a farewell dinner to Rennell Rodd who had been acting for him. Portal, presumably half-facetiously, but so much in character as to

[1] McDermott, *IBEA*, p. 298 ff. I am indebted to Mr. Anthony Low for some valuable comments upon this question. He is less inclined than the writer to believe that Rosebery had any hand in revising the report and considers the long delay in the decision supports this view.

justify quotation, eulogized the climate of Uganda " where fine open country and grassy uplands would afford innumerable playing fields for such English sports as football and perfect pitches for cricket." These would refresh his jaded countrymen in Zanzibar and—here came the revelation—" if by any means he had helped to place this country nearer the reach of the latter he would indeed feel that his work had not been in vain." There was much pleased laughter in the audience at this indiscretion which at once revealed Portal's bias and anticipated his report. " How in the face of *that*," declared Lord Lorne, " the government can ever get out of Uganda, I don't know."[1]

Earlier Lugard had written two long letters, or rather one long letter in two parts, printed on successive days in *The Times*. In these he poured scorn on the plan—which he suspected Portal would recommend—of trying to administer from a small island a mainland 450 times as large. This was a " stalking horse " policy, a " bamboozling " policy. Zanzibar finances were too weak to bear the strain and Britain might as well subsidize Uganda directly as indirectly. Zanzibar should be annexed since Britain was paying out between £100,000 and £200,000 a year on a naval patrol to check the islanders' illegal activities in the slave-trade. For a fraction of this Britain could administer East Africa, with its immense possibilities of development. With a practical administrator's contempt, he broke through the not altogether honest obscurities which have always been woven round the word " protectorate ". " It matters not whether we call East Africa a ' sphere ' or a ' protectorate ' or whether some diplomatic genius shall invent a brand-new phrase which shall defy definition." All that was needed was that those who were to administer the country should have the legal power to act.[2]

In January Lugard showed that he was not so dominated by the Uganda issue that he could not deal with other colonial matters. In an article in *Blackwoods Magazine* he took the government very seriously to task on three counts, firstly for its feeble attitude towards the continuance of slavery in Zanzibar; secondly for its policy of raising revenue in West Africa out of a vast trade in liquor—an abhorrence that was to play a large part in his life; and thirdly for allowing Mr. Rhodes to confuse the status of Nyasaland by accepting his

1 *Pall Mall Gazette*, 15 December 1893.
2 *The Times*, 28 and 29 November 1893.

subsidy.[1] He proceeded to attack the government elsewhere for their delay over Portal's report. "Not content with the procrastination involved by sending an extremely expensive expedition into the heart of Africa to obtain information which was not needed, Mr. Gladstone, after the lapse of over a year, is still unable, apparently, to offer a decision."[2]

It might have been thought that the government would have liked to be rid of this critical and embarrassing presence in the country. It is therefore significant that at this moment the Foreign Office asked the War Office to extend his leave again as he was needed in England.[3] Clearly, he was still in Rosebery's favour and of use to him.

On January 25th Portal, young, handsome, popular, successful, and just ascending to the height of what promised to be a brilliant career, died of fever which he had contracted in Uganda. The news, following the death of his brother in Uganda, was a great shock. " To lose two dear sons," the Queen wrote to the mother, " in so short a time from illness contracted in serving their Sovereign and country is terribly hard . . . ."[4] Gladstone expressed " deep grief " at this catastrophe and eulogies were spoken in parliament.[5] These deaths, two among a long list of such sacrifices to Africa, bring out that one of the most important qualifications for success in that continent was the sheer ability to survive, and to survive vigorously under the strenuous conditions of work in Africa. This capacity Lugard possessed in the highest degree.

The death of the author should surely have allowed of the immediate publication of the report which he, at least, could revise no further. But this was not the view of the government.[6] February passed with the report still withheld, in spite of French and parliamentary pressure. But then this January and February were the weeks of Mr. Gladstone's last and most unbearable bout of indecision as to whether or, rather, when and how to resign because of his disagreement with most of his Cabinet about increasing the naval estimates. He alone, in an issue not wholly unconnected with that of " imperialism " which Uganda

---

1 ' East and West Africa in Parliament', *Blackwoods Magazine*, vol. CLV, January 1894.
2 *Pall Mall Gazette*, vol. LVIII, 20 January 1894. The article is unsigned but its authorship is patently clear.
3 Rosebery to War Office, 25 January 1894, F.O. 83/1309.
4 *Q.V.L.* III, vol. ii, p. 358.
5 *Parliamentary Debates*, 13 February 1894, IV. 21. 390.
6 *Ibid.* 12 February 1894, IV. 21. 286.

had raised, was clinging to the anti-militarist doctrine of the old Liberalism. And while Gladstone hesitated to relax the grip of his old hands upon the premiership, his colleagues went through the unhappy back-stage manœuvrings which should decide the succession. It requires a psychologist as much as a historian to explain why this Liberal Cabinet, already at war with the Lords, accepted as Prime Minister a peer, a wealthy breeder of Derby winners, the man who was defeating them over the Uganda issue and was known to stand very uncertainly upon the main Irish plank of their platform. Looking ahead for a moment, the record of Gladstone's part in the Uganda question may be rounded off by a reference to his final bitter remarks upon his relations with Rosebery. In a "catalogue of errors" which he left behind in his papers, and which was probably written in 1896, he includes in these the over-large size of his 1892 Cabinet.[1] "Another and perhaps even worse error was the appointment of Rosebery to the Foreign Office." He was imbued with the spirit of territorial grab. "But the fatal element in this appointment was his total and gross misconception of the relative position of the two offices we respectively held, and secondly his really outrageous assumption of power apart both from the First Minister and from the Cabinet." As an example of this Gladstone mentions Rosebery's anger at Waddington's direct approach to Gladstone which occurred over the compensation for the alleged losses inflicted by Lugard. The Grand Old Man's bitterness was one part of the price paid for the retention of Uganda.

On March 6th Lord Rosebery took office, Lord Kimberley taking from him the Foreign Office. It only remained now for Rosebery to bring to a conclusion the policy for which he had worked with so much patience and tenacity. But he had to wait while Kimberley settled down into his new chair, and he had still his colleagues and their past promises to consider. And the exact form his policy would take was still open. So the delay continued.

On March 13th Sir Edward Grey promised that there should be a debate on Uganda after Easter and that the report would first be presented to parliament.[2] A supplementary vote for Foreign Office expenses overseas allowed the radical wing to attack again one of "these plundering companies" and the perjured ministry which

[1] B.M. 44791, f. 30.
[2] *Parliamentary Debates*, 13 March, 1894, IV 22 141.

supported them. The effect of Lugard's campaign was clearly seen. Sir Richard Temple, declaring that religious opinion was now in favour of retention, warned the government that a " halting or retrograde policy " would bring upon them a renewal of agitation.[1] A Scottish Liberal retorted upon his radical colleagues from Caithness with the reminder that " Captain Lugard nowhere had larger or more enthusiastic meetings than those which were held in the large commercial centres " of Scotland.[2] In order to keep up the posture of indecision Sir Edward Grey insisted again that the policy of the government was merely a policy of enquiry. Their freedom of choice was still absolutely open.[3]

Lugard redoubled his efforts, working not only to make sure that Uganda should be annexed but annexed in the manner he favoured. His own case with regard to his actions was coming up towards its decision by the Cabinet, yet he continued to do all he could to stimulate and criticize the government. Upon news coming in that Colonel Colvile, who was now holding Uganda pending the decision as to its fate, was at war with Kabarega, he wrote to *The Times* to explain the background of this event. He took the opportunity not only to point out that Portal's removal of Lugard's outlying Sudanese garrisons was probably the cause of war—Lugard was too ardently sure of the rightness of his own dispositions to refrain from attacking those who reversed them—but also to appeal again to remind the public that " the forces of anarchy, of lawless butchery, of slave trading and of savage despotism are face to face with the march of civilization " and to condemn the government's " dilatoriness " and " laxity " in appreciating Britain's imperial duty.[4]

At long last, on April 10th, the Uganda report was presented to parliament. The problem of its genesis was not much enlightened by its being dated from Zanzibar on November 1st 1893, received December 6th.[5] Two days later the following announcement was made in both Houses.

" After considering the late Sir Gerald Portal's Report and weighing the consequences of withdrawal from Uganda on the one hand and on

---

[1] *Ibid.* 15 March 1894, IV. 22. 395.
[2] *Ibid.* IV. 22. 400.
[3] *Ibid.* IV. 22. 401–405.
[4] *The Times,* 26 March 1894.
[5] C.7303 (1894). The report fills pp. 29–55.

the other of maintaining British interests there, Her Majesty's Government have determined to establish a regular administration, and for that purpose to declare Uganda to be under a British protectorate. The details of the arrangement to be made are under consideration."[1]

The final decision will cause as little surprise to the reader as it did, by the date of issue, to most of the British public. The reaction of *Punch* is reproduced opposite. We need not dwell for long upon the report because its connection with the decision was not one of real causation but rather of political artifice. There are, however, some matters which affected Lugard, both personally and politically, and the margin of his copy of the Blue Book is pencilled with marks and with comments that are not always complimentary.

The report, vigorously written, summarized all the reasons for retaining Uganda that have already appeared in these pages. Of various forms of retention, Portal opted in rather nebulous terms for a connection with Zanzibar which should allow Britain to charge that small, but now—partly as a result of Portal's own rather drastic reforms—solvent island, to carry some of the distasteful costs of the new annexation. But this meant that the Company must be entirely bought out; and it was suggested that the sultan should pay them compensation for relinquishing their concession with its improvements. A railway to Uganda or at least to Kikuyu—a feeble second-best—was essential.

Lugard, being fully human, was first struck by the lack of any recognition in the report of all that had been achieved, especially in Uganda and especially by himself. There was one admission that " to the founders of the Company belongs the sole credit of the acquisition, for the benefit of British commerce, of this great potential market for British goods " and Portal went on to assert, with an exaggeration, verging upon *suppressio veri*, especially as regarded the Kikuyu and Banyoro, that it was an acquisition achieved, "in marked contrast to the neighbouring European colonies in establishing their influence, without bloodshed."[2] Yet, with an inconsistency noted by Lugard in the margin, almost all the other references to the Company were depreciatory. Lugard felt himself implicated by the condemnations of the Company's administration as a failure, for Portal spoke of " the attempted administration of the country .... and the publicly

[1] *Parliamentary Debates*, 12 April 1894, IV. 23. 180; IV. 23. 223.
[2] C.7303 (1894), p. 35.

THE BLACK BABY.

Mr. Bull. "WHAT, ANOTHER!!—WELL, I SUPPOSE I MUST TAKE IT IN!!!"

acknowledged failure of the attempt."[1] But there were also a number of specific criticisms that pointed directly at Lugard. These concerned the importation of the Sudanese; the lack of control over them; the making of treaties which could not be implemented; and the impression created that these were made by imperial authority. Yet, as Portal went on to say, it was just these two last factors which made evacuation so difficult. Of all Lugard's strokes and comments in the margin none is more interesting than the one word " Rot " written beside the remark that the new Commissioner would not need " to interfere in the details of the administration." Lugard's idea of the " indirect " principle was never to be based upon the old aloof, limited liability methods followed in the Indian states.

Parliament was eager to discuss the report and especially to consider how the bald decision about a protectorate was to be carried out. But, as the ministers were still undecided about this and as there was much financial business to transact, the promised debate was again put off. The delay gave Lugard his chance to round off all he had contributed to the future of Uganda by contesting the policy of ruling it through Zanzibar. By now he had easy access to the highest political levels. He had, as we saw, been Lord Salisbury's guest at Hatfield; he was, of course, in close touch with Lord Rosebery, Sir Percy Anderson and other officials of the Foreign Office where he was helping to draw up details for the future administration of East Africa. He spent much time educating influential members of both Houses and of both parties in the complexities of the East African situation. Even Labouchere now came to him for advice upon this subject in which, the main decision being taken, they found some common ground as to the method of its fulfilment. But perhaps his most important pupil was Chamberlain, whose mind was at this time awakening fully to the importance of the colonial empire and its significance for Britain's economy. The correspondence shows how often Lugard was asked by Chamberlain for advice and information in preparation for the coming debate. They met either in London or by Lugard staying week-ends at Highbury. But Lugard made impartial use of either party for his ends. He admitted to his brother that he was playing with edged tools. On the one hand he was the agent of Rosebery and the Foreign Office, for whose service he had been seconded.

[1] Ibid. p. 29.

" On the other hand I am quietly going to Chamberlain to coach him how to embarrass the government if they don't run on my lines." (L. to E. J. L. 27 March 1894).

He busied himself equally in the journalistic side of politics. He was in close touch with Moberley Bell and Flora Shaw of *The Times*, helping to write leading articles. " I've gone tooth and nail ", he told his brother, against " Portal's policy [of ruling Uganda] through Zanzibar . . . . Had Portal lived, he and I would have had to fight— or compromise! As it is, all England mourns his loss, as one of the greatest men of the century. A movement is on foot for a Portal memorial, and Gladstone has just conferred a special pension on Lady Alice. So no one is the worse and we can all join in the shouting ' *De mortuis nil nisi bonum*.' (L. to E. J. L. 27 March 1894). His hopes and his ideas developed rapidly. A week later he was telling his brother, with reference to the Portal plan, " My book and letters in *The Times* have been uncompromisingly against it and I believe I've won. Now I am going all I know for a huge scheme. Abolition of our slave-trade suppression at sea (our policy for 50 years) and devoting the money to inland protectorates. Abolition of Sultanate and incorporation of all Brit. E. Africa including Sultanate, Witu and up to Uganda in one single Protectorate. Of course I shan't win, but I daresay I shall make a notch somewhere." If the Conservatives should come in " I may go near winning. It's an interesting game." With Lugard, as with most men, his political views were naturally taking colour from his own interests and experience. Just as Portal, posted at Zanzibar, saw the future in terms of an extension of power from that station, so Lugard, 'hoping to return to Uganda, willed the rule of the interior to be strong and independent. So he went on, not only lobbying but writing, sometimes under his own name, sometimes anonymously, not scrupling, in the latter case, to advertise his own book and refer appreciatively to his own views.[1]

In all this campaign Lugard had worked very closely with Kirk, who was much distressed by the general attack upon the Company with which he had so closely associated himself. Moreover the Zanzibar scheme, which Lugard had persuaded him to abandon and even to

[1] See signed articles, ' East and West Africa in Parliament ', *Blackwoods Magazine*, vol. CLV, January 1894; ' British Interests in East Africa ', *Pall Mall Gazette*, vol. LVIII, 20 January 1894; and unsigned, ' The Uganda Protectorate ', *Chamber of Commerce Journal*, vol. XIII, April 1894; 'The East African Question ', *Pall Mall Gazette*, vol. LVIII, 8, 10 and 12 May 1894.

attack, had originally been his own. But Lugard needed the much respected wisdom and immense authority of Kirk, now sixty-two years old, in partnership with his young energy and adventurous reputation. He was able to express towards Kirk the filial sense of devotion which he could not wholeheartedly feel towards his own father who, all the more with increasing age, depended upon him for help and guidance.

The great debate on Uganda, long postponed, was at last fixed for June 1st. Lugard was busy writing and coaching speakers, and especially Chamberlain and Lowther, every day. He had stuck to his two main purposes: to secure the abandonment of the Zanzibar scheme and to insure that the legal status of slavery, still recognized in the sultan's dominions, should be abolished. He and Kirk went together to Westminster. The House of Lords was debating the same subject and it was upon that day that Lord Stanmore, who initiated the debate, spoke his panegyric of Lugard, which has already been quoted, and urged that he should be chosen for the task in Uganda.[1] It seems that Lugard, torn between the two Houses, spent most of his time in the Commons.

The House was meeting in Committee of Supply upon a vote for £50,000 for Uganda expenses. Sir Edward Grey began by stating at last what the government meant to do with Uganda. They would set up a commissioner for Buganda only, with a sub-commissioner to administer communications through the intervening country, which was still regarded as no more than the great block of land dividing the coast and Lake Victoria. They would buy out the Company. And they would not build the railway. The reasons given for this throw interesting light on the conceptions held about colonial policy. Firstly Britain could not afford it. Secondly, it was the tradition that private enterprise undertook all such development of new lands. (Here Grey referred rather reprovingly to the constant and urgent *political* pressure of all the chambers of commerce with regard to East Africa though, on the *commercial* side, they were leaving it entirely to German firms to prospect for openings.) Thirdly, he said, because " public opinion has before now ebbed and flowed in regard to African affairs," a cold fit might succeed the hot, as it had in West Africa a generation ago.[2]

[1] See above pp. 371–2.
[2] *Parliamentary Debates*, 1 June 1894, IV. 25. 181–94.

Sir Charles Dilke followed. This brilliant and widely travelled man spoke against the retention of Uganda, as a costly, jingoistic gamble. He spoke ably, reproaching the government for eating their words, ridiculing arguments about the importance and value of Uganda. He was especially scathing about the obligations of honour created by the treaties. Had not Lugard, defending himself from Portal's accusation, insisted that he had made his treaties in the name of the Company and' not of the government![1] Dilke was severe in his references to the methods used in Uganda and Lugard's defective old Maxim was dragged once more on to the parliamentary stage for reprobation. Dilke suggested " that the only person who has up to the present time benefited by our enterprise in the heart of Africa has been Mr. Hiram Maxim." Again, referring to the missions, " if Augustine had landed in Kent with Maxim guns, the members representing the Church Missionary Society who are going to support this vote would have been Pagans now."[2]

The speech, eloquent, sometimes mordantly amusing, went on and on. Lord Randolph Churchill, himself rather indeterminate about the whole question, grumbled that it had gone on for an hour and fifteen minutes and had been both too long and too strong.[3] Chamberlain certainly found it strong: he left his seat and went up to the gallery to find Lugard and to get from him answers to some of the points in it.

While he was there, Labouchere was on his feet repeating all his old arguments against retention but bringing in a new one, to which Lugard in the gallery listened approvingly, for he heard Labouchere repeating his own lesson about slavery in Zanzibar and the need to abolish the legal status. The next speaker, Lowther, was another of Lugard's pupils and he and Kirk listened with special satisfaction to his long speech in which he put forward every point in Lugard's case, not forgetting to condemn the plan of taking over Buganda and leaving all the surrounding country outside British control. Mr. Pease, the Quaker philanthropist, who followed, had also been in close touch with Lugard: he quoted his book and showed much technical knowledge of the slavery issue. He concluded by quoting a verse of the humanitarians' poet, Cowper, which is aesthetically so uncongenial

---

[1] See, for example, *Morning Post*, 12 April 1894.
[2] *Parliamentary Debates*, 1 June 1894, IV. 25. 194–208.
[3] *Ibid.* IV. 25. 208.

to modern taste as almost to negative the effect of its genuine philanthropy:

> *Fleecy locks and black complexion,*
> *Cannot forfeit nature's claim*
> *Skins may differ, but affection*
> *Dwells in White and Black the same.*[1]

Shortly afterwards Chamberlain rose, masterful and cool, and made
a hard-hitting speech, rebuking the government for giving bad reasons
for doing the right thing, and for doing the right thing so badly and
incompletely. At times, Lugard seemed almost to be speaking through
him, as when he condemned the absurd administrative plan; the refusal
to annex outside Buganda, or to build the railway; or when he defended
the Sudanese troops or urged the need to abolish the sultanate of
Zanzibar and its attendant slavery, and use the naval patrol vote to
finance the interior. But at other times it is the authentic Chamberlain
introducing the new imperialism with a ringing confidence not heard
in the House for more than a century, the unabashed imperialism of
which Lugard himself was at once a major advocate and a spear-point.
It was Britain's " manifest destiny " to be " a great colonizing and
civilizing power." " Proceeding upon that principle we have grown
to our present greatness."[2] He broke with the idea that development
must be left to private capital, " either the government must make the
railway or it will not be made at all."[3] Colonization, his argument ran,
cost money and cost lives, but it saved both in the end. Should Britain
allow " this great estate in Central Africa to fall into the hands of our
rivals? "[4]

Lugard listened in deep excitement. He felt the impact of Chamberlain's oratorical power in the crowded House. Yet, he told his brother,
" Chamberlain's speech was purely the result of our conversations.
He had never seen Kirk." He could not help exulting in the knowledge
that he had helped to convert Chamberlain to his realization of Africa.
Had he not been told so on the best authority? " Miss Shaw, the
specialist of *The Times*, told me that the conversion of Chamberlain
was indeed notable; that in 1890 he had twice taken her in to dinner,

[1] *Ibid.* IV. 25. 241.
[2] *Ibid.* IV. 25. 253–4.
[3] *Ibid.* IV. 25. 265.
[4] *Ibid.* IV. 25. 255.

and he was quite half-hearted about Africa, now he is the leading enthusiast and goes further than anyone else in the House." (L. to E. J. L. 3 June 1894).

Chamberlain finished speaking and Bryce wound up for the government. Here, too, Lugard could find cause for pride. Not only did Bryce show how much the attack on the Zanzibar plan and "Legal Status" had gone home, but also, directing his remarks mainly towards his opponents in his own party, he asked what else could the government do about Uganda when "from every quarter, whether on behalf of missions, commerce or humanity, there came Petitions and Memorials against our abandoning the obligations we had undertaken."[1]

The vote was taken. Fifty-two Liberals followed Dilke and Labouchere against their leaders but Conservative and Unionist supporters, though convinced the Liberals were half-hearted in their policy, helped to swell the government majority.

Kirk and Lugard found they had been in the House for ten hours. It had been a great day for Lugard. It was typical of him that his greatest satisfaction was to have contributed to *knowledge*, detailed, realistic knowledge of the African question. "The debate on Uganda pleased me excessively," he wrote to his brother. "Contrast the intimate knowledge shown by the whole House on the question—on technical subjects such as the commercial treaties—the tenure of the Sultanate—the slavery question—the 'Legal Status'—the naval suppression, etc., etc., with the crass ignorance of two years ago"; the extraordinary knowledge, too, of Uganda. He believed that his "ceaseless efforts there and in England *have* produced a wonderful result." But for these, "I doubt if there would have been so full a House, so many speakers (and *many* more crowded out for lack of opportunity to speak) so well-informed, on any possession of the British Empire as there were about this little country in the centre of Africa."

But nothing pleased him more than to have contributed something towards the struggle against slavery. When he first came home slavery had been "a *fad* represented in the House by a small set of Quaker faddists. When they spoke the House emptied. Last Friday saw the *grandest* denunciation of the Legal Status—a clear exposition of the whole slavery policy . . . ." To his brother, and his brother alone,

[1] *Parliamentary Debates*, 1 June 1894, IV. 25. 267.

he need not hide the sense of personal triumph. " This is a success I'm proud of. Had speaker after speaker got up (as Lord Stanmore did in the other House) and praised *me*, it would have been very nice, but what would it have been worth in comparison to the knowledge in one's own mind that one had established these great points . . . . and had established them as subjects of National Importance . . . . . You'll be delighted, Ned, I know, for you know how hard I've worked and, my boy, this debate to my mind is the greatest triumph I've ever scored." (L. to E. J. L. 3 June 1894). "This," so this same brother told the writer fifty-four years later, " was undoubtedly Fred's finest hour."

Yet Lugard admitted that his success had not been won alone. As they left the House together, Kirk turned to him and said " What would that debate have been but for you and me? " " The knowledge and brains are *all* Kirk's," said Lugard to his brother, " but it is *I* who have made his views known and have got hold of men like Chamberlain." The next day, at a dinner-party, Chamberlain drew him aside and said he would ask in the House any question Lugard cared to send him and " that all his knowledge and his speech (a magnificent one) in the debate was solely derived from my book and conversations with me!" (L. to E. J. L. 5 June 1894).

Lugard was right to think he had contributed much to the unwilling conversion of the Liberal government and so to the retention of Uganda. We can see in review that his influence had been tireless and pervasive. It had also been many-sided in character—by his actions in Africa and by making his actions known by his reports; by writings of several categories from his large book down to letters and articles; by speeches in his country-wide campaign and to the distinguished audiences at the Royal Geographical Society and elsewhere; and by his unceasing interviewing and correspondence directed towards those who wielded power at the centre. But much of this effort would have been useless or even harmful to his cause if all he did had not been commended by what he was—single-minded, courteous, and bringing into the lobbies of Westminster and the political drawing-rooms of Mayfair and of great country houses the living evidence of the endurance and faith in his mission that had carried him through all the unknown dangers and difficulties of equatorial Africa. It would seem to strain the evidence of these chapters to state that he was modest.

But part of his confidence at this and all through his life lay in an unusually complete identification of himself with his chosen task. Such
identification, where the essential element of ego overbears that of
service, can be dangerous. In Lugard there was at this time a fair if not
a constant balance between the two. Had it been otherwise he would
not, as the chapters on his accusation and defence have shown, have
risked his whole future by challenging authority politically just when
it was judging him professionally.

Yet we must not err by estimating too highly the part he played in
the Uganda issue because of our necessary selection in these pages of
his activities out of the whole broad event. We can see now, looking
backwards, that while Lugard certainly helped to accelerate the movement of the current on the surface—an acceleration that *may* have been
all-important for the immediate timing and method of the Uganda
annexation—yet far deeper and wider forces were at work which were
rousing the British people to a more positive and combative assertion
of their own interests in a world which was becoming increasingly
dangerous. From this more fundamental view the Uganda issue is
closely linked with the simultaneous question of Ireland and naval
expenditure and, indeed, with the whole range of Britain's attitudes
and actions in external affairs. A rapid shift of opinion must cause
equally deep and often very painful party adjustments. It was because
it was upon the Uganda question that the adjustment on the imperial
aspect of the change had to be made that it became so prominent and
gave Lugard his chance to perform on the front of the political stage.
Upon the question as to whether the cause he supported, the one which
gained the day, was in the long run the morally superior or even the
more expedient cause, those who read this book will differ, for the
question is still open and in 1955 Uganda itself has become again a
place of controversy.[1] But at least a full survey of Lugard's part in the
Uganda decision, bringing together events on the equator and the
conflict of ideas about them in Britain, may furnish evidence which
should help towards a judgment.

The settlement of Uganda was by no means finished but we cannot
follow it now beyond the point where Lugard was obliged to abandon
any close connection with it, though, as he never lost interest in East

[1] For a full discussion of the public morality of the annexation and of Lugard's methods see
Woolf, *Empire and Commerce*, pp. 228–302.

Africa, we shall distantly consider this region again from time to time. But there is one further part of Lugard's activities which can be distinguished from the main issue and in which Lugard's contribution leads to a wider perspective in which to see his work and especially the next task he was to undertake.

References have been made from time to time to the international background. For Lugard the nearest part of this background was a jealously active France. Western historians have themselves characterized the process in which the nations clashed as a " scramble ", and though Salisbury was a participant, his detached mind saw it in much the same light. In a world still almost unregulated by international law, it was a matter of " us or them ", with few holds barred except, it was hoped, the grip of war, with its incalculable costs and results.

National methods of competitive acquisition varied, and here there was room for the play of intellect, character and even of morality. The French, surveying the map of Africa in the early 1890's, thought they had reasons for an indignation which was an extra spur to action. They bitterly resented Britain remaining, with repeated excuses, in Egypt. They had reason to believe that it was possible to manipulate the Nile waters from Central Africa and for this and other reasons they wanted to reach the river. They also—a point which will recur— viewed with dismay the Cape-to-Cairo idea. It was generally the French, and not the British, whom history showed going in for such large bold visions as this: here the cosmic mind of Rhodes was out of character with his nation. His longitudinal axis threatened to cut across France's latitudinal dream of an African empire stretching from their western acquisitions to their new foothold in Somaliland. They were still resolved to race Britain in filling the vacuum on the Upper Nile, which Britain was trying, in the name of Egypt, to keep empty, when they were suddenly confronted at the end of 1893 by the intervention of a third party, Belgium, in the form of a large expedition planned to thrust to the Nile near Wadelai, some 200 miles north of Lake Victoria. The Foreign Office, suddenly realizing the penalty of Britain's long inertia, was perturbed and the French were very angry. The famous French explorer, Major Monteil,[1] who was playing in France somewhat the same part as Lugard in Britain, that of African action and

---

[1] Monteil, Parfait-Louis, 1855–1925; officer, explorer and author; 1890–2 travelled from Senegal to Say, Lake Chad and Tripoli; 1893 in French Congo; 1895 in Ivory Coast.

metropolitan advocacy, strongly urged an expedition to the Upper Nile. This would at once cut off Britain to the north, threaten her control of the Nile and so of Egypt, and link the two sections of France's African empire. Fashoda was the key-point on the river at which to aim.

Rumour of Monteil's activities reached the Foreign Office. How could they be verified? Relations with the French were strained and the matter was delicate. While Sir Percy Anderson was pondering over this Lugard walked in. It appeared that he had made friends with an American, Poultney Bigelow, who was himself a friend of Monteil. The latter had told Bigelow that he was a great admirer of Lugard, though Lugard's name was at the moment anathema to the French. Anderson made a lightning plan out of this. " But," Lugard protested, " I don't speak a word of French and I don't see how I can conduct a very delicate matter like this and worm all Monteil's secrets out of him." That was Friday night—on Saturday Lugard went to a late party at Bigelow's, where he had a talk with Bryce. His host told him he was off to Paris next morning *en route* for a trip in North Africa. Monteil was in Paris. Would Lugard come? It was then midnight. On Monday, March 3rd, Lugard was in Paris, having thrown over half a dozen important engagements, including a meeting with the Duke of York, to get there.

The expedition gave Lugard at once his first taste of Parisian entertainment and of international diplomacy. With the help of his American friends he managed to make contact with Monteil. Enemies politically, the two men were drawn to each other personally. There was a first interview, in which Lugard flattered himself that he had got hold of some information. The evenings were spent at the Moulin Rouge where the frugal Lugard was appalled at the cost. " But we really had some fun. I felt for a moment as if I had rolled off 16 hard years and was the boy I was when I first came to London Town— *but not quite*. But I think it did me good. These ladies of Paris take life so *very* lightly. They are so happy and so bright! "

Monteil asked him to dinner and the two bronzed travellers fenced again. Lugard judged the meeting " fairly successful. It was diamond cut diamond but he did *not* get much out of me. If he alluded to Uganda, I affected to have paramount interests in Nyasa, but I drew him out fairly well, in spite of his reputation for diplomacy. We afterwards went to a real ice-skating rink. I *think* you might take your aunt there if she was keen on seeing ' life '."

It would be interesting to read Monteil's side of the story. Back in London, when Lugard reported on his encounter, Anderson professed himself delighted and got Lugard to put it all in a memorandum. " He was really quite strong in his praises, said I had done ' capitally ' again and again and that I had handled Monteil admirably—I was really quite proud, for it is my first diplomatic mission." When Lugard was asked to put in for the expenses of this mission, Anderson was astounded to get a claim for the price of the ticket and 4s. 2d. a night in Paris. He told Lugard he really could not ask for less than a pound a day. " So I did, and my bill will pretty nearly pay for all my follies in Paris. Not bad eh? " (L. to E. J. L. 10 March 1894).

Long before this mission Lugard had been warning his countrymen of the danger that France would cut off their advance in Africa. He had all the treaties and the diplomacy at his finger-ends and one of his main arguments for occupying Uganda was that the way north up the Nile was open. Not Belgium only but France, who was bound by no treaty recognizing Britain's claims in this part of Africa, was eager to reach the Nile, and the idea, in face of this threat, to abandon Uganda and then re-occupy was an "absurdity". " The whole history of the French acquisitions on the West Coast has been marked by extreme energy and a desire to push eastwards. Thus France may at any moment unite her Senegal and Congo possessions in the ' hinterland ' behind English and German intermediate (West) Coast possessions, and pushing this empire eastwards, establish herself on the Nile, while as usual British diplomacy is too late."[1]

British diplomacy was certainly clumsy. We cannot follow the maze of negotiations which filled the summer of 1894, with Leopold treating secretly with both Britain and France, with Britain making a treaty to encourage Italy against France in Ethiopia, and Germany watching grimly to snatch advantages, territorial or diplomatic, from the inevitable embarrassments. The main event was the conclusion by Britain of a treaty with Leopold by which Britain leased to him for life the so-called Lado Enclave, a region stretching from Uganda north up the Nile to Fashoda, which she had failed to occupy herself and now wanted Leopold to hold in order to keep out the

[1] Lugard II, pp. 570-1.

French. For his part Leopold leased to Britain a corridor leading from the north of Lake Tanganyika to Lake Edward, thus gaining that important section of Rhodes' all-red route, her possession of which Germany was known strongly to oppose.[1]

France was naturally enraged by these two treaties. She drew close to Germany, and Leopold was so intimidated by the two of them that he was forced to give way and abandon his occupation, which in any case was largely illusory. Britain was obliged, in the face of German protests, to abrogate the clause giving her the corridor and so lost all hope of the Cape-to-Cairo line. The whole incident, which brought us to the verge of war with France, backed by Germany, was one of great humiliation to Britain.[2] Its interest here is that Lugard threw himself with indignation and ability into the controversy. He wrote two articles for *Blackwoods* in the summer of this year, in which he showed his mastery of the whole subject, diplomatic, geographical, strategic, and political. He also showed courage in attacking the government for, though the articles were unsigned, their origin was clear to all the people who mattered.[3] In the second article, especially, he censured the ministers for their timidity in refusing to follow up his work and his advice and occupy the whole of Uganda northwards up the Nile, and for showing " blindness and ineptitude " in the actual handling of the affair. He ridiculed the Cape-to-Cairo idea as " claptrap "—we know that he was never an admirer of Rhodes—and " a mere sentimental jargon," since " the commercial watershed radiates to the east and west." Now Monteil, " the best man the French have " had been sent out to open the way to the Nile, and Fashoda would be the object. With a foresight which is being proved substantially valid as this is written, Lugard warned Britain that if " we occupy the Sudan as an Egyptian province, our tenure is dependent only on our occupation of Egypt and ceases with that occupation." Summarizing the position, with a sting of personal pique, he spoke scathingly of the government's policy of " reserving "

1 Hertslet, *Map of Africa*, vol. ii. p. 578. ff.

2 A full well-documented account of this not very creditable diplomatic adventure of Britain will be found in W. L. Langer, *The Diplomacy of Imperialism 1890-1902*, 2nd edition (New York 1951), p. 124 ff; A. J. P. Taylor, ' Prelude to Fashoda: the Question of the Upper Nile, 1894-5', *English Historical Review*, vol. LXV, 1950; and by the same author, ' Les Premières Années de l'Alliance Franco-Russe, 1892-5 ', *Revue Historique*, t. CCIV, July-September 1950. See also Gardiner, *Life of Harcourt*, pp. 310-23.

3 *Blackwoods Magazine*, vol. CLV, June 1894, ' Imperial Interests in East Africa ', and vol. CLVI, July 1894, ' The New African Crisis with France and Germany '.

their action in Uganda in 1892. " What that reservation meant we now know—two years of vacillation; the systematic discrediting of the Company so as to buy them out cheap; the replacement of Captain Lugard and his officers by those who have not borne the burden of the task; the adoption of a policy of disintegration in East Africa by which Uganda alone is declared a Protectorate, and is to be left ' in the air ' unconnected by a railway with the coast; the neglect to deal with the slavery question . . . and now a treaty to endeavour, by a smart trick, to recover the ground lost during the two years of indecision, a treaty which has set both Germany and France against us, and brought us perilously near to war! " There was nothing left now but to hold all Uganda or " *to eat dirt with dishonour.*"

This was exactly what Britain had to do: the treaty collapsed, Britain giving way to Germany and Belgium to France. But, for the moment, it was the last matter of high politics in which Lugard was able to act at the centre; another disappearance into the African bush was to silence his voice for a time.

PART FOUR

The Niger 1894-1895

CHAPTER XXII

THE SETTING OF THE COURSE

1894 : Aet. 36

DURING HIS twenty-two months in England Lugard had certainly enlarged his view both of Britain's domestic politics and of the rapidly changing total map of Africa as seen from Europe. But if his mind was enlarged his heart was still in East Africa and it was with dismay, as he approached the end of a second year of ceaseless activity upon its affairs, that he began to realize that the way back to that region might be barred to him.

The cup of fame, sweetened as it had been by success in his public cause, was therefore turning rather sour by the summer of 1894. And there was nothing in his personal life to give him solace. He had, indeed, very little of such life, almost the whole of his time and thought being given to Africa. Yet there were moments when the thought of returning to its only too well-known hardness and loneliness daunted him. Gordon had said of himself that men of his kind should not marry and, looking at the life and death of the wife of Livingstone, it seems doubtful whether that inspired traveller should have asked so much of a woman. But exceptionally hard and strenuous men are not necessarily relieved by a kindly providence from an intense longing for the joys of domestic life and Lugard had an unsatisfied craving to give and, to a lesser degree, to be given, affection. His half-sister Emma, Mrs. Brayne, was still his very good friend and helper, working hard collecting and pasting cuttings and doing some of the many drudgeries connected with the writing and publishing of a book. There was some intimate comfort here. Even closer to him was his brother to whom, to the great ultimate profit of his biographer, he wrote long and unreserved letters. But Edward was a soldier and was much in India at this period. During 1893, however, they were together in England, and Edward made a very happy marriage to

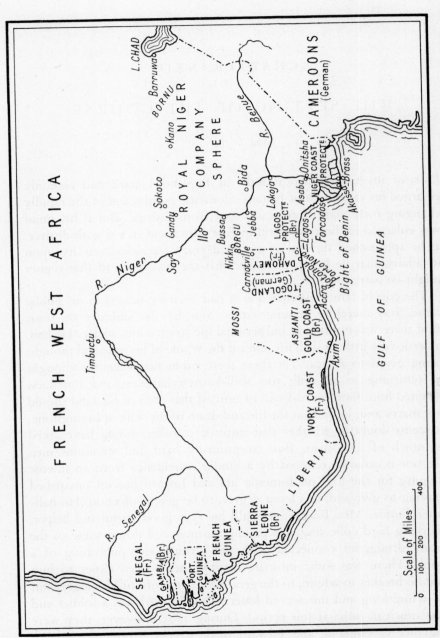

FRENCH WEST AFRICA

L. CHAD

Barruwa

BORNU

Kano

Sokoto

Gandu

Saya

ROYAL NIGER

COMPANY

SPHERE

R. Niger

Ilo

Bida

Bussa

R. Benue

CAMEROONS
(German)

Nikki

BORGU

Jebba

Lokoja

Onitsha

Asaba

Carnotville

DAHOMEY
(Fr.)

LAGOS
PROTECTE
(Br.)

Lagos

NIGER COAST
PROTECTE

MOSSI

TOGOLAND
(German)

Porto Novo

Forcados

Brass

Akassa

Timbuctu

ASHANTI

Accra

GOLD COAST
(Br.)

Bight of Benin

GULF OF GUINEA

R. Senegal

IVORY COAST
(Fr.)

Axim

LIBERIA

SENEGAL
(Fr.)

GAMBIA (Br.)

FRENCH
GUINEA

PORT.
GUINEA

SIERRA
LEONE
(Br.)

Scale of Miles

0   100   200   400

West Africa 1894

his cousin, Charlotte Eleanor (Nell) Howard. Lugard had the great joy of being his best man. But with the joy came the added sense of his own loneliness, also of his professional and financial insecurity. Nor had he ever been able to throw off the old sorrow which had so deeply afflicted his life. " I do wish I was not dependent on my commission for my daily bread and butter," he told his brother. " If one had but a house and an *anchor* of one's own, but I suppose I am destined to be a rolling stone and gather no moss year after year—while the old raw "—he was not thinking here of his physical injury—" still chafes and at times becomes a very very painful wound!—Well, . . . I've run off the line and gone on a siding which leads downhill. I'd better pull up short. The big hand of the clock nears 2 a.m. and I must be off. God bless you and your wife and give you the happiness you both deserve." (L. to E. J. L. 20 December 1893).

He told Emma, who was herself happily married, that " there is little probability of my marrying I should think and it would be best for the *general* interest that I should not, I think. We can't all find such ideal wives as you are, dear Emma—and some of us make mistakes."

His reference to the general interest meant the financial interest of the family. In spite of his wanderings and his poverty Lugard always gave the most generous response to the family needs. And they were heavy. His father, as always, was in difficulties and Lugard was much worried as to whether he should help him directly, so as to enable him to retire from the Norton living, or give money to his sisters. But Lugard himself had nothing but what he could earn and his prospects were always quite uncertain. In giving himself to his African work he had, with almost monastic devotion, not only to abandon family life but to embrace poverty. For himself such austerity was bearable: African conditions themselves generally imposed it. But it is remarkable that, because of his determination to be, and to seem to be, free of all personal interest in his public work, he refused, as we have seen, to accept any salary from the Company from the moment he landed in England. He also, for the same reason, refused an offer from Christy's well-known lecture agency of the payment of thirty-five guineas a lecture, no small fee in 1892. There are men who have found it possible, in order to retain their independence and integrity, to endure poverty themselves but have recanted in face of the needs of their families. But Lugard struggled on, living as best as he could, allowing for his family expenses, upon the salary of £500 a year which had been paid him by the Company for his service in East Africa, much of which had accumulated while he had been away. He was still a soldier and knew that, if all else failed, he would have to go back to his profession, even though it was at that time almost impossible for a man without private means. He became so accustomed to asking for leave and obtaining it that he was caught by surprise when suddenly ordered to India with his regiment by the War Office. Lord Rosebery obtained a further secondment, but all this time he drew no army pay and was even losing pension rights.

It was urgent that he should find some way to live. There was no money in being a public figure; rather was it an expense. He had hoped not only that he would return to East Africa, but that his next work would be in government service. It was natural that with the general acclaim for his achievements and his close relations with politicians and senior officials, he should have counted upon this. Lord Stanmore, as we have seen, had pleaded for his reappointment and many newspapers, when they were reviewing his book had emphasized his obvious qualifications. He counted especially upon Kirk, who was so close to Rosebery, and upon Lowther to help him. He had an offer, of which more presently, from Sir George Goldie, head of the Royal Niger Company, to go to West Africa, but he kept putting off the decision, hoping to the last that the longed-for offer to go east would come. Surely it would be at the great debate of June 1st on Uganda, which he had done so much to stage-manage! But then, he reminded himself, he had been so outspoken about the government's feeble slavery policy and their favourite Zanzibar scheme that they could hardly employ him: Anderson and the permanent officials must, as he said, be " quite savage " with him. Rosebery and Anderson, whom the records now reveal as being an official with a policy—one of expansion[1]—might use Lugard's daring in action and on paper to advance their aims, but they had no intention of risking the official employment of that daring. So the dismal decision had to be made. " I am pledged to West Africa," he wrote to his brother two days after the Uganda debate, " and apart from West Africa, my *life* is pledged to Africa. I would not chuck my life's work. Moreover, as I said, my destiny is *Africa* and I should be wrong to chuck that. Since

1 See especially his memorandum on Uganda, F.O. 84/2258.

I am kicked out of any chance of East Africa or Nyasaland, it means that I must go on these roving expeditions." And two days later he wrote, struggling with his depression, " I confess I feel very sorry to find that I am to be excluded from going on with my work in East Africa now that the time draws near for me to begin all over again elsewhere. And it is disappointing to find other men are to continue that work *under government auspices*—which I have worked so hard to secure!—there is my little grumble, and it's over now."

Even when he wrote this he had not quite given up all hope. He appealed once more to Lowther and Lowther went to Sir Edward Grey. The answer was the final blow. " Grey is very anxious that you should not think that your work there has been imperfectly recognized by the Foreign Office." On the contrary it was very highly appreciated, certainly by Grey himself. But—and this was just what Lord Stanmore had prophesied in the Lords debate—" Lord Kimberley is anxious to find a Commissioner who will start with a blank record, so far as African experience is concerned . . . ." (Lowther to L. 9 June 1894). In view of the strained relations with France, Lugard wrote in a retrospective note " Lord Rosebery considered that my return would be regarded as an affront to the French government and he would not allow me to return."

Yet Lugard still hesitated to close with Goldie. If the desired government service in East Africa was denied him, there was still the Company. But the days of the Company were numbered, and Kirk, who had had to bear so much from the vagaries of imperial policy, was, though sympathetic, sunk in gloom. Writing before the Uganda debate he had said, " I wrote two notes in acknowledgment of yours of the 26th and tore them up. I feel so strongly the shameful conduct of the government in the way they have and are dealing with the East African question, with the Company and with you, that I wrote intemperately." He was certain that " the government have no intention of using you unless they are compelled to," and as they were engaged in " hunting the Company to death," they would probably order him to rejoin his regiment if he again took service under the East Africa Company. In any case " the poor I.B.E.A. Co." might find it hard to give him the proper remuneration which the more prosperous Niger Company could afford. (Kirk to L. 28 April 1894). Warned in this way, Lugard refused Mackenzie's offer of the post of

Administrator under the Company which the directors made to him. By this date, July 5th, Lugard was, he said, "fully pledged to the Niger Company."

He might have said he was fully pledged to Sir George Goldie, for Goldie was the Niger Company. We must pause to consider both the Company and the man who, with his strong hand, now intervened to transfer Lugard to the opposite side of Africa, for Goldie was to be a large influence in Lugard's life.

Goldie was the creator of the first Chartered Company which undertook, in advance of the government, to occupy negro Africa. He was in effective action before Rhodes and Mackinnon. If, as we have seen, British governments of both parties hesitated to penetrate or annex African lands in the nineties, how much less was any forward official action possible in the seventies, when Goldie began to move!

Something has already been said of the lateness of Europe's penetration into the central and eastern block of the African continent.[1] Upon the western side European contact with the coast had been made some three centuries earlier than in the east. The slave-trade had taken Britain and other European nations to the west coast upon which they established posts, called factories. From these they collected, for transport to the New World, the human merchandise conveniently brought down to them from the interior. This being almost the only trade, Britain had little cause, after her abolition of it in 1807, to linger along this unhealthy and uninviting coast except for the humanitarian motive of finishing her task of putting it down. But this prevention was for long attempted only by means of a maritime patrol; the vast interior was still unopened. True, it was in 1796 that the exhausted, half-starved Scotsman, Mungo Park, struggling in alone from Senegal, had knelt down to drink the water of " the long sought for, majestic Niger, glittering to the morning sun, as broad as the Thames at Westminster, and flowing slowly to the *eastward*."[2] But nine years after this lone discovery he and all his forty-five white companions perished in the attempt to find the further course of the great river. Explorers sent out from Britain carried on the dangerous work. Clapperton and Denham travelled south from Tripoli to the kingdoms of Bornu and Sokoto in 1822; Clapperton and Lander went up to Kano from the

[1] See above p. 75 ff.; the writer's book, *Native Administration in Nigeria* (1937), contains some introductory chapters on the history of Nigeria.
[2] Mungo Park, *Travels in the interior districts of Africa, 1795-7* (1799), p. 194.

Guinea coast in 1825, and revealed the Muslim cities and states of Hausaland. In 1831 the Lander brothers at last found that Mungo Park's great river turned *south* to flow into the Atlantic.

Heroic explorers might force their way into western Africa to uncover its secrets, but the barriers they surmounted were not thrown down. A pause followed the discoveries. It was still believed that the demands of commerce and humanity, fluctuating a little but never quite dying away, could be satisfied, like the preceding slave-trade, by action from ships and coastal stations. Not only did the interior of Africa, as visible from these, appear primitive and unhealthy, but Britain was deliberately pledged against what seemed the expensive and quite unnecessary step of annexation. The disastrous expedition of 1841, promoted by the anti-slavery group, with the object of replacing the slave-trade by " legitimate " trade, in which 48 out of 145 white men died on a voyage up the Niger, discouraged the humanitarian motive for penetration. When, in this mood, parliament reviewed the position in West Africa in 1865, it was with regret that its members faced the fact that Britain still possessed coastal footholds at the Gambia, Sierra Leone and the Gold Coast, while, mainly in pursuit of her anti-slavery policy, she had actually acquired Lagos as lately as 1861. There was also an isolated consul posted to keep watch against the slave-trade, some 300 miles up the Niger at Lokoja. A parliamentary committee passed the famous resolution that as anti-slave-trade action was now the main purpose of these settlements, and the trade was diminishing, it was " inexpedient " that Britain should make " any further extension of territory or assumption of government," but on the contrary the natives should be so trained and encouraged that Britain could withdraw entirely from West Africa. Sierra Leone was the only " probable " exception from this, because it had been founded as an anti-slavery venture by private philanthropists.[1]

Some years earlier, the great German traveller Dr. Barth, sent by the British government, had returned after spending nearly six years visiting the cities of Hausaland and bringing a full account of their trade and culture.[2] Abandoning interior exploration, the British concentrated, not very energetically, on trade with the coast. Trade,

[1] Report from the Select Committee on the state of British settlements. *Parliamentary Papers* (1865), v. i.
[2] Dr. H. Barth, *Travels in North and Central Africa* (1857).

mainly in palm-oil products, halting and meagre though it was, had slowly increased up to the mid-century, thanks largely to the enterprising Scotsman Macgregor Laird (1808–1861). It was carried on mainly from hulks anchored near the river mouths. The French now took over the lead in exploration, pushing in from the western side up the Senegal river which led them on to the beginning of the Niger valley. Then, with the Franco-Prussian war, their efforts were distracted. In 1869 Britain withdrew the Lokoja consul. Thus, in 1877, when Goldie first began to take a serious interest in this region, there was still, as he said himself, " no foreigner, whether trader, soldier, missionary or traveller, in the entire basins of the Niger and Lake Chad, between the French colony of Senegal on the extreme west of Africa and the valley of the Nile on the extreme east, or between the seaboard factories on the Gulf of Guinea to the south and the Algerian and Tunisian frontiers on the north."[1] In other words, a really astonishing fact, this immense interior block of Africa, so close to Europe, and apparently so accessible, both by camel from the north and up the rivers from the south, was still, more than three-quarters of the way through the nineteenth century, inviolate from the footsteps of a single European.

Goldie meant to change this, and to change it in favour of Britain. He knew he had to work against time. He began by patiently combining the several British firms trading on the coast in the Niger region. This took two years, and another two were needed—an example the East Africa Company should have noted—to build up capital to £1,000,000, and develop the trade before the government would grant a charter. Then French traders, supported by their government, appeared on the Niger and they, too, had to be amalgamated, a much more difficult task. There were also treaties to be made with tribes and states along the river.

In 1884–5 the powers met at the West African Conference in Berlin. It had been called at a moment when, in the incessant and subtle process of bartering " friendship " and support between the major European powers, Germany had drawn towards France against Britain. It was therefore all the more vital for Britain to go with the strong case that only practical achievement could give her. Goldie just managed to conclude two years of very hard bargaining with

---

[1] Dorothy Wellesley, *Sir George Goldie* (1934), pp. 19–20.

the French companies as well as numerous treaties with riverain chiefs before he went, as an unofficial delegate to the Conference, to support Lord Granville in his claim that only the British flag flew on the Niger.

The government itself had suddenly shifted from its settled non-annexation policy. This was because it had had to face two unpleasant facts. One, as we saw in Chapter V, was that it must abandon its long cherished hope that it could continue trading with uncivilized lands without annexing them. The other was that its supplanter, if it hesitated, would be France, and to oppose and anticipate France in colonial expansion had become, from long historical experience, almost automatic. So the Liberal government plunged into hectic treaty-making activities along the Niger coast from Lagos, their earlier isolated annexation, to the Cameroons, now claimed by Germany, and finished the process only a few days before the Conference began.

At the Conference, into the intricate diplomacy of which we need not enter,[1] a shift on the part of Bismarck away from France helped Britain to get most of what she wanted, and above all the recognition of her position on this part of the West African coast. She was able to avoid the extension to the Niger of the International Commission which was established over the Congo river. The same freedom of navigation for all nations was declared for both rivers but on the Niger the British were themselves to ensure this freedom. This duty, with all other powers of administration, the government passed on to the Niger Company, in the next year, 1886, when it was at last given the Royal Charter for which Goldie had so long worked.

To charge the Company, and one ruled by Goldie, who had done his best to get the government to grant a monopoly, with the duty of ensuring freedom of trade for the ships of all nations was rather like employing a cat to ensure the safety of mice. The Company, the trade of which was supposed to be on an equality with that of all other traders, was allowed to raise a revenue for its administration of £90,000 a year by charging dues which must not discriminate, and also to issue and enforce any regulations which were necessary to ensure safety and order and the proper use of the posts and installations it provided up

---

[1] For a short account of the Conference see Crowe, *The Berlin West African Conference*. On the diplomatic background see Taylor, *Germany's First Bid for Colonies*.

the river.[1] The Company so exercised these powers that, to the great anger of the French and of British traders, especially in Liverpool, it did exercise a practical monopoly. Yet, Goldie declared, his enemies were never able to prove any technical breach of the Berlin Act, and he defended the level of the dues and fees on the grounds of the heavy cost of opening up trade in the vast territories reached by the river, and of administering them.[2] It must already be very clear that the western Company received very different treatment from the government as contrasted with that meted out to the eastern. For this there were four main reasons. Firstly, the Niger offered a well-proved trade; secondly, it was accessible from the sea; thirdly, the main rival here was France. The fourth reason was Goldie.

Goldie was the first of the three men who used the refurbished seventeenth-century instrument of the Chartered Company as a means to annex great blocks of tropical Africa for Britain. Representing, like them, the human embodiment of the later, rather confused Marxist concept of economic imperialism, he is well worth study, all the more in these pages as Lugard was to identify himself with his purposes. As a character, in strength of will, he stands with Rhodes in contrast with the gentle, self-sacrificing Mackinnon who had achieved his aim—or half of it—almost in spite of his own limitations, for which the practical and political energy of Lugard had done something to compensate. Lugard's new master remains a somewhat mysterious figure, partly because of his seemingly contradictory character in which something close to arrogance was mingled with a sensitive pride, and partly for the simple reason that his Company was a commercial Ishmael. He swore all his Company employees to silence; he burned all his own papers and threatened to haunt his children if they broke their promise never to write anything about him or to help anyone else to do so.[3] Thus, though his great solid achievement is plain in the records, the man himself, even so soon after his death, remains obscure and this gives a special value to the light which the records of his association with Lugard throw upon him.

Goldie was a Manxman. He was born in 1846, the fourth and

---

1 *General Act of the Conference of Berlin.* Africa No. 3 (1886), C.4739, chapter V. For the provisions of the Berlin Act covering the Niger see Hertslet, *Map of Africa*, vol. ii, pp. 481-4.
2 Proceedings at the fifteenth ordinary general meeting of the Royal Niger Company, 19 July 1895. L.P.
3 Wellesley, *op. cit.* p. ix.

youngest son of Lieutenant-Colonel John Taubman Goldie-Taubman of the Scots Guards, who was Speaker of the House of Keys. As a boy he went to the Royal Military Academy at Woolwich and was commissioned in the Royal Engineers in 1865. Two years later he resigned his commission and travelled for some years in upper Egypt and the Sudan. He first visited West Africa in 1877, and from then until 1900 devoted his life to establishing British control over the trade of the Niger basin. After his Company had surrendered its charter on January 1st 1900, his connection with West Africa ceased. He visited China, served on two royal commissions in South Africa, and went to Rhodesia at the invitation of the Chartered Company to study the question of self-government. In 1905 he became President of the Royal Geographical Society; in 1908, Alderman of the London County Council, and was chairman of its finance committee until 1919. From that date until his death in 1925, ill-health forced him to spend his time abroad. He had married in 1870, and had one son and one daughter.

Those are the main facts and dates. But we can get some intimate views of his life from the recollections of Lady Gerald Wellesley (the Duchess of Wellington). As a child she had a deep friendship with Goldie, then in his later middle-age. He, recognizing the courageous mind of the future poetess, seems to have talked without reserve, and with great powers of self-dramatization. A few of these fragments of recollection may be strung together to indicate the man. Speaking of his youth, he told her, " I was like a gun-powder magazine. I was blind-drunk when I passed my final examination for the Engineers. Two years later a relation died, leaving me his fortune. I was so excited by the freedom that this gave me, that I bolted without sending in my papers, and leaving all my belongings behind. I went straight to Egypt. There I fell in love with an Arab girl. We lived in the desert for three years. Garden of Allah! She died of consumption. I came home to lead a life of idleness and dissipation."[1] Of how his life's work began, he said, " All achievement begins with a dream. My dream, as a child, was to colour the map red. In 1877 I left England (largely to escape from private entanglements) to explore the interior of Nigeria with my brother . . . . On the journey back I conceived the ambition of adding the region of the Niger to the British Empire."[2]

[1] Wellesley, *op. cit.* p. 94.
[2] *Ibid.* p. 93.

Upon another occasion he revealed that when he went to the Niger "Rajah Brooke was a great hero in my eyes—I was very young then." When he saw what the climate was he realized that he could not repeat the Brooke experiment in West Africa, since " its administration to be successful must be at home."[1]

His vision, upon a much more modest scale, was thus of the same kind as that which Rhodes conceived in this same time when he made his first will arranging for the extension of the British Empire throughout the world. Goldie shared with Rhodes this combination of vast and distant aims with the power to pursue them in detail steadily, competently day by day through the most realistic methods. Both believed that money was the instrument by which dreams could be made into realities. But Goldie, in body and character, was taut and compact where Rhodes was sprawling and vulnerable. There was a more quick and cutting edge to Goldie's brain. Typical of this difference was his comment upon Rhodes' Cape-to-Cairo dream. "Trade seeks the sea by the shortest route." In Africa, he added, the natural lines of intercourse run across, not lengthwise. Further, Africa, taken crosswise, is homogeneous; lengthwise, heterogeneous.[2]

Goldie was probably a better judge of men than Rhodes. He picked the great explorer, Joseph Thomson,[3] and brought him from East to West Africa to make treaties in 1885 with the ruler of Sokoto, who was a kind of suzerain over the other Hausa states. Since then, working steadily year by year, his Company established its trade and its peace and made hundreds of treaties and established some forty trading stations along the Niger and the Benue. It survived an enquiry by a British commissioner sent, in view of the clamour of its enemies, to report upon its activities; it braved, at immense cost of angry diplomatic correspondence, three attempts by France to send in ships to break into its preserve, and—perhaps most surprising of all—it paid its shareholders a fairly steady dividend of 6%.

But by 1893 a severe crisis was threatening from the west. To understand Goldie's problem and why his observant eye marked down Lugard as his ideal man for what had to be done, we must see the map as it appeared to the two men in that year.

1 From notes of an interview with Lord Darwin in 1898 kindly supplied by Lord Scarbrough.
2 Wellesley, *op. cit.* p. 23.
3 See above p. 151.

The Setting of the Course

It is important to remember that in 1894 there was no Nigeria. There was the small colony of Lagos, centred upon that port; north of this lay the several large pagan chieftainships into which the culturally-advanced Yoruba-speaking group was divided. Into this region British authority had not yet penetrated far northwards from Lagos. Eastwards from Lagos the forested coastland held a heavy population of very primitive but high-spirited people, mainly of the Ibo group, living mostly in small kinship units. This region, declared British under the name of the Oil Rivers Protectorate, and later called the Niger Coast Protectorate, was, like Lagos, under the imperial government but as a separate unit. By later standards of administration, however, very little was done north of a narrow strip which could be reached from the few coastal and river stations. Through the middle of this region, from north to south, flowed the great Niger river, reaching the Bight of Benin through a wide muddy delta. The lower reach of the river was, at least nominally, under the control of the Niger Company.

So far, so good. But westwards and northwards much was uncertain. The huge squarish block of modern Nigeria is trisected by the Niger and its great tributary, the Benue, which meets it at Lokoja. North of this confluence the country changes, becoming drier and less wooded until it merges into open plains and semi-desert in the north. It is in this drier region, within the triangle of which the branching rivers almost form two sides, that the great Hausa states—great in their size and semi-civilization by comparison with most African societies—and the non-Hausa state of Bornu had developed as a group of Muslim principalities centred upon large cities. The Hausa states owned a loose allegiance to the sultan of Sokoto. We shall have occasion to look more closely at these interesting states later, in the second part of Lugard's life. Now we need only observe that, for all its large claims to this northern country and the treaties it had secured from some of the leading emirs, the Company had little or no continuous contact with any states that lay away from the river.

The Company, when chartered, had no boundaries, not even as regards the two British governments of Lagos Colony and the Oil Rivers, with which it will easily be believed its relations were not very cordial. In 1893 a frontier on the east with the German Cameroons was agreed. But to the north, and even more to the west, frontiers were non-existent and the Company's expansion was threatened by France.

There is no more clear and striking expression of the different character of the French and British peoples than their way of going about the business of colonial expansion. It has been the same story in India, North America and Africa. In France, centralized and authoritarian, though of course private individuals and groups played some part, it was the government which provided most of the initiative and drew up the plans for expansion. In Britain, private individuals and companies made the running and dragged their government after them. From this all other differences follow. The intelligent French statesmen and generals pondered over their maps of the new continents; British traders pushed in week by week from the coasts and established themselves piecemeal where trade was to be got or settlements made. The next stage was obvious: the French, with logical minds and large political and military objectives, would conceive a wide master plan which should shut in all these small, independent, separate, short-sighted British commercial beginnings and win mastery on a continental scale. They would send out soldiers and officials vowed to uphold the glory of France and to carry further the torch of culture she received from Rome.

West Africa in the late eighties and early nineties seemed an ideal setting for such large action by France. Britain's isolated coastal positions on the Gambia, Sierra Leone, the Gold Coast, Lagos and the Niger, were simply asking for the truncation and enclosure which the first three of them received. France was already established on the Mediterranean coast to the north, and at Senegal on the west. She had only to strengthen some intermediate positions she held on the coasts in between the British settlements, push northwards inland from them and meet the other inner line of advance where her agents were cutting straight from west to east inland along the Senegal and upper Niger valleys—she had reached the mysterious Timbuctu in 1894—and the whole vast mass of the western bulge of Africa would be French except for a few isolated British enclaves. Nor was this all. The map suggested an even grander vision. As we have seen, France believed she could move on into the still unoccupied interior and so right across Africa to join up with her Red Sea annexation, cutting the Cape-to-Cairo axis, straddling the Nile, shutting in Uganda and developing against Britain and Italy her relationship with Egypt and Ethiopia. It was an intoxicating vision and Lugard's position in the forefront of those warning the country of its dangers has already been remarked.[1] We must, however, confine ourselves here to that part of it which immediately threatened Goldie who had his own visions and his strong, single will to back them against the government of France.

In the game of scrambling for Africa, the competing powers paused now and then, as if to draw breath, and had a conference or made a treaty before they resumed their activities. France and Britain made such a treaty in 1889. In this they agreed, among other matters, upon a boundary line between Lagos Colony and the neighbouring French Dahomey. On the rather vague hinterland principle, a meridian was drawn straight northwards from this point on the coast as far as the 9th parallel, which was still outside the occupation of either power.[2] But this meant that the north was wide open and here the race might be to the swifter. The following year both countries made another agreement dealing with the whole region from the north. France had made great play of her indignation at not having been consulted over the 1890 colonial agreement between Britain and Germany which had ignored her position in relation to Zanzibar. This anger had to be soothed by recognition of her disputed position in Madagascar. Britain also recognized France's sphere of influence to the south of her Mediterranean possessions as stretching down to a latitudinal line some 700 miles long drawn from Say on the upper Niger (a point in the region where France coming from Senegal and the Niger Company groping up-Niger were just meeting), to Barruwa on Lake Chad. But all " that fairly belongs to the kingdom of Sokoto "—a difficult point of allegiance not yet determined—was to be in the sphere of the Niger Company and it was recognized that this would mean a northward bulge of the line near Sokoto itself. Commissioners were to be appointed to determine the spheres of the two countries " to the west and to the south of the Middle and Upper Niger."[3]

Unfortunately this treaty gave only a disputable definition of the

[1] See, for example, Lugard's articles ' Imperial Interests in East Africa', and ' The New African Crisis with France and Germany ', *Blackwoods Magazine*, vols. CLV and CLVI, June and July 1894.

[2] *Correspondence respecting the West African Agreement between Great Britain and France of August 10, 1889.* Africa No. 3 (1890), C.5905, p. 7.

[3] *Declarations exchanged between the Government of Her Britannic Majesty and the Government of the French Republic with respect to Territories in Africa.* Africa No. 9 (1890), C. 6130.

no-man's land into which the agents of the two nations were advancing in the attempt to forestall each other. A glance at the map will show how much turned upon the question as to whether this Say-Barruwa line was meant to be only the *southern* boundary of France's Mediterranean territories, to the further south of which she could expand from her western or southern occupations, or whether it was also the northern boundary of the Niger Company's sphere. If the latter, it would then cover the area enclosed by lines drawn straight south from these two named points. In this case, the large, still unexplored state of Borgu, lying westward of the great Niger bend, would fall to Britain.

This was how France, to judge by her newspapers[1] and other evidence, accepted the delimitation at the time. So did Lord Salisbury in announcing it though unfortunately, in defending what appeared to be such an immense extension of French territory on the map, 1,500 miles south of the Algerian coast, he explained that it was, after all, " what agriculturalists would call ' very light ' land," an indulgence in his natural irony in describing the Sahara desert which enraged the French.[2] " No doubt," said the wounded French ambassador, Waddington, " the Sahara is not a garden . . . . but your public reminder of the fact was, perhaps you will allow me to say, hardly necessary. You might well have left us to find it out."[3] Three years later, however, France changed her mind. She had now begun to push north from the Dahomey coast, to fight the warlike chief Samory in the interior and to realize that she could fan out from the south; cut off the German Togoland and the Gold Coast hinterland; link up with her Upper Niger territory; and scoop Borgu out from behind what the Niger Company thought was its boundary line south from Say to the Lagos border. In December 1892 she declared a protectorate over Dahomey. Soon the Foreign Office was complaining that France had begun to treat the Say-Barruwa line as confining the British to the north but not confining the French to the south.[4] Another advantage to France, at a time when waterways seemed the all-important means of communication, was that by annexing Borgu, she would get access for her new interior annexations to the Niger below the Bussa rapids where it was

1 See Goldie's speech in Proceedings at the fifteenth ordinary general meeting of the Royal Niger Company, 19 July 1895. L.P.

2 *Parliamentary Debates*, 11 August 1890, III. 348. 459.

3 Cecil, *Life of Salisbury*, vol. iv, p. 324.

4 *Memorandum on the claims of Great Britain and France in the Basin of the Middle and Lower Niger.* C.O.C.P. African (West) No. 539, pp. 17–18. L.P.

then navigable to the sea. This, to Goldie, was more important than so many square miles, more or less, of land. "If ever the French get a port on the Niger," he told the Foreign Office in his uncompromising way, "I will sell up the whole business and clear out."[1]

The period between the summer of 1893 and that of 1894 was, as we have already seen, a time of growing tension between France and Britain.[2] Goldie, by threatening drastic action against a French officer, Lieutenant Mizon, who had gone up the Niger twice in 1891 and 1892 in armed ships, forced the British government, on the second occasion, to insist upon the intruder's recall. The French public, treating him as a hero, were furious at this humiliation, while the French ambassador reported that British opinion on this point was "*douloureux enflammé*".[3] France was also very angry about the British Congo Agreement with Leopold, to which reference has been made.[4] By June 1894 Sir Clement Hill of the Foreign Office African Department could talk to a French embassy official about the possibility of war.[5] The Uganda dispute was still dragging on as the compensation for the "atrocities" had not yet been settled so that, when Britain flung the name of Mizon at the French, that of Lugard was thrown back in retaliation. And it was becoming likely that France now meant seriously to challenge Britain with expeditions to both the Niger and the Nile.

The most immediate point of danger was Borgu. When Goldie controverted the French interpretation of the Say-Barruwa line the French replied, as they had in East Africa, that they did not recognize commercial companies and, in any case, this one had broken the terms of the Berlin Act by denying free navigation on the Niger. And they evolved the ingenious theory that though they must not actually *cross* the line from north to south they could *edge* round it from the south. When Goldie claimed that he had made a treaty with Sokoto, they retorted that Sokoto's power did not cover Borgu and in any case their Monteil had made later and better treaties with Sokoto and with Gandu, an emirate which lay between Sokoto and Borgu. When Goldie flourished two treaties—of 1885 and 1890—with the king of

---

[1] Quoted in Everett to Hill, 31 December 1896, F.O. 27/3301.
[2] See above pp. 467–9.
[3] D'Estournelles to Develle, 1 December 1893, D.D.F. X. p. 665.
[4] See Langer, *Diplomacy of Imperialism*, pp. 124–41 (with illustrative map).
[5] Decrais to Hanotaux, 22 June 1894, D.D.F. XI. p. 173.

Bussa, on the Niger, claiming he was lord of all Borgu, the French denied this, and their explorer Captain Toutée went to Bussa and reported that the Company had no effective occupation there or even in the whole surrounding area. They also asserted that the overlord of Borgu was not the king of Bussa on the Niger but the king of a place called Nikki in the still unexplored centre of Borgu—" king " being an inflated title for these chiefs. The Germans, moreover, might send an expedition there to protect or extend their Togoland hinterland.[1]

Goldie realized that only rapid action could save Borgu for Britain and that he must take it himself. Such information as he had was to the effect that Borgu was inhabited by fierce and formidable pagans who had closed their country to all strangers. They must indeed be formidable to have kept out the mounted slave-raiding expeditions from the powerful Muslim Hausa states, for these harried all the surrounding pagan areas. It appeared that no white man had entered Borgu: certainly no white man had come out of it alive. Some agent, at once strong, courageous, respected and politically able, must make a dash into Borgu, get there before the French, and obtain a treaty with Nikki. Goldie had watched Lugard's career and he saw in him the man for the job.

Goldie first approached Lugard in April, 1894. This was before he realized the full urgency of the task he proposed for him. At the first meeting both men impressed each other. Goldie looked the eagle of a man that he was. Herkomer's portrait of him shows his strong large head, with the high brow, pronounced nose and confident, indeed arrogant and mocking, look. (Lady Gerald Wellesley aptly nicknamed him Rameses.) He was fair with blue eyes that could probe as fiercely as Lugard's dangerous-looking brown ones. He was not a patient man but he knew how to wait for what he wanted and he could understand Lugard's unwillingness to burn his East African boats, and his desire to work this time for the government and not again for a Company.

" You are," he wrote, " emphatically and undeniably the man for Uganda; I would not, if I could, take you away so long as there is any chance of your appointment there. Uganda is your own child." (24 April 1894). The matter, therefore, hung fire. But Goldie wanted

---

1 The whole question, which covers a vast area of diplomatic documentation, was summarized in *Memorandum on the Claims of Great Britain and France in the Basin of the Middle and Lower Niger* by Colonel W. Everett. C.O.C.P. African (West) No. 539, November 1897. L.P.

a decision one way or the other, and wanted it soon, while Lugard wished to delay binding himself to the last minute. Moreover he felt very doubtful about the expediency of the West African adventure. He knew that the whole question of frontiers was being discussed between the embassies in Europe. "It appears to me", he told Kirk on June 12th, "a futile thing for me to start on a filibustering expedition into this territory at the very time when the frontiers are being settled in Europe. I should not be there until about November when in all probability the matter would be settled. Then I should be disowned and discredited and my work would be useless." During May and June the matter still remained in suspense. For all his sympathy with Lugard's desire to keep open a loophole in case he should be asked to go to Uganda, Goldie made it clear that time was pressing and that he expected a firm decision. His clear mind and strong will are expressed in every letter. "I like *les situations nettes*," he told Lugard, "and I feel confident that your clear and practical mind will agree with this desire." (3 May 1894).

After the Uganda debate was over and Lowther had destroyed Lugard's last hopes, Kirk advised him to accept Goldie's offer. "Goldie has acted most generously to you, I must say, in never pressing you or taking advantage of your engagement—up to the last leaving you free as far as he was concerned." Goldie wrote on June 26th pointing out that if he were going he must sail in a month's time. So, reluctantly, Lugard turned his back upon East Africa and agreed to set out for the west coast.

He found himself under dominant and experienced command, very unlike that of the I.B.E.A. Company. Goldie had already laid down, in a letter of May 3rd, that Lugard had better travel with a very small escort of soldiers. "Presents and soft words are more effective with these *West* African rulers than a force, sufficient to arouse alarm but not strong enough to overawe. Besides, we want treaties and not conquest." So Lugard rapidly drew up his detailed estimates of the Europeans and natives required for a modestly sized caravan with the necessary equipment.

Goldie then sent him a formal letter in which he drew attention to the obligation imposed upon all employed by the Company to maintain secrecy. This pointed out that the Company was a government and was only exacting what all governments required of their servants.

The Company was attempting a task which most people believed to be impracticable. " The Company believes it to be practicable on one condition; namely, that, in view of the difficulties resulting from the climate, the difficulty of access to West Africa, the barbarism of the population and other abnormal causes, abnormal energy, persistence, patience, and above all, discipline, should be displayed by all the officials of the Company from the Governor and Council down to the junior customs clerk." The two great dangers in England were the general apathy about West Africa and the excitability for short periods when public opinion was led astray, on some popular hobby, by one-sided or exaggerated reports, so, " . . . . You will understand that in the complicated game which the Company is playing every move of which has to be calculated with the greatest care, it would be intolerable that any individual should be allowed to be the judge oː what he might (directly or indirectly) publish or communicate to other persons than the Council of the Company." Lugard was therefore asked to sign an undertaking which was to cover his period in the Company's service and five years afterwards, to preserve secrecy and not to publish books or deliver addresses except after revision of the text by the Company. Most employees were obliged to enter into an agreement to pay £1,000 damages if this contract should be broken but it appears that in Lugard's case this clause was omitted. He would certainly not have been in a position to make the pledge.

Lugard did not like this bond any more than he had liked the less precise obligation he had accepted under the East Africa Company. " I could not have signed such a letter," he told Goldie, " had I not the most *absolute* trust and confidence in yourself . . . I somewhat regret that there should be any necessity for a written bond between us on such a subject." (3 July 1894). " I feel sure," replied Goldie, " that you have done right in acceding to our request," and he added characteristically: " What is wanted in Central Africa is action and not discussion—of which there is already more than enough." (3 July 1894). Goldie knew of Lugard's energy as a writer and speaker and there could have been few employees whose voice and pen he was more anxious to control.

There was nothing more to be done except for Goldie to arrange for Lugard's further secondment—without pay—from the army and for Lugard to collect his equipment hurriedly and catch his ship.

The Company was to pay him at the rate of £1,000 a year, giving him £50 for his personal outfit. He did not enter the service of the Company as a regular employee: his was a single, special task. Very careful instructions were drawn up for him by Goldie; these included the possibility that at the last moment he might be ordered by telegraph to go to Lake Chad to control the situation upon the extreme north-east, where a powerful adventurer from the eastern Sudan, Rabeh, was reported to be invading Bornu, instead of to the west of the Company's territories. But it was expected that he must hurry with all speed to the heart of Borgu. All the arrangements for his expedition were already being made by the Company's officials on the Niger. He was given a wide discretion but the main object was to discover who were the rulers of Borgu and to make treaties with them, above all with Nikki. He was then to go on westwards—" the further west you penetrate the more successful your journey will be from a diplomatic point of view "—to visit Mossi, north of the Gold Coast, and to make treaties with what Goldie believed to be a number of independent tribes there, ignoring the claims of Monteil who had gone in to make a treaty with their supposed overlord. He was " to zig-zag a good deal, so as to run networks of treaties across and between the few treaties obtained " by Monteil and Binger, the other great French West African traveller, for France. He was to collect the fullest information about Borgu; to oversee the survey work of his assistant, Mottram; to note all trade and look out for gum trees, rubber vines etc. and news of minerals. But he was " to remember, above all, that diplomacy and not conquest is *the* object of your expedition westwards . . . the exercise of force cannot further your objects, but must on the contrary prevent them being attained." (Goldie to L. 24 July 1894).

Lugard sailed from Liverpool on July 28th. It seems that it was only at the end that Goldie realized the full urgency of the mission, for he wrote a few days later to tell Lugard that a Frenchman, Captain Decoeur, was actually in the field. It had been given out that he was to work only in Dahomey. " If this is not true and if the French Colonial Office are sending him to counteract your work, I am not likely to get any information about it." (Goldie to L. 2 August 1894). Actually Decoeur had left Marseilles on July 24th, four days before Lugard left Liverpool. His secret destination was also Nikki.

By disembarking on the Dahomey coast and going up to France's new station at Carnotville where the Governor, M. Ballot, was waiting for him with his caravan ready to start, he had a very much shorter journey than Lugard who had to go all the way round by the Niger to Jebba, 530 miles from the river mouth, and then plunge into Borgu from the eastern side. Not only that. A German expedition under a Herr Grüner was also being launched. The French press, certain of the success of their secret plan, was already triumphantly claiming that Nikki was the real capital of Borgu and that the kingdom would fall to the first man to reach that place. " It was," said the leading French colonial paper, when the news came out, " a veritable steeplechase in which France, England and Germany are engaged "[1] to win what the French called the " *boucle* ", or loop, of the Niger.

1 *Politique Coloniale*, 19 January 1895.

CHAPTER XXIII

FROM LONDON TO NIKKI

1894 : Aet. 36

THE ATMOSPHERE of the west coast, new to Lugard, closed around him as soon as he embarked upon the ship. There was the usual gossip about the character of the governors, the defects of their policies, the faults of the Africans and the dismal record of the white man's health. But Lugard was not the man to treat a sea voyage as a leisured interval and he set to work at once. He began two diaries in large ledgers which allowed the pages to be torn out while their inter-leaves remained as carbon copies. One of these diaries was private but the other he had decided—a striking testimony to the relations he had established with his new master—to send in confidence to Goldie. He began by writing several close-packed foolscap pages for each day, but it is not surprising that later, when he began his trek into the bush, he found that as he was then busy with map-making and the maintenance of a log and various other records, he could only keep up one full diary.[1]

The two diaries were not his only task on the ship. He had brought with him a number of books on West Africa, and he concentrated especially upon the classic records of the great traveller Barth.[2] He also studied the recent French travel books, including that of his friendly rival, Monteil, who was already in the field before him with his eyes fixed on Fashoda.[3] The most valuable book for his immediate purpose, however, was the record of Binger, a very impressive report, crowded with maps and lively pictures.[4] As he had not studied French since he was thirteen years of age, he found himself obliged to look up every tenth word in the dictionary; these

1 This and the next chapter are based largely upon Lugard's diary and other papers left by him.
2 Barth, *Travels in North and Central Africa*.
3 P.-L. Monteil, *De Saint-Louis à Tripoli par le lac Tchad* (Paris 1895). See above p. 465.
4 L.-G. Binger, *Du Niger au Golfe de Guinée par le pays de Kong et le Mossi, 1887–89* (Paris 1892).

he wrote over the printed word while he also made a full précis of all he read. In this way he gradually worked up to forty pages a day. He felt a great admiration for Binger's book. " The amount of information it contains is absolutely marvellous and puts one altogether out of conceit with oneself." From this reading he turned to work upon Hausa grammar, to study the existing maps, and to prepare sheets for his own. Like Livingstone upon his first voyage to Africa, he learned much from the very friendly captain of the ship about the use of the survey instruments he had obtained and the taking of observations. He had with him on the voyage a young medical student, G. N. Mottram, who was to accompany him upon the expedition and whose special duty was to help in plotting out the map with astronomical observations. They had brought with them two lively bull-terriers; these relieved the monotony of the voyage by fighting each other and by tackling sheep and even bulls when taken ashore at ports of call.

At Sierra Leone Lugard was appalled by what he heard from the doctor of the figures for mortality and sickness among the British. " Almost all the officers in the mess were the colour of a dirty table-cloth. They can't leave the house in this driving rain and they drink continual cocktails (I believe) and smoke and sleep." (Diary, 12 August 1894). He asked them why they did not make a racquet court and when he heard that they greatly wanted one but that government would not supply it, he set his practical and indignant mind to work upon the details of a plan by which they could, with the minimum of work and material, succeed in getting one made by their own efforts.

In spite of all his hard work on board he had some time to review his position and prospects. August 13th he noted as the day he got his captain's commission nine years before. " I haven't been doing very well for myself either in pay or promotion these last 7 years (it is just exactly 7 years since I left Burma). I am still a Captain on about £190 a year, with no hope of promotion, and I have added nothing to my medals or decorations in these years. *All* were got 7 long years ago! But I think I've learnt a *lot* in these 7 years, and I would not exchange my work and its results for all the decorations, or the biggest salaries available. Perhaps it's a tall thing to say, but I think I have learnt to look for a *better* recompense than any such. Gordon affected to despise most heartily all such acknowledgments—yet I have heard it said that

Sir George Goldie, from a portrait in the National Portrait
Gallery by H. von Herkomer, 1899

he was a disappointed man because he had not got them! May heaven preserve me from ever being that most paltry of all objects 'a disappointed man!' At least if I *have* a disappointment—and a feeling that I have failed to secure success where most I would prize it—it is *not* in the direction of personal emoluments or honours, I think." (Diary, 13 August 1894).

They passed Liberia, where the usual passenger stories were exchanged about the absurdities and enormities of the African government there. They came to the Gold Coast, where he heard very depreciatory comments upon the Governor: he went ashore at Cape Coast Castle and here he continued his education upon slavery by seeing the underground dungeons, " where in the old days the *British* crammed *thousands* of slaves awaiting shipment. . . . On one side were piled up a large number of ready-made coffins, ready for the poor devils of white men who die like flies in these parts." (Diary, 17 August 1894). By August 19th, twenty-three days after leaving Liverpool, they were off Lagos, where at that time, before the deep-water harbour was made, it was impossible to land because of the sand-bar. On August 23rd the ship turned into the Forcados river, the westernmost of the many mouths of the Niger. Lugard formed a very good impression here of Warri, the Niger Coast Protectorate station, with its excellent houses and its hospitable vice-consul, Mr. Crawford. Here he observed the well-trained servants and good food and learned that the officials adored their chief, Sir Claude Macdonald.[1]

He ran here, on August 25th, into a harsh reminder that, even though it was much more closely in touch with Europe than the eastern coast, this was the real Africa to which he had returned. He came across the naval launch, *Alecto*, sent to make a reconnaissance of the position held by a strong and obdurate slave-raiding chief, Nana, who had 5,000 slaves in his stronghold and had rejected all invitations to parley. The naval officers entertained Lugard and Crawford pressed him to go up-river with them. It seemed to Lugard that it was a somewhat light-hearted expedition that was being prepared. He had been suffering from fever and decided the weather was not very

[1] Macdonald, Rt. Hon. Sir Claude Maxwell, P.C., K.C.B., G.C.M.G., G.C.V.O., 1852–1915; 1882–4 Egyptian campaign and Suakin expedition; 1882–7 Military Attaché to British Agency in Cairo; 1887–8 Acting Agent and Consul–General at Zanzibar; 1889 sent by F.O. on special mission to Niger territories; 1891 Commissioner and Consul–General in Oil Rivers Protectorate; 1896–1900 Envoy Extraordinary and Minister Plenipotentiary at Peking; 1900–12 Ambassador at Tokyo.

R

promising for the trip. The party of officers and bluejackets went off in high spirits. Not very long after the *Alecto* returned, her decks stained with blood, and conveying a cargo of dead and wounded. The ship's pinnace had run into heavy fire from a masked battery from Nana's fortified position on the bank of the river. Lugard's pleasant host, vice-consul Crawford, with part of his leg shot away, was carried ashore to endure amputation. Captain Lawler only kept silent in his agony by biting upon a handkerchief held between his teeth and was covered with blood where he had bitten his tongue to control himself. Lugard followed the dead, wrapped in the Union Jack, to the place of burial and, as an old soldier, he remarked sadly upon the shock these inexperienced men had suffered. " These young chaps see what *war* means—they were *horrified* and I fancy it has choked off their martial ardour a good deal and they no longer ' hope to goodness Nana won't give in without a fight after all our preparations,' as they said to me before." (Diary, 27 August 1894). It was later discovered that Nana had twenty-three heavy cannons behind the creeks, forest and stockades of his slaving stronghold and it later took a large expedition to storm it.

The incident, in which he had been so nearly involved, led him to analyse his own attitude towards fighting in words that may seem surprising after all that has been recorded of him. " This ' *ardor pugnandi* ' is wholly absent from my own composition, or at any rate has now been for many a long year. Nature seems to have implanted in some dispositions a positive love of fighting for fighting's sake, as in the bull-dog. One can understand it somewhat, where men stand up and receive and give blow for blow, or fight with swords—but to stand up and be shot at, with the knowledge that you may at any moment get a bullet in the jaw, which may render you a loathsome spectacle, and a burden to yourself, or disable you for life, is *not* compensated for by shooting down others, at least not to me. The ' lust of carnage ' does not come over me—I do not care to kill men, though I know the strange feeling as one sees them fall, and knows one's hand and eye and judgment sent that poor devil to eternity. But to me it remains an act of defence. I have no wish to kill *because he is against me*—only because I know he is coming to kill me, or because as we are fighting it is necessary to kill in order to win. Strange (it seems to me) that this kind of feeling is I believe altogether an exception. My experience is so. It is (like very much else about me) a *woman's* character. If I had gone with Crawford to the *Alecto*, I wonder what would have happened? " (Diary, 27 August 1894). It is interesting to contrast here the opinion of one of Lugard's military contemporaries, Lord Wolseley, who has believed that " all other pleasures pale before the intense, the maddening delight of leading men into the midst of an enemy . . . . That rapturous enjoyment takes a man out of himself to the forgetfulness of all earthly considerations."[1]

Lugard had now to turn his thoughts to his own expedition. As his ship moved eastward along the coast towards the Niger entry he felt himself getting "warm". There was news of the expedition to Sokoto which Mr. Wallace, Agent-General of the Niger Company in Africa, had just completed in order to confirm the Company's relations with that all-important ruler. He heard that Rabeh had been checked in his advance into Bornu. The telegram that might have diverted him to that region had not come, though Lugard had again dreamed great dreams of marching further east to emancipate the Sudan from the Mahdists in alliance with the famous leader, Zebehr Pasha, Rabeh's foster-father. The ship went on, with Lugard deep in a book about the influence of Buddhism upon Christianity, and touched at the Niger Coast Protectorate port of Brass. This was the home of vigorous native traders, deeply resentful of the control which the Company imposed from its neighbouring river-mouth station at Akassa.

At this port Lugard made his first contact with the main coastal station of the Company. He was much impressed. He compared both the scale and the purposeful character of its installation with those of the East Africa Company. Sir George Mackenzie had sadly anticipated this impression in a letter written to him just before he left England. " I fancy you will find the Niger run on more *practical lines* than our Company. They have proved themselves wiser in their generation . . . . " But then, as Lugard remarked, his new employers had, in palm oil, a real trade to deal with. Here at this port " ocean steamers call to pick up a thousand casks of valuable exports at a time (brought down by the fleet of river steamers) and a strong serviceable wharf alongside which they anchor expedites the shipment . . . . I was greatly struck with all this, it is after my own heart, practical, workmanlike and free from gas and bunkum." (Diary, 29 August 1894).

[1] Quoted in Langer, *Diplomacy of Imperialism*, p. 89.

He was impressed, too, by his own reception. The Company's staff, at once traders and administrators, were posted at the stations established along the river. Mr. Wallace had passed him as he went southwards on leave but the acting-head of the Company in Africa, Mr. Flint, showed that he was fully ready for him and that preparations for his expedition were well advanced. Lugard's relations with the regular Company officials were excellent, whereas, in his position as the leader of a temporary and independent mission, responsible direct to Goldie and imposing a good deal of work upon them, they might have been difficult. He remarked that few of them were gentlemen but that did not matter to him who, like St. Paul, was " all things to all men." The next day, August 30th, he and Mottram left the *Niger*, embarked upon the river-steamer *Nupe* and started with Flint up the river. Here again Lugard made comparisons with East Africa. He was deeply struck by the width and volume of the great waterway, filled with islands. Here was a river such as East Africa could not boast! The banks were walled with tall forest trees, many of them bearing great scarlet flowers, while orchids and ferns grew on their boughs. Sometimes they passed villages and he saw the naked women and the strong, well-made men fishing or paddling their little canoes. He was told they were cannibals. On September 2nd he went ashore at Onitsha to visit a coffee and rubber plantation. At Asaba he called on the Company's Chief Justice and admired the excellent jail. Observing that the Company was beginning to develop a timber trade, he wrote to them to advise the use of elephants, on the example of Burma, and sent full details as to their training, management and food.

But though he was both interested and impressed he had so far found nothing to appeal deeply to him in his first view of West Africa. Certainly, to most people coming from East Africa, there is—or there was—something menacing about the Niger coast at first contact. The frequent heavy rain from dull skies; the contorted mangrove trees with their fantastic roots writhing out of the mud of the delta; the dark forests; the vague sense of their hiding a brooding witchcraft and cannibal practices; the vast numbers of people at once blacker, more negroid, assertive and strident than the easterners; all these create a nostalgia for the contrasting conditions of the east. Lugard certainly felt this and it chilled his spirits long before he reached his base.

Lokoja, the important station upon the Niger-Benue junction, was reached on September 5th and Lugard began to get to grips with his problems and to discuss the number and equipment of his caravan. He saw Hausa troops being drilled; the northern Muslim Sudanic people were regarded as better soldiers than the southern pagan tribes. Lugard was provided with thirty Hausas and ten Yorubas and asked the doctor, before passing them, to examine them very carefully for syphilis and for the condition of their feet. He did not like to ask for more than forty, as Goldie had strongly advised him to take a very small escort.

On September 8th, the *Nupe* reached Jebba, then the northernmost station manned by the Company on the Niger, and impressively marked by a great hump of rock rising out of the river. From here Lugard was to start his march westwards into Borgu in search of Nikki, and here his loads were being prepared and porters enlisted. There was none of the East African difficulty of obtaining a sufficiency of these. He decided that, while the equipment and loads were being prepared, no time would be lost if he were to make a quick march up the river to see the king—he found that the pettiest chiefs were all called kings in West Africa—of Bussa. In case it were true that this man should turn out after all to be the real king of Borgu, it was necessary to get into touch with him and obtain guides and also passports in the form of letters to the other kings of this country. He arrived in Bussa on September 16th, after marching for six days alongside the Niger in pouring rain. Yet he could congratulate himself that it was only fifty-one days since he left his club. His first interview with a West African potentate was not impressive. He found the king a very disappointing and dilatory person. It greatly irked Lugard's impatient spirit and pride of race that he must follow the Company policy of what he called " abasement before these petty African chieflets." He put on the scarlet coat emblazoned with gold lace— " I detest this mummery . . . . " The king of all the Bussas turned out to be " a specially dirty and mean-looking savage seated on a filthy, and greasy carpet . . . . the doorways were blocked with gazing crowds of naked girls . . . . " (Diary, 17 September 1894). The king, who drew a subsidy of £50 a year from the Company, promised to send letters to his brother kings of Kiama and Nikki, and provided messengers in return for powder and flint-lock guns. But he kept

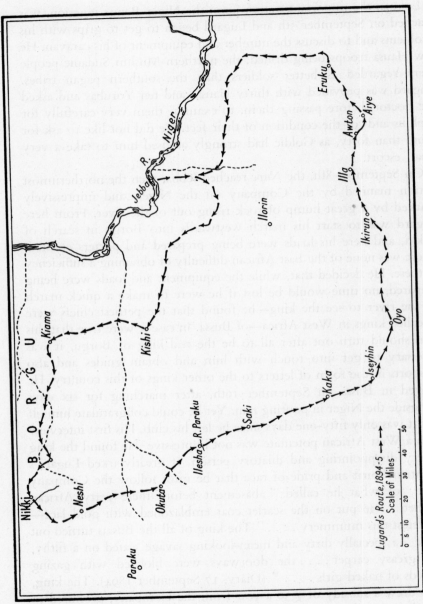

The March to Nikki, 1894–5. Based on the map to illustrate F. D. Lugard, 'An Expedition to Borgu on the Niger', *The Geographical Journal*, vol. vi, 1895

Lugard waiting while he went through some pagan rites, first making him move his tent from the sacred ground which he claimed was necessary for these ceremonies.

After this dreary and humiliating excursion of 200 soaking miles, Lugard hurried back to Jebba, shooting down the rapids, which break the Niger below Bussa, in a canoe in torrential rain. He had so far had little time for observation, but he did conclude, as he saw some of the northern Muslim people in their flowing and embroidered gowns, meeting and greeting each other with the most courtly obeisances, that here, at least in parts, was a standard of civilization very much higher than that of East Africa. He also questioned in his mind the propriety of the Company officials combining administrative and commercial duties; in his view there should have been two separate cadres for the two functions.

He got back to Jebba on September 24th. The hope upon which he was gambling was that Decoeur, still unaware that he was out to race him, would not attempt to start until the end of the rains which made travel almost impossible in this region, though not, he decided, for himself. Every day was therefore of value. He hurried on with the final preparations. There were a hundred jobs to be done, checking the weight and content of the loads, and the equipment of the caravan; inspecting the men; drawing up the instructions and allotting tasks; arranging the order of the march and sending off the final mails. The total caravan consisted of 320 men, forty of whom were soldiers while the rest, Nupe, Hausa and Yoruba, were porters. There were three Europeans, Lugard, Mottram and a young Company man, Reynolds; two southern negro interpreters, Joseph and Robinson, and two headmen. The most disappointing and unhappy part of the caravan were the forty donkeys, which since, as Lugard remarked, they were about as useless in rain as brown paper, began to crumple up even before the start was made, and so cast their loads upon the already overloaded porters.

As Lugard struggled to get ready for the first day's march and as he went exhausted to bed on the night before the start, he was very depressed. He was unable to speak to any of his men, as he did not know their languages. Yet he could not delegate any responsibility to the white youngsters, since the one was straight from England and the other did not himself know any native language. Both were keen and willing, but each had the work of three or four men to do and he feared they would not stand the strain. The two negro interpreters he found inefficient and pretentious, demanding their own train of servants and wholly without the weight and dignity which would have allowed him to give them any supervisory functions. He longed for his excellent assistants of Uganda days, especially for Dualla, whom at one time he had even thought of bringing over for the expedition. In addition to the interpreters he had only two headmen for 320 porters and soldiers, whereas in East Africa he would have had seven with about twenty-five other men of intermediate rank in charge of small groups. Almost more serious if danger should arise, his forty soldiers turned out, according to his high standards, to be the rawest of recruits, undisciplined and untrained, while their numbers would be wholly inadequate to protect porters strung out for a mile or more along forest tracks. He decided that he faced the hardest task of his life and his expectations were gloomy. The common idea that men of endurance and heroic action have nerves of steel and suffer from no temperamental torments was wholly untrue of Lugard; his quality lay chiefly in the strength of will which mastered not only external difficulties but those of his own imaginative nature. But upon the eve of an enterprise, perhaps for the very reason that he could foresee the immense demand it would make upon his physical and mental energy, he tended towards a deep depression which was generally dispersed by action.

The expedition set out soon after dawn on September 28th. The direct westward line into Borgu was regarded as impracticable so the first march was due south as if away from Borgu and towards the Yoruba centre, Ilorin. Lugard noted the number of people along the track, and the many villages and the courtesy and orderliness of the Yoruba people, who, in this northernmost of their districts, were Muslims. He tried to reduce his caravan to some kind of order, but as the men disappeared at night to sleep in the villages and were late in the morning, and as the three tribal groups of porters, Hausas, Yorubas, and Nupes, fought each other over the loads, he was unable even to attempt his strict East African standards of order. Heavy rain poured upon them, yet there was great heat, always an unpleasant combination in Africa. There were swollen streams to be swum, where the poor enfeebled donkeys had to be unloaded and forced across. The equipment was soaked. His two European colleagues went down at once with fever; Mottram was especially bad and Lugard had to nurse him, doing the most intimate services for the sick youth. In spite of all difficulties, handicapped almost to desperation by his inability to speak directly to the men—he could not even call orders to them because so many answered to the same name!—Lugard by sheer tenacity of will drove forward his almost unmanageable crowd of soldiers and porters.

Turning northwards, he struck out for the frontiers of Borgu. The population began to thin out as this dangerous kingdom—if kingdom it was—drew near, and Lugard struggled to get his caravan into better shape preparatory for such defence as it could put up. On the Yoruba-Borgu border, over 100 miles from Jebba, he was met by a great welcome at the last Yoruba town of Kishi, which he reached upon October 11th. Once again, looking back with the knowledge of all the changes the first European was to set in motion we may remark the poignant interest in these first encounters. This king sent a series of messengers to meet Lugard on the road. He said that the British had put the country to rights and done great good; already the Borgu raiders who were troubling him were beginning to run away at the very news that a white man was approaching. Lugard camped outside the town and sent a message to say that he would entertain the king or come to see him as the king wished. The king's reply was that he was not Lugard's equal and that therefore it was for him to come and call, but as, if he did, the whole population would get up and follow him, he would ask to be forgiven if he asked the distinguished stranger to visit him. When they brought this communication the messengers prostrated themselves flat on their faces before Lugard. " A wonderfully gentlemanly speech " was Lugard's comment. He noted with admiration the formal courtesy of the people; their flowing robes dyed dark blue from a local dye; the excellent cultivation; the houses with their square, walled courtyards, and the broad, clean roads. For the moment his impression of West Africa brightened.

The next day Lugard put on his scarlet coat and paid a state visit to the king. It appeared that Kishi, which was not yet under British occupation as the authorities at Lagos—which, it will be remembered, was the headquarters of the Colonial Office territory—had not yet reached the country, was tributary to the leading Yoruba potentate further south, the Alafin of Oyo. It was much harassed by Borgu raiders. The king whispered to him that he would like to see him alone. The Yoruba, it appeared, had a devotion for democracy and publicity, which sometimes had its inconveniences. Lugard readily agreed. Making an act of faith, he went alone to the king's house where he found him waiting with a small council. One of the councillors, a fine and intelligent looking man, got up and made a speech. " He thanked God for our coming with great fervour, said that three days ago you could not have seen a man 300 yards from the town without bow and arrow; now all went unarmed. The British had introduced law and order into all Yoruba and at last it had come to them. They were on the very frontier of Borgu. Fifty yards from my camp was Borgu territory. They lived in daily dread of them and they raided constantly and carried off people for slaves. They prayed God my coming was the beginning of peace; all they desired was peace." (Diary, 12 October 1894).

Lugard made a suitable speech in reply. He realized that he had a chance of making a treaty here for the Company and he explained clause by clause, in his conscientious way, what this agreement would mean. Even as he had the standard treaty form translated, Lugard admitted to himself that it was " pretty stiff". It asked for the cession of the territory to the Company with full rights of jurisdiction while offering in return a very qualified protection. However, the councillors listened eagerly to each word of the treaty—how much of its meaning, even with the explanations, could they understand?—and agreed that it was all good and Lugard went back to his camp at midnight by the light of the moon well pleased with his night's work. This was peaceful occupation indeed.

Next day, in front of large crowds, the treaty was signed and witnessed. Lugard was much worried by the streams of people of all grades of importance who came to give presents, mainly of food. It was the custom to give in return a present of cloth. Lugard did not want the food. He had a regular system of paying his men in cloth with which they in turn bought their own food. But he could not offend the people who made the gifts, and so his economical soul was anguished at having to watch the drain upon his loads of cloth, every yard of which he might need in the difficult journey, the length and duration of which he could not yet foresee, which lay before him.

The caravan got away from Kishi on the morning of October 15th, having first been warned that the Borgu were already planning to attack. On the credit side, however, Lugard received useful letters of introduction sent to Kishi for his use by the important Emir of Ilorin and addressed to Kishi, Kiama and Nikki, while a very welcome guide from Bussa arrived to offer his services. The art of writing had been introduced as a result of Muslim penetration from the north, and letters were objects of great value as passports. There were generally one or two Muslims, Hausa traders, or wandering scribes or mullahs, who could interpret them to illiterate pagan chiefs. The Ilorin letters were to prove of great value to Lugard.

The caravan now set out to cross the frontier into the dreaded Borgu. Everything possible had been said about its people to make Lugard's flesh creep. The first Borgu town they must approach, Lugard learned, was called Kiama. It was a very agreeable disappointment when, instead of a rain of arrows, they were met in the track by a messenger, mounted and grandly dressed, bringing a welcome from the king. Then the king himself, gorgeously and voluminously robed and accompanied by two naked young women, one of whom carried his sword, came out to meet the strangers. Lugard, astonished at this unexpected reception, and alert for treachery, looked hard at the man's face. He was middle-aged, with fine clear-cut features and a fearless bearing. Lugard camped a little way off the town, forcing his men for the first time to camp together within a stockade of branches. The king sent him at once exceptionally good presents of food. There followed a private message asking Lugard if he would meet the king secretly in the night near a stream, bringing only one attendant. Lugard might justly have hesitated. The almost suspiciously friendly welcome from the first ruler to be encountered in the dreaded Borgu would easily be explained if it were leading up to a trap. But there had been something about this king of Kiama which made Lugard, whose life had often to depend upon his quick judgment of men, decide to trust him. He therefore sent back a message to say that he would keep the appointment. If the invitation had been a test it must have satisfied the king: he now said that he would come himself to Lugard's camp that night. " So I received him there. He was *most* friendly. Said that now he had seen me he was my lifelong friend . . . . and I was as safe here in his country as in my own—as for him he would

507

like even to sleep in my tent to show his confidence in me. I replied
that we dealt as men with men, he feared not to come alone to my
camp at night, nor I to go into his town unarmed by night to see him;
therefore I believed that we should not deceive each other, for that
was the resource of thieves, and men who feared to meet each other
openly; he would find the British staunch to the word &c., &c. All
this and more had an obvious effect." (Diary, 18 October 1894).
Most valuable of all, the king gave his version of the political structure
of Borgu.

> " The king said his main object in coming was to ask my destination
> and purpose of travel. He was afraid he could not allow me to go beyond
> Nikki (if such was my purpose), as the country was most dangerous, in
> fact he had come to warn me that the Nikki people were very bad and in
> especial very treacherous. His elder brother was King of Nikki, and he
> was in a sense under Nikki, but paid no tribute to him, in fact was
> independent. He said Bussa (the eldest of the three and looked up to by
> all), Kiama and Nikki were all independent kings, and the only kings of
> Borgu. Seven days beyond Nikki the Borgu country ended. There was,
> he said, in especial, a man whom he named (on the way to Nikki) who
> was evilly disposed, and he feared would make trouble."
>
> (Diary, 18 October 1894).

Lugard learned that while the rulers and the older men were
peaceable, the young "princes" and their bands of followers were
fierce and uncontrollable.

Lugard did not actually raise the question of a treaty at this interview,
but he prepared the way. He was indeed a little puzzled as to what
inducement he could offer in return. This king was in no need of protection; as a Borgu potentate he was feared by all and nothing but a
very large present, which Lugard could not give, or the promise of a
subsidy which he had not been empowered to make, would be an
adequate return for the cession of sovereignty.

The interview had, however, been such a success as almost to bear
out the truth of Kipling's bold, romantic and almost contemporary
assertion :

> " *But there is neither East nor West, Border nor Breed nor Birth,*
> " *When two strong men stand face to face, tho' they come from the ends*
> *of the earth.*"

" We parted in great good fellowship. Learning that I am by profession a soldier, and by practice (for 17 years) a hunter, he was delighted. I like the manly tone and bearing of this king—he has good features— a thin, hard, wiry-looking man."   (Diary, 18 October 1894).

Apart from his relations with the king, things were not happy in the British camp. Mottram was down with fever; the Nupe porters were forever quarrelling with everyone else; the cloth was running away all too rapidly in presents, while Lugard himself was suffering from a most painful cyst on his mouth which he cauterized ruthlessly, and which—this was " a purgatory "—denied him his beloved pipe. He also had opthalmia which tormented him the whole of the trek and made his night work by lamp or candle over maps and the writing up of records and diaries a most painful effort, though one he never allowed himself to neglect.

Next day, " doing the peacock in my scarlet coat," Lugard visited the king, and found him in state, sitting under a large spreading tree in the middle of the village, upon a dais draped with cloths. On this he sat " and his naked girls cuddled close up to him and fanned him and peeped shyly at us." Lugard was relieved to find here " no pressing crowd tumbling over each other and every now and then driven back with sticks (as at Kishi), but a small, quiet and *very* orderly few, mostly apparently people of standing. These Borgu are not at all inquisitive, less so than any Africans I have met." (Diary, 19 October 1894). The king returned the visit later in the day, accompanied by trumpeters who, as Lugard had already observed at Bussa, blew deafening peals through trumpets six feet long right into the king's ears.

At night Lugard, accompanied by only one interpreter, went secretly to the king's house. Only one or two confidential councillors were present. " Quick work for Africa—three visits in one day instead of in 3 weeks." As before he (the king) " expressed his joy and delight at the visit of Europeans to Kiama. It would be recorded in the history of his country that it was when he was king that this great and long-wished-for event had taken place. Now we were one—and intimate friends, and he wished me well, &c., &c., and he then went on to question me about my going to Nikki, and to caution me against ' trouble '. He said that the Borgu people were extremely treacherous, that on no account must I allow them in my camp, or consent to meetings by night like this, alone and unarmed . . . . The

more I see of this man the more I like him." (Diary, 19 October 1894).
Certainly in the history of African exploration, there can have been
few such meetings as this, in which a chief even warned a stranger
against the character of his own people.

Lugard raised the question of the treaty and the king accepted all
its clauses except, as he had his own flag, the flying of the Company
flag. Three days later, on October 22nd, the treaty was signed by the
king, his sister, and all the senior chiefs. Lugard made ready in the usual
storms of rain to set forward. He sent back to Jebba, in charge of a
strong party, his reports, and copies of his two treaties. A rich present,
mainly of red and yellow plush, worth £20, was sent to the king.
The king gave another proof of his sincerity by producing six men who
had been sent from Jebba to catch up with Lugard bringing him
loads and mails. These had been plundered, stripped and tied up by
the king's men. The king had recovered all their loads and now
returned them to Lugard.

Just as he was preparing to leave, the king sent for him again.

" I went, and after very many strong expressions of friendship he told
me he had got certain news that a man named Bekin Yaki of the village
of Basoro (of whom he had spoken to me before) who was his enemy
and raided his country, had determined to attack us in force and loot
our caravan. He said his numbers would be about 400 with 60 horsemen, and if his ' War-Captain ' was there, there might be more. Either
they would lie in ambush in a very thick place, or the crossing of a river
or a swamp (and he told me the exact places), or else they would attack
by night. They were armed with spears, and mostly with bows and
poisoned arrows. This news was absolutely reliable, he said, and I have
found him so extremely friendly, and so quiet and self-possessed, that I
believed it as implicitly as if told me by a European. He is moreover a
warrior himself, I am told, who leads his men in war in person, so I did
not regard him as easily scared, and likely to repeat idle reports. He told
me in a quiet and dignified way, and said that any harm which happened
to me was the same as if it had happened to him; he had told me the news,
now I must decide. If I was strong enough to fight these people he and
everyone would rejoice if I defeated them—if not I had better turn back,
and he would help me in every way to reach Jebba safely."

(Diary, 24 October 1894).

Lugard felt keenly the responsibility of the decision he had to make.
His knowledge of bush fighting and his vivid imagination showed him

the exact picture of his 300 unarmed, dispersed porters being attacked in dense bush by showers of poisoned arrows, the uselessness of his forty almost untrained, so-called soldiers attempting to defend such a long line and probably unable even to see the enemy. He had come to the conclusion that since the country of the Borgu people was flat and did not seem very defensible, their strength lay largely in their use of poisoned arrows, the secret of the poisons and still more of the antidotes being jealously guarded; in their habit, unusual in Africa, of attacking by night; and also in the reputed strength of their witchcraft by which they could demoralize their foes. Dismally Lugard reviewed his own forces. He had still failed to reduce his horde of porters and soldiers to the discipline and handiness he desired; he found them almost useless at building bridges or stockades, and as his sentries went to sleep at night, he had to be constantly on patrol or at least on the alert himself. A night attack upon his camp would be almost as deadly as an ambush by day.

The decision, however, was to go forward. His two young Englishmen were prepared to go on with him; to go back was to abandon their whole purpose. The king sent him an excellent letter to the king of Nikki and, in a final act of generosity, presented him with a first-class horse, a valuable gift in these parts. As he marched on he began to impose a firmer discipline upon his men. The Company officers, in his view, had allowed a number of slack and over-indulgent traditions to grow up in their trekking routine and it was the more difficult for him to enforce his own high standards upon men accustomed to easier ways. Before leaving, he began by threatening to flog the men who had not used the cloth allocated to them to pay their debts in Kiama and who now cheerfully announced that he would pay up for them. The debts were promptly paid! Next he ordered thirty lashes for a Nupe porter who had shed his load. This was the first punishment of its kind. " Much as I abhor flogging," Lugard commented, " if it has to be done I mean it to be in earnest—thirty lashes laid on so that each one leaves its mark for a week or more."

It is easy for the critic, remote from the period and the conditions of such an enterprise, to condemn this form of discipline. But finding himself again outside all law, Lugard had to face the need for sanctions. It must be repeated that there can be no understanding of the work and character of a man like Lugard unless the severity which he was ready to show to himself and to others in order to carry out his difficult purposes is appreciated. The lives of all these men depended upon the discipline they kept. To lose loads was to lose the power to obtain food and that might mean starvation. To wrong the peoples through whose lands they were passing would do more than destroy the British reputation for justice and fair dealing; it would give them enemies and a bad name that might well lead to their own immediate destruction. When Lugard had done all that reason and positive leadership could do there were no other effective sanctions left to him but to cut a man's rations or to flog him. We have considered this before, but it is naturally a recurring theme. From what we know of the records of other caravans in Africa in this century, it is certain that, in comparison with Lugard, few white men got them through to their destinations with less harshness to their own men and less injury to the peoples along the track.

The long file of porters and soldiers was now entering upon the most dangerous stage of their journey. Lugard was beginning, more-over, to be anxious about the time factor. What if Decoeur had also braved the rains? He had maddening visions of his rival reaching Nikki just ahead of him. The delays he met wore down his patience. Between Kiama and Nikki a small chief held him up demanding a leisurely exchange of civilities and grumbling at the size of his presents. But worse followed. He was met by a messenger from Nikki to say that the pagan medicine men had told the king that if he looked upon a white man he would be dead in three months: the stranger was there-fore forbidden to come to Nikki. Lugard made a bold psychological gamble. He affected not to be at all put out by the prohibition. Nikki was not the only place in Africa and if he did not get a message by the day after tomorrow he would march in another direction and the loss would be Nikki's. He guessed that this might change the king's attitude, especially as there would most probably be a party which wanted the novelty, the presents and the prestige which would accompany the first visit from a white man.

Lugard passed, however, a very uncomfortable three days waiting for the upshot of his gambler's throw. The whole success of his mission depended upon it. On November 2nd a messenger came back from the king to say that he would allow the strangers to come. The messenger, it is interesting to note, took the most elaborate precautions against witchcraft, even spitting into a bamboo container round his neck, lest he should leave behind part of his own essence through which power over him might be exercised.

While waiting to set out for Nikki, Lugard enjoyed the first hour of complete rest which he had taken since the expedition started. It was, however, rest of his own kind. He lay on his camp-bed and read all the newspapers which had caught him up in the recovered loads at Kiama. Here he read news of Nyasaland and confided to his diary a long criticism of the policy followed by Sir Harry Johnston and endorsed by the Foreign Office in subsidizing the Arab slavers Jumbe and his old enemy, Mlozi. He indulged in a burst of cynicism. " The good old coach of Foreign Administration will lumber along, and its representatives in Parliament will continue to shew great emotion over questions re the slave-trade, and to demonstrate that never was a government which did so much to repress it—and will vote the whole thing a ridiculous ' Fad ' in private, and in Africa lives will be sacrificed, and by neglect of the ' stitch in time ' much money will have to be expended till Mlozi and Co. and Jumbe and Co. are finally ' dealt with '—and British methods are British methods, and he is an infidel or a lunatic who would think of disputing that in all circumstances and under all conditions they are the very best imaginable—and if inaugurated by the F.O.—they come little short of a Divine sanction." (Diary, 3 November 1894). Time was to prove him only too right. We have already seen that before long Johnston had to storm Mlozi's fortress and hang Lugard's old enemy, loaded with his multitudinous murders, in the presence of the long-oppressed Nkonde.[1]

But the realities of the west soon recalled Lugard from speculations about the east of Africa. On November 4th the caravan started on the last stage to Nikki. All three white men were knocked up, Lugard himself being ill with fever. But " 10 grains antipyrine and 13 miles marching in a blazing sun, in a perfect bath of perspiration, put me right." Mottram's dog was a bag of bones—his own had died of heat-apoplexy on the first day's march; of the thirty-four donkeys which left Jebba only fourteen were alive and they were manifestly dying; the horses—which he never rode himself—were emaciated and covered with sores. The soldiers and the porters, however—and this was the best testimonial to Lugard's leadership—were all in good health.

[1] Johnston, *British Central Africa*, p. 139 ff.

On November 5th the caravan, having so far seen no sign of the expected enemy, marched right up to the walls of Nikki. There were no signs of the French. At this crisis of the enterprise, while waiting for the king's first move, Lugard characteristically sat down to bring all his records up to date—first the map, then the log-book, then his elaborate analysis which he called " the present state " of the caravan, with the records of all the men, the stocks of cloth, of barter goods and treaty presents and cowries (the little shells which were used as a currency in the region), upon which the analysis was based. With these records, kept by himself, he would be able to account for every man, every item of goods and every cowrie he had taken from Jebba.

As the hours went by it became clear that Nikki was not going to be an easy proposition. When Lugard sent messengers the reply was that the king would not even see them until he had first received a present. This Lugard refused; he was not a trader; the king had invited him to come; he did not mean to stay long and would doubtless, if all went well, give a present before he left. Meanwhile his men found that they were unable to buy any food with their cloth. Lugard learned that the king was very old and blind and that the real power at court was the Muslim missionary, the *liman*. While he noted down these points in his diary he little guessed how each item would for four years be the subject of solemn and protracted exchanges between the diplomats and newspapers of London and Paris. Finally, the *liman*, a garrulous and shrewd old man, was induced to come secretly to the camp at night. He said that the people fully believed the prophecy and were determined not to lose their king as a result of his seeing a white man. The *liman* asked the very natural question: " If, after I have persuaded the king to see you, the sick old man should die in the course of three months, what would happen to me?" Lugard applied the same question to himself. Doubtless the people of Borgu would rise and kill them all; hence the sooner he got away from Nikki the better. But not without his treaty.

By November 8th Lugard's position was getting serious. It was the custom in this region for a king to give official welcome and recognition to strangers by sending them " the king's water " and food. The king of Kiama, for example, had sent forty women with huge water pots to supply the camp. But, as the king still neglected to do this, the people in their turn refused to sell food to the camp. Moreover, a long-standing issue between Lugard and his men flared up at this time of tension. On top of all the other problems Lugard had to calculate the changing rate of the cowrie currency in goods; he had also to note the variations in the amount of food which a given measurement of cloth could buy. Naturally, as the travellers moved further away from the trade-routes, cloth went up in value until it might possibly buy four times as much as it could near Jebba. Lugard therefore cut down proportionately the issue of cloth to the men. They objected, asserting that the custom was to give the same measure throughout. Had Lugard done this he would have run out of cloth before the expedition got home. As if these were not problems enough, some of his men began to steal from the local people. When one of them was caught red-handed, Lugard had him publicly flogged and sent a crier round the camp to publicize the warning.

It may have been this which at last touched the king, for he sent a message to say that this news had come to him and that " he was astonished and said that it was indeed true that Europeans were quite different in their methods from other people and it was wrong of him to [keep] such people waiting." (Dairy, 8 November 1894). He therefore sent the water and a present of food—a very poor one—with it, while crowds of acquisitive " princes " and courtiers came with derisory gifts of food for which, to the distress of the thrifty Lugard, they had to be compensated with gifts of cloth which would not be beneath their rank.

The next day, November 9th, Lugard, as was his custom, went through the proposed treaty, clause by clause, with the *liman*, to whom he had given a handsome present, and with two councillors who, after long discussion with the king, had been selected to represent him. The words were translated into the Hausa and the Borgu languages, and the *liman* kept " saying ' Keoh ' (good, excellent) with the air of a man calling for three cheers." Thus, with apparent ease, with an air almost of anti-climax, the famous treaty was obtained. This document was to be one of international controversy and for that reason, and as an example of the paper instrument by which much of Nigeria was brought under British rule, it may be interesting to give its more important clauses.

" TREATY made on the 10th day of November, 1894, between the King of Nikki,

(which is the Capital of Borgu) on the one hand, and the Royal Niger Company, Chartered and Limited, for themselves and their assigns, for ever, herein-after called ' the Company,' on the other hand.

1. I, Lafia [also called Absalamu, son of Waru Kura], King of Nikki and of all Borgu country, with the view of bettering the condition of my country and people, hereby give to the Company and their assigns, for ever, full criminal and civil jurisdiction of every kind over all foreigners to my country, ...

2. I bind myself not to have any intercourse, as representing my tribe or State, on tribal or State affairs with any foreigner or foreign Government other than the Company, but this provision shall not be interpreted as authorising any monopoly of trade, direct or indirect, by the Company or others, ...

3. I recognize that the Company, as a Government, represents Her Majesty the Queen of Great Britain and Ireland, and I accept the protection of the British flag, but I understand that such protection against the attacks of neighbouring aggressive tribes can only be afforded as far as practicable."

[Clause 4 gave sole mining rights to the Company and in Clause 5 the Company promised to respect native laws and customs, consistently with order and good government.]

6. " As a pledge of their good faith, the Company have this day paid the said Lafia, King of Nikki, a donation, receipt of which is hereby acknowledged.

This Treaty having been interpreted to us (the representatives deputed to act for him by the above-mentioned Lafia, King of Nikki and of Borgu), we hereby approve and accept it for the King and for his successors for ever.

[Signature of Native Ruler.]
[Arabic signatures.]

Attestation:
Witnesses to all signatures:
    (Signed) T. A. Reynolds.
              Guy N. Mottram.

I, Captain F. D. Lugard, for and on behalf of the Company, do hereby approve and accept the above Treaty, and hereby affix my hand.
(Signed) F. D. Lugard, Captain,
           Commanding Borgu Expedition."

[Then the African interpreter made his testimony.]

" I certify and solemnly declare that I was sent to the King Lafia by Captain Lugard to carry to him a present from the Company, and that at that interview, in accordance with my instructions, I asked the King myself, in the presence of various Chiefs and people, whether he had himself deputed the Liman and Sirkin Powa and Naimin to act for him in the matter of this Treaty, and that he thrice declared to me that he had done so.

(Signed) J. F. Joseph.

Witnesses:
(Signed)   T. A. Reynolds.
             Guy N. Mottram.

Declaration by Interpreter.

I, J. F. Joseph, native of Sierra Leone, do hereby solemnly declare that I am well acquainted with the Hausa language and that on the 10th day of November 1894 I truly and faithfully explained the above Treaty to the representatives deputed by the said Lafia, and that they understand its meaning.

Signature or mark of Interpreter:
(Signed) J. F. Joseph.

Witnesses to the above Interpreter's mark or signature:
(Signed)   T. A. Reynolds.
             Guy N. Mottram.

Done in triplicate at Nikki, Borgu, this 10th day of November 1894.

The King, being blind, and also having a superstitious dread of personally meeting any European, has deputed the Liman and the Sirkin Powa to be his representatives and proxy, and to sign the Treaty on his behalf. In the presence of these and other important men the Treaty has been translated, word by word, and fully explained in Hausa—many understanding that language—and translated again, sentence by sentence, into Borgu dialect.

(Signed) F. D. Lugard, Captain,
Commanding Borgu Expedition."[1]

We should note here that the form Lugard used for this treaty was headed " (FORM NO. 12.) (FOR MOSLEMS.)"

On November 10th this treaty was formally signed and presents were sent to the king and the *liman*. The following day Lugard sent

[1] The treaty is in C.O. 96/282.

the interpreter Joseph to make sure that the king fully understood what had been signed by his representatives.

" Joseph took the present to the king, and I instructed him to ask the king if he had in reality deputed the 3 men to act for him in the matter of the treaty. The king, who is old and blind, was behind a screen. He was very cordial, and said that never before had Europeans entered Borgu. Now he thanked God that it was in his lifetime they had first come, and even if he died tomorrow that fact and honor would remain. Now we had made a treaty of friendship, and from North to South and East to West, whichever direction we wished to go in at any time, the country was open to us and we were welcome. Guides and envoys would be provided, both to precede us and to go with us, and make us welcome everywhere. I sincerely and most earnestly hope after the treaties that I have made, which are *thorough* and not a farce—that the Company will never 'swap' or abandon Borgu to France but get it included in the British Empire eventually."   (Diary, 11 November 1894).

We may naturally ask why, in contrast with Buganda, and some other parts of Africa, these Borgu and Yoruba rulers seemed so anxious to receive and make treaties with men of a race never seen before. The answer is probably that the Niger region was a restless place, with conflicts between its southern, mainly negro, peoples and the Hausa states of the north, between Muslim and pagan, between slave-raiders and the weaker tribes. In 1894 while much would be known in the interior about Europeans, who had so long been visiting the coast, it would be mainly to their credit as traders, rather than to their discredit as conquerors. It was probable that the treaties were assumed to be alliances, to confer prestige, possibly to bring protection and certainly to promise a supply of guns and trade goods.

Thus, neither by coercion nor trickery, but by speed of movement, by open and temperate negotiations, Lugard, the first European to reach Nikki and the heart of Borgu, obtained the treaty. But it is to be remarked, that in all this negotiation, as far as Lugard was concerned, the much-sought, mysterious king had remained invisible. Decoeur reached Nikki sixteen days after Lugard left it.

CHAPTER XXIV

FROM NIKKI TO LONDON

1894-1895 : Aet. 36-37

THE TREATY signed, Lugard had to consider what his next step should be. His instructions, though in very open terms, directed him to go much further west, as far, if he could, as some 600 miles or so west of Jebba. But he found that reports of countries outside Borgu were extremely vague; he therefore decided first to march south, bearing an excellent letter from the king, and preceded by a royal messenger, and to beat the bounds of the state where it bordered upon Dahomey. He first sent back a copy of the treaty to Goldie—one copy was left with the king—by the hands of two Kiama guides who had played an important part in helping him to win the confidence of the Nikki people and who agreed to take mails back to Jebba. He received a very warm message from the king, or at least purporting to come from him through the *liman*, which said that all the people were now glad of his visit and were impressed with the impeccable behaviour of the whole caravan. He left Nikki on November 12th.

The next days were spent observing the trade and production of the country. He found that it was not true that no trade came that way. Kola nuts, slaves, horses, linseed and gunpowder passed through. Lugard again had great difficulty, because of the eager desire for his cloth, in struggling to hurry past "kings" of villages to whom it was a matter of custom and indeed of prestige to keep him waiting about for the exchange of presents and for guides. The "kings", for all their dilatoriness, performed the proper courtesies of the road, but Lugard began to become increasingly uneasy at rumours, confirming the king of Kiama's warnings, that he and his valuable loads were not to be allowed to leave Borgu, and that a large-scale attack was being planned. It appeared that the attackers were likely to be the young war-chiefs and warriors who could not bear to see white strangers, appearing for the first time, cross their country and take out of it that long string of precious bales. It is, of course, possible that the kings themselves were in the plot and that this explained the ease with which they had signed the treaties. This cannot have been true of the king of Kiama, who had so earnestly warned Lugard against the great dangers into which he was heading. The king of Nikki, on the other hand, just before parting, had sent a message begging him not to believe the rumours of an ambush. The behaviour of the kings and people of Borgu, as revealed by Lugard, is very interesting evidence of the politics and psychology of an isolated, pagan people. It is clear that they shared many of the universal values of right and wrong, even when they were unable to live up to their own standards.

On November 16th, Lugard made a long march to a village called Neshi. The sun had been blazing hot, and all the men and Lugard himself came in very done up. Their guide, who seems to have become attached to them, warned them that an attack was really imminent now and that men from a number of towns through which they had passed had collected to make a considerable attacking force. The king of Neshi himself sent a message to say that he had utterly failed to dissuade the leaders of this war-party not to attack. They would do so either in the night or on the road next day. Unfortunately, in their weariness and heat, the men had already scattered to seek shade and the result was a long rambling camp. Lugard issued warnings and instructions, but, as we have seen, he lacked any reliable interme-diaries, sergeants or headmen, between himself and the rank and file. He therefore stayed up himself all night to keep guard and took the precaution of sounding the reveille half an hour before dawn at the first cock-crow. Nothing happened and the caravan started, crossed a stream near by and then began to climb some rising ground beyond it. Suddenly they saw a large crowd of men drawn up near the village, marshalled by some horsemen . . . . " They had chosen an open place the far side of a large tobacco field. Two or three mounted men were marshalling them into order. Tho' there was no earthly doubt in the matter, I was unwilling as I am always to fire the first shot and waited to see. Perhaps it was a pity, for I could I think have dropped one of the horsemen with my own rifle and as it was their bowmen crept up in the long grass on each side and fired many arrows before I was aware and gave the order to fire. The soldiers were a mere excited rabble—they blazed off their guns as fast as they could stick in cartridges, firing from the hip or anywhere—vaguely into the sky. A steady advance was impossible—the shouting, yelling, and firing were deafening. As I advanced the men rushed forward, and the mass of porters huddled up behind the firing line, and would *not* keep back for threats or curses or blows. Joseph, my only medium of communication, was rushing about like a pea in a drum, off his head with excitement." (Diary, 17 November 1894).

At considerable risk to himself Lugard managed to get in front of the wild line of men. They were still firing off as fast as they could without looking what they were firing at. Lugard felt something strike him on the head and concluded he had been grazed by a bullet from one of his own men who were blazing away behind him. Mottram came running up and Lugard asked him to help him to get his men into line, saying that one had hit him in the head already. He tried to take off his helmet to get at the wound, but found it was somehow held back. Mottram told him it was transfixed by an arrow. One of the Hausas came up and tried vainly to wrench it out. Then Lugard's hunter, Mallum Yaki, came up. He was an excellent fellow, very skilled in jungle craft and an expert with the bow and arrow. He managed to get the helmet off and then wrenched, without result, at the arrow. It was firmly fixed in the head. With Lugard sitting in the sandy soil, the hunter dragged him along at the end of the arrow in the attempt to pull it out—the fight meanwhile going on all around them—and it was not until he braced his foot against his master's that he got it out. As there was still a piece of skull attached to it Lugard expected to find it heavily barbed; it was, however, a straight piece of iron which had penetrated the skull three-quarters of an inch. It was poisoned. Mottram produced the stuff, looking like sawdust, which they had been given as an antidote in Kiama, but they could not know if this were the antidote to this particular poison. Lugard ate some of it and the hunter gave him another kind and also chewed up some of it to put into the wound. Another man came up with a piece of root; this also Lugard took and it filled his mouth with a glutinous paste and turned the saliva to jelly.

Lugard, incredible to record, did not hand over the command. He advanced with his men upon the village into which the enemy was now fleeing. The cease-fire was sounded, and leaving a rear-guard kneeling with their rifles ready, Lugard sent the caravan forward. At this moment Bio, the guide, turned up. He was much disturbed to hear the news of Lugard's wound and he produced out of various bags hanging upon his person a number of other remedies. Although half an hour had passed since the arrow struck, Lugard ate these filthy messes, but when Bio started some magical incantations he told him to drop that. Bio then went and dug up still another root, with a very bitter and stringent taste. The native experts told him that if the poison was going to take effect he would begin to feel dizzy at the end of two hours, and that he would not be safe for twenty-four.

There could be no lingering in this hostile country even though they must now march under the heat of a particularly intolerable sun. They marched thirteen miles. Lugard managed to keep going but arrived utterly exhausted and slept like a dead man. He awoke in the morning refreshed and with no ill-effects from his wound, nor from the filthy collection of antidotes which he had consumed. One of these may have saved him, though why they did not at the same time give him abdominal poisoning is not easy to understand.

He recorded in his diary his intense disgust at the useless and panicky behaviour of his soldiers and at his being provided with such a small number of improperly trained men. Forty riflemen were lost when strung along a procession of over 300 porters. Had the attack been at night or from ambush it must have succeeded. The king of Neshi sent to say he was very sorry about the attack. It seems that thirty of the assailants were killed, but this had not damped the determination of the Borgu war-parties and it was reported on all sides that they were determined to get the caravan before it could march out of their range of action.

By November 23rd Lugard was nearing the important town of Ilesha, which was subject to Nikki. It was at this point that he heard the first news of his rival. A French caravan was reported in the neighbourhood of Paraku, due west of Lugard's position, a place where he had indeed meant to go himself. The rumour was that the people there had been subject to Borgu, but that the kingdom of Dahomey, in the French sphere, was now asserting authority over them. This had resulted in heavy fighting in which the Frenchmen were said to have intervened.

Lugard had a difficult time at Ilesha during the last days of November. This was not the fault of the city. Though the king, who was said to be a brother of the ruler of Nikki, would not see him because his suzerain had not done so, he found the authorities very pleased with the treaty he presented to them and ready to sign a declaration that they fully accepted it since they were under Borgu sovereignty and would eat sand if ordered to do so by the king of Nikki. (Diary, 23 November 1894).

The difficulty lay in the problem of the next move. He wanted to obey his orders to go further west. There were, however, a series of obstacles to any advance in this direction. His Hausa and Nupe porters refused to go on the grounds that it meant certain death. " We are but poor unarmed porters ", the men said to him, " working for our daily food, we are no fighting men . . . . it is death to go on." He felt deeply for these weary and dejected men, but he hardened his heart and said that never yet had he been dictated to by those he had been sent to command. Yet he was at that moment a very perplexed commander. Between Ilesha and the sphere of Oyo, the great Yoruba centre to the south, there was certain to be a dangerous section of the route, but to turn back into Borgu might be fatal, since, in addition to the Borgus' determination to rob the caravan, they now had the blood of thirty men to avenge. Lugard's first thought was to let all who wished turn back to find their own way home, but this meant that they would almost certainly be enslaved or murdered before they could reach the Nupe country. Moreover he had not sufficient barter goods to carry him much further west and it was not worth encountering all the dangers and difficulties, which included running into a strong French party, if he could not hope to reach any useful objective. A junction with British forces in the Gold Coast hinterland was quite beyond the resources of his caravan. Perhaps the strongest reason for turning back was that it had been arranged that a party bringing a supply of cloth for currency and other necessaries should come and try to find him near the Yoruba border. This way was thought to be safe for Africans with proper guides and letters but Lugard now realized they were certain to be wiped out by the southern Borgu raiders and he would have their blood on his conscience. He must, therefore, try to meet them. Yet he felt there was something humiliating in turning back with his full task unfinished. He was feeling very ill at this time and the strain of responsibility for the safety of the caravan, in the face of continual warnings of attack, with perpetual night watching because of the complete unreliability of the sentries, wore down even his energy and made him doubtful of his own judgment.

On November 26th a sudden alarm that an attack was coming enabled him to judge the demoralized state of his men, especially the fatalistic resignation to death shown by the porters. After this episode he spent a very bad night. Neither Mottram nor Reynolds could help him to make the decision. "I spent a horrible night of doubt—reasons for going back and for going forward seemed so evenly balanced. Shall I be ashamed to add in my private diary that I *earnestly* sought assistance in my dilemma from a Higher Source?" (Diary, 26 November 1894).

In the morning his mind was made up. He would abandon the journey further west. First he led the caravan back on the dreaded road to Paraku, where it was certain that the bands were ready in ambush. Then suddenly whispering to a guide whom he trusted the word "Saki", the name of an important Yoruba town to the south, he swung the whole caravan on a circuit through thick grass—and African grass in the rains can hide men of six foot or more—until they gained the Saki track. The king of Ilesha's grandson, who was acting as a guide, naively admitted that his own men were among the waiting band, and that they were now completely "sold". Lugard's stratagem must have duped his enemies for they ran into no hostilities and as they approached Saki they were met by messages of welcome from the king, who was astonished that they had come through alive. This Yoruba ruler sent them pigs and obligingly added bundles of firewood with which to roast them. Lugard had their throats cut at once to stop them squealing, and the whole party settled down to a good feast and to the first night of untroubled sleep for many days.

They were now marching into the real Yoruba country through that part which lay between the southern region already annexed by the British to the Lagos Protectorate and the borders of Borgu. Lugard was greatly impressed by the standard of culture in Saki contrasted with that of Borgu. It was shown in the ceremoniousness of their reception, the prevalence of clothes, the trading activity and the richness of the presents sent to him. The king even had a broad road cleared the whole two miles from his house to the camp, so that Lugard should not " tread on dirt." Saki appeared to be an independent town, though it owed the general Yoruba allegiance towards the superiority of Oyo. After several days of discussion with the king, on December 1st a treaty was signed with Saki. Lugard was rather uncertain as to whether the British government in Lagos would not consider that he was treading on their preserve even though they had still failed to reach so far north.

Lugard discovered that the men of Saki lived in perpetual fear of Borgu. He had indeed been a little premature in thinking he was now clear from danger from this state. The king of Saki told him that the Borgus raided all round their town and that Lugard was not safe even in his present camp two miles outside the walls. This was a nasty shock and Lugard felt it all the more as he was again feeling very ill. Mottram, too, was ill and the chief interpreter, on whom so much depended, now undermined Lugard's whole position as he had often done before, by being drunk and incapable. Entries in Lugard's diary show how hardly even his iron will and physical constitution were strained. " It was not till late I got the first burst of fever over, and I had a weary night. It is mere purgatory to be down with bad fever when you are in a tight place and all depends on yourself. Then things begin to look hopelessly bad, and in one's fever nightmare one dreams and fancies all kinds of disasters; and the long hours seem to move up, as though each minute were an hour, and one gets nervous and at last by the mere strain on the nerves one begins to fancy every noise in the night to be the premonitory sounds of an attack! and one wonders how on earth one will see it thro' when one's head is bursting and one's strength all gone. Fever is bad anyway—but when things are awkward it is mere hell. All today I kept off a relapse by piling on waterproof sheets and blankets, and closing my tent tho' the temperature must be close on 100° or more at midday. The idea did occur to me too, of course I am giving the King [of Saki] time to collect all his strength, and if he *should* mean treachery it would be bad for us." (Diary, 3 December 1894).

He had the greater cause to fear treachery as news had come that an agent of the Lagos government, one Captain Bower, had just come up north into the region of Oyo. As this and the neighbouring cities were still independent both of Lagos and of the Niger Company, there was much speculation and uneasiness about this rumour. The idea seemed to have got about that this white man from the south meant to bring war to the large Muslim Yoruba city of Ilorin. This fear and suspicion might find easy vent in an attack upon Lugard as a vulnerable white man who might be in league with the other. Moreover, as a servant of the Company, he had his own reasons for being disturbed by the news. Where would the border run between Lagos and the Company's sphere? Was Lagos trying to " jump " the Company's rights and future claims in this still unoccupied region? The relations of the imperial officials of Lagos and those of the mainly commercial Company were not very cordial and the future of the city of Ilorin and of the whole borderland between their spheres, bound by its Muslim faith to the northern states, rather than to the rest of pagan Yorubaland, had for long been in dispute.[1] It was therefore with some perturbation that Lugard contemplated the possibility of crossing the road of this Captain Bower. Yet he felt that as the only representative of the Company in the region it was his duty to attempt a meeting and, if necessary, defend his employers' interests.

The king of Saki, far from taking any advantage of Lugard's position, begged him to go on to Oyo to report upon his journey to the pagan Yoruba potentate there, the Alafin. Lugard, in view of the danger from Borgu raiders even in that part of the route, hesitated to go in a defined direction known in advance to his possible enemies. The king of Saki, however, offered him a large escort for his protection and soon after he had started there came up an imposing array, led by the chief minister, of some 500 Yoruba warriors. They were armed with guns and many of them were riding upon horses with high built saddles. They were dressed in flowing garments, festooned with chains, and they were enlivened on their way by a band of drums, whistles and pipes. In this dressy Yoruba country, Lugard felt the incongruity of the respect paid by these impressive delegations to his small, ragged, unimportant-looking self. He was indeed nicknamed in these parts, " the man with his sleeves rolled up " as it was in this guise that he marched. The escort showed him where only last year the Borgu raiders, who were even now camped beside the route waiting to pounce, had attacked a European and seized all his goods, while he, wounded by a poisoned arrow, escaped only to die of its effects. Lugard was deeply appreciative of the generous and active help of the

1 See map on p. 474.

king of Saki in sending this large escort and it was therefore especially unfortunate that one of his men should have chosen to run away with the chief minister's wife. There was no defence and Lugard had him publicly flogged in front of the Saki escort.

On December 8th Lugard, moving south into greener, more hilly country, where the oil-palm began to abound, reached another important Yoruba town, Iseyhin, with its walls of fifteen miles' circumference, and a population reckoned at 60,000. Here too, he had a courtly and hospitable reception and met the first fringe of advancing European influence in the person of some native Methodist missionaries who, in this half-pagan, half-Muslim town, were pioneers in teaching Christianity.

Three days later he entered the venerated Yoruba town of Oyo and as he marched in he saw a white woman, the first he had seen since he left the Canary Islands, watching from a doorway. She was the wife of a pioneer Wesleyan missionary. Lugard learned, with little satisfaction in view of his past and present adventures, that French Roman Catholic Fathers were also at work. Putting on his scarlet coat, white trousers and sword, and taking an escort of twenty soldiers with fixed bayonets, he set out to call upon the semi-sacred Alafin of Oyo. Here he saw a sight almost identical with that presented to the writer when, following Lugard's route in this region nearly forty years later, the successor of this same ruler was visited.

" The King, seated under a kind of straw dome which formed part of the verandah, was got up in the height of his magnificence, but in the dark background it was hard to gauge all the splendour of his presence and belongings—we could only distinguish outlines of gold and velvet and plush draperies, and a hatting which was unique. Its gold and parti-coloured fringes drooped over the royal countenance and hid its lustre from the vulgar gaze. Grouped around the royal presence were masses of people arranged like a Whitechapel group on Margate sands waiting to be photographed, and in front of the King, sitting alone and bolt upright like a Hindu idol was—I presume—a princess of the blood royal! In front of all this pomp and glitter of savage king-dom a scarlet cloth was laid and between it and the presence were men bearing gigantic umbrellas of crimson and plush, and velvet with fringed and tasselled edges—the things being some 8 ft. across and 8 ft. high. Around the large open space was a dense mass of humanity. All the sightseers who had been gazing open-mouthed at us outside had now flocked in thro' the big gate. They formed a dense ring of very orderly folk and 7 umbrella bearers stood on each side. I came forward and was asked to stop just short of the scarlet cloth—my chair was placed and a man with umbrella summoned to shield me from the sun." (Diary, 11 December 1894).

The Alafin complimented his visitor upon safely traversing Oyo and expressed his sincere thanks that he had warned the Borgu rulers against continuing their turbulent conduct to the injury of peace and trade. He then asked for his help in negotiating with Captain Bower, whose demarcation of the frontier between Ilorin and Ibadan, the great Yoruba city with which the Alafin was beginning a long and vexatious rivalry, was not accepted by either Ilorin or Oyo. It seemed that Bower had the reputation of being a hasty man and his anger was feared. This and much more Oyo gossip Lugard learned from the French Fathers with whom he dined, a somewhat embarrassing experience as he had to talk of his affairs without revealing exactly where he had been and what he had been doing, lest Goldie should first learn of it from a telegram in a Paris newspaper.

On December 16th, as he left Oyo, he met Bower riding towards him. He found him at first a little high-handed, claiming that Kishi and Saki, the towns with which Lugard had made treaties " belong to us." Lugard also noted with shocked surprise, but also with a little justifiable complacency, that Bower made no attempt to impose Lugard's standard of discipline upon his men, leaving them to get provisions as best they could from the local people with resulting irregularities that were a bad example for his own men. He also considered that he showed rather less than proper civility to the courtly Yoruba representatives with whom he had to deal.

For what little remained of the year 1894 Lugard and Bower went about the country lying along the Ilorin-Ibadan border endeavouring to trace between the two groups a fair boundary which would also demarcate the Protectorate and Company spheres. Lugard came in the end to like and respect his companion, an officer who impressed himself deeply upon the Yoruba and whose name is still well remembered there. He had, however, to hear from Bower some very severe criticism of the Company, which he had not yet the knowledge to dispute. Bower said that the Company did not fulfil its obligations to

Sir James Willcocks
From his book *From Kabul to Kumassi*, 1904

govern the regions it claimed and that unsatisfied litigants found themselves obliged to appeal to the Lagos officials who in turn had to send them on to Lokoja upon a fruitless search for justice.

On Christmas Day Bower insisted upon Lugard coming to his camp for dinner. Lugard realized that this would be the first time he had left his men for a night, and he was most reluctant to do so. When he came back to them in the morning they turned out to welcome him and said that they had felt like orphans while he was away, but now they would sleep soundly again. He was surprised and touched by this demonstration.

" I am a bit foolish on this point, I daresay. I live with my men and *never* leave them. I never leave camp even for an hour—on the march I walk with them, in camp I am never away for five minutes even to collect insects etc., as I am always *intending*! .... They are queer devils—they *fear* me, I know, and I am equally sure that they like me, for I don't think I am ever hard on a man without good cause." (Diary, 25 December 1894).

Early in January, having made their demarcation and completed the maps, Bower and Lugard parted company, and Lugard marched north to Jebba. On the course of this return journey, circling east and north, Lugard visited a number of Yoruba towns, Ikirun, Illa, Awton and others, and was everywhere impressed by the high standard of civilization and the courteous reception given him at each place. On his way up through the edge of the Nupe country he heard much of the slave-raiding by the Muslim rulers of the emirate of Nupe among the neighbouring Kabba and Yagba pagan tribes and how the attempt of the latter to pay their customary tribute in produce, instead of in children, had led to cruel reprisals. Lugard was much troubled, as this was happening in Niger Company territory and he held that the Company should either govern or clear out. He does not seem to have known that Goldie was already planning an expedition that should put an end to the great " slave-sweeps " carried out annually by the Emirs of Bida and Ilorin in this region.

The river opposite Jebba was reached on January 13th. Here he learned that, because of the Nupe " war ", his supply party had never been sent. He could not, therefore, have gone on, without immense delay, on his western march. This helped to salve his unhappy conscience. His caravan had marched 700 miles in 107 days, many of which had not, because of the many difficulties and delays, been marching days. Both the young men, Mottram and Reynolds, arrived in very bad condition, riding the two remaining horses, but Lugard, in spite of all his strain, fever and eye trouble, not to speak of the poison and its antidotes, marched in on his feet, weary but in excellent form. After paying off his men and, despite his choleric references in his diary, parting from many of them with great regret, he checked off the stores, and embarked on a river steamer. After calling at Lokoja, he had time to write full and very frank reports on his expedition for the Company which he handed in at the river-mouth station at Akassa.

Although he did not know it he was by no means out of danger. Finding Akassa hot and feverish, and having received a cable telling him to await orders, he decided to do the waiting in a healthier spot. He therefore left Akassa and went back up-river to Lokoja on January 26th. The very next night a number of canoes left Brass, carrying the native traders who resented the Company's interference with their traditional system of trade, and at dawn on January 29th they attacked and destroyed the Company station at Akassa and massacred or captured all who were there. The Acting Agent-General and the dozen or so white men who were with him just managed to escape. The event was made peculiarly horrible in that the Brass chiefs, sophisticated traders though they were, captured and later mutilated and butchered in cold blood their forty-three African captives and had a great feast upon their bodies, an end which might have been Lugard's if he had not chanced to leave the day before. Even a young man educated at a college in England was seen by a Roman Catholic priest jumping around naked and painted white with pieces of human flesh hanging to him. Only a few Christian chiefs with their followers refused to join the party. Lugard volunteered his services as a soldier, but they were not accepted and he confessed to his brother that he felt little enthusiasm for the beastly job of fighting with cannibals in the mud and mangrove swamps of the delta. After waiting for some two months at Lokoja, he received the order to return home. He left the Niger early in April and arrived in Liverpool on May 9th having been away for nine months.

CHAPTER XXV

DIPLOMACY AND DISAPPOINTMENT

1895-1896 : Aet. 37-38

LUGARD RETURNED to London to find how inappropriate was the metaphor of a steeplechase which the French had applied to the rivalry over Borgu: a game of chess would be more appropriate. In this game he had been no more than the most advanced pawn, and he now had to find out how the nations at play had been disposing of the rest of the board. The hostility between the contestants had increased, though it must be remembered that as the always " rising indignation " of their people was one of the main diplomatic weapons which ministers flourished against each other, this ever mounting indignation was not always quite what it was reported to be in the dispatches. Drawing back, as often happened, upon the edge of conflict, Lord Kimberley and the French Foreign Minister, M. Hanotaux,[1] had agreed, even before Lugard left England, to " enter into a general review of all pending African questions."[2] But this did not stop either power from pressing on in the field, since every position gained, even if it could not be held, was valuable for bargaining.

The employment of Lugard was, for Paris, one of the most exacerbating items in the controversy. His alleged crimes in East Africa had not yet been atoned before he appeared on the other side of Africa to injure France on the Niger. It is interesting to observe that though the officials of the Foreign Office would not employ Lugard themselves because of the provocation to France, they were content to allow the Company, for the acts of which its Charter made them ultimately responsible, to engage him. Such were the fine shades of responsibility

1 Hanotaux, Albert-Auguste-Gabrielle, 1853–1944; 1879 Secretary in Ministry of Foreign Affairs; 1886 elected Deputy; 1894–8 Minister of Foreign Affairs, except for one short break, May–June 1895; 1921 delegate to League of Nations Assembly.
2 Dufferin to Hanotaux, 6 June 1894, *D.D.F.* XI. p. 204; and Hanotaux to Dufferin, 9 June 1894, *D.D.F.* XI. p. 207.

in which foreign ministers dealt! Early in September, Phipps,[1] who was the British expert on African affairs at the Paris embassy, was told to inform Hanotaux that Britain would only continue negotiations if assured that French officers would not be allowed to make any treaties in Borgu. Sir Percy Anderson, like a farmer waiting to see if he should call his dog off an intending trespasser, minuted on this that " the Niger Company have Lugard at Akassa ready, but if satisfactory assurances were given would stop him. There is, however, no time to be lost."[2] It was then too late. The French competitor was already well on the way.

Attempts to call off the race had therefore failed and all that remained was for both sides to await the emergence of their champions from the dangerous silence of Borgu. In France there was acrid comment upon the name of the British agent. " As for the English," ran an article in *Débats*, " it was learned the day before yesterday that Captain Lugard, the conqueror of Uganda, engaged in the service of the Niger Company, has left Bussa . . . . and, at the head of an exceptionally strong mission, is advancing to the West . . . . With the known character of Captain Lugard, it can be foreseen how he will fulfil his mission."[3] The choice of Lugard, said the same paper ironically, a few days later, seemed only *médiocrement heureux* considering the acts committed by him in Uganda which were still a cause of litigation between the two nations.[4] His famous Maxim made a provocative reappearance in the French press. And *Le Temps* insisted that the Company was really acting for the Foreign Office, and that Lugard was " above all, an English officer."[5]

Lugard, as we have seen, had got first to Nikki but, as had happened in Uganda, because of the shorter communications the other side got its news, that of the French treaty, to Europe first. This was in mid-December. At once the claim was made that all Borgu was now under French protection.[6] In sending their news from Borgu the

---

1 Phipps, (later Sir) Edmund Constantine Henry, G.C.M.G., C.B., 1840–1911; 1858 entered Diplomatic Service; 1881 Consul-General at Budapest; 1890 First Secretary at Paris; 1893 Minister Plenipotentiary at Paris; 1893 British delegate on West Africa Commission; 1894 Minister Plenipotentiary at Brazil; 1900 Minister at Brussels.

2 Minute by Anderson on draft dispatch, Kimberley to Phipps, 3 September 1894, F.O. 27/3183.

3 *Débats*, 8 October 1894.

4 *Ibid.* 14 October 1894.

5 *Le Temps*, 14 October 1894.

6 *Ibid.* 16 December 1894.

French officers, or at least those who relayed their report, made no reference at all to Lugard's prior arrival though it was, of course, known to them. The British ambassador was at once instructed to inform the French government that Borgu was in the Niger Company's sphere.[1]

When Lugard, emerging into the edge of the known world, sent news of his treaty, Goldie, always brief and apt, telegraphed " Bravo, Lugard." This comforted Lugard's distress at having turned back. Goldie sent the news to the Foreign Office on January 25th.[2] The French at once met it with the retort that Lugard's claim was a lie, that he had run away from Nikki upon hearing of the approach of the French and, according to the king himself, had never seen that potentate or obtained any treaty.[3] Goldie wrote to *The Times* on March 1st to assert that Lugard's treaty, the text of which had now arrived, was in proper form.[4] The controversy in the press continued, with the French elaborating their case against Lugard. They were not content with a verbal campaign. They followed it up with action. As against Lugard's single, numerically weak mission, representative of a Company which could not afford expensive expeditions to ward off foreign powers, the French at this time sent in no less than five officially-supported and strongly-manned military missions, though, with one of the devices common during the scramble, they often turned, on diplomatic notepaper, into purely private or scientific and exploratory expeditions.

Lugard sent to his brother from Akassa his own account of the controversy as far as he then knew it:

" Moreover the French have made a treaty with Borgu, 16 days later than mine, and say they have a declaration from the King that he had made no prior treaty, so Goldie wants me home to confute them. The French papers were in such a pother about the " Race for Borgu " and, thinking themselves certain to win, shoved it down everyone's throat that Nikki was the one and only capital of Borgu and whoever got there first took the cake. Then (as they had counted on for certain) they got news that Decoeur had waltzed in. Now they are rabid because the infamous adventurer, Capt. Lugard, claims to have won. It's very funny, and the way they blackguard me is absurd. I will send you a few cuttings presently. Of course Nikki made a treaty and swore anything they wanted

1 Dufferin to Dupuy, 1 January 1895, *D.D.F.* XI. p. 509.
2 Goldie to F.O., 25 January 1985, F.O. 27/3256.
3 *Politique Coloniale*, 31 January 1895; *Le Temps*, 30 January 1895.
4 *The Times*, 2 March 1895.

in the face of an expedition of 300 or more soldiers armed with magazine rifles, followed by a second, presumably also of great strength. I believe the idea is that I had not as yet succeeded in making a treaty when I heard of the French coming and bolted incontinently . . . . The French were clean mad at my going to make a treaty, ... and they contemplated that Monteil, who has an army to fight Samory and Co., would come for me and wipe me out . . . . *P.S.* I see the French had *five* expeditions in the countries I was to traverse!! Monteil has a large *army*,—Decoeur a very powerful expedition. Alby 5 officers and 300 men with repeaters. (4) Capt. Toutée I don't know [his] strength. (5) Lt. Baud.—A pretty warm quarter for me! " (L. to E. J. L. 23 March 1895).

Later, when he heard that the French papers spoke of it as " a veritable steeplechase," he found another reason for rejecting the description. " But then, the French have such imaginations! Had the editor changed places for a day with Mr. Mottram and the donkeys, he would have modified his metaphors."[1]

It may be recorded in passing that Monteil's expedition had come to grief. He had never started for the Nile. He had been badly wounded in fighting Samory's men north-west of Borgu in February 1895.[2] He had fallen back and returned incapacitated from further adventures, and the subject of some criticism at home from the fickle public who goaded on their pioneering champions. But he was still generous enough to feel a friendly interest in his rival: the two corresponded, Monteil sent him his book and they met to exchange experiences. Lugard never crossed the path of the German expedition which, under Dr. Grüner, struck out well to the west and north of Lugard's route, cutting in to make a treaty with the Hausa state of Gandu. This achievement delighted the German press and the *Kölnische Zeitung* of October 3rd claimed that this was a journey as clever as Carl Peters' dash to Uganda, and hoped it would prove a more successful weapon against " our colonial hereditary enemy, England." Grüner, who appears to have almost equalled Peters in brutality, returned home to the kind of reception that was now a ritual in all three countries for such travellers, and to make his offering to his nation of treaties, lectures and maps.[3]

1 F. Lugard, ' An Expedition to Borgu, on the Niger ', *The Geographical Journal*, vol. VI, September 1895, p. 205.
2 H. Labouret, *Monteil* (Paris 1937), p. 237 ff.
3 Sir Edward Malet (British ambassador at Berlin) to Salisbury, 3 October 1895, F.O. 64/1358.

Part of the French expedition, after leaving Nikki, moved north up to Say, then came down the Niger and again overlaid Lugard's work by making their own treaty with Bussa. Another expedition under Captain Toutée not only went right across Dahomey but reached the Niger, and early in 1895 actually built a port there only a few miles north of Jebba. This was called Arenberg after the prince who was a leading political opponent of Britain's claims. This last defiance especially disturbed the Foreign Office. It was known that Hanotaux had opposed it and it seemed to prove that the extreme colonial party had gained the upper hand.[1] They were certainly very active in a full dress three-day debate at the beginning of March, when the fear was expressed that in spite of all their large expeditions, Britain, having at her disposal Captain Lugard, " one of the leading men in their African colonies," would still beat them in the Niger bend. The Prince d'Arenberg, though in private frankly appreciative of British colonial methods, demanded an assertive and forceful policy, and there was much bitter self-criticism on the grounds of ministerial instability, feeble commerce and feeble colonization by comparison with Britain, who was at once envied, hated and admired.[2]

Goldie, in his exposed position as head of the Company, had to take the brunt of the onslaught and ward it off the government. Not only had the Brass men destroyed his Company headquarters but the event was being used as an occasion to attack the Company in parliament, on the grounds that its monopoly was not only injurious to British merchants but also oppressive to Africans,[3] while a strong Aborigines Protection Society delegation carried similar complaints to Lord Kimberley.[4] Goldie pointed out to the Foreign Office that he could hardly be expected to deal with all his enemies, French, Hausa and 1,600 Brass men armed with rifles, on the limited revenue he was allowed to levy.[5] He stood by the Lugard treaty, and he sent a copy of it with extracts from Lugard's report to the Foreign Office.[6]

The government, still very far from being ready to spend any public money upon the Company's sphere or to send troops, tried to secure

---

1 Minute by Sir C. Hill, 24 November 1894, on Dufferin to Kimberley, 23 November 1894, F.O. 27/3187.
2 J. O. (Ch.), 28 February–4 March 1895, pp. 589–724.
3 See for example *Parliamentary Debates*, 26 February 1895, IV. 30. 1571.
4 Copy of memorandum, 22 March 1895, L.P.
5 Goldie to Kimberley, 4 March 1895, F.O. 83/1375.
6 Royal Niger Co. to F.O., 5 March 1895, F.O. 27/3257.

Lugard's gains and to fend off French expeditions by the weapons of diplomacy. Lord Kimberley called on M. Courcel, the French ambassador,[1] who had been appointed as likely to conciliate the British, and both he and Sir Edward Grey spoke very gravely of the report of French activities in Borgu. This was British territory and the government meant to stand by the Company.[2] At the same time, in the House of Commons, when Grey made his famous statement that, if the reported French expedition should enter the Nile valley it would be viewed as " an unfriendly act ", he went on to speak very seriously of the activity of the French expeditions into the Niger territory. These were to be regarded as being not only of local importance but from " the much more serious point of view of their effect on the relations of two great European Powers."[3] Courcel was firm in the face of this strong attack. He defended France's right to send expeditions into territories which were not effectively occupied—and here the Company was vulnerable—and he went on to reproach the two British Ministers because their information as to what had happened on the Niger came only from the reports " . . . . d'une société ambitieuse, qui emploie à son service le trop célèbre capitaine Lugard."[4]

On May 11th the French ambassador reported to Hanotaux that this same celebrated captain had arrived back in England on the previous day and he sent various newspaper cuttings on the event. Interviewed on arrival at Liverpool, Lugard appears to have begun with a very correct protestation of reticence which he then went on to break. He gave his own account of the " steeplechase " and remarked that as Decoeur's expedition had been large and well armed, the king of Nikki had not improbably considered it judicious to go through the form of signing a treaty.[5] The *Pall Mall Gazette* which held no brief for the Company, protested that ministers and not " claim-jumpers " should decide the issue and the familiar formula appeared that British patience " has its limits, and that they have been nearly reached."[6]

1 De Courcel, Baron Alphonse Chodron, 1835–1919; 1881–6 Ambassador in Berlin; 1894–8 Ambassador in London.
2 Courcel to Hanotaux, 28 March 1895, *D.D.F.* XI. p. 629.
3 *Parliamentary Debates*, 28 March 1895, IV. 32. 405–6. For an interesting comment on this see Langer, *Diplomacy of Imperialism*, p. 265; Taylor, ' Prelude to Fashoda ', *English Historical Review*, vol. LXV, 1950, pp. 76–7.
4 Courcel to Hanotaux, 2 April 1895, *D.D.F.* XI. p. 650.
5 *The Times*, 10 May 1895.
6 *Pall Mall Gazette*, 10 May 1895.

Diplomacy and Disappointment

Lugard was now able to take a part in the European side of the controversy. But, while he was advancing his education as a student of international relations, he can have had but a very limited idea of the extent and intricacy of the work of diplomacy perpetually being woven between the main chancelleries of Europe, and in which the Niger issue was but one single recurring thread. It would be beyond the proper limits of our subject to unravel this web, though much of it can be sorted out in the archives now open to students. In these we can see how Germany was perpetually playing off France and Britain; how restless France was in her Russian alliance and how, in spite of flirtations with Germany, the memory of 1870 and the loss of Alsace-Lorraine prevented any real reconciliation between these two old enemies. France was thus, in spite of her enmity with Britain over Egypt, Siam, the Niger and many other questions, generally unwilling to go too far in antagonism to Britain. Her ministers therefore played a dangerous game of unleashing the ready hostility of the colonial interests and the energies of colonial agents abroad, while trying, as diplomatic occasion demanded, to bring them to heel.

It is interesting, in view of his then imminent appointment as Colonial Secretary, to see how Chamberlain reacted to Lugard's expositions of these West African events. " The intervention of the French, especially on the Niger," he wrote to Lugard, " seems matter for grave anxiety. If they do not take care they will some day go too far and find themselves forced to retreat or to go to war. I am convinced they do not mean the latter, but they have a way of bluffing which is very dangerous and which may easily lead to serious trouble." (Chamberlain to L. 1 June 1895).

The European nations at this time were not unlike a lot of greedy, quarrelsome children in a school playground; none quite big enough to dominate all the others, kicking and then making up to each other, sulking, coaxing, telling each other secrets and then " splitting ", combining for a moment and then breaking up. Britain was the rather aloof child in the corner, a little superior, unwilling to join whole-heartedly in the rough games and yet warily watching lest too many of these quarrelling schoolmates should suddenly combine against her.[1]

[1] See J. D. Hargreaves, ' Entente Manquée, Anglo-French Relations, 1895–96 ', *Cambridge Historical Journal*, vol. XI, 1953; A. J. P. Taylor, ' Les Premières Années de l'Alliance Franco-Russe, 1892–5 ', *Revue Historique*, t. CCIV, July-September 1950; also his ' Prelude to Fashoda: the Question of the Upper Nile, 1894–5 ', *English Historical Review*, vol. LXV, 1950.

To Lugard, of course, the core of the whole international issue was the validity of his treaty. And this did, indeed, play no small part in the diplomatic negotiations of 1894 to 1896, as it was being debated privately in the chancelleries and stridently in the press. The French, as Lugard pointed out in letters to *The Times*,[1] shifted their ground. They first claimed, as we saw, that Lugard had never got to Nikki at all. Then the returning Decoeur honestly admitted that this was untrue. As for the second line, that the treaty was made with the religious head without the knowledge of the king, Lugard showed that this was wholly impossible at an African "court" where all the inhabitants, and even neighbouring chiefs, knew everything that was going on. The French officer, Alby, was sent back to Nikki to get a certificate from the king to support the French argument. Lugard's comment on this was that the French had forces sufficient to intimidate an African chief into doing whatever was asked of him, whereas he himself had gone with a small force, in a pacific and reasonable manner.

The controversy continued all the summer and autumn of 1895 after his return with Salisbury taking over the cudgels from Rosebery in June. The French certainly had a case. It was not only that Lugard had, in fact, never seen the king. There was also the fact, for which he was not responsible, that he had been able to do no more than reach Nikki and hurry away, leaving Borgu once more entirely empty of any Englishman. The French, on the contrary, had sent several agents back and forth and their Captain Toutée was at this time calmly building himself into a fort right on the Niger and south of Bussa. As Sir Percy Anderson admitted in the secrecy of a Foreign Office minute, it was " impossible not to be struck with the admirable way in which these numerous French expeditions are conducted by capable officers. On our side we oppose to them our one negro, Ferguson " (he referred here to a remarkable coloured agent who was trying to maintain the Gold Coast hinterland) " . . . . and Lugard's journey. It is not surprising that the French claim to have more interest in the ' boucle du Niger ' than we have."[2] Moreover, he was personally a little dubious about the British case over the Say-Barruwa line, in view of the clause about commissioners arbitrating the frontier near the Niger

[1] *The Times*, 22 and 31 August 1895.
[2] Minute by Anderson, 18 September 1895, on Dufferin to Salisbury, 14 September 1895, F.O. 27/3232.

to the south. But this only made Lugard's achievement the more valuable. " . . . . our right to Western Borgu [is] dependent on Lugard's recent hardly-won and disputed treaty."[1]

Salisbury agreed with his officials that the British government would stand fast by Lugard's treaty. Lord Dufferin and M. Hanotaux politely exchanged their copies of the two Nikki treaties, each claiming the other's was worthless.[2] With Goldie threatening to attack Toutée on the Borgu reach of the Niger, the Foreign Office, after months of protest, at last got the intruding Frenchman recalled and he left, publicizing the absence of any single Company representative in the whole region. The French also hit back by supporting the claim of Germany to Gandu, as being independent of Sokoto.

It was indeed a bad time for Goldie. His sphere was harassed by the French and Germans on the west, and by the raiding Rabeh on the north-east. The Liverpool merchants were agitating about Lugard's treaties with the Yoruba towns lest they should go under his Company with its hated monopoly, instead of under the Lagos government. His credit at the Foreign Office had suffered from the revelations of Captain Toutée. And now Kirk, who had been appointed to report upon the Brass raid, had sent an advance report to Salisbury, in which he justified the grievance of the Brassmen against the Company, though not of course their horrible revenge.[3] Goldie's problem was the same as Mackinnon's, the need to thrust out and occupy expensively vast areas of land for political reasons when the commercial interests of the Company demanded a slow, cautious advance from the coastal bases of trade. The difference was, of course, that the Niger Company really had a flourishing trade but, almost equally important, it had Goldie. This can be appreciated from the unpublished records which show how Goldie, simply by being efficient, fearless and quick to act, frequently imposed his will upon a hesitant government. It can also be read in the fighting speech directed against all his enemies and critics, which he made to his shareholders in the summer of 1895. This was also the public occasion he used to compliment Lugard in the warmest terms upon an achievement in which, Goldie said, he had " fully sustained his previous high reputation which is

[1] Memorandum by Sir Percy Anderson on the International Situation East and West of the Niger, 31 August 1895, F.O.C.P. 6783: Niger Territories, No. 65.
[2] Hanotaux to Dufferin, 18 July 1895, D.D.F. XII. p. 122.
[3] Kirk to Salisbury, 25 August 1895, F.O. 83/1382.

too widely known to justify our attempting to do more than allude to it."[1]

If the antagonism of two nations which might end in war, and the destiny of many Africans, had not been bound up with this event, in the scramble for Africa, it would have had as its main theme an element of the ridiculous, as it certainly had of the undignified. Sir Percy Anderson's minutes show that he felt this. And his chief, Kimberley, assured Courcel that the French already possessed the most valuable parts of Africa and the rest was not worth bothering about.[2] Even the combative *Politique Coloniale* had its moment of doubt about this flag and treaty game. " Shall the rights of these great powers be determined merely by the speed shown by explorers who carry the flags of each country? And what, in any case, is the value of these scraps of paper which are triumphantly brought back by all the travellers who take the trouble to ask for them? .... Lugard, Decoeur, Alby, Ballot— all have such papers! "[3] This was a view of the event which Lugard could hardly be expected to take. No man could force his way through the unknown of such a country as Borgu unless he were buoyed up by a sense of the nobility and high importance of his mission.

Lugard was not to see the end of the Borgu controversy before he again left England for Africa. When ministers on both sides saw that the question was pushing them to the edge of a breach, they drew back a little. Lord Dufferin felt he would like to get Anglo-French relations upon a better footing before he left Paris, and Hanotaux who, for all his deep interest in the colonial question, seems to have tried, if not always with success, to keep a steadying hand upon his more intemperate compatriots, was ready to respond. It was time for sanity. Courcel, from London, wrote that a settlement was more possible now than it had been in 1894 when " opinion had become infatuated through the polemics of the press, pursued with increasing intemperance and excitement on both sides. The public had come to believe that France and England .... were advancing to an inevitable rupture. Even the official world had allowed itself to be won over by this spirit. ... The English," Courcel continued, " with that

1 Proceedings at the fifteenth ordinary general meeting of the Royal Niger Company, 19 July 1895. L.P.
2 Courcel to Hanotaux, 10 January 1895, A.A.E. vol. 900, f. 68.
3 *Politique Coloniale*, 3 September 1895.

practical spirit which characterizes them when they are not carried away by their pride " recognized that France did not want war. Now the time seemed to have come when the governments really wanted to solve the outstanding questions. The problem of the Niger bend would sort itself out, and it would not be prudent for France to insist upon the matter of compensation for Lugard's action in Uganda " outre mésure ou intemperativement."[1] As a result of this *détente* the African question was, before the end of the year, again confided to the Niger Commission, a body of British and French experts set up in 1890, following the Convention of that year, and which had met intermittently since that date.

We must turn now to look more closely at Lugard and consider his activities with regard to Borgu and other matters during his period in England. He had, of course with Goldie's approval, played a very active part in the verbal struggle that had followed his physical struggle on the Niger. In addition to letters to *The Times*, he wrote articles for monthlies which were illustrated with instructive maps; he addressed the usual important bodies; he wrote endless letters and interviewed all the most effective officials and politicians. The close friendship and harmony of ideas which he developed with Goldie meant that it was easy for him to get his permission to speak and to write.

Lugard pursued all these activities in no very optimistic mood either about his own prospects or about the success of his mission. He had met enough letters and newspapers even on his way home to convince him of this. From the Canaries he communicated his gloom to his brother.

" I see little prospect of my getting anything whatever in Africa—even if the Conservatives come in. I can't go abegging to Ld. Salisbury—and he is a curt despotic man who would not wish it. Meanwhile there is no doubt that I have got the permanent officials (who are *all-powerful*) against me. It is wholly my own fault, if you like to phrase it so—I cannot expect them to like me after what I wrote in my book and in monthly magazines &c. At best they might give me a small Consulate in some out of the way post . . . . I think that this last business of mine—though I have scored off the French very handsomely—has done me no good for that very reason. The French are *mad* with me,

[1] Courcel to Hanotaux, 29 September 1895, A.A.E. vol. 907, f. 234.

and almost each day in *The Times* there is some by no means flattering reference to me from Paris. This will of course form an excellent reason for the Govt. to declare it impossible to give me any African appointment. Even Chamberlain agreed to that. To give me anything is to insult France! and as we love to eat dirt, it is not likely they would do that to oblige *me*! " (L. to E. J. L. 1 May 1895).

Lugard had learned as soon as he landed that Kirk had been given the commission to inquire into the Brass raid upon Akassa, and was to sail the very next day, so " I bolted to Sevenoaks and talked half the night to him." Goldie afterwards reproached him for this; he did not think that Lugard understood the situation on the lower Niger. The result, so Goldie believed, was that Kirk, who had promised to keep an open mind, set out with one coloured by Lugard's erroneous views and so failed to appreciate the case for the Company.[1]

Goldie, however, was a man of too powerful and detached a mind to allow this or other points upon which he disagreed with Lugard to affect his warm appreciation of the man who from being the Company's agent became, during this leave, his close personal friend. Lugard told his brother that Goldie was enthusiastic about the Borgu mission and had been using all his influence with the Foreign Office to get him the appointment in East Africa upon which his heart was set. But he failed. Lord Rosebery, in spite of his appreciative knowledge of Lugard, was, it appeared, determined not to employ him. He had more than one reason for this, but the most important was that he was objectionable to the French.

" Really," Lugard exclaimed to his brother, " the French excuse is *too* paltry for a nation like England—independently of oneself, it makes one quite indignant that the British Government should plead such a miserable, cowardly excuse, while the French simply deify anyone who insults us or aggresses in British territory." (3 June 1895).

Meanwhile, without taking a day for relaxation, Lugard once more threw the same passion of energy into each twelve hours of his London days as he had in the wilds of Borgu or Uganda. He joined with a doctor, one Crosse, in rooms at 63, Jermyn Street, " *perfect* diggings, we own a sitting-room—*such* a pretty one." He had met this man on

---

[1] See *Report by Sir John Kirk on disturbances at Brass*. Africa No. 3 (1896), C.7977.

the Niger and developed a rapid intimacy with him, talking philosophy far into the night, as they steamed up the great river. The relationship had, indeed, led him to wonder how women were willing to allow such a man to remain unmarried and he reflected sadly that it was the showy, dominating males who succeeded in attracting women and often the quiet, sterling men who would have made women much happier never found the opportunity to win themselves wives.

It is interesting to look out for a moment from our preoccupation with the single West African theme, one among the crowded events of 1895, and consider to what sort of London Lugard had returned after his harassing disappearance into the bush and rocks of Borgu.

The May in which he landed was leading on towards the blazing summer of this year and to a London season crowded with political and social events and starred with famous personalities. There was tension with France, tension in South Africa, but as yet no full realization of danger. The Queen's reign was rising towards the climax of the 1897 Jubilee. In Westminster the political tournament was between the two brilliant peers, Rosebery and Salisbury, each supported by an able group of proved or rising supporters. It was the London of gaslight and hansom cabs in which Sherlock Holmes was conducting his investigations. On the bookstalls the *Yellow Book* and the green *Westminster Gazette* had just begun to appear, while among the new novels lay *The Amazing Marriage*, Kipling's second *Jungle Book*, and a rather startling scientific story, called *The Time Machine*, by a new writer. On the stage the abundant productivity of Gilbert and Sullivan had just run down but London society could see itself in the gilded parodies of Oscar Wilde, whose scandalous fall in the height of his fame was the sensation of the year.

Lugard cared for few of these things. To study his activities upon this leave is to observe again the combination of a man of action in the strongest sense with the persistent, voluminous writer and industrious student. He had a rare, and to ordinary mortals, an alarming power of concentration. Men who can work half the night as well as during the day and who never need an interval of relaxation have a great advantage over their fellows, though the erratic genius may, with some justification, cling to his belief that their work will never attain to the heights which he can reach in occasional inspired bursts of activity. An overmastering interest is a quick teacher and he soon learned that Britain was beginning to turn towards an assertive imperialism, but was not yet quite convinced about it and, even where convinced, was far from being instructed. The Uganda retention campaign had been, for him, much more than the Nyasaland question, an exciting adventure in democracy and he continued to speak over the heads of politicians and officials to a public which at this time was eager to hear about the new Africa, both the west and east of which he could now describe.

The writings listed which are below[1] reveal where Lugard believed Britain's imperial interests and duties lay in 1895 and how he thought he could best commend them to those influential thousands who then read *The Times* and the monthlies, and who crowded to attend meetings at the Royal Colonial Institute and the Royal Geographical Society.

Several dominant ideas can be distinguished in what he wrote and said.

There was an urgent call for British expansion and assertion in Africa, in the interests of trade. He drew vivid pictures of the vast reaches of the continent which he had travelled. He enlarged upon the crops which could be found ready for marketing or which could be

---

[1] It is interesting, as an indication of the extent and character of Lugard's industry, insofar as it was expressed in print, to enumerate the pieces of writing that can be traced to his pen during the nine months that he spent in England.

(1) 'British West African Possessions', *Blackwoods Magazine*, vol. CLVII, June 1895.
(2) 'England and France on the Niger, The Race for Borgu', *The Nineteenth Century*, vol. XXXVII, June 1895.
(3) 'British East Africa and Zanzibar' (3,600 words), a letter to *The Times*, 13 June 1895.
(4) 'An Expedition to Borgu, on the Niger', *The Geographical Journal*, vol. VI, September 1895 (paper read on 1 July 1895).
(5) 'England and France in the Nile Valley', *National Review*, vol. XXV, July 1895.
(6) 'Routes in Africa', *National Review*, vol. XXV, August 1895.
(7) 'The Borgu Treaties', a letter to *The Times*, 22 August 1895. (This gave extracts from the treaties and correspondence with native chiefs). A further letter on this subject followed on August 31.
(8) 'New British Markets, Tropical Africa', *The Nineteenth Century*, vol. XXXVIII, September 1895.
(9) 'A Journey in West Africa and some points of contrast with East Africa', *Scottish Geographical Magazine*, vol. XI, December 1895.
(10) 'The Extension of British Influence (and Trade) in Africa', *Journal of the Royal Colonial Institute*, vol. XXVII, December 1895 (paper read November 12).
(11) 'The Massacre by the Masai', a letter to *The Times*, 30 December 1895.
(12) 'Slavery under the British Flag', *The Nineteenth Century*, vol. XXXIX, February 1896.
(13) 'Slatin Pasha and the Sudan', *National Review*, vol. XXVII, April 1896.

Those who wish to look up some of these articles will probably find those numbered 4 and 10 in this list the most important and interesting.

developed and the minerals, proved or possible, that might be worked. He warned the British that their whole economy was in danger; that the world had not followed their easy-going free-trade system but was hemming them in with aggressive tariffs and that they must open up new markets and new sources of raw material or face a decline of wealth. This last was a theme which Chamberlain, the new Colonial Secretary, could expound from the metropolitan viewpoint, but Lugard could paint in the colonial side of the picture in freshly mixed colours which the politician could not match. He had, moreover, as he did not hesitate to point out, developed this argument before Chamberlain made his famous House of Commons speech about investment in " the undeveloped estates."[1] Lugard regretted unashamedly that Britain had not occupied more of the lands to which she could have made some claim and he rang the alarm bell vigorously about the threat from France. From the dramatic conflict of claims in the bend of the Niger, in which he had been the protagonist, he again drew public attention to the other side of Africa, to the designs of France against the vital region of the Upper Nile, with their danger to Britain's position in Uganda and in Egypt.

His second theme was the need for effective administration and development. Occupation must not be on the map only. Here he could give substance and particularity to the words which others were beginning to use in a general sense: he could explain exactly how the capital Chamberlain demanded should be spent, and where railways should run; what administration meant in terms of men and money; how and how soon local taxation could begin to meet the cost of government, and many other matters of sober fact by which he made the rather heady, romantic revelation of Africa a subject for serious men.

What of the moral theme, and the interests of the peoples? We have seen already over the Uganda controversy that the scruples of Gladstone and Harcourt had little or no meaning for Lugard. He had not changed since then. To him the question as to whether the Africans had the same interest in being annexed as Britain had in annexing them could not be seriously formulated. It was necessary to use many arguments to convince Britain of her interest in annexation, but that of the interests of the African peoples was to him so self-evident that

[1] See p. 544, n. I, no. 8.

it took up few words of the argument. That, after all, was the view of almost every European who had penetrated the continent from the time of Livingstone; the critics of empire at this time, and for long after, were mostly at home. Nor, as Lugard's writings this year insisted, did the alternative for the Africans lie between annexation by Britain and their old freedom, stagnant as it was, but between annexation by Britain or by some other power, and in this issue he saw no room for any argument. There was, however, no taint of hypocrisy in Lugard's advocacy of expansion. As he told a very influential audience at the Royal Colonial Institute:

"It is essential to bear in mind that this annexation of Africa by the white races was no outcome of missionary or philanthropic zeal. It was the natural outflow of the nations of Europe into the waste places of the earth, following the law which has guided and, indeed, formed the history of the earth . . . . In our own case the hostile tariffs imposed by other nations upon our industries, the competition of foreign-made goods, and the depression of trade, have driven us to seek new markets and new fields for our surplus energy. Settlers driven to seek their fortunes in new Colonies, by motives such as these, do not embark for Africa with the primary object of benefiting the natives, but of benefiting themselves . . . ."[1]

Lugard detested hypocrisy and sentimentality and, in spite of his warm admiration for individuals amongst them, he had some prejudice against missionaries, and much more against critical armchair philanthropists. These sentiments may have tempted him sometimes to play down his country's motives to too low a note. His interpretation certainly did not wholly cover his own behaviour. In the next breath with such avowals as these Lugard would break into strong appeals for a vigorous policy in suppressing slavery. The bitterness of his attacks upon the lethargy of the Foreign Office in East Africa, if dictated partly by his longing to take charge of the situation there himself, sprang equally from his loathing of an institution which he, like Livingstone, had seen in its horrifying reality along the Arab slave-routes and the hunting grounds of Nupe. The same passionate hatred for the abuse of the weak was turned upon the liquor traffic of West Africa. Here, too, if the complexity of his motives is to be dissected, his indignation was reinforced by partisanship for his friend,

[1] See p. 544, n. 1, no. 10.

Goldie, who had prohibited the trade from which the neighbouring British governments to the south drew the bulk of their revenues. Again, his sense of justice drew from him a forcible letter to *The Times* defending the Masai, following a report of a so-called massacre of an expedition by them. The letter was a striking example of the value of sympathy combined with knowledge in judging remote colonial events. He showed convincingly that the blame must have rested not on the Masai but on the white men concerned. The letter prompted by his indignation and distress was not likely to promote his fortunes with the Foreign Office.

" The friendship ", he wrote, " which already three years ago had begun to prevail between this brave tribe and the British has led to the hope that their raiding propensities might be suppressed without bloodshed and their indomitable courage and warlike instincts used to advantage in the service of the administration. We have but ourselves to thank if these hopes are now nullified."[1]

It is strange that Lugard, in writing to his brother about his first articles, could claim that they were " moderate." " I've not trod on the F.O. toe much." (3 June 1895). All these articles from first to last were written in the tone of one having authority, and that not only in the description of territories where his evidence was sometimes unique, but in advising upon policy at the highest level of national and international affairs. More than this, he freely criticized the work of the Colonial Office and the Foreign Office, demanded a better allocation of duties between the two departments and asked for a department and a Secretary of State for Africa. He took up this question seriously, pointing out the immense advantages of harmonizing British policy in Africa.[2] He discussed the question with the London Chamber of Commerce. His view was that an influential council on Africa, composed of the leading experts, might induce the government to consider setting up a separate department for Africa. But he was well aware of the difficulties which have continued to stand in the way of such a measure.

With all his practice Lugard had made little progress as an orator. He always remained better in the reading than the hearing. Not that

1 *The Times*, 30 December 1895.
2 See p. 544, n. 1, no. 10.

he attempted brilliance in writing any more than in speaking. It was his character and his special power that he turned away from these arts to base nearly every sentence four-square upon his own experience or upon a principle of action which was itself drawn directly from that experience. The result was a convincing solidity: Lugard had no brilliance as a propagandist but there was a hammering force in much that he said or wrote. He could see so clearly the African territories as they could be, peaceful within settled frontiers, living under a just and ordered administration; exporting their products—and he could already prophesy with some foresight what these would be—along a network of roads and railways and importing British textiles and hardware; freed from slavery, cruelty, raiding and the drink traffic; the virile tribes trained in the arts of peace or, as legions of the new African empire, of war. This was not only the Africa—the British Africa—that could be, but the one he meant *should* be, and that very soon and, moreover, he would have a large hand in making it! These talks and writings were, from first to last, like those of his French opposite number, Lyautey, *paroles d'action*, and of urgent action at that.

There were some other features of Lugard's views at this time which are worth remarking because of their relationship with the opinion of his maturer years. He strongly advocated white settlement in that regrettable, nameless 800 miles of partly empty country which lay between Uganda and the coast, which was one day to be Kenya. He was, however, insistent from the first that the settlers must be of the " right sort ", that is, hardworking farmers, and also that they must be strictly controlled as to their allotment and utilization of land and use of labour. Another point to remark was that, rather surprisingly, his conviction that it was right and proper for Britain to annex as much of Africa as possible was not combined with any complacency about her past or future behaviour in that continent. There was much, as we have seen, that he boldly and strongly criticized. Stranger still, his nationalism was not so blind that he could not, even at this early date, grasp the contribution which internationalism could make to the interests of the African. To him the Berlin and, still more, the Brussels Acts were no mere humanitarian façade for European earth hunger; the Conventions with regard to slavery and the traffic in arms and in drink should, he urged, be strictly honoured and called into play even against Britain where she defaulted. This was to be for him a strong and continuous principle. Another anticipation was his condemnation of British neglect of African languages, especially upon the west coast.[1]

This account by no means covers all Lugard's work during this period in England. Among many other things he drew up, at Chamberlain's request, a full scheme for the administration of East Africa as a single state, dealing at once with principles—he advocated "indirect" methods of rule—and with the smallest facts and figures of staffing and expenditure. He helped the Foreign Office to deal with the delicate matter, the summary execution of the trader Stokes by a Belgian officer, on a charge of supplying arms to the Arabs. He worked with Kirk upon slavery questions, especially in Zanzibar. He followed the development of the Uganda question, instructing members of parliament, as the Liberal government moved, still divided on the question, towards the more positive policy which the facts of East Africa demanded.

It was at this time, in the long drawn-out agony of the Imperial British East Africa Company's demise, that a decisive step was taken. The government, turning a deaf ear to the indignant protests of the Company, which find much place in Kirk's letters to Lugard, bought out its rights and properties for £250,000, a transaction which Anderson himself felt it was a little difficult to justify.[2] As the sultan of Zanzibar had to pay £200,000 of this to buy back his concession to the Company of the ten mile coastal strip, the transaction meant that Britain secured East Africa at the bargain price of £50,000. The Cabinet refused any compensation for the acquisition of Uganda or any consideration of all the political and imperial responsibilities which the Company had been obliged to take at the cost of its commercial interests. It may be asked who *did* pay for the acquisition. The shareholders, whose claim to be predominantly philanthropic had been jeered at as "philanthropy plus five per cent," lost 10/- in the pound on their investment.[3] The lives of many of their officers had been lost. But perhaps, as we have seen, the Africans paid most.

[1] ' The Extension of British Influence (and Trade) in Africa', *Journal of the Royal Colonial Institute*, vol. XXVII, December 1895, p. 27.

[2] Anderson to Rodd, 5 April and 14 July 1893, Rodd Papers.

[3] See *Correspondence respecting the Retirement of the Imperial British East Africa Company*. Africa No. 4 (1895), C.7646; also Annual Reports of the Company for 1893–5, available at the Royal Empire Society; McDermott, *IBEA*, pp. 378–90; and *Parliamentary Debates*, 13 June 1895, IV. 34. 1086–1142.

Cheap occupation, however well intentioned, of primitive lands is always dear in its inevitable inhumanity, and the colony of Kenya, including the Kikuyu, are still paying part of the price. That Uganda, above all Buganda, paid so much less is due partly to its own relatively advanced society and partly to the good work of many men from Mackay onwards, making a list in which Lugard's name must have a high place.

Lugard did not, in order to achieve all this writing, shut himself up in his Jermyn Street lodgings. As upon his last leave he flung himself into the main stream of social life in the capital, but not for social reasons.

"I have been a bit in the 'Vortex' of late . . . . My object is to be in the swim and so meet the men I want to influence. Am working the press a little—also a few M.P.'s—it's all interesting." (L. to E. J. L. 3 June 1895).

The picture of the strong, ascetic, explorer would be more in character if he could be portrayed as scorning the pleasures in which, for his overriding purpose, he chose to join, but in his letters to his brother there is still the ring of genuine pleasure as well as triumph which marked the period of his Uganda campaign.

"Dined to meet 3 Royalties on Friday—a huge party of 26. I had to talk to Princess Christian most of the evening. Also Princess Louise wished me to dine, but I hadn't landed. A dance (!) at Duchess of St. Alban's;—dinners, Lord Camperdowne, Lord Falmouth, Mrs. Chamberlain, etc., etc., and yet I made no calls at all . . . . Spent two 'Saturdays to Mondays' on the best house-boat on the Thames at Henley—had *real* good times. Scenery from paradise, but the society preferable to angels . . . . I am to dine with Seymour Hicks and his wife (that lovely little girl, Ellaline Terriss). The latter is as charming as pretty . . . . they give us a box at the theatre afterwards—they are *the* success of London just now, spite of Equatorial weather you can't get standing room at the theatre."
(L. to E. J. L. 3 June 1895).

On July 2nd, 1895, Lugard was awarded the C.B. Congratulations came in from all sides. In the press they were led by *The Times*. But amongst a wide circle of acquaintances they were coupled with indignation that the honour was inadequate. *The Times* of July 2nd remarked that to see " Captain Lugard's name . . . . among a crowd of C.B.'s was to regret that any rule of progressive advancement should limit the reward of his labours to this modest honour." The *Spectator* of the same week was even more outspoken:

" Colonel Colvile[1] is made K.C.M.G., and Captain Lugard a C.B. As Burke said, ' We live in an inverted order.' No one will grudge Colonel Colvile his honour; but if he who followed in Captain Lugard's footsteps in Uganda deserved a knighthood, what did Captain Lugard deserve? Captain Lugard, however, is one of those men who would probably escape decoration, even if it rained stars and ribbons from Heaven."

Shortly after his arrival Lugard dined with the Prime Minister, Lord Rosebery, who had awarded him this minimum decoration, and this although he had never solicited such entertainment by calling upon him.

" He was excessively affable—said it ' beat ' him to realize I had been in Central Africa and done things since we met last year. I looked as if I'd never stirred out of England. I thanked him for C.B., and he said he had *long* wished to confer it, but knew there would be an outcry in France and so had delayed—now, as he was going out of office, he had no option. Fancy a Prime Minister telling the recipient of a decoration that it had in his own view long been due, but withheld thro' fear of France, isn't it *too* humiliating! Lord Roberts wrote to congratulate me; and Chamberlain at the Levée shook hands heartily and said with special emphasis that he hoped this was the *commencement*."

(L. to E. J. L. 10 July 1895).

He improved his relations with Sir Edward Grey who, after Rosebery, seemed the member of the government most sympathetic towards his views. Grey especially drew upon his views of the Nile question.

" I breakfasted with him and he took me to see him play tennis (you know he is nearly amateur champion)—*not* lawn tennis, and I palled with Lady Grey a good deal. Grey is a *first-rate* fellow, *thoroughly sound* in his views, but hampered of course by his colleagues. All this is very strange and significant when you recall that my *Times* letter on morning of Uganda debate (13th) was a knock-down blow (as everyone said), and its points were hammered into Grey in the debate by Lowther,

1 Colvile, Major-General Sir Henry Edward, K.C.M.G., 1852–1907; 1893–5 served in Egypt and the Sudan, Acting Commissioner, Uganda; 1894 commanded Unyoro Expedition; author of several books, including *The Land of the Nile Springs* (1895).

Balfour and others. Grey explained in confidence why he had not been able to adopt my view. Of course it was *France* again!—but I gave him substantial replies (Kirk's)." (L. to E. J. L. 10 July 1895).

Grey had, indeed, defended Lugard when his name came up, as usual, in the East African debate of June 13th, shortly before the ministry fell.

The record seems to show that, if his official decoration were inadequate, Society, political and non-political, had confirmed the unofficial status of lion which it had given him on his last period in England. He was, however, increasingly impatient to obtain more solid recognition. But he was still a difficult man to employ. He was no neutral or adaptable agent whom any British government could use. He was by now the perfect instrument for a forward policy; the question remained as to whether Britain was quite ready yet to use him. The rather doctrinaire, anti-expansionist principles for which Gladstone and his older colleagues had stood were now ceasing to commend themselves to Britain as they did not seem to fit the more dangerous world which was rapidly taking shape. They were left as the property of a small minority among the Liberals until the new Labour party should take them up. Home, Irish, foreign, and imperial affairs were so closely fused at this time that it is misleading to isolate any one from the other three: all were beginning to conform to a single pattern of British policy, in which the chief aims were strength, unity, assertion and organized development rather than peace, isolation, retrenchment and *laissez-faire*.

There can be no doubt that Lugard did much at this time, when a new national attitude towards colonial expansion was developing, to influence the form it should take towards Africa. He was not, of course, single-handed in this effort. In their different ways, he and Goldie, Kirk, Johnston and Horace Waller; Rhodes and Stanley in their more dramatic fashion; Flora Shaw at her influential, anonymous post on *The Times*, contributed varied but mutually supporting ideas; carried them forward with the public and offered them as material which Rosebery, Salisbury and Chamberlain could use in the construction of policy.

The general election in June which followed the defeat of the unhappy and divided Liberal government showed Britain in more decisive mood. The Conservatives were sent back with a majority which they were to keep for the next ten years. The country was now ready for a very serious stock-taking of assets and liabilities, and among the former the unity of the empire and the strategic and material value of undeveloped or unannexed Africa were seen to be important items. Chamberlain, who had led his liberal-unionists into allegiance with Salisbury, confirmed this view and began a new chapter of imperial history by refusing the Exchequer in favour of the once despised Colonial Office. As he was almost in the position of a co-Prime Minister, his assumption of this office at once gave it the highest importance.

Lugard recognized at once what " Joe's " arrival at the Colonial Office might mean to him. It is difficult, looking back, to realize what a revolution it meant in colonial affairs that the minister in charge should be ready to apply government capital and initiative to colonial expansion. Flora Shaw, who had the entrée to the large room on the first floor with the maps and the globe, was, as *The Times* colonial expert, one of the first to feel the impress of the new minister.

" The change at the Colonial Office was marvellous;" she said, " it was a total transformation; the sleeping city awakened by a touch. Everyone in the department felt it, and presently everyone in the Colonial Service felt it to the furthest corners and the loneliest outposts of the Queen's Dominions."[1]

But Lugard was not to feel it yet. Chamberlain entered his office on July 1st; the election followed at once; by the beginning of August he was surely seated at his new desk, but as the days of the hot summer passed, Lugard's hopes once more began to sicken. The letter he wrote to his brother is worth quoting at some length as it throws interesting light not only upon Lugard's problem but also upon Chamberlain's view of his own position.

" The change came. A gigantic majority for the Unionists, and out of it all Mr. Chamberlain emerged as one of the strongest and most influential men in the country. Now you may know that I have had a great deal to do with him, and perhaps I am not wrong in saying that the very prominent part he has taken in African questions, and the intimate knowledge he has shewn regarding them, is due in a very large measure to myself. I was staying at Highbury at the time of the elections, and he

[1] J. L. Garvin, *The Life of Joseph Chamberlain* (1934), vol. iii, p. 11.

asked me where I would like to go, and what I would do if I were sent there—what scheme I would put forward for the practical working of the thing, &c. At the same time he warned me that he had no power as regards East Africa. It is under the F.O., and no-one except the Foreign Minister and the Prime Minister, could touch it . . . . To be frank my view is that the Foreign Office is a *monument* of incompetency. As Moberley Bell said, there is not a single official in it who is up to the standard of a second-rate or third-rate appointment on *The Times*. The heads of the departments (re Africa at any rate) are men who strike you as being absolute fools, even in the first 5-minutes conversation. The Colonial Office I have always heard is much abler. Consequently as ignorance and ineptitude is invariably accompanied by jealousy and pettiness, you may imagine that any encroachment on their domain by the Col. Office is keenly resented by the F.O. officials. So J.C. is hampered. He dare not even suggest, for to do so is to trespass beyond his own Dept., and already the criticism about him is to the effect that he *will* shove himself where he has no business—so he *has* to be cautious. In effect all he could say was this—a *non possumus*. I know he hated saying it, for I have misread his character wholly if he is not *thorough*, and a man of his word, but I do not see what else he *could* say . . . . My next move is to work the Press a little, so as to bring some pressure to bear on the questions I advocate, and to force the reforms and the scheme I suggest upon Govt. Also I may see Curzon, &c. Goldie is the one man who is desperately strong on my behalf. He wrote privately to Chamberlain urging my claims, and has worked in season and out of season as though his whole interest lay in my advancement and employment. I enclose a letter of his to shew you—I hear from him *daily* in the same sense . . . . I hear rumours that they intend after all to shelve the slavery question.[1] J.C. is firm on this subject. I gave him the cue, and I am now about to prepare a Memo for him on the subject. I shall do it *con amore* . . . . What the spring may produce—goodness knows. I must do something, for I am living at present mainly on savings plus a few occasional dollars for magazine articles . . . . " (L. to E. J. L. 19 August 1895).

Thus, by the late summer, Lugard again found himself obliged to face the fact that he would not be given the government employment he so desperately wanted. For some time Goldie had considered the possibility of sending an expedition to Lake Chad to deal with the militant intruder Rabeh and with the French, who seemed to be threatening to encroach upon his sphere in that region. He would, it

1 That is, the government's delay in abolishing slavery in Zanzibar.

appears, have offered Lugard command of this. But the plan fell through. Other plans were considered but Lugard's determination, shown so strongly in East Africa in his relations with Sir Francis de Winton, never to serve except in sole command, did not make it easy to find him an appointment he would accept. There can be no doubt that he envied " little Johnston " in his governorship of Nyasa-land and Mr. Arthur Hardinge,[1] another Foreign Office man, who had been appointed consul-general at Zanzibar.

At the end of August the War Office—which seems to have been a very long-suffering and indulgent department where Lugard was concerned—asked him when he would return to regimental duty. This sent Lugard to the Foreign Office to interview Sir Percy Anderson, whom he always suspected of being hostile to his employment. To his brother, whom he had been greatly hoping to bring over from India to Africa as his assistant in some post, he wrote as follows:

" He then went on to tell me that there was no prospect of my being employed ' at present,' but held out chances of my getting one of the minor billets in East Africa at present held by clerks or what not taken over from the Company! The Company long ago asked me to go out and be Administrator *over* all of them. Otherwise perhaps some frontier delimitation might be given me as a small job. I said nothing till he got embarrassed . . . . Later I saw Chamberlain; there's no nonsense about *him*. He's as straight as they make 'em. He had deferred a definite talk to me, to see if he could get East Africa under the Colonial Office. Lord Salisbury won't agree at present. So then he spoke straight and told him what he thought of me—and I *know* it was pretty thick. I find he has also been cramming Balfour in the same way, and also Curzon! He managed to get the latter to accept my Memo [i.e. on East Africa] and read it. But such is the jealousy of the Foreign and Colonial Offices, from the highest to the lowest, that he told me frankly if he tried to do more he would only damage my interests! He hinted at my accepting something on West Coast (under him) if it offered, but I don't much jump to that. He told me candidly that Lord Salisbury, for motives of policy quite unconnected with my personality, would not give me *any* administrative appointment in Africa. So *that* bubble is bust . . . . Lord Salisbury is a great Unapproachable—few men have commanded such an awe as he does. He is a veritable Henry VIII and his word is law. He is engrossed with

[1] Hardinge, Sir Arthur Henry, P.C., G.C.M.G., K.C.B., M.A., 1859–1933; 1884 entered diplomatic service; 1894–1900 Consul-General at Zanzibar; 1900–5 Minister at Teheran; 1906–11 at Brussels; 1911–13 at Lisbon; 1913–19 Ambassador at Madrid.

China, Armenia, Siam, and France. After all *the* great and only African power is Percy Anderson—and he, though effusive, is against me, as I have long known, and I am utterly and wholly opposed to him and have fought him over the Slavery question for years. We won on that, but now it is to be shelved. Whereupon I put Chamberlain on to it, and then had an hour's talk with A. J. Balfour, and also with Curzon, and doubtless I shall win (with Kirk), but Anderson will have his revenge. It is *not* the Slavery question in the main however. It is that Anderson dislikes my independence, and fears my press and literary connection . . . . There's a remarkable feeling in my favour in the country and in the Press, and doubtless I could easily bring pressure to bear and get myself ' written up,' but I can't do that, old boy, *even for your sake.*"

(L. to E. J. L. 29 August 1895).

The rebuffs and disappointment did nothing to diminish Lugard's belief in himself. He refused, for example, an offer to command the troops in Uganda; he would not take a military command where he had hoped to be the first governor. He was scornful about the suggestion of a boundary commission in Northern Rhodesia. He did not hesitate to go on putting his problems and ambitions before Chamberlain and it was not until September that a letter from the Colonial Secretary advising him to accept other work finally extinguished his hopes.

Goldie was giving him the same advice. During the summer the correspondence which punctuated the frequent meetings between the two men reflects Goldie's great faith in Lugard.

" I should be a bad imperialist if I did not try to support you to the utmost. I look upon you as a very hardly used man—a victim to the present desire to make things pleasant for France at all costs. This weighed with me when you first came to see me and the conviction has grown with time." (Goldie to L. 12 June 1895).

In August Goldie still had hopes that Lugard would get his heart's desire, and go to East Africa as "the influence of independent men, who have nothing to gain by recommending you, will be on your side." After dealing with some confidential matters of his own, he goes on to reveal his friendship towards Lugard, confessing that he had told him " much that surprises me after our comparatively short friendship, but I have unlimited confidence in your straightness, capacity and friendly feelings to myself. I can number on my fingers—almost on one hand—the number of men whom I really trust after nearly half a century of life—hundreds whose honesty I trust but not their discretion." (Goldie to L. 6 August 1895).

The attention Goldie gave to Lugard's affairs during this summer was the more remarkable in that he was working with hardly time to eat or sleep, as he felt that Kirk's report would rally all the many enemies of the Company, and that his life's work was in danger and with it the interests of his shareholders. He, however, continued to do what he could to press Lugard's chances at the Foreign Office until, on September 2nd, he wrote to say he had come to the conclusion that the government really had no post of a status that Lugard would accept. He therefore advised him, as Chamberlain was doing at the same time, to close with an offer from a wholly unexpected and surprising quarter, that of the newly-formed British West Charterland Company.

PART FIVE

The Kalahari 1895-1897

CHAPTER XXVI

THE PRELIMINARIES

1895-1896 : Aet. 37-38

LUGARD DID not easily bring himself to accept employment by yet another company. He had now led expeditions for three different companies in three widely separated regions of tropical Africa, all of them highly dangerous places, difficult of access and, in greater or less degree, unexplored. Each time, as a spear-point of expansion thrust far beyond the frontiers of the government of his own or any other nation, he had carried the heavy responsibility of being a law to himself. The companies had gambled with their capital but he had had to gamble with life as well as fortune. The stakes had appeared to be high enough to warrant the risk. There were large regions to be gained and fame to be won for the man who helped to gain them. But even if life were not lost on the throw, reputation, or at least career, was always in peril. A false move might involve his company and indeed his nation in grave difficulties or even in war. If the expedition were successful, as far as it lay in his power to make it so, he might yet, by some turn in the diplomatic situation, come back to meet a cool or controversial reception and to find all he had won by endurance and daring in Africa surrendered as a counter in the international game. Yet, much as Lugard longed for the greater dignity and certainty of an official appointment, and continued to the last moment to work for one, there were some attractions in the new proposition.

The British West Charterland Company had been formed by a group of very wealthy city men, some of them British and some foreign. Chief among them were Mr. Julius Pam, Mr. Felix Bruch and Mr. Oakley Maund, an Englishman who was the moving spirit. Their object was to prospect for gold and diamonds in Ngamiland in the Kalahari desert. The Company had a capital of £100,000 in cash and £50,000 reserve shares under option at £2 per share. The project was an exciting speculation. The immense riches discovered in the diamond fields of Kimberley and the gold of the Rand had drawn the attention of European financiers to South Africa. The frontiers of this troubled and complex country were swarming with concessionaires. One of these, named Hicks, and his associate Nicolls, had obtained in 1889 a concession from Moremi, chief of the scanty Tawana tribe, who claimed the great square of semi-desert and swamp of which Lake Ngami was the centre. This concession had been bought from Hicks by Maund and his friends and formed the basis for their British West Charterland Company. If the rich mineral-bearing strata further east should continue into this forbidding and little-known land, as there seemed every possibility they would, then incalculable wealth lay within the grasp of the new Company.

But these potential minerals lay at a great distance from the Company's offices in St. Swithin's Lane, and the way to them was obstructed by a number of natural and political barriers. It was clear that the man who should lead the initial prospecting expedition would need an unusual combination of qualities. First of all he must be able to organize and lead a gruelling trek through the desert. Secondly, in a region where he would be responsible to the Colonial Office and under philanthropic scrutiny from Britain, he must be capable of dealing justly and effectively with Africans and especially with a chief of the power and standing of Khama, chief of the Ngwato tribe, whose domain bordered Ngamiland and who was at odds with Sekgoma, the young chief who had succeeded Moremi. He must bring to a new Company, whose concession was somewhat ill-defined, a personal standing and experience that would enable him to negotiate authoritatively with the Colonial Office at home and with its representatives in South Africa and also, if necessary, hold his own with the British South Africa Company and its Cæsarean master. Furthermore, because the directors had hopes of obtaining a charter to administer the country they wanted to find a man to whom the government would be willing to entrust such a responsibility.

So perfectly did Lugard measure up to these qualifications that the Company directors were willing to go all lengths to secure him. His genuine reluctance to accept only enhanced his value. He was offered a salary of £6,000 a year, an astonishing figure for 1896, and this was to be paid into Consols to await his return. He was to be allowed to nominate his beloved brother as his second-in-command, also at a princely rate. He was to be given an absolutely free hand in running the expedition and in handling the Company's money and was assured of their complete trust. He was to join the board at once, and be its managing director in Africa. Finally—and to him most important of all—he was to be free to resign from the Company's employment immediately if he were offered a government post which he desired to take.

Thus limited and defined, the post had its attractions. Among these an important place must be given to the money. Lugard's youth had been harassed by poverty and his adult life had seen him pass from the almost impossible position of a subaltern with no private means to a seconded officer, living from hand to mouth on intermittent appointments while, as a result, his small prospective army pension of £200 was being cut down by £5 for each year that he continued upon secondment. His father and other members of his family, as we know, needed help which he loved to give; and there was always Celia, whom he could never quite abandon and with whom he was now in correspondence, requiring assistance. Then he had a great longing to buy for himself some dwelling-place, however modest, with a small patch of the earth of his country which, in the way of his wandering kind, he loved all the more because he so often had to leave it. He worked out that by living sparely he could save enough during the expedition if, in spite of his other and higher hopes of government employment, it should last for three years, to invest and provide himself with a yearly income of £650, half of which he would set aside for those dependent upon him. The other half would serve something more than his own material needs. It would—and it is wonderful to recall what could be expected of £325 per annum in 1895—

" render me independent of the army or of other restricting ties when my time here is done. This is a *great* matter, for I would be free to take my own line on Africa, on the slave question etc., careless whether or not I quarrel with my own bread and butter."   (29 November 1895).

There is little sign that he had up till then suffered from any great restraint in expressing his views, but independence was something of which Lugard could never have enough.

His pride remained, however, a little uneasy about the financial aspect of his new employment. He felt he had to justify it to Flora Shaw, whose private opinion he valued and whose public judgment, as *The Times* colonial editor, was of great importance to him. They saw a good deal of each other at this time and it seemed natural for him to write at length justifying himself to her. He told her of the Company's "absurdly liberal offer". As for the gold-mining venture, "it doesn't appeal to me in any way, except, of course, that I am quite poor." All his interest was centred upon the prospect of the Company getting administrative powers. (L. to Flora Shaw, 11 November 1895).

In addition to the solid attraction of the money there was the great joy of helping his brother and sharing the adventure with the one partner he could completely trust. There was the interest of seeing a new part of Africa and of overcoming great and novel difficulties. Finally, though city men were a strange new species to him, he was impressed, even touched, by the generosity and confidence with which he now found himself treated. The directors, he decided, were no mere money-grubbers. Mr. Maund, the prime mover, was a man with wide views who wanted to make the venture " an Imperial success " and wished to take over the administration of this great block of Africa. The directors renounced all idea of allowing the shares to be a medium of speculation, declared their intention of devoting their capital to the *bona fide* development of the country and assured Lugard that they endorsed his well-known views upon African races and were inviting him to work not only in the interests of the Company, " but generally in the interests of the British Empire." When the news of his new appointment came out, the press congratulated the Company rather then Lugard. " Seldom does it fall to the lot of . . . . a pioneer Company to be able to engage such a leader—a man full of experience, knowledge of African affairs and possessing the confidence not only of the present government but also of the opposition."[1] The *Westminster Gazette* blamed the government for failing to recruit him for official service and wondered how a man of his great adventures would take to " spotting mineralized regions, and keeping in order gold-miners on the outskirts of civilization . . . . "[2]

Lugard soon found that he was booked for a country which had a most indefinite status and future, and one where he was almost certain

[1] *Financial News,* 7 December 1895.
[2] *Westminster Gazette,* 7 December 1895.

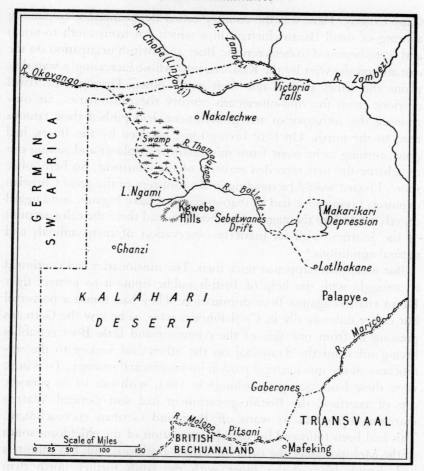

Bechuanaland Protectorate 1896

to cross once more the path and the interests of Cecil Rhodes.[1] Ngamiland had first to be looked up on the map. Like most of the places to which he found his way, the mapping was as yet very sketchy. It was, however, a little less *terra incognita* than the other regions into which he had forced his way. Nor was it, like them, very far beyond any recognized frontier. It was part of the still undemarcated British sphere which lay in the arid centre of the sub-continent north-west of

1 See above pp. 150–2.

Cape Colony. Here was the country called Bechuanaland, containing a string of small Bantu chieftainships which ran from south to north and were hemmed in between the Boer and British occupation on the east and on the west by the Kalahari, into whose increasingly waterless plains the tribes pushed out their cattle posts. Through the tribal corridor from the mid-nineteenth century the missionaries, far out-running the authority of any government, had pushed their famous road to the north. Up here Livingstone, harassed by the Boers, had gone, turning as he went from missionary to explorer and setting out to achieve the first recorded traverse of the continent. So here, once more, Lugard would be treading in the footsteps of the great Christian explorer. Livingstone had in 1849 discovered Lake Ngami, and Lugard eagerly turned up the pages of his book to read there the calm account of the journey with its masterly observation of men, animals and natural conditions.[1]

But much had happened since then. The missionaries had continued to struggle with the help of British public opinion to protect their Bantu charges against Boer domination. They had found a powerful but rather dubious ally in Cecil Rhodes who, as he saw the Germans pressing in from one side of the continent and little Boer republics hiving off from the Transvaal on the other, had woken to the sig-nificance of the missionaries' road in his continental strategy. To whom were these lands going to belong? In 1885, with one of its periodic acts of assertion, the British government had sent General Warren marching up north to warn off Boer and German encroachment. This had been followed by British annexation of the chiefdoms south of the Molopo under the name of British Bechuanaland, but ministers had shrunk from doing more with the lands further north than declaring the chieftainships up to and including half of Khama's country, to be under British protection. In 1889 Rhodes' Company was granted a charter which promised, in very vague terms, to confirm any jurisdiction, rights etc. it should acquire over lands lying north of British Bechuanaland and west of Portuguese dominions.[2] The next year saw Britain, in the Anglo-German Convention of July, recognize German South-West Africa and the following year an Order of Council, again in the vaguest terms, included Ngamiland in the British

[1] D. Livingstone, *Missionary Travels and Researches in South Africa* (1857), pp. 53–73.
[2] Clauses 1 to 4 of the B.S.A. Co. Charter, 29 October 1889. This is printed in *British South Africa Company's Territories* (1898), C.8773, p. 4.

Protectorate under the High Commissioner for South Africa, and provided legal basis for its administration. This, as far as concerned Ngamiland, a region substantially larger than England and Wales, was by 1895 to consist of nothing more than two white police officers with some two dozen policemen, Basuto and European, and these stationed in the extreme south of the area at Ghanzi. The Resident Commissioner, nominally responsible for the two Bechuanalands and for Ngamiland remained—and, surprisingly, still remains—in a head-quarters at Mafeking, well outside the borders of his inhospitable territory.

Rhodes, his "immense and brooding spirit" now hovering over all southern Africa, was determined to have all these lands for his Company. He wanted them as a segment in his all-red Cape-to-Cairo axis. He wanted them more immediately as the route to Matabeleland which he was just acquiring for his Company. He was planning, through a subsidiary company, to push a railway from Vryburg to Mafeking and on to Bulawayo, right through the tribal lands. He had also a more private reason for very urgently needing a position under his control as close as possible to the eastern border, near the Transvaal Republic and Johannesburg, where the cosmopolitan and gold-mining Uitlanders were chafing against Kruger's rule. In the autumn of 1894 he wrote to the Colonial Secretary, Lord Ripon, to remind him that it was "thoroughly understood" when the charter was granted that the Protectorate would be taken over by the Company, and only on this assumption had he embarked upon the railway. Lord Ripon, the British government being in one of its acquisitive moods, agreed almost by return of post.[1]

This was in 1894. But now fate, which had favoured Rhodes, seemed to turn against him on the very threshold of success in his sweeping cartographic designs. The first blow was that Salisbury succeeded Rosebery, with Chamberlain at the Colonial Office. Although Chamberlain was so much more freely and frankly expansionist than Rosebery, he was bound to come into conflict with Rhodes, now at the height of his power and influence, because Rhodes thought he could use the "imperial factor" as an instrument for his own designs, and discard it when ready to act independently. Chamberlain was a Unionist in more contexts than that of Ireland, and he was

[1] A. Sillery, *The Bechuanaland Protectorate* (1952), p. 66.

reluctant to go into partnership with a local imperialist, especially a man whom he distrusted. The second event was that Khama and two of his fellow chiefs, horrified at the idea of passing from British to Company rule, hurried to England in the summer of 1895, and called at the Colonial Office in top-hats. Chamberlain listened to them and in November promised, to Rhodes' fury, to retain their lands under a direct British Protectorate and to give the Company only the probable reversion of Ngamiland, and the narrow railway strip. Rhodes did, however, manage to get control of the small but all-important block of land he wanted on the Transvaal border.

Rhodes now found the new British West Charterland Company suddenly appearing in his path, a minor obstacle but one which threatened the commercial aspect of his plans. His Company had obtained a mineral concession from Khama but not from Moremi. His charter carried an obligation to recognize any concessions in the promised area which had been gained before the date of incorporation. And the Nicolls-Hicks concession, which the British West Charterland Company were buying, qualified for this right by a month. Moreover, it appeared to cover an immense area. Rhodes wanted to sweep it from his path and in 1895 his Company claimed to possess *all* rights. Only after Nicolls and Hicks had in February brought an action for slander of title against the B.S.A. Company did the latter sign an agreement recognizing the Moremi concession and also promising, when they took over the administration, to assist the concessionaires to open up the country. This was in February 1895 and the next month the Colonial Office also recognized the validity of the concession.

But this did not dispose of the difficulties of the Charterland Company. Lugard was desperately anxious for it to get administrative powers not only because of the interest and dignity they would add to his task but also because the War Office rules made it difficult to second military officers to purely commercial posts. But, in view of the promises to the B.S.A. Company, Chamberlain, for all his friendship with Lugard, could only inform him that the whole of the country, outside that which he had reserved a week before to Khama and his fellow chiefs, was promised to Rhodes' Company. "The promise was made long ago by my predecessors and I have not felt that I could treat it as open to reconsideration." He advised him to treat directly with Rhodes for a delegation of administration. (Chamberlain to L. 16 November 1895). But, Chamberlain told Lugard, Rhodes was " furious " with the Charterland Company and this meant that even his own advocacy for Lugard's appointment would probably fail though he was, rather generously, willing to risk this rebuff. (L. to Goldie, 16 December 1895).

Lugard realized gloomily that he would have to try to treat direct with Rhodes. He and Goldie were both agreed in their strong dislike of the great man, though they shared much with him in their interests and their qualities. Yet Goldie, like Chamberlain, advised Lugard that he must make suit to Rhodes, for neither Lugard nor his Company could make headway if Rhodes, now at the summit of his power in Africa and his influence in Britain, were against them. So Lugard turned to the distasteful task of asking Rhodes for a delegation of those powers which, in fact, Rhodes' Company did not yet possess, as they were still suspended on the wings of a promise somewhere between the Company's office and Downing Street. But neither Rhodes nor his agent, Dr. Harris, was interested. " Nothing in the world ", Harris told Lugard, " would induce Rhodes to part with his powers." Harris would not even dare to send a cable of enquiry as it " would put Rhodes in a rage," though Rhodes might possibly agree to appoint Lugard himself, as his name would carry great weight with him. Lugard believed that Rhodes preferred to appoint his own creatures. (L. to Chamberlain, 22 November 1895). Yet he felt obliged to ask Flora Shaw, who, as a mutual friend, was the link between him and Rhodes, to write to Rhodes and ask him to treat Lugard " in a friendly manner and with consideration " during the expedition. But in an exchange which throws interesting light upon the two correspondents as well as upon their subject, he tried to shake Miss Shaw's faith in her friend.

" I am strongly opposed to serving under the B.S.A.C." he wrote. " I know you think very highly of Rhodes and his subordinates, *so far*, at any rate. I do *not* . . . . because men I trust (and whose opinion would carry far greater weight with you than mine) all seem to mistrust . . . . I can see for myself, in correspondence I have read, that they are " smart "—*very* smart . . . . I would *greatly* like to hear the other side, but if you think that my opinion is worth anything, believe me there is a *great* deal to overlook . . . . Under these circumstances I naturally prefer that Ngamiland should be wholly free of ' Charter ' and Rhodes' influence and I even feel that, if placed under his control, I would *very* greatly dislike to go out."

By contrast he praised his own employers, Messrs. Hanau, Maund, Pam and Bruch. " All enquiries I have instituted have resulted in no word against any one of them . . . . They all strike me as being perfectly straight." (L. to F. Shaw, 9 November 1895).

But not even from Lugard would Miss Shaw hear a word against Rhodes, for whom she was shortly to dare and suffer so much. The letter written by the woman who was to become the chief influence in Lugard's life is worth quoting fully because it is so frank and self-revealing, and because in it she set him her standards for public men.

Nov. 7/1895   130 Cambridge Street,
Warwick Square, S.W.

DEAR CAPT. LUGARD,

. . . .

I think that you will have to work in friendly relations with the B.S.A. Co. if anything is to be achieved. I feel the force of all you say and the weight of the opinion which you quote. I cannot help thinking, however, that if you were brought into personal touch with Mr. Rhodes and could realize as I do the absolutely unsordid and unselfish nature of the devotion which he gives to the Imperial cause you would acknowledge the ennobling influence of a great conception and much of your prejudice would disappear. I have met now most of the English public men of my day and the impression conveyed to me by Mr. Rhodes is of an unselfishness of aim greater and more complete than I have ever recognized before. He appears to me to seek nothing for himself. He cares neither for money, nor place, nor power, except in so far as they are a necessity for the accomplishment of the national ideal for which he lives. He has no personal life and the aloofness from personal motive which I observe in him does not strike me as the ordinary renunciation of good men. It is rather, if I may so describe it, a passionate extension of aim which so far outstrips personal success as to leave the thought of it where most of us have learned to leave some at least of the toy dreams of early youth. If I interpret his character rightly he has not renounced himself he has passed beyond himself, and this is the surer form of conquest as it implies a growth which can never be undone.

She ended by asking to be allowed to bring him and Rhodes into contact so that he could answer the question " Can I work with or under this influence, believing it to be of the noblest but disliking as

I do many of its accepted methods? It is a question which each man must answer for himself."

Rhodes himself seems to have been speaking here through his admirer. It is worth remembering that in the brief letter he wrote shortly after this, when going into acute danger among the Matabele, to his critic Harcourt, he used the word " sordid " no less than three times in his rejection of it as an adjective to apply to himself.[1]

Lugard read her friendly exaltation of Rhodes with great dubiety. He felt able to pass it on to Flora Shaw's other great friend, Goldie. The comment of the man who founded Nigeria upon his contemporary who founded Rhodesia is worth quoting. Its cynical tang breaks in so harshly against Flora Shaw's pæan that it is difficult to understand how they could have been intimate friends.

Nov. 11, 1895.   11 Queen's Gate Gardens,
                                                              S.W.

My Dear Lugard,

As you say you will be back in town tomorrow, I now return you Miss Shaw's letter which is, as you say, remarkable.

I fully believe in her view that " The God in the Car " cares nothing for money except as a means to an end. What man of sense can, provided he has wholesome food, warm clothes, shelter from weather, a few favourite books & a pipe? Women, as a rule, still love luxury, ostentation & rivalry. It is the fault of their education & a useful vice for the progress of civilization. As to love of power, no man in a civilized community has any power worth exercising. Men in power today are slaves of work & of the public, & not masters—even of themselves.

So far I can go, but no further; yet I strongly advise you to accept Miss Shaw's offer. I have always told you that your Ngami people must, in the end, arrange with the Company; why not at once?

Yours very truly
George Taubman Goldie

This was written on November 11th. The month before Rhodes' Company had succeeded in saving one vital strip on the Transvaal frontier from the wreckage of their hopes achieved by Khama and Chamberlain. Dr. Jameson was posted there as Administrator with a force of so-called mounted police. Flora Shaw, privy to the plot to aid a rising of the Uitlanders in Johannesburg against Kruger's government, was busy writing leading articles in *The Times* in support of

[1] Gardiner, *Life of Harcourt*, vol. ii, p. 392.

their case.[1] She was in telegraphic communication with Rhodes by secret code and when, on December 29th, Jameson started out from Pitsani on his raid without waiting for an Uitlander rebellion, she published in *The Times* the next morning the manifesto the Uitlanders *would have* issued if they had risen, a copy of which Rhodes' agent had prematurely telegraphed to her. The Raid was a military fiasco but it was a political earthquake. Among the results of interest to this story, the chief one is that Rhodes, overthrown in one night by his friend's impetuous act, fell from power and ceased to be a problem to Lugard and his directors, for there could now be no serious thought of making any further concession to a Company which, like its head, rocked on the edge of disgrace. They were helped, as regards British opinion, by the Kaiser's letter of congratulation to Kruger. As for Flora Shaw she too was on trial, both within the privacy of Printing House Square, the reputation of which she had endangered and, later, publicly before the parliamentary Committee of Enquiry, on the evidence of her secret cables to and from Rhodes.[2] One effect of the raid, as Kirk, who called it " The most stupendous piece of folly ever attempted," told Lugard, was to make the government unwilling to grant administrative powers to any other Company in the region.

Before leaving for South Africa, Lugard had discussions and correspondence with Sir Percy Anderson about the possibility of his being given a post in East Africa. Their negotiations led at last, in February 1896, to the definite offer by Anderson, on the instructions of Lord Salisbury, of the post of Deputy Commissioner in East Africa, but only if this post were created. The post was to be held outside Zanzibar and the coastland, presumably somewhere between the coast and Lake Victoria. The salary, £1,000 a year, and the pension were agreed. As to the powers, Lugard would be under the authority of the British agent in Zanzibar, a relationship which he and Kirk agreed would be highly inconvenient as well as uncongenial. He almost certainly hoped to get this plan changed when he took up the post. In the meantime he defined his peculiar views frankly to Anderson. " I know myself

---

1 See especially the leading article of 10 October 1895; also her weekly article of 16 and 30 December 1895.

2 See the official account of the enquiry, *Report of the Inquiry into Incursion into South African Republic etc.* (second report), H.C. 311, *Parliamentary Papers*, 1897, ix. 5; also E. Moberley Bell, *Flora Shaw, Lady Lugard, D.B.E.* (1948); *History of " The Times "* (1947), vol. viii, chapters 7 and 9; and Jean van der Poel, *The Jameson Raid* (1951). The last book gives an interpretation of Flora Shaw's evidence damaging to Chamberlain.

sufficiently well to know that I can do a hundred times better work if I am in command. I do not fear responsibility, though I think I realize more fully and acutely than many men its full weight and extent. I have for so many years been in sole command in whatever I have had to do (actually since '87 and practically since '84), that I dread lest I should fail should my judgment and action be curtailed by local intervention." (L. to Anderson, 13 February 1896). He was quite ready to resign his " comparatively light duties " in South Africa, and their princely emoluments when, by the end of the year, he should have led the expedition to its destination.

Once the decision to go to South Africa was taken, all went smoothly. Mr. Chamberlain used his influence with the India Office to obtain the secondment of Lieutenant Edward Lugard, then in India, and with the War Office to obtain the extension of Lugard's own secondment. The proposal was first made to Lugard in August 1895, and the agreement was signed on January 1st 1896. While waiting to set out Lugard followed his usual course of making a thorough study, historical, geographical and commercial, of the country in which he was to work.

The directors gained their first return for the faith they had put in Lugard when he proposed that Sir John Kirk should join the board. Kirk, who with Livingstone had first explored the far northern fringes of this region, brought his great reputation and experience of Africa to the Company, while Lugard's position was made still stronger by having his most trusted friend as one of the directors. Lugard was also of great help in negotiations with the Colonial Office over the relations between the two Companies and the controversy about the concession which depended upon the limits of the chieftainships of Khama and the Batawana chief Sekgoma. Lugard then set about collecting the elaborate equipment needed for the expedition, which included tents, rifles, survey instruments lent by the Royal Geographical Society, drugs and a small collapsible boat. A code of mining regulations was worked out. There was also staff to be engaged. With the help of his medical friend, Sir Alfred Fripp, Lugard selected a young, newly qualified doctor, Spon, " a capital boy who enjoys life to the utmost and enters on this expedition as on a huge picnic," and an R.E. sergeant surveyor. But the key man of the expedition was of course the mining engineer, one " Colorado Browne " from the Middle West.

The party set sail for South Africa on February 22nd 1896, Kirk and some of the other directors coming to Waterloo station to see them off. " I shall sorely miss you," ran Kirk's final note before Lugard left. " I have few confidants . . . . if any man will pull it through you are the man . . . . it will need even more delicate management than anything you have had before." (Kirk to L. 20 February 1896). Lugard spent the voyage in his usual way, reading blue books, writing letters, and going over the proposed mining regulations with the engineer. On March 9th he had his first view of Table Mountain and the southern corner of the continent, the outpost of a land over which the political sky was already darkening. Armed with a letter of introduction from the Colonial Secretary, the two brothers called upon leading imperial authorities in the colony. There was the Commander-in-Chief, General Goodenough. Then there was Admiral Rawson, " a man whom one can see at a glance is a man to be trusted." The Admiral, with a command stretching right round Africa from the tropical east to the tropical west, had from his maritime angle as wide a conception of the affairs of the continent as had Lugard from his terrestrial experience.

Lugard was less impressed by the chief representative of Britain, the High Commissioner, the old and weary Sir Hercules Robinson (later Lord Rosmead),[1] lately back from his humiliating embassy to the triumphant Kruger, and by the Imperial Secretary, Sir Graham Bower. This was partly, perhaps, because they had some authority over him and because they reflected, he thought, the hostility which, in spite of Chamberlain's friendship for Lugard, the Colonial Office had from the first shown to his enterprise. He took " no kind of fancy " to Bower; his eyes were never still, " his fingers twitched nervously "— perhaps the after-effects of the strain of the Jameson Raid.[2] " He announced with what almost seemed satisfaction that cattle disease had spread as far south as Palapye . . . . " (Diary, 11 March 1896). When Lugard talked of his mission and the Moremi Concession covering Sekgoma's territory of Ngamiland, he was at once told that Sekgoma's claim to the whole of this land was very far from being admitted, and that his frontiers had still to be settled. Lugard claimed that the B.S.A. Company at least had admitted his Company's rights to a defined

1 See above p. 147.
2 See van der Poel, *op. cit.* where Bower is said to have accepted the role of scapegoat for the Raid. See especially pp. 160-3, 209-10.

territory between Long. 25° and 21° east, and Lat. 22° and 18° south. While his right to prospect was accepted, he was made to realize the complex position with regard to land rights between Sekgoma, his neighbour Khama, the B.S.A. Company and the government. He on his side, already a firm and punctilious upholder of international regulations in Africa, was shocked to learn in the course of the conversation that the Brussels Act prohibiting the sale of fire-arms to natives was not being properly observed. He did not see Rhodes nor, it seems, did he try to see him.

He now set to work with all speed to make the final arrangements for his expedition. There were prospectors and transport riders to be engaged, vehicles and oxen to be collected, more equipment to be bought, rations to be worked out and stores to be obtained. And there was everything to learn about the South African base from which he had to operate. It was a deeply unsettled base. The Jameson Raid had happened only ten weeks before he landed. The ship bringing Jameson home as a prisoner for trial berthed just before his own left. The Boers in the Transvaal were arming feverishly and the possibility of war between the two European groups hung over the country. There were other unfortunate events which concerned Lugard's enterprise more immediately. It had appeared that this journey, which he was by no means the first to make, was to be one of the easiest he had carried out. Now, as if fate had decided that his peculiar gifts should not be allowed to be idle, a combination of misfortunes suddenly made the journey appear not only difficult but almost impossible.

The first and greatest disaster was the rinderpest. While in Capetown Lugard learned that this dreaded cattle disease had reached the Bechuanaland Protectorate. This was the same disease which had strewn his track up to Uganda in 1890 with buffalo corpses. Since then it had been working its way slowly and fatally southwards through the tribal cattle and wild game of Africa for 1,500 miles to meet him on arrival at the Kalahari. The plans for his expedition were based upon the universal South African method of transport, the great waggon with its span of twelve to sixteen trek-oxen. There seemed no other means of dragging all the men and equipment for hundreds of miles through a country of heavy sand and scant water. Moreover, the disaster to these largely pastoral tribes of the region had made them restless and suspicious.

Lugard, who had come to regard almost every expedition as a race, had intended to get away in April, a month before his promise, and he raged furiously against this check. To his diary he admitted that " difficulties only exist to be overcome and I should almost prefer to have some—in reason." But there was nothing reasonable about rinderpest, and there were emergency restrictions which checked his wild notion of breaking through with his ox-waggons and braving the plague. He hurried up to Kimberley on March 17th to get nearer to his problem. There three more severe blows were dealt him by fate. First he learned that unprecedented flights of locusts were destroying every green thing—and there were not many—in the north-west. Secondly, this always arid land had been hit by so severe a drought that there could be no knowing how many of the rare wells might not have dried up, or the *vleys* (pans of rain-water) be empty, and these uncertainties might mean death to travellers on the Kalahari tracks. Thirdly, responsive to the unsettled conditions following the raid, and ruined by the rinderpest, the newly-subjected Matabele had risen and were said to be wiping out Rhodes' first settlers, men, women and children. This meant frantic efforts to get together an expedition which must pass up Lugard's route on the north road and which in passing would lay hold of every man, animal, vehicle and store of food in the area.

It seemed as though Lugard would at last have to admit the existence of the word " impossible ". At Kimberley he was able to get into direct touch with the problem through men who knew something of the conditions further north, and at this point it will be well to look a little more closely at the map, largely blank and very inaccurate, which lay before him as he gazed at the problem it presented.

The place which he meant to reach as the centre for the prospecting was the lake—if this piece of capriciously appearing and disappearing water could be called a lake—Ngami. It was not only a central point, it was near Sekgoma's headquarters and his first task, a familiar one by now, was to get for his Company a new agreement from this chief which would prolong the Hicks concession. Lake Ngami lay some 700 miles from the railhead at Mafeking. It would be necessary to trek north with animal transport along the so-called " Great North Road " (along which Rhodes' railway was even now being built) and then to diverge north-westwards into the desert at Palapye, the headquarters of the Ngwato chief, Khama. This place lay almost 400 miles from Lake Ngami, but it was not so much the distance as the deep sand, interspersed with stones, which must make this part of the journey so slow and hazardous. Here were long stretches without any water, aptly called " thirsts ". Even when, about two-thirds of the way to Ngami, the Botletle river would be reached, only one problem would be solved. The track still remained extremely difficult in parts, while, since the northern Kalahari carried a dense scrub, it was often blocked with thorn-trees.

Far from being wholly arid, Ngamiland possessed a freakish and most unhelpful water system. The heights of Angola to the north feed three large rivers which flow south-east. The first of these is the great Zambezi, which skirts the corner of Bechuanaland, leaps over the Victoria Falls, and after many other adventures finally reaches the Indian Ocean. The second river is the Chobe or Linyanti, which just enters the corner of Bechuanaland and, turning sharply away, joins the Zambezi. The third river is the Okovango. This brings into the Protectorate a heavy volume of water, until after about one hundred miles it breaks up into a delta of several branches and finally loses itself in an immense swamp. In very wet years some of its water seeps into Lake Ngami, while some runs into the Botletle, a seasonal river which loses itself in the Makarikari Depression about 200 miles east of Lake Ngami. This river is fed from one of the branches of the Okovango river system, the Thamalakane river. Very interesting investigations and dramatic proposals have been evoked from time to time by the exasperating spectacle of great rivers wasting themselves to the north of a desert which cries out for their waters.[1] But Lugard was concerned with minerals and not with irrigation and he was interested only in finding sufficient water to allow his men and animals to make their way into and about this uncongenial wilderness.

The word desert may, however, give too harsh an impression of the land he was to traverse. The northern Kalahari was no great expanse of barren sand. The rain was just sufficient to nourish a meagre cover of thorn scrub and of grass. But normal human beings—Bushmen being excepted—could only survive in the area, and make use of the

---

[1] See D. Reitz, *No Outspan* (1943), pp. 196–201; ' Waters of the Kalahari ', *The Times*, 25 August 1945; F. Debenham, *Kalahari Sand* (1953); and *Report of a Mission to the Bechuanaland Protectorate to investigate the possibilities of economic development in the Western Kalahari, 1952,* H.M.S.O. (1954).

poor pasture, where they were within reach of its ill-dispersed permanent or seasonal water. So the small Tawana tribe,[1] an offshoot of Khama's Ngwato, were based upon the lake and the southern rivers—the northern swamps being barred by tsetse—and wielded their paupers' lordship over still poorer and weaker groups who herded and hunted for them on the fringes of their moving villages. Their cattle were rivals for the capricious water with crocodiles, lions, elephant and many other animals, while still further out the more enduring creatures, giraffe, ostrich and many species of antelope, shared this thirsty land with their hunters, the tiny Bushmen, who had no houses and who sucked up moisture through reeds out of damp patches of sand.

This, then, was the setting for the transport problem which Lugard set himself to solve. The alternatives to oxen, he decided, were to be found in horses, mules and donkeys. Horse-sickness ruled out the first as the main draught-animals. Mules were also liable to it, but were regarded as hardier. But mules were much inferior to oxen. Whereas oxen could feed themselves on the grass, mules needed grain which had to be carried, and they needed more water. They were, by comparison, very ineffective where the going was heavy. Donkeys needed rather less food and water and were immune from horse-sickness. But they were very slow (a grave handicap in the conditions) and were too light to be of much use in heavy sand. It was impossible to take all the fodder needed for the animals; the mules even on half rations would have consumed the entire weight of any load they could haul long before the end of the journey. It was the uncertainty of food or water for the animals under the drought conditions which spelt the gravest peril for the caravan. Moreover—and this was a really serious point—whereas almost everyone in South Africa understood how to handle ox-transport, it was more difficult to find anyone, black or white, capable of using mules and donkeys for heavy trekking. Instead of using local natives it was necessary, therefore, to hire expensive Cape-boys who demanded rations and equipment of an almost European standard. As all the food for the men, both for the journey and for months afterwards, had to be hauled for many hundred miles, some very anxious arithmetic was necessary before the scale

[1] Major E. J. Lugard estimated the Tawana as being only about 1,500 in 1896. See his Introduction to ' The Flora of Ngamiland ' by N. E. Brown, *Bulletin of the Royal Botanic Gardens, Kew*, No. 3, 1909, p. 84.

of rations, the weight and distribution of loads and the minimum numbers of men and animals required could be ascertained.

It was the opinion of all the local men of experience that to attempt the expedition in the face of all these obstacles would be madness. There was a unanimous view that it must be abandoned. Lugard thought otherwise. For this most questionable decision he could find reasons with which he could at least convince himself. It was necessary to substantiate his Company's claim by action; to gain an extension of the concession from Sekgoma; to be at hand while Sekgoma's boundaries and perhaps the future fate of the Protectorate were being decided, and also to cut short a delay which, he reckoned, was costing his employers £40 a day. Moreover, the Company had left him full responsibility and the decision lay with himself alone, in itself an additional spur to his will.

He had the advantage of having in his company one man who had been in Ngamiland. This was the Hicks who had been concerned in getting the original concession from Sekgoma's father, and who had joined the expedition at Cape Town. Not only did he know the local language, Sechuana, but he was an effective and socially congenial person. With the help of other advisers and agents Lugard rapidly collected stores, and sent his mining engineer to the Transvaal to buy mules, saddlery, light carts and prospecting gear. Donkeys were purchased, though at very high prices. By the end of April the preparations were well advanced and Lugard wrote and dispatched his first quarterly report to the directors from Kimberley and then went on to the railhead at Mafeking. Here, at prices rapidly rising because of the demands of the Matabele war, he completed his purchases. He found that, as he could not rely upon obtaining anything at Palapye, where he must leave the route to Rhodesia, he had to reckon Mafeking as his supply base and set off fully equipped from there, though it was nearly twice as far from Lake Ngami as Palapye.

At Mafeking he spent some useful hours in conversation with Mr. Newton, the Resident Commissioner for the Protectorate. These were somewhat dramatically interrupted by the arrival of Earl Grey, who had succeeded the fallen Jameson as Administrator of Rhodesia, and whom Rhodes had dispatched north to organize resistance to the Matabele. Grey, as we have seen,[1] had known Lugard in England and

1 See above p. 445.

he was astonished to encounter him in Mafeking. His astonishment gave way to the exciting conviction that Lugard had been found and sent by Providence to help him to deal with the Matabele rebellion. " You must come with me at once to Bulawayo," he cried and offered him command of all the native forces. When Lugard told him about his own expedition he swept it aside. He would cable the directors; they should be compensated for the loss of his services.

As Lugard gave demure answers to Grey's excited and emotional appeals, in his introspective way he looked into his own mind to discover the real reasons why he was unmoved. He judged that the immediate danger to European life, and especially that of women and children, was over so that the plea that had moved him to plunge into the conflict in Nyasaland had no force here. But he came again to the conclusion, as after the *Alecto* incident on the Niger, that he was no longer attracted as he had once been, by the excitement of battle.

" Grey wants, he says, a man of ' great dash,' which means that he wants a man to hurl himself and his raw Basuto recruits on to the Matabele and get butchered to cause a diversion from the white contingent. There are Irishmen, and others I believe, who have this ' death-or-glory' mania. I had it myself when I was under twenty-five, and perhaps even later. I have not got it now . . . . I regret to write this; I regret the mad soldier's ambition which has gone from me, but so it is. As I marched past on a Sunday, a young cadet at Sandhurst, and the band played, ' The British Grenadiers ', I could feel my soul expanding till it nearly burst my tunic and I keenly regretted the absence of ' a cannon's mouth ' that I might walk up to it and get blown to glory. Courage is an affair of age, and of the liver and of various other things prosaic . . . . 'Tis pity 'tis true and pity 'tis 'tis true"." (Diary, 13 April 1896).

His actions and his further musings showed that he had not lost his courage but that he had brought it under the control of his reason and his reason did not approve its employment upon Grey's enterprise. He had doubts of the efficiency, the justice and the humanity with which action against the Matabele would be conducted. Above all, there was his distrust of Rhodes and Jameson. In this matter he continued, as he collected more South African evidence about these two, to disagree ever more strongly with Flora Shaw. He had learned much in South Africa about both men and about the Jameson Raid which had set out so recently from near Mafeking. " What between the two—well, I'd sooner run my own apple-cart and have only myself to blame if it upsets."

What he heard locally of Jameson was:

" a bitter, ironical comment on *The Times* article (by Miss Shaw?) I read only last night saying what brilliant things had been done by Jameson . . . . I believe Dr. Jameson to have been a single-hearted, honourable man above lucre and personal gain, but surely England will begin to doubt if he was the Heaven-born Administrator he was boomed to be . . . . from all I hear it seems the general opinion that Jameson & Rhodes hatched this plot against the Transvaal deliberately for months— well, we shall see."   (Diary, 28 March 1896).

And again, as Flora Shaw's opinions were following him up to Bechuanaland:

" The attitude of *The Times* and its blind partisanship is pitiful. I am a literary dabbler and as an Englishman feel the degradation of our great paper keenly. I argued with Miss Shaw before I left, but she is a blind enthusiast for Rhodes and Jameson. A woman's emotions always will dominate her intellect. In that I think a man shows more control. However stirred his emotions are he can—if he is a *man*—project himself outside of them to some extent and ' see things as others see them ' and act logically—at least more than a woman does."   (30 March 1896).

So when Grey came back reiterating his appeal, Lugard was firm in refusal and continued to prepare his own expedition. Here a new difficulty of a most embarrassing kind was threatened. Lugard was beginning to find it most difficult to co-operate with the other key-man of the party, the mining engineer. In that phrase in which Lugard would sum up a man who was the extreme opposite of his own orderly and reliable self, he described his colleague as " a good fellow but sketchy to a degree." The engineer, upon his side, undoubtedly put his finger upon Lugard's greatest weakness as an administrator when he accused him of trying to deal with everything, even petty details which were not worth his attention. Lugard, with great honesty, admitted to himself that the man was right.

" I know this to be a fault of mine and I lose much of the important issues of life by over-attention to detail. For instance, I never read the important books of the day which I long to read, because I simply cannot skim through my *Times* and I lose the valuable for the ephemeral."
                                                                 (Diary, 26 April 1896).

581

Confession did not lead to amendment; Lugard retained this major failing to the end of his life, as well as the special fault to which he refers. Certainly *The Times* never had a more thorough and unfailing reader.

Lugard saw the danger of a breach with his expert and resolved to avoid it, though "I would rather take a waggon-load of Bengal tigers to Ngamiland than this man!" However, in spite of all difficulties, both those which had been overcome, and those still to be surmounted, Lugard, with the congenial companionship of his brother, was now ready for the trek and determined to go forward. This itself, in the circumstances, was a considerable achievement.

CHAPTER XXVII

THE TREK

1896-1897 : Aet. 38-39

IT WAS on May 4th 1896, that the expedition pulled out of Mafeking.

To meet the situation created by the rinderpest and the drought, the original numbers of men and material had been cut down by half or even more. Every man, animal, vehicle, or pound of equipment had to be considered and reconsidered in an expedition which was above all a problem of transport. The total caravan was now as follows:–

Vehicles and transport animals.

4 light tented wagons each drawn by 12 mules with 2 spares.
3 lighter vehicles each drawn by 18 donkeys.
3 buckboards drawn by 10 donkeys each.
1 cart drawn by 12 donkeys.
1 water cart with 6 mules.
The total number of mules taken was 62 and of donkeys 110.

Men.

11 Europeans.
27 Africans—mainly " Cape-boys " to attend the transport.

Material.

The total load carried weighed 35,000 lbs. It was made up largely of food stores (canned beef, flour, biscuits, salt, rice, compressed vegetables, soup in solid cakes, and lime-juice). There were also tents, medical supplies, prospecting gear, photographic apparatus, goods for barter, rifles and ammunition, and a collapsible boat.

As Lugard could get no reasonable and reliable contract for sending up further supplies, arrangements were made for a subsidiary expedition to come up later with an assistant mining engineer.

The trek north was marked by the carcases of thousands of oxen putrifying in the hot sun. The rinderpest appeared to induce a frantic thirst, and as the dying beasts had mostly managed to struggle to the nearest water in which they had collapsed, all the water-supplies were contaminated. The edge of the Marico river in the Transvaal, beside which they marched for a time, was studded with corpses. It distressed Lugard, with his passion for order, to see these carcases unburnt and the rivers uncleared. The flies were terrible; the waggons were black with them. After ten days' trekking four mules, two horses and three donkeys had died on the road. The trek was made the more gloomy by increasing difficulties with the mining engineer. He overloaded his waggon until it broke down; he then broke the axle in trying to mend it. His driver deserted and none of the other men would take his place. Upon an expedition of this kind the man's incompatibilities were as bad as criminal tendencies. Finally he declared himself to be very ill and, viewing the undoubted dangers that lay before them, became convinced that he would never return from this journey. This allowed the contract to be broken on medical grounds, but though the man's departure was a personal relief to Lugard, it meant that he must proceed upon a mining enterprise without a mining engineer. Too much hung upon the post for Lugard to risk making a new appointment in South Africa so, in passing Gaberones, he cabled to his directors. Meanwhile he felt he must push on as there was much preparatory work he could do even though the main purpose of the expedition could not be pursued.

At Gaberones they were told that northwards to Bulawayo there were 4,000 waggons stranded, their 64,000 trek oxen lying dead on the road beside them. This was, of course, in addition to the immense numbers of the tribal herds which had died. The natives were skinning them and dealers were trading in the diseased skins. Lugard carefully collected all the evidence he could about the character of the disease, its movements, its effect upon different species of animals, wild and domestic, and many other points, and sent all the information back to England, where little was as yet known about this scourge.

On June 1st he arrived at Palapye, the headquarters of Chief Khama. There were three chiefs in South Africa in the nineteenth century who wrote their names in large letters into the history of the sub-continent: they were Chaka of the Zulu, Moshesh of the Basuto and Khama of the Ngwato. The first was a destructive force while the other two were constructive African statesmen. Perhaps the most remarkable thing about Khama was his Christianity. As a youth he had heard about the teaching of the great men of the London Missionary Society, Livingstone and Moffat, and had come under the influence of Mackenzie, and had been baptized with his wife thirty-four years before. As a chief among a primitive people, and surrounded by physical and political dangers he had, to an astonishing degree, acted upon his new religion. He prohibited the white man's liquor which was demoralizing his tribe and expelled the traders who refused to obey his law. Now he was just back from his visit to England where he and two other chiefs had worsted Rhodes, discussed his affairs with Chamberlain— ("Mwatlhodi," the Man who Rights Things)—impressed the British public and been presented to the Queen. ("It is humiliating to be utterly beaten by these niggers," was Rhodes' comment, "They think more of one native, at home, than the whole of South Africa.")[1]

As soon as Lugard arrived in Palapye, being largely dependent upon this masterful African chief, he went to see him and to ask for permission to outspan. Khama courteously came round himself to see his party and said they could outspan wherever they liked. The two men, who had met briefly in London when the Duchess of Westminster invited Lugard to meet this unusual visitant, took an immediate liking to each other. This was the more remarkable as Lugard was on his way to Khama's enemy and neighbour, Sekgoma, with whom the chief was in bitter conflict over boundaries and he must have known that Lugard, holding a concession from Sekgoma, had an interest in supporting his rival's claims to the full. It was, moreover, a very anxious moment in Khama's life. Head of a pastoral tribe, from being rich in cattle, he had been ruined almost overnight by the plague. His own herd of 10,000 cattle had gone. The fate of his country, which he had fought so hard to keep under the Queen, might still be in doubt. Just across the Transvaal border a few miles away his scouts reported that the Boers were ceaselessly engaged in rifle-fire. When Lugard asked why, Khama replied, "They are training their eyes in case of war."

Yet at such a time he did everything he could to help the passing white man. Lugard was much impressed. He was no negrophil in the sense in which that word is sometimes used to describe those to whom it is a matter of doctrine to exalt and defend all black men in their

[1] Garvin, *Life of Chamberlain*, vol. iii, p. 50.

contact with white. Lugard had not travelled in Africa for nearly ten years beyond the frontiers of civilization without knowing the meaning of savagery, yet he never, like so many other men of like experience, grew dull of response to cruelty or injustice in Africa, whether committed by black or white. The very day before he met Khama he had sternly rebuked a Rhodesian frontiersman who had gloated over the destruction of a whole *impi* (regiment) of the Matabele and had said he rejoiced at the extermination of every murderous savage. Lugard had pointed out that they were a fine, brave race and were only fighting for their country. If they had to be displaced they should be helped to settle in new lands beyond the Zambezi. With the same sensitivity he could receive the impress of a black man's character. Though few Africans in his experience, and in a period of strong class-distinctions, could yet be admitted to social equality, he quickly distinguished Khama with words that in his mouth were the highest appreciation he would give to any man. " He is a thorough gentleman." He praised his manners, and spoke gratefully of his cordiality and kindness. With his special views of the liquor traffic, not to speak of the strain of puritanism, or at least of asceticism, in his own nature, he found Khama a kindred spirit and warmly approved his measures.

There was much to discuss with the chief. More than once Lugard invited him to lunch. " I am not in favour of eating with black men. My own prospectors, of course, do not lunch with me and they are men of my own race and colour." But Khama he could treat as an honoured guest, and be proud to entertain him. " He is such a gentleman—so unobtrusive and yet so thoroughly well-bred and at his ease . . . . he is proud of being a black man and he is most anxious not to appear to ape the white man. For this reason he lives in a native hut and in all his ways is one of his own people." On one occasion when Khama turned up unexpectedly at the camp and Lugard invited him to lunch, Hicks, who usually interpreted, was absent, so the black loose-limbed, grey-headed chief and the compact Englishman ate their meal together in silence and Khama, his host remarked, as he looked at his broad, benign face, " obviously enjoyed himself."

The question of boundaries was thrashed out. Khama made no difficulties for Lugard and said he would not object if the prospectors strayed over his frontiers. That would be more a matter for the B.S.A. Company which had the mineral concession over his lands. Nor, though Sekgoma and he were at odds, did Khama speak of him with any rancour. Sekgoma had threatened to take up the boundary beacons and drive back Khama's men.

"What will you do?" Lugard asked him, "Have you told me these things because you wish me to take any action?"

"No," replied Khama, "I have told you these things merely out of friendship and that you may know something of the country into which you are going."

"Then what will you do?"

"Nothing," Khama replied, "I shall take no action upon mere threats. Sekgoma can do as he likes. I rest upon the undeniable justice of my claims."

(Diary, 5 June 1896).

The way in which he said this made a deep impression upon Lugard, his manner was so quiet and dignified, his attitude so statesmanlike and controlled.

Khama was able to do his visitor a very great service. It was essential that some arrangement should be made by which Lugard could keep up communications with the world. This would have been difficult to arrange under the best conditions, but as things were, it seemed almost impossible. He had made an attempt to come to terms with the Post Office at Cape Town, but its officials had suggested onerous and, indeed, absurd terms. Khama now came to the rescue, engaging to send runners every week and—a point which Lugard appreciated as being very unusual with an African chief—payment for their services could be made directly to the men and not through Khama. Finally, in the great dearth of labour, the chief lent as donkey attendants six men who proved excellent workers. At Lugard's request, he also sent two of his subordinate chiefs to point out the boundaries he claimed.

On June 15th began the second and most difficult part of the trek. Lugard had no accurate map to show the route, or, still more important, the position of water. Even where this was indicated there was no information to be had as to whether in this exceptional season the water had not dried up. Moreover, they were now in Bushman country and the little men would never reveal water and even, wherever possible, hid or plugged the wells against intruders. To Lugard their clicking speech and appearance seemed hardly human. "They are the most ghastly, hideous animals I have ever seen on this

earth. Pot-bellied, spindle-shanked, misshapen and hideous in face."
In addition to the absence of water there was the presence of sand.
There were long stretches of the route, perhaps a third of the whole,
where even by the most exhausting efforts and with mules and donkeys,
urged up to and beyond their strength, the caravan could only cover
three or even two miles in a whole day. There were hills of loose sand
where the mules had to rest after each four or five yards of struggling,
flogging and yelling, of pushing behind the waggons and of digging
wheels out of sand. Sometimes stones were the obstacle and Lugard,
with the rest, had to pick up and remove thousands of stones and shovel
soil into the holes between those remaining. At other times thick thorn
trees blocked the track and Lugard went ahead with any spare men to
hack a way through them. Everything that grew in the Kalahari had
armed itself with thorns in fierce self-protection. The sun was fiercely
hot by day, but the bitter cold of the desert came upon them at night
and left ice on the water. Lugard's hands, hard though they now were,
became at once chapped with the cold, burned by the sun, cut with
thorns, and blistered with hauling and digging.

At this moment his old wound began to give trouble and night after
night he sat up cutting little splinters of bone out of his arm. Often,
what with digging out choked wells, attending to the exhausted
animals and rising early to get the caravan ready, barely three hours
were left for sleep. He complained that he had no time to keep up with
his log or to read the heavy post and batches of his staple literary diet,
The Times, that the mail runners brought. Yet, once more, night after
night, the foolscap pages in the big interleaved diaries were covered
with the tiny, level writing, with copies for Sir John Kirk, until by
the end of this relatively brief expedition, four full volumes with
800 pages of writing had been filled. He was, of course, also drawing
up immensely detailed quarterly reports for his directors, keeping
elaborate records and accounts and maintaining his old invention of the
" Present State " of the caravan, in which he kept a detailed, up-to-
the-day record of every man, his health, pay etc., and the account of the
stores. Add to this that he had a very scratch lot of men, mostly
unknown to him, many of them unused to mule and donkey transport
and, at a moment when labour was almost unobtainable, of very
independent spirit. They must all have known, as they fought their
way forward at a rate of a few miles a day, and beast after beast fell

dead in its tracks, that their race with time might very easily turn out to be a race with death. As they approached a halt called Lotlhakane, unbearable sun alternated with a howling gale which swept over a salt-pan area so white that Lugard could not bear to open his eyes for more than a moment at a time. It took them three hours to cover two miles, and as they struggled through the sand Lugard remembered what had happened to another expedition formed by a group of Boers who had tried to reach this place in 1878.

" This is the fateful place where the Boer trek of 1878 suffered so fearfully from thirst. The maddened oxen rushed down and fell into the pits and could not be got out and were cut up and taken out piecemeal, and the blood and water and filth left in the pit was doled out. Women kept their children alive with blood and vinegar. A wretched remnant only escaped."
(Diary, 27 June 1896).[1]

Such were the joys of African travel, the same joys of pitting human intelligence and endurance against the obstacles set by nature which have taken men to polar regions and unscaled mountains as well as to tropical jungles and deserts.

It was not until early in August that the caravan reached the supposed borders of Sekgoma's Ngamiland. By this time a third of the mules and nearly all the horses were dead. Others were failing. Some had to be lifted on to their feet in the morning. Gruelling work, lack of food and water had reduced most of them to bags of bones. But shortly after this they reached the Botletle river and gazed at the almost incredible sight, after the " thirsts " of the desert, of " a broad and very deep river, rolling silently along with a fair current," before it lost itself in a salt-pan. The collapsible boat was unpacked.

" I have launched my boat and *sculled* on the Botletle! It is a brilliant success, and last night I took Ned out at sunset and returned by the full moon, for an hour's enjoyment. Ned could hardly contain himself for pleasure. The contrast of the placid-flowing river from the deep sand, dust and thorns we have lived in, is like another world. I christened her ' The Kitty '—the first white man's boat which has ever been on the waters of the Botletle (for it has no outlet to the sea), and we drank a little toast to its success in its new career."

---

[1] In his careful way Lugard noted the source of this information. H. A. Bryden, *Gun and Camera in Southern Africa* (1893), p. 416.

Here he heard the song of the sedge-warbler

" always one which to me conveys (more than the song of any other bird I know) an impression as though the songster were brimful of happiness .... The nightingale is proverbially sad—the robin reminds me of dark and depressing November days and I *hate* it—it is a pugnacious song. The blackbird and thrush sing of the country and are charming, their song is didactic and though beautiful, lacks pathos. It is what narrative poetry is to lyrical. But the blackcap, the sedge-warbler and the nightingale are the lyrical songs par excellence."

(Diary, 21 August 1896).

He had need of the comfort of such thoughts—though how had this wanderer from England found time to mark and to meditate upon the songs of English birds?—for the arrival at this strange river did not solve any other problem but that of water. And water brought its own problems. There were now mosquitos and also lions and hyenas to seize or scatter the transport animals at night, so that, although there was some harsh spiky grass which the hungry animals could eat, they had to be folded at night for safety. The alternative of grazing by day and trekking by night could not be followed because the men were too terrified by the lions to march in the darkness. This meant that the extra work of cutting grass had to be undertaken. Lugard, with that foresight which was one of the many qualities that went to make up his greatness as an African traveller, had included sickles in his sparse equipment. But the sand and thorns on the track were now worse than ever: there were still days when only two and a half miles could be made. The caravan could not travel together; there were no longer sufficient teams to pull all the vehicles, so that the advance had to be made in relays. The flies grew worse; they covered the body and crawled into eyes and nostrils. The men were coming to the end of their endurance and Lugard began to fear mutiny or desertion.

At last, on September 13th, driven by the unresting will of the leader, the expedition reached what, until they could find a suitable headquarters, might be regarded as their goal. This was the point in Ngamiland's fantastic river-system, as the map will show, where the Thamalakane from the north flows almost at right angles into the river, or river-bed, of the Botletle flowing to the east, with a channel to the west linking it with Lake Ngami. Here the river, as Livingstone pointed out,[1] might divide and flow both to east and west (which is said to have occurred in 1899). Lugard, however, found the lake arm at this time a mere reed swamp. It was here that the native drivers gave notice in a body. They had, they said, no grievance against Lugard, it was only the intolerable conditions, and above all the sand, that had at last broken their spirit. Now they had reached their destination, they held a decidedly low view of the country, a matter about which anyone would have agreed with them. Higher pay might tempt them, they intimated, but Lugard, aware how an excessive rate of pay once granted in the pioneering days, sets the standard indefinitely and may play a large part in holding back the development of a backward country, refused to consider this. A day or two later the men returned and signed on again, an action that reflected some credit upon them and much upon their employer.

At the Thamalakane-Botletle junction Lugard paused for a few days to take stock. He and the surveyor had measured and surveyed their route. They had marched 670 miles from Mafeking and 365¾ from Palapye. On the first part, counting halts, they had averaged 11 miles a day; from Palapye—though hardly daring to halt at all—they had averaged 4⅙ miles a day. Out of 66 mules, 44 had survived; out of 135 donkeys, 102 remained, but only 4 out of 12 horses were still alive. Lugard worked out for the directors most ingenious schemes for improving the system of transport. Then, as though hardly convinced by his own reasoning, he ended on a note of daring hope. " I observe that there is a movement for the adoption in England of ' Motorcars ' or self-propelled vehicles. If such vehicles could be procured, capable of burning wood as fuel, they would be invaluable. Wood fuel abounds and such vehicles would be independent of forage, of water (except at long intervals) and of lions." He strongly urged their adoption in Africa.

Lugard could not rest so long as any task remained to be done. His troubles had been sweetened by letters of great appreciation of his achievement up to this point from Kirk and the other directors. He was able to smile cheerfully over a letter from Chamberlain who wrote that he understood that his attempt to get into the country had failed. He was amused again a little later to hear that he and his brother had been reported missing—the third occasion in his career—though he

[1] Livingstone, *Missionary Travels*, p. 67.

591

hoped that his father, now eighty-eight years old, had not heard the report. A new mining engineer, a German, was on the way up and a young overseer, a man he greatly liked, was also moving up, with great difficulty, from Palapye. Meanwhile, he decided to press ahead and get into touch with Sekgoma, the chief of the Tawana.

He had heard little that was good of this young man. Khama had spoken with restraint, though they had disagreed about his daughter: one story was that Sekgoma had jilted her, the other that Khama refused to allow his daughter to marry a man of Sekgoma's character. One of the missionaries had told Lugard that Sekgoma was "a monster of cruelty" who, with all his Tawana, ill-treated the subject people known as the Masarwa. (These, upon a visit to this region in the thirties, the writer found to be still in a serf-like dependence). A " truculent youngster " was another description. Yet Lugard had to try to establish good terms with this chief who might otherwise make his position very difficult. Above all, he had to review and revise the concession upon which the very existence of his Company depended. Supposing Sekgoma should refuse a new concession or even repudiate the existing one? Had he not been told at Mafeking that he was on a fool's errand?

He set off on September 16th, taking with him only Hicks, as interpreter, and one or two natives. He liked Hicks, who in spite of his shy, nervous manner was a good hunter and horseman; he liked his tall, lean, fair good looks and he accorded to him the title of gentleman. But Hicks, the indispensable, the expert, chose this moment to be ill. Lugard, who when the occasion demanded was always cruel to himself could be a little ruthless with others. Refusing to wait, he made up a kind of bed for Hicks in a light cart, while he rode one of the remaining horses. Sekgoma's headquarters, Nakalechwe, lay north-east of the lake, some hundred miles from Lugard's camp. They rode along the dry bed of the "Lake River." By a shrinking pool of water Lugard shot a huge crocodile and as the great reptile thrashed about on the bank, his fox-terrier swam frantically across the pool to retrieve it. The sun grew hotter, the sand looser and it became clear that Hicks, lying in the jolting cart, was becoming dangerously ill. Then they ran into thick acacia forest in which Lugard had to hack a way with an axe. At night the cold was more bitter than anything they had experienced. What with cutting bush, surveying the route and nursing

Hicks, Lugard had a busy time, but he pushed on as fast as he could. When they reached the lake, " this fine-looking sheet of water " where Livingstone " could detect no horizon,"[1] not a drop of water was to be seen: it had been dry for two years. There was only a vast waste of reeds. The floor of the "lake" was full of the ash of burnt vegetation which the wind whirled upon them until they and their bodies and clothes were black. Going on by night along the lake shore, Lugard saw the sun go down a crimson globe as if in a London fog, but the fog here was made by a haze of dust and sand which stung his eyes and choked his nostrils. At night the moon came up and it seemed strange to go through this place of a dead lake and dry rivers where, unbroken by the chirrup of an insect or the cry of a bird, there was a stillness which could be felt.

At Nakalechwe, Lugard found there were two Europeans, a trader, Muller, easily recognizable from his appearance and guttural voice as a German, and a young Englishman bent on trade, who, strangely enough and without any qualifications, was acting as a doctor to the natives. Lugard summoned him urgently to Hicks who now appeared to be almost *in extremis*, and was pleased with the way the young man (" A smart, likely-looking fellow ") set about the sick bed. But his report was grave and next day the " doctor " carried the sick man to his own shack at Nakalechwe to nurse him.

The next day was Sunday and the ever impatient Lugard fumed when he discovered that the graceless young chief kept the day as rigidly as Khama and would be engaged in hymn-singing. With Hicks apparently dying, Lugard was obliged to risk asking Muller, who appeared to be Sekgoma's friend and adviser, to be his interpreter and to help him to get what he wanted. It was very common at this period for chiefs in South Africa to have a white man, missionary or trader, as a friend and counsellor. It was not a very safe step to take, but Lugard, in his quick way, judged well of Muller's honesty, and took the risk.

The *kgotla*, or chief's council, was fixed for September 25th. On these occasions Lugard generally awoke very resentfully to the need of dressing himself in proper fashion. Unfortunately he had brought only one coat with him on the expedition; this was now in rags from the thorns and, as a result of this and of his washing it, it had shrunk

[1] Livingstone, *op. cit.* pp. 65–6.

so that it looked " something between an Eton jacket and John the Baptist's shaggy garment." His boots also had " paid out." They were worn through, so that his feet were sore and the toe of one boot was flapping loose. However, he reflected, they had not done too badly— a thousand miles walking in West Africa and now another thousand in South Africa. " I make my personal effects last pretty well." So he might, but once more we are bound to record astonishment that Lugard's efficiency as a traveller seemed to break down over his own wardrobe. He managed to produce a pair of white flannel trousers he had been saving for such an occasion, a cotton shirt and a neck-tie. Thus arrayed, he went to the council.

He found the chief seated, according to custom, among his councillors and elders on their stools. He looked quickly at Sekgoma and noted that he was " a little man—a mere boy—with the appearance of a well-educated and very well-dressed monkey." Muller introduced Lugard and then interpreted his speech, to which all the councillors listened intently. Lugard reminded them of the concession which Moremi had given to Nicolls and Hicks. He explained that his Company had not, like others, come for land or for the right to govern, but only for minerals. It would be their interest to uphold Sekgoma's just claim to his boundaries as these also bounded the Company's rights: as an independent party he could advise the tribe in its relations with the B.S.A. Company. He would open up roads so that goods could be sold more cheaply. But he wanted three things—that the concession should be renewed for ten years; that instead of the waterless site that had been arranged for a headquarters, a better one should be granted; and that, instead of a royalty of 2% on minerals, £400 should be paid down when minerals were found. Meanwhile, as soon as the new concessions were signed, £400 would be paid. It is not easy to defend these financial revisions by Lugard's employers. Finally, he handed over his presents. These—a writing case and some of his own notepaper stamped " Ngamiland "—were not very rich by West African standards, but they seemed to please. He knew too much about African palavers to expect an immediate reply. So he was not surprised when Sekgoma said that he must consult the ex-regent who was not there and that he would reply on Monday.

When, however, Lugard returned, there were difficulties. First Sekgoma kept him waiting half an hour at the *kgotla*. Then he came and said he could not sign. He must wait at least until the evening to explain the matter further to his people: an appeal to democracy was probably a reality and not a subterfuge. Although Lugard was much disappointed, he pretended not to care. He was willing to wait for days in the boiling sun to achieve his object, but he pretended he had no time to spare. He had, as we know, devised a special technique for these occasions, that of assuming indifference and of being resolved to go at once whether the chief signed or not. But he threw out that Sekgoma was being given a capital chance and would be a fool to lose it.

Whether or not Lugard was right about the effectiveness of the tactics upon which he prided himself, Sekgoma began to weaken. It is interesting to speculate as to whether the chief could know what this concession might mean to himself and his people for good or ill? And, however excellent Lugard's intentions and those of Kirk and the others, could even they know how it might turn out? Where would the Tawana be if another Kimberley or another Johannesburg should spring into existence in their wretched, but to them precious, wilderness? Years afterwards in this country the writer was to hear Khama's son, Tshekedi, declaim passionately against the possibility that the B.S.A. Company should be allowed to open up gold-mining in the lands of his tribe. They preferred to be poor—his hand indicated the boulder-studded waste almost as unpromising as Sekgoma's country— they would rather continue to exist thus in their own way than be swept into annihilation as a tribe by the onset of the white gold-miners. Perhaps some dim fears of this kind were fighting in Sekgoma's mind against the immediate attraction of the cash and the other advantages this masterful and resolute white man might bring him.

" Sekgoma gave a *terrible* amount of trouble—almost as much as Mwanga in Uganda! I spent hours this afternoon and did not get the paper signed in triplicate till after sundown. At the last moment he kept jibbing and smelling his pen and shying at the paper and fooling and asking rotten questions . . . . But I played my role—assumed an air of *ennui* and indifference . . . . and smoked cigar after cigar, first through my mouth and then my nose for a change and I out muled this most obstinate and suspicious of natives. At last all were signed, and I made three leading chiefs sign as witnesses, also Muller, and I made Muller sign a stiff certificate about having fully and clearly and thoroughly explained and interpreted it so that he understood every word before signing . . . I need hardly say that after 8 days of suspense and worry over this matter, I feel pretty pleased tonight! . . . . "   (Diary, 28 September 1896).

Next day Lugard was off before sunrise, having packed the recumbent Hicks, who was now, astonishingly, beginning to recover, into his cart. He hurried across a dangerous stretch of sand in order to examine the new site Sekgoma had granted him. It was waterless and the little party had a struggle to get back to the camp alive. Lugard contracted dysentery, but as both his servants and two white prospectors who came out to meet them, went down with sunstroke, he was forced to keep on his feet, and it was a wretched company which at last crawled in at the end of the journey. But he had at least succeeded in his object.

Lugard's next task was to find a suitable headquarters for the expedition where men and stores could be housed and from which the long-awaited, all-important mining engineer could work. He settled finally upon the site Hicks had established a year or two earlier on some low hills about twenty miles south-east of the lake. Here he was able to take over a store-house and some huts formerly erected by Hicks, and he set to work to build a small house for himself. Water was the main problem and he was fascinated to find ancient wells piercing the solid rock and driven by men who must have had either amazing knowledge of hydraulics or power of water-divining. Unfortunately, in this unprecedented drought, only one of the wells showed water, and that a very little, so drilling and blasting went on feverishly in the hope that these hills, named Kgwebe, the only promising site in the whole horrible region, might be taken as the base for the Company's operations.

These were trying days for Lugard. Periods of relative inaction always irked him. By the time he had got his little hut tidy; arranged his books; put all the accounts into perfect order; written his report; read up all the old copies of *The Times*; given Sekgoma, who was now a frequent and friendly caller, a lot of good advice; worked out a scheme for settling the Armenians in East Africa, and written an article upon the liquor traffic, there was nothing much left to do but wait for his men to dig down to water and for Dr. Passarge, the German mining expert selected by the Company, to arrive. Nor was the Bechuanaland scene, as viewed from the Kgwebe hills, very promising.

The Trek

The heat was intense, and it was accompanied by a constant gale which drove clouds of dust through the air and broke into tornados, but never brought rain. On November 4th, the rinderpest reached Ngami and almost immediately the pools in the dry river beds were choked with dead and dying oxen. On November 6th, the locusts arrived. Cloud after cloud came over the hills. A little patch of maize below the hills disappeared as they looked at it and the trees round the camp, stripped of their leaves, ceased to give any shade from the intolerable sun. The transport animals again began to die, this time from sheer starvation. Restlessness and dissatisfaction now appeared among the white men, and some of them asked to go. The death of one of their number upset them: this was no place in which to die. There was no specific grievance. Lugard was reminded of similar moments in Karonga when a sudden loathing of the hard conditions and a fear for their own survival would run through his company.

In the middle of November the rains broke at last. Africa does not take long to respond to their coming, and after a long drought this response is a sight not to be forgotten by those who have seen it. Lugard and his brother, a keen botanist who was collecting useful information for the Botanical Gardens at Kew, walked out observing with delight, and also with scientific precision, new flowers and insects, new birds in song, and trees and bushes bursting into green life. Within a few days the khaki-coloured sand, all dust and dead sticks, was throwing up a carpet of lilies.[1] The *vleys* filled and, a little more slowly, grass came. But there is often treachery as well as harshness in Africa's nature, and the longed-for rains brought sickness to men and animals. Mules, horses and goats died and only the patient little donkeys stood up to the conditions. At one time all the native servants were ill at once, while the whites also suffered.

Lugard was the more depressed as he had to part with his brother, sending him to the Cape, as the man he could best trust, to purchase a new stock of stores and equipment. His presence on the expedition had been the greatest comfort and joy to Lugard, who reported upon him in laudatory words to the directors. Lugard's great powers of affection were able to find an object in this younger brother, whom he had hardly known in boyhood; not, indeed, until about 1886, when Edward, at the age of twenty, was entering the army. From the first

1 E. J. Lugard, *Bulletin of the Royal Botanic Gardens, Kew*, No. 3, 1909, p. 85 ff.

Edward had responded with affection charged with an admiration that was almost hero-worship. As Lugard confessed in a letter to a friend in England,

" Ned starts in a few days, and I am oppressed by the thought of losing him. He is my ' alter ego '—and my right hand. How I am to live quite alone without him I don't know—how I am to get through the work without him I don't know. It is a depressing thought, for he is the apple of my eye. I am, I know, irritable, imperious, and difficult, especially when I am ' not quite myself' or overworked, but Ned has the patience and the self-negation, and unselfishness of a woman and an angel. There was never anyone like Ned. He has every good point that partial critics can discover or invent in me doublefold, and he lacks all my *many* and most serious and palpable faults. And his love for me is like that of David for Jonathan."   (12 January 1897).

Before his brother set off, early in February, the long-expected mining engineer arrived. In spite of all the help and information Lugard had been able to send him, he had suffered greatly on the road. Lugard made a cautiously favourable report on his first impressions of this important person and commended especially the speed and energy with which he started the work which was the whole object of the expedition. Unfortunately the overseer who arrived a few days later, a friend of Kirk's and a young man of whom Lugard thought highly, proved to be in a very nervous condition. The day after his arrival, following a late dinner in which the newcomer kept everyone in continuous laughter, Lugard was called out in the early morning to find him lying in the bush in a huge pool of blood which was pouring from his throat which he had cut " in a most decisive manner." Africa had remorselessly found the weakness of a highly strung temperament. The anxiety of the trek and of the young man's over-conscientiousness about his work, added to worry about a love affair with a forbidden cousin, had led him to this act. The sight shook even Lugard's nerve and stayed for long in his mind. As he buried him in a deep grave near the camp under a thick tree he murmured to himself: " God forgive him his deed—I at least have no fears on that score."

There were other matters beside the shock of this suicide to depress the expedition. The first months of 1897 were not much of an improvement upon the final quarter of the last year. There was a certain sense of anti-climax after the strenuous achievement of reaching the goal, to sit and wait while the chief engineer and his team journeyed hither and thither with little immediate result. All the white men except Lugard himself had some bad periods of illness. One of the white men died in camp, and another on his way to Palapye; one of the Africans was blinded in a blasting operation, while others suffered as much from the climate as the Europeans. Lugard, who had anxieties of his own which will be discussed presently, grew unbearable in this hated inactivity, and knew it. There was a severe shortage of labour, since Sekgoma, though otherwise most amenable, chose this moment, Bantu-fashion, and probably in pursuit of water, to move to a new " capital " and all the available labour of his sparse tribe was conscripted for this operation. Then the mails, which meant so much to Lugard and which Khama, true to his word, sent up punctually every week by runners, suddenly stopped. Week after week went by without a word from the outside world. Then, after eight weeks' isolation, it was learned that six mail-men sent up had died on the road and one had been eaten by a lion, after which Khama had stopped sending the mail. Finally, after Lugard with great difficulty had collected at fancy prices some " salted " oxen (that is, beasts from among the few which had recovered from the rinderpest), new diseases, gall-sickness and lung-sickness, attacked them.

In spite of all this, Lugard kept the morale of his little band fairly high. He busied them, in his orderly, constructive way, with building most carefully-designed quarters for men and animals. These included, more for reasons of propriety and convenience than comfort, a managing director's house or cottage. Besides well-digging and prospecting, he set his men to make roads or rather tracks radiating out from the Kgwebe hills, especially to Ghanzi in the south-west and another in a straight line south-east in order to meet the route to Palapye—reached about this time by the railway—at Sebetwane's drift. This shortened the route and avoided the feverish stretch along the Botletle.

In all his reports to the Company he could speak well of his men. But in the record of the diary he naturally sometimes confessed less complete satisfaction. He certainly asked a great deal of men undergoing Africa's rigorous test of strength of character and soundness of education. Lugard's character was so close in texture, not only on the surface but right through, that no adverse influence seemed able to penetrate or erode it. In fundamentals, what he had been at No. 31, Saint Paul's Square, York; at his school; and again, what he was in London, this he remained in Borgu and Ngamiland. Leading rough men through rough conditions, within the limits of the possible, he did not change or even adapt his standards; he retained them as they were and imposed them as far as he could upon others.

He had plenty of opportunity to do this. Passarge, his new German colleague, had hardly set off on his first prospecting expedition than one of his African men came back and complained of ill-usage.

"I sent him back at once with a note to P. . . . In reply I got a huge long letter from P. It was a regular German's letter. 'The discipline' must be upheld—the men under him must be made to obey orders and so on . . . . I hope it will never be said of me that I am one of those men who always take a bias against the white man and in favour of the black, yet I admit I *do* think it is generally the white man's fault . . . . But I will not flog a boy unless I am *convinced* he deserves it, and what is more I will not let *any* other man do it. Negrophile or not—I care not for terms—but I care for justice as I conceive it." (Diary, 1 January 1897).

He absolutely forbade any white man to take the law into his own hands and strike a native. If punishment there had to be, it must be decreed by him formally and publicly after investigation. A few days after this a group of natives came back refusing to work under the engineer. Lugard's sympathy was with them, but to one, who was brought to him as having raised a stick against the engineer, Lugard felt obliged to award twelve strokes.

"I *loathe* a flogging, and this is absolutely the first time a man has been touched, not even a cuff or a blow has been given before this."
(Diary, 26 January 1897).

It is worth repeating that, among travellers of the last century, few besides Livingstone could have said so much.

Holding these ideas Lugard was distressed and ashamed when he heard of any instance in which his own countrymen had fallen below what he held to be the British standard of justice and humanity. He believed this to have happened in the suppression of the Matabele rebellion, in which, he heard, packets of dynamite had been left about on the veldt, and he understood that Chamberlain had defended this on the grounds that it was no worse than mines or torpedoes. Another

M.P. had defended the effect of the Lee-Mitford rifle because "the desideratum of a rifle and bullet was to be an effective man killer." Lugard's comment on the lowering of standards which this represented marks vividly the further distance the world has travelled since then.

"I have always understood that the desideratum was to put a man out of action without of necessity so shattering his vitals as to preclude the possibility of his ultimate recovery when the war was over. We are progressing in these days, and I am becoming an old-fashioned soldier."
(Diary, 3 July 1896).

Later news of the shooting down of Matabele "rebels" deeply angered him. It was the white man's injustice and folly he believed that often led to such risings.

"The way of some of our Boy-Administrators are past finding out, but they are all very, very good because they are BRITISH—and because they are mostly told [so] by themselves! I am a trifle bitter, perhaps, but it is enough to make a man bitter who has any sense of right feeling and justice. Africa seems to rub off all the angularities of justice and tone it down to convenience and even to the right of might. And the secret of it all is that the wrong class of man is so often pitchforked into a place where he has infinite power of doing harm." (Diary, 22 October 1896).

He remembered that he had approved Johnston's execution of his old enemy, the cruel and persistent slaver, Mlozi, but regarded that as a very exceptional case.

"Men who are isolated in the heart of Africa must be just and merciful gentlemen—but they must also be self-reliant above all things and willing to accept responsibility."
(Diary, 12 August 1896).

If the little company of white men perched on the Kgwebe hills above the flat Ngami desert remained reasonably contented, it was not because they found any relief in easy living. Quarters were cramped and food often sparse and monotonous. The leader of the expedition himself lived with the greatest simplicity. The sickness of native servants and their shortage often left him to carry out all his own household tasks himself. He patched his tattered clothes. He baked his own bread out of such flour as he could sieve out from among the weevils and it was voted the best in camp and could be made to last for ten days before it went mouldy. When the one wandering police officer who represented British government in this immense area arrived one day, Lugard happened to be ill, but he got up and cooked the dinner himself, soup, mince, compressed vegetables and dried apples and, having laid the table with the best crockery he could get together, he brought it in and served his guests and then went to bed dinnerless himself. On one occasion a sick and injured German drifted in, and Lugard nursed him. The man's jaw being hurt, he could not bite and was starving. Lugard was equal to the situation.

> " I got some mutton (boiled and cold) and minced it in a mincer. Then I got 2 eggs which I found in the nest and beat them up in a cup of milk with some salt and Worcester sauce and some dried mint. . . . This I poured into some boiling fat in the frying pan and made a sort of lovely rumble-tumble and while stirring it up and fizzling I poured in the mince-meat and made it all one mass. I tasted it and it was *deuced* good! "
>
> (Diary, 6 July 1897).

To this he added some Brand's pea-soup. The patient, however, failed to play his part, and gave a genuine or a polite reason for recoiling from Lugard's confection—" I haf ge-eaten nosing, my toad (tooth), he too sore is."

The first half of 1897 came to an end. Edward Lugard returned bringing—strange though it may seem in view of the harsh conditions —his young wife and child. They had come out to South Africa to be near him and, rather than face further separation, they decided to take the risk. Mrs. Lugard had already roughed it in India and as a botanist and an artist she was not likely to find even the Kalahari uninteresting. Transport to the camp was now properly organized. Lugard gave up his cottage to them and shewed his delicacy by refusing to make a fourth at their table. The return of his brother meant much to him: he had missed his trusted co-operation as well as his company.

He was beginning to be very anxious about his continued inability to report any mineral discoveries or even promising geological conditions to his employers. Expeditions were made according to a careful plan in all directions. Lugard waited upon the expert's reports with increasing impatience and gloom. From these it appeared that most of the volcanic rocks were felstone-porphyrite which rarely contains gold. The non-volcanic areas were covered with deep shifting sands of unknown depths, so that prospecting in them was like dredging in the

open sea on the chance of striking a treasure ship on the bottom. Some
of the rocks and slates associated with diamonds had been found, but
even here the prospects were not very favourable.

It was a new experience for Lugard, after he had done all that lay
in his power against heavy odds to make the expedition a success, to
face the possibility that for reasons outside his control it might turn
out a complete failure. He was comforted when Kirk wrote that he,
personally, had never been very sanguine. On the other hand Maund
had been most hopeful and, as a mere soldier, Lugard was astonished
that business men could be so unbusinesslike.

" I have *always* in my own mind looked upon it as a marvellous and most
curious undertaking. To exploit a country like this till lately 750 miles
at the nearest point from a railway . . . . with an almost impassable desert
intervening, with no food and little local labour available . . . with above
all this vast deep coating of flying sand, this absence of water, this climate
which has proved so fatal . . . ."   (Diary, 29 July 1897).

He comforted himself with one certainty. The absolute trust which
the directors had given him, reinforcing his own strong bent, had led
him to impose a most rigorous economy upon himself and all others,
and he could thus calculate that while many leaders would have
spent £500,000 upon the expedition and have found reasons to justify
this cost, he had spent only some £7,000 in non-recoverable expenditure. His long penury had not bred in him any personal avarice:
worried about the high salary paid to him after the first year, now that
the really exacting and dangerous work was coming to an end, he
wrote to the directors asking them to reduce it.

He could do no more than he had done, and as he reviewed the
arduous work of the last eighteen months he had to teach himself a
fatalism and a moderation neither of which were natural to him.

" Inshallah we may find these blessed diamonds! It would make one's
work *appear* successful, though as a matter of fact the finding or not
finding is no part of the success of my work, which is the organization
and control of the means to the end—simply that." (Diary, 29 July 1897).

As he wrote this his work in Ngamiland, though he did not know it,
was almost at an end.

CHAPTER XXVIII

THE RECALL

1896-1897 : Aet. 38-39

THE STORY of the expedition has been told in terms of sand and mules, rinderpest and locusts, the physical efforts and achievements of the days and weeks in the Kalahari. All this was written into his diary and when, according to his practice he wrote over copying paper and sometimes tore out the top sheets and sent them to Kirk, these were accompanied with an apology.

> " A Diary always gives a false perspective and acts as a microscope . . . . and to you reading it at home, we appear to be veritable Hannibals crossing the Alps, instead of very humble ordinary folk leading donkeys across a plain." (4 January 1897).

Here he was referring to the chronicle of the day's exertions and mile by mile advance. But all the time there was for Lugard another story, in some ways more real and important to him than anything he could see with his sand-inflamed eyes and grasp with his roughened hands. It concerned the affairs of the world he had left so far behind him, his special world of personalities and urgent, intense interests and, beyond it the African continent and the world in general, as it was revealed to him, mail by mail, in letters and in the bundles of *The Times* which Khama's strong runners brought at intervals. As he surveyed this distant, exciting world, though he found in it other and nobler themes, that which chiefly dominated him was the frustration of his driving ambition to take a strong hand in its affairs.

The evidence of the diary upon this aspect should be used with the same discrimination and understanding which Lugard asked for upon his chronicle of events. Most keepers of private journals have two selves, the one which by act and word they show to the world by day, and the one they restrain and hide, giving it relief at night in the safe intimacy of secret writing. Which is the truer self and by which kind of evidence should a man be judged? Lugard knew well the value and the temptations of the diarist. He would sit alone at midnight and long after, when all the camp was asleep and through the heavy air came the voice of the grasshopper, the cricket and the bull-frog, and write in his small, level, neat hand into the big ledger-shaped book on his knee:

"A journal is a fine institution. One can ease one's mind and have a fling—be a philanthropist or a Puritan, or a fool—which is the same thing—and then return to one's daily work refreshed. *Only* no-one should read it but the writer for there is nothing so deceptive or which gives so false a colouring and perspective as a journal which gives vent to opinions and passions, instead of chronicling small beer and events only."

(Diary, 4 January 1897).

Lugard was ambitious. To some the word itself stands for a fault. But all depends upon the contents given to the word. The great dramatist of ambition could present it as the sin to which Wolsey confessed and from the imputation of which Cæsar had to be defended, but which, under the name of honour, the heroic King could proudly claim to covet more than all other men. The men who achieve things seldom do so by accident rather than by design; they desire with the whole of their strong natures to achieve them and they believe, often before anyone else shares their faith, that they *can* achieve them. "I suffer absurdly," wrote André Gide, "from the fact that everybody does not already know what I hope some day to be, what I shall be . . . ."[1] In this the man of action does not differ from the man of letters. When men have this inner conviction and believe they are being denied the opportunity to prove their powers, and when they feel the precious months and years of their prime passing, they may become restless and thwarted.

So it was now with Lugard. As a man conscientious in the highest degree he gave all of himself that was needed to make a success of the Kalahari expedition, but there was no need to give his whole mind or any of his heart. His heart was still in East Africa, his mind set upon the problem of slavery which he had studied and tried to solve, and upon the fortunes of the Baganda. He longed to return there to take up his work in the dignity and scope of an imperial appointment

[1] André Gide, *Journals*, tr. Justin O'Brien (1947), vol. i., p. vi.

and with the freedom of sole command. As the eagerly awaited mails arrived with their letters and newspapers all the world they revealed was to him a vast backcloth of a stage: the play was in East Africa, and the scene was waiting for its chief player. But still the promised call from the Foreign Office did not come.

Apart from *The Times* and other papers it was from Kirk that Lugard derived most of his news and in some matters, so great was his esteem for his friend, his views. They discussed the balance of power in the Cabinet and the relations between Salisbury, authoritarian and often inscrutable, who, as Foreign Secretary, was in charge of East and Central Africa, and Chamberlain, who wished to add these territories to the Colonial Office sphere. Together the two friends began at this time to have serious doubts about the character of Germany.

" I suppose," wrote Lugard in his diary, " millions of Englishmen feel as I do—looked on the Germans as our nearest continental kindred and natural allies; and now, disgusted by their low scurrilous abuse and invective of their press . . . . feel a great revulsion of feeling towards them as a nation, and would not be sorry to see them humiliated . . . . "

(Diary, 8 May 1897).

Carlyle was among the few authors represented in his hut, but now he began to detest him. Both he and Kirk received the news of Menelik's victory over Italy at Adowa with very different feelings from those which most people, taught by the developments of the intervening years, now regard it. The Italians were, after all, said Kirk, " the only possible allies we can have," and both feared that Abyssinia would now become the catspaw of France or Germany. The entry of a Russian Red Cross mission on to this exotic setting also roused Lugard's suspicions. " It is not *Italy*, they are aiming at. It is *England* and the Nile Valley and the Massawa-Kassala key." He found more cause for satisfaction as he shifted his gaze north, and rejoiced to observe Kitchener's preliminary movements towards the conquest of the Sudan. He had often suffered from what appeared to be Salisbury's negative policy but now he could admire the Prime Minister's courage in launching such a bold venture at a difficult moment in international affairs.

Nearer at hand Lugard felt, even in the remoteness of his desert, the growing tension in South Africa. He made an impressive list of the troubles hanging over the country, and this included some remarks upon the problems of labour. " The white man is a gentleman here who thinks that God made Kaffirs to do all the menial and manual work and made him a superior being to supervise." Always critical of Rhodes and Jameson, his own sense of having been shelved sometimes gave a rasping edge at this time to his comments upon other men. He and Kirk competed in the severity of their judgment upon the Jameson Raid and Lugard studied with excited interest the evidence about it which was brought out in the enquiry. He agreed with Kirk that, even after all that happened, and the near-disaster to her own career, " Miss Shaw was still as bound up in faith in Rhodes as ever." He regretted her newspaper's continuing bias in favour of Rhodes, for which she was in large measure responsible, and continued to wonder why so much should still be made of the fact that the purposes of Rhodes, a millionaire, were " so unsordid ". Nor was this an academic subject, for Kirk wrote to him that " Rhodes is fully informed that diamonds are to be found in Ngamiland " (11 October 1896), and it was reported to Lugard—it is not clear on what evidence—that Rhodes was determined to get him out of the country.

Lugard's recent experiences in West Africa naturally kept his attention alert in that direction. Goldie and he corresponded and Goldie commented with appreciation upon Lugard's new adventures and his adverse circumstances.

> " But I know no one so competent as yourself to overcome them or, at any rate, to do all that is possible. I often comfort myself with the lines from ' Cato.' ''Tis not in mortals to command success—We have done more, Sempronius, and *deserved* it.'" (12 August 1896).

" That is the true ring," commented Lugard in his diary when he read it, " of a man who has lived his life with an object and an ideal." (15 October 1896). Goldie told him of Niger Company affairs and of his fear that the government might turn against his creation. Kirk and Goldie began to make plans to meet the threat, which was to have an important influence upon Lugard's life, but Kirk, from long and bitter experience, was sometimes pessimistic.

> " Goldie is living in a fool's paradise, but I have given him a hint that he is no match for the F.O. and that if he does not now protect his assets he will come to grief." (Kirk to L. 20 May 1896).

But Goldie's self-confidence was untouched by his friend's doubts.

"Kirk always takes a rather gloomy view owing to the treatment of the I.B.E.A. Co. by H.M.G.; but the conditions are different—so long as I live and keep my fighting powers." (Goldie to L. 12 August 1896).

Presently Kirk could report that

"Goldie sails to-morrow to the Niger to conquer Nupe by force. If he succeeds he will be in a still stronger position than he is now to defend his rights." (Kirk to L. 4 December 1896).

"A deuced good business" is Lugard's comment with an angry thrust at the Foreign Office since

"they intend to throw over the interests of the Empire, to cringe to France and Germany and to treat as a bargainable asset the life's work of Goldie." (Diary, 21 January 1897).

And a little later he is recording

"Goldie of course completely successful on the Niger. He is not likely to bring back his troops without first doing something worth going for. I wonder if he will precipitate the 'Armageddon' as he called it to me and tackle Sokoto himself! I think not." (11 March 1897).

But he was wrath with *The Times* for giving a misleading account of the event by exaggerating the extent of the victory and claiming that slave-raiding was "the one thing the Company could not tolerate." Lugard, for all the depth of his own feeling against slavery, hated any attempt to exaggerate British humanitarianism and he remarked acutely:

"The difficulty of the Indian law courts is to prevent a man who has right and fact and truth on his side from lying to such an extent in order to try to better his case as to almost obliterate the truth—we as a nation partake of the same failing." (15 March 1897).

In this instance the Company *had* long tolerated the Nupe Emirs' slaving because it was too busy to attend to it; it had moreover its own interests in destroying a threat to its power and communications. Honesty, Lugard believed, was the best policy even in justifying imperialism.

608

If East Africa should be denied him, would the call be to West Africa? Goldie had hopes, if his schemes succeeded, that he would be able to offer him a purely administrative post, though he was doubtful if he could make it worth his while, " if the magnificent pay of the Ngami Co. is not exaggerated by report—as I hope it is not." (Goldie to L. 12 August 1896). This meant Company service once more. True, Lugard had been offered the Niger Coast Protectorate by the government, but he had refused and Goldie approved. " I am very glad you did not accept the N.C.P. and sink into a Coast Customs Collector." (Goldie to L. 12 August 1896). Lugard himself had a revulsion from that region.

" Thank Heaven I did not go to that thrice accursed place. I think I would sooner undergo penal servitude. Everything connected with the N.C.P. revolts me, its liquor-traffic, its so-called ' Administration,' its climate, its cannibals, and the spirit of its officers." (Diary, 15 March 1897).

There was no doubt as to which part of his adopted continent drew him. It is characteristic of the colonial administrator to love best the place of his most effective achievement; the inner glow of pride and joy in good work irradiates the people who were served and the very scenery of the country. Uganda was especially high in Lugard's affections. He had letters from his old lieutenants there, especially from Wilson, and he loved to hear both that his name was remembered and that the country he had done so much to win for the empire was progressing well. He had always thought highly of the Baganda.

" Everything is *couleur de rose* in Uganda and the place is going ahead wonderfully. How I wish I could have had a hand in this development, which from my knowledge of that very remarkable people I foresaw . . . " (Diary, 13 December 1896).

Some of these remarkable people had been able to recognize *his* quality and be grateful for his services. Lugard was not effusive or forthcoming in personal relations; his standards of character were high and he exchanged friendship only with those who measured up to them. But when he did give his regard or friendship they were worth having. We have seen his instant trust in the king of Kiama and his respect for the great chief of Palapye. Now he learned that his old friend, Zachariah of Uganda, still cherished "Kapelli's" friendship.

He had become an Anglican priest and he now used his newly acquired use of the pen in writing letters to him, which sometimes ran to eight quarto pages.

" I think," he wrote, " your ears and your heart are always ready to hear the words and the condition of Uganda." (" And," Lugard commented, " he speaks of the peace now in the country in terms almost poetical! ") " Husbandmen in truth are the soldiers of the country who guard our land, the hoes with which they till the soil are its cannon and its rifles— now there is naught but peace throughout all our land of Uganda."

" All that I said," Lugard continued, " (about the freedom of religion) he says is now fulfilled. Then he asks me to send them some seeds of fine English trees which they will plant close to the King's house in memory of me." (Diary, 4 November 1896).

He had other letters from Uganda, including one from the king of Toro, whom he had restored, while many more, who could not write, sent him warm messages telling him how right he had been in what he had tried to do for them and how well the country was progressing. Nothing touched him more than messages from Malia whom, as a little girl, he had adopted while her father was in arms against him. He longed to be back amongst them again. Even one of the French priests wrote to him a warm and friendly letter. He could not help wondering what those foreign critics who had called him murderer, some of whom had said that his C.B. should mean Commander of the Bath of Blood, would have thought if they could have read these letters.

It was anguish for him to think that Macdonald whom, it will be remembered, he condemned for personal and public reasons, should be in charge of the work he had begun so well. Yet, as we saw, he had refused without any hesitation an offer to go back to Uganda in command of the troops, with the right to deputize in the Resident's absence; it was not soldiering he wanted now, but administering and that from the top.

But if he felt an intimate and personal concern for Uganda, the land to which the controversial and expensive railway was now being painfully extended, he had another interest in the coast where the railway had its base. Here, it will be remembered, he had confirmed his boyish interest in slavery. The evil which he had been led to fight physically in Nyasaland, he had met on the East African coast as a complex social problem to be dealt with by skilled administration. Since he had left East Africa he had fought a long campaign in England in close alliance with Kirk. The succession, which Kirk had inherited from Livingstone, was now falling upon Lugard, and once again it was being handed on through friendship and co-operation and personal experience of the hated thing. Lugard condemned the Foreign Office bureaucrats, the East African officials, and the " Anti-Slavery Faddists " impartially for the way they were failing to carry on Kirk's work, but he was refreshed to see

" one solitary *Man*—the one upright, honest man with convictions and without fear and withal with an intellect that dwarfs their united purblind foolings. Dear old Sir John—it is my greatest pride and my greatest pleasure that I may call myself his friend and though I can't rival his ability and intellect I can—and I trust *do*—follow in his own fearless line in these matters."

(Diary, 3 March 1897).

Their letters to each other and Lugard's diary were largely taken up with a commination in which the sins of the High Commissioner of East Africa, Sir Arthur Hardinge,[1] were the reiterated refrain. It would be too large a task to explain all the counts in the indictment against him. It will be enough to say that both Kirk and Lugard were eager to see Arab slavery eliminated gradually without compensation by the abolition of its legal status. They considered that Lord Salisbury and his Foreign Office advisers and agents were defaulting from the fine traditions of Britain and showing far too much concern for the interests of the Arab slave-owners and too little for their human property. Kirk, who knew as much as any man about Zanzibar and its Omani dynasty, would have seen the sultanate abolished rather than that consideration for its interests should stand in the way of Britain's anti-slavery policy. In the end the legal status of slavery was abolished abruptly in April 1897 but with compensation to the Arabs.[2]

There were other charges against the East African administration. Here Lugard, who had vivid memories of his happy relations with the tribes on the way to Uganda, and especially with the Kamba and Kikuyu groups, was distressed to hear of continuing punitive expeditions, and of Indian troops being used against the Swahili " rebels "

[1] See above p. 555.
[2] See L. W. Hollingsworth, *Zanzibar under the Foreign Office, 1890–1913* (1953), pp. 132–43.

and inland tribes. " It makes me wild to think of it." With knowledge and sympathy, he believed all this repressive action would have been unnecessary.

It may be assumed that neither Kirk, as an elder statesman, watching those who had taken up his life's work, nor Lugard, who was criticizing a governor whom he was burning to replace, were wholly impartial in their judgments. Lugard was so certain that he—and perhaps, as his friends suggested, he alone—could carry East Africa, " the finest country in the Empire" through this difficult formative phase, dealing justly and sympathetically with all interests, and above all, keeping high Britain's reputation for humanity. There were times when the news brought to him gave him such a longing to seize hold of events in East Africa and shape them in his own way that he recoiled from the work upon which he was engaged. He writhed at the thought that by his present appointment he had lost at least one good opinion which he valued and which meant much to him.

" Chamberlain, I know, thinks I have been bought for this job. He thought me disinterestedly keen about East Africa and doubtless now smiles cynically when he learns (as he supposes he has) that I had my price . . . . I confess that my petty and despicable pride is hurt that my reason should be so misconstrued."   (Diary, 11 November 1896).

In East Africa, he thought, " I might do a lot of good . . . . Anyway I chafe at the thought that I am hunting for this damned gold and pebbles when I might be roasting Hardinge!" (Diary, 4 January 1897). This mood persisted into February.

" I have worked as though an Empire's fate was at stake. I have written a report of 48 pages of quarto very small writing, an annex of 8 more etc., etc., and I have time to look up and I ask myself with some considerable misgiving, is it worth the postage? . . . The fact is I am considerable depressed and with good cause, and a worry and anxiety absorbs my mind and drives me mad."   (Diary, 19 February 1897).

There were times when, spurred to the sudden need to carry out some task, to make things " ship-shape," or when warmed by the directors' trust or Kirk's commendation, he found some satisfaction in what he was doing. Then the unrest would come again. " It seems a terrible waste of time and I am capable of a higher class of work than this."

We have seen that he always had great respect for anniversaries, and on May 11th he noted that he had completed nineteen years' service .... " North India, Central India, Afghanistan, Burma, and the Soudan, Nyasaland, East Africa and Uganda, West Africa and Borgu and now South Africa .... I have *lived* these 19 years." But was he living now?

He felt that he was forgotten. He read of speeches on Nyasaland by Harry Johnston and by a director of the old African Lakes Company.

"Neither mentioned my name .... And yet I saved that Company and held the place for a year. I never took a cent from them .... and it is the same now re Uganda. These things are a just rebuke to one's self-importance."

(Diary, 20 March 1897).

And when the newspapers came in—" It is these glimpses of the great world outside Ngamiland—and the recollection of the great things that are to do in it which stir the rotten ambition in one's veins and make one feel cramped in this God-forsaken desert .... " (Diary, 30 January 1897). He would carry out to the full his obligations to his " most generous and kind employers. But *after* that I long to be back in a position of less freedom and more responsibility—a higher class of work, with greater results, the building up of an Empire." But close upon the conception would come, almost inseparable from it, the longing to continue his attack upon the thing he loathed—African slavery. " I have a longing," he confided to a friend, " to be once more an instrument in the creation of a future Empire—to have the moulding of some of the earlier work and to make the mark of my own personality and my own views on those beginnings." (29 November 1896). For this he would at once and gladly sacrifice the money, the freedom and what, according to his peculiar standards, he regarded as the *ease* of his present life.

He seems to have been quite certain that Sir Percy Anderson of the Foreign Office would keep his promise to appoint him to East Africa.[1] As time went on he almost began to dread that he would have to work with or even under Hardinge. Even if he did not detest his policy, could he ever again serve under another man?

" I have much misgiving that I am not suited to work under *any* man! It is a sad confession to make, but I know it to be true. I am headstrong

1 See above pp. 572-3.

and independent. I don't care a curse for much that I suppose I ought to value and I have 'run my own show' for so many years, and that 'a show' which demanded often no ordinary charge of responsibility and initiative and self-decision, that I am as unsuited (to compare small with great) as was Gordon to do bottle-washer to Ripon in India. I fear that in my desire to go back there and pull the chestnuts (viz., the slaves) out of the fire, my case will be as great a fiasco as was his. Yet how can I refuse? " (Diary, 17 January 1897).

A few days later, after a period of intense preoccupation with this longing (during which even his devoted brother told him his " manner was unbearable ") he came to his decision. " I *must* go . . . . is it not my duty to stand in the breach—a thankless task—and do what I can for East Africa." (Diary, 21 January 1897). The day after this—his thirty-ninth birthday—he felt much more himself because he had made up his mind. He was, like Kirk, absolutely certain that the offer would come from the Foreign Office. Even the news of Sir Percy Anderson's death did not bring serious doubts that the promise would be affected. On this day, therefore, he wrote to Maund, asking for leave to come home to England in order to discuss the East African appointment with the Foreign Office.

A few days later an exhausted runner from Khama came in with the mail. There was a letter from Kirk to say that he had been brought face to face with Hardinge, in the presence of Chamberlain and Balfour. " You might as well pit an inflated frog against a bull " was Lugard's comment followed by his delighted conclusion that " Hardinge was *crushed*." Then he looked at the rest of the post. There, at last, was the long-expected letter from the Foreign Office, franked by Lord Salisbury and bearing his own " S " in red-ink. Lugard's hand trembled as he opened it; his whole future life, he told himself, depended upon its contents. In polite and evasive terms, in which he was thanked by Lord Salisbury for his willingness to give up " your present lucrative appointment ", he was informed that " a somewhat costly scheme for strengthening the British Administration of East Africa " had been abandoned and there was now no call upon his services. (Diary, 27 January 1897).

Lugard was astounded. He had Anderson's letter offering him an appointment at a later date and his own acceptance. It was a severe blow to his pride as well as his hopes, especially as the letter contained no hint of any future appointment. " I am sorry—very sorry—that apparently I am to be ousted altogether from East Africa." Anderson, doubtful ally though he had been, was dead and " A new king has arisen who knows not Joesph." What lay behind the decision? It is difficult at this date to be sure. Had Lord Salisbury cherished some prejudice, however faint, against the name, ever since it had been flung at him in 1888 when he had refused to annex the lands round Lake Nyasa? And had that prejudice been fostered in that cool detached mind by the energetic controversial activities abroad and at home connected with this same name in the succeeding years? Or was he simply supporting his own Foreign Office nominee, Hardinge, against the criticism of Kirk and the intrusion of his friend, especially as Hardinge's cautious policy with regard to slavery must have had Salisbury's full confidence. Or was this, only half-consciously perhaps, a defensive action against Chamberlain, who coveted his East African domain and who had pressed Lugard upon him? It seems certain that if East Africa had at that time been under the Colonial Office Lugard would have been sent there. Not only would this have greatly changed his own career; we may wonder whether he might not also have influenced the future of East Africa. No one man could have wholly exorcised the profound difficulties that were just beginning to develop in East Africa but it may well be wondered whether the sense of order, the administrative energy and the sure touch of a strong African administrator, moulding the still malleable clay of the future Kenya's racial and land problems, might not have given that country a better and fairer start than Sir Arthur Hardinge and his immediate successors had it in their power to give.

Though Lugard felt at once a relief from the strain of anxiety about making his own decision, he was also bitterly disappointed and hurt. He found some comfort in that most sterile of achievements, a cutting and ironic reply to the government department concerned. But he would not have been his mother's son if he had not treated himself to the appropriate sermon, even if it no longer had a Christian text:

" Man has got but one life to live and the approval of his own consciousness is the highest reward his reason confers, let who will argue
to the contrary. So there's my bit of moralising, the inevitable resort and
consolation of the disappointed—since the days of Æsop and the fox and
sour grapes."
(Diary, 2 February 1897).

Meanwhile, having cabled to his employers cancelling his request for leave, he threw himself with a more single mind into the work that lay to his hand on the Kgwebe hills.

It was not to last for long. One evening in August, Lugard was sitting with his brother in one of the little wooden huts of the abandoned mission station they had taken over. Above them rose the summit of the hill, studded with large, rough boulders. Below here and there on the slopes stood immense baobabs, those most distorted of trees with vast trunks and puny branches. Beyond them in all directions stretched the vast level plains, a sea of grey, flat-topped acacia thorns. The brothers sat at a table made of packing-cases. Lugard's firm chin was hidden by a dark brown beard and his slight figure was clothed in patched and ragged clothes. They were calculating the losses of the new oxen from lung-sickness. " I scheme and plan all day to reduce expenses," grumbled Lugard, " and then the animals die off and £1,000 is lost in a few days."

Presently Mrs. Lugard called them to a tent near by, where she had been preparing dinner, for this, being Sunday, was the day when Lugard dined out. She had cooked a dinner of several courses, and with the help of some china a passing missionary had left behind and some linen she had brought, it was served as nearly as possible as dinner, by their standards, should have been served. As they sat eating someone blundered heavily over the tent ropes and a weary white sergeant of police, a new and strange apparition, was seen in the doorway holding a large envelope. Lugard took it. Inside was an official letter, plastered all over with huge seals and marked secret. In this was a cable from the Colonial Office to the British High Commissioner in South Africa. It ran as follows:

" From Secretary of State for Colonies to High Commissioner, Cape Town. London, July 30/97. It is the intention of H.M'.s Govt. to raise without delay a West African force of 2,000 or 3,000 men to occupy important places on the Hinterland of Gold Coast and Niger territories, which are within the British sphere of influence and which otherwise may be occupied by the French. Forward this information by letter in the most sure and secret manner, if possible in cipher, to Major Lugard, and in the name of H.M.'s Government offer him the command of this force at a salary of £1,500 and with the title of Commissioner and Commandant of the forces with the local rank of Lieut. Colonel. If he accepts he must immediately come home to receive instructions. In any case he must keep the matter absolutely secret."

Lugard's first feeling on reading this was that of having received a blow, and his first thought: " How can I decline? " Now that he was offered a military command he realized in a flash that he detested the idea of soldiering and felt that he had neither the will nor the competence for the task. He saw at once that it was another of these highly difficult and delicate expeditions. Then he remembered how his uncle, Sir Edward Lugard, had told him that on his Persian campaign he had conducted the operations while his chief Outram[1] had kept all the political work. " If I can find a man as capable," thought Lugard, " I would act as Outram did. ' *Si licet in parvis exempla grandibus reti.*' " For he knew that in spite of his first distaste for the job and the region he must accept. " Yes, I *must* go through with it." (Diary, 22 August 1897).

The decision taken, he set about preparing for an early departure and a swift journey. It was, he now found, not easy to go, in fact it was " a horrible wrench." It was only when faced with this wrench that he realized that this last year, with his brother's company, his absolute freedom, and his relief from money worries, had been in some ways the happiest in his life. Those whom he was leaving felt it too. His brother's wife, as she heard he was going, exclaimed half to herself words that were a very just tribute, one which many others would feel in the future, that when he was there, " there was a feeling of someone so strong behind." Rapidly he gave to his trusted brother all his papers, his advice, and most earnest good wishes.

He set out at once with little attendance and only 300 lbs. of baggage, intending to dash to Palapye at the highest possible speed. As he hurried south-east, he had to send back one by one exhausted mules and unprofitable servants who were slowing his pace until he faced the " thirsts " between the last water and Palapye with only two boys, one mule and one horse. It was necessary to send back all but the barest minimum of flour and water and papers, and much of these, with his gun, he had to carry himself. All depended in the last spurt

---

[1] Outram, Lieutenant-General Sir James, K.C.B., Commander-in-Chief of the Persian Campaign, 1856-7. Sir Edward Lugard was his Chief of Staff. See Major-Gen. Sir F. J. Goldsmid, *James Outram* (1880).

upon the party being able to keep moving almost without rest so as not to eat up their provisions. Everything went wrong. Trudging in the deep hot sand Lugard wore the soles off his boots, and his men the skin off their feet. They were visited by lions and stung by swarms of vicious bot-flies; some water they found in a *vley* all but poisoned them and to his horror, Lugard detected the beginnings of dysentery. He dosed himself heavily according to his usual drastic self-treatment, with chlorodyne and ipecacuanha. His nine-year-old wound in the wrist began, as often in hard moments, to eject splinters of bone. Again, but now exhausted and untended, he endured the burning heat of days and the cold at night. The last hundred miles of struggle across the waterless sand, flogging on the exhausted animals, very nearly saw the end of the three men. It was only when they had almost won through to Palapye that they met an escort with eight splendid mules sent out by Khama to bring them in. It had not been expected that Lugard would start two days after the runner arrived and move so quickly.

At Palapye those who had seen him before were shocked at his appearance after his trek. There was a warm meeting between Lugard and Khama. They had new reasons to respect each other. Lugard had been impressed by the way Khama had kept his difficult promise to send up the mails and Khama by the tales the men had brought back of generous and courteous treatment. But there was an awkward little matter to be settled between them. One early morning on the trek, sleepy and still exhausted, Lugard had suddenly come upon what he thought were two zebra standing against the rising sun, which shone level over the plain straight into his eyes. He had bagged them with a right and left and hurried forward to find a horse and a mule lying on the ground. In his mortification he could hardly bear to look at them. The mule, it appeared, was one which had run away from his caravan on the way up, but the horse belonged to one of Khama's tribe. For this murder he was accountable to Khama. The chief, it need hardly be said, took it in good part, and allowed Lugard to assess the damages himself. This he did, buying for £10 another horse for the owner.

From Palapye he cabled for permission from his directors to resign and, having received this, he cabled acceptance of Chamberlain's appointment and hurried on to Cape Town. It was indeed a quick change of scene and of life. He found himself a guest at Government House attended by two A.D.C.'s who had been with him at Sandhurst, and by another, young Wood, the son of Sir Evelyn, "a very nice, merry boy." There was Table Mountain, "gauze on its mighty limbs" above him, around him exquisite gardens with running streams, roses, violets and hedges of plumbago, and, best of all, deep talk with the High Commissioner, Sir Alfred Milner, "the same charming, utterly unaffected and shrewd and able man I have always known." It was an intense pleasure to talk to a man so intelligent and responsive. He put before him all his views about Bechuanaland and its administration with the case for his Company. He complained about the hostile behaviour towards it of the Colonial Office, and he came away feeling he had proved his points. Milner was especially pleased with the road-making and other useful work he had done in Ngamiland.

He sailed from Cape Town on October 6th. On the voyage, for once, by his own assertion, he "slacked," a treatment that was most certainly needed. The German Governor of South-West Africa was on board and his face ("the most repulsive evil face it is possible to conceive"), his behaviour and his reputation for brutality confirmed his new opinion of the Germans and decided him not to speak to the man during the voyage. In this conduct he was reinforced by what he had heard of German cruelties over the border during his time in Ngamiland.

The night before he reached Southampton, as he walked round the deck gazing into the rough autumn night, his not unusual tendency to gloomy prognostications had him thoroughly in its grip. "I feel myself in as disagreeable and awkward a position as any I can remember in my life." The mood was not altogether unwarranted. As the ship came into Madeira he had been given a foretaste of the condition to which he was returning. According to his diary, a friend wrote to tell him his belief that not only Kirk, but the directors officially were dismayed at his sudden return, since:

> "your secession practically settles them, for no one with two grains of sense in his head will believe that you have thrown up a magnificent salary and position for the mere fad of serving under a Govt. that has outraged you in every way. The opinion of the City will undoubtedly be that you have thrown the Company over because as an honest man you could not serve it."
> (Diary, 20 October 1897).

This, thought Lugard, was absolutely intolerable. He would be received after his hard work, not with a welcome, " but as a renegade and traitor who has injured those who trusted him and ruined the interests committed to his care." (As it turned out the Company lost nothing by his resignation. He continued to fight for its interests against the Colonial Office and other opponents after his return and the search for minerals, though unsuccessful, was carried on for the following two years, under his brother's direction, until the Boer War broke out.) Almost worse was the news which met him at Madeira about the expedition he was to lead. The secret had been lost: the French, having wind of it, had already sent 500 Senegalese troops to Nikki, and he would have to meet " these fiends under French officers " with his hurriedly collected, raw levies.

The longed-for imperial appointment had come at last, only to be given this strange reception. " The task before me ", he decided that same last night on the ship, " is one from which I shrink and which I detest." (Diary, 23 October 1897).

PART SIX

The Niger Again 1897-1898

The Niger Again 1897-1898

CHAPTER XXIX

IMPERIAL APPOINTMENT

1897 : Aet. 39

IT HAD been in a spirit of urgency that Chamberlain had recalled Lugard. While Lugard had been surveying Ngamiland, Anglo-French rivalry in his old arena in the bend of the Niger had been working up again to the level of international conflict.

Much had happened in West Africa since Lugard had taken up his work for the Charterland Company, and this must be reviewed if the significance of his appointment is to be understood. Just as he left England, Goldie, having decided to tolerate no longer the rivalry of a slave-raiding emir in the very heart of his commercial dominion, had organized a campaign which, like most things to which he put his hand, had been swift, efficient and decisive. The directors of Chartered Companies in the nineties did not conduct their operations from an office chair, and just as Rhodes had gone almost alone in the summer of 1896 among the rebellious Matabele, a phial of poison in his pocket, so a few months later Goldie, carrying, it was said, the same precaution, himself marched with the Company's forces. These seemed absurdly small for their task. The result showed once again what European weapons and discipline, employed with resolute purpose and aided in this case by a navigable river, could achieve in Africa. It was something very different from the issue of that other battle fought the same year by the Italians at Adowa upon the opposite side of the continent where the Africans had not only European weapons but a great leader and a great tradition. Even on the Niger the vast hosts of the emirs, had they been led with determination and been prepared to face the cost of initial casualties, could have smothered the little European-led force. A few white officers and some 500 of their trained Hausa soldiers were engaged against their fellow Muslims in two battles. In the first, 30,000 of the enemy were defeated with the

623

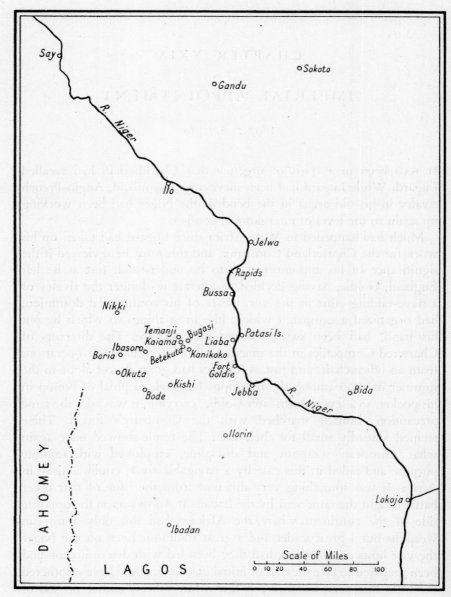

Say

Sokoto

Gandu

R. Niger

Ilo

Jelwa

Rapids

Bussa

Nikki

Temanji
Kaiama
Ibasoro
Boria
Betekutd
Okuta

Bugasi
Liaba
Kanikoko
Fort
Goldie

Patasi Is.

Kishi
Bode
Jebba

R. Niger

Bida

Ilorin

Lokoja

D A H O M E Y

Ibadan

Scale of Miles

0 10 20   40   60   80   100

L A G O S

The Niger Bend 1897-8

loss of eight men on the Company's side, while in the other, some 10,000 were routed without any casualties to the victors.[1] The important Muslim centres of Ilorin and Bida submitted to Goldie, and he used his power to preserve the emirates, because—a remark worth noting in view of Lugard's later administrative methods—" The Company, following the example of the East India Company and the Government of India, desires, as far as practicable, to rule indirectly through native feudatory princes." But " slave-raiding . . . . is at an end for ever."[2]

But this efficient little campaign, though it opened up for occupation an important block of the vast area which the Company claimed on the map, lay well to the south-east of the scene of Lugard's former operations, into which the French at this time were trying to pierce more and more deeply with a number of small but very nimble expeditions. It was, indeed, a continuation of the same story that was recounted before, only with the action growing rather more tense.

The French were alarmed by Goldie's sudden military incursion. There were critical references to it in the press and in parliament. Was this, it was asked with barbed sarcasm, going to be a new Jameson Raid into French territories? If so, as it proved successful, it would not on *this* occasion, be disavowed in London.[3] Lord Salisbury reassured the French ambassador as to the area of the campaign,[4] but the French took the opportunity of Goldie's distraction to send a naval officer, one Bretonnet, from Dahomey to occupy some hundred miles of the right bank of the Niger from Ilo to the long-claimed Company station of Bussa, at which post their representative took the title of " Resident de France au Moyen Niger."[5] Other expeditions continued the French fanning-out process further west into Gurma and Mossi, the latter cutting into the natural Gold Coast hinterland. Lord Salisbury wrote to the British ambassador in Paris requesting an explanation of the French action and asked that a copy of his dispatch be sent to the Foreign Minister, M. Hanotaux.[6] But,

[1] *Report by Sir George Goldie on the Niger Sudan Campaign to the Earl of Scarbrough, Deputy Governor, R.N.C.* (1897), pp. 14–21, C.O. 147/124.
[2] *Ibid.* p. 6.
[3] J.O. (Ch.), 7 December 1896, p. 2046, col. 2.
[4] Courcel to Hanotaux, 17 December 1896, A.A.E. vol. 921, f. 137.
[5] Salisbury to Monson, 15 April 1897, F.O. 27/3335.
[6] Salisbury to Monson, 12 March 1897, F.O. 27/3335.

V

with their missions advancing daily, it paid the French to delay, and it was not until April 23rd, after two reminders, that M. Hanotaux answered and then only to say that he had referred the matter to the Colonial Minister.[1]

The French case must be understood. It was now again in the hands of that very able Frenchman, Gabriel Hanotaux, who became Foreign Minister in April 1896.[2] He had held this office three times in the preceding years, but on this occasion he was a member of the unusually strong Méline ministry, and the period during which it held office, the two years April 1896 to June 1898, was also unusual in its length. Hanotaux combined the experience of a professional diplomat with those of a politician and a historian, one, moreover, of marked literary merit who has left us his own account of his diplomatic struggle with Britain.[3] He had made a study of the English temperament; he was subtle and tenacious in his policy but knew when moderation, or the appearance of it, could pay. It was the French view that the agreement of 1890 with Britain, and especially the Say-Barruwa line,[4] had been a disgraceful act of weakness for France and there was a determination in colonial circles to revise it by action. We have seen how their attempt to claim all Borgu by a treaty with Nikki was challenged by the Niger Company through Lugard in the race to Nikki; challenged but not, in the French view, defeated. The long story of Nikki was by no means ended.

Hanotaux defined French opposition to British claims and directed it but, as his ultimate purpose was a satisfactory settlement with Britain, he also tried to keep it in check. For the Niger grievance was, of course, always subsidiary to the rankling wound of Britain's continued occupation of Egypt. The Marchand expedition to the Upper Nile, a project about which Lugard had warned his country,[5] was already on the way. But in the meantime the Niger region was the place where Britain was most open to a counterstroke. On the morrow of the Jameson Raid, Britain, in European eyes, seemed to have over-reached herself, especially in Africa. Hanotaux, playing on the old deep French impression that all over the world and at every time Britain

---

[1] Monson to Salisbury, 23 April 1897, F.O. 27/3338.
[2] See above p. 531.
[3] G. Hanotaux, *Fachoda* (Paris 1909).
[4] See above pp. 487-8.
[5] See, for example, his article 'England and France in the Nile Valley', *National Review*, vol. XXV, July 1895.

stood in the path of France's imperial ambitions, was determined this time to assert France's rights. He characterized Britain's African policy as one of reckless assurance. She had, he believed, a triple design—to inherit Portugal's possessions; to destroy the South African republics; and to instal herself permanently in Egypt and on the Suez Canal. " A conception, a gigantic formula, worthy of the imagination of the compatriots of Shakespeare, crowned this fascinating project: ' the Cape-to-Cairo railway.' The British had christened Africa ' The Black Indies '."[1] Hanotaux knew the difficulty of the task he was setting himself. " Anglo-French negotiation ", he stated, " is the supreme test of diplomats . . . . " The English language itself was a barrier, " elle affirme, elle n'explique pas."[2] He believed his only hope was to confront Britain, not with arguments but with facts, the solid facts of possession. This was the last thing Britain wanted. The policy of the Niger Company was to work its way gradually outwards from its main bases as commercial opportunities and communications allowed, and not to be rushed into rapid, unremunerative annexation for the political and military reasons which dominated French and German minds.

There were two fields of contest—the hinterland of the Gold Coast and the Niger Company's sphere. We are concerned with the second of these. Here it was still the old question of the great triangle of Borgu within the Niger bend, and whether this was covered by the extension south from Say of the 1890 Say-Barruwa line. If not, it was a free-for-all scramble. And if that what, if any, were the rules of the game? There were three possible rules for deciding the winners: firstly, that of treaties with chiefs; secondly, that of effective occupation; and thirdly, that of the right to the hinterland behind an occupied coast. But none of these was defined beyond question in international agreements, still less accepted. It was a game in which the players on each side changed the rules to suit their position at any given time in the field and, as there was no umpire, confusion and bad temper, with the possibility of something worse, were the inevitable results. The French even invented new rules in the middle of the game: the typically Gallic ones that the planting of the French flag at any time[3]

---

[1] Hanotaux, *op. cit.* p. 80.
[2] *Ibid.* p. 85–6.
[3] Gosselin and Everett to Gosselin, 29 October 1897, F.O. 27/3340; and Salisbury to Gosselin. 11 November 1897, F.O. 27/3336.

or the shedding of French blood in any place gave her a sacred right to its possession.[1] The British worked under the handicap of administrative division between a Company and a government, and that a government which was dealing with the region through two departments of state, one of which, the Colonial Office, had two colonial governments as its agents in the region, those of the Gold Coast and Lagos, the Niger Coast Protectorate being under the Foreign Office until 1899. Whereas the French were still building up a single area from the Mediterranean to the Gulf of Guinea, and from Senegal to Chad and beyond, the British areas, extending inland from the coast, were now clearly becoming separate enclosures in this encircling sweep of the French advance.

The conflict which now entered upon an intensive phase took place at once upon several different planes. At the top, coming increasingly into action, were the principals, the Ministers, Foreign and Colonial, upon each side, both pairs suffering from acute private difficulties over their own departmental frontiers. Below them came their respective ambassadors, in London the able Baron de Courcel, sincerely anxious to attain peace and, in Paris, Sir Edmund Monson,[2] handicapped by a profound lack of confidence in his country's case. Below the ambassadors, acting as a sort of sub-committee, was the Niger Commission of experts, which had wrangled throughout most of 1894, had broken off in despair and had resumed their sessions in February 1896. Alongside these official antagonists, acting for the most part in diplomatic privacy, were the vocal elements of press and parliaments. The former became increasingly clamorous as the months passed, though this time the French press was rather less provocative than the British. *The Times* of 1897 carried a number of articles, most of them written by Flora Shaw, summarizing the whole diplomatic position at a length that is impressive to our generation, while it also printed editorials and long letters on the subject as well as the day-to-day news of the movements of the game. *Le Temps* answered *The Times*, while the voices of the *National Zeitung* and the *Kölnische Zeitung* could be heard in the background. Large and excellent, if somewhat provisional, maps appeared in the daily press and in the monthly journals. Finally, since

1 See below p. 699.
2 Monson, Sir Edmund, G.C.M.G., G.C.B., 1834–1909; 1858 entered Diplomatic Service; 1865 retired and stood unsuccessfully as Liberal candidate at Reigate; 1869 re-entered Diplomatic Service; 1893 Ambassador in Vienna; 1896–1904 Ambassador in Paris.

negotiation in Europe put no veto upon "scrambling" in Africa, there was the frontier conflict where the French expeditions, well on into 1897, were doing all the scoring.

In diplomacy the French showed themselves extremely versatile fencers, circling all round the unhappy Monson and pricking at him from every quarter. This Bussa treaty of the Niger Company—they regarded that as merely a commercial contract with no political significance. In any case Borgu was not under Bussa; it was a conglomeration of independent chiefdoms which they were at liberty to appropriate piecemeal—as indeed they were doing. And they did not recognize the Niger Company's treaties unless they were confirmed by the British government. They would certainly not recognize any treaty made by a native agent. These and many other thrusts were followed by two which were aimed at the heart. Firstly, did not the Berlin Act lay down that occupation to be valid must be effective? And could it be said that the Niger Company had effectively occupied when not a man of theirs was to be seen away from the river? Had not the Commandant Toutée searched in vain for any sign of the Company even 100 kilometres south of Bussa? All he could find was a single negro, who called himself Sir Byron Macaulay, and said he was the representative of the Company and stole the French mission's sugar.[1] And secondly, did not the Berlin Act also guarantee freedom of navigation on the Niger? This freedom, thanks to the Niger Company, was as much a minus quantity on the river as were effective occupation or valid treaties away from it.[2]

The British used all their heavy diplomatic ammunition which expended itself harmlessly in Paris while the French in Africa, well out of its range, continued their process of effective occupation. After May 1896, when the negotiations of the Niger Commissioners had been broken off, the French were pressing on north of the Gold Coast, while French officers with their Senegalese soldiers wandered at will about Borgu. They were reported to have seized Kiama, terrorizing Lugard's old friend there into submission, and even to be taking short cuts across the corner of Lagos territory on their way from the Dahomey coast to Borgu. They had actually occupied Kishi, which, it will be remembered, was an important Yoruba town with which

[1] J. Darcy, *Cent Années de Rivalité Coloniale* (Paris 1904), pp. 244–5.
[2] It is impossible to give all the references in support of this paragraph. See especially F.O. 27/3335–42.

Lugard had made a treaty, and which lay between Borgu and the Lagos Protectorate.[1]

In Togoland, the Germans, far less experienced in African travel than the other two nations, were under the same threat of restriction as the British, but they came to terms with the French and consoled themselves for losing a hinterland from Togo territory up to the Niger by helping to embroil the two main contestants. But there were German voices which protested that, in face of the strangling policy of France, " Togoland's dreams are at an end."[2]

In Borgu, as elsewhere, the Africans, at first hostile and suspicious, then bewildered and finally overawed, watched the strange doings of the mutually hostile intruders. The mere presence of firearms, once it was known what they could do—and Goldie's campaign had been a large-scale exhibition of that—was an overwhelming negative argument against resistance, while cloth and other valuables were very positive inducements to sign or scrawl a mark on a paper, the full significance of which not even the best-intentioned explanations could convey to them. It is not surprising that one impressionable chief in West Africa made exclusive treaties in six months with the agents of the three different nations.

It is usual in our day to treat the whole of this proceeding with moral censure. The word " scramble ", which has been applied to this competition in annexation, does not evoke very dignified pictures and these West African episodes surely represent the most headlong scrambling of all. We are conscious today, in a way that our grandfathers could hardly be, of the Africans as a third party, grandfathers of today's African ministers and judges, conscious, individualized and destined, at a speed unimagined in the nineties, to move towards political self-expression and to a criticism of imperialism which they would learn to condemn from repentant imperialists, rather than from their own standards. It is natural to wish now that the process of African civilization had begun with more order and dignity. But in the absence of effective international law, control or even co-operation, Africa, the vast and inert prize, was divided up in a headlong competition which, thanks largely to Salisbury, did not lead to war. Under these conditions the constructive processes of civilization could

---

[1] McCallum (Governor of Lagos) to C.O., 4 August 1897, C.O. 147/116.
[2] *Kreuz Zeitung*, 31 July 1897.

not begin until these tattered, moustachioed and bearded white men, supremely convinced of racial superiority and of the national and humanitarian mission of their own nations, had walked their hundreds of miles in the bush under rain and sun, swum their rivers, shot their game, planted their flags and sweated or died of malaria in their little tents.

Could France be checked on the Niger? If this were to be done it would be an energetic and risky task. Lord Salisbury, nearing seventy, if not the man to make tame surrenders, was not likely to push matters to extremes in what was to him a minor area of conflict. He was much more interested in the Nile than the Niger. Kitchener was now on his way up-river against the Mahdi, and across Africa at right-angles to his path Marchand was *en route* for Fashoda. What would happen when they met? The question was seldom out of Lord Salisbury's mind. And the view from all the Foreign Office windows on to Europe was of British isolation. The Kaiser's telegram to Kruger had chilled Anglo-German relations. There was a crisis over Port Arthur with Russia. Salisbury told his daughter that he did not think that Britain could fight Russia and France together. In March 1897, though very unwell, he actually made a private call on Hanotaux in Paris, and tried and failed to arrange a treaty of arbitration to deal with the many Ango-French difficulties.[1]

But if the Foreign Secretary were inclined to emphasize the east side of Africa at the expense of the west, and rate the Nile above the Niger, the new Colonial Secretary was fully capable of redressing the balance. We must look back a little to see what he had been doing during 1897 while the situation worsened. It took him some little time to master the quickly changing West African map. There had been plenty of more urgent matters on his desk since he had gone to the Colonial Office in the summer of 1895. Indeed, they had been more than urgent for they had been a challenge to his reputation and even to his personal honour. The Jameson Raid, the Kaiser's telegram, the Jameson trial and the enquiry into the Raid—these had filled the year 1896 and run into the spring of 1897, and over them all had hung the suspicion—it was believed that only Flora Shaw knew the whole truth—that the Colonial Secretary had been privy to the Raid.[2] And

---

[1] A. L. Kennedy, *Salisbury* (1953), pp. 280–2.
[2] Garvin, *Life of Chamberlain*, vol. iii, pp. 82–3.

Cecil Rhodes, in the part of the fallen but unrepentant Lucifer, had not been an easy man to deal with. From these disturbing arraignments Chamberlain had plunged into the Queen's Diamond Jubilee, which had reached its climax in June with its pageant of empire, of which he had been pageant master. And this was followed by the Colonial Conference.

The social and political pressure and the excitement of the summer months must have been almost intolerable for the Colonial Secretary. In May, however, he had found time to get into contact with Goldie. Directors of Chartered Companies and the ministers to whom they were rather ambiguously responsible tended, as we have seen, to be almost natural opponents. Mackinnon had finished up by having his heart broken by Rosebery. Rhodes and Chamberlain had been embarrassingly linked in co-operation and in conflict. In some ways Goldie, his Company always at bay to its critics and in danger of being sacrificed to them by the government, proved the most difficult to handle. The position was complicated because his Company, like the others, was responsible to the Foreign Office, which administered the Niger Coast Protectorate, while the Colonial Office was responsible for Lagos Colony and Protectorate. He also became much more fully informed upon West Africa than was his chief and Foreign Minister, Lord Salisbury. His colonies and the Company must co-operate, and yet he could only deal with Goldie direct with that chief's permission. Chamberlain's first interview with Goldie in May was abortive and Goldie wrote a curt note afterwards to say he had been surprised at being so cross-examined at the Colonial Office. His underlining of the last three words was, to say the least, unkind:[1] Goldie was no respecter of dignitaries and he wrote equally brusquely to Salisbury at the way he was sent about between the two departments, without getting from either the information that was due to his shareholders. Lord Salisbury, who cannot have been used to such treatment, called this " a curious letter."[2]

The evidence of the records is that Chamberlain hesitated before he finally made up his mind to act. On June 4th he sent a dispatch to the Governor of the Gold Coast which had in it the germ of the later " chessboard " policy. It suggested he should take any still untaken

[1] Goldie to Chamberlain, 28 May 1897, C.O. 147/127.
[2] Goldie to Salisbury, 28 May 1897, S.P. vol. 127 (Miscellaneous D-L).

places within his reach and said that more forces would be sent if the Company would help with recruits. This force would also be available on the Niger and " would be in effect a small West African army."[1] And two days later his studies of the dispatches and the maps led him to exclaim to Salisbury, " We have thrown away all our cards," to receive the rather resigned reply " None but the irrecoverable."[2]

Was it because Chamberlain doubted his power to carry the Prime Minister and the Foreign Office with him that a few weeks later a rather confused and irresolute memorandum came to Goldie from the Colonial Office? Though not over Chamberlain's signature, so important a statement must clearly have emanated very directly from his mind. In it is noted that the idea to which both the government and the Company had clung for so long, that the French would respect treaties, must now be abandoned. The result of British inactivity had been that each time we went to negotiation it was to find that the actual position on the ground was weaker than it had been before. Three possible courses were reviewed. It was decided that the bolder ones would lead to war or to too great expense, and that we must now sacrifice a portion of our claims in order to obtain a final settlement, allowing the French to take the right bank of the Niger down to Liaba, a point thirty miles south of Bussa. For, in words which later events make interesting, " There can be no question of going to war with France on account of Bussa or Mossi." The hope was, the document concluded, " that the present policy of drift, which has already had such disastrous consequences, may be finally abandoned."[3]

By the terms of this letter, Chamberlain laid himself open to the retort of a man who felt he had little cause to love or respect the government. Goldie replied, two days later, that the " policy of drift" had never been that of his Company. On the contrary it had been entirely due to its efforts, sustained by the dues which had made it so unpopular, that the Niger hinterland had not been entirely whittled away like those of the other British colonies on the west coast. As for the policy of surrender, the anti-climax to which the firm introduction had so weakly led up, " A landed proprietor will not usually submit to a small but valuable portion of his estate being occupied by a

[1] Chamberlain to Maxwell, 4 June 1897, C.O. 96/302.
[2] Garvin, *op. cit.* vol. iii, p. 204.
[3] C.O. to Goldie, 1 July 1897, C.O. 96/308.

neighbour, even if the legal expenditure necessary to protect his rights exceeded the value of that portion." The French, whose press he studied carefully, showed that France believed Britain would never fight. He advised that he should be allowed to attack the French, the navy blockading by sea; " I would, of course, personally direct the operations." He asserted that the prime object must be to keep the French out of the navigable Niger below the rapids; once there, they would ruin the Company's trade. For this, he was even prepared, if necessary, to see the entire northern part of the Sokoto Empire—which he had yet to occupy—bartered away. He reiterated his belief that Bussa was a single powerful state—stretching from Say to Ilorin—and therefore controlled by his Bussa treaty.[1]

Following upon these letters, Chamberlain's Colonial Office began to press upon Salisbury's Foreign Office possible plans for dealing with the French encroachment. The physical impotence of the government, unless it were prepared for the undignified policy of relying entirely upon the Company as its military agent, was the clearest lesson of the long negotiations with France. The unpleasant logic of this—and we have seen how British governments at this time shrank from serious military expeditions in remote countries—was that an official force must be sent out to stiffen the soft frontier into which the French were so busily probing. In August, on the same day as it happened that Monson telegraphed that Hanotaux had refused to evacuate Bussa, Chamberlain sent his plans to Salisbury in some detail and the War Office was, of course, brought in to advise.[2] The preliminary steps for the creation of a force of some 2,000 African soldiers were now taken. But the possibility of so delicate and dangerous an enterprise in such a region could not be carried very far without a decision as to the man who should be chosen for the dual part of Commissioner and Commandant. It did not take Chamberlain long, considering all that he knew of him and all that had passed between them, to think of Lugard. The fact that at last the government was ready to employ a man with such a reputation in France strikingly advertised the change of policy. This was the story which lay behind the dispatch of the cable of July 30th.

After this, Chamberlain went off for a well-earned holiday in

1 Goldie to Chamberlain, 19 July 1897, C.O. 96/308.
2 C.O. to F.O. 14 August 1897, C.O. 147/124; and C.O. to W.O., 17 August 1897, C.O. 147/116.

Switzerland. There it rained incessantly, and this may have led him to spend more time than he otherwise would have done upon his West African geography and diplomacy. He now learned from his papers the full extent of the French occupation of Borgu, which was still a continuing process. Moreover, on August 13th, Hanotaux at last made his definite reply to the protests about Bussa. He firmly rejected them. He gave up some half of a long dispatch to a further detailed attempt to invalidate Lugard's Nikki treaty.[1] Chamberlain now shed whatever might still be left of the mood in which Goldie had been approached earlier in the summer. A harder, stronger tone issued from the Colonial Office. The plans for raising an imperial force, which was soon named the West African Frontier Force, were hastened. On September 28th Chamberlain telegraphed to Selborne, his Parliamentary Under-Secretary, that the Gold Coast and Niger hinterlands were to be saved " even at the cost of war." Two weeks later he returned to England. " I think it was time I came back ", he wrote to his wife, " . . . . we shall gain our point although it will be a near touch and we move only just in time."[2] Ten days later Lugard landed and all the chief British players for the second act of the Borgu drama were assembled in London.

They were all uncompromising characters, and their relationships now were one more illustration of the fact that it is not without clash between strong minds and wills that the policies of nations are built up. The front of the stage was taken by the Colonial Secretary. As the holder of his office he had not, in a matter of foreign policy, been cast for the chief part but he took it because he was so sure he knew how to play it and it was he who, in the end, dominated the scene. Lord Salisbury was disinclined, in this matter, to go all the way with Chamberlain; he knew better than his colleague the world-wide dangers of his country's position and he was responsible for their avoidance. He never experienced moods of pugnacity in which he forgot the weaknesses of the British case. And he was, in his own quieter way, a masterful man who did not like to employ agents who might get out of control. The relationship between the two chief men in what the German Emperor called the " double headed " government naturally affected the conduct of the affair.

[1] Hanotaux to Monson, 12 August 1897, enclosed in Monson to Salisbury, F.O. 27/3339.
[2] Garvin, *op. cit.* vol. iii, p. 208.

Chamberlain was much more than Salisbury's Colonial Secretary; he was the leader of the Liberal Unionists and the most dominating politician in the country. There was little intimacy between men so diverse in temperament but they learned how to work together. Even so it was sometimes difficult for Chamberlain to carry his chief and the Foreign Office step by step along his forward path in a race with time. Salisbury seems to have retained as much of African affairs as possible under the Foreign Office because he had such a deep personal interest in them. Chamberlain wanted to take them over for exactly the same reason. In West Africa they had to share responsibility. This did not make for an easy partnership in this region. The French, quick to observe any wedges it would be profitable to hammer, gave hopeful attention to this one, not hesitating to caricature Chamberlain as a disrespectful nephew expecting to inherit his uncle's property.[1] Hanotaux, who had reason to know, said that the government was visibly subject to two influences; sometimes that of Chamberlain was dominant, at other times " l'autorité—plus sereine " of Salisbury asserted itself.[2]

If Chamberlain had no easy task with his chief, he did not find even the instruments of his policy very easy to handle. Goldie was as decisive and wilful a man as himself, and at this juncture he was also a man with a grievance. As head of his Company, his own laborious creation, brought into being for the large imperial objects for which he lived, he had always had every man's hand against him. There had been bitter exchanges with the government. The Liverpool merchants vehemently accused him in a ceaseless plaint to the Foreign Office and the public; the coastal Africans attacked his Company by word and deed; the French hated him and his Company. A deputy in the Chamber could even call it a band of rotten merchants and brigands who dishonoured the flag of a civilized nation.[3] Now it had been said openly that the days of the Company were numbered and that the government would soon be taking it over, but the how and when had still to be settled.[4] When, therefore, Chamberlain suggested that the Company, which had long been held back by the government from dealing with the French, should now bestir itself more, hold the

1 Garvin *op. cit.* vol. iii, p. 218.
2 Hanotaux, *Fachoda*, p. 14.
3 J.O. (Ch.), 26 March 1898, p. 1400, c.2.
4 *Parliamentary Debates*, 24 May 1897, IV. 49. 1111–13.

situation in the interval before Lugard could come into action with the proposed Frontier Force, and lend troops, Goldie in turn held back and began to bargain. Why should he spend the shareholders' money to retain assets their future tenure of which was so uncertain? But Chamberlain had a temper too.

" Now Goldie seems refractory," he told Salisbury on September 19th, " and practically refuses to move . . . . I should like to tell him that the British Government do not understand the contract with the Company as he does, nor do they agree that he is to take all the profits and that we are to spend hundreds of thousands or possibly millions in securing his claims against the French, and that he is then to step in and enjoy without cost all the security that we have gained for him.

If this is his view our best course will be to expropriate him, lock, stock and barrel, paying the capital value of his property but allowing nothing for goodwill or future profits since these are altogether dependent on the expeditions we are to make. In fact I should take a very high line with him and tell him that in this crisis he must be with us or against us, and that we cannot allow him to dictate terms."[1]

From Lugard, at least, Chamberlain, ignorant perhaps of his close friendship with Goldie, must have expected perfect compliance, that of the greyhound slipped at last for the course. After landing on October 12th, he made an early call upon the Colonial Office. He was told that Chamberlain was most anxious to see him, but that first he had better read up all the information about the situation. He was given a great stack of blue books and documents containing all the diplomatic and other history of the West African question and told to make himself thoroughly acquainted with it. Those who thought it necessary to give these instructions did not know their man. Sitting in his rooms in Jermyn Street, he set himself at once not only to read the material— and few records are more voluminous and repetitive than the day-by-day diplomatic *ipsissima verba*—but, in his own painstaking, conscientious way, to make a full analysis of them on paper. Meanwhile he had the work of winding up of his stewardship of the B.W.C. Company—a task he was not inclined to scamp even for Chamberlain —and this entailed writing a summary of all his Ngamiland reports, and quarrelling with the Colonial Office about a vexed question concerning the limitations of this Company's mining rights. He was,

[1] Garvin, *op. cit.* vol. iii, pp. 209-10.

moreover, besieged with correspondence and invitations from all his friends and relations and from applicants for jobs in the new Force.

It was a bad start. He had not learned, he never learned, how to spare himself. The amount of work to be done, the number of hours in the day and night to be allotted to it, were to be decided by the amount of work, never by the powers of the body. For his body he had less consideration than a brutal muleteer who flogs on his animal as if it were a machine and not made of flesh and blood. Perhaps it was for this reason that he started upon this enterprise tired, a little at odds with himself, a little inclined to be refractory with others.

On November 12th he had his first interview with the Colonial Secretary. It did not begin very well. Chamberlain, with his famous monocle, was a formidable person to interview. " When he screwed his eye-glass," Lugard once said, " you felt as if you were going to be sifted to the marrow."[2] Chamberlain started by pointing out that he had not forgotten him and that he had given him the first post that offered itself. Lugard said "Thank you", politely, but he was angry at this attempt to put him on a footing of obligation. Had he not given up not merely a post with four times the salary of the new one, but, what he valued far more, his partnership with his much-loved brother? Quietly watching him as he talked, he made mental disparagements of the great man: he found him abrupt and domineering, acting the commanding officer. He seemed changed from the man he had known before. It is possible to reconstruct their conversation.[1]

" When will you be ready to go? " Chamberlain asked.

" Whenever I am ordered," was the correct reply.

" You had better go at once. Nothing will be done until you get out."

" Certainly," Lugard replied, " But I hardly yet know what I am to do."

Chamberlain launched at once into an exposition of what Lugard called his " chessboard " policy. Lugard knew about this, for immediately upon his return he had foregathered with his friends, Goldie and Kirk, and the three had already discussed and condemned the policy. Goldie had, indeed, been invited by the government to

---

1 This is based upon the very full account which Lugard wrote in his diary on March 13th 1898, when he used the opportunity of the voyage to West Africa to bring his diary up to date. But, in view of his methods, it is almost certainly based on notes taken at the time.

2 Garvin, *op. cit.* vol. iii, p. 16.

carry it out and had replied he was quite prepared to turn the French out but not with these infiltration methods. Forearmed thus against Chamberlain's persuasions by his two friends, Lugard listened coldly to his emphatic sentences. He was ordered to occupy country where the French held their posts, infiltrate around and behind them, and if they held a village he was to hold one alongside, cutting off their communications, proving to the Africans that we were as good or better fellows than they and so show them that their occupation policy was futile. But—and this was the prime command—on no account were Lugard's men to be the aggressors; " but if through them a collision should occur, ' tant mieux ' and we can go for them." Lugard did not put his objections. He sat silent. " As J.C. went on I purposely showed in my face and manner my strong dissent—as he became domineering, I grew very obstinate and reserved." Lord Selborne was sitting in the room and remarked Lugard's manner, as Lugard meant that he should. Chamberlain now referred to some place which Lugard said he thought had already been given up on the Lagos side.

" Who told you so? " said Chamberlain.

" Antrobus." This was the head of the West African section.[1]

Chamberlain rang the bell and sent for him and ordered Lugard to repeat what he had understood Antrobus to have said. The official looked scared, " but he is a *real* good fellow and a plucky fellow, and he stood by me."

" A *concentrated* force could enter the country," said Chamberlain.

" That would be *better*," said Lugard, and went on to ask if he was to have the use of the Royal Niger Company troops and all their resources.

" Yes," replied Chamberlain. " Three hundred troops and all their resources."

Here, however, Antrobus intervened to say that Goldie had just stated that he could not now carry out all he had promised. This made Chamberlain very angry.

" Goldie is always changing and I never know where he is. He had agreed definitely and even made other proposals regarding his own future which I am prepared to consider." (Lugard knew that

[1] Antrobus, (later Sir) Reginald, K.C.M.G., C.B., 1853–1942; 1877 entered Colonial Office after first open competitive examination; 1880–9 private secretary to successive Colonial Secretaries; 1889–90 acted as Governor of St. Helena; 1898–1909 Asst. Under-Secretary of State for the Colonies; 1909–1918 Senior Crown Agent for the Colonies.

he was referring here to an idea of Goldie's that he might start a new Chartered Company in the Nile Valley.) " Well, anyway you will have 300 of their men."

" I have had a note from Sir George," Lugard interrupted, " who says he is probably resigning the Governorship."

" If the Niger Company do not help, it will be the worse for them," retorted Chamberlain (" who was now," Lugard says, " fairly angry "). " Anyhow we have all their resources. You are to raise a small West African army to go anywhere in Africa and do anything."

" Such a force," Lugard remarked, " would not be available for eight months or a year; until then it would be only an armed rabble."

" I don't expect you to do anything for a long time," replied Chamberlain (thus, Lugard noted, contradicting his earlier demand); " you are to advise the government of all the requirements of such a Force. Expense is no object—plenty of guns and everything. Two gun-boats will be there, practically under your orders. Where will you have your headquarters, I wonder? "

" Lokoja " replied Lugard promptly. The answer was significant. It was not only, as he confessed to himself, that he thought Lokoja was healthier, already furnished with rifle ranges, and on the Niger waterway. " My *main* reason was to be out of the jurisdiction of Lagos and its Governor." Here once more, and stronger than ever, was Lugard's determination to serve only in complete independence of any other man. This did not suit Chamberlain at all, since Lokoja was outside his sphere, while, from a base in Colonial Office territory it would be much easier for him and his department to control the campaign, the government forces operating from Lagos on the right bank of the Niger and the Company on the left. Lokoja, under the Company and so under the Foreign Office, was doubly unacceptable to the Colonial Office. To Lugard, it was the region of his friend.

The conversation went on while Chamberlain explained that he thought the negotiations with France would probably be broken off and what he thought should be done then. Here the watching Selborne broke in and suggested that Lugard should be asked what *he* thought was best. Lugard looked Chamberlain straight in the face and asked if he might speak frankly. Chamberlain had to say yes.

" Then," said Lugard, " send an ultimatum to Paris saying that unless they withdraw from Bussa, about which, unlike the rest of

Borgu, there can be no dispute, there will be a collision. Then advance, occupying the banks of the Niger, without going inland, since the river is the strategic base. Give Hanotaux a sop by the cession, as suggested by Goldie, of the Sokoto Empire north of latitude 12, provided the Nile Valley question is settled simultaneously."

This was bold advice for a soldier to give to a minister. It also showed Chamberlain that Lugard was in close contact with the difficult Goldie, and that both were prepared to sacrifice the important but still unconquered sphere in the north in order that both banks of the Niger up to the rapids could be saved. But Chamberlain had moved far beyond the hesitations of his June letter to Goldie. He had, the documents testify, learned much from Goldie, but only what he chose to learn, and he had now no intention of parting with Sokoto. He was prepared to stand fast against the French, and was determined to impose both his policy, and also what appeared his questionable method of applying it, upon Goldie and Lugard, the men of action, and to carry his own doubting Prime Minister with him. At this time both he and Selborne were writing memoranda and minutes of increasingly determined tone, telling the Foreign Office that Britain should be ready to break off relations with France and even prepare for war rather than surrender any more territory.[1] There is, however, a rather curious document in the Salisbury Papers dated September 12th 1897 in which Chamberlain writes to Selborne (who could not have needed the instruction) almost like a schoolboy repeating a lesson, that a question likely to lead to a European war " must be decided ultimately by the Foreign Office, which knows better than we do the nature of our relations with France, and by the Prime Minister, who is responsible in a peculiar sense for all questions of peace or war. Accordingly I should in any case yield to Lord Salisbury's wishes," although wishing to put before him " my reasons for differing from the course he proposes."[2] It almost looks as though, as the possibility of a rift developed, Salisbury may have insisted, in order to clarify the position between himself and Chamberlain, and between their two departments, that Chamberlain should make this admission in writing.

Lugard's suggestion must at once have surprised and angered him. " Vehemently and angrily," in Lugard's words, he scouted the idea.

[1] Minutes by Chamberlain of 9 November and 1 December 1897, and by Selborne, 30 November 1897, C.O. 537/13.
[2] S.P. vol. 134 (Colonial Office 1895–1900).

He said he " would *never* be a party to giving up our country in order to get what is already ours. The Nile question was not my business or his." True it was Salisbury's but then so was most of the Niger question. He then held forth about his constructive plans for the future. The imperial government could do for these countries what " no small company " could do. He brushed aside the idea of even a minor surrender. He reiterated that we could always have more money behind us than the French and hence spend double and have a larger force till they gave in. And Lugard said to himself, "The Birmingham Screw Policy!"

It was not a promising beginning for the enterprise and it is not surprising that Selborne took Lugard down to his own room and tried to soothe and reassure him. He told him that it was much more than a military task; that the government would attend to his advice, but that it was useless to ask the French government to cede Bussa, as they would be turned out of office if they did. As for the chessboard policy, the French would be in the same boat as the British and would not dare to attack. The Company, he thought, would be bought out *in toto* and at once.

Lugard went back to his rooms hardly knowing what to do. He was disappointed with Chamberlain and he had no faith in the policy. He decided to resign the post which had hardly yet been defined. But, though Goldie had helped to arm his mind against Chamberlain's influence, he was still anxious that Lugard and no one else should be sent out to Borgu on this difficult mission. It was almost impossible that the commanding officer should not get at odds with the Company both at home and in Nigeria, as he would take command in *their* territory and give orders to *their* troops and this at a time of bitterness and uncertainty about the whole future of the Charter. But Lugard was his friend even if the wary and steely Goldie did not return the wholehearted devotion and admiration which Lugard was then giving to him. So when Lugard sat down impulsively to write his resignation, Goldie was at hand to check him. Lugard was steadied. " I am certain of his utmost support," so he assured himself, " and he is a legion in himself and will lead the others or compel them." The letter of resignation went into the waste-paper basket. With the gloom and doubt with which Lugard entered upon most of his enterprises, he decided to accept the task of taking over the creation of a West African military force and of leading it to its first assignment.

CHAPTER XXX

MEN, WOMEN AND MEASURES

1897-1898 : Aet. 39-40

ONCE THE decision to accept the post of Commissioner and Commandant of the proposed West African force had been taken, Lugard did not allow his doubts to prevent him from throwing himself into his new task with his usual concentration and appetite for detail. But hard work did not dispel his dissatisfactions.

One of these was that he had to take up a plan which had been devised by others and already partly carried out. There were to be two battalions in the new force and some of the officers had already been appointed. Over this a struggle at once began when Lugard announced that he would appoint the rest; the War Office authorities were indignant at his trying to ride roughshod over them. Lugard said he was not going to have his force made a cesspool into which the bad characters and scum of the army could be shot. One of the colonels, T. D. Pilcher, had already begun to "organize" the force—the inverted commas were put in angrily by Lugard—and to appoint officers. While Lugard took to him very much personally, he was a man who had never seen active service, a Staff College officer and an expert on the German army. According to Lugard, his idea of recruiting for the force was to tell the War Office to supply so many officers, N.C.O.s, and doctors, to have them "inspected" and sent off to Africa. He was a wealthy man and much interested in the sartorial side of the force, down to the design of the buttons, and he drew up a list of things needed by the officers which, Lugard remarked, were enough for a three years' campaign with elephants for transport. Lugard soon changed all this. Remembering the story of his soldier uncle and of Outram, he had already cabled from the Cape that he wanted his old transport chief from India, Colonel Willcocks,[1]

1 See above p. 46.

appointed as his second-in-command. He now found that this had not been done. Lugard insisted that the War Office—" the most incompetent department in the Empire "—should cable for him. They sent off a confused message and it was only when Lugard cabled himself, and made his friend understand that he was to serve under *him*, that the offer was at once accepted.

Lugard set to work to engage his other officers. He chose a Colonel Fitzgerald to command the 2nd battalion, a man seven years his senior. Even the doctors he put through a rigorous examination with the help of his surgeon friend, Fripp, rejecting some already chosen. He decided to have two affiliated batteries with his two battalions, and he went very carefully into the question of their guns which, to suit him, had to be specially manufactured with a view to human transport. The heaviest part of his eight-pounders was not to weigh more than 150 lb. There were to be six of the very newest 75 mm. Maxim-Nordenfeldt guns as reserve artillery. When he demanded portable huts for the white men because of the rains, he was told they would cost £20,000, and would take months to make. He drew up the specifications himself; found a firm that was prepared to make them; got them delivered in fourteen days, and only paid £9,000 for them.

To anticipate here the final result of Lugard's labours, and summarize the facts which represent the birth of the West African Frontier Force, each of the two battalions, to be composed mainly of Hausa and Yoruba, was to be about 1,200 strong, with 29 British officers and 44 N.C.O.s each. The use of European N.C.O.s was an interesting new experiment. There was an engineer company with Royal Engineer officers and N.C.O.s; a telegraph company; two R.A. field batteries and one reserve twelve-pounder battery; an accounts branch; a transport department; one base and two field hospitals. In addition to Lugard's own new force of nearly 3,000 men, he was to take over if he could—for this was to be a difficult point with Goldie—any Company forces already in western Borgu with another 300 Company troops; about 250 Lagos Constabulary and a detachment from the West Indian Regiment. Lugard spent £140,000 on the equipment and the annual salaries bill was some £120,000. Two Royal Naval gun-boats were to operate on the Niger " more or less under my orders, though it is supposed to be impossible for Naval officers to operate under anyone's command except that of a Naval officer; however, I suppose it will pan out all right." (L. to E. J. L. 3 December 1897).[1]

Night after night Lugard worked until 4 or 5 a.m. drawing up his lists of all his requirements " down to a tin-tack," for the force was an entirely new creation; it had to be completely self-contained from its tents and huts down to its lamps, rations and stationery; it was to operate in a severe, wet, tropical climate under difficult and still partly unknown conditions, 500 miles up-river from the coast. And all this recruiting, planning, requisitioning and financing had to be done at the highest possible speed and, according to his evidence, against the lethargy, conservatism or genuine ignorance of War Office officials. Fortunately, on January 3rd, Willcocks arrived and Lugard had a man after his own heart, above all the man of his own choice, with whom to work. Willcocks afterwards told the story, so characteristic of his former subordinate, that when, having abandoned his own work and crossed half the world at highest speed in answer to his summons, he hurried to his room, Lugard, absorbed in his calculations, looked up vaguely and indicated to him to sit down and wait until he had finished what he was doing. Even Willcocks was astonished at the amount of detail Lugard had covered in these months, and the innumerable tables, regulations, and orders which he had prepared. " Of all the men I have ever met," he exclaims, " I never knew one who equalled Lugard as a persistent hard worker. He has his own hours, which do not suit everybody, and he has his own methods of work; but if you wish to succeed with him you must adapt yourself to both."[2] Willcocks soon learned to sit up into the morning hours.

But this is to anticipate. Much had been accomplished before Willcocks arrived. The twenty British officers and forty N.C.O.s of the 1st battalion were got away on November 27th, less than a month after Lugard had started reorganizing them on his own lines. Their duty was to raise and train the native recruits at Lokoja. Lugard had an immense amount to do before he could follow. In addition to making out the full requisition for the expedition and raising the British members of the 2nd battalion, he had to settle the plan of operations with the Colonial Office and the War Office. As regards

[1] See also *West African Frontier Force: statement of annual establishment charges,* C.O. 445/1.
[2] Sir J. Willcocks, *From Kabul to Kumassi* (1904), p. 162.

the latter, it may be assumed that Lugard was less explosive over this question in person than he was in his diary, where he could hardly find terms strong enough for the ignorance and incompetence of this department when it came to planning military action in West Africa. It seems to be a peculiarity of British public life that the heads of administration, military and civil, are able to engage in the fiercest internecine warfare without any fatal injury to the projects they have been jointly commissioned to execute. It is, perhaps, by this strenuous test, at the cost of routine and conventional standards of efficiency, that men of great ability win the powers they are fit to exercise and the freedom to use them.

The contacts and clashes between the leading personalities and between the departments continued during the last months of 1897. The parts played by the main characters have already been given. Willcocks had now come on to the stage as a loyal and devoted second to Lugard and the cast was completed by two notable female players. It would have been unusual at any time to find women playing such an important part in public action. But this was 1897. However, the common twentieth-century conception of Victorian England, as regards the position of women, has occasionally to accept some startling inconsistencies and recognize some female eccentrics. So in this affair of high politics, of annexations and the threat of war and, even more surprising, of little-known and savage Africa, we find two women playing leading and most effective parts.

The first of these, Flora Shaw, has already entered these pages upon several occasions. We have good reason to study her, not only for her close co-operation with Lugard at this time but because of the part she was to play in his career as his wife. Since their last contact, she had become even more of a public figure. Reference has already been made to the dramatic and hazardous part she had taken with regard to the Jameson Raid. She had come through the parliamentary enquiry of May 1897 with astonishing success, and Lugard found her still at her old post as colonial editor of *The Times*. She was deeply interested in the affairs of West Africa, anxious to learn from him all she could about them, and, with her strong faith in Britain's imperial mission, ready to use her personal and professional services to advance her country's interests in the area of dispute. Before she went off in 1898 upon an adventurous journey into the Klondyke gold-fields, she gave much time to her two friends, Lugard and Goldie, and did her best to keep the peace between Chamberlain and his intransigeant men of action.

At forty-four years of age, a little older than Lugard, she was a woman of beauty, slender, fair, distinguished by a fine carriage of head and possessed of a nature glowing with sympathy, intelligence and humour. Working with Goldie and Lugard, in close touch with Chamberlain and the Colonial Office, she did much, as part of her work of educating public opinion in the great opportunities offered by the empire, to spread knowledge of the facts and issues of West Africa. She wrote a series of articles in *The Times* upon the West African question. She instructed her readers to see Africa as a whole. " The question of Central Africa stretches from ocean to ocean, and it cannot be touched in one of its parts without rousing the sensitiveness of the whole."[1] She sketched clear, broad pictures of the geography and conditions of West Africa. Deeply interested in its peoples and their problems, she told the history of the old Muslim Emirates and how Kano had been founded when William the Conqueror was building the Tower of London. It was she who formally proposed that the Company's territory should be named Nigeria,[2] since Goldie, with his peculiar mixture of pride and self-effacement, emphatically refused to follow Rhodes' example and allow it to be called Goldesia.[3] She played her part in seeing that West African news was given a large place in her paper, and that well-informed editorials supported Britain's claims against France. Indeed, the French later made diplomatic protests that secrets of the Commission sitting on the Niger question were finding their way into *The Times'* articles.[4] She described the Bida campaign as a success due to the foresight and powers of organization of Sir George Goldie. She was heart and soul with her three friends, Chamberlain, Goldie and Lugard, with regard to the forward policy, for however much the three might differ as to the methods and the exact limits of British action on the Niger, they were all determined to keep the flag flying on the middle reaches of that river, and as far as possible to the west of them.

---

[1] *The Times*, 7 March 1897. For other articles see January 1 and March 30; also April 17 and April 19 of the same year. These articles were, of course, unsigned.
[2] *Ibid.* 8 January 1897.
[3] Wellesley, *Sir George Goldie*, p. 98.
[4] Monson to Salisbury, 15 February 1898, F.O. 27/3411.

The other woman was, like Flora Shaw, a famous traveller and writer; like her she combined intellectual gifts with great physical courage and political initiative, and was possessed of a generous and kindly temperament; like her again, she was still unmarried. While Flora Shaw found her way to the bleak Yukon with the gold-diggers, and tried vainly to gain permission to enter the Mahdist Sudan, Mary Kingsley in her trailing skirts and bonnet, had waded through crocodile-infested rivers and was on familiar terms with the cannibals, snakes, gorillas and " palm-oil ruffians " of West Africa. In her talk and writings, laughter, mischief and extravagance broke like a spate of foam over the deep current of seriousness which ran beneath. By the end of 1897 her travels, writings and public speeches had made her a public and, indeed, an astonishing figure in Britain.

Both these women were unqualified admirers of Goldie. Flora Shaw was bound to him by a strong affection. In the public tributes, by which the two women helped him at this critical stage of his work, there was little to choose in emphasis. *The Times* printed Flora Shaw's account of the history of the Niger Company[1] and of Goldie's Bida campaign,[2] and an editorial which went so far as to compare his achievements with the establishment of British power in India.[3] Mary Kingsley's book declared that his Company showed " how great England can be when she is incarnate in a great man, for the Royal Niger Company is so far Sir George Taubman Goldie."[4] " For nearly twenty years," she wrote, " the natives under the Royal Niger Company have had the firm, wise, sympathetic friendship of a great Englishman who knew them personally."[5] Goldie, who was intensely interested in women, returned her admiration. " She had the brain of a man," he wrote at her death in 1900, " and the heart of a woman."[6]

The two writers were also agreed in their admiration for the energy and the policy of Mr. Chamberlain, " who alone," wrote Mary Kingsley, " of all our statesmen saw the great possibilities and importance of western Africa." But Mary Kingsley, who had the courage to be just to all parties, was also the champion of the unchartered traders on the west coast and as, like Flora Shaw, she was a peacemaker

1 *The Times*, 17 and 19 April 1897.
2 *Ibid.* 30 March 1897.
3 *Ibid.* 19 April 1897.
4 Mary Kingsley, *West African Studies* (1899), p. 279.
5 *Ibid.* pp. 360-1.
6 Stephen Gwynn, *The Life of Mary Kingsley* (1932), p. 252.

and clung to her seemingly incompatible friendships with Goldie, Chamberlain and the Liverpool merchants, she could but regret the " dissensions, distrust and misunderstandings which have raged among these three representatives of England's majesty and power."[1] She also tried to be just to the French and—though she found this more difficult—to the missionaries, and as she laid about her with startling vigour in the cause of justice, it may easily be imagined that there was nothing placid about her career as a colonial expert. Her defence of the merchants who sold spirits to the Africans landed her in conflict not only with Goldie, who detested the liquor trade and—at immense sacrifice to the Company's revenue—prohibited it in the Company's territories. She soon had to defend herself from a flank attack from Goldie's ally Lugard, who continued to support Goldie in this issue with almost the same passionate conviction which he brought to his hatred for slavery.

The controversy had begun in 1895. Lugard had, as we have seen, spoken and written much in that year, and he had gone out of his way to brand the liquor traffic as a crime for its demoralization of the fine peoples of Africa and had praised the Niger Company, and above all Goldie, for their prohibition of this traffic.[2] This implied attack upon her friends and herself as their champion brought Mary Kingsley into the ring. She gave her side of the story to a friend.

" Liverpool, as I daresay you know, hates the Royal Niger Company like the devil. The R.N.C. has got its back against a door, fighting France. I, from my statements on this liquor traffic, Liverpool's backbone, have a certain influence with L., and that influence I threw into getting the Liverpool merchants not to harry the Company while it was in this trade row. I had succeeded beautifully, Liverpool was behaving like ten saints rolled into one, when down in the middle of it comes Major Lugard's article, praising the Company up to the skies for its anti-liquor policy—pitching into me and Liverpool right and left. My flock broke away at this and I have had a pretty scratching time of it, getting them into the fold again, and have only done it by saying I will answer Lugard. This I have only just got through and sent it to the printer. It is fire and brimstone for me when it comes out, and all Liverpool can

1 Kingsley, *op. cit.* p. 307.
2 See especially 'New British Markets, Tropical Africa', *The Nineteenth Century*, vol. XXXVIII, September 1895, p. 445; and 'A Journey in West Africa', *Scottish Geographical Magazine*, vol. XI, December 1895, pp. 622-3.

do is to put up a memorial window to me . . . . a West African ju-ju
hung round with square faced bottles."[1]

When he knew that she meant to make a public attack on Lugard,
Goldie went to her and, in her own words,

"tackled me . . . . I admire and honour him and Lugard . . . . But deliberately and cold-bloodedly—after what Sir George had said—I sat down and
thought the thing out quietly . . . . and I decided that though I must lose
by it what I valued greatly, it was my duty to do it . . . ."[2]

At first sight, this intensely humane woman's defence of the gin-
traffic is hard to understand. But she was almost the first of a new
species, that of women of science, and because in her travels she could
see no evidence that the liquor trade had brought drunkenness and
demoralization to the west coast, ascribed the fierce hostility towards
it to the prejudice of missionaries and temperance cranks and defended
her Africans and her traders against them. She even had the trade-gin
analysed and disproved the charge that it was deleterious. Her controversy with Lugard became public, but Mary Kingsley, incapable
of personal bitterness and fully appreciative of Lugard's great services,
made a direct approach to him in her own unique and famous
style.

" . . . . *Now* I have been and upset you in some way or another. I am totally
unfit for the higher forms of cultured intelligence, in consequence of having been brought up among pathologists—and Biblical critics—awful
warlike tribes—and then spending my old age among West Coast traders
—mind I do not say that a West Coast trader is anything like so savage
or unprincipled in his methods as either the champion of a pet microbe,
or a Biblical critic, but they are all three singularly alike and cultivate,
in a nervous and retiring person like myself, a tendency to shoot at sight,
and to disregard ' the Times ' &c. My dear Sir, you have attacked me so
it's no use asking a person of my limited thinking power to think that
you have not, but I hastily beg to say I do not mind being attacked . . . .
but with black or white I must fight fair, though as aforesaid I don't dislike fighting in itself in the least. What you have done is to say that I
and the Liverpool merchants are liars just as I said the Bishop and his
followers were liars . . . .

1 Wellesley, *op. cit.* pp. 38–9.
2 Gwynn, *op. cit.* pp. 187–8.

The whole position in which I am put by you and by the Liverpool men is frankly ridiculous; who in the world am I to be talked of by such as you as a 'high authority'!—I see why it is done by the Liverpool men. When I say anything that suits their side I am everything that's great and glorious, when I don't, as in re the Royal Niger Company, I am a misguided woman who has fallen under the personal fascination of Sir George Goldie . . . . I am only an honest observer who has had a very hard scientific training and who fights down any personal prejudice when dealing with facts—personally I would very much rather be on the side of such great gentlemen as you and Sir George— but I am outcast from you . . . . Of course my experience is nothing to yours, but no one who know me on the coast will give me a good character for keeping out of bush villages or native quarters of coast towns—in the factories I have stayed at—I have always bribed the watchman not to start a concert on his bell and rouse the house when I came over, or through, the stockade after hours, and the amount of brilliant burglaries I have committed getting into my quarters which have been locked up by careful stewards when I have been down town o'nights should place my name alongside C. Peace's . . . . I cannot help thinking I must have seen, going on as I did, something of the evils of the liquor traffic had it been so fearful and so prevalent . . . . I have seen drunkenness of course here and there but very rarely—never anything like what I have seen in the Vauxhall Road or the East End or Clerkenwell . . . . The African will keep on surviving the amateur empirical experiments tried on him and will ultimately reach his highest possibility in culture and then fade away like the rest of us, but we have a chance now of giving the African a similar help forward that Greco-Latin civilization gave the Teutonic tribes and we shall not do it in the way we are trying to now . . . .

I do not like to ask you because I know you have so many better places to go to and are so busy but if, at any time you could spare time to come here and have a quiet chat about anything you like I should be very honoured . . . . "   (19 December 1897).

To this he replied affirmatively and their friendship grew with their meetings and a correspondence, on her side, in her staccato and racy style.

There was nothing in Lugard, who was completely self-confident in those spheres which he regarded as his own, and as completely humble in other matters, to make for anti-feminism. He had a deepening friendship with Flora Shaw, and he would not let public controversy prevent him from making personal friends with Mary Kingsley. He was able to learn much from both these remarkable women. They were utterly different from that other woman for whom, in spite of that almost fatal blow of disenchantment, he still felt a sense of respon-. sibility with its attendant anxiety and restlessness.

We must return to the three principals and their strange, three-cornered relationship. It was not surprising that there was continued tension between Goldie and the uncompromising minister who was dependent upon his co-operation and who was at the very same time planning to bring his life's work to an end. What was surprising was that Lugard, who was to enter Goldie's kingdom as the chosen agent of this same minister, should have been able to keep Goldie as friend and ally through these difficult months. If, as has already been suggested, one clue is found in the value Goldie placed upon having a friend in such a position, the other may be found in the increasing devotion and admiration Lugard felt towards Goldie, one very hard to square with the loyal obedience to Chamberlain which his position demanded. Lugard's confidence was not easy to win, but the few to whom he gave it received it in full. " I am *absolutely* at one with Goldie," he told his brother, " and if they attempt arbitrary confiscation, will fight on his side all I can (though necessarily secretly)." (L. to E. J. L. 16 November 1897).

The position of the Company at the moment and its future were closely bound up with all Lugard's plans. He remarked the public hints and assumptions that the Company would be taken over. There was constant pressure on the government from Liverpool, which was electorally important, and there were fulminations from Paris. The long-drawn-out and troubled demise of the Imperial British East Africa Company, the causes of which were not easy for the public to understand, and the association of the British South Africa Company with the Jameson Raid, had turned chartered companies, recently such favoured agencies, into objects of suspicion to the British public. It did not matter that the indictment of each of the three companies must be framed upon quite different grounds; the prejudice had been born and it flourished. This public was now disturbed by the incessant assertions that Goldie's conduct of the Niger Company was high-handed and monopolistic. But Goldie was not the man to run away from the position he had defended so successfully for many years. Combative and contemptuous of his enemies, he was still certain that, even if some new settlement must be made, it would be largely according to his will.

There was, however, as Lugard saw it, a new danger for the Company on the horizon. Unlike his predecessors, Chamberlain had some very positive and personal reasons for ending its administration. The Colonial Secretary had declared in 1895 that the colonies were in the condition of undeveloped estates " which can never be developed without Imperial assistance," and he had reiterated this new theme.[1] He must now make good his words and show his skill as a dynamic and productive bailiff for the nation. West Africa, with its large population and its tropical products, had caught his imagination. Mary Kingsley, in the mood of over-estimation often found in pioneer tropical travellers, announced it to be " the richest feeding grounds in all the world for England's manufacturing millions."[2] Northern Nigeria, with its large semi-civilized population and considerable internal trade, appeared to have a most valuable economic future. Chamberlain at this time aimed at taking over increasing responsibility in Africa from the Foreign Office. " So Joe," remarked Lugard, " is determined to play the role of Ahab with this Naboth's vineyard."

Lugard, indeed, judged his new master very hardly over this. He set down his ideas on the subject with some formality in his diary. They undoubtedly reflect the mind of Goldie, with whom he was in such close sympathy and contact at this time. Yet though Goldie and Kirk were the men who most influenced Lugard, his mind was no passive reflector of other men's ideas. Chamberlain, in his view, was appropriating the life's work of another man with little or no justification. It was Goldie who, in thirty years of ceaseless effort, had built up the Company's position on the Niger, had bested two foreign powers, had kept his hinterland when the imperial colonies along the coast had lost theirs. He had risked his life in a brilliant campaign which he alone had conducted. He had staked his whole future, his credit and reputation to preserve his creation. Now, at the end of thirty years of effort, just when the moment had come at last when the result of all this work might be harvested, Chamberlain was stepping in to rob him of his life's interest and achievement. On the question

[1] Garvin, *Life of Chamberlain*, vol. iii, p. 19.
[2] Kingsley, *West African Studies*, p. 307.

of compensation, which Goldie must fight on behalf of his shareholders, Chamberlain could evade the issue on the grounds that he was himself a shareholder, and that it was not proper for him to give any opinion on the point.

Lugard was anxious, too, about the future of this large territory. True, imperial resources *could* develop it more rapidly than was possible for the Company. But was a country in which human sacrifice, cannibalism and slavery still flourished ready to be opened up to exploitation and rapid development by rival merchants and foreign traders? And would the nation be prepared to pay the large recurrent costs that would be needed if the government were to take over this vast country and put down slavery and cannibalism? His own small force would cost £120,000 a year and Chamberlain was intending to double it. " Parliament has had no voice in the matter— it is Joe's scheme." And what of the future administration? If Goldie did not go out as administrator then " his thirty years of experience and his marvellous personal capacity . . . . may be lost to the Empire." It certainly would be were it not for his passionate devotion to " his child ", which Lugard felt would compel him to continue to work for it.

Lugard's cogitations carried him further, or rather, step by step nearer and nearer to himself. He admitted Chamberlain's energy and his present interest in Nigeria, but he had the whole empire on his hands and—here he foresaw rightly—his intention might at any moment be distracted, or he might fall from power. Everything, therefore, would depend upon the man sent out by the imperial government to govern Nigeria. " Who will this be and will he be competent? Will he be carried away by a sense of self-importance and power or will he listen to wisdom from Goldie's years of experience? " His own future position inevitably came into his mind. " Joe has chosen me to begin with, as Commissioner and Commander, and I am proud that where he has so much at stake—his own credit and his own theories—I am the man selected to be his agent in the task, though I think Goldie, too, had a voice in it." But would he be the man to carry on the administration?

Before facing up to his new commitment, Lugard threw one more nostalgic glance back to East Africa, from which had come news of the Uganda mutiny with the deaths of British officers and of the

severe treatment of the Muslims.[1] He believed that the tragic business
was the result of his old opponent Macdonald's mishandling, and he
fought one more battle in his Uganda campaign. He was in close
touch with the relatives of those officers murdered in the mutiny;
he briefed Flora Shaw for *The Times*, and lobbied before the debate
on Uganda in the House of Commons on March 3rd.[2] All this added
much work and worry to days that were already over-full. Lugard
seldom hated, but was a good hater once his mind was made up.
He did, however, set himself limits. "I do not want to make a personal attack on Macdonald while he is fighting in Uganda and in a
difficult and onerous post. I have myself suffered in a similar case."

But as that Foreign Office region seemed to be unattainable to
Lugard, his friends were pressing him to stick to his decision to go to
the west. Flora Shaw admitted that he would be the right man for
Uganda but she also urged that he was wanted even more in West
Africa and could not be spared from there. Kirk was in the con-
spiracy, detached, judicial and wise. Goldie, of course, was insistent,
and he succeeded.

Working closely together under Goldie's leadership, and keeping
a wary eye on Chamberlain, like men trying to manœuvre a powerful
and capricious bull into the pen which they had prepared for him,
the four of them hatched a very pretty plot. The Company was to
give up the commercial functions which had made it so unpopular
and retain its administrative powers. Since the Colonial Office, according to Goldie, could never be "permanently creative" but only act as
"the control, the governor of the steam engine, not the boiler," there
ought to be a policy-making council for West Africa in Britain on
which, it was to be inferred, Goldie would be the moving spirit.[3]
Goldie, though such a good businessman, was much more interested
in the political than in the commercial aspect of his creation; like
Rhodes and Mackinnon he cannot be fitted into the communist
pattern of the economic imperialist. Lugard would go out as administrator; Goldie, aided by Kirk, would run the British side. This,
Lugard recognized, would be a great sacrifice for Goldie, but then

---

[1] See Sir H. Johnston, *The Uganda Protectorate* (1902), vol. i, pp. 236–42, and Jackson, *Early Days in East Africa*, pp. 302–15.

[2] *Parliamentary Debates*, 3 March 1898, IV. 54. 504–77.

[3] Goldie to C.O., 21 July 1897, C.O. 147/127. See also unpublished section of Kirk's report on the disturbances at Brass, F.O. 83/1382.

Goldie, who " has extraordinarily strong Imperial instincts and a truly wonderful Patriotism " would accept this solution " if he had full confidence in the Administrator appointed by government " and could still influence its affairs. He would like an official position from which to do this, but failing that, " through his vast influence with the press and in parliament, he could *force* his will on the Secretary of State. *Provided that*, and here lies the whole point—the Administrator out there saw eye to eye with him and worked hand in glove." His speculations had now alighted upon this subject: he himself was to be the man, or, as Goldie wrote in one of his brief, strong letters, " Not you administrator nor I—but *both*—each doing our share and working together for Imperial ends." (Goldie to L. 26 January 1898).

Lugard tried to understand himself as he stood before the choices that seemed to be open to him. He was fully aware of the psychological interest of this encounter between strong personalities. He tried to pierce " the true inwardness of each man's action," first Chamberlain's, then Goldie's, and now his own. It was certainly surprising that, with his passion for independence, he was prepared to serve under the control of so masterful a man as Goldie. He tried to answer the question himself. Why was he ready to accept this plan? " Is it not enough for me that my two ideal men, Kirk and Goldie, are its authors, and that I should be their Agent? Such is Goldie's view, but he is the most eminently practical man I have ever met in my life. That and his high standard of honour are the sources of his influence over me. He wastes no time on Ideals, but accepts facts and works on them. Idle regrets form no part of his stock in trade. Therefore since Joe is the most powerful factor in the situation, his policy is to guide Joe and make the best of his good points."

How far was " Joe " aware of these plans for his own management? If he were, he would not have been much troubled. His self-confidence was as superb as Goldie's, and his will set to go in exactly the opposite way from the one designed for him. The Colonial Office files reveal what neither Goldie nor Lugard could know at the time, the strength of Chamberlain's determination to cancel the Company's charter at the earliest possible moment. He had become increasingly angered by the way in which Goldie was making play with the one strong card left in his hand, his possession of the only seasoned troops on the spot and his command of the transport needed to reach that spot. Day by day, Goldie refused to act according to Chamberlain's plans, and the Foreign Office and Monson in Paris declared that he had deceived them as to the extent of the Company's occupation, and yet was quite ready to risk a rupture with France for his own interests.[1] In fact, as Goldie angrily informed Salisbury in October, it was impossible what with the extent and remoteness of this still almost unexplored region, to know *where* the French were, especially as they were always on the move, fighting, setting up flags, requisitioning food and over-awing the people.[2] It must be noted that Goldie's ignorance constituted an admission that Borgu was not effectively occupied by his Company. Chamberlain became so indignant that he consulted the Law Officers of the Crown as to whether he could act against the Company at once, but they advised him that such action might allow the French to claim, with an opportunist reversal of their former argument, that the validity of the treaties with Africans lapsed with the Charter.[3] This incident allowed Monson in Paris to say with some satisfaction of the Colonial Office, " Verily they have been like the Scriptural party who invoked the assistance of Balaam "—for Monson and the Foreign Office were almost as critical of Chamberlain's department as they were of the Company.[4]

The conspirators, ignorant of the true position, used bold methods. The Chancellor of the Exchequer, Sir Michael Hicks Beach, was in Lugard's view (though in such high matters he probably accepted that of Goldie), a man who could easily be put at odds with Chamberlain. Not only was he an aristocrat who found his Birmingham colleague socially uncongenial, but he was a man of very independent character, which was inclined to rub against that of the wilful Colonial Secretary. Most important of all, he was the guardian of the public purse and, already disturbed by the heavy drain of the Colonial Office for East and West Africa and the West Indies, would probably jump at " Kirk's scheme " as being much more economical than Chamberlain's plan of the government taking over the incalculable expenses of administering Northern Nigeria.[5] Goldie was in close touch with Hicks Beach.

[1] Monson to Bertie, 20 August 1897, F.O. 27/3339.
[2] Memorandum by Goldie on the local situation in Borgu, enclosed in Goldie to F.O., 11 October 1897, F.O. 27/3372.
[3] Report by Law Officers on the validity of Royal Niger Company Treaties, 29 December 1897, C.O. 537/14.
[4] Monson to Bertie, 14 November 1897, F.O. 27/3340.
[5] Lady Victoria Hicks Beach, *Sir Michael Hicks Beach, Earl St. Aldwyn* (1932), vol. ii, p. 47.

W

When, therefore, Lugard left England he could believe that the issue about the future of Northern Nigeria was still undecided. " Who will win? " he wondered, " Joe or Hicks Beach? Joe is *absolutely* determined," (Lugard drew a rare double underlining), " but if Goldie puts out all his force and if the Chancellor takes a decided line, even Joe may be defeated."

There were thus two issues at stake, the forestalling of the French and the future government of Northern Nigeria, in both of which Lugard's own future was now bound up. But in this complex story there were two minor plots as well as two major ones.

The first minor plot affected the immediate conduct of the operations to restore the British hold upon Borgu, and concerned the question of strategy raised by Chamberlain's chessboard policy. In spite of Lugard's criticism, in which both Kirk and Goldie supported him, Chamberlain showed no sign of weakening upon this. The matter remained undecided while Lugard went on with the organization of the force, and sent off stores and batches of men piecemeal as they were ready. But on January 22nd 1898, he received a detailed memorandum from a certain Major Barker of the War Office Intelligence, in which the chessboard strategy was worked out in detail. Lugard sat down at once and wrote a criticism tearing the plan to pieces, beginning with its " petty inaccuracies " and ending by the remark that for an officer without experience of active service, who knows nothing of the country, or local conditions, " it was hardly compatible with the legitimate scope of his functions " to lay down the military details in advance.[1]

He then proceeded to reiterate the former arguments against the chessboard policy. These were mainly that cutting lines of communication was an act of war; and that ten natives carrying a French flag, and knowing we dare not fire on it, could turn back three hundred British soldiers. Once more he urged that if war were to be entered upon, it should be by the will of the Cabinet and the nation and not because a junior military officer made a mistake or some individual Frenchman courted self-advertisement. It would be more in accord with the dignity of the nation that this issue should be brought to a crisis in Europe, not in Borgu.

1 Memorandum dated 8 February 1898, L.P.

Behind all Lugard's detailed objections to Chamberlain's plan of operations there appears to be one which he never clearly formulated even to himself. It arose from that antagonism in co-operation, so especially acute in democracies, between the soldier and the politician. Lugard's life, health and energies had for long been committed to enterprises which were at the mercy of politics and diplomacy. Now it seemed to him that, in spite of his official appointment, he was again to go out in an ambiguous position in which he must take decisions which were the proper responsibility of ministers in Whitehall. The soldier, we have lately been told again by Lord Montgomery, works with a precise machine and should have a clearly defined purpose; the politician works with different but far less clearly defined objects, and must be subtle and compromising. " Many battles have been fought for political and not for military reasons and these have been the graveyard of many a soldier's reputation."[1]

The strategic plan was a matter of absolute disagreement between the Colonial Secretary and the War Office on the one side and, upon the other, the commanding officer who was to carry out their instructions. Lugard was therefore beginning to wonder again whether he would be able to go out at all when Chamberlain called him for another interview.[2] He went to the Colonial Office on January 27th, and entered the now familiar big room, with its globes and maps and handsome fireplace.[3] He found Lord Selborne and Mr. Antrobus there with Chamberlain, and later Mr. Edward Wingfield came in.[4] Lugard, realizing that strategy would be the main issue, had asked if he might bring in Willcocks, but Chamberlain said there was a personal matter to be settled first.

Lugard noticed at once that Chamberlain had dropped his domineering air of the last interview but that he had not forgotten the matters of their former disagreement. Yet, if he spoke in a quiet and conciliatory tone, his opening words were no more hopeful.

" The Memorandum from the War Office " (the one Lugard had torn to pieces in his comments) " was *my* policy, and I agree with

[1] A. Moorehead, *Montgomery* (1946), p. 237.
[2] The description of the conversation which follows is based almost word for word upon Lugard's own account which he wrote the same day, and upon his diary, written up on board ship, 13 March 1898.
[3] Now, unfortunately, replaced by a very commonplace room in Church House.
[4] Wingfield, (later Sir) Edward, K.C.B., 1834–1910; 1878 Assistant Under-Secretary of State for the Colonies; 1897–1900 Permanent Under-Secretary of State.

every word of it. Are you prepared to undertake this task? Or must I find another man? "

There was a pause during which Selborne and Antrobus waited with obvious eagerness for the reply. Lugard answered very slowly and distinctly.

" If *you* desire me to go, Mr. Chamberlain, I go. But the policy is, in my opinion, wrong and it is unpracticable."

Lugard's record of the interview shows that he was quite able to relish, perhaps to heighten, the dramatic side of it. He observed—or liked to think?—that this defiance of their masterful chief electrified the three men who were watching. Chamberlain himself seemed taken aback.

" I cannot," he said, " send a man to carry out a policy in which he does not concur. Let me hear your objections. I conclude they are military ones."

He added the warning that if he appointed someone else this would prejudice Lugard's future. To this Lugard at once replied that his personal position must not weigh in the matter at all, as what became of him was of no consequence. This was a proper gesture, but Lugard knew when he made it that Chamberlain could not very easily discard him at this point. He had recalled him from South Africa, causing him to resign a very highly paid job. His appointment and its significance had been discussed in the press in France as well as in England, and if he were now to resign on a question of policy, with men of the status of Kirk and Goldie to come out in public support of him, even Chamberlain would be embarrassed. " In fact," Lugard decided to himself, " I should smash his policy, even though he smashed me. So I had strong cards and the strongest was that I hated the whole business. I had come as no suppliant. I suppose I am ambitious—one hardly knows—but I was not at all inclined to sacrifice my independence of judgment or to bow my knee to him in order to obtain any possible honours he could give."

They then plunged into an argument about the chessboard policy.

" I shall go into this country with my hands tied," Lugard said, " while the French have their hands free."

Chamberlain stopped him at once by asking him what he meant by the French having their hands free.

" They are free because they are unscrupulous, especially the men who are there. They know very well that they would have the whole applause of France if they attacked me. They would say that I had attacked first . . . . The young officers on the spot in Borgu will be all the more anxious to attack if I personally am in command, since my name is hated in Paris."

He went on to say that the French had much larger forces than the British would have. Every convoy must have an escort in that country. If he ordered a French escort to turn back and they refused and he could not force them to turn, he would become a laughing-stock and the natives would go over to France.

" In this memorandum," he went on, " there is a great deal about cutting their lines of communications. What is that, Mr. Chamberlain, but an act of war?"

" Well, perhaps ' cutting communications ' is wrong," admitted Chamberlain, " I would rather use the phrase, ' sitting on their lines of communications'."

Chamberlain, following up this politician's refinement, then said it would be no disgrace if an overwhelming French force called upon them to evacuate a post and they did so. But this, Lugard replied, was a contradiction of what he had said before, that with ten men the British could defy a host, because they knew the French had just as positive orders not to attack as we had. " In fact," Lugard commented to himself, " they are quite at sea. There is no logic in their policy."

When told again that Goldie was making difficulties about sending his promised 300 soldiers to join the imperial force, " Joe waxed very warm and said it would be the worse for the shareholders if they refused assistance," but in the end he was obliged to ask Lugard to use his influence with Goldie to bring him to reason, a request he cannot have enjoyed making.

" You know Goldie and are his friend, you have served with the Royal Niger Company . . . . I have tried and failed, you had better see what you can do."

He realized the new force would not be ready for months, but all the other available troops, plus the West India Regiment and the Lagos Constabulary, which it had been decided to add to the force, would be under his command.

At the end, very deliberately and thoughtfully, as though taking account of the fact of Lugard's unbending opposition to his plan of action, Chamberlain said,

" Well, I would like you to go, Lugard."

" All right, sir," Lugard replied.

In this strange way the interview ended. It would be interesting if we knew Chamberlain's side of the situation and why he kept to his decision to send out upon such a delicate mission a man who disagreed so obstinately with his instructions. It is possible to speculate but it may be better to do so later with the help of that wisdom which comes after the event.

As for Lugard, he had one more struggle with himself. When he got back to his flat and reviewed his conversation he felt that he could not go. He was especially disturbed by Chamberlain having said to him that he knew he could count upon him to carry out his policy loyally if he went. That seemed to make it a point of honour to execute a policy of which Lugard had shown his disapproval. He sat down and wrote a letter to say that he must resign because he could not put his whole heart into the work. This, he knew, would be the end of any employment by the government. He went round and showed the letter to Goldie. " One word of concurrence from you and this goes in." Again, Goldie begged him not to send it. He and Lugard thought alike upon this question and once Lugard was gone Goldie would work the press and parliament and upset this folly of the chessboard policy.

Shortly after his interview with Chamberlain, Lugard dined with him and his wife. It was a small party and among the guests were the Duke of Devonshire and Mr. George (afterwards Lord) Curzon. A social engagement was, to Lugard, generally a chance to continue his work by other methods, and he was certainly not idle upon this occasion. He took the chance to discuss Macdonald and Uganda with Curzon and Chamberlain as well as with the Duke. Chamberlain " very emphatically condemned Macdonald and said if Uganda were under him he would have recalled him at once." Lugard, if pleased at this, was also shocked.

" Joe is extraordinarily indiscreet. Such language must simply revolt a man of the Duke's temperament."

Chamberlain went on to say that all this showed the incompetence of the Foreign Office to administer protectorates and that they ought to be transferred to the Colonial Office.

" He used almost the *very words* and the identical arguments I had used a few days before to Miss Shaw, so much so that I feel convinced that she had repeated them and that they had sunk into Joe's mind. I was, of course, delighted."

After his long interview with Chamberlain, Lugard wrote, as he had promised, to Goldie to ask for the military help of the Company. Goldie replied by return, giving Lugard in two sentences what he had so long denied to Chamberlain, and what he had written to Lugard a few days before to say was impossible in view of his obligations to his shareholders.

" I am never surprised at anything . . . . Try and give me as exact details of men and stores as you can, so that I can wire exactly what is wanted."
(Goldie to L. 28 January 1898).

He was, as usual, as good as his word. Further, the Colonial Office having alleged that his Company was refusing to ship their Royal Engineers' mission up the Niger, at a word from Lugard all the necessary arrangements were made.

So much, at least for the moment, of the working-out of one of the minor plots. The other, which had emerged at the interview with Chamberlain, came again to the surface very soon; it concerned the Lagos base. Goldie and Lugard were determined that the new Frontier Force should operate against the French from bases in the Niger Company territory. This had the great merit for Goldie that it would make Chamberlain dependent upon the Company's co-operation for the success of the enterprise and so give him a hold over the Colonial Secretary at a moment when the Company's fate was being decided. It would also allow Goldie and Lugard to work closely together. For Lugard it offered the advantage, indeed for him, the necessity, of an independent command. " Have as little as you can to do with McCallum," said Goldie. Lugard did not need this warning against the Governor of Lagos as a man impossible to work with, for the man's character was irrelevant; it was his status and location which mattered. Lugard decided, with the same emotional intensity he had shown in his relations with de Winton, that he certainly would have as few contacts with Lagos as possible. There can be little doubt that the decision was militarily sound. The Niger base at Jebba put the Frontier Force in the very heart of Borgu and from the standpoint of military psychology, the movement of troops and gun-boats up and down the desired and disputed waterway, instead of overland from Lagos, was likely to impress both the French and the Africans.

This question had come up during Lugard's last interview with the Secretary of State when Chamberlain argued for the Lagos base.

"This did not suit me *at all*," was Lugard's comment, "I am of course fully in co-operation with Goldie, and have taken a delight in embarrassing the Government so as to force them to a statement of their intentions re the R.N.C., but neither he nor I want to lose our lever by transferring back to Lagos, and *my* position with the Governor McCallum would be an impossible one."

On February 1st Lugard received a long and formal letter from the Colonial Office, and signed by Edward Wingfield, giving him his instructions. The chessboard policy was now translated—not, we may be sure, without difficulty—into official orders. Lugard was to push detachments boldly forward in Borgu and to thrust them where possible across the French lines of communication. But:

".... you are in no case to act on the aggressive, although if you are yourself attacked, you have full authority to take such measures of defence as you may think necessary."

This, unpalatable though it was, had been expected. But more followed. The advantages of conducting the campaign from the Lagos Protectorate were set out against the inconvenience of conducting it from the Niger, since "no arrangement has been made with the Company," and there was the possibility of divided responsibility. The Governor of Lagos was already effectively conducting operations along his own border. Therefore, although the possibility of a parallel advance from the Niger was not ruled out, Mr. Chamberlain was sending a dispatch to the Governor of Lagos "as to the instructions to be given to you as Commissioner and Commandant in the British protected territories of the Niger." It was pointed out that Lieutenant Colonel Northcott, who was carrying out exactly similar operations in the northern part of the Gold Coast, had been placed in the same relationship with Sir W. Maxwell, the Governor of the Gold Coast.

Lugard was not only astonished but he was also very angry. He had understood that his insistence upon an absolutely independent command of a higher status than Northcott's had been fully accepted. He at once suspected that Chamberlain had realized his mistake in sending him out after that unbridged disagreement upon strategy and was using this method of forcing his resignation on a personal question of Lugard's status, which would seem to put Lugard rather than himself in the wrong. He sat down at once and wrote a very stiff letter asking if he was to understand that nothing in his instructions was irreconcilable with the independent command he had been promised. The response was a verbal message from Lord Selborne asking him to come and talk it over. He replied that he preferred to have an answer first to his official letter. Antrobus now sent round his private secretary to beg him to come round. He went, but in a very angry mood. He was now prepared to throw up the appointment and yet—the thought came even as he went, for he was beginning to know himself—

" The task was a great one and I well know what I should feel once I found myself kicked out and the work on which I had been engaged entrusted to another, I should feel it very keenly, for had I not been through the experience in the case of Uganda and East Africa? "

He found Selborne, Antrobus and Wingfield all waiting for him and another official, a man whom he knew and despised. Angry though he was, Lugard was impressed by Selborne's remarkable tact, his clear head and conciliatory manner. Selborne pointed out the difficulties of dealing independently with Lugard who would be away in the wilds and out of touch, whereas McCallum was already operating on the indeterminate Lagos frontier, was under the Colonial Office and was also on the now northward extending telegraph line. Lugard had his answer for every point and then turned on his heel and examined a map on the wall. He realized that his attitude bordered on bad manners, but he tried to be scrupulously deferential and polite to Selborne, of whom, indeed, he had never had so good an opinion as at this interview. The official, the fourth man in the Colonial Office team, now said pompously—we must remember that this is Lugard's account— that the relations of a commander in the field and the governor of a colony were laid down in the regulations. " The infernal ass! " was Lugard's private comment, " why could he not have been content with the natural assumption any stranger would arrive at from looking at his face, instead of proving it beyond doubt by braying." Aloud he said:

" Yes, that is so, but the only flaw in your argument is that we are not dealing with a colony at all, but with a country outside the jurisdiction of any colony."

The argument went on. Lugard left no doubt of his attitude, but to make quite sure he went down afterwards with Antrobus to his room and said:

" I *think* I spoke clearly enough, Mr. Antrobus, but in case I did not I would like to know whether you understand that if I am placed under Lagos I resign at once."

" Oh, yes, clearly," was the answer.

" Did Lord Selborne understand too? "

" Quite clearly," Antrobus replied.

Lugard passed two wretched days. Even though he recognized that he had been unbearable to deal with, he had no intention of giving way. He continued doing his office work every night until 4 or 5 a.m., rounding off his responsibilities to the West Charterland Company, of which he was still a director; mixing in Uganda affairs; and dealing with the press. It was Willcocks, working most closely with him, who received the chief hurt from his uneasy temper and the backwash of his troubles with the Colonial Office. But Willcocks, though his own interests were now bound up with the enterprise, gave a steady support and loyalty to his chief in the stand he was taking. Indeed, in a set of subordinate negotiations, in which he was sounded by the officials, he was as uncompromising as Lugard. Antrobus, who dreaded that Lugard should resign, pumped Willcocks more than once about this. Willcocks said bluntly:

" You have got the best man in the Empire for this job, the only man whom Goldie and his Niger Company will lift a finger to help, and now you are breaking faith with him by trying to take away the appointment for which he has resigned a very good post. ' I'll serve under no-one else,' he concluded, ' and if Lugard resigns I'm off!' "

" Do you think he will resign? " Antrobus asked again.

" I can't say what Lugard will do, but I know I would if so treated, and he is a stronger man than I am."

The result of all this conflict of policies and will was that two days after his interview with Selborne and the rest, Lugard received a letter which gave him the independence of Lagos for which he had fought. This was a clear sign of the value Chamberlain put upon his services.

While Chamberlain and his advisers in the Colonial Office were trying to prepare men and measures for the military side of this international game of poker, the diplomatic round of the game was being vigorously played a little further up Downing Street, where Lord Salisbury, as Prime Minister and Foreign Secretary had offices upon both sides of that short *cul-de-sac*. But the diplomatic struggle was not only a foreign war; a little civil war was also breaking out in this street. It was largely hidden from the public and even from Lugard and Goldie, and only fully revealed by the opening of the records. Chamberlain now began to lead his Colonial Office into a final struggle against Salisbury and his Foreign Office over the West African issue. Fortunately it will not be necessary to follow all the moves of these involved transactions, external or internal.[1] The telegrams and letters with their enclosures were passing daily and sometimes more than once a day between the British ambassador, Sir Edmund Monson, and the Foreign Secretary; between the Foreign and Colonial Offices and the Niger Company. To increase the amount of paper, though not to speed up the result, the Niger Commission had resumed its sessions in Paris on October 29th, 1897, a few days after Lugard had arrived from South Africa. Colonel W. Everett and Mr. M. Gosselin were the British commissioners. It was a long-lived Commission, having been first appointed in 1890, but its subsequent sessions had been intermittent.

The delegates now began to argue at great length about the general interpretation of international treaties and the special validity of African ones; of the exact powers and spheres of this or that chief, and especially the undiscoverable lord of Borgu; of effective occupation, spheres of influence, hinterlands, and freedom of commerce under the Act of Berlin. Bronzed soldier explorers, with names that were then famous, were called upon to expound the maps they were making. Mary Kingsley, who was a very much interested onlooker, was perhaps a little captious when she remarked that the amount of probity in diplomacy " is a thing that would not at any time cover a threepenny bit." Her next remark, however, was rather less extreme, and might

---

[1] The opening of the French archives beyond the present date of 31 December 1896 will make it possible to compare the complementary diplomatic theme in full.

be allowed to apply to this episode in the scramble. " It is a form of war that shows no blood, but which has not in it those things which sanctify red war, honour and chivalry."[1]

Meanwhile the diplomats could not concentrate rigidly upon their work round the table. They had to keep an eye upon the movements of the forces in the Nigerian and Gold Coast hinterlands, where both nations were trying to reinforce diplomacy by manœuvrings and occupations which presented the distracted diplomats with an ever-changing situation about which to negotiate. The French were still doing all the scoring in Borgu, while the British were more active in the Gold Coast hinterland. And while the diplomats behaved with some attempt at dignity and discretion, speaking almost apologetically in time-honoured terms of their inability to answer for the strong feelings of their people, the press of the two countries shouted accusations at each other over their heads. Before the end of October Hanotaux was reported to be taking note of the serious British preparations for military reinforcements on the Niger and was making the customary protest that Britain was trying to provoke a conflict.[2] Salisbury was devoting a good deal of attention to supporting the wavering morale of Monson, condoling privately with him " on this task for it is a very disagreeable one," but encouraging him to believe that, tense though the situation would become, it could not lead to war, for neither nation would risk this " for the sake of a malarious African desert."[3] And a few days later, approving the stand made by Monson, he wrote " If he [Hanotaux] talks about the fury of the Chamber and the probable violence of the press, tell him that we have a democracy quite as unreasonable, and that our newspapers can use very bad language if they try."[4]

During November 1897, the two sides had been mainly concerned with stating their claims in the Commission. Chamberlain considered the British delegates much too feeble in the stand they took, and he set to work to stiffen their diplomatic offensive in harmony with his military advance. On the 15th of this month they reported that the Commission was at a deadlock, and Chamberlain minuted on the following day that both the ambassador and the commissioners were

---

1 Kingsley, *West African Studies*, p. 280.
2 Monson to Salisbury, 22 October 1897, F.O. 27/3340.
3 Salisbury to Monson, 19 October 1897, S.P. vol. 107 (France 1895-1900).
4 Salisbury to Monson, 22 October 1897, ibid.

" easily discouraged and inclined at every check to fall back on their ingrained inclination for what they call compromise—which means in every case giving up something which we believe to be ours and getting nothing in return."[1] In December he found himself rejecting a French claim for a corridor from their part of Borgu—however that should be defined—to a port of their own on the navigable Niger near Jebba.[2] Salisbury seemed inclined to accept this, and there were others who were recoiling from the uncompromising position taken up by Chamberlain. Kirk wrote his own misgivings to Lugard:

> " I cannot but think this is one of the most dangerous games of bluff ever played. But it amazes me to think that we are playing into the German hand, and if we have a rival in Europe, it is Germany, not France. ' Joe ' is a Brummagem shop-keeper and no diplomat. Bluff will do between rival ' screws,' but he may be taken too seriously on the other side in diplomacy." (undated).

But Chamberlain *was* serious. In the same strong letter to Salisbury, of December, he regretted that he was unable to agree with him over the French corridor, and insisted that in these negotiations doubtful claims should be exchanged for doubtful claims. But the French only proposed to yield theirs for our undoubted rights. " I do not think," he finished up, " that we ought to yield a jot to threats." On this occasion Salisbury repeated this almost word for word in his instructions to our embassy in Paris dated December 30th.[3] But to Selborne Chamberlain wrote that Lord Salisbury's behaviour was

> " most discouraging. I thought he was entirely with us and now he is prepared to give away everything and get nothing. I am more than sorry to differ from him, but I cannot stand it."[4] (1 December 1897).

January saw the negotiations becoming more dangerous as the stiffening which Chamberlain had injected into them began to be felt by the French. A number of apparently isolated pieces of news came in to be fitted into the pattern of international conflict. The French were reported to have finally put down a prolonged rising against them in Borgu, to have re-occupied Nikki and to have seized its king.

---

[1] Minute by Chamberlain, 16 November 1897, C.O. 537/13.
[2] Chamberlain to Salisbury, 1 December 1897, C.O. 537/13.
[3] *British Documents on the Origins of the war 1898–1914*, ed. G. P. Gooch and H. Temperley, vol. i (1927), p. 132.
[4] Garvin, *Life of Chamberlain*, vol. iii, p. 213.

They were reported to be intriguing in Sokoto. They continued to demand a corridor to the navigable Niger, below Bussa. The Marchand expedition was known to be moving across Central Africa.

But the tide of action was now just beginning to show signs of turning. On January 8th, *The Times* announced that the two British gun-boats had been pieced together at Forcados and were proceeding up the Niger. On the 17th the news came that the British operating from Lagos had occupied Okuta, from which they would be able to prevent the French taking short cuts across the southern corner of the British Protectorate. On the same day the Prime Minister received a grave communication from Sir Edmund Monson in which he analysed the restless and abnormal mood of France, where the Dreyfus case was in progress, and warned his government that unless they made concessions there would probably be war.[1] There was, he said, irritation in the army and a lot of combustible material lying about. Chamberlain was unmoved. When the British commissioners put up a paper pointing out " the indubitable strength of the case against us," Chamberlain, in a circular note to the Cabinet, characterized their paper " as an admirable document if it were written by French officials as a brief for a French minister."[2]

Later in the month the French soldiers, having now fully regained their hold upon rebellious Borgu up to the Niger, re-opened their diplomatic attack upon Lugard's treaty with Nikki, both in the Commission and in the press. His competitor in the famous steeple-chase, Captain Decoeur, was called before the Commission and this time asserted that Lugard had been the victim of a plot, that a group of unauthorized people had tricked him into signing a treaty with them for the sake of a present, and that he could testify that, contrary to Lugard's report, the king was not blind. Lugard turned aside from his military preparations to draw up an emphatic and indignant defence of his achievement. Had not his interpreter, Joseph, heard the king repeat three times that the signatories were his representatives? He had explained his treaty publicly before the assembled people, as he always did. No presents were given before the treaty was signed. If the king was not wholly blind, his eyes were very weak. Of course, a European using strong force could have coerced him into seeing a

1 Garvin, *Life of Chamberlain*, vol. iii, p. 213.
2 Memorandum by Chamberlain, 25 January 1898, C.O. 537/14.

white man, and Decoeur had 130 fighting men to his 24. He regarded the matter as a point of honour; he had never expected his treaty to be questioned. Was it likely that Decoeur, new to Africa, would have succeeded in getting a treaty if he, Lugard, with all his experience, had been fooled? Lugard sent in one long explanation after another. The French even tried to score a point on the grounds that they had found on Lugard's treaty the mark " Form 12. For Muslims." Lugard explained that this was merely an appropriate form for an important potentate. He was then accused of having lodged with the Muslim plotters. He retorted that here, as everywhere, he had camped outside the native town.[1] For a time Salisbury stood by Lugard's Nikki treaty[2] but as the months of wrangling over it went by, even the Colonial Office began to fear that in form, though not in fact, Lugard's treaties were assailable, and to wish he had taken those pains with them which he would have taken " if he had known how minutely they would be criticized in Paris."[3] This was not the end of the Nikki controversy. The travellers, the delegates, the diplomats, and the politicians continued a discussion that consumed months of negotiation about the precise actions that had taken place in Nikki and their significance.

During February it was clear that the crisis was taking a graver turn. There was hardly a day in this month when *The Times* had not some news to print, some message from Paris, quoting the French press, or some comment to make upon the issue. There were, for example, editorial articles upon the question on February 21st, 22nd, 23rd and 24th. On the last day a whole page was given up to an impressive map showing the exact distribution of places with the dates of the treaties made with them, and dotted with flags to show the position of the forces stationed at the various posts. Both nations were kept fully informed day by day about the negotiations and the actions in that distant region which the great French traveller, Binger, brusquely told the Commission, was worthless.[4] It was, however, with every week that passed, gaining in value as an object upon which the wills of two determined nations were set.

[1] Gosselin and Everett to Monson, 3 February 1898, containing extracts from Lugard to Everett, 8 November 1897, F.O. 27/3411.
[2] Salisbury to Monson, 26 November 1897, F.O. 27/3336.
[3] Minute by Chamberlain, 31 May 1898, C.O. 537/15.
[4] Gosselin and Everett to Gosselin, 11 November 1897, F. O. 27/3340.

The Niger Again 1897-1898

On February 8th, Chamberlain read out in the House of Commons two telegrams. One reported the arrival of a party of French Senegalese at Boria, a post the British Hausas had reached a few days earlier. They had called upon the British to haul down the flag. Upon their refusal the Senegalese camped close to the town. The second telegram announced a French advance in the Gold Coast hinterland.[1] The House was said to have listened in tense silence but Lebon,[2] the French Colonial Minister, described Chamberlain's manner as one of " calculated emotion " and part of his plan for deliberately inflaming British public opinion against France.[3] Not many days after this, the report came that the French had dispatched a force into Sokoto, which, if yet unoccupied, was by still unchallenged treaty in the British sphere on the east of the Niger. It was also Goldie's sphere. He did not hesitate for a moment. He immediately ordered a Niger Company force to march north under Wallace, the Company's Agent-General, to compel the French to recross the Niger, but not to attack until " extremely courteous written summonses " had been refused. It was characteristic of Goldie that he sent the order first and then informed Chamberlain. At this moment there was no rebuke.[4]

Kirk was not the only man to doubt the wisdom of Chamberlain's persistence. The editor of *The Times* found it necessary to write to Flora Shaw to say that he could not publish an article of hers, presumably supporting the British case, as he had trustworthy information which convinced him that the Niger Commissioners were right to be " profoundly dissatisfied with our case." Then, writing obviously of Chamberlain, he went on " It would be absurd for our friend to resign because the government will not press to the point of war a case their own delegates do not believe in." (G. Buckle to F. Shaw, 14 February 1898). Yet the line Flora Shaw wanted to take was not wholly reversed.

On February 21st *The Times* in a leading article reproved the French press for the levity with which they were treating this intermingling of outposts which the British determination made a very serious matter. At any moment some of these armed bands roaming

---

1 *Parliamentary Debates*, 18 February 1898, IV. 53. 1183–4.
2 Lebon, André, 1859–1938; 1884 professor at Ecole des sciences politiques (Paris); 1893–8 deputy for Deux-Sèvres; 1895 Minister of Commerce in Ribot cabinet; 1896–8 Minister for the Colonies in Méline cabinet; 1932 President of the Paris-Lyon-Mediterranean railway company.
3 A. Lebon, *La Politique de la France en Afrique, 1896–8* (Paris 1901), p. 73.
4 Garvin, *op. cit.* p. 214.

about this region might bring on a disaster. " The peace of the world ought not to rest upon the ability and inclination of a number of youthful officers to control their native troops." For the British the limit of concession had now been reached. " It would be wrong and foolish to minimize the gravity of this fact." Hanotaux denied that a French force had been sent to Sokoto and blamed the Niger Company for trying to make bad blood between France and Britain.[1] The French newspapers, however, added that " all Africa must not be included in the term Sokoto," and chorused their disapproval of the excitement shown in the English press at matters which could be settled by negotiation. " Therefore, Messieurs les Anglais, a little more calm and patience, if you please."[2] While the French were still advancing and consolidating, this cool advice was rather hard to follow. There had already been an acid reminder that Lugard's treaties had to convince the Niger Commission, not *The Times*.[3]

On February 24th Chamberlain came to the House of Commons for provision for the West African Frontier Force and a general debate upon the situation in West Africa took place. The unwearying anti-imperialist Labouchere, with the usual Irish support, attacked Chamberlain for risking war with France for unwanted strips of territory in Africa. Chamberlain answered with a long exposition of British policy in West Africa. It had been his hope that Britain could have occupied the territories assigned to her gradually and economically, but France had forced our hand. He justified the raising of the Frontier Force, which would be necessary for the policing of the country even apart from French encroachment. He spoke of Lugard's appointment. He denied Labouchere's shrewd assertion that the Cabinet was divided upon the matter.

" The Cabinet is absolutely united—and, I believe, that in this they have the whole country behind them—in the determination that while they will exhibit the most conciliatory disposition in dealing with disputed matters, and will be ready even to make concessions of what they think to be their rights, in order to secure the friendship of the great nation with which they desire to remain in cordial unity; on the other hand, they will not allow the important interests of this country to be sacrificed."[4]

[1] Monson to Salisbury, 24 February 1898, F.O. 27/3411.
[2] *Le Matin*, quoted in *The Times*, 23 February 1898.
[3] *Bulletin du Comité de L'Afrique Française*, December 1897.
[4] *Parliamentary Debates*, 24 February 1898, IV. 53. 1628.

Sir Edward Grey, from the front opposition bench, supported Chamberlain. Labouchere could muster little support on a division except from the Irish vote, and the debate and the voting justified *The Times* in its statement the next day that " the whole nation with the exception of a few ' cranks ' " supported the government's policy. Lugard could feel that in his new task he had the support, not only of a Minister, or a party government, but of parliament as a whole.

March saw no settlement in sight. The French continued to demand their corridor in the face of reiterated refusals and they continued monotonously to pick holes in Lugard's treaty with Nikki. They were reported to be occupying the remaining small towns in Borgu. Lord Salisbury sent a firm note to Paris to say that the British would make no further concessions.[1] A broad survey of the whole Sudan position from east to west, from Khartoum to Uganda and from the Nile to the Niger, written by Flora Shaw—but not over her name— was published in *The Times* the same week. She ended by referring to the departure of Lugard for Nigeria, counting the strength of his forces with satisfaction and concluding with assured words about the prospects of her friend's enterprise.[2]

This was the position of affairs in Europe when, at last, on March 12th Lugard sailed. Two days before, Chamberlain summoned him for a farewell talk. They were quite alone this time and the Minister was most friendly. He said he could not give Lugard very precise instructions, but asked what he meant to do upon arrival. Lugard explained that hitherto a forward move would have been impossible. This was because the river between Lokoja and Jebba was too low, and if all the light draught vessels had been employed up there, there would have been a dearth of transport for the men collecting in the delta, who would have died like flies. Further, he went on (encroaching again upon Chamberlain's political sphere), as he understood that the choice of himself had been made partly with a deliberate view as to its effect upon the French, it would have lost half its effect if he had hung about at Lokoja, or had sent Pilcher ahead to Jebba. Now he could go straight ahead and also meet the new recruits marching up from Ibadan and be ready to act at once.

" What will you do next? " asked Chamberlain.

---

1 Monson to Salisbury, 1 March 1898, S.P. vol. 104 (France 1898).
2 *The Times*, 7 March 1898.

Lugard said that if they could get the huts erected at Jebba before the rains came on, they would do devilish well. If he wanted them to attempt to go on at once and operate in the rains, he personally could do it, but Chamberlain must understand that there would be enormous mortality with the raw men from England. With the satisfaction of a soldier facing the politician with the cost of his policy, Lugard observed " Joe, of course, squirmed at this."

If Lugard thought, however, that his chief had repented about the chessboard policy, he was mistaken, " for once more he began in his sketchy way to talk at large about thrusting ourselves across the French communications, and planted his thumb on names marked on the map at huge distances off, and suggested their occupation and so on." Lugard had the sense to say little to all this, discussing it in an abstract way and being careful not to seem to agree to it as an actual plan.

" The conversation was very social and friendly and he was his old self entirely, with the personality which I like and admire. For him, when he is *natural*, I have a great admiration, and I would do much, but his hectoring role did not come off with me and only made me hesitate on the verge of resignation."

" Now suppose it came to *war*," Chamberlain asked, " what would you do? " and, answering himself, suggested the withdrawal of all troops from Borgu and an attack in Dahomey itself. Lugard concurred entirely, but said that a man-of-war must anchor off Porto Novo and prevent reinforcements coming in via Dahomey. Upon this one rather grim item of agreement, Chamberlain shook his hand cordially and wished him luck. He had one more word to say, to give him permission to write to himself or Selborne unofficially and tell him everything more freely and fully than could be done in an official capacity. Goldie, " who always puts his finger on the really important point," was very pleased to hear this and said that " coming from Joe it was a very high mark of confidence and friendship." (Diary, 13 March 1898).

Thus, the parting between the two men was more harmonious than their meeting five months before. But it had done nothing to square the unresolved difference between them as to the practicability of the instructions which the politician had imposed upon the soldier.

675

CHAPTER XXXI

CONFLICT AND SETTLEMENT

1898 : Aet. 40

ON MARCH 12th Lugard and Willcocks boarded the S.S. *Benin* at Liverpool. Lugard had been working nearly all night and day coaching members of parliament for a Uganda debate; rounding off his requisitions; drawing up memoranda about his Borgu treaties for the Niger Commission, taking leave of his friends and winding up his private affairs. Now, although he told his brother that he had enough work to do on board to occupy a voyage round the world, he had at least some time to take stock of his position in the brief marine interval between the preparations for action and the action itself. The same anxious, industrious ordering which he gave to his public duties he turned upon the affairs of his mind. They too had to be listed, classified and adjudged.

He decided that he had good reasons, on the whole, to be satisfied. As far as his private life was concerned he had come away warmed by the affectionate farewells of his friends. His father, who had been ill, was now better. His sisters had sent their offerings, a revolver and an air-tight box, designed by himself, for keeping cigars. Even his landlady in Jermyn Street had produced a small work-box fitted with every kind of appliance for repairing clothes. His brother, still in Ngamiland, had sent good news about himself, his wife and child and also about his work, though the expedition had still failed to strike either gold or diamonds.

Most comforting of all, perhaps, was his hope of fulfilling that dream he had cherished from his days in Uganda, which he shared with so many English wanderers in the tropics, of possessing an acre of his own and a little house in England. The poverty which had hung over him since as a boy he could first feel its restrictions, had been lifted as a result of his Ngamiland expedition. In spite of the family calls upon him, which he so quietly and generously met, and which included substantial help for educating the children of his half-sister Emma, he had now put away what he called " a considerable sum of money." The sum was probably about £3,000, since, with what he meant to save in West Africa, he felt able to contemplate spending £3,500 upon a house and nine acres. The house was at Blackdown, near Haslemere, in a valley facing south and 700 ft. up in the Surrey downs. He had meant to spend only £600 upon one acre and the wooden cottage he meant to build upon it, but the beauty of the place and the persuasions of his friends had led him to consider this great extravagance. As he did not think he would marry, the little property would go to Edward and his son. " It is a fascination to me and I devote all my leisure thoughts to it and picture the site in my mind and devise plans for laying it out." From his house his thoughts ran over his friendships, and especially his satisfaction at his happy relations with the Waller family (who lived near the desired property). But, best of all, " I became on terms, I think, of closer friendship with Sir George Goldie, a man I admire and like *immensely*. I value his friendship very greatly." (Diary, 13 March 1898).

So much for his private life. In public matters—though Goldie's friendship, he thought, belonged to both sides of his life—he could also reckon up a good credit balance. He had spoken his mind to Chamberlain and in spite of that had kept his appointment and his chief's confidence. He had created a new force, as far as this could be done in London, and had won the right to choose his own officers. He had defeated a plan to deprive him of his independence and to change the base that guaranteed it. Yet, there should have been two unfavourable items in the reckoning. He was going out to execute a plan with which as a soldier he disagreed. And he was very tired, though the country and the conditions in which he was going to work demanded a man's fullest energy.

This may account in part for something which is not easy to explain. Lugard had some reasons, which have been given, for delaying his departure. As early as November 1897, he wrote defending this delay against Chamberlain's urgent wish that he should get away as quickly as possible. The impatience was not confined to the Colonial Office. " When is Lugard going out? " wrote Gosselin from Paris in February. " I cannot understand the long delay which has occurred in getting him under weigh; is his health doubtful? "[1] The diplomats may have had no faith in the hand they were asked to play but at least they wanted some strong cards with which to play it, and hoped that Lugard and his force would be some sort of ace. It would seem that, with all the diplomatic alarms in Europe and the military excursions in Africa, with news coming in almost daily of French encroachments, a man of Lugard's ardent temperament would at least have chafed against delay, even if his better judgment enforced it. There is no hint of this in his diary or any of his letters. We are reminded of a similar delay in an equally urgent enterprise when he went up to Uganda. The reason was the same; it was something additional to the need for the adequate organization of the new force and the rise of the Niger flood which would give access to the Jebba base. It was his unwillingness to carry out any project except under what he regarded as the conditions favourable to his own command of it. There are hints in his letters that he delayed at least partly in the hope of some change in policy or in the situation by which he could get his way. His friends seem to have encouraged him in this course, and in his lack of faith in the enterprise.

Goldie warned him that:

" they would have thrown me over if I had accepted the chessboard (futile) policy, as they will throw over you, Willcocks, Pilcher, Fitzgerald etc., if you *do* anything beyond bluff." (26 January 1898).

Had not the far-seeing Kirk told him that Chamberlain's game of bluff was dangerous, and:

" the longer you are here to see how the question shapes, the better for you. You will go out in the end ready to do the work for which you are really needed, namely the organization of the whole country." (28 October 1897).

There can be little doubt that when Lugard finally went out though he was, of necessity, ready to carry out his distasteful orders, he still hoped either that Goldie would succeed in upsetting Chamberlain's chessboard policy or that some diplomatic event would bring either real peace or real war. He already had his eyes upon a further and a wider horizon than that represented by the Borgu foreground, and upon a different profession from the military.

[1] Gosselin to Hill, 4 February 1898, F.O. 27/3408.

The voyage was dismal. The Elder Dempster steamer carrying him aroused all Lugard's hatred for inefficient and untidy methods. The deck was stacked with coal and the life-boats choked with baggage. At Sierra Leone he found an ancient colonel of the West Indian Regiment, who was not sure whether he or Lugard was in sole command of all West African forces and whose troops had just retreated before a native rising against the payment of taxation. Off Axim the ship grounded and, in view of her unready life-boats, there was a bad quarter of an hour. Here, too, he passed some of his non-commissioned officers, already being invalided home from his force. At Accra he lunched with the Governor and, as a believer in official formality, disapproved of the way in which he chaffed a native cook he was engaging for Lugard. While he loathed pomp and self-importance, Lugard was a believer in form and dignity, especially in relation with Africans who, he believed, shared his taste.

Willcocks was rash enough to go ashore at the French port of Kotonou in Dahomey, the base of the expeditions they were to encounter. He voted it a miserable post. When held up by the French official in charge for a landing fee of 15 francs he decided at any cost to refuse payment and gave as his explanation of himself that he was on his way to Borgu with Colonel Lugard, an excuse hardly likely to endear him to the French authorities.[1]

Lagos, Lugard feared, might well offer him a delicate situation in view of his rejection of the Governor's control. It was true that he had told Chamberlain, when he was struggling out of what he regarded as a noose, that it should be unnecessary to assure him " that no effort will be omitted on my part to maintain cordial relations with the Governor of Lagos," and he added, perhaps a little too confidently, but with an important proviso reminiscent of St. Paul, " I trust that my past career under somewhat varying and difficult conditions will prove that, as far as in me lies, I am the last man to incur friction with constituted authorities." However, on arriving at Lagos on March 31st, he found the Governor was away in the north and the rumour was at once brought to him that he had gone away in order to avoid meeting him. It might more charitably have been assumed that the operations warding off the French from the northern border of his Protectorate

---

1 Willcocks, *From Kabul to Kumassi*, p. 165.

required the Governor's presence. Lugard was informed that Government House had been left at his disposal, but found it without servants or food and full of workmen. He was further disgusted by what he regarded as the unbusinesslike methods exhibited by the officials whose duty it was to present him with the official telegrams sent out from Whitehall since his departure. He was still further enraged when this, in his view, inefficient Governor wrote to warn him that the administration and practical work of the Royal Niger Company—Goldie's Company!—was a farce. An invitation from the Governor to come up and meet him at Ibadan—" a very civil and nice letter " he had to admit—at once roused Lugard's horror of subordination. " He wants to make it appear, I suppose, that I am his puppet, who is to dance to his tune." He found an adequate reason for refusal in that he must hurry on to Lokoja to see about the erection of the permanent hutting before the rains should come.

The arrival of Lugard in Nigeria was, of course, noted in France, and noted with anxiety. As *The Times* Paris correspondent wrote:

" ever since the events in Uganda that officer has symbolized for them the fierce and grasping spirit of perfidious Albion. He is for them the stuff of which legends are made."[1]

The French paper *Débats* reassured itself by remarking that whatever his orders were they could not be to capture French posts. " It is too clear, in fact, that there would be but one issue of an adventure of this sort. Everybody knows that France has not the temperament of China."[2] *Le Temps* had already reminded its readers that Lugard was the man who massacred the Catholics in Uganda.[3]

Lugard and Willcocks left Lagos on April 4th. They now went on to Forcados to board a Company launch there to go up the Niger. As usual, Africa gave Lugard no welcome. The rain fell heavily; a tornado hit the boat; the steering-chains, rattling and clanging, passed through Lugard's and Willcocks' rooms; the twin-screws were frequently tossed out of the water to grind in the air. Even Lugard could not work in such conditions and was driven to read one of Conan Doyle's new Sherlock Holmes stories, a rare indulgence for him. Up the Niger conditions grew worse. There was ceaseless rain,

1 *The Times,* 19 April 1898.
2 *Débats,* 18 April 1898, quoted in *The Times,* 19 April 1898.
3 *Le Temps,* 13 January 1898.

which came through the roofs of the cabin and it was so cold that Lugard had to wrap himself up in a Jaeger blanket. He caught a chill and both he and Willcocks suffered from violent toothache. The ship was overloaded with stores for trade in addition to their equipment and they grounded on a bank; the vibration of the screw in the small ship was almost intolerable and the whisky had been forgotten. Willcocks, though used to the comfort and highly organized routine of Indian travel, was a man of cheerful temperament and he took his first introduction to Africa without flinching. There were, after all, some compensations—the sense of freedom; the almost boyish thrill he could still feel in pioneering; the importance of their venture. He had no doubts about that, and no reserves, in 1898, against confessing it. " Did we not feel we were the pioneers of a new Force; could we not realize the fact that we too were taking our share in Empire building? " Clearly, Lugard had been careful not to infect his buoyant friend with his own gloom. And, in spite of rain and discomfort, Willcocks, repeating Lugard's earlier impressions, could admire the Niger, the noble Black River, up which they steamed. Its muddy ripples ran against them; hippos grunted and submerged themselves; hundreds of parrots shot over the steamer like showers of loose silver, while on the banks stood immense trees deep in ferns and hung with creepers.[1]

There were also, despite exasperations at almost every turn, some compensations. Lugard found that most of the stores had been pushed upstream and the rest he took in hand himself. If he had any doubts about the kind of relations which, with his imperious nature, he would be able to establish with the senior service, these disappeared when he caught up with the gun-boats under Commander Melville, R.N., and he soon had the Navy humbly towing up his precious wooden huts. Goldie, moreover, had more than kept his promises: the Niger Company officials were most co-operative and he found that the fastest launch on the river had been assigned to him for his personal use.

On April 16th they arrived at Lokoja, the main base of the expedition. The 1st battalion, now half-trained, paraded 1,070 strong, and Lugard and Willcocks took stock of the men, the officers and the camp. All through the expedition Willcocks' comments are kinder than those of his chief: he had an optimistic outlook and a friendly

1 Willcocks, *op. cit.* p. 167 ff.

eye. He had, in the best sense, a simple nature, and he was as happy as a schoolboy in the adventure whereas Lugard had a divided mind and he was much fatigued.

He found, moreover, that he was not altogether content to resume the profession of arms, upon which he had turned his back ten years before. The rough pioneering work he had done since he left his regiment might have been expected to breed an indifference to regimental routine. But though he abhorred " spit and polish " as ends in themselves, his perfectionist standards led him to give almost too much time to the minutiæ of organization. The military instructions he issued to his force upon arrival are extremely comprehensive. Some of their most interesting sections refer to discipline and these are inspired both by his African experience and his humanity. Great leniency towards new native recruits is enjoined: example rather than punishment is the best teacher. " The continual exhibition of patience, tact and firmness combined with kindness and justice, will assuredly produce the best results possible." Troops were ordered to avoid " causes of offence to the native population and to treat them in a courteous manner." This was especially true of troops on the march with regard to looting, theft of crops and interference with women. " It has been our pride that British expeditions, in respect of their treatment of native populations, have borne a character throughout Africa which has contrasted greatly with those of other nations," and this new force was to uphold British traditions. (Instructions to his troops, 31 March 1898).

Lugard and Willcocks inspected the officers. Some of them would die by the Niger and others very shortly afterwards in Ashanti or South Africa. They were a keen and able lot of men, all volunteers, and coming from many territories and regiments to join the new force. They were ready for rough conditions and active service. But Willcocks' buoyant spirits sank as he looked for the first time at the black faces of his Hausa and Yoruba soldiers. Soon, however, he changed his mind about them, until the day came when he could honestly say that " if I had my choice once more, nowhere would I sooner serve than with my faithful Hausas and Yorubas, whom I learned to admire, and whose reputation is very precious to me."[1]

Lugard, however, was very critical of much that the colonel of the

[1] Willcocks, *op. cit.* p. 172.

1st battalion had done before his arrival. He considered he had been
wasting time and energy in building a large parade-ground: he had
put the soldiers' quarters on land above the officers' site, so that in the
rains all their drainage and refuse would run down on to them. Lugard
also found the office work in a confusion that distressed his orderly
mind. Uncertain whether to have his headquarters at Lokoja or at
Jebba, he went upstream to the latter and found the same elaborate
type of parade-ground had been constructed there.

He now began to consider how he should implement the policy
he had been told to carry out. The 1st battalion was, as we have seen,
at Lokoja. The 2nd battalion was on its way under Colonel Allen,
cutting across country from Ibadan, the great Yoruba city, where it
had been recruited. The telegraph also was being carried up from
Lagos to Jebba as quickly as possible. He was in command of all forces
and could order up a company of the West India Regiment, though
neither he nor the Lagos authorities had a high opinion of this force,
mainly because the men insisted upon having so much kit that it took
nearly 1,000 porters to move 100 men. As for contacts with the French
it was hoped that as a first move their garrison in Kishi, where men
and officers were accused of great excesses, would be turned out by a
native rising and that, under cover of this, a British force would march
in. This would probably mean a French counter-stroke elsewhere and
Lugard was horrified to find that small garrisons of seven to ten men
were scattered about, tempting the French to action. There was a
shortage of soldiers because the Royal Niger Constabulary had called
up so many of their men for the expedition to turn out the reported
French intruders into Sokoto. Now this relatively large force came
marching down and Wallace reported that, as far as they could
discover, the French had never entered this forbidden sphere and their
expedition had been in vain. Chamberlain, however, thought it had
been a very useful demonstration of strength and resolution.

Wallace's return embarrassed Lugard. He was now camped with
Willcocks at his advanced base at Jebba on a bank standing 200 feet
sheer above the Niger, with the strange "Ju-ju" rock humping out
of the river a mile away, and the familiar unprofitable wilderness of
Borgu stretching away to the west. Here he could face his problems
in full actuality. In the absence of any seasoned troops—for the first
W.A.F.F. battalion were still hardly ready for anything but guard and

escort duties—he had felt obliged to wire for West Indian troops. Now that Wallace had brought back his force, these were unnecessary and had to be countermanded. But, much more serious, the return of the Company troops, and the removal of fears for Sokoto to the north, left him with no reason to delay carrying out the operations he so much disliked. He had hoped by now that Goldie would have succeeded in upsetting the chessboard policy. " I do sincerely hope he has succeeded," Lugard confessed in his diary, " for otherwise I am in the dilemma of having to carry it out, impossible and mad as it is." (14 April 1898). It certainly seemed no less mad to him now he was actually on the edge of the potential battlefield. He found that no British post now remained away from the line of the Niger. The French lines faced the river from the west and he could only move by going between and behind the French as Chamberlain had ordered. He looked across at his friend Willcocks, with his clear honest face. Here, in every way, was a man after his own heart. Yet the character of this friend was now almost a danger. He thought to himself, " He is so brave and straight a soldier he cannot and *will* not understand these crooked paths of diplomacy." Aloud he asked him, given the conditions, how he would act. The answer—the only possible answer from such a man—came back like the crack of a rifle.

" If the French come south of any post I am in command of, I *must* attack or I shall be a branded coward. If we go behind them, they will, for the same reason, attack. Of this I am *positive*." (14 April 1898).

Lugard said nothing. He did not agree about the French, but he knew that nothing he said could convince his friend. He knew that the French were at Bussa just upstream and again higher up at Ilo. He would propose, according to his instructions, that Willcocks should interpose himself between these points. But that, Willcocks believed, would be an act of war and the French *must* attack. Lugard had to gamble on Chamberlain's conviction that they would not, and on that gamble the issue of a great European war might hang. If, as Lugard expected, the French then interposed themselves between Bussa and the new British post, how would the British be any better off? No, the nearer he got to this game of chess, the less faith he had in it. And with an unsubtle soldier like Willcocks, the risks of an early clash seemed high.

Lugard, though it was well perhaps that he did not know it, had authoritative support for this view. Not long before Monson had written to warn Salisbury that the chessboard policy must lead to local hostilities " which could hardly fail to develop into something far more extensive." And Hanotaux was saying that " the hot temper of any individual officer may precipitate a war." Six weeks later, referring again to the effect of the Dreyfus affair on the French attitude, Monson spoke of the danger of war as " the French public and the French Army have lost their heads."[1]

These two men, Lugard and Willcocks, pondering their action on the banks of the Niger in the spring of 1898, showed how various are the forms of courage, even the courage of the successful soldier. To most minds the unswerving, intense will to action of the second-in-command, without physical fear or psychological complexities, represent the true type of military courage. Lugard was very differently constructed. He had a mind which must foresee every difficulty and danger and weigh them, indeed sometimes overweigh them, in his anxiety to provide against them all to the full. In Uganda and on his former journey through Borgu, his vivid imagination had conjured up every detail of the disasters that, by all the odds, seemed certain to befall him and his men. So now, it was by visualizing, even expecting, the worst that he made his preparations. Yet so far, whether in Nyasaland, Uganda or in Borgu, in spite of this mental struggle going on step by step with the extreme physical endeavour, he had brought each difficult and dangerous enterprise to success.

It says much for Lugard's strength of mind that, tired and anxious as he was, and with the affectionate intimacy in which he and his second-in-command had passed the last months, he seems never to have communicated to the other man all the doubts of his own mind which was ranging over wider and more distant fields than those of the immediate operations. As Lugard used his diary as a safety-valve for the expression of his anxieties, grievances, and physical weakness, it is likely that his officers saw a very different man from the one revealed there. Even so, it is surprising that Willcocks, writing a year or two later, could use these words of the happy moment when at last Lugard slipped the leash and ordered him to go.

[1] Monson to Salisbury, 14 January and 1 March 1894, S.P. vol. 104 (France 1898).

" Needless to say, the cup of my joy was full to overflowing when he asked me to go in command; and although I knew my absence would throw an immense amount of extra work on him, I, of course, felt pleased to have such an important charge; and also I felt sure I was better acquainted with his wishes, and could therefore better carry out his plans, than any other officer there . . . . In Lugard we had a man who would never withdraw except under compulsion from home; and fortunately for our prestige the Colonial Office had no intention of directing him to do so; on the contrary, I received orders to advance rapidly westwards from Fort Goldie until I came in contact with the French outposts; then to move on into the interior, avoiding towns or villages over which the Tricolour was actually flying, and which were guarded by soldiers properly armed and in uniform; but barring this, I was free to occupy any place and hoist the Union Jack, and once that was accomplished I was to consider it British territory, and to act accordingly in case of anyone being of a different opinion. The orders were clear, concise, and exactly to my wishes."[1]

This was pure chessboard. Before these orders could be given, however, there was much to be done. Firstly, there were some very delicate negotiations to be carried out with Wallace, the head, in Nigeria, of the Company, and with Major A. J. Arnold, a fine regular officer who had been lent to the Company to command their troops. When these two came down from their abortive expedition to Sokoto, Wallace had received a surprising cable from Goldie telling him to occupy Ilo and also that Lugard was in supreme command of all the British forces. The first order puzzled Lugard, as it looked as though Goldie had utterly failed to upset Chamberlain's policy, and even that he now endorsed it. The second upset Wallace who believed himself to be curtly demoted in his own sphere. Lugard, who was ill with fever, had to exert all his diplomacy to soothe Wallace and Arnold and insisted upon interpreting the cable as meaning that he was in supreme command of troops north of Lokoja, but only with regard to their dispositions. For all other purposes they would remain Company Constabulary under Wallace and Arnold. It was agreed that of the 920 Company soldiers now available, 509 should go down with Wallace and Arnold to carry out campaigns south of Lokoja, 191 should be used to hold Fort Goldie, Liaba, and Patasi Island (the highest point up the river the British would hold at the moment) while

1 Willcocks, *op. cit.* pp. 184-5.

220 should be lent to Willcocks for his projected march. Willcocks, indeed, could hardly be held back. Ever since the prospect of action appeared, " he had been quite on the rampage " and having thrown over all doubts, he was now longing to seize Ilo and indeed all Borgu.

From his bed, in a high fever, Lugard drew up his plans. The mail had come in from England and to his astonishment there was no word from Goldie. So, his last hope of a change of policy having gone, he had no choice but to act. He ordered Willcocks to establish a line curving south-west—here the map on page 624 should be consulted—through Bugasi, Ibasoro and Okuta to the Dahomey frontier. This would be an advance and would engulf some French posts which, it was hoped, would be squeezed out as untenable. Then Lugard, lying in a bath of perspiration under a mass of blankets, proceeded to answer his immense English mail, to write dispatches to the Secretary of State; to draw up plans for a new camp at Fort Goldie; to give Willcocks full and final instructions; to scold the Governor of Lagos for holding up wire for the telegraph which had halted forty miles south of Jebba; and to deal out orders to the various officers in charge of garrisons, stores and transports. It was after midnight when he gave way to his fever, with the conclusion he generally voiced at such times: " One earns one's pay, I think, in West Africa."

Lugard and Willcocks now parted—it was April 24th—Willcocks going to Fort Goldie, ready to set out upon his march a few days later, while Lugard went south on the fast-shrinking waters of the Niger to tackle the confusion of administration and transport at Lokoja. Ill as he was, he fell upon the base camp with formidable impact. His own ill-health gave an extra edge to his strictures. The Royal Navy, whose smart little gun-boats on the remote African river thrilled Willcocks with the romance of empire, were sources of annoyance to Lugard when their officers began to tie up when they had fever, bulged their plates on sandbanks or grumbled at being turned into common carriers up and down river. As for the Colonel of the 1st battalion, it was fortunate that Lugard liked him personally, as professionally he had hard words—probably much too hard—for a man whom he found, though a correct parade-ground staff officer, " the most sketchy of fellows," piling up illegible papers while he used his coolies for fancy work or sent out the officers to draw contours. Next it was his R.E. officer who came under the lash. It was useless that he worked unsparingly, exposing himself to the sun. " *This* is not what I want." He had not carried out his orders with the exactitude Lugard demanded. " The fact is that like so many R.E.s he thinks he can always go one better than his orders. They seem to think that God made R.E.s first and then, if not with their assistance at least with their approval, made the rest of the world. I am therefore of the poorer clay, but I'll have my orders obeyed nevertheless . . . . " (Diary, 28 April 1898). Even the three women nurses whom Lugard, rather daringly, had sent up to this advanced post, got into trouble. The white men were going sick; one had committed suicide, others had died. But Lugard found the nurses living in Wallace's house, while its owner camped in a grass hut. " Meanwhile fellows are dying and these excellent nurses I see going out for an evening stroll! I shall wheel them into line tomorrow! " These three pioneer nurses later received decorations which Lugard must have recommended or at least approved.

Lugard was always quick and confident in his judgment of people, but the sickness and anxiety of this expedition made him sum up the men with whom he was working with almost violent abruptness. Of one Company officer he encountered at Fort Goldie he writes: " There was a young gentleman here . . . . He was an Ass and the poor devil was aware of the fact." Asked about his contact with Goldie, this man was foolish enough to reply: " I thought him a very genial man," and so disgusted Lugard further with such a wildly ill-chosen adjective. By contrast, another young man strikes him at once as being " a particularly good class of fellow, keen, smart and soldierly." Of another young officer it is noted that " He comes in for orders and to carry them out, not to tell me how it ought to be done . . . . and that is the kind of man I like." Wallace, too, is a " most admirable fellow, obliging to a degree and so prompt." But, for the Governor of Lagos and his crowd—" Lagos has kept up its character for utter incapacity in every branch. *Never* have I seen such chaos." And once more Lugard evaded going down to see the Governor before this much-abused functionary went on leave and handed over to Lugard all his military responsibilities on the Lagos frontier.

Lugard was, indeed, submerged in military administration. He had no proper staff, and only one clerk, though an excellent one, Mr. C. E. King,[1] and even his A.D.C. could not draft letters and could take a day and a half to decode a telegram. The Force, as we saw, was estimated to be spending about £120,000 a year, and Lugard had to teach his officers not to spend without sanction and also the meaning of orders, indents and vouchers. His work was all the more difficult as the Colonial Office had then no experience of raising troops or running campaigns and there were many mistakes and delays at the Whitehall end. There were great difficulties in buying fresh food from the natives yet Lugard set his face against forcible requisitioning, of which he accused the French. Fortunately, an able young Guards officer, Captain the Hon. Richard Somerset, employed his leisure in running a farm on Jebba Island, and without doubt saved the lives of many white men by his supply of fresh meat and vegetables. There were difficulties with the naval boats which continued to go aground as the river, the tiresome habits of which were not yet accurately on record and which was, in any case, new kind of water to the sailors, continued to fall. Lugard had intermittent bouts of malaria and the perpetual office work made him an unromantic casualty with writer's cramp. A soldier's judgment on all Lugard's activities at this time would be the most valuable, yet even the uninitiated may ask whether, in his state of health and mind, he did not, on this expedition, take too gloomy a view of the situation and of some of his colleagues, and also allow his love of order and pursuit of detail to become almost an obsession. For in this present mood he found it more than ever difficult to delegate.

How their commanding officer appeared to one of those under him is shown by the remarks in Captain Somerset's diary.

" Lugard told Morland the other day that he had never been in such a tight place in his life before as he was now, and no wonder. The situation is *very* queer. . . . It is all kept frightfully secret from us, though doubtless everything is in the papers at home . . . . Lugard rushes up and down the river or starts and returns or is ' in readiness,' while Willcocks and others appear and disappear mysteriously."

That was in June. In August, to look further ahead, he noted:

[1] Mr. King kindly supplied the writer with some material.

x

" Lugard has been very seedy; he is frightfully overworked, as he *will* do everything himself, even writing memos to me about the farm."

And later in the same month:

" Lugard was frightfully ill . . . . He leads the most extraordinary life; gets up late and sits up all night and has very sketchy meals at odd hours. I never saw a man look worse."[1]

It seems that in most campaigns there are always two wars, the war with the enemy and the war between the several branches of the army in the field and the departments at home, not to speak of the wars already discussed, between the soldiers and the politicians. Lugard's position seemed almost to necessitate for him, in addition to these, a war with the Niger Company officials. His friendship with Goldie had at first warded off this danger and he set himself to defend the Company against the accusations of Lagos and the exactions of his own force. But towards the end his happy relations with the Company were wearing a little thin, and he was listing all the things with which they had been unable to supply him: recruits, meat, transport vessels, horses, clerks, artisans, or planks with which to make coffins for his dead officers. Then, checking himself, and remembering perhaps that he might show Goldie his diary, he admits that the Company is absurdly under-staffed and cannot manage its own work, let alone his.

The history of these operations is not, however, the history of the river-bases, even though these made the action possible, and though it was here that the Frontier Force had its first training. Just as Lugard was the physical projection of Chamberlain's policy in Nigeria, so Willcocks was the agent of Lugard, and his action in the field was the purpose and the climax of all this weary work of transport and administration. It has been recorded that Willcocks left Lugard at Jebba on April 24th. He first went up by canoe to Fort Goldie.[2] Here he received a telegram, addressed to Lugard, from the Governor of Lagos to say that the French garrison had quitted the important town of Kishi and that some of the British native troops had walked in. What should be done? Willcocks knew that the British had encouraged

[1] Diary of Capt. the Hon. R. F. Somerset, Grenadier Guards, Adjutant, 2nd batt. West African Frontier Force; privately printed, L.P.

[2] The account of operations that follow is based largely upon Willcocks, *From Kabul to Kumassi*, pp. 185-227.

a native rising against a small French Senegalese force, and without hesitation took the responsibility of ordering a white officer to move in and occupy the place with more force. Thus the French lost this important town and were very bitter about the means used to expel them.

On May 1st Willcocks sent out an advance party under Captain Welch with instructions based closely upon the chessboard policy. It turned out—as Chamberlain had foreseen—that the French had been given exactly the same orders against fighting as the British commanders, so that it became a question as to which side could best restrain its soldiers under intense provocation. Welch marched straight forward through uninhabited and unexplored country until he reached the village of Kanikoko on May 2nd. He found a French N.C.O. in charge who sent a runner back to Willcocks with an angry letter accusing him of breaking all the rules of civilized countries by invading French territory in time of peace. Next day Willcocks himself marched to Kanikoko. He halted 300 yards from the village where he saw the tricolour floating from a high pole and a crowd of soldiers with rifles. He found that Welch had gone alone and unescorted for the three miles further on to Kiama and had walked straight into that town, finding his way without a guide. In the circumstances this was a very cool act, as anything could have happened to him, whether at French instance or not, in the bush, and his death would have been a matter of controversy.

The next day Willcocks again followed up and occupied a village two miles from Kiama where he raised the Union Jack. A second French letter of warning followed this action. On May 5th a French N.C.O., very smartly dressed, came over to see him with twelve Senegalese soldiers carrying the French flag. The meeting was conducted upon both sides with the formality of the parade-ground. The Frenchman saluted and said, " *Mon Colonel*." Willcocks did the same and as the French flag was raised he turned to salute that. The Frenchman in turn saluted the Union Jack. At this rather embarrassing moment a diversion occurred. Lugard's old friend, the king of Kiama, came riding up at the head of a big and showy cavalcade.[1] Willcocks summed him up with a quick glance. A very fine specimen of an African chief, he decided, as Lugard had done before him. He looked

1 See above pp. 507–11.

a thorough soldier. The king made a speech in which he said that a few years before he had met and made friends with a great white man who had made promises to him and had then gone away and he had heard no more of him. What could Willcocks say? The king had been put in an utterly false position since Lugard's treaty had never been followed up, and he had been left ever since completely defenceless against the domination of the French. Willcocks could only say that this same white man had now returned and was at that moment only a hundred miles away.

But his main argument was with the French. The N.C.O. accused him of violating the law of nations by forcing his way into country over which the French flag was flying. Willcocks stated that the flag had no right there, but could get no answer except:

" You have insulted our flag. The history of Borgu shows how England has overridden all treaties."

" The history of Borgu," Willcocks objected, " has surely yet to be written."

This seemed rather apt. But as a retort the Frenchman produced from his haversack a large bundle of manuscript and said that this was the complete history of Borgu. Willcocks, with difficulty keeping his face straight, replied that this was the French version and that as it had not yet been translated the English were as yet ignorant of it. The Frenchman laughed at this, and the generous Willcocks at once decided that he was a " thorough gentleman with a nice way of putting things." But this interlude of pleasantries could make no difference to the grave clash of their orders. Further defiance was therefore exchanged, after which Willcocks settled into his camp and began to survey the surrounding country.

There followed a visit from the king's son, and then Willcocks called upon the king. Willcocks refused even to listen to his talk of a ruse by which the French might be evicted. His code of loyalty to his own race, even in the circumstances, was inviolable. With his own soldiers he always spoke as if they would have to fight only against other Africans and not with white men. So he merely exchanged with the king kind greetings and friendly wishes. Those of the king included riches, a big family, sleep, drink, food and victory. The Englishman then departed amid the booming of drums.

Two days later, leaving a post at the camp, Willcocks set off due south from Kiama to Kishi, a distance of thirty-six miles. He located a number of French posts on the way. The rains had broken and at times their way was through an almost impassable swamp. Willcocks was then able to appreciate the cheerfulness and endurance of his Hausa and Yoruba troops. On one occasion they camped close to a French post in pouring rain. They had no food and they could not even light a fire to boil a kettle. The French corporal first formally protested against their presence and then brought them food and water.

As Willcocks approached Kishi he saw the French flag still flying at a small camp near the town guarded by a handful of soldiers. " I touched my hat to the emblem of a powerful nation for whom I had always had the highest regard and passed on."[1] At Kishi he met the West Indian soldiers for the first time, marked their burly type and strength but questioned the utility of bringing men of their race, who demanded most of the conditions and equipment of white men, to do service in Africa. From Kishi he marched on twenty-seven miles to Bode, through the burning heat of a waterless forest, and on to the British station at Okuta, which had recently been taken over from the French on the frontier of Lagos Protectorate.

So far Willcocks had found the British flag at many of the villages he had passed, but as he now doubled back and returned upon a more northerly line in the direction of Ibasoro, he found villages which were unoccupied. At all of these he left the Union Jack. He then passed right through the line held by the French, marching round their posts and arrived on May 17th at a village called Betikuta. This was a " British " village but in the night a French sergeant and six men had crept up and planted the tricolour 400 yards from the post. It looked as if Betikuta might provide the inevitable testing point.

Willcocks wrote a letter to the French officer in charge of Kiama, which was nearby, to say that unless the French flag were removed from Betikuta in forty-eight hours he would advance to Kiama and plant the Union Jack 400 yards from the French flag there. This was a serious threat since, as we know, Kiama was an important place with a king and population who well understood the rivalry between the two white nations, who were known to prefer the British, and would be impressed by this action. Meanwhile Lugard had dispatched Major Arnold into this area with some Company troops and he had occupied

---

[1] Willcocks, *op. cit.* p. 196.

several villages which lay between Kiama and the French base at Nikki. Some of his men had actually occupied one place, Temanji, by forcing and shoving their way through a barrier of Senegalese soldiers. Upon another occasion a small French force tried to stop a British force with two officers by using fixed bayonets. The British had walked round them and had been followed for a mile by men spitting at them and cursing. By a miracle of restraint on both sides the rifles had not gone off though the native troops and some of the officers were longing for this unnatural tension to break into honest fighting.

Willcocks himself was now convinced that the situation at Betikuta *must* lead to hostilities. He employed the forty-eight hours of his ultimatum in preparing a fighting column, and put in a day at practice with the Maxims and with volley firing. The French commandant at Kiama wrote and asked for a week's grace to enable him to consult his headquarters at Nikki as to what action he should take. To this Willcocks, very much the gentleman, agreed and used the interval himself to cover the ninety miles between Kiama and Jebba to consult Lugard. This was to turn out to have been a providential delay.

Willcocks found his chief in very poor condition. He had just come up from Lokoja and had been really ill on the river but, as his one clerk was down with fever, he was struggling with the accounts and correspondence. Fortunately, Colonel Fitzgerald, the commander of the 2nd battalion, who had now brought his troops up across country from Ibadan in a very fine march, made a good impression as one who " means business, not theory." On Lugard's return to Jebba, though he had been disturbed by an outbreak of fighting between the imperial and the Company soldiers, he at once began to organize a tidy office.

Willcocks arrived in the middle of the night and came into Lugard's room shouting his name. Lugard was delighted to see him. He heard the whole story of the march and they discussed the general situation. Lugard had just received a cable from Chamberlain authorizing him to occupy a position on the Niger between Bussa and Ilo. Lugard was averse from this. Formerly regarded as a reckless fire-eater, he was now in the strange position of being the most cautious man of all those concerned in the business. He had consistently taken a more serious view of the French forces in Borgu than Chamberlain, Goldie or Willcocks. He now feared that if he shifted the rivalry up north of Bussa the French would this time really cross the Niger and stir up against him either the important ruler, the Shehu of Sokoto, or the Shehu's pagan neighbours, who were in a restless state. And near Sokoto was another potentially hostile Muslim state, Gandu. Although the Company expedition had left Sokoto after finding no French party there, Wallace had sent a Resident with a small escort to the city. In spite of a long-standing treaty between Sokoto and the Company, he had been turned back and the Company had done no more than establish a small post at Jelwa, just off the east bank of the Niger, some fifty miles north of Bussa. Even this post was threatened. Lugard feared that if, without having command of this stretch of the river, he endeavoured to establish a British post between the French posts, and opened up the whole formidable problem of Sokoto, he would not have the forces to deal with the situation. He therefore wrote a long dispatch to Chamberlain giving " a resumé from every point of view," (the Colonial Office can never have been kept better informed!) and later he also sent a £100 telegram saying that if he were to take on the French north of Bussa, with the possibility of having to deal with Sokoto, he would need two or, at the least, one Sikh regiment from India.

The course of action so far in Borgu had not made Lugard relish any more than before the position in which he found himself in relation to Chamberlain. He had hardly drawn up his dispatch and sent his telegram when another long cipher telegram arrived from the Secretary of State urging him to occupy a place right up in the French hinterland, as they had occupied one of ours (Bussa). He was to do this in case the Paris negotiations should fail. The bitterness between the man who is in the field and the minister who handles him from a safe distance flared up for a moment angrily in Lugard. " It is all very well," he exclaimed, " for Chamberlain to sit at home and ask these questions." The rains were now breaking in earnest, yet the river was still so low that he could hardly get any supply ships up it. The guns had not yet arrived, nor any arms for the 2nd battalion. It was hard enough to keep even Jebba supplied, still less to keep more advanced forces in the field. " Yet he wishes me to bring on a collision and to fight the French."

On May 24th, the Queen's birthday, Lugard, with Willcocks still with him, watched a parade of the 2nd battalion. The proceedings were saddened by the news of more British deaths; among them was that of one of the naval commanders and a young officer who was drowned while bathing. But Willcocks' visit was a great stimulus to his overstrained chief. " Dear old Willcocks was as full of almost boyish good spirits as ever and he pleased me by his keen appreciation of my work." Willcocks had thought that his experience in Indian frontier wars would have fitted him to run any show, but he had had no idea of what would be entailed by practically having to create, against every conceivable obstacle, a new force while at the same time trying to use it in the field with no staff, no proper base and no officers trained in the departmental work required. Willcocks was indeed shocked at the change in Lugard and at the crushing load of work which his own high standards and his inadequate assistance placed upon his shoulders. Before he left he wrote a private letter to Antrobus at the Colonial Office to say that Lugard was simply killing himself.

Willcocks went off again early on May 26th. Whatever doubts Lugard had about the whole issue and especially about starting other operations further north, there was no hesitation now about the orders he gave Willcocks at this crisis of the whole enterprise. He was to hoist the flag at Kiama if the French had not withdrawn theirs at Betikuta. Willcocks was back for his fateful rendezvous in good time. He received a strong letter from the chief French Resident in Borgu, accusing him of being an unauthorized invader of French soil, whose evil deeds would soon raise a " cry of horror throughout the land." He was formally called upon to evacuate the invaded territory and warned that in future all relations between them would be governed by the *service en campagne*.[1] Willcocks prepared to act, fully believing that he would have to fight and so perhaps bring about a general war between Britain and France. He observed that the French officer had used the delay he had asked for to bring up considerable reinforcements, but, in his tolerant way, he did not blame him, since all was fair in war. But for himself, the last relics of the old code of military chivalry still survived in 1898, at least in Africa.

Willcocks set his men to erect a palisade round his camp and to dig a trench. His men had brought no entrenching tools—who was to blame for this omission?—but with spoons, cooking pots and sharp pieces of wood they produced an amazing result and soon a small, rough fort came into being. Ceaseless torrents fell upon them and they

[1] Willcocks, *op. cit.* p. 199.

had only one set of clothes and one blanket each. On the morning of May 30th he sent off Major Arnold with a company of infantry to march the two miles to Kiama, while he walked round the fort, talking to the men and officers and preparing a reserve to follow Arnold the moment he heard that he had been opposed. " I have seldom," Willcocks confessed, " spent a more anxious hour." The distance to Kiama was two miles. He sat, pretending to write, his ears straining for the sound of a shot. As he learned afterwards there were many in Europe anxiously waiting for news from Betikuta, for by now the name of this obscure village, or at least the issue which hung in the balance there, had been telegraphed to the European capitals. Lugard had, of course, been waiting with the same anxiety. On June 11th a telegram reached him to warn him—and this only a few days after Chamberlain's earlier telegram desiring him to advance north into the French hinterland—that an agreement was imminent. Lugard could have only one thought: " It may be too late—the collision may have occurred! " He went out and called the officer whom he considered most reliable. There was no moon, but he set him off upstream the thirty miles to Fort Goldie. From there mounted messengers were to race the sixty miles to Willcocks at Betikuta. That would take forty hours.

Meanwhile events were going forward at Kiama. A messenger came hurrying back to Willcocks to say that the flag had been planted. As Arnold approached Kiama all the Africans had retreated into the town, which he saw was now flying a number of new tricolours. As he neared the main gate a French guard fell in and stood to arms. He saw that sentries had been posted in the trees. Everything pointed to a fight. But as Arnold with his flag reached the named distance of 400 yards, the French officer advanced and made a formal protest and then he said that he would offer no resistance. Chamberlain had guessed right: Lugard and Goldie had guessed wrong.

The position was, however, still tense. At Kiama or elsewhere a " regrettable incident " could still occur. But two hours after Arnold ran up his flag an urgent message, arriving earlier than Lugard's courier, reached the French officer at Kiama to say that a Niger Convention between Britain and France was on the verge of being signed and that he hoped this was in time to prevent the imminent conflict at Kiama.

To understand how this Convention had been attained we must turn back to the diplomatic struggle which had been conducted simultaneously with the manœuvres of defiance on the Niger for they were two sides of the same operation.

Soon after Lugard sailed for West Africa the two governments got to the point of drawing up draft agreements. Each side then proceeded to reject the other's draft.[1] But the Colonial Office began at last to agree with the Niger Commissioners that Lugard's treaties, largely because of the wording of the official forms which he had used, were vulnerable to French attack; this meant that Nikki might have to be sacrificed.[2] March and April saw Chamberlain taking an increasingly high hand both with the French and with the Foreign Office. His Under-Secretary, Selborne, declared himself ready to go to war over the Say-Barruwa line.[3] Chamberlain bargained over every point: when he was obliged to cede anything he demanded a counter-concession; he never once admitted, as even Selborne did, that things were going well. He was ready to threaten to break off negotiations. He was confident that with Lugard and his new force in action, " in six months [Britain] ought to have posts all over . . . . the Dahomey hinterland."[4] He could hardly confine his indignation with Monson and even more with the commissioners within anything like official language. He agreed to the suggestion that Goldie, even though he " has not been kept acquainted with our proposals as to the Niger " should be sent to Paris to see our Niger commissioners. His intransigeance might supply a tonic to men who " have not enough stiffening in the lot to hold up a paper collar."[5] Three days later he fumed that they "perfectly revel in the character of advocates for the French . . . . I have no faith in Colonel Everett and Mr. Gosselin. They are excellent men to arrange an unconditional surrender."[6]

The British embassy which, on the grounds that it had so much Niger work now, had had to ask for a new typewriter, sank into deeper gloom as Chamberlain, strengthened by Lugard's reports from the Niger, grew more uncompromising. Monson urged his government to sign the agreement before the Méline Cabinet should fall when

[1] Salisbury to Monson, 24 and 29 March 1898, F.O. 27/3408.
[2] Minute by Antrobus, 29 March 1898, C.O. 537/15.
[3] Minute by Selborne, 31 March 1898, C.O. 537/15.
[4] Minute by Chamberlain, 25 May 1898, C.O. 537/15.
[5] Minute by Chamberlain, ibid.
[6] Minute by Chamberlain, 28 May 1898, C.O. 537/15.

all the value of the years of hard bargaining with the intelligent and relatively moderate Hanotaux would be lost.[1] On May 13th Chamberlain made a speech in Birmingham on foreign policy, so belligerent in tone, especially against Russia, and so confident of the greatness of the British empire in amity with the United States, that there was a fall on the Paris Bourse and *Le Matin* prophesied war in a month. Courcel, whom Monson met at a party, took a very gloomy view of the outcome because of the extreme nearness of the two forces in the Niger bend and the stiffening of the British press since early April.[2]

It is unnecessary to follow here all the points upon which the final haggling turned. They included to the end the significance of the Say-Barruwa line and the French corridor to the navigable Niger. They were also concerned with positions on the Gold Coast hinterland, especially with a place called Bona. Salisbury appears to have been dragged unwillingly along by his Colonial Secretary; his own eyes were still strained towards the Nile valley where Kitchener, advancing south, had won the battle of Atbara on April 8th, and towards which Marchand, lost now to view, was slowly but surely making his way.

At the very end Chamberlain had to rely entirely upon strength, as represented by Lugard's force, and very little upon diplomacy to gain his ends. Both sides, however, were now beginning to feel that a settlement must be made. Chamberlain felt strong enough to make some small concessions, especially with regard to Nikki and access to the Niger, in order to achieve it. But he was also strong enough to stop abruptly at his chosen point and this led to a final struggle with Salisbury. Hanotaux, at the beginning of June, declared himself ready to accept the terms, but made a special plea for Ilo, where a French officer had been assassinated, and which had therefore a sentimental value. Monson telegraphed " Fate of negotiations hang on Ilo."[3] Salisbury wished to give way. Lugard's doubts about the military situation, revealed in his grave £100 telegram, seemed to give him at least a chance to weaken his unbending colleague.

---

[1] Monson to Salisbury, 15 May 1898, F.O. 27/3413, and minute by Salisbury, 29 May 1898, F.O. 27/3409.
[2] Monson to Salisbury, 22 April 1898, F.O. 27/3412.
[3] Garvin, *Life of Chamberlain*, vol. iii, p. 218, and Gooch and Temperley, *British Documents*, vol. i, pp. 155-6.

" . . . . I think we have come to a critical point in the West African negotiations and must consider our further course carefully . . . . I cannot find that we have any claim to Ilo by treaty *eo nomine* . . . . On the other hand Lugard's telegram (received by me this morning) of the 31st May is very grave. It means that we cannot take any measures for meeting the French concentration at Ilo, without finding ourselves at war with Gando and Sokoto. It will be a war in which we shall be very far removed from our base and in which we shall have to meet the two most powerful principalities of those regions. We know so little about those countries that we cannot discern what sort of difficulty it will be that this contingency will open to us—but it may be very grave and its cost will certainly buy out the value of Ilo a hundred times over. I say nothing about the quarrel with the French—for that is familiar ground. I therefore should confidently counsel the abandonment of Ilo."   (2 June 1898).[1]

Chamberlain was unmoved by this. He was neither wearied by the negotiations nor disturbed at the possibility of their breakdown. He had full faith in the new imperial force on the Niger and even seemed ready, if necessary, to take up Lugard's request for some Indian troops to make more ambitious operations possible. He felt that Britain had already lost a hundred miles of her original claim on the Niger, the reach from Say to Ilo. Therefore he opposed his chief in a letter which illustrates clearly the place Lugard's operations played in his diplomacy:

"I have very anxiously considered your letter, as I feel that a wrong decision may lead to momentous consequences . . . .

I cannot agree with you that the cession of Ilo would not be a climb-down.

From the first the Colonial Office have always attached the greatest importance to the retention of this place . . . .

As regards the future it is becoming clear that the so-called empire of Sokoto is in a state of dissolution like that of the Great Mogul in the time of Clive. I imagine that in accordance with that precedent a small European force, with perhaps Indian auxiliaries and modern armaments will be able to establish our authority, but we shall have a very great responsibility for the future government of this vast country . . . .

Although, therefore, I am most anxious to meet your wishes, I have reluctantly come to the conclusion that I have gone to the extreme limit to which, as specially charged with these interests, I am entitled to go, and that on the side of the Niger at any rate, I could not defend any

1 Garvin, *op. cit.* vol. iii, pp. 218–19.

further surrender . . . . I think that we shall not be the greatest losers even if the present negotiations, fall through. In that case I hope we may take steps to put ourselves in a better position before they are resumed. There is no reason why we should not follow the example of the French and occupy places in *their* hinterland which would give us something to exchange when they are tired of the danger and expense of the present situation . . . . "   (2 June 1898).[1]

Salisbury yielded, but he took the occasion to write a characteristic comment, one which also showed his preoccupation with the other river.

" I am wholly unconvinced of the value of Ilo; and I cannot discover on what our claim to it rests. But I should prefer giving up Bona to giving up Ilo because our title to Bona seems to me positively bad. It will be a pity if we break off the negotiations, for it will add to our difficulties in the Nile Valley . . . . If we are to send British or Indian troops in the hope of fighting another Plassey with Lugard as our Clive and Sokoto as our Bengal, the prospect becomes very much more serious. Our Clive will be in no danger of being astonished at his own moderation. There is no loot to get except in Goldie's dreams. If you wish to come to terms it would be prudent to do so before we take Khartoum. We shall get nothing out of the French Assembly after that event."   (3 June 1898).[2]

Chamberlain, therefore, got his way. He was right once more and the French did not break off the negotiations over Ilo. But these exchanges were followed by the climax of tension near the Niger which had, of course, its reflection in London and Paris. Lugard telegraphed to Chamberlain from Jebba on June 7th that there was an acute danger of fighting[3] and Chamberlain, with the Convention now all but signed, telegraphed back that he was to avoid a collision at all costs.[4] The Convention was signed on June 14th. On the very next day the Méline Cabinet fell.

The Convention laid down the lines the Anglo-French frontier was to follow. It will be seen from the map on the next page that in Borgu the line represented a compromise. The British were pushed down the Niger a hundred miles from Say, their 1890 claim, to Ilo and from there the frontier, running south-south-west, gave them a

[1] *Ibid.* pp. 219–20.
[2] *Ibid.* p. 220.
[3] Lugard to Chamberlain, 7 June 1898, C.O. 445/1.
[4] Chamberlain to Lugard, 9 June 1898, ibid.

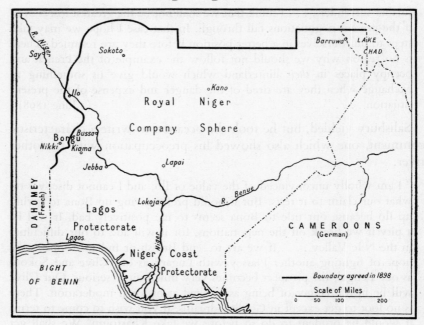

The Niger Region according to the Anglo-French
Convention of 1898

slice of the controversial, triangular, but somewhat indeterminate
entity, Borgu. The French got the notorious Nikki, but not Kiama.
The northern frontier described an arc a hundred miles from the city
of Sokoto, and then ran straight partly along the 14° parallel and partly
along the 13° 20 parallel to Lake Chad. The exact delimitation of these
lines was to be carried out on the ground by boundary commissioners.
In the meantime both sides were immediately to withdraw their
troops approximately behind the new frontiers. The French succeeded
in gaining their access to the navigable Niger in the form of two
stations, one at the mouth and the other just south of the Bussa rapids,
near Liaba. It was agreed to discuss further the regulations governing
commerce on the Niger.[1] Further west the French secured Mossi.

The Convention had still to be ratified, a conclusion that was for
long by no means certain, and which the French postponed in 1899 to

[1] See *Convention between the United Kingdom and France* . . . . C.9334 (1899); and also
Hertslet, *Map of Africa*, vol. ii, pp. 785-96, for the text of the agreement and maps.

the last possible moment. In addition to the divided views in France about the merits of its terms, the Niger crisis was followed by the Nile crisis, generally named after Fashoda, the uninteresting village on the Upper Nile, which was at last reached by the Marchand expedition just as Kitchener was fighting his way south down the middle reaches of the great river. The more clear-cut and dramatic character of the second crisis, and the more ambitious and surprising nature of the French intrusion into the British-Egyptian sphere, tended to draw public attention and the later interest of historians away from the long-drawn-out struggle over Borgu, which seemed no more than a curtain-raiser to the Fashoda incident. Yet even though the Nile, linked as it was with Egypt, was of far longer and deeper significance to both nations than the Niger, an incident might have occurred on the western river that France, in her uncertain mood, would have not ignored, and it seems a valid assumption that the same possibility of war with France had hung over the marching columns of Lugard and Willcocks as over the much larger forces commanded by Kitchener.

After such a long and spirited conflict carried out both in Africa and in the two capitals, it is natural to ask which side had won the greater advantage in the Niger Convention.

Its reception in France was very mixed. There was a good deal of bitterness at what was regarded as the high-handed behaviour of the British government and especially of Chamberlain, and of the intemperance of much of the British press, led by *The Times*, in the usual campaign of intimidation. The colonial enthusiasts were loud and long in their indignation.[1] In the Chamber of Deputies, M. Etienne thundered against Britain's policy of using threats and force in Africa right up to the Niger Convention. Lugard was cited as an example. Even after, he said, in Uganda massacre had succeeded massacre under the eyes of an English officer who had since won great authority in England, that country continued without scruple to use his brilliant qualities. " I have named Captain Lugard."[2] But Hanotaux, as one of the chief artificers of the Convention, defended his own work,[3] as did the Colonial Minister Lebon, who described it as a triumph for neither side but " du moins à leur satisfaction respective suffisante."[4]

1 Monson to Salisbury, 24 June 1898, F.O. 27/3413.
2 J. O. (Ch.), 6 March 1899, p. 682, col. 2.
3 Hanotaux, *Fachoda*, pp. 122–3.
4 Lebon, *Politique de la France*, p. 75.

Certainly the British claims had receded considerably from those made when the rivalry first opened, when it had been hoped to draw a line due south from Say to the sea, to incorporate Mossi into the Gold Coast and even to prevent the French linking up Dahomey with their Upper Niger territories. But for the work of Goldie, Britain would never have been able to advance such claims. But the Niger Company had failed to turn claims into occupation; to occupy Borgu away from the river; to follow up Lugard's dash to Nikki and to implement his treaties. This failure had allowed the French to extend their position until the British were forced back to the Niger south of Bussa. The vigorous diplomacy and military action inspired by Chamberlain had since done much to retrieve British fortunes from this diminished position. The recovery of a large part of Borgu, the pushing back of the French to Ilo, the refusal of a corridor to the navigable Niger, and the French acceptance of our claims to Sokoto, which even Goldie and Lugard had been prepared to sacrifice, were all to be counted gains when viewed against the position at the beginning of 1897. Sir Edmund Monson, who had been obliged, in spite of all his emphatic warnings, to recognize the effects of Chamberlain's resort to forceful arguments, confessed himself astonished at the degree of success Britain had gained. This was especially true of Nigeria. The Gambia had been pressed in almost to the river banks and Sierra Leone restricted, while the surrender of Mossi had truncated the Gold Coast. The Nigerian hinterland, as a glance at the map will show, makes by contrast a striking projection to the north.

This projection, we may conclude, can be credited partly to Goldie and partly to Chamberlain, both using Lugard as their agent. The French compensation in the form of the leased stations on the Niger, and the reform in the transit regulations on that river, which were so eagerly debated in 1898, once gained, proved of very little practical importance, as railways relieved commerce from dependence upon the seasonal facilities of the Niger. And though, as Binger so frankly remarked, Borgu itself was not very valuable territory, that, as Goldie taught Chamberlain and Chamberlain had persuaded Salisbury, was not the issue. Borgu was the place where Britain chose to stand against further French pressure, which was being applied not only on the Niger but on the Nile and elsewhere. The determination shown by

Britain over this dispute may possibly have helped to break the full force of the French resolution over Fashoda; the other side of the same coin may have been that their recent successful stand on the Niger encouraged the British to call French bluff on the Nile. Yet this point must not be over-emphasized; for both countries the Nile represented an older and a deeper issue than the Niger.

There was one further substantial gain from the Niger crisis. In the course of defending Borgu, Chamberlain had set Lugard to the fashioning of a new colonial force which was to be an instrument of annexation and order in West Africa and play a most honourable part in two world wars, not only in West and East Africa, but on distant Asian battlefields.

If the Convention meant for the British a happy ending of the long-drawn-out international rivalry, the hero of the last part of the story is not Lugard, still less Goldie, but Chamberlain. This is the strong impression that comes from a reading of the official records upon the question, above all from the diplomatic material. At least from the midsummer of 1897 when Chamberlain first came to understand in full the realities and possibilities of the situation in West Africa, he decided upon an objective, difficult to visualize, and still more difficult to attain, from which he never wavered. To gain this by his own forceful methods, he had to struggle not only with the French but with his own Prime Minister, with Goldie, with Monson in Paris, with the British Niger Commissioners and even with his own chosen subordinate, Lugard. All these he bent to his will. In the face of their doubts his purposes and his methods were stamped with success, largely due, it must be admitted, to the crude use and threat of force, but also to a political flair which made him judge more exactly even than Salisbury, whose beard had grown grey in the conduct of foreign affairs, the limits to which the French would go. It was also due to his success in popularizing the new assertive colonial policy and linking it clearly with the economic interests of the masses. He could thus rely upon almost unanimous support in the nation, whose opinion, nourished upon many converging interests and ideas, was rising to the high water mark of what the old Liberals had condemned as jingoistic imperialism.

As for Lugard, uncertainty of mind and persistent fever had combined to cloud his own satisfaction in this enterprise, which must have come as something of an anti-climax after the dramatic and autonomous adventures in which he had been engaged for the last decade in Nyasaland, Uganda and Borgu. This time he did not even conduct the actual operations in the field. Yet it was for what he had done and for what he was that Chamberlain had chosen him for a task of great importance and difficulty, and he had carried it through, however unwillingly, just as the Minister had required. Are we to think that Chamberlain judged Lugard better than Lugard could judge himself, and that he knew that once he was on the Niger he would carry out his orders, however distasteful, with thoroughness and determination?

For the soldiers in West Africa, the signing of the Convention relieved the worst of the tension, but made little change in their immediate duties. The French in Borgu were greatly embittered by the orders to evacuate gains they had made by such great and prolonged efforts. For the rest of the year the Frontier Force had to be always ready, especially as the Fashoda crisis developed, for the possible outbreak of hostilities. The officers of the Force, such being then the training and nature of soldiers, had been disappointed at having been denied the active service for which they had volunteered. They received, however, their baptism of fire in an expedition directed at the instance of the Company against the emir of Lapai, in order to stop him slave-raiding, and in other action further south for which they were lent to the Company and in which they met with some losses.

In the two months between the signing of the Convention and his departure from Jebba on August 29th *en route* for England, Lugard's health became still worse. According to the perceptive Somerset he went home looking like a ghost. The last words in his diary, which breaks off abruptly in June, because he was too ill to keep it up any longer, are significant: "I am not myself. It is a harassing and anxious time and sometimes one almost thinks that obscurity, rest and the meagre victuals that content me would be a good exchange, but such moments are rare and only when one is out of health and overworked." That was the man revealed in the diary. The man the force knew was the commanding officer, who thought of everything and did everything himself, from planning operations to the small—perhaps the too small—details about their health and discipline. It was he whose energetic directions transformed the barren island of Jebba into a most habitable advanced headquarters, with houses, hospital, drill-grounds, and offices. He handed over his command to Willcocks, who felt able to take on this charge because " I had the immense advantage of Lugard's experience to guide me for some months."

Lugard's last weeks were largely taken up with writing his dispatches upon the whole of the operations to the Secretary of State and—a familiar exercise—rebutting the bitter French complaints about his conduct.[1] They claimed that they had been wronged and insulted, especially at Kishi. Mutual accusations were indeed an almost inevitable accompaniment of the frustrating rivalry under the trying physical conditions both sides had endured. Lugard's dispatches are full of condemnations of French methods. Willcocks was a much more tolerant critic and his personal chivalry and courtesy—he even supplied the French with cloth to mend their torn flags—may have contributed much to preventing the spark of antagonism between the few men at the explosive point of contact from igniting. But Willcocks, like Lugard and the other Englishmen, declared that the French did not pay for their food but lived on the countryside with all the oppression that this made possible, and, indeed, in view of the shortage of food supplies, inevitable. Lugard accused the French of using high-handed and oppressive methods in dealing with the Africans, which led to risings and punitive action. In confirmation of this Willcocks described how upon one occasion when, upon his approaching a village, the whole population fled into the bush at the appearance of white men, he had the happy thought of running up the Union Jack. At once the people emerged from the trees and rushed to this symbol. Upon another occasion he had the satisfaction of seeing slaves in a Muslim trader's caravan break from their file, rush to his flag, and seize the staff in the classic pose of claiming liberation under its folds.[2]

The French on their side extolled the humanity of the soldiers and gentlemen who opened up Africa for France by contrast with the ruthless commercial elements of some other powers. The act of evacuation imposed upon the French officers in Borgu by the Convention was most painful and was postponed as long as possible. Willcocks, who felt the closeness of the bond between himself and the men of his own race and religion, as contrasted with the gulf between himself

[1] The official report is in C.O. 445/1; the military report is printed in *Reports on the West African Frontier Force of the Niger for 1897-8* (1899), C.9046-28.

[2] Willcocks, *From Kabul to Kumassi*, pp. 225-6.

and the Africans, did all he could to spare them unnecessary humiliation. He did not march into Kiama until two hours after the French
evacuated. Before they left he entertained the officers in his camp;
arranged to dine with them in London and Paris; staged a formal
salute of the two flags and then watched the tricolour gradually
disappearing down the track through the forests where for four years
it had flown unchallenged.[1]

The two white nations might understand each other upon a deeper
level than that upon which they were in conflict. But it was not
surprising that the Africans were bewildered by the strange form of
conflict they had witnessed. There was the case of the unfortunate
king of Kiama. He had first, as we have seen, pledged himself in the
spirit and the letter to the first white man he had seen, towards whom
he had felt a respect and trust that had been mutual. This stranger had
promised him protection, but the king soon found himself overrun
by another and probably less considerate and friendly kind of white
man with a different flag and armed with another treaty, to which he
was compelled to agree. The pagan king had indeed done his best to
keep faith. In his perplexity he had sent a letter after Lugard—it will
be remembered he had some Muslims at his court who would have
the art of writing—to explain his difficulties. It was addressed:

" From the King of Kiama to his friend, his good friend, to his brother,
to the man whom God sent to him, to the one who gave him presents
and advice—Salutations and greeting."

In the letter he told him:

" the Frenchmen came to me three times after your visit . . . . they came
into this country as if it was a heathen country. I told them to leave and
they refused, and I told them a second time and they still refused and they
left me in anger."

Later they returned:

" I did not agree to it. I do not know what country they came from, or
what people they are; they are too strong for me and I pray that you will
come between me and them; this is what I want to say to you. I send you
one sheep as present; this is all. Salutations."[2]

[1] Willcocks, *op. cit.* p. 227.
[2] *The Times*, 22 August 1895. Lugard sent this letter in one of his own in which he defended
his claim to have reached Nikki before the French.

Lugard at the time could only send an inconclusive reply to this pathetic appeal, and it was not until four years later that a white man of the same tribe as the first appeared in the person of Willcocks. The king had been forced by his French " protectors " to tell this man that he loved France, though secretly he had declared himself ready to keep his first pledge of loyalty by turning out the French. But the man of white tribe number one had gone away only to return later to place his tribal emblem beside that of the king's French master. The next thing that happened was that he was told that the first white men were coming back and the second were going. Convinced that the British would revenge themselves upon him for having broken his treaty and admitted the French, he fled with his wives into the bush. This gave the " French " Senegalese soldiers time to loot his town very thoroughly before they left. When Willcocks arrived two days later, he found the town altogether deserted. Forty-eight hours later however, he was woken up at midnight to find the king had come to his camp clearly expecting the worst that could happen. " It was sad," Willcocks said, " to see this really fine chief in such a position." How, he asked Willcocks, could he tell who would eventually own his country? The Englishman reassured him and entertained him with food until the formal evacuation should allow him to resume his town. The next day a French officer came to see Willcocks. He was accompanied by a man carrying a tricolour, and when the king saw the two men and the two flags together he assumed they had now combined to revenge themselves upon him for his double betrayal. He took once more to the bush. When the French had gone, he re-appeared, and dismounting from his horse, knelt at Willcocks' feet and asked him for his forgiveness. " How are the mighty fallen! " was this officer's comment. " I raised him and offered him a seat and from that hour his kingly dignity returned and we became very good friends." So the story that began with the astonishing acts of mutual trust between this king and Lugard, had a happy ending.[1] And the day was to come when his first white friend would visit him in state and confirm his power.

Who was to judge between France and Britain in this long African rivalry? Claims and counter-claims could be discussed upon numerous and shifting rules—the Niger Commission took forty-six meetings of

[1] Willcocks, *op. cit.* pp. 207–8.

its last session to discuss them—but at bottom the clash was absolute. It was between the wills of two nations, with interests and reputations bound up with the struggle. On his side, Hanotaux, reviewing the whole situation, could say " The seeds of Empire have been sown in all parts of the world. By God's grace they will grow . . . . Who will regret that more of France has been spread through the Universe? "[1] To which Chamberlain's words that " The British race is the greatest of governing races that this world has ever seen," can be taken as a reply, with his slightly more modest belief that " we are predestined by our defects, as well as by our virtues, to spread over the habitable globe . . . . "[2] Yet behind the colonial rivalry the two nations had good international reasons for co-operation. France, however, had more need of peace than Britain. Her external perils and her own instability were greater. It was because French ministries knew this that, for all their bold acts and words, it was France in the end which tasted some of the bitterness of surrender over the Niger and much more, a few months later, over the Nile.

In the half-century since these years of acute rivalry in Africa we have seen the long friendship and partnership with France which began, surprisingly, very soon after them. We have seen, too, great wars and a development of the methods of war which have taught us and some other civilized peoples to regard war as a crime. We have also changed or rather developed our conception of empire. From this new historical perspective many of those who constitute themselves judges of their forerunners will, when presented with this record, condemn the British government and especially the mainspring of its policy, Chamberlain, for his readiness to go to war in order to insure that a certain slice of African territory should belong to us rather than to France. And from this standpoint the men who risked their lives and reputations in the heat and rain and fever of an almost unknown stretch of Africa, as the agents of this policy, may not appear figures which posterity should honour. The historian who himself sees darkly through the glass of his own age knows that the moral evaluation of the past is an essential exercise in the moral activity of the present. But it follows that he at least will not allow either omniscience or absolute moral validity to his own or to any age. He must do what he

---

[1] Hanotaux, *Fachoda*, pp. x, xii.
[2] Garvin, *Life of Chamberlain*, vol. iii, p. 27.

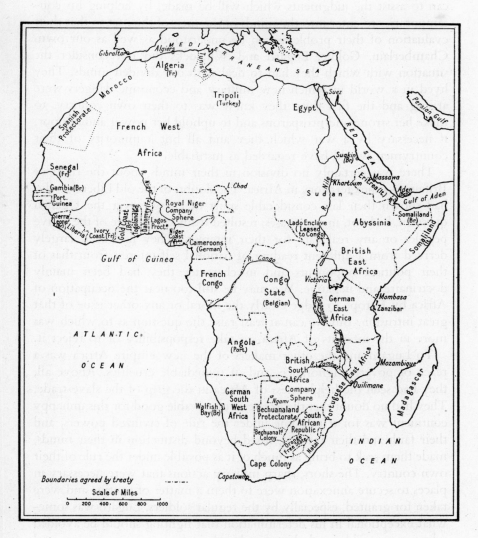

Boundaries agreed by treaty

Scale of Miles

0   200   400   600   800 1000

Africa 1898

can to assist the judgments which will be made, by helping his contemporaries to enter into the minds of the men of the past so that their evaluation of their problems can be understood as well as our own. Chamberlain, Goldie, Lugard and Willcocks did not consider the situation with which they had to deal with our divided minds. They lived in a world in which new military and economic dangers were arising and the first duty they knew was to their own country, to make her strong and prosperous and to uphold her power and honour, if necessary by a war which they and all but a minority of their countrymen would have regarded as justifiable.

There was certainly no division in their minds about the right of Britain to annex territory in Africa. The doubts of the old Liberals, who had shown their last considerable spurt of energy over the Uganda question, had not, in most cases, resulted from knowledge of the native peoples or any real care for their interests. They had been largely derived from a different reading of national self-interest from that of their political opponents and in character they had been mainly doctrinaire and negative. We may be still too near the occupation of Africa by Europe to judge clearly the moral or any other issue of that great intrusion. But we can at least raise the question as to which was more in the interests of Africa, to take responsibility or to reject it.

To Lugard and the other makers of the new empire Africa was a place of poverty, ignorance, and of remediable cruelties. Above all, they had seen the helplessness of Africa in the grip of the slave-trade. They had no doubt that the greatest conceivable good for this unhappy continent was for it to come under the rule of civilized powers, and their faith and their interest, fused beyond distinction in their minds, made them seek to bring as much of it as possible under the rule of their own country. The short, sharp military actions that were necessary in places to secure annexation were to them a matter of routine and were taken for granted, especially by the regular soldiers. Lugard was somewhat exceptional in his determination that fighting should be avoided whenever possible, and always reduced to the minimum in time and scale. That physical force was required in such small measure, and by no means everywhere, only seemed to show that Britain's power was for the most part entering a vacuum that would certainly be filled, if not by Britain, by some other European nation, or by something worse—uncontrolled adventurers, white, brown or black, armed with invincible weapons. The big question-mark that could be drawn over the still almost blank map of Africa, as the nineteenth century ended, was not *whether* the great tropical mass of the continent would be annexed by the European nations, but *by which* of them.

We leave Lugard as he embarked for England, a very weary man, in August 1898. At the age of forty he stood mid-way in his career, and at the entrance of the second and very different half of his life. He has struggled through one adventure after another, still keeping not only his life but his health and a will which events had served to strengthen and instruct. His life was now to take a turning somewhat away from the past, from unofficial adventuring towards government employment; from fighting to administration; from effort to success; from loneliness to marriage and love. Lugard's life has been shown hitherto to be bound up with three large themes. The first of these is action along the advancing frontiers of the empire. The second concerns that inter-weaving of the action with the ideas of the British public, parties, parliament and ministries, ideas by which colonial policy was created. The third theme is the international framework within which these national activities had, with difficulty, to be fitted. In the second half of Lugard's life, the theme of frontier fighting and annexation merges naturally into that of administration. Lugard, as a governor, was to be in some ways even more autonomous and original than as an adventurous pioneer. He had played a large part in urging his countrymen to take up the absolute power over Africa which lay ready to their hands, and had himself done much of the actual taking. The next question, a much more difficult one, concerned the use that would be made of that power. During the next forty-seven years Lugard was to do more than any other man to answer that question.

CHRONOLOGY OF LUGARD'S LIFE

Chronology of Lugard's Life

1903	Expedition against northern Nigerian emirates
1907–12	Governor of Hong Kong
1911	Founded the University of Hong Kong. Created G.C.M.G.
1912–13	Governor of Northern and Southern Nigeria
1914–19	Governor-General of Nigeria
1914	Amalgamation of Nigeria proclaimed
1914–16	Campaign in Cameroons
1919	Retired from the Colonial Service
1920	Made a Privy Councillor
1922	Publication of *The Dual Mandate*
1923	Appointed British Member on the Permanent Mandates Commission of the League of Nations
1924	Appointed British Member of the International Slavery Committee
1926–45	Chairman of the International Institute of African Languages and Cultures
1927	Appointed to the International Labour Organisation Committee of experts on native labour
1928	Raised to the peerage as Baron Lugard of Abinger
1929	Death of Lady Lugard
1930	Member of the Joint Select Committee on Closer Union in East Africa
1945	Died at Abinger, Surrey

List of Sources

I. UNPUBLISHED MATERIAL

A. OFFICIAL PAPERS

Archives des Affaires Etrangères; at the French Ministry of Foreign Affair (by permission).
Colonial Office Records; at the Public Record Office.
Foreign Office Confidential Print; at the Foreign Office Research Department (by permission).
Foreign Office Records; at the Public Record Office.

B. PRIVATE PAPERS

Anti-Slavery Society Papers; at the Bodleian Library, Oxford.
Cawston Papers; at Rhodes House, Oxford.
Church Missionary Society Papers; at C.M.S. headquarters, Salisbury Square, London, by kind permission of the Secretary.
Gedge Papers (the diary and letters of Ernest Gedge); by kind permission of Mr. Cuthbert Gedge.
Gladstone Papers; at the British Museum (Additional Manuscripts; Cabinet notes by permission).
Lugard Papers; (these are now in the possession of the author, but will be deposited at the Bodleian Library after the publication of Volume II of this biography).
Mackinnon Papers; at the School of Oriental and African Studies, London University.
Portal Papers; at Rhodes House, Oxford.
Rodd Papers (letters of the first Lord Rennell of Rodd); by kind permission of Lord Rennell.
Salisbury Papers (bound volumes); by kind permission of the Marquess of Salisbury.

II. PUBLISHED MATERIAL

A. OFFICIAL

Documents Diplomatiques Français, Première Série, 1871–1900 (Paris 1929–51).
Journal Officiel de la République française, débats parlementaires, Chambre des députés et Senat.
Parliamentary Debates (Hansard).

List of Sources

Parliamentary Papers:

C.4361 *Protocols and General Act of the West African Conference.* Africa No. 4 (1884–5), C.4361. lv. 133.

C.4739 *General Act of the Conference of Berlin; signed 26 February 1885.* Africa No. 3 (1886), C.4739. xlvii. 97.

C.5428 *Correspondence relative to the Slave Trade, 1887.* Slave Trade No. 1 (1888), C.5428. xciii. 283.

C.5603 *Further correspondence respecting Germany and Zanzibar.* Africa No. 10 (1888), C.5603. lxxiv. 255.

C.5905 *Correspondence respecting the West African Agreement between Great Britain and France of 10 August 1889.* Africa No. 3 (1890), C.5905. li. 1.

C.6046 *Correspondence respecting the Anglo-German Agreement relative to Africa and Heligoland.* Africa No. 6 (1890), C.6046. li. 19.

C.6130 *Declarations exchanged between Her Majesty's Government and France with respect to territories in Africa, 5 August 1890.* Africa No. 9 (1890), C.6130. lxxxi. 511.

C.6375 *Treaty between Her Majesty and His Majesty the King of Portugal defining respective spheres of influence in Africa, 11 June 1891.* Portugal No. 1 (1891), C.6375. xcvi. 417.

C.6555 *Papers relating to the Mombasa Railway Survey and Uganda.* Africa No. 4 (1892), C.6555. lvi. 599.

C.6560 *Papers respecting the proposed railway from Mombasa to Lake Victoria Nyanza.* Africa No. 2 (1892), C.6560. lvi. 585.

C.6817 *Papers relating to Uganda.* Africa No. 8 (1892), C.6817. lvi. 753.

C.6847 *Further papers relating to Uganda.* Africa No. 1 (1893), C.6847. lxii. 335.

C.6848 *Further papers relating to Uganda.* Africa No. 2 (1893), C.6848. lxii. 391.

C.7109 *Further papers relating to Uganda.* Africa No. 8 (1893), C.7109. lxii. 501.

C.7303 *Reports relating to Uganda by Sir Gerald Portal.* Africa No. 2 (1894), C.7303. lvii. 641.

C.7646 *Correspondence respecting the retirement of the Imperial British East Africa Company.* Africa No. 4 (1895), C.7646. lxxi. 189.

C.7977 *Report by Sir John Kirk on the disturbances at Brass.* Africa No. 3 (1896), C.7977. lix. 361.

C.8773 *British South Africa Company's Territories; Charter 1889; Order in Council 1891; Order in Council 1894* (1898), C.8773. lx. 157.

List of Sources

C.9046–28   *Reports on the West African Frontier Force of the Niger for 1897–8* (1899), C.9046–28. lxii. 341.

C.9334   *Convention between the United Kingdom and France for the delimitation of their respective positions to the West of the Niger, and of their respective possessions and spheres of influence to the East of that river, 14 June 1898* (1899), C.9334. cix. 837.

Report of Select Committee on the State of British Settlements on the Western Coast of Africa (1865), v. i.

Special Report from the Select Committee appointed to inquire into the origin and circumstances of the incursion into the South African Republic by an armed force and into the Administration of the British South Africa Company, etc. 1897 (64), ix. i.

Second Report, 1897 (311), ix. 5.

B. Books Mentioned in the Text

The Rev. R. P. Ashe, *Chronicles of Uganda* (1894).

Sir S. W. Baker, *The Albert N'yanza* (1866).
   Ismailia (1874).

Dr. H. Barth, *Travels in North and Central Africa* (1857).

C. F. Harford Battersby, *Pilkington of Uganda* (1898).

E. Moberley Bell, *Flora Shaw, Lady Lugard, D.B.E.* (1948).

L.-G. Binger, *Du Niger au Golfe de Guinée par le pays de Kong et le Mossi, 1887–9* (Paris 1892).

W. S. Blunt, *My Diaries*, 2 parts (1919, 1920).

H. A. Bryden, *Gun and Camera in Southern Africa* (1893).

G. E. Buckle, *The Life of Benjamin Disraeli, Earl of Beaconsfield*, vol. vi (1920).

T. F. Buxton, *The African Slave Trade and its Remedy* (1840).

Lady Gwendolen Cecil, *Life of Robert, Marquis of Salisbury*, vol. iv (1933).

R. F. Clarke, *Cardinal Lavigerie and the African Slave Trade* (1889).

H. E. Colvile, *The Land of the Nile Springs* (1895).

R. Coupland, *Kirk on the Zambesi* (1928).
   East Africa and its Invaders (1938).
   The Exploitation of East Africa 1856–90 (1939).
   Livingstone's Last Journey (1945).

Lord Crewe, *Lord Rosebery* (1931).

Lord Cromer, *Modern Egypt* (1908).

J. Darcy, *Cent Années de Rivalité Coloniale* (Paris 1904).

F. Debenham, *Kalahari Sand* (1953).

List of Sources

L. Dècle, *Three Years in Savage Africa* (1898).

H. Drummond, *Tropical Africa* (1888).

W. Furness, *The Centenary History of Rossall School* (1945).

A. G. Gardiner, *The Life of Sir William Harcourt*, vol. ii (1923).

J. L. Garvin, *The Life of Joseph Chamberlain*, vol. iii (1934).

André Gide, *Journals*, trans. Justin O'Brien (1947).

Major-Gen. Sir F. J. Goldsmid, *James Outram* (1880).

G. P. Gooch and H. Temperley ed., *British Documents on the Origins of the War*, vol. i. (1927).

S. Gwynn, *The Life of Mary Kingsley* (1932).

S. Gwynn and G. M. Tuckwell, *The Life of Sir Charles Dilke* (1917).

A. J. Hanna, *The Beginnings of Nyasaland and North Eastern Rhodesia* (forthcoming publication).

The Last Journals of Bishop Hannington, ed. E. C. Dawson (1888).

G. Hanotaux, *Fachoda* (Paris 1909).

Sir E. Hertslet, *The Map of Africa by Treaty*, 3 vols. (3rd edition 1909).

Lady Victoria Hicks Beach, *Sir Michael Hicks Beach, Earl St. Aldwyn*, vol. ii. (1932).

S. L. Hinde, *The Fall of the Congo Arabs* (1897).

C. W. Hobley, *Kenya from Chartered Company to Crown Colony* (1929).

L. von Höhnel, *Discovery of Lakes Rudolf and Stefanie* (London 1894).

L. W. Hollingsworth, *Zanzibar under the Foreign Office 1890–1913* (1953).

Sir F. Jackson, *Early Days in East Africa* (1930).

H. A. James, *School Ideals* (1887).

A. Johnston, *The Life and Letters of Sir Harry Johnston* (1929).

Sir H. Johnston, *British Central Africa* (1897).

  The Colonization of Africa (1899).

  The Uganda Protectorate (1902).

  The Story of my Life (1923).

Père J. Mercui, *L'Ouganda, La Mission Catholique et Les Agents de la Compagnie Anglaise* (Paris 1893).

Sir Apolo Kagwa, *Customs of the Baganda*, trans. E. E. Kalibala (New York 1934).

A. L. Kennedy, *Salisbury* (1953).

Mary Kingsley, *West African Studies* (1899).

H. Labouret, *Monteil* (Paris 1937).

W. L. Langer, *The Diplomacy of Imperialism 1890–1902* (2nd edition, New York 1951).

R. Laws, *Reminiscences of Livingstonia* (1934).

G. Leblond, *Le Père Auguste Achte* (Maison Carrée, Alger 1912).

List of Sources

A. LEBON, *La Politique de la France en Afrique 1896–1898* (Paris 1901).

D. LIVINGSTONE, *Missionary Travels and Researches in South Africa* (1857). *Narrative of an Expedition to the Zambesi and its Tributaries* (1865).

W. P. LIVINGSTONE, *Laws of Livingstonia* (1921).

F. D. LUGARD, *The Rise of our East African Empire*, 2 vols. (1893).

J. R. L. MACDONALD, *Soldiering and Surveying in British East Africa* (1897).

P. McDERMOTT, *British East Africa or IBEA* (2nd edition 1895).

F. MOIR, *After Livingstone* (1923).

P.–L. MONTEIL, *De Saint-Louis à Tripoli par le lac Tchad* (Paris 1895).

A. MOOREHEAD, *Montgomery* (1946).

A. NICQ, *Le Père Siméon Lourdel* (Paris 1895).

Notes on Uganda, or an Analysis of the various reports etc. issued on the late wars between the Imperial British East Africa Company and the Catholics of that British dependency (London 1893).

R. OLIVER, *The Missionary Factor in East Africa* (1952).

MUNGO PARK, *Travels in the interior districts of Africa 1795–7* (1799).

F. PENNY, *The Church in Madras* (1922).

M. PERHAM, *Native Administration in Nigeria* (1937).

CARL PETERS, *New Light on Dark Africa*, trans. H. W. Dulcken (1891).

A. PHILIPPE, *Au Coeur de L'Afrique* (Paris 1929).

J. VAN DER POEL, *The Jameson Raid* (1951).

SIR G. PORTAL, *The British Mission to Uganda in 1893*, ed. Rennell Rodd (1894).

D. REITZ, *No Outspan* (1943).

N. J. ROBINSON, *The History of Smith Mackenzie and Co. Ltd.* (privately printed 1938).

G. SCHWEITZER, *Emin Pasha, his Life and Work*, 2 vols. (1898).

A. SILLERY, *The Bechuanaland Protectorate* (1952).

CAPTAIN THE HON. R. F. SOMERSET, *Diary* (privately printed, no date).

J. H. SPEKE, *Journal of the Discovery of the Source of the Nile* (1863).

D. STANLEY, *Autobiography of Henry M. Stanley* (1909).

H. M. STANLEY, *In Darkest Africa* (1890).

E. STOCK, *History of the Church Missionary Society*, vol. iii (1899).

A. J. P. TAYLOR, *Germany's First Bid for Colonies* (1938).

The History of "The Times" (1947).

The Second Afghan War, 1878–80, the abridged official account (1908).

The Letters of Queen Victoria, Third Series, ed. G. E. Buckle, vol. ii (1931).

H. B. THOMAS and R. SCOTT, *Uganda* (1935).

E. J. THOMPSON and G. T. GARRATT, *Rise and Fulfilment of British Rule in India* (1934).

J. P. THOONEN, *Black Martyrs* (1941).

A. R. TUCKER, *Eighteen Years in Uganda and East Africa*, vol. i (1908).

List of Sources

"VINDEX", *Cecil Rhodes, His Political Life and Speeches* (1900).

H. WALLER, *The Last Journals of David Livingstone* (1874).

D. WELLESLEY, *Sir George Goldie* (1934).

A. WEST, *Private Diaries* (1922).

F. R. WINGATE, *Mahdism and the Egyptian Sudan* (1891).

SIR J. WILLCOCKS, *From Kabul to Kumassi* (1904).

L. WOOLF, *Empire and Commerce in Africa* (1920).

C. ARTICLES MENTIONED IN THE TEXT

N. E. BROWN, "The Flora of Ngamiland", introduced by Major E. J. Lugard, *Bulletin of the Royal Botanic Gardens, Kew*, No. 3, 1909.

SIR J. GRAY, "Mutesa of Buganda", *Uganda Journal*, vol. I, 1934.

"Early Treaties in Uganda, 1888–1891", *Uganda Journal*, vol. XII, 1948.

"The Year of the Three Kings of Buganda", *Uganda Journal*, vol. XIV, 1950.

"Sir John Kirk and Mutesa", *Uganda Journal*, vol. XV, 1951.

J. D. HARGREAVES, "Entente Manquée, Anglo-French Relations, 1895–1896", *Cambridge Historical Journal*, vol. XI, 1953.

SIR R. HILL, "The Suakin-Berber Railway, 1885", *Sudan Notes and Records*, vol. XX, 1937.

F. LUGARD, "Lake Nyassa and Central Africa", *Manchester Geographical Society Journal*, vol. V, 1889.

"Nyassa-land and its Commercial Possibilities", *Proceedings of the British Association*, 42nd meeting, section E. 1889.

"The Fight against Slave-Traders", *The Contemporary Review*, vol. LVI, 1889.

"A Glimpse of Lake Nyassa", *Blackwoods Magazine*, vol. CXLVII, 1890.

"British Officials and French Accusations", *Fortnightly Review*, vol. LVIII, 1892.

"Travels from the East Coast to Uganda", *Proceedings of the Royal Geographical Society*, vol. XIV, N.S. 1892.

"Characteristics of African Travel", *The Scottish Geographical Magazine*, vol. VIII, 1892.

"East and West Africa in Parliament", *Blackwoods Magazine*, vol. CLV, 1894.

"An Expedition to Borgu on the Niger", *The Geographical Journal*, vol. VI, 1895.

List of Sources

"British West African Possessions", *Blackwoods Magazine*, vol. CLVII, 1895.

"England and France on the Niger, the Race for Borgu", *The Nineteenth Century*, vol. XXXVII, 1895.

"England and France in the Nile Valley", *National Review*, vol. XXV, 1895.

"New British Markets, Tropical Africa", *The Nineteenth Century*, vol. XXXVIII, 1895.

"Routes in Africa", *National Review*, vol. XXV, 1895.

"A Journey in West Africa and some points of contrast with East Africa", *Scottish Geographical Magazine*, vol. XI, 1895.

"The Extension of British Influence (and Trade) in Africa", *Journal of the Royal Colonial Institute*, vol. XXVII, 1895.

"Slavery under the British Flag", *The Nineteenth Century*, vol. XXXIX, 1896.

"Slatin Pasha and the Sudan", *National Review*, vol. XXVII, 1896.

[F. LUGARD], "The Uganda Protectorate", *Chamber of Commerce Journal*, vol. XIII, 1894.

"Imperial Interests in East Africa", *Blackwoods Magazine*, vol. CLV, 1894.

"The New African Crisis with France and Germany", *Blackwoods Magazine*, vol. CLVI, 1894.

"British Interests in East Africa", *Pall Mall Gazette*, vol. LVIII, 1894.

"The East African Question", *Pall Mall Gazette*, vol. LVIII, 1894.

R. OLIVER, "Some factors in the British Occupation of East Africa, 1884–1894", *Uganda Journal*, vol. XV, 1951.

J. STEVENSON, "The Arabs in Central Africa", *Manchester Geographical Society Journal*, vol. IV, 1888.

A. J. P. TAYLOR, "Prelude to Fashoda: the Question of the Upper Nile, 1894–5", *English Historical Review*, vol. LXV, 1950.

"Les Premières Années de l'Alliance Franco-Russe, 1892–5", *Revue Historique*, vol. CCIV, 1950.

H. B. THOMAS, "More Early Treaties in Uganda, 1891–96", *Uganda Journal*, vol. XIII, 1949.

H. WALLER, "The two ends of the slave-stick", *The Contemporary Review*, vol. LV, 1889.

Also articles from the *Anti-Slavery Reporter* and the *Church Missionary Intelligencer*.

Note: The articles under [F. LUGARD] appeared anonymously.

723

INDEX

problem of conversions, 242–3; L.
asks for Resident for, 246; comes
within British sphere of influence,
248–9; and Fransa-Ingleza rivalry,
261; and enmity with Bunyoro, 262;
Imperial British East Africa Company's suzerainty of, 309; L.'s farewell to, 319–20. *Mentioned*: 258, 259,
260, 287, 288, 291, 298, 315, 316. *See
also*: Baganda, The

Bukoba: 212, 263, 305, 306, 310

Bulawayo: 584

Bulingugwe Island: 217, 218, 302,
303–4, 351, 359, 381

Bunyoro: 212, 213, 222, 247, 248, 254,
260, 262, 285. *See also* Banyoro,
The

Burdett-Coutts, W.: 346, 435

Burma: 53–5

Burmese Wars, The: 53

Bushmen: 577, 578, 581–8

Busoga: 207, 223, 246, 305, 306, 310,
317, 319

Bussa: 490, 501–3, 625, 633, 634, 635,
640, 642, 694, 695, 704

——, King of: 489, 502–3, 535

—— Rapids, The: 489, 702

Buxton, Sir Thomas Fowell: 77, 78, 82,
83, 165, 168, 290

Cambridge, Duke of: 416

Cameron, Cdr. Lovett: 146, 151

Cameron, Dr.: 110

Cameroons, The: 481; (German), 485

Campbell-Bannerman, Sir Henry: 356

Cape Coast Castle: 497

Caravan, African, author's description
of: 194–7

Carnotville: 494

Casimir-Périer: 362, 373

Cather, Col.: 54, 55

Catholic Union of Great Britain: 293,
344

Cavignari, Sir Louis: 42

Cawston, George: 152

'Celia': 61–2, 64, 67, 253, 563

Chad, Lake: 487, 493, 554, 702

Chamberlain, Sir Joseph: opposes German methods in Africa, 88–9, 149;
praises Lugard, 346–7; speaker in
Uganda debates, 434, 439, 460, 461–
2; seeks L.'s advice, 457–8, 459, 463;
and colonization, 461–2, 545; sympathy with L.'s view of events in
West Africa, 537; becomes Colonial
Secretary, 553–4; opposes Rhodes'
claim to Bechuanaland, 567–8; unable to give L. administrative powers,
568–9; obtains secondment of L. and
his brother, 573; offers L. military
command in W. Africa, 616–17,
618; his many African problems,
631–2; relations with Salisbury, 632,
633, 634, 635–6, 641, 667 ff; adopts
stronger tone towards French, 634–5;
interview with L. about W. African
mission, 637–42; his intention to take
over Royal Niger Company's work,
652–4, 656–8; his "chessboard"
policy for Borgu, 638–9, 658–62, 675,
678–684, 686, 691; condemns Macdonald's policy in Uganda, 662–3;
his uncompromising attitude to
French claims, 668–70, 672; expounds
his W. African policy in Parliament,
673; L.'s farewell interview, 674–5;
authorizes occupations on Niger,
694; instructs L. to occupy French
territory, 695; his Niger negotiations
with French, 698–701; his belligerent
foreign policy speech in Birmingham,
699; refusal to surrender Ilo to the
French, 700–1; criticised by French
for high-handedness over Niger
Convention, 703; success of his
policy, 704, 705. *Mentioned*: 571,
591, 600, 612, 615, 655, 664, 665,
690, 691, 694, 704, 710; and Flora
Shaw, 647; and Mary Kingsley,
648–9

Chamberlain, Col. Neville: 54, 55, 63

Chambers of Commerce, 426, 459

tiations, 365–7; Salisbury questions her claims in Uganda, 368; threatens British interests on the Upper Nile, 404, 413, 545; and scramble for Africa, 465–9; and West African exploration, 480, 481; her methods of expansion, 486; in W. Africa, 486–90, 493–4; her anger at Anglo-Belgian Congo Agreement, 489; in Paraku, 522; opposition to L.'s employment in W. Africa, 531, 532; Franco-British rivalry in W. Africa, 532–41, 668–74; supports German claim to Gandu, 539; and Chamberlain's "chessboard" policy, 638–9, 658, 660–1, 683, 684, 685, 691; and the Niger Convention negotiations, 698–70; 703, 704, 706; her methods in Nigeria, 707; evacuates Borgu, 707–8; and rivalry with Britain, 709–10

Fransa Party, The: 222, 239–42, 247, 256, 261, 284, 286, 293, 294, 295, 296, 297, 298, 301, 302, 303, 306, 311, 316, 317, 357–8, 360, 381, 382–3. *See also* White Fathers, The

Free Church Mission, The: 84, 92–3, 108 (and n.), 111, 116

Fripp, Sir Alfred: 573, 644

Fuladoyo: 178

Futabangi, The: 293, 296, 303, 305, 311

Gaberones: 584

Gabunga, The: 293

Gambia, The: 479, 704

Gandu: 695

—— Emirate of: 489, 534, 539

Gedge, Ernest: 175, 226–7, 231, 353

George, Lake (Ruisamba): 266, 269, 283, 285

German Colonization Society: 404

German East Africa Company: 92, 130, 172–3

Germany: in Africa, 87–92, 94; Anglo-German blockade of East African coast, 130, 138; and the rebellion in

its sphere, 170, 171; threatens Imperial British East Africa Company's expedition to Uganda, 172–4, 179; signs Anglo-German treaty (1890), 204–5, 222; and White Fathers, 305; learns of the fighting in Uganda, 328, 329; and British expansion, 388–9, 404; opposes Anglo-Belgian treaty, 468; expedition to West Africa, 494; Lugard's suspicions of, 606; Kaiser congratulates Kruger, 572, 631

Ghanzi: 567, 599

Giriama, The: 178

Gladstone, W. E.: opposes Beaconsfield's policy in India, 42–3; gives up Kandahar on returning to office, 44; held responsible for Gordon's death, 48–9; and the Sudan campaign, 51–2; and German claims in Africa, 88–9; praises Lugard's character, 331; avoids Government responsibility for Imperial British East Africa Company, 338; disagrees with Rosebery, 339; his cautious reception of L.'s defence, 345; confirms Macdonald's appointment as investigator in Uganda, 346; hesitates to judge Uganda issue, 361; opposes proposed subsidy for Uganda railway project, 399–401; abstains from voting in debate, 401; returns to office, 402; opposes retention of Uganda, 405–6, 407, 408, 410–11; favours return of mainland to Zanzibar, 417; opposes Commission to supervise evacuation, 418; changes his mind, 428; and Portal's appointment as Commissioner, 430–1; replies to Labouchere in Commons, 433; and Portal's report, 450; his indecision, and resentment of Rosebery, 453–4

Gold Coast, The: 479, 486, 497, 616, 625, 628, 668, 672, 699, 704

Goldie, Sir George Taubman: creator of first chartered company in tropical Africa, 478; develops trade in

CHARACTER:

Influence of mother and Christian upbringing, 23; at six years old, 17–20; influence of Dr. H. A. James, 33–4; at twenty years old, 38; subsequent development, 168, 189, 227, 236, 245, 341, 446, 463–4, 605–6; "decidedly eccentric" (de Winton), 188; "too self-confident" (de Winton), 206; "over-sensitive" (Mackenzie), 245; his "morbid sensitiveness" (Kirk), 414; "a curious, cranky fellow" (Mackenzie), 415; Stanley's view of, 414–15. *Tributes to:* 116 (Dr. Laws); 126 (Rev. D. G. Scott); 134 (Henry O'Neill); 139 (Dr. Cross and Monteith-Fotheringham); 315 (Père Achte and the Mujasi); 321 (Mwanga); 330 (Labouchere); 330–2 (Salisbury, Chamberlain and Harcourt); 346, 412 (Burdett Coutts); 346–7 (Chamberlain); 371–2 (Stanmore); 373 (Dècle); 374–5 (Bishop Patterson); 384 (The Kabaka, Daudi Chwa); 394, 412 (Rev. H. Waller); 435 (Lowther); 556–7 (Goldie). *Friendships:* 446–7, 609, 652; and 'Celia', 61–3, 188–9, 253–4, 563, 652; and Flora Shaw, 443, 458, 564, 569–71, 580, 581, 646–7, 651–2, 655; and Mary Kingsley, 649–52. *Health:* 43, 54–5, 62–3, 101, 119, 123–4, 126, 182–3, 247, 250, 275–7, 282–3, 317, 447, 453, 513, 521–2, 525, 588–96, 687–9, 694, 696. *Personal appearance:* 416, 423, 437, 490. *Self-analysis:* 136, 190, 237, 253, 254, 504. *Industry and attention to detail:* 46, 47, 52, 53–4, 61, 103, 118–19, 145, 238, 266, 275, 282, 312–13, 440–1, 545, 588, 689–90, 706. *His economical nature:* 150, 265, 313, 506; and money, 474–6, 562–4, 677. *His humanity and justice:* 102, 198, 237–8, 272, 281–2, 358–9, 435–6, 600–1, 682. *As leader and organiser of expeditions:* 115, 178, 194, 197–9, 206, 237–8, 240, 250, 260, 272, 280–2, 504–5, 599–600.

HIS VIEWS ON:

Africans: 585–6, 600, 679; Mwanga, 208, 228, 229–30, 231–2, 240–1, 302, 306, 307–9, 320–1; King of Kiama, 507–11; Khama, 585–7. *British expansion:* 140–1, 145, 220, 240, 370, 398–9, 404, 408–9, 412–13, 416–17, 421, 426, 440–1, 457, 458, 464–9, 547. *Fighting:* 498–9. *Flogging:* 198, 202, 238, 363, 511–12, 515, 527, 600. *Liquor traffic:* 452, 546, 586. *Looting:* 121–2, 263, 272. *Native Society:* 101–2, 136, 193, 198, 202–3, 230, 236, 240, 281–2, 324, 359, 503, 505, 529. *Slavery:* 64, 102, 103–4, 111–26, 135, 140–1, 144–5, 191–2, 201, 310, 318, 459, 460, 462–3, 497, 546.

PUBLIC LIFE:

Appeals to public opinion: 141, 142, 144–5, 152, 411–13, 415, 416–17, 423–4, 435–6, 439–42, 445–6, 453, 455, 458–9, 463–4, 547–8. *As diplomat:* 467. *Relations with Missions:* 112, 113–14, 116, 126, 224, 227–9, 230–1, 232–3, 242–3, 249, 296–8, 300, 302–3, 304, 306–8, 309–13, 341–5, 383, 527, 528. *His speeches:* 421, 423–4, 451. *His writings:* 145, 152–3, 159, 295, 330, 412–13, 416–17, 432, 435–6, 452, 455, 458, 544–7; *The Rise of our East African Empire,* 439–44.

Lugard, The Rev. Frederick Grueber (Lugard's father): antecedents, 4–5; born, 5; education, 5; ordained, 5; sent to India, 5; life and character, 5–8; letters to his family, 16–17; returns to England, 22; financial difficulties, 24, 45, 136, 137

Lugard, Lt.-Col. Henry (Lugard's uncle): 36

Lugard's Col. H. T. (Lugard's cousin):
114
Lugard, Henry (Lugard's half-brother):
47
Lugard, Capt. John (Lugard's grandfather): 4–5
Lugard, Lucy (Lugard's half-sister):
3, 6, 14, 24
Lugard, Mrs. Mary Jane (Lugard's mother): 3; antecedents, 4; joins C.M.S., 4; marries, 4; character and influence, 7–8; journey home from India (1863), 11–12; settles in York, 13; letters to husband, 14–16; her religion, 15–16; ill-health, 20–1; death, 22
Luwambu: 260, 286, 305
Lytton, Lord: 41, 42

Macaulay, "Sir" Byron (native agent):
629
Mbogo: 252, 316, 317, 318, 319
McCallum (Governor of Lagos): 663, 664, 665, 679–80
McDermott, P. M.: 289, 390
Macdonald, Sir Claude: 479
Macdonald, Capt. J. R. L.: 318–19, 322–6, 334–6, 352, 353–4, 359, 363, 364, 365, 376–7, 378–9, 610, 655; *and see* Macdonald Report, The
Macdonald Report, The: reaches England, 348; charges against Lugard's administration in Uganda, 349–51; circumstances of its compilation, 352–5; its reception by Cabinet, 355–6; L.'s reply to, 356–9; fate of, 365, 367, 368–9; weaknesses of, 378–9; Hirth's view of, 381
Machakos: 175, 176, 188, 201–2
Mackay, The Rev. Alexander: 166, 197
Mackay, Capt.: 184, 188, 191
Mackenzie, Bishop C. F.: 83
Mackenzie, Sir George: his first encounter with Lugard, 168, 169; asks L. to survey Sabaki route, 176; insists on secrecy about affairs of Imperial British East Africa Company, 177–8; his relations with L., 179–80; stresses importance of reaching Uganda before the Germans, 181, 182; defends L. against de Winton, 183–4; his confidence in L., 244; warns Foreign Office about French in Uganda, 404–5; his opinion of L., 415; plans campaign with L. against evacuation of Uganda, 421; compares I.B.E.A.C. with Royal Niger Company, 499. *Mentioned:* 172, 181, 185, 245, 256, 258, 265, 285, 290, 387, 393, 413
Mackinnon, Sir William: and proposed British occupation of East African mainland, 165–6; his failings as a business man, 167; urges Government co-operation in Uganda, 388–9, 391; his anxiety about Imperial British East Africa Company's finances, 395–6; Kirk's view of, 397; reproaches Salisbury for failing to support I.B.E.A.C., 401–2; L.'s visit to, 413–14, 415; his proposal for subsidy rejected, 428–9. *Mentioned:* 172, 180, 190, 205, 261, 313
McNeill, Sir John: 50
Macpherson, Dr.: 238, 250, 257, 259, 266, 282, 302
Madagascar: 487
Madras: 5, 6
Mafeking: 567, 579
Mafia: 90
Mafutaa: 303
Mahdists: 48, 49, 52, 70, 132, 222, 247, 254, 276, 278, 394, 631
Makalolo, The: 105, 154
Makanjira, Chief: 129, 134
Makarikari Depression: 577
Makongeni: 178
Malet, Sir Edward: 205
Malia: 296, 307, 315, 320, 610
Malindi: 176
Mallum Yaki: 521
Malombe, Lake: 115
Mambwe tribe, The: 121